When a man is tired of London, he is tired of life;
for there is in London all that life can afford.

Dr Samuel Johnson 1777

Ph. Gajic/MICHELIN

Travel Publications

38 Clarendon Road - WATFORD Herts WD1 1SX - U.K.
Tel. (01923) 415 000
www.michelin-travel.com
TheGreenGuide-uk@uk.michelin.com

Manufacture française des pneumatiques Michelin

Société en commandite par actions au capital de 2 000 000 000 de francs
Place des Carmes-Déchaux – 63 Clermont-Ferrand (France)
R.C.S. Clermont-Fd B 855 200 507

No part of this publication may be reproduced in any form
without the prior permission of the publisher

Based on Ordnance Survey of Great Britain with the permission
of the Controller of Her Majesty's Stationery Office © Crown Copyright 39923X
Reg. User No. 01/3373

Printed in France 02-01/3.1

Typesetting: APS-CHROMOSTYLE, Tours
Printing and binding: MAME, Tours
Cover design: Carré Noir, Paris 17e

THE GREEN GUIDE:
The Spirit of Discovery

The exhilaration of new horizons, the fun of seeing the world, the excitement of discovery: this is what we seek to share with you. To help you make the most of your travel experience, we offer first-hand knowledge and turn a discerning eye on places to visit.

This wealth of information gives you the expertise to plan your own enriching adventure. With THE GREEN GUIDE showing you the way, you can explore new destinations with confidence or rediscover old ones.

Leisure time spent with The Green Guide is also a time for refreshing your spirit, enjoying yourself, and taking advantage of our selection of fine restaurants, hotels and other places for relaxing.

So turn the page and open a window on the world. Join THE GREEN GUIDE in the spirit of discovery.

Contents

Antique shop, Portobello Road

Globe Theatre

Sights   91

Inner London

Outer London   295

Practical information   381

Millennium Dome

Trooping the Colour

Maps and plans

COMPANION PUBLICATIONS

City plans
Michelin Plan of London **34** (Scale 1 : 8000 – 1cm : 80m), also available as a spiral-bound atlas, includes main thoroughfares, one-way streets, main car parks, post offices and the most important public buildings in the city, an alphabetical street index and maps of the underground network

Regional maps
Michelin map **404** – South East Midlands East Anglia (Scale 1 : 400 000 – 1cm = 4km – 1in : 6.30 miles) covers the main regions of the country, the network of motorways and major roads. It provides information on shipping routes, distances in miles and kilometres, plan of London, services, sporting and tourist attractions and an index of places.

Country maps
The Michelin Tourist and Motoring **Atlas** – Great Britain & Ireland (Scale 1 : 300 000 – 1cm = 3km – 1in : 4.75 miles) covers the whole of the United Kingdom and the Republic of Ireland. It provides information on route planning, distances in miles and kilometres, over 60 town plans, services, sporting and tourist attractions and an index of places.

Internet
Users can access personalised route plans, Michelin mapping on line, addresses of hotels and restaurants featured in The Red Guides and practical and tourist information through the internet:
www.michelin-travel.com

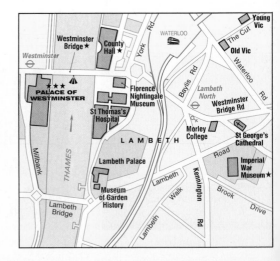

LIST OF MAPS AND PLANS

Plan of museums and monuments

Using this guide

● The summary maps are designed to assist at the planning stage: the **Map of Principal Sights – Inner London** at the beginning of the guide and the **Map of Outer London** identify the major attractions according to their star ratings.

● It is worth reading the **Introduction** before setting out as it gives background information on history, the arts and traditional culture.

● The main natural and cultural attractions are presented in alphabetical order in the **Sights** section.

● The clock symbol ⊘ placed after the name of a sight refers to the Admission times and charges chapter in the **Practical information** section, which also includes useful travel advice, addresses, services, information on sightseeing, a calendar of events and bibliography.

● For a selection of hotels and restaurants, consult the **Travellers' addresses** chapter and the **Michelin Red Guide London**, which also contains town plans.

● To find a particular place or historic figure or event or practical information, consult the **Index**.

● We greatly appreciate comments and suggestions from our readers. Contact us at :

Michelin Travel Publications,

38 Clarendon Road, Watford WD1 1SX, UK

Tel 01923 415 000

Fax 01923 415 250

TheGreenGuide-uk@uk.michelin.com

www.michelin-travel.com

Little Venice

Key

★★★ **Highly recommended**

★★ **Recommended**

★ **Interesting**

Tourism

⊙	Admission Times and Charges listed at the end of the guide	►►	Visit if time permits
	Sightseeing route with departure point indicated	AZ B	Map co-ordinates locating sights
	Ecclesiastical building		Tourist information
	Synagogue – Mosque		Historic house, castle – Ruins
	Building (with main entrance)		Dam – Factory or power station
■	Statue, small building		Fort – Cave
†	Wayside cross		Prehistoric site
◎	Fountain		Viewing table – View
	Fortified walls – Tower – Gate	▲	Miscellaneous sight

Recreation

	Racecourse		Waymarked footpath
	Skating rink	◆	Outdoor leisure park/centre
	Outdoor, indoor swimming pool		Theme/Amusement park
	Marina, moorings		Wildlife/Safari park, zoo
	Mountain refuge hut		Gardens, park, arboretum
	Overhead cable-car		Aviary, bird sanctuary
	Tourist or steam railway		

Additional symbols

	Motorway (unclassified)		Post office – Telephone centre
❶ ①	Junction: complete, limited	✉	Covered market
	Pedestrian street		Barracks
	Unsuitable for traffic, street subject to restrictions		Swing bridge
	Steps – Footpath		Quarry – Mine
	Railway – Coach station	B F	Ferry (river and lake crossings)
	Funicular – Rack-railway		Ferry services: Passengers and cars
	Tram – Metro, Underground		Foot passengers only
Bert (R.)...	Main shopping street	③	Access route number common to MICHELIN maps and town plans

Abbreviations and special symbols

C	County council offices	**M 3**	Motorway
H	Town hall	**A 2**	Primary route
M	Museum	**a**	Hotel
POL.	Police		London wall
T	Theatre		City boundary
U	University	● ●	Pub
			Underground station

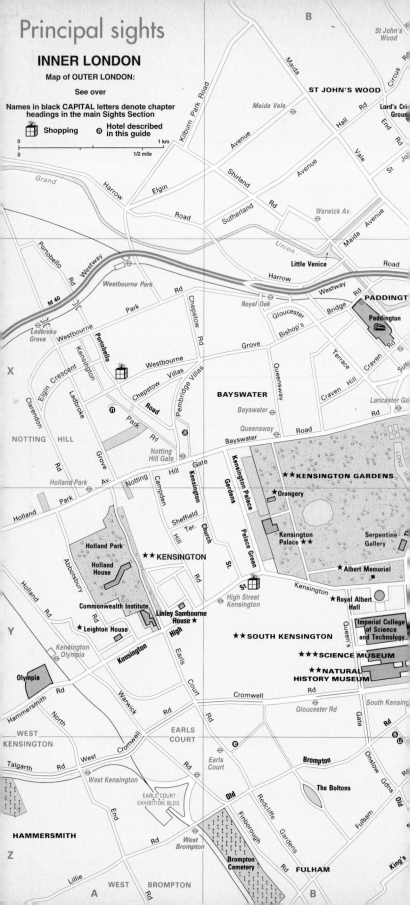

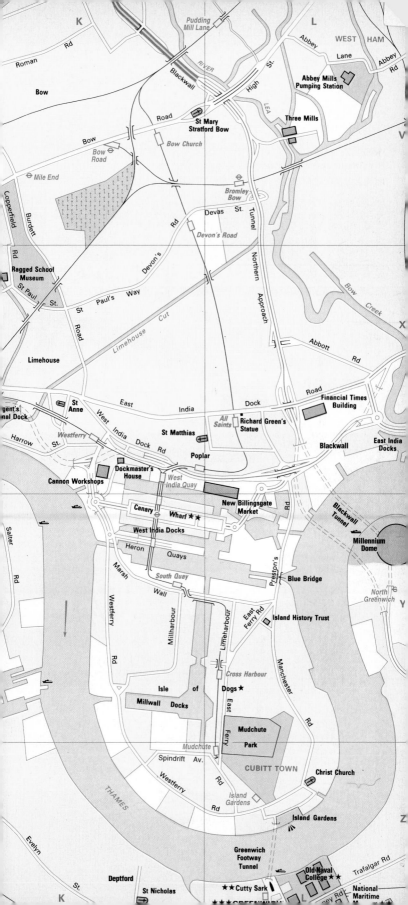

The Gates of Buckingham Palace

Introduction

History

1536-39	**Reformation:** Papal authority rejected by the English Church; suppression of the monasteries.
1547-58	Reigns of Edward VI (1547-1553) and Mary I (Bloody Mary) (1553-1558).
1555	Execution at Smithfield of 300 Protestants. Founding of the Muscovy Company.
1558	Population 100 000.
1558-1603	Reign of Elizabeth I (Good Queen Bess, the Virgin Queen).
1567	First Exchange established in the City.
1581	Founding of the Turkey (later Levant) Company.
1599	Inauguration of the Globe Theatre in Southwark.
1600	Charter of incorporation granted to the East India Company.

House of Stuart

1603-25	Reign of James I (James VI of Scotland).
1603	Population 200 000.
1605	The **Gunpowder Plot** was hatched by a group of Roman Catholics seeking religious toleration: Robert Catesby, Thomas Winter, Thomas Percy, John Wright and Guy Fawkes intended to blow up the House of Lords, the king and queen and heir to the throne. They rented a cellar extending under Parliament and enlisted Guy Fawkes, a little-known individual from abroad, to plant the explosive in the cellar: at least 20 barrels of gunpowder camouflaged with coal and faggots. Seeking to recruit additional support, Catesby approached Francis Tresham, who warned Lord Monteagle, his brother-in-law, not to attend Parliament on the fateful day. Monteagle alerted the government and Guy Fawkes was discovered in the cellar late on 4 November. Under torture on the rack he revealed the names of his fellow conspirators. Catesby and Percy were killed while resisting arrest. The others were tried and executed on 31 January 1606. Parliament declared 5 November a day of public thanksgiving.
1615	Inigo Jones appointed Surveyor of the King's Works.
1616	Queen's House at Greenwich, the first Classical building in England, designed by Inigo Jones.
1625-49	Reign of Charles I.
1635	Covent Garden Piazza built.
1642	Beginning of the **Civil War**: Charles I opposed by Parliament; Royalists confronted at Turnham Green by City trainbands (citizen militia); Charles I deterred from attacking London.
1649	**Execution of Charles I** on Tuesday 30 January 1649 outside the Banqueting Hall in Whitehall. He was buried a week later at Windsor. He had been brought to trial on 20 January in Westminster Hall on a charge of high treason and 'other high crimes against the realm of England' before a specially constituted high court of justice, which he refused to recognize on the grounds that 'a King cannot be tried by any superior jurisdiction of earth'. He maintained that he stood for 'the liberty of the people of England' and refused to plead. On 27 January he was sentenced to death as a 'tyrant, traitor, murderer and public enemy'. He claimed that he was a martyr for the people.
1649-60	**Commonwealth.**
1653	Cromwell appointed Protector of the Commonwealth.
1660	**Restoration.**
1660-85	Reign of Charles II (the Merry Monarch, the Black Boy).
1660	Royal warrants granted permitting theatres in Covent Garden.
1661	Design of Bloomsbury Square, the first London square.
1665	**Great Plague:** records give the total mortality as 75 000 out of a population of 460 000, rapidly spreading through London from St Giles-in-the-Fields and causing the most deaths in the poorest, over-crowded districts on the outskirts of the City (Stepney, Shoreditch, Clerkenwell, Cripplegate and Westminster). In June 1665 the king and the Court left London, only to return the following February; Parliament met briefly in Oxford. A vivid account of events is given by Daniel Defoe in his *Journal of the Plague Year (1722)*.
1666	Publication of the first London newspaper.
1666	**The Great Fire of London** was the worst in the history of the capital; it lasted three days (2 to 5 September) and destroyed four fifths of the City: St Paul's Cathedral, 87 parish churches, most of the civic buildings and 13 000 houses. The Monument was erected near to the point

where it began in the king's baker's house in Pudding Lane near London Bridge; it ended at Pie Corner near Smithfield. The flames, fanned by a strong east wind, raged throughout Monday and during part of Tuesday; on Wednesday the fire slackened and on Thursday it was thought to be extinguished. When it burst out again that evening at the Temple, adjoining houses were demolished with gunpowder to prevent it spreading further. People escaped with what they could carry by boat or on foot to Moorfields or the hills of Hampstead and Highgate. The most vivid account is told in the Diary of Samuel Pepys.

1666-1723	Reconstruction of St Paul's Cathedral and the City churches by Sir Christopher Wren.
1670	Founding of the Hudson Bay Company.
1682	The Royal Hospital in Chelsea is founded for veteran soldiers.
1685-88	Reign of James II.
1685	Arrival of Huguenot refugees from France following the Revocation of the Edict of Nantes.
1688	**Glorious Revolution**: flight into exile of James II; crown offered to William of Orange.
1689-1702	Reigns of William III and Mary II until her death in 1694 and then of William alone.
1694	Founding of the Bank of England.
1700	Population 670 000.
1702	Publication of the *Daily Courant* newspaper.
1702-14	Reign of Queen Anne.

House of Hanover

1714-60	Reigns of George I (1714-1727) and George II (1727-1760).
1750	Construction of Westminster Bridge.
1753	British Museum established.
1756-63	Seven Years War.
1760-1820	Reign of George III.
1775-83	American War of Independence.
1780	Gordon Riots against Roman Catholics.
1801	First census: population 1 100 000.
1811-20	Reign of the future George IV as Prince Regent.
1812	Regent Street created by John Nash.
1820-30	Reign of George IV.
1824	Opening of the National Gallery.
1828	Founding of University College, 'that Godless institution in Gower Street'.
1830-37	Reign of William IV.
1831	Founding of King's College.
1832	Reform Bill.
1836	**University of London** incorporated by charter as an examining body.
1835-60	Reconstruction of the Palace of Westminster (Houses of Parliament).
1837-1901	Reign of Queen Victoria.
1851	Great Exhibition in Hyde Park. Population 2 700 000.
1852	Founding of the Victoria and Albert Museum.
1856-1909	Building of the South Kensington museums.
1860	Horse-drawn trams introduced.
1863	First underground railway excavated.
1894	Opening of Tower Bridge.
1897	First omnibuses (buses) introduced.

House of Windsor (Saxe-Coburg until 1917)

1901-10	Reign of Edward VII.
1901	Population 6 600 000.
1909	Establishment of the **Port of London Authority** (PLO) to manage the docks.
1910-36	Reign of George V.

Queen Victoria

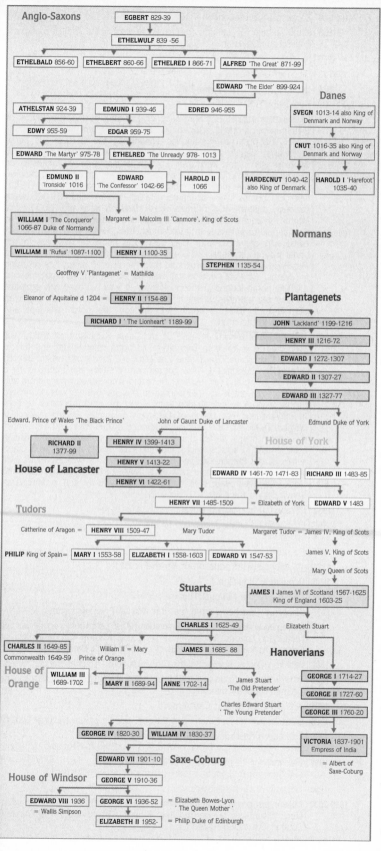

Anglo-Saxons

EGBERT 829-39

ETHELWULF 839 -56

ETHELBALD 856-60 | ETHELBERT 860-66 | ETHELRED I 866-71 | ALFRED 'The Great' 871-99

EDWARD 'The Elder' 899-924

Danes

ATHELSTAN 924-39 | EDMUND I 939-46 | EDRED 946-955

SVEGN 1013-14 also King of Denmark and Norway

EDWY 955-59 | EDGAR 959-75

CNUT 1016-35 also King of Denmark and Norway

EDWARD 'The Martyr' 975-78 | ETHELRED 'The Unready' 978- 1013

EDMUND II 'Ironside' 1016 | EDWARD 'The Confessor' 1042-66 | HAROLD II 1066 | HARDECNUT 1040-42 also King of Denmark | HAROLD I 'Harefoot' 1035-40

WILLIAM I 'The Conqueror' 1066-87 Duke of Normandy | Margaret = Malcolm III 'Canmore', King of Scots

Normans

WILLIAM II 'Rufus' 1087-1100 | HENRY I 1100-35 | STEPHEN 1135-54

Geoffrey V 'Plantagenet' = Mathilda

Eleanor of Aquitaine d 1204 = HENRY II 1154-89

Plantagenets

RICHARD I ' The Lionheart' 1189-99

JOHN 'Lackland' 1199-1216

HENRY III 1216-72

EDWARD I 1272-1307

EDWARD II 1307-27

EDWARD III 1327-77

Edward, Prince of Wales 'The Black Prince' | John of Gaunt Duke of Lancaster | Edmund Duke of York

RICHARD II 1377-99 | HENRY IV 1399-1413 | **House of York**

HENRY V 1413-22

House of Lancaster | HENRY VI 1422-61 | EDWARD IV 1461-70 1471-83 | RICHARD III 1483-85

HENRY VII 1485-1509 = Elizabeth of York | EDWARD V 1483

Tudors

Catherine of Aragon = HENRY VIII 1509-47 | Mary Tudor | Margaret Tudor = James IV, King of Scots

PHILIP King of Spain= MARY I 1553-58 | ELIZABETH I 1558-1603 | EDWARD VI 1547-53 | James V, King of Scots

Mary Queen of Scots

Stuarts | JAMES I James VI of Scotland 1567-1625 King of England 1603-25

CHARLES I 1625-49 | Elizabeth Stuart

CHARLES II 1649-85 | William II = Mary | JAMES II 1685- 88 | **Hanoverians**

Commonwealth 1649-59 | Prince of Orange

House of Orange | WILLIAM III 1689-1702 | = MARY II 1689-94 | ANNE 1702-14 | James Stuart 'The Old Pretender' | GEORGE I 1714-27

GEORGE II 1727-60

Charles Edward Stuart ' The Young Pretender' | GEORGE III 1760-20

GEORGE IV 1820-30 | WILLIAM IV 1830-37 | VICTORIA 1837-1901 Empress of India

EDWARD VII 1901-10 **Saxe-Coburg**

= Albert of Saxe-Coburg

House of Windsor | GEORGE V 1910-36

EDWARD VIII 1936 | GEORGE VI 1936-52 | = Elizabeth Bowes-Lyon 'The Queen Mother'

= Wallis Simpson | ELIZABETH II 1952- | = Philip Duke of Edinburgh

17

1914-18	Zeppelin raids on London.
1933	Establishment of London Transport to coordinate public transport: underground, bus and railway.
1936	Accession and abdication of Edward VIII.
1936-52	Reign of George VI.
1938	Establishment of the **Green Belt.**
1939	Population 8 610 000.
1940-41	**London Blitz** (aerial bombardment of London) during the Battle of Britain began in 1940 after the British retreat from Dunkerque (Dunkirk). The first heavy raids on London by the German Air Force (Luftwaffe) began on 7 September; for 57 consecutive nights 163 bombers per night flew over London dropping heavy explosive or incendiary bombs. Only adverse weather conditions brought respite. During the eight month bombardment, which ceased in May 1941, 190 000 bombs were dropped; 43 000 civilians died, 61 000 were seriously injured; 404 firemen were killed on duty and 3 000 were injured; 1.25 million houses in the London region were damaged. At first people took refuge in Anderson shelters, which were effective but damp and crowded; later they spent the hours of darkness in the underground stations, where bunks and sanitary facilities were installed; only three underground stations received direct hits resulting in deaths. St Paul's Cathedral was hit twice: on 12 September a 1 000lb bomb lodged in the clocktower; it was removed and exploded on Hackney marshes where it created a crater 100ft in diameter; on 16-17 April 1941 a bomb fell through the north transept and exploded in the crypt.
1951	The **Festival of Britain**, an echo of the Great Exhibition of 1851, was promoted as a 'tonic to the nation' to bring colour, light and fun to the postwar scene. The theme *The Land and the People* was presented in pavilions designed in new contemporary styles and materials by a team of young and untried architects and embellished by sculptors and painters. The small site (27 acres) on the South Bank was dominated by the Skylon, a cigar-shaped vertical feature which appeared to float in mid-air, and the Dome of Discovery (diameter 365ft), a circular pavilion made of steel and aluminium. Between May and September 8.5 million people visited the Festival where they learned about British achievement in arts, sciences and industrial design and enjoyed themselves at the **Pleasure Gardens** in Battersea Park: fireworks, Music Hall shows, a vast single pole tent as a Dance pavilion, sticks of Festival Rock, the tree walk, the crazy Emmett railway and a Mississippi Showboat on the river.
1952	Elizabeth II is crowned Queen.
1958	First women peers introduced to the House of Lords. Gatwick Airport opened.
1966	Founding of the City University.
1971	15 February: introduction of decimal coinage.
1975	Population 7 million.
1976	Opening of the National Theatre.
1979	Margaret Thatcher elected the first woman Prime Minister.
1981	**London Docklands Development Corporation** (LDDC) set up to regenerate the redundant London Docks. First London Marathon run. Marriage of Prince Charles to Lady Diana Spencer at St Paul's Cathedral.
1982	Barbican Centre opened in the City of London; Thames Barrier raised.
1986	Deregulation of trading on the Stock Exchange. Abolition of the Greater London Council.
1988	Jets begin landing at City Airport.
1995	50th Anniversary of Victory in Europe. Launch of the National Lottery.
1996	The queen celebrates her 70th birthday. After 700 years the Stone of Scone is returned to Scotland
1997	Inauguration of the British Library, St Pancras. 1-6 September: London mourns Diana, Princess of Wales.
1998	Opening of Globe Theatre.
1999-2000	Millennium projects completed: Dome (Greenwich), Jubilee Line extension, Millennium bridge and Tate Modern (Bankside), British Airways London Eye (South Bank).
2000	Election of Mayor of London.

URBAN DEVELOPMENT

Site – London straddles the estuary of the largest river in Great Britain, in the southeast corner of the country, near the Channel ports and links with the continent. Although the Romans established their capital first at St Albans (Verulamium) and then at Colchester (Camulodunum), they recognised the importance of the site of London as a bridgehead and trading port.

By the 13C, however, the **City of London** had become a rich port and the **capital** of the kingdom. The **double centre** of London – a unique feature – was created by **Edward the Confessor** who, on being elected king by the people of the City of London, went upstream to **Westminster**; here he rebuilt the abbey and constructed a royal palace; since then the monarch and parliament have been separate from the business community in the City.

Physical expansion – After Boadicea's attack in AD 61 the Romans encircled the City with a defence wall. In the Dark Ages assaults came chiefly from invaders sailing upriver and the wall fell into decay. It was rebuilt in the Middle Ages largely on the original foundations with an extension to the west; ruined sections are visible at London Wall and by the Tower.

In 1643, during the Civil War, earthworks were thrown up: on the north bank from Wapping via Spitalfields and St Giles-in-the-Fields to Westminster and on the south bank from Rotherhithe to Lambeth. At no time did any of these barriers prevent the expansion of London; in 1598 Stow was describing 'the suburbs without the walls'.

Queen Elizabeth, in whose reign the population doubled, passed the first of many acts prohibiting the erection of any new houses within 3 miles of the City Gates.

The reason for the royal alarm was twofold: it was feared that the newcomers, poor country people, might easily be led into rebellion and that water supplies, sewerage and burial grounds were inadequate. These and later decrees were, however, largely ignored or circumvented. Knowing that their houses were liable to be pulled down, the poor builders resorted to jerry-building using the cheapest materials; the rich usually bought a licence or paid compensation for their projects.

From the 16C fashionable society migrated westwards resulting in the development of the **West End** with its life of elegance and leisure. By contrast successive waves of immigrants from home and abroad tended to settle east of the City in dockland which by the 19C was known as the **East End.**

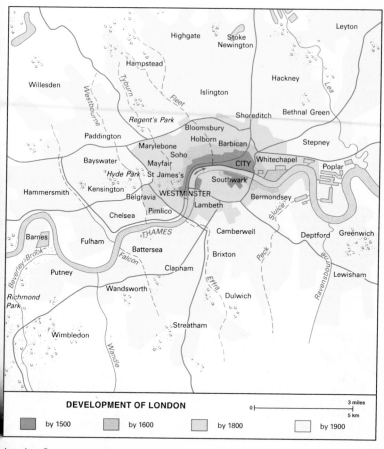

DEVELOPMENT OF LONDON

0 |————————| 3 miles
|————————| 5 km

■ by 1500   ■ by 1600   ■ by 1800   □ by 1900

Industrial Revolution – As the London merchants established trading posts abroad, great changes were simultaneously evolving at home as a result of the Industrial Revolution. By the mid 18C people hitherto employed in agriculture were moving into London and the towns of the North and Midlands to work in the new factories; textiles and other products poured out on to the home and export markets.

Improved methods of transport were developed for the carriage of goods and raw materials: **canals** were excavated; Turnpike Trusts were established which by the mid 19C had constructed 20 000 miles of good **turnpike roads** and nearly 8 000 toll gates (including one in Dulwich, at Marble Arch, Hyde Park Corner); **railways** were constructed. All roads and railways, both literally and metaphorically, converged on London. Easier travel led to the development of the **London Season**, as men coming to London on business brought their wives and particularly their grown-up daughters who required husbands. Socially this practice was endorsed by the Reform Bill of 1832 which introduced a new type of Member of Parliament: unlike the City businessmen, they accumulated their wealth from industry and had no feudal manorial connections.

London Today – At the end of the 20C London is still evolving. The double centre remains the City of London for business and Westminster for politics. To the outward eye the villages may have coalesced into a great urban sprawl but they are claimed with local pride by their residents. During the Second World War, the City and the East End suffered greatly from bombing but, as in previous periods, new commercial and residential premises, schools, museums and concert halls have risen from the ruins: new amenities in tune with the age. The docks, which stimulated the growth of the city, are being replaced by modern industries driven by the latest technology.

Mercers   Grocers   Drapers   Fishmongers   Goldsmiths

City Livery Companies and Ancient City Guild Halls

There are in existence 100 guilds of which 12 make up the so-called Greater Companies: Mercers, Grocers, Drapers, Fishmongers, Goldsmiths, Skinners, Merchant Taylors, Haberdashers, Salters, Ironmongers, Vintners, Clothworkers. Most are successors of medieval religious fraternities, craft or social guilds, some of which adopted uniforms and were thus styled livery companies. The number of their halls has been reduced to 25 by the Great Fire, local fires, changes of fortune and incendiary bombs – the Master Mariners have adopted a floating hall, the frigate *HMS Wellington*, which is moored in the Thames off the Victoria Embankment below the Strand.

New guilds are created by the modern professions. The Worshipful Company of Information Technologists, which ranks number 100, held its first meeting in 1992 in Guildhall. The requirements for a new livery company are a minimum of 100 freemen, £100 000 in charitable funds and a record of charitable and educational good works.

Although in 1523 Henry VIII 'commanded to have all money and plate belonging to any Hall or Crypt', many halls have collections or pieces dating back to the 15C which they either managed to hide from the king or re-purchased. Notable collections reside at the Mansion House; Clothworkers' Hall *(Mincing Lane)*; Founders' Hall; Fishmongers' Hall; Tallow Chandlers' Hall *(Dowgate Hill)*; Skinners' Hall *(Dowgate Hill)*; Innholders' Hall *(College Street)* – salts and spoons; Vintners' Hall *(Upper Thames Street)*; Mercers' Hall *(Ironmonger Lane)*; Haberdashers' Hall *(Staining Lane)*; Ironmongers' Hall *(Aldersgate Street)*; Barber-Surgeons' Hall *(Monkwell Square)*.

Vintners   Clothworkers   Apothecaries   Watermen & Lightermen   Barbers

It is, of course, the inhabitants of London who make 'London town': Londoners born and bred, adopted Londoners from the provinces, refugees from political persecution abroad (14C-17C Flemish and French Huguenots, political theorists such as Marx and Engels, post-war ex-monarchs, 20C Chileans and Ugandan Asians) or economic immigrants attracted by a higher standard of living (from the Commonwealth) men and women who achieve international recognition and the nameless millions who ply their daily trade with wit and humour.

THE CITY – CENTRE OF TRADE AND COMMERCE

The City of London and its port developed in parallel until the latter half of the 20C when the port shifted down river to Tilbury.

Roman Londinium – When the Romans invaded Britain, a Celtic fishing village had already existed since the 5C BC on the north bank of the Thames by a gravel strand which was the first ford and later the first bridging point across the river. The Romans built on the twin hills above the river crossing; the community grew into a major town containing some of their largest buildings north of the Alps, complete with a permanent stone bridge over the Thames and defended by walls after the assault by Boadicea and her warriors in AD 61. Archeological remains of a basilica and forum (60 acres) extended between Cornhill, Leadenhall Street and Fenchurch Street; a large amphitheatre stretches under the Guildhall; important villas built of Kentish stone with mosaic floors have been found below Poultry; to the west was the Temple of Mithras *(see CITY – Queen Victoria Street)*; to the south on the Thames foreshore stood the governor's palace.

Legionaries and merchandise came ashore in the auxiliary Kentish and south coast ports or in London itself and passed through the city on their way to the Roman capital (at St Albans or Colchester) or to cities and settlements in the north. Much of Roman London was destroyed by fire in AD 125, and occupation finally gave way in the mid-5C.

Medieval City – Trade continued throughout the Dark Ages, despite the siege and fire of Germanic and Danish invasions. Although there is no mention of London for scores of pages in the *Anglo-Saxon Chronicle*, in the 8C it was recognised as the

Armourers
& Brasiers

'mart of many nations by land and sea'. Under Alfred for a brief period the kingdom was united and London was constituted a major city but an attempt to establish the metropolitan see in London was unsuccessful.

Slowly the **City** developed into an ordered and rich community: in 1016 the assembly (gemut) of London elected Edmund Ironside as King. When his successor, Canute, exacted tribute, the citizens contributed £10 500, an eighth of the total paid by the whole of England.

Two months after the Battle of Hastings (1066), the citizens of London submitted to William I, who built the Tower of London, Baynard's Castle and Mountfichet Castle on the river east and west of the City, less to defend it against future invaders than to deter the citizens from reconsidering their submission. The City requested and obtained a **Charter**, the first of several to be granted by the monarch, whereby government, law and dues devolved directly upon the citizens themselves. In 1215 under King John Londoners were empowered to elect annually their own mayor (elsewhere a royal appointee) who had only to submit himself formally at Westminster for royal approval; this was the origin of the Lord Mayor's Show *(see CITY – Mansion House)*.

The City merchants grew rich; they loaned or gave money to Edward III and Henry V for wars on the continent and, apart from the risings of Wat Tyler in 1381 and Jack Cade *(see index)* in 1450, kept clear of strife, even during the Wars of the Roses. Indeed, the City never encroached on Westminster; with a few notable exceptions, citizens held no office under the Crown or Parliament. Many of the merchants, insurance brokers and bankers who later took over from the commodity dealers, were related to landed families; younger sons, such as Richard Whittington (d 1423) and the Hanseatics, who had arrived by 1157, were sent to seek their fortune in the City: they traded in everything and anything particularly wool and cloth, building great timber-framed and gabled mansions and buying country estates in the West End and the outskirts of London. Tall oversailing houses lined the narrow streets.

Richard Whittington

Religious Houses – Many monasteries and magnificent churches were erected in the City of London by the religious orders. The Dominicans, who arrived in England in 1221 constructed Blackfriars in 1276; the Franciscans (1224) began Greyfriars Church in Newgate in 1306; the Carmelites (1241) had a house off Fleet Street; the Austin friars (1253) settled near Moorgate; St John's Priory, the London Charterhouse and Rahere's priory with St Bartholomew's medical school were established on the north side of the City. At the **Dissolution of the Monasteries** (1539) Henry VIII seized their riches, destroyed the buildings and nominated himself as refounder of the hospitals – St Bartholomew's and Bedlam; this did not spoil his relations with the City, which became the home of the royal wardrobe. Under Edward VI St Paul's Cathedral, one of the great Gothic cathedrals of Europe, was stripped of its holy statues and remaining riches.

| Cutlers | Founders | Innholders | Stationers & Newspaper makers | Tallowchandlers |

Elizabethan London – Queen Elizabeth contrived that her merchant adventurers were financed more often by the City than from the royal coffers and tried vainly to curb the growth of suburbs outside the walls. James I, however, subsidised the New River scheme which brought fresh water to the street standards. Charles I was always forcing loans, applying restrictions to trade and requiring gifts, ship money and tonnage; he worsened relations to such a degree that, when he went down to Westminster in 1642 to search out five Members of Parliament, the City gave them sanctuary. The Jews, who had been banished in the late 13C, returned in strength under Cromwell during the Commonwealth (1649-60).

In the 16C, during the Age of Enlightenment, the city began to develop from a community of merchants, bankers and craftsmen, into a forum for men of letters and the arts.

Overseas ventures – In the age of exploration the City raised loans and fitted out and financed merchant venturers. The Elizabethan navigators were knighted by Queen Elizabeth but the funds for the voyages of Drake, Frobisher, Hawkins and Raleigh (to sail the Spanish Main with the **Golden Hinde**, singe the King of Spain's beard, defeat the Armada and to sail to Virginia) were raised by the City. The aim of the adventurers was to make their fortune, of the City to establish trading posts. The result was a world-wide empire.

In 1600, under a charter of incorporation, Queen Elizabeth I granted a monopoly of trade between England and India to a new undertaking, the **East India Company**; by the 18C the larger part of India was being ruled by the company; after the Indian Mutiny (1858) administration passed to the Crown. The founding in 1670 of the **Hudson Bay Company** with a monopoly that lasted until 1859 in the fur trade with the North American Indians led to British rule in Canada. The head offices of all such companies were in the City.

Fire of London – The Great Fire (1666), which burned for four days, destroyed four fifths of the buildings within the City walls. Within five days, on 11 September a sketch plan for rebuilding the City was submitted by Wren; on 13 September a second was submitted by Evelyn. In fact the city was rebuilt more or less according to the old street plan but the Act for Rebuilding the City of London of 1667 stipulated that all future structures, houses included, should be of brick and thus reduce the risk of fire.

Eleven out of 87 City churches survived undamaged and it was decided to rebuild only 51 on former sites, often amalgamating several parishes which before the fire covered on average 3 1/2 acres each. Money for rebuilding the churches was granted under acts of parliament which increased the dues on coal entering the Port of London. The prisons, numerous and insanitary, corrupt and cruel, were also rapidly rebuilt.

| Skinners | Merchant Taylors | Haberdashers | Salters | Ironmongers |

Victorian Improvements – In the 19C as more bridges were built and traffic increased, new wide streets were created to relieve congestion: King William Street (1829-35) as a direct route from the Bank of England to the new London Bridge; Queen Victoria Street (1867-71), the first street to be lit by electricity.

20C City Corporation – The City is governed by the Corporation of London, which acts through the Court of Common Council. The latter, numbering 25 Aldermen and 159 Councilmen, who represent the different wards, is presided over by the Lord Mayor and meets in Guildhall. It has its own police force; the helmet is different from that worn by the Metropolitan Police who patrol the rest of London. Territorial boundaries are marked by the winged dragon of St George and street signs bear the City coat of arms.

Financial Centre – In the 1950s the importance of the Port of London faded: her smog-inducing industries were relocated and the demands for warehousing and docking dwindled. Instead efforts were concentrated on the service industries: company administration, banking, commerce, insurance.

Ph. Gajic/MICHELIN

Success, affluence and tradition pervade the streets of the City where dark-suited employees of international corporations, private institutions and merchant banks jostle with traders in jockey-like coloured cotton coats from the **LME** (London Metal Exchange Ltd for base metals: lead, copper, zinc, tin, aluminium – the precious metals silver, gold and platinum are traded directly by financial investors) and **LTOM** (London Traded Option Market for share and stock options). London, strategically placed between Tokyo and New York attracts the lion's share of the world's business turnover conducted during European trading hours.

Another important institution is BIFEX which trades in freight-forward cargo and container ship-space. This business thrives in part because of London's pre-eminent insurance and under-writing business.

Big Bang – In 1986 the Financial Services Act was passed in order to simplify share dealing in London. Since 1812, the Stock Exchange had employed jobbers to transact trading business on the open market on behalf of brokers; the reform now made prices openly and immediately available to financial investors by computer. The sudden demise of the middle-man and the implementation of government-appointed regulators to monitor share transactions and investment business was nicknamed 'Big Bang'.

Black Monday – In October 1987, shortly after Margaret Thatcher's re-election to a third term in office, share prices reached an unsustainable high. Then, when American trade and budget deficits were published on Black Friday, confidence in the US economy plummeted provoking the collapse of market prices: the following Monday, the repercussions hit the London Stock Exchange. Fortunately, the country was not plunged into deep recession as had been feared.

WESTMINSTER – CENTRE OF GOVERNMENT

The Realm – Great Britain is composed of England, Wales, Scotland, the Channel Islands and the Isle of Man. The United Kingdom which is ruled from London's Palace of Westminster however, comprises England, Wales, Scotland and Northern Ireland but does not include the Channel Islands and Isle of Man which have their own parliaments and are attached directly to the Crown. Major recent constitutional reforms include devolution of some powers to a Scottish Parliament and to a Welsh Assembly.

Monarchy – The United Kingdom is a constitutional Monarchy, a form of government in which supreme power is vested in the **Sovereign** (king or queen): in law they are the head of the **executive** (government elected by a majority, headed by a Prime Minister and implemented by civil servants), an integral part of the **legislature** (the Houses of Commons and Lords responsible for deciding upon matters of law), head of the **judiciary** (Criminal and Crown Courts of law), commander-in-chief of the armed forces, temporal head of the Church of England and symbolic Head of the Commonwealth. In practice the role is strictly a formal one, reigning supreme but acting on the advice of government ministers. During the reign of Queen Victoria (1837-1901), the monarch's right in relation to ministers was defined as 'the right to be consulted, to encourage and to warn'.

Imperial State Crown

Parliament – The United Kingdom has no written constitution as such, but several important statutes underpin the institution and conventions of government: the **Magna Carta** (1215) sealed the king's promise to refrain from imposing feudal tax save by the consent of the Common Council of the Realm and instituted a fundamental human right: 'To no man will we deny or delay right or justice'; **the Petition of Right Act** (1628) confirmed that no tax should be levied by the king without the consent of Parliament and that no person be imprisoned or detained without lawful cause; the **Bill of Rights** (1689) ensured ultimate supremacy of Parliament; the Act of Settlement (1701) established the independence of the law courts and regulated the succession to the Crown of England; the **Race Relations Act** (1968) aimed to prohibit prejudice on account of race, colour or ethnic origin; the **Representation of the People Act** (1969) gave the vote to all persons over the age of 18 listed on the electoral register save acting members of the House of Lords and those incapacitated through insanity or imprisonment.

The supreme legislature is Parliament, consisting of two bodies: the House of Commons and the House of Lords within the Palace of Westminster *(see WESTMINSTER)*. In the Middle Ages, the king would meet with his lords; the common people were rarely summoned and had no regular meeting place until 16C. Regular Parliament meetings were assured after the Bloodless or Glorious Revolution (1688) when Parliament repealed James II's rule by 'divine right' and appointed William III and Mary; both houses were dominated by 'landed gentry' until the 19C (MPs were paid a salary from 1911).

Much of the traditional London pageantry and ceremony has its origins in royal protocol, military routine or the customs of the City of London. The annual sequence of events proceeds from November to July: when the season is over, Parliament goes into recess and the queen retires to Balmoral (Scotland) for the summer.

House of Commons – Since the 17C, two major parties have been predominant in Parliament (Her Majesty's Government and Her Majesty's Opposition) with Tories and Whigs, Conservatives and Liberals, Conservatives and Labour vying for power; representatives of other parties contribute to debates and may be lobbied for support by party whips to carry motions when opinion is equally divided.

Since 1992, the United Kingdom has been divided into 651 constituencies calculated to hold approximately 65 000 voters. Members of Parliament are elected by a majority vote secured at a General Election to appoint a new government or at a by-election if the seat falls vacant in the interim. Government term is for a maximum of five years. General Elections are traditionally held on Thursdays.

The House is presided over by the Speaker, appointed at the beginning of each session. MPs sit on parallel benches: members of the government cabinet sit in the first row opposite the members of the shadow cabinet (front-benchers) while members of their respective parties sit behind (backbenchers). Their combined function is to decide upon legislation: each act is subjected to two Readings, a Committee and a Report Stage and a Third Reading before going to 'the Other House' and obtaining Royal Assent.

House of Lords – 1 193 peers make up the second House: the largest number consists of the **Lords Temporal** who hold hereditary titles (Dukes, Marquesses, Earls, Viscounts and Barons), followed by the **Life Peers** who include the Lords of Appeal (Law Lords) and distinguished persons honoured for service to the Land (since 1958); finally, the **Lords Spiritual** are the archbishops and bishops of the Church of England.

This body of the legislature made up of experienced professional men and women from all walks of life debates issues without the bias of party politics. It also acts as the highest court of appeal in the land, although only the Law Lords are involved in such proceedings. The main body of the legal establishment, the Royal Courts of Justice and Chambers reside between Westminster and the City, where the Strand gives way to Fleet Street. The role of the House of Lords as well as the withdrawal of voting rights from hereditary peers are under scrutiny.

Local Government – Constituency responsibilities for education (excluding the universities), personal welfare services, housing, public health, environmental planning, traffic management is handled by regional county councils.

ADMINISTRATION OF LONDON

Governing Bodies – Since the early Middle Ages the City has been administered by the Corporation of the City of London. After the Dissolution of the monasteries (1539) Westminster and Southwark, the other urban districts, were given into the care of newly-appointed **parish vestries**, which differed in character and probity. Their powers overlapped and were insufficient to control, even where they thought it necessary, the speculators engaged in jerrybuilding in the centre and on the outskirts of the City. The builders erected tall houses with inadequate sanitation, which thus polluted the water supplies, and let off each room to one or often several families. Hogarth illustrated the scene in the 18C, Mayhew and Dickens described it in the press in the 19C. Conditions were not, of course, uniformly bad – the 'good life' was led with considerable elegance in St James's and Whitehall, in Mayfair, Marylebone, Knightsbridge, Kensington and westwards beyond.

By the 19C reform began, spurred on by traffic congestion and the dangers of poor sanitation. In 1855 the Government established a central body, the **Metropolitan Board of Works**, with special responsibility for main sewerage. It was also to act as coordinator of the parish vestries (now elected), which were left in charge of local drainage, paving, lighting, and the maintenance of streets.

Slum clearance began as new roads were built to ease traffic congestion: Victoria Street, Northumberland Avenue, Trafalgar Square, Shaftesbury Avenue, Charing Cross Road, New Oxford Street, Queen Victoria Street and Southwark Street. Through its chief engineer, **Joseph Bazalgette**, the board reconstructed the drainage system for central London, removed the outflows into the Thames and, as part of the scheme, built the embankments – Victoria (1864-70), Albert (1866-69) and Chelsea (1871-74).

In 1888 the County of London was created with the **London County Council** (LCC) as the county authority with responsibility for an area equivalent to the present 12 inner London boroughs.

Further road building was continued in the 1920s and 1930s by the LCC, following bomb damage during the war and the large-scale demolition of terrace housing in the 1960s. Municipal (council) housing is a 20C phenomenon; the first council flats were built under the LCC and its successor the GLC and the London boroughs.

In 1965, in the newly defined area of Greater London, the LCC was superseded by a regional authority, the **Greater London Council** (GLC). Greater London comprised the former County of London and former local authority areas surrounding London, in all a total of 610 square miles, with a population of about 6.7 million.

Following the 1983 general election the government was committed to reforming the structure of local government and the necessary legislation was passed for the abolition of the GLC and other metropolitan councils on 1 April 1986. The GLC's functions were devolved largely to the borough councils. New statutory bodies were created to take over control of local services such as transport, fire, drainage, waste disposal and flood control to be provided on a wider basis. For more than a decade London has been without a voice and this unsatifactory situation has brought about conflicts of interests and a lack of direction. Under the present Labour government, a referendum in 1998 proved overwhelmingly in favour of an elected mayor for London. Elections will be held in 2000.

Local Taxation – In 1601 a statute was passed requiring householders to pay **rates** to provide a dole for vagrants and the destitute, since the traditional almoners, the monastic foundations, had been suppressed by Henry VIII in 1539. For centuries the major part of the levy was employed for the relief of the poor; in 1813 out of £8.5 million raised nationally, £7 million went in relief and only £1.5 million on all other local necessities.

In 1993, the 1991 **Community Charge** was replaced by the **Council Tax**, which was based on the sale value of a property, with a reduction for single occupation, and collected locally through the borough councils and City Corporation. It is supplemented by the **Block Grant**, a government subsidy distributed to the borough councils and the statutory bodies. The latter are also funded by specific government grants and subsidies, payments for services and a proportion of the council tax.

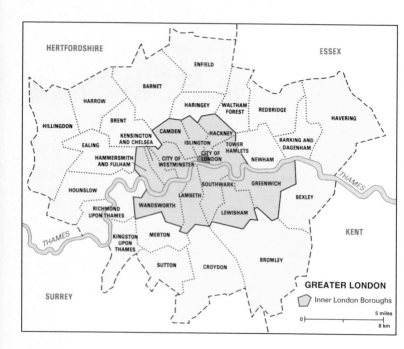

Urban improvements – The so-called **Improvement Acts of 1762** began the transformation of every street in the capital. Many were in a worse than medieval condition, while others, although fine and handsome, were rough surfaced and ill-lit.

Paving became the responsibility of the parish vestries *(see above)* who found it in their interests to relay the streets which previously had been the responsibility of individual householders, each paving his frontage (or not) with stone or rubble at a level convenient to his house without regard to the general course.

The vestries replaced the deep central drains (kennels) with shallow underground sewers and lateral gutters. They provided scavengers and sweepers to clear the streets of night soil and garbage which were still thrown out of doors.

By the 17C houses were being built of brick and tile; the practice of advancing the upper storeys and thus bridging over narrow alleys, was abandoned; new streets were wider. Legislation called for the removal of balconies and projections, of coal shoots and lean-tos at pavement level and of house, inn and trade signs. The small stagnant alleys and courts, however, were not reformed; slaughterhouses remained adjoining private dwellings; the problems of the overcrowded burial yards persisted; in non-epidemic as well as plague years the open pits (poor's holes) were not earthed over until full. In all but the worst areas, however, the streets were cleaner; the squares were cleared of accumulated refuse and were enclosed and planted.

The same 1762 Acts also instituted **house numbering** and **street lighting**. Since 1416 householders had been required to burn a candle at night outside their doors; since 1716 those in the City had been ordered to burn lights on the 18 dark nights of each winter moon but snuffers and lampholders outside the 18C houses of St James's and Mayfair are a reminder of how pedestrians carried their own flaming torches and link boys walked ahead of sedans and carriages. Change began in 1738 when the vestries installed 15 000 oil-fed lamps with cotton wicks which burned from sunset to sunrise in such main thoroughfares as Oxford Street. In 1807 there was a second advance when after a preliminary demonstration outside Carlton House, 13 gas lamp-posts were set up in Pall Mall. Seventy years later (1878) electricity was available and the first major street lighting project was inaugurated with the illumination of the Embankment.

The inner boroughs are now responsible for 895 miles of metropolitan thoroughfares and the outer boroughs for 6 800 miles of local roads. They liaise with the Departments of Transport and of the Environment regarding traffic and road planning.

The corollary to the 1762 Improvement Acts came with the passage of the **Clean Air Acts** (1956, 1962) controlling the burning of coal in furnaces and open grates, so banishing the notorious London pea-soup fogs.

Education – A century ago there were in the capital only the schools of ancient foundation such as Westminster (1371) and St Paul's (founded by the Dean, John Colet, in the cathedral churchyard in 1510), charity schools, Sunday schools and a few groups run by the Ragged Schools' Union organised by Lord Shaftesbury in 1844. The government had the right of inspection in 258 of these institutions and in 1854 reported attendance by 57 000 pupils, an estimated 12.5 % of the child population.

Dolpin lamppost

The Education Acts of 1870 and 1876 provided schools and laid upon parents the duty of seeing that their children 'received elementary education in reading, writing and arithmetic' (the 3 Rs). Responsibility later devolved on the LCC (1903) and subsequently (1965) on the Inner London Education Authority (ILEA) for Inner London (the old LCC area). When ILEA was disbanded in 1986 education in inner London became the responsibility of the individual boroughs as it is in outer London. Under later legislation some schools opted out of local authority control.

Open Spaces – London is a very green city endowed with at least five million trees (excluding those in private gardens): cypresses (12.8 %), sycamores (6.7 %), ash (3.5 %), plane and cherry (2.6 %).

The Royal Parks – St James's, Green Park, Hyde Park and Kensington Gardens lie at the very heart of Inner London while Regent's Park, Greenwich Park, Richmond Park and Bushy Park extend beyond.

The ancient commons – London's open spaces are further boosted by some 3 500 acres of 'common land' despite continual encroachment by peasants, manorial farmers, larger landowners and, in the 19C, by land speculators, builders and local authorities constructing roads. Ringing the urban sprawl north of the river are Hackney Marshes (340 acres), Hampstead Heath (792 acres), Wormwood Scrubs (200 acres reduced by construction of the prison), while on the south side there is Wimbledon Common and Putney Heath (1 200 acres), Clapham (205 acres), Wandsworth (175 acres reduced by the prison), Streatham (58 acres), Tooting Bec (218 acres) – these last four were probably continuous originally and, further east, Peckham Rye (64 acres), Plumstead (104 acres), Woolwich (240 acres) and historic Blackheath (271 acres).

Lounging in Regent's Park

Others – Most parks are tended by the borough councils and some have more than local interest: Kenwood (English Heritage), Lesnes Abbey Woods (Bexley), Crystal Palace (Bromley), Alexandra Park (Haringey) and Jubilee Gardens (South Bank Board). These, besides stretches of gardens, natural or landscaped features and flowers, have sports facilities: football and cricket pitches, bowling greens, golf courses, tennis courts, bandstands, children's summer zoos and playgrounds.

In 1977 the first **ecological park** was created out of inner city wasteland, turning it into a renewed natural refuge where urban wildlife could thrive, bringing nature to the city-dweller for serious study or simple enjoyment; similar in purpose are the **city farms**. Only in the 1930s was a visionary solution proposed and enacted (1938): a **Green Belt** (840 sq miles) was designated to run through the home counties encircling London at a radius of 20 to 30 miles. Although in some sections the belt has disappeared completely and exceptional buildings have been erected on it in others, it has had some success in defining the limits of London and halting the metropolitan sprawl.

The City – There is little room within the square mile for parks but since 1878 superb tracts of land 'for the recreation and enjoyment of the public' have been acquired: Epping Forest (6 000 acres), Burnham Beeches (504 acres), Coulsdon Commons (430 acres), Highgate Wood (70 acres), Queen's Park in Kilburn (30 acres), West Ham Park (77 acres), Spring Park and West Wickham in Kent (76 acres). The Corporation has also converted Bunhill Fields into a garden, it maintains a bowling green at Finsbury Circus, and has created gardens and courts in churchyards (Postman's Park by St Botolph's) and in the shells of blitzed or deconsecrated churches: 142 patches of green with over 2 000 trees.

Architecture

Roman City Wall and Gates – None of the city gates has survived but their existence is recalled in the names of the modern streets or neighbouring churches: Ludgate, Newgate, Aldersgate, Cripplegate, Moorgate, Bishopsgate, Aldgate.

The wall was built by the Romans c AD 200. From the 12C to the 17C large sections were rebuilt or repaired. Demolition began in the 18C and by the 19C most of the wall had disappeared. The line of the old wall can be traced by excavated outcrops, usually consisting of an upper area of medieval construction resting on a Roman base (Barbican, St Alphage Church, All Hallows Church, Sir John Cass College and the Tower of London). The street known as London Wall more or less follows the line of the Roman Wall between Aldersgate and Bishopsgate; Houndsditch marks the course of the old ditch outside the wall.

The **London Wall Walk** *(just under 2 miles; about 2 hours)* between the Museum of London and the Tower of London is well mapped out with 21 descriptive panels.

Materials – A variety of materials are used in various forms of construction. Timber for a long time was the cheapest option. Stone, quarried in Kent or imported from Normandy was brought up river to the Tower of London; Portland stone was first

> Secular architecture can be divided into two categories one answering to the public domain under royal or corporate patronage, and the other for the private sector, both in and out of town.

brought to London for St Paul's Cathedral (17C); Yorkshire stone for the Houses of Parliament (1835-60). Bricks were made locally in Kensington and Islington. In the City roofs were for the most part thatched until the 15C or 16C and were not uniformly tiled or slated until after the Great Fire (1665).

Norman – Edward the Confessor grew up in exile in Normandy before assuming the throne of England (1042-66), it was therefore natural for him to model his designs for Westminster Abbey on the Abbey at Jumièges as a symbol of the Church Militant. The best examples of Norman architecture are to be found at St Bartholomew-the-Great, St John's Chapel in the Tower of London and the extant parts of Westminster Abbey rebuilt by Edward the Confessor before the arrival of William the Conqueror.

The boldness of design and sheer scale of the Norman style are reflected in the White Tower built by William I, and in Westminster Hall – the largest to be built north of the Alps (238ft long), which was constructed by William Rufus and given its great hammerbeam roof by Richard II.

Tudor and Jacobean – The greatest examples in the public domain are St James's Palace and Hampton Court, which have the typical multi-storey gateway. At Hampton Court are preserved decorative chimney stacks, internal courtyards and the great hall with its hammerbeam roof. The first and most impressive (spanning 68ft) is that in the hall of the Palace of Westminster, while other examples survive in the Middle

Temple Hall (Elizabethan), Charterhouse and Eltham Palace (c 1479); decorative pendants used at Hampton Court also survive at Crosby Hall in Chelsea. Tudor brickwork with diaper patterning is visible at Charterhouse and Fulham Palace.

Gothic – Gothic arrived in England from the continent in the 12C with the expansion of the Benedictine and, in the north, of the Cistercian Orders. It remained the predominant style for 400 years, evolving in three main phases.

Early English emerges as a distinctive style at Salisbury and is confirmed at Westminster (1220) where the fabric of the building was essentially conceived as a framework for traceried windows. When in 1245 Henry III assumed the financial burden for re-modelling the Westminster church to his taste, the king assumed the role of pre-eminent patron of architecture in the country – an example continued until the reign of Henry VIII. While in the country abbots and bishops were obliged to rely upon local materials and building expertise which forged insular regional styles, the king, in London, could select the best craftsmen from home and abroad. The result is an English interpretation of French Gothic: Westminster never aspired to heights reached at Amiens or Beauvais, but was consolidated nonetheless with flying buttresses (cloister side of the nave). The elevation consisted of a high arcade, narrow triforium and tall clerestory; rose windows were modelled on St Denis (on the outskirts of Paris) where they had recently been invented. However, what is distinctively English is the window tracery, so delicate and fluid as no longer to be considered stone masonry as such; the use of polished stone column shafts; the overall richness of applied decoration and the use of iron tie-rods as an alternative to flying buttresses; shallow doorways are adopted instead of deeply recessed porches and a centrally planned vaulted chapter-house is contrived as a function-room for cathedral canons and clergy.

Decorated emerges in the late 13C and may be distinguished by the decorative richness and wealth of design in geometrical and later curvilinear tracery; as from the 1290s, lierne vaulting becomes widespread. In essence, a spirit of experimentation and variety of approach pervades this transitional phase.

Perpendicular, which overlapped with the previous style for 50 years, inspired architects, on occasion, to abandon the quadrangular in favour of the polygonal, thereby giving greater visual play to the windows and the illusion of a more coherent space. In some cases this led to the use of timber rather than stone for roofing. At St Stephens, begun by Edward I after a long visit to France, structural and decorative elements become homogenous: civil engineering know-how is applied with esthetic considerations. Unfortunately, the Royal chapel was destroyed in 1834, as was the chapter-house of Old St Paul's built in the 1330s. Relying therefore on the contemporary building of Gloucester Cathedral choir, the new style may be identified by the use of panels of decoration to articulate structure – the effect is one of order and clarity. These visual patterns, repeated 7in three dimensions, precipitated fan vaulting, which, it has been suggested, may have been used in Old St Paul's.

During the 15C financial and human resources were drained by the Hundred Years War and the War of the Roses: when peace was restored by Edward IV, the Crown returned to being the leading patron leaving us the three Royal chapels in southeast England: St George's, Windsor (1474 crossing and aisles); King's College, Cambridge (1446, 1508-15) and Henry VII's Chapel, Westminster Abbey (1503-19) – the most cluttered and over-ornamented of them all.

Otherwise, this Perpendicular phase was the great age for secular building and for Parish Churches. Alas many of the London churches were damaged by the Reformation and/or destroyed in the City by the Great Fire (1666). Over the 45 years that followed, St Paul's Cathedral and 51 of the City's Parish churches were rebuilt to designs by Sir Christopher **Wren** (1632-1723), marking an end to the evolution of Gothic architecture and the dawn of a different continental influence.

Andrea Palladio (1508-80)

Andrea Palladio evolved a distinctive Classical style that was formulated upon a strict sense of proportion. His profound appreciation and understanding of Antique architecture was derived from a detailed analysis of architectural theories outlined by Vitruvius (1C BC), reinforced by the study of surviving buildings in Rome.

Primarily, Palladio advocated that buildings should be designed to suit their purpose, that they be adapted to their situation, and be practical to use and/or comfortable to live in. Secondly, he advises structural simplicity; rooms should be arranged symmetrically, harmoniously proportioned one to another and one to the whole, preferably planned as interdependent, basic geometric volumes of space (cube, sphere and pyramid). He conceived the villa almost as a piece of sculpture, carefully positioned in the landscape so as to be seen and admired from all sides, the main front slightly grander than the garden or lateral facades. This consideration was later taken up and developed in the context of garden design by the 18C English exponents of Palladianism (Campbell, Burlington, Kent, Adam, 'Capability' Brown and the like).

Early Classicism or Palladianism – The turning point in the evolution of English architecture comes in the mid-16C when the Duke of Northumberland sent a certain John Shute to Italy 'to confer with the doings of the skilful masters in architecture'. His findings together with Serlio's *Regole generali di architettura*, however, were superficially assimilated into decorative designs applied to rambling Elizabethan country houses.

At the turn of the century, **Inigo Jones** (1573-1652) emerges as the first British architect with a definable personality: this was moulded not only by his education according to the Renaissance Humanist ideal but also by his comprehensive understanding of Italian architecture, contained in Palladio's *I Quatro Libri dell'Architettura* published in Venice in 1570, and from personal experience gleaned on visits made to Venice (1601 and 1605), Padua and Rome (1613). Important projects undertaken for the Crown by Jones to survive include the Banqueting House completed in 1622 *(see WHITEHALL)* and the Queen's House *(see GREENWICH)*.

Classical Baroque and the Classical Revival (17C-18C) – In the wake of Jones comes **Sir Christopher Wren** who is perhaps one of the three or four greatest Englishmen: the dome of St Paul's is a masterpiece worthy of comparison with Shakespeare's greatest drama. Wren left England only once for Paris in 1665 where he met Bernini the famous Baroque sculptor, architect and designer from Rome who was engaged on designs for the Louvre Palace at the behest of Louis XIV. On his return to London, Wren drew up a series of designs for the rebuilding of the Old St Paul's inspired by Lemercier's dome at the Church of the Sorbonne. These were accepted on 27 August 1666: a week before the Great Fire destroyed the old Gothic cathedral. His plans to rebuild the City on a grid of long straight streets punctuated with open piazzas and such focal points of interest as the Cathedral and the Exchange were impractical, impossible even given the complex system of freehold land holdings. In the event houses and shops were rebuilt at their owner's expense more or less where they had stood before the fire: public buildings were paid for by the City and the Livery Companies; the churches were financed out of the proceeds from a tax on coal.

Sir Christopher Wren

National Portrait Gallery

The City Churches – Although only a few of the parish churches were drawn in detail by Wren, most were planned by the Royal Surveyor, and later supplied with steeples. What is important is that each church be distinctive in appearance and suitably adapted to suit the new Anglican liturgy and the need for the congregation to hear and see the preacher; a bonus is their fine acoustics. The most complete Wren churches to survive include St Bride, St Mary le Bow, St Stephen Walbrook, St Vedast, St Clement Danes and St James's on Piccadilly.

The City churches are usually symmetrical and rectangular in plan, orientated as far as possible in the cramped and awkward sites available. The choir played a reduced part in the new Protestant Service which hinged rather on long sermons: large open galleries were therefore provided to accommodate extra seating, while side-chapels, transepts and side aisles were eliminated. The prototype for these light, spacious and airy hall-churches derived partly from Dutch Calvinist models and partly from Jesuit churches where the altar was placed against the east wall. Exceptions are centrally planned as a cross in a square (St Martin Ludgate, St Anne and St Agnes, St Mary at Hill), as a vaulted octagon or a domed square (St Mary Abchurch) – perhaps the most original experiment is St Stephen Walbrook which achieves a truly Baroque spirit hitherto unknown in Puritan England.

St Paul's Cathedral – What is remarkable is that Wren lived long enough to see the completion of his masterpiece (1675-1710). The original plans were undoubtedly inspired by Michelangelo's drawings for St Peter's as the Great Model would indicate. However Wren realised that it would be more practical to design his building in such a way as to allow the construction to be put up in stages: the Warrant Design not only allowed him to resolve any structural engineering problems encountered as the dome was erected but would have safeguarded the project should financial resources be suspended. The result with its rich variety of detail and carefully contrived combination of elements has long provided later generations of architects with inspiration and solutions to design problems.

Wren continued to be engaged upon other projects while St Paul's was progressing: besides Trinity College Library (Cambridge) and Christ Church (Oxford), he worked on Hampton Court Palace (south and east wings), the Chelsea Hospital and the Greenwich Hospital, now the Old Naval College – in imitation of the Hôtel des Invalides in Paris, where he was certainly assisted by Hawksmoor and Sir John Vanbrugh (1664-1726) – the attribution of whose work may be confusing at first sight as both use Classical elements with boldness and imagination to dramatic effect.

City Churches

There have been churches in the Square Mile since Saxon times. By 1666, there were 100 of which 88 were destroyed by the Great Fire – 53 were re-built under the supervision of Wren, more were constructed by Hawksmoor.

By 1939 the construction of new roads in the 19C and 20C had reduced the number of City churches to 43 of which 32 were by Wren. Nearly all were damaged and several totally destroyed during the war, but as the floor plans survive, it was possible for some to be reconstructed. Today there are some 39 City Churches, 11 are pre-Fire and 23 by Wren; 6 of the 9 free-standing towers are by Wren. 24 continue to be parish churches, 15 have become guild churches some are both. Most city churches are open weekdays and hold midday services; many also organise recitals, debates and counselling.

For detailed information apply to the City Information Centre or enquire at the churches themselves. If you wish to provide voluntary help or contributions to the upkeep of these monuments, contact Friends of The City Churches, 68 Battersea High Street, London SW11 3HX.

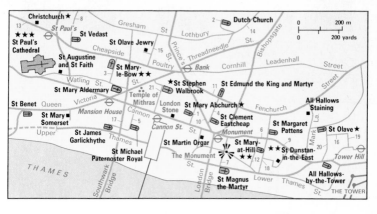

1 Abchurch Lane	8 Foster Lane	15 Old Jewry
2 Austin Friars	9 Great Tower Street	16 Pepys Street
3 Bow Lane	10 King William Street	17 Queen Street
4 Clement's Lane	11 Lombard Street	18 St Mary at Hill
5 College Hill	12 Lovat Lane	19 Savage Gardens
6 Eastcheap	13 Newgate Street	20 Seething Lane
7 Fish Street Hill	14 Old Broad Street	21 Walbrook

The Clerk of Works who followed Wren, **Nicholas Hawksmoor** (1661-1736) was less well-acquainted with the formal implementation of the Classical vocabulary and therefore developed his own form of English Mannerism (St Mary Woolnoth in the City; St Alfege in Greenwich; St Anne, Limehouse; St George-in-the-East, Stepney; St George, Bloomsbury; west towers of Westminster Abbey).

Neo-Classicism – The rise of a new aristocracy together with the Duke of Marlborough's great military victories provided new opportunities for patronage and travel to the Continent. The Grand Tour took young gentlemen to France, Venice, Florence, Rome and Naples; it aroused a new interest in Vitruvius and provoked an obsessional urge to collect, acquire and accumulate works of art that were sent home to England. During the first decades of the 18C, **Colen Campbell** (d 1729) published *Vitruvius Britannicus,* a compilation of British buildings in the Antique manner – a veritable manifesto for Palladianism; the other two mainstays of the movement were **Lord Burlington** (1694-1753) and **William Kent** (1685-1748), who together went on to forge a powerful partnership that provided architectural designs, interior decoration and layouts for extensive gardens-cum-parks in the manner of Palladio's Brenta villas (Chiswick Villa).

The man who bridges the gap between Wren and the new surge of Palladianism is **James Gibbs** (1682-1754), the architect of St Martin in the Fields. Gibbs had studied under Carlo Fontana in Rome and came back to London a great sympathiser of Wren – his St Mary-le-Strand a sympathetic call from Wren's St Clement-the-Danes up the Strand. St Martin's shows an audacious use of Classical elements that to this day jar with purists: for when did a steeple ever grace a Classical portico in Antiquity. But as success relied inherently on the political climate of the day, the Scot lost several commissions: his reputation therefore rather hinges on his published writings – *A Book of Architecture* (1728) and *Rules for Drawing the Several Parts of Architecture* (1732) – which were well received and proved most influential in America.

Georgian – The next generation of eclectic designers working in the Classical vein is dominated by two rivals: **Sir William Chambers RA** (1723-96) an upholder of tradition, and the more innovative **Robert Adam** (1728-92).

31

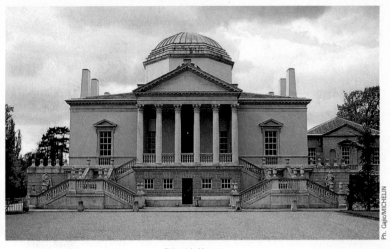

Chiswick House

Chambers was born in Sweden and educated in England before embarking with the Swedish East India Company to the Far East. After publishing a book about his observations on China, he was asked to re-model Kew Gardens and embellish them with exotic temples and a pagoda. He acquired particular favour from George III which allowed him to exercise his taste and judgement in such important commissions as Somerset House *(see STRAND)*.

Adam also travelled extensively, to France, Italy and Dalmatia where he meticulously measured and drew the ruins of the Palace of Diocletian (284-305). His intention was to explore the Classical style outside the confines of Imperial Rome as studied by Palladio, and to draw inspiration direct from the example of Antique domestic architecture. In interior decoration he borrowed extensively from descriptions of Pompeii and Herculaneum which had recently been discovered, from artefacts excavated from Palmyra and Greece, most especially from Greek vase painting – he developed a light touch and delicacy that having found favour at Osterley Park and Syon House, was quickly assimilated into 18C esthetic movements. Few Adam town-houses survive intact: Home House at 20 Portman Square, the south and east sides of Fitzroy Square, single houses in St James's Square *(no 20)*, Chandos Street and behind the Adelphi.

English **Neo-Classicism** evolved into an informal reinterpretation of the Antique: in its purest form it is limited to architecture, its spirit however affected all the decorative and applied arts. Patrons were painted by **Reynolds** adopting the stance or pose of Classical statues, silversmiths modelled their shapes upon Antique vases, **Wedgwood** created his Etruria ware, carpets were woven to echo coffered ceilings, furniture to accommodate the latest fashion in clothes, fixtures and fittings like sconces and tripods reflected the influence of objects brought to the British Museum. Multi-disciplined designers like Adam and Chambers were content to accommodate other revivalist styles in the form of follies, bowers and band stands. Gothick which was promoted by Walpole's Gothick novels was limited to private houses (Strawberry Hill); Chinoiserie to garden pagodas (Kew); Rococo to follies or pleasure gardens (Vauxhall); the Picturesque contrived to imitate untamed Nature, as depicted in painting – dead trees were planted and 'ruins' were artificially assembled in gardens.

By the late Georgian period architects had begun to freely adapt the principles of the Classical style as is evident in **John Nash's** All Souls, Portland Place (1822-24).

Regency (1811-1830) – The key figure of this phase is probably **Henry Holland** (1745-1806) who designed Brooks's Club in St James's, the headquarters of the Whigs favoured by the Prince Regent. The main thread of the Regency style came from pre-Revolution France, copied from picture books and interpreted by continental craftsmen.

The period up to the death of George IV is dominated by three men. **Sir John Soane** (1753-1837), a professional and eclectic architect of the first generation to emerge from the Royal Academy Schools, and whose principal legacy was the Bank of England, now largely destroyed. **John Nash**, favourite architect of George IV, urban planner and visionary responsible for laying out Regent Street, the terraces of elegant residences for Members of Parliament surrounding Regent's Park (1810-11), for designing the grand and monumental Carlton House Terrace, Buckingham Palace – although much changed, the Brighton Pavilion and various country houses.

7 Adam Street

33

Wilton Crescent

Thomas Cubitt, quality builder and property developer, worked from George Basevi's designs to create Belgrave Square and other large sections of Belgravia (1825), Pelham Crescent (1820-30); other squares, crescents and streets stretch from Putney and Clapham to Islington, Kensington to the Isle of Dogs.

Victorian (19C) – Social changes resulted from greater affluence and industrial expansion. A population explosion provoked a huge demand in urban housing that in turn necessitated a change in building practices that saw the demise of the individual craftsmen and the rise of the power-wielding contractor. Materials began to be industrially manufactured (iron in the late 18C, plate glass in the mid-19C, by the 1840s whole buildings were being pre-fabricated, concrete was being tested in the 1860s) and transported cheaply by rail. The middle-classes became versed in matters of taste with the advent of travel and increasingly sophisticated education. The main phases may be identified as **Early Victorian,** characterised by earnest historicism and the use of plainish materials, **High Victorian** (1850s-1870s) which reacted against archeological correctness with strong colour, contrasting materials, and strong sculptural effects and **Late Victorian** which reverts to smooth contours and soft textures, intricate decoration and delicate colour.

A key figure who straddles all three phases was **Sir George Gilbert Scott** (1811-78), the son of a clergyman who regarded himself as an architect of the multitude. Not only did he restore buildings (notably Westminster Abbey in 1849) he applied his confident Gothic style as easily to religious buildings (St Mary Abbotts, Kensington) as to secular developments: St Pancras Station and Hotel, Albert Memorial, Broad Sanctuary west of Westminster Abbey; the new government buildings in Whitehall are forged in a rather staid, unimaginative civil-service Renaissance style. His son **Sir Giles Gilbert Scott** (1880-1960) proves himself to be a far more sensitive and inspired product of the Late Victorian age, bequeathing such individual landmarks of the post-industrial age as Battersea Power Station (1932-4), Waterloo Bridge (1939-45) and Bankside Power Station.

Functional cast-iron building became an art in itself (Palm House at Kew, Paxton's Crystal Palace, Lewis Cubitt's King's Cross Station), while in other domains, fashions for eclecticism and revivalist movements continued: turrets, gables, pointed windows and stained glass proliferated in the neo-Gothic architect-designed estates and the anonymous streets of the expanding suburbs.

Red-brick developments were instituted by the London County Council who drew inspiration from **Philip Webb** for Bethnal Green and Millbank. Another successful exponent of this practical, unfussy style was **Richard Norman Shaw** (1831-1912) who

Cadogan Square

designed Lowther Lodge in Kensington (1873 now the Geographical Society), Swan House in Chelsea (1876) and four houses in Cadogan Square (60a, 62, 68 and 72) which inspired the 20C nickname 'Pont Street Dutch'. At Bedford Park near Turnham Green, Norman Shaw, assisted by E W Godwin and Eden Nesfield (1835-88) designed various functional 2 to 3 storey houses each with its own garden in the red brick Queen Anne style with tile-hanging, rough-cast rendering and white woodwork, a church, shop and inn. The interior decoration and furnishings were left to the firm of the socialist **William Morris** (1834-96) and as such soon became identified with the **Arts and Crafts Movement**, of which Ruskin (1819-1900), Philip Webb, C F A Voysey and W R Lethaby were members. Against the tide of mass production, came a revival of craftsmanship in architectural sculpture, stained glass, practical hand-made furniture, block-printed fabrics and wallpapers.

While **Alfred Waterhouse** (1830-1905) designed the Natural History Museum combining naturalistic observation with fantastic imaginary beasts applied to some great Germanic Romanesque fabric, De Morgan tiles and Morris screens spurned the development of Art Nouveau.

Ecclesiastical building – A surge in church building was provoked by demand to serve the new suburbs. Perpendicular spires spiked the sky as a new interest in Gothic architecture was born out of a profound respect for the past and painstaking erudition – promoted by **John Ruskin** and culminating in the new designs for the Palace of Westminster. The detailed designs of Gilbert Scott and Augustus Pugin included every element accurately and skilfully executed. As in the 18C, fads and fashions proliferated prompting a revivalist taste for neo-Norman, neo-Early Christian and in the mid century for neo-Italian Romanesque.

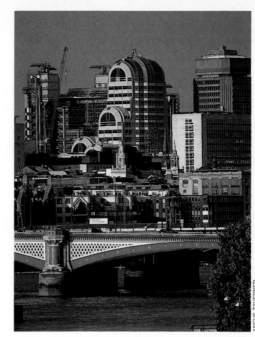

The City

20C Post-war – The International Style formulated by the Belgian **Henri van der Velde** (1863-1957) and the German **Peter Behrens** (1868-1940) – both painters turned designers and architect were followed by **Walter Gropius** (1883-1969) in wanting to deny the impact of historical antecedents and any recognisable association of style with function (cast-iron construction being synonymous with railway stations and tropical palm houses). They nevertheless advocated quality in building and practical functionality – factories and power-stations should not be dressed to look like schools or cathedrals. Meanwhile, steel-frame construction (Ritz Hotel by Mewes and Davies 1904) and the use of concrete led to ever shorter building time-frames.

Churches – Not until the 1920s was the neo-Gothic tradition broken when Edward Maufe provoked a change of direction by building truly modern churches: St Columba's in Pont Street, St John's in Peckham, the churches of the Annunciation and Resurrection in Beckenham, and beyond London the new cathedrals of Coventry, Guildford, Bristol RC and Liverpool RC.

Residential developments – Distinctive modern housing is rare: 64-66 Old Church Street in Chelsea (c 1934) by the International Modernist Mendelsohn and Chernayeff, the Sun House in Hampstead (1935) by **Maxwell Fry**, Highpoint One and Two in Highgate (1936-38) by the reclusive Berthold **Lubetkin** and Tecton, **Goldfinger's** custom-built 2 Willow Road and Cheltenham Estate (Kensal Rise) which includes London's most popular high-rise Trellick Tower. Lillington Gardens, Pimlico (1960s) and Aberdeen Park in Islington (1980s) by Darbourne and Darke show that council housing need not be unattractive. 'Persistent sharp and invigorating' are the terms used to describe the architecture of Thamesmead. Today, important contemporary developments abound on the South Bank, in the City, Docklands, around Heathrow, Gatwick and Stansted airports, while imaginative conversions proliferate along the Thames and within London's mainline railway stations and disused markets (Billingsgate, Smithfield, Spitalfields). Notable landmarks on London's skyline include Centre Point, the South Bank Complex, Barbican, Telecom Tower, Richard Rogers's Lloyds Building, Nat West Tower, Chelsea Harbour, Vauxhall Cross, and 1 Canada Square – known simply as Canary Wharf. The Millenium Dome adds a futuristic note to the riverside at Greenwich.

Technical architectural terms

Acroterion: ornaments placed at the apex and ends of a pediment of a temple.

Ambulatory: continuation of the aisles around the east end sanctuary.

Apsidal or radiating chapel: apsed chapel radiating from the ambulatory or sanctuary.

Archivolt: continuous architrave moulding on the face of the arch, following its contour.

Axial or **Lady Chapel:** chapel radiating or extending from the sanctuary dedicated to the Virgin Mary.

Barrel vaulting: most basic form of tunnel vaulting, continuous rounded or pointed profile.

Basket arch: depressed arch common to late-medieval and Renaissance architecture.

Bay: single unit of elevation between piers or columns.

Blind arcading: decorative frieze of small, interlacing, arches and intervening pilaster strips; typical of Romanesque architecture in Lombardy and West Country Transitional.

Buttress: a structural member placed along the exterior wall to reinforce and counter side thrust of a vault.

Capital: head or crowning feature of a column. In Classical architecture there are four orders: Doric, Ionic (with volutes), Corinthian (leaf decoration) and Composite (Ionic and Corinthian). Other forms include a Cushion capital (Romanesque cut from a cube) and a Crocket capital (decorated with stylised Gothic leaves terminating in volutes).

Caryatid: female figure used as a column (atlantes are male caryatids).

Clerestory: upper section of the elevation containing large windows.

Coffering: vault or ceiling decoration consisting of sunken panels.

Column: tapering shaft of stone comprising a base, shaft and capital, designed to support the entablature.

Corbel: projecting block (stone) that supports a beam or other horizontal member.

Crypt: underground chamber or chapel.

Depressed arch: three-centred arch sometimes called a basket arch.

Exedra: niche, usually semi-circular, with a bench around the wall.

Fan vaulting: all the ribs have an identical curvature resembling a fan.

Flamboyant: latest phase (15C) of French Gothic architecture; name taken from the undulating (flame-like) lines of the window tracery.

Flame ornament: ornamentation used in classical art representing a vase spewing flames.

Flying Buttress: buttress of masonry decorated with pinnacles.

Foliated scrolls: sculptural or painted ornamentation depicting foliage, often in a frieze.

Fresco: mural paintings executed on wet plaster.

Gable: triangular part of an end wall carrying a sloping roof; the term is also applied to the steeply pitched ornamental pediments of Gothic architecture.

Gallery or **tribune:** an upper storey over an aisle, opening onto the nave.

Gargoyle: waterspout projecting from the parapet often ornamented with a grotesque figure, animal or human.

Groined vault: produced by the intersection of two perpendicular tunnel vaults of identical shape.

Keystone: central stone of an arch or a rib, sometimes fashioned as a boss.

Lierne: a tertiary rib, one that neither springs from the main springers nor passes through the central boss.

Lintel, transom: horizontal beam or stone bridging an opening of a door, window.

Mullion: a vertical post dividing a window.

Obelisks: tall tapering shaft of stone (granite).

Ovolo moulding: egg-shaped decoration.

Pediment: low pitched gable over a portico, usually triangular, in Classical architecture.

Peristyle: a range of columns surrounding or engaged to the façade of a building.

Pier: solid masonry structural support as distinct from a column.

Pilaster: engaged (attached) rectangular column.

Pinnacle: small turret-like decorative feature crowning spires, buttresses.

Piscina: basin for washing the sacred vessels.

Portico: a colonnaded space in front of a façade or in an interior courtyard.

Quadripartite vaulting: one bay subdivided into four quarters or cells.

Rib vault: framework of diagonal arched ribs carrying the cells.

Rood screen: carved screen separating the chancel from the nave; rood was the Saxon word for a cross or crucifix and this might be flanked by figures of the Virgin and John the Baptist.

Rose or **wheel window:** circular Gothic traceried (stained-glass) window.

Rustication: large blocks of masonry often separated by deep joints and given bold textures (rock-faced, diamond-pointed...); commonly employed during the Renaissance.

Segment: part of a ribbed vault; compartment between the ribs.

Semicircular arch: round-headed arch.

Spire: tall pyramidal, polygonal or conical structure crowning a tower, turret or roof.

Steeple: a tall tower with a spire together; also a term applied to curious lanterns or spires in the form of a crown.

Stucco: mixture of powdered marble, plaster and strong glue; used for decoration.

Terraced houses: a continuous row of houses in a uniform style.

Thatch: a roof covering composed of straw or reeds.

Tracery: intersecting stone ribwork in the upper part of a window.

Transept: transverse section of a cross-shaped church bisecting the nave.

Transverse arch: separates one bay from another, running perpendicular to the nave axis.

Triforium: arcaded wall passage running the length of the nave above the arcade and below the clerestory.

Triptych: three panels hinged together, chiefly used as an altarpiece.

Voussoir: wedge-shaped blocks of masonry making an arch or vault.

Term: sculpted ornament consisting of a carved bust tapering to a square base pillar.

Painting

Tudor patronage – **Hans Holbein the Younger** (1497/8-1543) first came to London in 1526 with an introduction to Archbishop Warham and Sir Thomas More from the Humanist scholar Erasmus; his return in 1532 was largely prompted by the unsettled religious climate at home caused by the Reformation – his great draughtsmanship, penetrating eye and delicate colour suggest the artist's concern for capturing an accurate resemblance of physique and personality – formal portraits show the master keen to emphasise the exquisite detail of a jewel, brooch, brocade, silken velvet, fur or other such mark denoting status (*The Ambassadors* 1533, NG) – much in the manner of the 15C master Jan van Eyck (*Arnolfini Mariage* NG). Holbein joined the court of Henry VIII as a goldsmith's designer and decorator; he was subsequently sent abroad by the king charged with painting prospective brides (*Duchess of Milan* NG). **Hans Eworth** who came from Antwerp in 1549, fused his own style (*Sir John Luttrell*, Courtauld Collection) with that of Holbein, in order to be promoted to court painter by Mary I, and influence the likes of British-born **Nicholas Hilliard** (c 1547-1619) who rose to become the most eminent Elizabethan portraitist in about 1570. Having been apprenticed to a goldsmith, Hilliard's jewel-like precise style was eminently suited to miniature painting: he further secured his position by writing a technical treatise on *The Arte of Limning* (first published in 1912) which records discussions on portraiture with Queen Elizabeth I (notably condemning the use of shadow) and outlines the intellectual dimension of this sophisticated art enhanced by the use of conceits copied from contemporary poetry (works in the Wallace Collection, V&A and Tate Gallery). His greatest disciple and later rival was **Isaac Oliver** (d 1617) who travelled extensively, either as a result of Huguenot persecution or in search of work, to London, France and Italy (Venice).

The Stuarts – A move away from the Elizabethan 'costume-pieces' came with a change in royal dynasties from the Tudor to the Stuart and a shift in artistic awareness: Thomas Howard, Earl of Arundel, Charles I and George Villiers, Duke of Buckingham emerge as three great patrons of the age: driven by their genuine love of art, they sponsored the architect Inigo Jones, and the painters Paul van Somer, Daniel Mytens and Cornelius Johnson before the arrival of Van Dyck in England (1632). Prince Charles's interest was sparked off by an impromptu visit to Spain to woo the Infanta (1623), accompanied by the Duke of Buckingham, the future king was enamoured by the power of paintings by such masters as Titian, Velasquez, Rubens – an experience that resulted in the king acquiring the great Mantua collection that included Mantegna's *Triumphs of Caesar.*

Religious troubles continued to provoke restlessness on the continent, and artists were obliged to seek patrons where they could. **Van Somer** settled in London in 1616 and quickly found favour at the court (*Queen Anne of Denmark*, 1617, Royal Collection); he is buried at St Martin-in-the-Fields. **Daniel Mytens** came to England in c 1618 from The Hague bringing a new sense of confidence both in his bold style of painting and the stances given to his subjects; he was appointed Painter to Charles I in 1625, who sent him back to the Low Countries to get acquainted with the current standards of Royal portraiture. To complement the public image, London-born **Cornelius Johnson** (1593-1661), a master of technique, painted in an honest, naturalistic way, setting his bust portraits in an oval like an intimate cameo. He, together with Mytens, was superseded in popularity by **Sir Anthony van Dyck** (1599-1641) whose full length official portraits project an air of gracious ease and elegance, synonymous with the Restoration of peace after the Civil Wars. Van Dyck's Baroque compositions are a symphony of colour and texture – shimmering silk set against a matt complexion, heavily draped curtains contrast with solid objects that might represent a distinctive attribute pertinent to the sitter (a sword for military might). His brushstrokes are less bold than those of his master Rubens for whom he served as chief assistant before coming to London in 1620, tempered, perhaps, by four years spent in Italy surveying collections in Rome, Florence, Venice, Palermo, Genoa and perfecting his technique. Certainly his portraits of the English royal family set a bench-mark for future generations perpetuated through Dobson, Lely, Reynolds, Gainsborough, Romney, Lawrence... (*Charles I in Three Positions* Royal Collection, *Charles I on Horseback* NG).

'The most excellent painter England hath yet bred', **William Dobson** (1610-46), was born in London and grew up to become a staunch Cavalier (Royalist). His portraiture is less refined than Van Dyck's whom he succeeded as court painter, his robust, natural style having been formulated from studying Charles I's collection of Italian pictures: for his portrait of *Endymion Porter* (Tate Gallery) he adopts Titian's pose for the Roman Emperor Vespasian; the attributes denote the sitter's patronage of the arts: spiritual (contemplative) inspiration of the Greek god Apollo, placed in the top left corner presides over Pallas Athene, the goddess of the arts and science (and of war), and allegories of Painting, Sculpture and Poetry represented by the frieze upon which Porter leans; in contrast, the opposite diagonal axis highlights the man's active prowess and accomplishments as a respected huntsman and keeper of the land.

Sir **Peter Lely** (1618-1680) was born in Germany of Dutch parentage. His early works (1640s) in England show him to be painting narrative religious pieces. At the Restoration he succeeded Van Dyck as Principal Painter to Charles II (1661). His studio expanded to produce endless stylised portraits which proliferated the image of languorous Beauty (*Windsor Beauties* at Hampton Court) or masculine Admiralty (*Flagmen* at Greenwich) so typical of that era: one celebrating virtue, the other victory in the Second Dutch War. Fame brought success and demand, his studio prepared the basic canvas according to a numbered formula and the master then filled-in the personality of his sitter's face and hands. His 'history' pictures meanwhile satisfied a less prudish market depicting the same modish voluptuous ladies (*Sleeping Nymphs* at Dulwich) in more sensual poses. He was buried at St Paul's, Covent Garden on 7 December 1680.

The reign of James II saw the appointment of a new Principal Painter, **Sir Godfrey Kneller** (1646/9-1723), who had studied in Holland under a pupil of Rembrandt's and travelled to Italy before settling in London (1676). Successive official portraits in the style of Lely are dignified if not beautiful in the Classical sense; well-executed, they conform to a taste for formality and noble bearing (42 portraits known as the Kit-Cat series showing the head and one hand, *see NATIONAL PORTRAIT GALLERY*). It should be remembered that the three monarchs (George I, II and III) under whom Kneller was to serve were famed not only for their lack of good looks but also for their lack of connoisseurship. Demand for portraits was such in the 18C, however, that large numbers of assistants were trained and employed in an organised studio that was to provide a prototype for the institution of a Royal Academy in 1711.

Decorative schemes – In 1635 **Peter Paul Rubens** (1577-1640) completed the ceiling of the Banqueting House in Whitehall: this was a complex allegorical painting commissioned by Charles I, the only decorative scheme undertaken in England by the painter-diplomat during his service as Court Painter to the Spanish Court of the Netherlands. Rubens evolved his highly energetic Baroque style from studying works by Titian, Raphael, Velasquez in royal collections in Mantua, Rome, Genoa, Milan, Madrid... he therefore epitomised the best of contemporary continental art: the impact on the English court of this bold political celebration of Charles's kingship should not be underestimated, nor should his influence on subsequent court painters be dismissed.

Lesser decorative schemes for stairways and panelled ceilings were undertaken by foreign artists, paid by the square foot: **Antonio Verrio**, a vulgar, pretentious and extravagant personality who prided himself on being a Neapolitan, is registered in the service of the Crown from 1676 until 1688 at Windsor, St James's Palace and Whitehall (later at Chatsworth, Burghley House) before returning to Windsor and Hampton Court where he died in 1705. **Louis Laguerre** was more reserved: born at Versailles, he was trained in the Classical French tradition before coming to England at the behest of the Duke of Montagu, special Ambassador in Paris, who was building Montagu House in Bloomsbury. **Pellegrini**, a follower of Ricci and brother-in-law of Rosalba Carriera, was invited to England by the Earl of Manchester, then British Ambassador in Venice to work at Castle Howard with Vanbrugh; he later became a founding member of the Royal Academy. The Venetian **Sebastiano Ricci** was responsible for the dome painting at Chelsea Hospital and a pair of large mythologies that hang in Burlington House. The great skill of these craftsmen, their ability to suggest luminosity and movement on a grand scale have secured their reputation as well as that of **Sir James Thornhill** (1675/6-1734), the British Baroque master of decorative painting who followed their example when engaged to undertake such important commissions as the Painted Hall at Greenwich, the Prince's Apartments at Hampton Court and the dome of St Paul's Cathedral (sketches in the Tate Gallery). Taste veered away from this French art in the manner of Lebrun only when the Neo-Classical designer **William Kent** managed to clinch the commission to decorate Kensington Palace with Lord Burlington's intervention.

Landscape – **William van de Velde** was an official war artist employed by the Dutch navy to document battles against the British fleet. Works at Greenwich confirm his ability to record precise detail – a quality that no doubt endeared him to the British authorities who persuaded him to switch sides and work for them; in 1674 he and his son William were given a studio in the Queen's House at Greenwich. Of the two, however, it is the younger William who left the more lasting impression on the evolution of British marine painting, happy as he was, to paint tranquil topographical riverside views as well as warships at sea (National Maritime Museum Collection). Meanwhile, other Dutch painters specialised in recording such social events as hunting scenes and the construction of major buildings; this generated a taste in sporting pictures, decorative still-lives with game and flowers, topographical landscapes: genres that were to flourish throughout the 18C.

18C – The Age of Enlightenment promoted connoisseurship in the Italian art of the Renaissance and Classical art from Antiquity either from travel to the continent to study the styles at first hand or from drawings, engravings and folios which proliferated at this time; another, less intellectual but no less accomplished influence, came from Versailles in the form of a highly decorative French Baroque. Taste was a matter for stimulated debate much as were the politics of the day; preference for a particular style, therefore, varied from patron to patron.

In 1757 this freedom of choice was reinforced as **Edmund Burke** published his treatise *A Philosophical Enquiry into the Origin of Our Ideas of the Sublime and Beautiful.* The **Sublime** was defined as an artistic effect that could provoke the mind to respond with the greatest emotional feeling: 'whatever is in any sort terrible or is conversant about terrible objects or operates in a manner analogous to terror is a source of the Sublime'. The impact of this work was considerable both in Burke's own life time and on subsequent generations. In the Romantic era it prompted a recognition of man's vulnerability and sensitivity to external forces; in the modern context the theory endorsed the artist's license to see his art (poetry, prose, visual art) as a personal expression of emotion, and therefore subject to his own sense of esthetics.

William Hogarth (1697-1764). Apprenticed as an engraver, Hogarth struggled to earn respect and recognition for his work: despite striving to establish what he called 'high art' or 'history' painting, it was his 'conversation' pieces like *The Beggar's Opera* that made him popular. In his treatise *The Analysis of Beauty* (1753) he upholds the importance of a national style at a time when foreign artists were achieving greater success; he propounded theories on naturalism, observing that figures conform to standard expressions, gestures and stances appropriate to age (the seven ages described by Shakespeare in *As You Like It* for example); he advocated the use of the serpentine line as a basis of artistic harmony and beauty in composition (inscribed on his palette in his self-portrait in the Tate). Although ill-received at home, his theories were translated into German within a month.

Perhaps Hogarth's greatest follower was **Thomas Rowlandson** (1756-1827), a fine caricaturist and supreme draughtsman who went to Paris at the age of 16 before enrolling at the RA School. An inveterate gambler, he dissipated the fortune left him by his Parisian aunt and was forced to turn his hand at producing pictures drawn from low-life and populist subjects. His talent is Rococo in its freshness, although the humour and wit are undoubtedly English.

George Lambert (1700-65). The precursor of Richard Wilson is widely regarded as 'the father of British oil landscape', although his pictures were often executed in collaboration with a figure-painter (Hogarth) or a marine-painter (Scott) who painted details into his landscapes as required. The practice was probably regarded as quite acceptable at the time as Lambert was engaged as a scenery painter at Covent Garden and regarded landscape as a picturesque artifice that was moulded and arranged to suit the subject: much as William Kent set out to order 'untamed' landscapes nurtured by Mother Nature into parks and gardens that provided bowers, vistas and mazes on a human scale.

> ### Antonio Canaletto (1697-1768)
>
> During the 1740s, the War of the Austrian Succession prevented British noblemen from undertaking the Grand Tour: Italian artists like Antonio Joli and Antonio Canaletto who had hitherto relied on their patronage decided therefore to come to England (1746-56). Engaged by the Duke of Richmond, Canaletto transposed the sparkle and lucidity of the Venetian landscape to reaches of the Thames (Canaletto pictures are to be found in the Sir John Soane Museum, and the collections of the Bank of England, Courtauld Institute, National Gallery...).

Richard Wilson (c 1713-82) was given a classical education by his father. When he arrived in London in the 1740s he came as a portrait painter although early landscapes survive from 1746 (Coram Foundling Hospital Collection). In 1750 he is recorded working in and around Rome, forging a new style in the tradition of **Claude** and Vernet illustrating idyllic landscapes composed of clumped trees and buildings that might be linked with serpentine paths or rivers and populated with figures (usually drawn from Classical literature or mythology). On his return to England, the Roman Campania gently gave way to views of his own green and pleasant land, noted and admired by Sir Horace Walpole – who had complained in his *Anecdotes of Painting in England* (1765) at the lack of good painters capable of recording England's 'ever-verdant lawns, rich vales, fields of haycocks...'

Sir Joshua Reynolds (1723-92) is a key figure in the development of British painting: the son of an educated Devon family, he was the first painter not to be a mere tradesman-cum-craftsman, but a respected figure associated with the circles of Dr Johnson, David Garrick, Goldsmith and Burke. He trained under Thomas Hudson, a rather provincial if prolific portraitist and drew inspiration from Van Dyck and the Old Master paintings known in England by engravings (Rembrandt self-portrait) or posing his sitters according to Classical statues from Antiquity (Apollo Belvedere). 1752-54 he spent in Rome with his friend Commodore (later Admiral Viscount) Keppel; there he was able to study the intellectual basis of High Renaissance Art. Returning to London via Venice, he resolved to merge the taste for the Italian 'Grand Style' with the demand for 'face-painting' at home.

In 1768 he was rewarded with the Presidentship of the new Royal Academy; over the course of the following 25 years he delivered his fifteen Discourses outlining in the most lucid terms the way a British School of History might be forged. He advocated devoted study to the understanding of the Rules of Art and the analysis of the ideas of predecessors in arriving at modern composition. The history-portraits he exhibited at the Royal Academy endorsed his theories (*Three Ladies Adorning a Term of Hymen – The Montgomery Sisters* in the Tate Gallery) and provoked a shift in fashion towards simple Neo-Classical 'nightdresses' rather than comfortable billowing gowns of damask.

At his death the position of Painter to the King was taken by **Sir Thomas Lawrence** (1769-1830). Lawrence was commissioned by the Prince Regent, later George IV, to paint portraits of all the leading men who had opposed Napoleon; a large collection of sovereigns and statesmen now hang in Windsor Castle.

Thomas Gainsborough (1727-88). Reynolds' principal competitor Gainsborough developed his own very natural style of portraiture, while painting landscapes and 'fancy pictures' for his personal pleasure. Shortly after he married (1740s) he returned to his native Sudbury in Suffolk before moving to Ipswich, to Bath (1759) and then to London (1774) in the wake of Fashionable Society. In Bath, his portraits become more assured, full-length, life-size and set in arcadian gardens. His landscapes meanwhile echo the Dutch style of Hobbema and Ruisdael, whose works he had been employed to restore during his early years in London. The rich palette used for his wooded country scenes, meanwhile, is evidently drawn from Rubens: at first glance these small pictures seem to exude naturalism although in reality, the composition is carefully contrived to accommodate pathways that open out into vistas, hence their collective classification as 'fancy pictures'. Gainsborough's textured rendering of foliage preempts Constable while his skilled technique of diluting oil paint into turpentine washes and using this medium to capture haze and flickering light foreshadows Turner.

George Stubbs (1724-1806) began as a portrait painter while studying anatomy in York, where he lectured medical students and published a book about midwifery. He visited Rome in 1754 in order to prove that the study of art was secondary to the observation of Nature; there he wit-

Sporting pictures

At this time as the fashion for stag-hunting waned, fox hunting gained popularity: from this evolved an interest in horse racing and the breeding of effective hunters and hounds, and so evolved a demand for animal portraiture.

nessed a horse being devoured by a lion, a scene that was to haunt him and provide inspiration for several works for years to come. On his return to England, true to the spirit of the Age of the Enlightenment, he applied himself to the study of the skeleton and musculature of the horse by minute observation, dissection and from Renaissance drawings with a view to publishing his *Anatomy of a Horse* in 1766. In 1795 he began an analytical and comparative Study of Tiger, Man and Fowl having fallen out with the RA authorities.

Stubbs painted in oils, but preferred to use enamels because of their assured durability, even if the medium demanded an exacting and meticulous technique more traditionally associated with miniature painting. Finding himself restricted by size when using copper plate, Stubbs turned to Wedgwood, the industrial potter, to help him develop a type of ceramic panel that would not warp when fired at high temperatures.

Mr and Mrs Andrews: Thomas Gainsborough

19C – By the turn of the 18C, American independence had been recognised, Parliamentary union of Great Britain and Ireland had been agreed (1800), in 1802 the Treaty of Amiens sealed a (temporary) end to war with France and in 1807 slavery was abolished throughout the British colonies: the age of reform and development had begun.

John Constable (1776-1834). Constable developed his personal style and technique from observation and experimentation: his landscapes suggest topographical accuracy *(Salisbury Cathedral, Hampstead Heath)* when in fact realism has been compromised for the sake of art: trees, perspective or other such elements are contrived to better the overall composition, which in turn is unified by *chiaroscuro* (patches of light and shade) much in the manner of Claude and Gainsborough. Constable refused to depend upon formal patronage, in his own words: 'my art flatters nobody by imitation, it courts nobody by smoothness... how then can I hope to be popular'. He therefore was able to explore a new almost revolutionary relationship between man and the landscape, contradicting the 18C view of Nature as a force to appease and tame rather than accept and admire for its own sake: in Constable's words 'We exist but in a landscape and we are the creatures of a landscape'. He considered how to convey the atmosphere of a pastoral landscape (*Hay Wain*, National Gallery) by comparison to the fear and dread of a storm at sea much in the way authors were reviewing their descriptions of Nature in literature (Burke, Austen, Wordsworth); it is interesting to note how, from 1828, after the death of his wife Maria, Constable seems to betray a fascination for sombre skies and disturbed seas almost as if in protest against the forces of nature. In this way Constable conveyed in landscape as much drama as any grand gesture or emotion in 'high art' (Painting is a science, and should be pursued as an enquiry into the laws of nature). He arrived at his theories by sketching from nature – in oil, a medium which took time to dry and therefore intensified his awareness of fleeting effects of light, ephemeral phenomena like rainbows and transient cloud patterns and formations. He began exhibiting work at the RA in 1802 but his work met with little success, he therefore resolved to compete in terms of size and embarked upon a series of 'six-footers' (*Flatford Mill* in the Tate Gallery) for which he was forced to make scale sketches. In 1816 he settled permanently in London, spending the summer months in Hampstead and capturing scenes of kite flying high on the heath.

In 1824 he was awarded gold medals for two pictures exhibited at the Paris Salon *(Hay Wain* NG; *View on the Stour)*, which provoked great interest from the members of the Barbizon School of outdoor painters and artists associated with the Romantic Movement, notably Delacroix who later came to England in 1825 to discuss with Constable his observations on his use of colour: 'Constable says that the superiority of the green in his meadows comes from it being composed of a multitude of different greens. The lack of intensity and life in the foliage of most landscape painters arises because they usually paint them in a uniform tone'... effects are further enhanced by splashes of red and flecks of pure white.

Watercolour is a medium that found particular favour with English artists who found it a suggestive means of capturing changing qualities of light or the distance through rolling green fields to a far horizon and blue sky; for travellers on the Grand Tour it provided an efficient way of recording atmospheric details to complement topographical pencil drawings or thumb-nail sketches before the advent of photography (hence **John Ruskin's** near-obsessional realism). Unlike continental predecessors, the English artists used opaque white paper which, if left blank, provided bright highlights. The leading water-colourists include Paul Sandby (1725-1809) – 'the only man of genius' capable of painting 'real views from Nature in this country', J R Cozens (1752-97), J M W Turner (1775-1851) and **Thomas Girtin** (1775-1802) who as a young man copied Canaletto and studied drawing with Turner under Dr Munro before travelling to Paris. The large panoramic view of London which he exhibited in 1802, *The Eidometropolis* is now lost, but a number of his sketches survive in the British Museum. After Girtin's death from asthma or tuberculosis, Turner is said to have remarked 'Had Tom Girtin lived, I should have starved'.

Drawings and illustration – Romantic poetry and sensitivity to the forces of Nature were popularised by translations of foreign literature: Winckelmann, Goethe, Voltaire, Rousseau, Baudelaire, Poe, while Beethoven and Wagner worked similar themes into music. In art, **Henry Fuseli** (1741-1825) explored the realms of the imagination, dreams and nightmares, full of drama and extravagant movement, stylised form in vivid if horrifying detail *(Lady Macbeth Seizing the Daggers)*: in 1787 he met the visionary poet **William Blake** (1757-1827) living in Lambeth, whose spirit contradicts the Age of Reason and heralds the advent of Romanticism. A large collection of Blake's works on paper is to be found at the Tate Gallery.

Joseph Mallord William Turner (1775-1851) – Born the son of a London barber, Turner showed precocious talent at painting topographical watercolours: by 1790 his work was hanging at the RA; six years later his *Fishermen at Sea* demonstrated his ability to handle oil and to show man in a natural world that was full of light, moving water and changing sky. Subsequent paintings confirmed his preoccupation with the same themes: *Snowstorm, Shipwreck* 1805; *Snowstorm, Hannibal and his army crossing the Alps.* Meanwhile he continued to produce atmospheric studies of landscape (*London from Greenwich* 1809).

41

He went to France and Switzerland visually cataloguing his impressions as he went for use later; in 1819 he journeyed to Italy, followed by subsequent visits in 1828, 1833, 1840... These sketch-books contain evocative studies of climate, as Turner managed to suggest reflected sunlight, its blinding brilliance, its translucence and somehow its transience *(Norham Castle, Sunrise)*. In 1842 his Romantic predisposition to experience 'atmosphere' at first hand before rendering it in paint was pushed to extremes: the drama captured in *Steamboat off a Harbour's Mouth* resulted from the artist insisting on being strapped to the mast of a ship pitching at sea in squally weather...

Turner also studied the work of Claude, the first artist really to attempt to paint the sun at dusk setting over rippling water: in his will he stipulated that his large canvases *Dido building Carthage or The Rise of the Carthaginian Empire* and *Sun Rising Through Vapour* or *Fishermen Cleaning and Selling Fish* be hung alongside two views by Claude entitled *Seaport with the Embarkation of the Queen of Sheba* and *The Mill – Landscape with the Marriage of Isaac with Rebekah* (as they do in the National Gallery).

Pre-Raphaelite Brotherhood – The initials PRB began to suffix Rossetti's signature in 1849 following discussions between the coterie of RA School artists **W H Hunt** (1827-1910), **D G Rossetti** (1828-82) and his brother William, **J E Millais** (1829-96), Collinson, the sculptor Woolner and Stephens. All young and Romantic in temperament, the Pre-Raphaelites considered the 15C Renaissance paintings by Raphael to be already too sophisticated and over-praised: they therefore sought to develop a style that might have predated Raphael insisting on serious subject-matter, elaborate symbolism charged with poetic allusion, strong colour (pure pigment applied to a white ground) heightened by outdoor natural light and meticulous detail. Instead of using ground pigment on wet plaster (fresco), they applied their paint to wet, white sized canvas. The key to their success came with Ruskin's defence of their art before harsh criticism from Charles Dickens (especially directed at Millais' *Christ in the House of his Parents*, better known as *The Carpenter's Shop*, Tate Gallery). During the early 1850s, the group was dissolved: Millais to aspire to President of the Royal Academy, Rossetti to associate with William Morris and Burne-Jones, and Hunt to travel to Egypt, Palestine and the Holy Land in search of topographical settings for his Biblical subjects (one version of *The Light of the World* hangs in St Paul's Cathedral).

Associated in style but independent of the Brotherhood is Sir **Edward Burne-Jones** (1833-98), a fine technician with an excellent sense of style and visual appeal honed by travels in Italy with Ruskin for whom he executed a number of studies of Tintoretto (1862); the influences of Mantegna and Botticelli are also apparent in his flat and linear designs for tapestries and stained glass windows. In a similar vein and as accomplished are the members of the Aesthetic Movement *(see Inner London: TATE GALLERY)* whose age was immortalised in **Oscar Wilde's** *Portrait of Dorian Gray*: Frederic, Lord Leighton (1830-96), Albert Moore (1841-1893) and Whistler.

Foreign Artists – **J A McNeill Whistler** (1834-1903) trained as a Navy cartographer, hence his etching skills, before going to Paris to study painting. In 1859 he moved to London and earned notoriety for falling out with his patron over the Peacock Room decor (now in the Freer Gallery, Washington), and later with Ruskin who accused the painter of 'flinging a pot of paint in the public's face' when he exhibited *Nocturne in Black and Gold* (now in Detroit): he won the court case that ensued and was awarded a farthing in damages but the costs bankrupted him and he was forced to leave for Venice. Having been influenced by Courbet, Fantin-Latour, Degas and Manet during his life in Paris, Whistler introduced new perspectives to Victorian England, notably in the form of Japanese art.

J S Sargent (1856-1925) was both talented and prolific: born of American expatriate parents in Italy, Sargent eventually settled in London to paint his vivid portraits and capture the elegance of Edwardian High Society with all its brilliance and sparkle.

French Impressionism came to England in the form of a large exhibition put on in London in 1883: the Impressionists used pure pigments to capture the effects of bright sunlight on coloured forms; vibrancy was achieved by contrasting complementary shades (green with red, magenta with yellow, orange with blue); texture and movement were suggested by bold brushstrokes. Simple family scenes, informal portraiture and landscape provided them with engaging subject matter.

The portrayal of circus performers and cabaret entertainers for what they are was explored by Degas, Seurat and Toulouse Lautrec, in turn they provided subjects for Walter Sickert and Aubrey Beardsley.

Rebellion – In 1886 the New English Art Club was founded to provide a platform for artists ostracised by the Royal Academy: Philip Wilson **Steer** (1860-1942) and **Walter Sickert** (1860-1942) went on to set up an alternative exhibition entitled London Impressionists, at the Goupil Gallery.

20C – In 1910, the critic and painter **Roger Fry** organised a major show of modern French art: *Manet and the Post-Impressionists* comprised 21 works by Cézanne, 37 by Gauguin, 20 by Van Gogh and others by Manet, Matisse and Picasso. In 1912 he organised another dedicated to Cubist art and large compositions by Matisse: *Second Post-Impressionist Exhibition*.

Augustus John's reputation as a leader in modern British Art hinged on *The Smiling Woman*, a portrait of his mistress exhibited in 1909: a famous series of contemporary luminaries followed.

Sickert conforms with the philosophy of Impressionism which he assimilated while living in Paris. In 1905 he moved back to London, settling at 8 Fitzroy Street and founding the Fitzroy Street Group in 1907 from no 19. Three years later, having been drawn back to his favourite areas around Camden and Islington, he produced a series of works depicting the Old Bedford Music Hall, painting its performers, stage and audience with sympathy much in the tradition of Degas and Toulouse Lautrec *(Ennui, La Hollandaise);* in 1911 he founded the **Camden Town Group** which attracted Robert Bevan, Spencer Gore, Harold Gilman, Charles Ginner. Bold colour, strong outlines and broad brushstrokes were dedicated to depicting the urban landscape.

The **Bloomsbury Group** collected together writers and artists: the biographer Lytton Strachey, the economist Keynes, novelist Virginia Woolf, her publisher husband Leonard Woolf, Clive Bell, Henry Tonks, Marc Gertler and the members of the **Omega Workshop**. Vanessa Bell, Roger Fry and Duncan Grant all used bright colour to delineate bold form in the manner of Matisse; by 1914 they were experimenting with abstraction.

The **Vorticists**, lead by Wyndham Lewis and acclaimed by Ezra Pound, responded to Cubism and the dynamics of Futurism in painting and sculpture – Jessica Desmorr, Epstein, Gaudier-Brzeska were later joined in spirit by David Bomberg. Strong axes, parallel lines, harsh angles, stepped geometric forms, lurid colours proliferate, mesmerising the eye.

Pure Abstraction inspired Nicholson, Moore, Hepworth, Nash who explored form in relation to landscape: they considered the impact of Stonehenge, rounded pebbles so suggestive of the power and expanse of the ocean, reinforcing the image of Britain as an island... In 1936 the International Surrealist Exhibition was held in London, a highpoint in London's avant-garde artistic circles which also included at that time Ivon Hitchens.

Among post-war artists are Graham Sutherland, painter of religious themes, landscapes and portraits as well as scenes of urban devastation; Sir Stanley Spencer whose visionary Biblical scenes are set in familiar surroundings and who explored eroticism as a means of exorcising the violence of war. Peter Blake, David Hockney and Bridget Riley were the exuberant exponents of **Pop Art** while the disturbing portraits and figures of Francis Bacon and Lucien Freud evoke a darker outlook. The Tate Gallery, Whitchapel Gallery and Saatchi Gallery put on shows by artists such as Gilbert and George, Paula Rego, Beryl Cooke, Julian Opie, Damien Hirst among others, exploring new idioms – collages, installations which challenge preconceptions and at times provoke strong reactions.

Sculpture

In sculpture the evolution from Gothic tomb effigies to modern abstract form begins with William **Torel**, citizen and goldsmith of London, who modelled Henry III and Eleanor of Castile (1291-92), and the visiting (1511-20) early Renaissance Florentine **Torrigiano**, who cast the gilt bronze figures of Henry VII (in the V & A), his queen Elizabeth and mother Margaret, Duchess of Richmond. After the Reformation, contact with Italy was suspended, dominant influences are therefore imported from France and Flanders.

Actual portraiture appears in the 17C in the works of, among others, Nicholas Stone (John Donne), the French Huguenot **Le Sueur** (bronzes of Charles I and James I) and **Grinling Gibbons** (statues of Charles II and James II). Gibbons is better known and celebrated as a wood-carver of genius and great delicacy, who often signed his work with a peapod.

In the 18C, as a Classical style began to appeal to graduates of the Grand Tour, the Flemings, Michael Rysbrack and Peter Scheemakers, the Frenchman François **Roubiliac**, the Englishmen John Bacon, John **Flaxman** and Nollekens executed hundreds of figures, many with considerable strength of character, until the genre became stylised and empty in the 19C. Many examples of their work are to be found in the nave and north transept of Westminster Abbey.

Vigour began to return in the 20C in portraiture and religious sculptures with works by Jacob **Epstein**, in human, near abstract and abstract themes by Henry **Moore**, and pure abstract by Barbara **Hepworth**. In the 1930s after Dada and Surrealism had swept through Paris touching all forms of artistic consciousness, a number of painters, sculptors and architects emigrated, several moving to Hampstead which hosted a new move towards pure abstraction: Roland Penrose, Lee Miller, Henry Moore, Barbara Hepworth, Ben Nicholson (the spirit of these times is best encapsulated at 2 Willow Road, at the private home of Erno Goldfinger).

Grinling Gibbons: Limewood wreath

Some fine contemporary sculpture adorns the open spaces created by modern town planning: the *Horses of Helios*, the Sun God, with the three Graces above, by Rudi Weller (corner of the Haymarket and Piccadilly Circus); *Boy with a dolphin* in bronze by David Wynne (north end of Albert Bridge in Chelsea and outside the Tower Hotel in Wapping); *Fulcrum* by Richard Serra (Broadgate); *Shepherd and Sheep* (1975) by Elisabeth Frink (Paternoster Square); a *Dancer* (Bow Street opposite the Royal Opera House); *Horse* by Shirley Pace (The Circle, Bermondsey); *The Navigators* by David Kemp (Hays Galleria, Southwark).

Collectively displayed along the embankments, Parliament Square (General de Gaulle, Winston Churchill) and Leicester Square (Charlie Chaplin).

Decorative arts

FURNITURE

Antique English furniture has long enjoyed favour. Distinctive types have evolved to suit changes in lifestyle and tastes in dress. Influences have been exerted by waves of craftsmen seeking refuge from Holland or France, and by the arrival of foreign pieces from Japan, China, India or other far corner of the Empire. The most complete display is to be found in the Victoria and Albert Museum, while most of the large houses provide period contexts in which original fixtures, fittings and furnishings may be appreciated (Ham, Osterley, Kenwood, Fenton).

The height of English furniture-making came in the 18C when the greatest transformation occurred: oak was replaced by imported mahogany and later by tropical satinwood, before a return was made to native walnut. These new woods were embellished not only with carving but also with enrichments of brass in the form of inlays and gilded mounts, hardwood veneers and marquetry.

A handful of names dominates English furniture of the period. **Thomas Chippendale** (1718-79), was the son of a carpenter. He married and settled in St Martin's Lane and is recorded as importing uncompleted furniture from France which his workshops then finished off (1769). His reputation as the pre-eminent cabinetmaker of his day, famed for a classical sureness of style, was secured by his publication of *The Gentleman and Cabinet Maker's Director* (1754). It illustrated a comprehensive range of household furniture, predominantly Rococo in style, cataloguing impossible concepts alongside prototypes poached from Continental and rivals' pattern books. Perhaps the most original Chippendale designs were made for the great Neo-Classical houses designed or remodelled by Robert Adam and his contemporaries, by the second Thomas Chippendale (1749-1822) who went on to produce an anglicised version of Louis XVI and archetypal Regency furniture. **John Linnell** (1729-96) also inherited his father's business. He began as a carver but soon expanded his workshops in Berkeley Square to include cabinet-making and upholstery. His reputation was secured by his association with William Kent, Robert Adam and Henry Holland (mirrors and chairs). The partnership of **William Vile** (1700-67) and **John Cobb** (1751-1778) produced the most

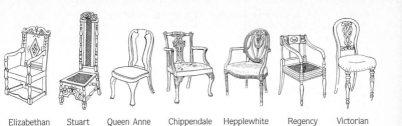

| Elizabethan | Stuart | Queen Anne | Chippendale | Hepplewhite | Regency | Victorian |

outstanding pieces, certainly better crafted than Chippendale if less original. He was a favourite of the Prince of Wales, who on becoming George III appointed Vile cabinet-maker to the Royal Household.

George Hepplewhite (d 1786) achieved widespread recognition two years after his death when *The Cabinet Maker and Upholsterer's Guide* was published. This codified 300 designs suited to Neo-Classical interiors: best epitomising, some say, the application of Adam's principles of uniting elegance with utility. As intended, it became the standard handbook for country gentlemen commissioning furniture from artisans. Hepplewhite pieces are therefore considered as country furniture, simple, rational, extremely elegant and stylish. Typical features include bow-fronted and serpentine chests of drawers, oval, heart-shaped and shield-back chairs usually with straight or tapered legs; Prince of Wales feathers and wheat-ear central splats are also characteristic.

Post-Hepplewhite but pre-Regency comes **Thomas Sheraton** (1751-1806) whose rectilin-ear designs dominate the 1790s, a perfect foil to Adam's delicate, intricate yet restrained interior stucco-work. His designs are recorded in *The Cabinet-Maker and Upholsterer's Drawing-Book* (1791-94) addressed primarily to the trade, and sub-sequently in two further less-successful publications. He particularly exploits and celebrates the grain and textures of wood with contrasting inlays, relief panels and highly polished surfaces. Inspiration is drawn from Louis XVI furniture, notably for such subjects as small, rather feminine worktables, beautiful sideboards, secretaires and full-height bookcases. He also produced many 'harlequin' or dual purpose items such as library tables containing hidden stepladders.

The Goliath of Victorian taste is undoubt-edly **William Morris** (1834-96) whose firm of Art Decorators at Merton Abbey supplied the full gamut of furnishings: furniture – mostly designed by Philip Webb, textiles, wallpapers, carpets, curtains, tapestries often in collaboration with Burne-Jones, tiles, candlesticks and brassware. Many designs were collated by Morris himself who drew his inspiration from historic pat-terns found in churches, paintings or book illumination and natural forms. Some Arts and Crafts work, which was based on craftsmanship and pre-industrial techniques, is on show at the William Morris Gallery *(see index)*.

In the following generation, Sir Ambrose Heal (1872-1959) became known for simple solid oak furniture, sometimes inlaid with pewter and ebony often associated with Charles Voysey. His niche market was supplying middle-class homes with inexpen-sive alternatives to flimsy reproduction or expensive Arts and Crafts furniture; a niche-market now supplied by Conran and Habitat.

CERAMICS

Tin-glazed earthenware – The **Lambeth Potteries**, founded in c 1601 are most often associated with a characteristic dark blue

John Adam: Etruscan decor at Osterley

earthenware with a raised white ornamentation thereafter known as **Lambeth delft**; during the 18C decoration was influenced by Chinoiseries – a European interpretation of Chinese designs.

The leading factory throughout the early 17C was the **Southwark Potteries**, founded by a Dutchman Christian Wilhelm in 1618. In 1628 he secured a 14-year monopoly for producing blue and white pieces fashioned in imitation of Chinese Ming, preempting the fashion for Delft in the 1660s. On the whole the painting is judged heavy-handed.

Porcelain – The **Bow Factory** (identified by a variety of marks – incised, impressed or painted in underglazed blue and/or red), together with that at Chelsea were the first porcelain factories in England. Its early history is uncertain; it was founded by an Irish painter Thomas Frye with a glass-merchant Edward Heylyn in the East End (Stratford Langthorne). In 1744 it registered a patent for wares crafted from a white clay (unaker) imported from America. Records show **soft-paste porcelain** being made by 1748 when Frye also patented the use of bone ash to make **bone-china** – a softer material than hard-paste, cheaper to manufacture and more durable than soft-paste. The height of production (1750-59) seems to come just prior to Frye's retirement. Early pieces include plain white figures, while receptacles appear to have been decorated with sprigs of flowers and foliage or painted underglazed-blue or enamelled with colour (Kakiemon quail pattern) or transfers. In 1775 the factory was bought by William Duesbury and amalgamated with the Derby factory.

The earliest pieces identified with the **Chelsea Factory** (incised with a triangle) are marked and dated 1745, most modelled on shapes then current for silver plate. The name 'soft-paste' derives from the texture and translucence of the material, similar to white glass, as demonstrated to the Royal Society in 1742 by one Thomas Briand. After the first manager Charles Gouyon departed, the concern was headed by Nicholas Sprimont, a silversmith of Flemish Huguenot origin (raised anchor period 1749-52 followed by the red anchor period 1752-58. The factory closed 1757/8 before re-opening with the gold anchor mark 1758-69). From 1750-70 the factory enjoyed great commercial prosperity, owing to the high technical quality of the product and the adoption of new colours, including a red tint known as claret: influence shifts from Meissen prototypes – attractive, animated figures, Sir Hans Sloane's botanical specimen plants to a taste for French Sèvres. Despite the flavour of Continental Rococo, the highly varied Chelsea wares (vegetable tureens, fruit containers, vases, chandeliers, figurines, busts, flasks etc) are somehow very English, their style painted decoration being highly naturalistic.

In 1770 the factory came under the ownership of William Duesbury and in 1784 the Chelsea business was moved to Derby (marked with an anchor, and the letter D during the Chelsea-Derby period 1770-84). For definitions of ceramic types *see* VICTORIA AND ALBERT MUSEUM.

METALWORK

Gold and silver – English gold and silversmiths were already known for their work in the Middle Ages and by 1180 they had formed a guild in London. In the Elizabethan period the pieces produced showed a bold and elegant line which gave way to greater austerity in the reign of James I. Pewter, considered as poorman's silver, followed the same trend.

The 17C was an extravagant period for London silver which was particularly influenced by Dutch Baroque. Under Charles II the French style predominated as highly skilled Huguenots (Protestant Calvinists) were expelled from France following the Revocation of the Edict of Nantes (18 October 1685).

Under Queen Anne, in the early 18C, Dutch silver design ceded to more sophisticatedly ornate designs – cut card work, strap design, cast ornaments with scrolls, escutcheons, boss beading, repoussé and chasing. The Rocaille style of Paul de Lamerie (1688-1741) was followed by more sober designs produced by William Kent (1684-1748) and others working within the delicate Adam style.

Important collections of silver plate (functional receptacles made of metal: tableware, church vessels, commemorative pieces etc) are on view at the Tower of London, the Victoria and Albert Museum, Apsley House, the Courtauld Institute of Art, Bank of England, the National Maritime Museum in Greenwich and the various military museums. Other significant private collections to which public access is restricted, survive at the Mansion House and in the halls of the City guild and livery companies (Drapers, Fishmongers, Tallow Chandlers, Skinners, Haberdashers, Goldsmiths, Ironmongers, Barber-Surgeons, Cutlers).

Iron – London offers many fine examples of decorative gates, railings, balconies and balustrades from the work of masters such as **Jean Tijou** (active 1689-1712) at Hampton Court to the modern design of the Queen Elizabeth Gates in Hyde Park.

Sword rest in St Magnus' Church

Hallmarking in a nutshell

The origin of the English hallmark dates back to the reign of Edward I when the king ordered the Worshipful Company of Goldsmiths to brand gold products with his seal, a **leopard's head**, as a guarantee of quality (1300) – this set gold at 19.2 carats, 'the Touch of Paris', and silver at the standard of contemporary silver pennies or 'sterling' currency ie 92.5 %. In 1478 the gold standard was reduced to 18ct and the leopard's head became crowned, the year in which wares began to bear a **date stamp** (running from 19 May, St Dunstan's Day) delivered by a government assay office (20-letter cycle A-U, omitting the J). **The lion passant gardant** appears in 1544, probably following Henry VIII's debasement of currency, to denote the maintained standard of plate.

In 1576, the gold standard was raised once more to 22 carat. In 1660, the annual change of letter was reset at 29 May to celebrate the Restoration of the Monarchy, King Charles II's birthday. All goldsmiths were then required to register their personal marks (1675). Large quantities of plate having been melted down in the 1640s to raise money for the Civil War, the process was reversed during peacetime: in 1697 the national coinage was reformed, new coins were given milled edges to discourage clipping, plate standards were raised and the marks changed to the seated Britannia and the lion's head erased (side view). Goldsmith marks were also altered. The mark of the Crown and the numbers 18 and 22 were introduced in 1798 and 1844 to counter ever increasing fraud. The **orb and cross** came into use for platinum on 2 January 1975, the quality of which is measured by atomic absorption spectro-photometry.

Today, the statutory function of hallmarking is upheld by the London Assay Office. It is also responsible for annually testing coins manufactured by the Royal Mint, a process known as the Trail of the Pyx (held in February).

Many City churches contain elaborate wrought-iron **sword rests** which date from the Elizabethan period (16C) at a time when it was customary to provide a pew for the Lord Mayor of London in his own parish church furnished with a sword rest where he could deposit the Sword of State during the service.

In the 19C design and iron casting complemented each other in the production of **street furniture**: the Egyptian-inspired bench ends along the Victoria Embankment by Cleopatra's Needle; the cannon ball and barrel bollards marking the Clink in South-wark; the beautiful dolphin lamp standards of 1870 which line the Albert Embank-ment; the pair of George III lamp-posts in Marlborough Road in St James's. The gold-crowned bracket lanterns at St James's Palace, made of wrought rather than cast metal, are of earlier date.

The first **pillar boxes** in London, fifteen years after the introduction of the penny post in 1840, were erected in Fleet Street, the Strand, Pall Mall, Piccadilly, Grosvenor Place and Rutland Gate; they were rectangular with a solid round ball crowning the pyram-idal roof. Subsequent hexagonal, circular, fluted, conical designs followed, flat-roofed, crowned or plain, most emblazoned with the royal cipher. A few hexagonal boxes (1866-79) survive, as do some from the 1880s 'anonymous' series which the Post Office forgot to mark with its name. Pillar boxes were promoted by Anthony Trollope and were first painted red in 1874.

Brass – From the Middle Ages until the 17C **brass tomb plates** were very popular, and a variety are still to be found in several London churches. The design was engraved with a triangular-headed graving tool and the groove was sometimes filled with enamel, or black or coloured wax. A study of these brasses shows how fashions in dress changed over the centuries. The oldest show warriors clothed in chain mail from head to foot, armed with a heavy sword and shield; next come knights in armour wearing a helmet. From 1463 the footwear has rounded toes in ac-cordance with an Act of Parliament prohibiting the toes of shoes to be more

The long-standing tradition and patronage of fine craftsmanship and design in London is maintained today by the **Chelsea Craft Fair** and the **Goldsmith's** show at the Guildhall where interna-tional buyers come to explore ideas that will launch new trends world-wide *(see PRACTICAL INFORMATION – Calendar of events)*.

than 5cm (2in) in length. The wives of such nobles range from the veiled simplicity of the 14C, via the rich dress and complicated headdress of the 15C, the plainer style of the Tudor period, to the ribbons and embroidery of Elizabeth's reign. In the 16C the brasses of the great churchmen were removed. In their place were rich merchants, with short hair and clean shaven in the 15C and beards in the Elizabethan period. **Brass-rubbing** is organised at All Hallows-by-the-Tower, St Martin-in-the-Fields and Westminster Abbey.

Music

The light airs of Tudor England (*Greensleeves* attributed to Henry VIII) developed into rounds, canons and finally a golden age (1588-1630) of madrigals by Thomas Morley – who published the first collection, John Wilbye, Thomas Weelkes, Orlando Gibbons and Thomas Tompkins. Much instrumental dance music was written with variations to display the performer's virtuosity; **John Dowland** excelled at solo songs accompanied by lute and viol. At the same time **Thomas Tallis** and **William Byrd** were composing religious music for the organ and voice in masses and anthems, set to the Latin and or English liturgy; only in Elizabeth's reign did a distinctive Anglican style emerge.

In the latter half of the 17C composers extended their range with *Te Deums* and secular airs, songs and incidental music for the theatre. **Henry Purcell** (1659-96), who despite his brief life dominated his own and subsequent generations, produced the first full-length opera *(Dido and Aeneas)* in 1689. Italian opera then became popular and was firmly established with *Rinaldo* (1711) by **Handel** who had arrived in England that year shortly before the future George I to whom he had been *Kapellmeister* in Hanover.

National Portrait Gallery

Handel

Handel settled in Mayfair, residing at 25 Brooke Street until his death in 1759: in that time he produced operas based on mythological subjects which were satirised by John Gay in *The Beggar's Opera* (1728), occasional pieces such as the *Fireworks* and *Water Music* (for evening pleasure boat-trips along the river) and a great succession of oratorios about religious heroes: *Esther, Israel in Egypt, Messiah, Judas Maccabaeus.* **Mozart** visited England as a prodigy of 8 in 1764 (composing his first symphony while residing at 180 Ebury Street and leaving his name to Mozart Terrace in Pimlico), **Haydn** in the 1790s when he was the greatest musical figure in Europe. **Mendelssohn** came early in the 19C, although the *Scottish Symphony* and *Midsummer Night's Dream* were not completed until some 20 years later.

English music entered an entirely new phase at the end of the 19C when it began to become widely popular. The Savoy operas – libretto by **W S Gilbert** and music by Sir Arthur **Sullivan** (1875-99) appealed to a wide audience. As radio became widespread in the 1930s, the BBC began to broadcast the **Promenade Concerts**, which had been inaugurated in 1895 by the conductor, Henry Wood, in the Queen's Hall. The programmes, organised by the BBC, include orchestral works and opera by classical and modern composers, performed by national and visiting musicians and conductors. Since 1941 these concerts have been held in the Albert Hall. The audiences continue to draw large numbers of promenaders, who stand in the gallery or in the central arena and make a spirited contribution to the Last Night, when traditional pieces are played *(Pomp and Circumstance)*.

The opening of the 20C also saw the appearance of a host of new British composers: Edward **Elgar** (*Enigma Variations* 1899, *Dream of Gerontius* 1900), Delius, **Vaughan Williams** (9 symphonies, the ballet *Job*) and Gustav **Holst** (*The Planets* 1914-16). They were joined in the 1920s by Bantock, Bax, Bliss (*Checkmate* 1937) and William Walton (*Belshazzar's Feast* 1931).

After the war they were reinforced by Michael **Tippett** (*A Child of Our Time* 1941, *The Midsummer Marriage* 1955) and Benjamin **Britten** who produced a magnificent series of works – *Peter Grimes* 1945, *Albert Herring, Let's Make an Opera, Billy Budd, Turn of the Screw, Noye's Fludde, Midsummer Night's Dream, The Burning Fiery Furnace, The War Requiem* and the operetta *Paul Bunyan*.

The second half of the 20C has seen the establishment of permanent centres of opera at Covent Garden and the London Coliseum, the construction of concert halls on the South Bank and at the Barbican and the birth of numerous provincial (Summer) festivals.

For details of exhibitions and other events taking place in London
Consult the weekly programme guides published on Wednesday (Time Out) and Thursday (Evening Standard).

Literature

Not all have felt with William Dunbar 'London thou art the flower of cities all' nor even with Dr Johnson that 'there is in London all that life can afford' but at some point in their careers many writers lived in London.

While some have detested the capital and some indulged in a love-hate relationship, others have known that for them it was the only place in the world to live. In consequence English literature from detective stories to diaries, from novels to biographies and histories, is permeated with scenes of London. The development first of radio, then of television and faster travel, has made it possible for late 20C writers to live and work outside the capital.

Despite their numbers there has been no regular forum for writers down the years: groups have shifted from the pubs near Blackfriars Theatre to those on Bankside and down the Borough High Street close to the Globe; to Highgate, to Chelsea and, for a charmed circle, to Bloomsbury; at the turn of the century a group around **Oscar Wilde**, which included Aubrey Beardsley and Max Beerbohm, and artists of the day met at the Café Royal. Since many have begun or earned a living as journalists, the first regular haunts were the coffee-houses around Fleet Street; Addison and Steel frequented the George and Vulture, then doing greater business in tea, chocolate and coffee than in ale, and subsequently Button's at both of which they wrote copy for the *Tatler* and *Spectator;* **Dr Johnson** called at many coffee-houses and taverns but nearest his own house was The Cheshire Cheese where, tradition has it, many of the great conversations took place.

Verse — **Geoffrey Chaucer** (1340-1400) was a courtier and diplomat; he draws on the rich tradition of contemporary French, Latin and Italian literature to recount his *Canterbury Tales* about pilgrims journeying between Southwark and Canterbury. The Elizabethan Age is encapsulated in Sir Edmund Spenser's *Faerie Queene,* a long poem populated with personifications of Justice, Temperance, Holiness, Chastity, etc conceived as a glorious allegory of his times. Artists were seduced by 'conceits': an intricately contrived sonnet as technically brilliant as a painted miniature. Skilled use of alliteration, assonance, rhythm and rhyme are inherited by the two great masters of theatre **Christopher Marlowe** (1564-93) and **William Shakespeare** (1564-1616), who used free verse enriched with powerful imagery and varied syntax.

Fashion in courtly poetry has dwindled so it is not until **John Milton** (1608-74) emerges that the genre heralds the Age of the Enlightenment. Intellectually provocative, modelled on Classical prototypes, Milton carefully expressed his Puritan anti-Royalist politics in prose and his views on the Fall of Man in verse *(Paradise Lost, Comus, Lycidas).* The first Poet Laureate, **John Dryden** (1631-1700) records contemporary events in his poetry, criticism, drama and translations: his verse is often judged 'occasional' in subject-matter, but clear and precise in style — heralding the rational climate of the period of **Alexander Pope** (the other Metaphysical poet), **Jonathan Swift** *(Gulliver's Travels)* and **Samuel Johnson** (compiler of the first Dictionary 1755).

Such **Romantic** poets as Blake, Burns, Wordsworth and Coleridge are great and distinctive figures but like Bronte, Hardy and Eliot wrote largely outside the London scene, turning instead to spirituality, Scottish patriotism, and Nature for inspiration. The quintessence of the movement exists in the tragically short life and inspired output of **John Keats** (1795-1821) who came to London to study medicine. The key to his spirit is provided by his own poetry: 'A thing of beauty is a joy for ever.' His verse is sensuous, rich in illusion and imagery, varied in form (sonnet, ode), spontaneous and yet meditative in expression. **William Wordsworth** mused on Westminster Bridge but lived in the Lake District; **Lord Byron** enjoyed high society.

For the Victorians, Imagination must reign over Reason — the Poet Laureate **Tennyson** *(Morte d'Arthur)* specialised in mellifluous poetry, **Browning** in more disjointed, exclamatory verse, and **Arnold** in descriptions of the moral dilemmas of life deprived of religious faith. Just as in Elizabethan times, Pre-Raphaelite poets such as **D G Rossetti**, his sister Christina, William Morris and **Swinburne** echo values explored by a movement in painting — imagery is pictorial, subject-matter is drawn from the timeless if archaic myths and legends, form modelled on the ancient ballads.

The **Aesthetes** of the 1890s, originators of the *Yellow Book* including **Oscar Wilde** (1854-1900), **Beerbohm** and **Beardsley** among others, were greatly impressed by the philosophical writings of Henri Bergson (1859-1941) and affected by Huysmans' Symbolist novel *A Rebours (Against the Grain* alluded to in Wilde's *Picture of Dorian Gray).* The counter-reaction this provoked was a move towards realism: Kipling drew on popular music-hall song for his endearing verse full of colloquial language, natural rhythm and vitality, a marked contrast to that of **W B Yeats** (1865-1939). The Georgian poets including T S Eliot *(Waste Land, Old Possum's Book of Practical Cats, Murder in the Cathedral),* D H Lawrence and Walter de la Mare, defined the transition to Modernism: their work is haunted by the devastating effect of war — poignantly captured by the War Poets (Sassoon, Owen and Brooke) who later rekindled their spirit of hope and celebration at having been spared. Form is carefully explored and blank-verse is found to be the more flexible.

The 1930s era of depression is recorded by **W H Auden**, **Cecil Day Lewis**, **Louis MacNeice** and **Spender**: contemporaries at Oxford, their verse is direct in appeal, colloquial in language and anti-establishment in politics. Metre and imagery are used with skill to enforce the topical concern that characterise the period, so different in emphasis from the preoccupations of **Dylan Thomas** (1914-53) who explores childhood and innocence and **Ted Hughes** (1930-98) who describes the inherent violence of Nature.

Light Verse – Truly English in quality is the light, humorous and entertaining light verse. Many of the major writers dabbled in it, but it is the likes of **Edward Lear** (1812-88 – *Book of Nonsense*) and **Lewis Carroll** (1832-98 – *Alice in Wonderland*) that have been the most enduring masters of nonsense and limerick. **Hilaire Belloc** (1870-1953 – *Cautionary Tales*) and A A Milne (1882-1956 – *Winnie the Pooh*) contributed their verse to *Punch* magazine – a venue that in the pictorial arts had already long perfected the parallel genre of caricature and cartoon. From this tradition stems the ballad-like sing-song verse of W S Gilbert that was successfully popularised by operetta when set to Sullivan's music.

Lord Henry laughed. 'I don't desire to change anything in England except the weather' he answered. 'I am quite content with philosophic contemplation.'

Oscar Wilde, The Picture of Dorian Gray

The Novel – 'The object of a novel should be to instruct in morals while it amuses' so observed Anthony Trollope. The first of a line of great novelists is **Daniel Defoe** (c 1661-1731), former political pamphleteer and author of *Robinson Crusoe*, and *Moll Flanders*, who managed to describe ordinary middle class characters in credible plots. Following Defoe comes **Samuel Richardson** (1689-1761), originator of the epistolary novel with *Pamela* and *Clarissa* which explores human thought and emotion, and the highly regarded playwright **Henry Fielding** (1701-54). *Tom Jones* is the history of a man of unknown birth who goes to London to seek his fortune: moralistic in tone, characterisation at times verges on caricature. At the turn of the century Oliver Goldsmith, Fanny Burney, Sir Horace Walpole found fame with single works prompting an interest in the Picturesque with the Gothic novel full of mystery and terror – a tradition which was to inspire Mary Shelley's *Frankenstein* (1818).

The Romantic movement is dominated by the prolific **Sir Walter Scott** (1771-1832), a specialist of the historical novel where high-born and more lowly characters seem powerless pawns before external political predicaments *(Waverley, Rob Roy, Ivanhoe)*. By contrast, **Jane Austen** (1775-1817) draws her six novels from personal experience – notably in matters of love and marriage; she writes with wry humour and sensitivity which give her novels an enduring popularity.

The Victorian chapter is dominated by **Charles Dickens** (1812-70), who animates his great catalogue of novels, set in and around London, with colourful characterisation, inventive plots, humour and pathos *(Pickwick Papers, Oliver Twist, Nicholas Nickleby, A Christmas Carol, David Copperfield, Bleak House, Little Dorrit, Great Expectations...)*.

Charles Dickens

Published as serials, his stories quickly found a large audience and stirred contemporary Humanists to reform social conditions for children, the poor and the deprived. **Thackeray** (1811-63) sets his *Vanity Fair* in Regency England, reproaching hypocrisy and double standards.

H G Wells (1866-1946) drew on his studies at London University to create scientific romances that preempt *The Day of the Triffids* and the science fiction of John Wyndham (1903-69).

Travel and free thought are the principal themes of a new phase in literature: **E M Forster** (1879-1970) explores the frailty of human nature; **Virginia Woolf** (1882-1941) saw herself as a rational and enlightened thinker, an artist retaliating against the narrow-mindedness of Victorian London; she is certainly one of the most discerning and psychological novelists. **Evelyn**

Waugh (1903-66) depicts social circumstances with wit, black comedy and farce that develop to realism in the face of the threat of war – a realism that pervades the work of **George Orwell** (1903-50) and his haunting images of a spiritless, futuristic age.

The 20C is marked by various versatile personalities living and working in London, who transpose their experiences of the provinces and travel abroad into their novels: Graham Greene, Kingsley Amis, Muriel Spark, Doris Lessing, Iris Murdoch, Anthony Burgess....

Theatre – During the Middle Ages plays were performed outside the city boundaries as the City of London authorities were steadfast in refusing to allow theatrical performances within their jurisdiction. The first regular 'public' performances were held in Clerkenwell and Shoreditch where **James Burbage** founded the first English playhouse, and then south of the river in Southwark.

Meanwhile, the courts of Henry VIII and Elizabeth I at Nonesuch Palace and Hampton Court attracted contemporary dramatists and entertainers for private functions. Masques were light amateur dramatic compositions enacted in elaborate costume and set to music often to celebrate a particular occasion. The legal fraternity also provided facilities for the performance of plays, masques and revels; in the late 16C *The Comedy of Errors* was staged in Gray's Inn and *Twelfth Night* was played beneath the hammerbeam roof of the Middle Temple Hall.

The true theatrical tradition as we know it today however is descended from the popular genre whose most famous exponents through the ages include **Christopher Marlowe** (1564-1593), **William Shakespeare** (1564-1616), Ben Jonson (1572/3-1637), Wycherley, Congreve, Sheridan, Oscar Wilde...

Until the Theatres Act of 1968, theatres were licensed by the Lord Chamberlain, an officer of the Royal Household. This title was bestowed in 1494 when the first Master of the Revels was appointed to supervise court entertainments. At the Restoration (1660) the Lord Chamberlain began to intervene directly in the regulation of theatres and in censorship, in those days on religious and political grounds. Under the Licensing Act 1737 and the Theatres Act 1843, he was empowered to censor all new plays or adaptations with reference to indecency, impropriety, profanity and seditious matter with the assistance of three readers in English and one in Welsh; he could reject any material without giving reasons.

Film

The Edison Kinetoscope opened in London in October 1894 at 70 Oxford Street. This American peep-show device ran continuous films – but Edison failed to have his invention patented in Britain... Two Greeks, therefore, sponsored Robert Paul, an electrical engineer from Hatton Garden, to develop his own moving pictures. In association with Birt Acres the first film was made and shown at the Empire of India Exhibition at Earl's Court in 1895.

Early films to survive are news reels, historical documentary material charting the 1908 Olympics at White City, riots, marches and rallies in the post-war years, life in the slums, building in the suburbs, the first Cup Final at Wembley (1923) and the Festival of Britain (1951). At that time the production and distribution companies, including **Pathé News**, were centred around the Charing Cross Road, with Cecil Court known as 'Flicker Alley'. The advent of Soho as the heart of the film industry came about in the 1920s.

The Studios – In 1927 the Government passed a Cinematograph Films Act to support the film industry at home which at the time was dominated by the imported American and French movies. The film studios of the Golden Age had to be located outside London, as far away from the threat of pea-soup fog as possible: **Ealing** (BBC studios since 1955; National Film and Television School from 1995); **Elstree** *(Star Wars, Indiana Jones);* **Pinewood** (founded in 1936); **Shepperton; Denham** (demolished 1981); **Hammersmith** (now the Riverside Studios); **Gaumont** in Lime Grove, Shepherd's Bush; **Stoll** in Cricklewood... During the war these large premises accommodated factories and food stores; Pinewood housed an annexe for Lloyds, the Stock Exchange and the Royal Mint.

LONDON ON SCREEN

1926 – The Lodger: A Story Of The London Fog tells the story of the unsolved Whitechapel Murders of 1888; directed by Alfred Hitchcock.

1928 – Pandora's Box (Die Büchse der Pandora) was a German film based on the evil story of Jack the Ripper; filmed in Germany; directed by G W Pabst.

1929 – Blackmail, directed by Alfred Hitchcock is considered as the first British talkie. **High Treason** creates a futurist vision of London in the 1940s; directed by M Elvey.

1941 – Dr Jekyll And Mr Hyde is evocatively set by Hollywood in London; directed by Victor Fleming.

1942 – Mrs Miniver, with Walter Pidgeon and Greer Garson, filmed in America, portrays London during the war; directed by William Wyler.

1945 – Pursuit to Algiers is an early tale involving Sherlock Holmes and Dr Watson, recreated by Hollywood. **Brief Encounter**, directed by David Lean, used the same sets at the Denham Studios as **Perfect Strangers.**

1946 – Great Expectations was carefully filmed in London after the war under the directorship of David Lean.

1948 – Oliver Twist with stage sets recreated by David Lean from Gustave Doré's illustrations to *London* (1870).

1949 – Stagefright with Marlene Dietrich singing *La Vie En Rose*, Michael Wilding and Jane Wyman set in London, directed by Hitchcock. **Passport to Pimlico** filmed in fact in Lambeth; directed by H Cornelius.

1953 – Genevieve is the name of a 1906 Darracq car that takes part in the famous London to Brighton veteran car run – made by Ealing Studios; directed by H Cornelius.

1955 – The Lady Killers set in Barnsbury, captures the Copenhagen Tunnels outside King's Cross on celluloid. **1984**, the first adaptation of Orwell's novel was partly filmed by London Wall under the directorship of M Anderson. **Witness for the Prosecution**, directed by Billy Wilder was set amongst the legal fraternity in and around the Royal Courts of Justice.

1964 – Mary Poppins, that archetypal British nanny envisaged by the Americans resides with her wards in St John's Wood; directed by R Stevenson. **My Fair Lady**, made by the Warner Studios in California, recreates an evocative if sentimental interpretation of the London class divisions, with Audrey Hepburn and Rex Harrison, costumes by Cecil Beaton after Bernard Shaw's *Pygmalion;* directed by George Cukor. **A Hard Day's Night** boosted sales of Beatles records; directed by Richard Lester.

1965 – Blow-Up set in the 1960s, a photographer on a fashion shoot accidentally witnesses a murder with David Hemmings, Vanessa Redgrave and Sarah Miles – the quintessential London movie; directed by Antonioni (featuring Maryon Park, Woolwich).

1966 – Alfie tracks Jack-the-lad, south-London-born Michael Caine and the easy life; directed by Lewis Gilbert.

1971 – A Clockwork Orange, Stanley Kubrick's banned cult film is about the terrors of anarchy, sequences filmed at Thamesmead.

1973 – The Optimists of Nine Elms shows Peter Sellers in the role of an old street busker; directed by Anthony Simmons.

1979 – The Long Good Friday charts the decline of the Docklands; directed by John Mackenzie.

1980 – **The Elephant Man** is a provocative story set in Victorian England, directed by David Lynch, starring John Hurt, Anthony Hopkins, Anne Bancroft and John Gielgud.

1981 – **The French Lieutenant's Woman**, with several scenes shot in Shad Thames; directed by Karel Reisz.

1985 – **My Beautiful Launderette** explores racial tensions in south London; directed by Stephen Frears.

1986 – **Sid and Nancy** exposes the true spirit of Punk with Sid Vicious played by Gary Oldman; directed by Alex Cox.

1987 – **Hope and Glory**, John Boorman's London in the Blitz. **Full Metal Jacket** about the war in Vietnam was in fact made by Stanley Kubrick in London's Royal Docks.

1988 – **A Fish called Wanda** starring John Cleese, Kevin Kline, Jamie Lee Curtis in and around London Town and Docklands; directed by Charles Crichton. **Buster** tells the story of the Great Train Robber 'Buster' Edwards who once sold flowers under the arches in Waterloo, acted by Phil Collins; directed by David Green.

1992 – **Chaplin** recreates the life of Charlie Chaplin in south London in the 1880s, directed by Richard Attenborough.

1994 – **Madness of King George**, Nigel Hawthorne in Alan Bennett's play about the mad monarch. Supported by Helen Mirren; directed by Nicholas Mytner.

1995 – **Richard III**, with a star-studded cast led by Ian McKellen exploits several famous London landmarks (Battersea and Bankside Power Stations, St Pancras).

1999 – **Notting Hill**, a romantic comedy with Julia Roberts and Hugh Grant set around Portobello Road; directed by Roger Mitchell.

The Thames

For information on boat services see PRACTICAL INFORMATION.

Main thoroughfare of London – Until the late 17C the Thames was the capital's main highway; the royal household, the City Corporation and the city livery companies had their own barges; ordinary citizens hired the services of the watermen who plied for hire at the many landing stages (Stairs); cargo ships and men o'war added to the congestion. The first regular steamer services began in 1816 and by mid-century were carrying several million people. On weekdays the boats were crowded with workers going into the docks and boatyards, the arsenal and south bank factories; fares were a penny from one pier to the next. At other times they carried families and friends out for an evening trip or for an excursion, often to the estuary and seaside towns of Herne Bay, Margate and Ramsgate.

Old engravings show craft of every size thronging the Thames in times past: it is now used chiefly for recreation. According to specialists, the key issue is the tides – too fast to maintain a reliable waterbus service and too high to harness and yet maintain fish and wildlife. Oarsmen train in rowing skiffs; marinas provide moorings for private craft; pleasure steamers offer evening excursions with music and refreshment or daytime excursions downstream to the Tower, Greenwich and the Thames Barrier or upstream to Kew and Hampton Court. The muddy banks at low tide are also frequented by archeologists and treasure seekers under the auspices of the Society of Mudlarks and Antiquarians and the Port of London Authority in search of discarded mementoes of broken engagements and old ship timbers...

Pool of London – London grew to importance as a port, owing to its location on the Thames, the major river in England (215 miles long). From the 16C to the mid 20C commercial prosperity of the city derived from the wharves and docks in the Pool of London and the shipbuilding yards downstream. Merchantmen unable to sail beneath London Bridge or to approach the wharves across the mudflats, moored in midstream and depended on a fleet of some 3 500 lighters for loading and unloading. This system provided many opportunities for pilfering by river pirates, night plunderers, scuffle hunters and mudlarks.

Commercial Docks – The first enclosed commercial dock, designed to cut down the opportunities for theft, was built early in the 19C. By the end of the century, there were four systems of enclosed docks, formed by the amalgamation of earlier smaller companies, extending over 3 000 acres with 36 miles of quays and 665 acres of dock basins: London Docks (1864), Surrey Commercial Docks (1864), East and West India Docks (1838), Royal Docks (1855-80).

In 1909 the whole docks enterprise, which was in urgent need of modernisation, was taken over by the newly-instituted **Port of London Authority**, which was granted jurisdiction over the tideway (94 miles) from the Tongue (opposite Margate in Kent) upstream to Teddington Lock, where high tide is 1 1/2 hours later than at London Bridge. During the Second World War the docks suffered severely from bombing.

By the 1960s decline in the use of the docks forced the PLA to begin closing them and cargo handling was transferred to specialised riverside wharves and the dock at Tilbury. With the ending of the Dock Labour Scheme in 1989 the port has revived and

Thames tributaries

Most now flow underground in pipes although some have been dammed to form lakes. There is little except the occasional street name to recall the course of these lost waterways. Among the northern tributaries are (from east to west) the Lea; Walbrook (short) from north side of the City; the Fleet (2 branches) from Hampstead and Highgate; Tyburn via Marylebone to Westminster (traced by Marylebone Lane); Westbourne via Paddington and Kensington to enter at Pimlico; Stamford Brook which enters at Hammersmith; River Brent which enters at Kew. Among the southern tributaries are (from east to west): the Ravensbourne which enters at Deptford Creek; Effra River which enters in Brixton; Falcon Brook which enters in Battersea; River Wandle which enters at Wandsworth.

is still the largest general cargo port in the United Kingdom, handling some 45-50 million tonnes of goods each year; of this some 6 million tonnes are handled upstream of the Thames Barrier.

During the 1990s, the docks have provided good facilities for various water sporting activities. Plans for Europe's largest aquarium are also afoot.

Water supply – In the Middle Ages water supplies came from the Thames, its tributaries and from wells (Clerkenwell, Sadler's Wells, Muswell Hill). After 1285 conduits of leather or hollow tree trunks were provided by the City fathers to bring water from the Tyburn, Westbourne and Lea to lead cisterns in the City where it was collected by householders and by water carriers, who later formed a guild. During the next 300 years these provisions were augmented by private enterprise. Six tidal water wheels were licensed under the northern arches of London Bridge between 1582 and 1822. The first pump driven by horses was set up in Upper Thames Street in 1594. The most elaborate undertaking, however, was the cutting (1609-13) of the New River.

The industrial revolution brought steam pumping, tried unsuccessfully in 1712 and gradually introduced from 1750 with cast-iron pipes: wooden mains could not sustain the higher pumping pressures. The widespread introduction of the water closet after 1820 resulted in sewage being discharged into the streams and rivers, polluting the water supply and bringing epidemics of typhoid and cholera (1832 and 1848). In 1858 the Thames was so foul that sheets soaked in disinfectant were hung at the windows of Parliament to keep out the stench.

Filtration (1829), the requirement to draw water from the non-tidal river above Teddington (1856) and chlorination (1916) made London's water safe to drink.

LONDON'S BRIDGES

1 Kingston
2 Kingston Rlwy
3 Richmond
4 Richmond Rlwy
5 Twickenham
6 Richmond Footbridge
7 Kew
8 Kew Rlwy
9 Chiswick
10 Barnes Rlwy
11 Hammersmith
12 Putney
13 Fulham Rlwy
14 Wandsworth
15 Battersea Rlwy
16 Battersea
17 Albert
18 Chelsea
19 Victoria Rlwy
20 Vauxhall
21 Lambeth
22 Westminster
23 Hungerford Rlwy
24 Waterloo
25 Blackfriars
26 Blackfriars Rlwy
27 Millennium
28 Southwark
29 Cannon Street Rlwy
30 London
31 Tower

● Piers

A HMS Wellington
B HMS Belfast
C Gypsy Moth IV
D Cutty Sark

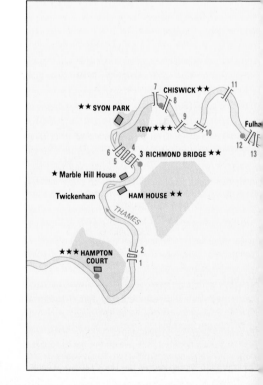

Aerial view of the Thames and the City

Today, supply is maintained by reservoirs situated on the periphery of London at Datchet (8 300 million gallons), Staines, Chingford and Walthamstow. In 1974 the Thames Water Authority was constituted to take over from the Metropolitan Water Board (1903). It levied its own rate and was responsible for the management of the Thames throughout its length and for London's water supply, sewage disposal and pollution control. Since 1989/90 the National Rivers Authority (Thames Region) has been responsible for flood defence and pollution control. By the 1980s pollution of the tideway was greatly reduced and many fish were descending the stream and re-entering the estuary. Licences for eel fishing are in demand and salmon have returned in quantity after an absence of more than 150 years; they were once so cheap and plentiful that apprentices complained of having to eat them every day.

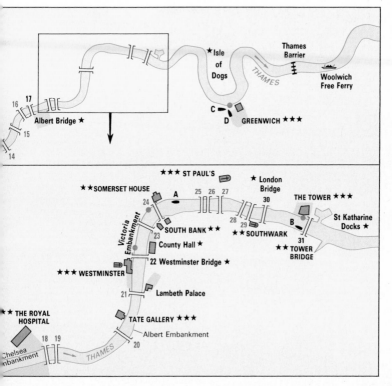

Travellers' addresses

Where to stay

London, a sprawling city which offers entertainment all year round, is an attractive holiday destination. It remains a firm favourite with visitors from overseas and, with the opening of the Channel Tunnel, it is easily accessible from continental Europe. The selection of hotels listed below have been chosen for their surroundings, character, excellent location and value for money. Hotels on the outskirts are included for motorists driving from the Channel ports who may prefer to leave their car and travel to town by underground or overground train. Prices are given for double rooms but are liable to change. It is advisable to contact the hotel for further details.

ON THE ROAD TO LONDON FROM THE SOUTH COAST

(CC): payment by credit cards accepted

SEVENOAKS (Kent) – 25 miles southeast of London by A 20 and A 224

Royal Oak – Upper High Street, TN13 1HY. ☎ 01732 451 109; Fax 01732 740 187. Parking. 36 rooms. £90-110 (VAT inc). (CC). *Restaurant*

BOROUGH GREEN (Kent) – 7 miles east of Sevenoaks by A 25

Stone Ridge – 168 Maidstone Road, TN15 8JD. ☎ 01732 882 053. Parking. £25-45. (CC).

MAIDSTONE (Kent) – 36 miles southeast of London by M 20

Grangemoor – 4-8 St. Michael's Road, ME16 8BS. ☎ 01622 677 623; Fax 01622 678 246. Parking. 47 rooms. £46-52 (VAT inc). (CC). *Restaurant*

Travel Inn – London Road, ME16 0HG. 2 miles northwest on A 20. ☎ 01622 752 515; Fax 01622 672 469. Parking. 40 rooms. £39.95 (VAT inc). (CC). *Restaurant*

REIGATE (Surrey) – 26 miles south of London by A 24 and A 217.

Bridge House – Reigate Hill, RH2 9RP. 1.25 miles north on A 217. ☎ 01737 246 801; Fax 01737 223 756. Parking. 39 rooms. £61-136 (VAT inc). (CC). *Restaurant*

Cranleigh – 41 West Street, RH2 9BL. ☎ 01737 223 417; Fax 01737 223 734. Parking. 9 rooms. £80-99 (VAT inc). (CC). *Restaurant (evening only)*

GUILDFORD (Surrey) – 33 miles southwest of London by A 3

Angel Posting House and Livery – High Street, GU1 3DP. ☎ 01483 564 555; Fax 01483 533 770. 16C coaching inn with 13C vaulted cellar restaurant. 14 rooms. £135-180 (VAT inc). (CC). *Restaurant*

Travel Inn – Parkway, GU1 1UP. ☎ 01483 304 932; Fax 01483 304 935. Parking. 87 rooms. £39.95 (VAT inc). (CC). *Restaurant*

DORKING (Surrey) – 26 miles south of London by A 24.

Burford Bridge – Box Hill, RH5 6BX. 1 mile north on A 24. ☎ 0870 400 8283; Fax 01306 880 386. Parking. 57 rooms. £165 (VAT inc). (CC). *Restaurant*

Travelodge – Reigate Road, RH4 1QB. 0.5mile east on A 25. ☎ 01306 740 361; Bookings: ☎ 0800 850 950. Parking. 54 rooms. £39.95-£59.95 (VAT inc). (CC).

White Horse – High Street, RH4 1BE. ☎ 0870 400 8282; Fax 01306 887 241. Parking. 69 rooms. £150-170 (VAT inc). (CC). *Restaurant*

REDHILL (Surrey) – 21 miles south of London by A 23.

Nutfield Priory – Nutfield, RH1 4EN. 2 miles east on A 25. ☎ 01737 824 400; Fax 01737 823 321. Parking. 59 rooms. £105-155 (service, VAT inc). (CC). *Restaurant*

Travel Inn – Brighton Road, RH1 5BT. ☎ 01737 767 277; Fax 01737 778 099. Parking. 48 rooms. £39.95 (VAT inc). (CC). *Restaurant*

BED AND BREAKFAST

For simple accommodation in family homes, contact the following agencies which specialise in bookings for selected homes:

London Home-to-Home – 19 Mount Park Crescent, London W5 2RN. ☎/Fax 020 8566 7976; stay@londonhometohome.com; www.londonhometohome.com

London Bed and Breakfast Agency Ltd – 71 Fellows Road, London NW3 3JY. ☎ 020 7586 2768; Fax 020 7586 6567; stay@londonbb.com; www.londonbb.com

Bed and Breakfast – 94 Bell Street, Henley-on-Thames, Oxon RG9 1XS. ☎ 01491 578 803; Fax 01491 410 806; bookings@bedbreak.demon.co.uk; www.bedbreak.com

Two small hotels which offer similar facilities are located near Regent's Park and Victoria Station:

Hart House CX (☉) – 51 Gloucester Place, W1U 8JF. ☎ 020 7935 2288, Fax 020 7935 8516. No parking. 15 rooms. £70-98 (VAT included). (CC). No restaurant.
A family-run hotel in a Georgian terrace originally occupied by the French nobility during the French Revolution.

Winchester – 17 Belgrave Road. SW1V 1RB. ☎ 020 7828 2972; Fax 020 7828 5191. No parking. 18 rooms. £85-100. (service, VAT included). No restaurant.
A well-kept, friendly hotel in a Georgian terrace conveniently located behind Victoria Station.

A SELECTION OF HOTELS

This small selection is no substitute for the Michelin Red Guide *London*, an extract from the current Michelin Red Guide *Great Britain and Ireland* which lists hotels in all categories. *See also Practical Information – General Information.*

Map references given immediately after the name of the hotel (except for those outside London) locate the hotel on the Principal Sights Map in this guide.

The selection covers three categories:

– **Moderate**: usually small, simple but comfortable hotels charging less than £60.

– **Mid-range**: hotels charging from £60 to £150. It is advisable to book in advance as there are usually few rooms at the lower rates.

– **Luxury**: pleasant, traditional hotels in a central location; the rates reflect the standard of the amenities.

Moderate Hotels

In Central London and on the outskirts the **Travel Inns** chain offers simple but comfortable hotels with rooms at a single rate of £40.95 – £69.95 (service, VAT inc; central booking: ☎ 0870 242 8000): **Euston** (Camden), **County Hall** (Lambeth, *see South Bank*), **Putney** (SW), **Kenton** (Harrow, NW), **Hayes** (Hillingdon, W), **Chessington** (Kingston-upon-Thames, SW), **Croydon** (S). **Travel Lodges** offer similar facilities at a single rate of £39.95 – £69.95 (VAT inc; central booking: ☎ 0800 850 950 (freephone): **Battersea** (SW), **City of London**, **Ealing** (W), **Hounslow** (W), **Heston** (W), **Tower Hamlets** (E).

Mid-range Hotels

Academy EX (☑) – 17-21 Gower Street, WC1E 6HG. ☎ 020 7631 4115; Fax 020 7636 3442. No parking. 49 rooms. £115-165. (CC). Meals except Sat and Sun.
The Academy comprises 5 Georgian houses in Bloomsbury, near Bedford Square, one of the best preserved squares in this famous area.

Henley House BZ (☉) – 30 Barkston Gardens, SW5 0EN. ☎ 020 7370 4111; Fax 020 7370 0026. No parking. 21 rooms. £75-112 (service, VAT included). (CC). No restaurant; however evening meal available by agreement.
A small comfortable hotel in Earl's Court located away from the busy main roads. Visitors can enjoy the "village" atmosphere of Earl's Court and South Kensington.

Aster House BYZ (❶) – 3 Sumner Place, SW7 3EE. ☎ 020 7581 5888; Fax 020 7584 4925. No parking. 12 rooms. £75-175 (service, VAT included). (CC). No restaurant.
A charming hotel with climbing plants decking the façade, within easy access to shops and museums in Kensington, Knightsbridge and Chelsea. Warm, family ambiance.

Five Sumner Place BYZ (❺) – 5 Sumner Place, SW7 3EE. ☎ 020 7584 7586; Fax 020 7823 9962. No parking. 13 rooms. £82-130 (service). (CC). No restaurant.
A pleasant hotel part of a Victorian terrace near shops and museums as above.

Durrants DX (❻) – 26-32 George Street, W1H 5BJ. ☎ 020 7935 8131, Fax 020 7487 3510. No parking. 88 rooms. £97.50-140 (service, VAT included). (CC).
For some two hundred years this traditional hotel has occupied 4 Georgian terrace houses behind Hertford House (see Wallace Collection). Dinner is served in intimate dining rooms; previously ladies were not admitted in one room decorated with nude paintings.

Luxury Hotels

Beaufort CY (❷) – 33 Beaufort Gardens, SW3 1PP. ☎ 020 7584 5252; Fax 020 7589 2834. No parking. 28 rooms. £165-295 (room service), bar and health club. (CC). No restaurant.
This elegant, quiet hotel is reputed for its convivial atmosphere and for its English floral watercolour collection. It is within walking distance of Harrods and famous museums.

Hazlitt's EX (❶) – 6 Frith Street, W1V 5TZ. ☎ 020 7434 1771; 020 7439 1524. No parking. 22 rooms. £140-175 (service included). No restaurant.
It is one of the few hotels in Soho and the decor is quite striking. The painter and writer William Hazlitt was born here.

Knightsbridge Green CY (❷) – 159 Knightsbridge, SW1X 7PD. ☎ 020 7584 6274; Fax 020 7225 1635. No parking. 16 rooms and 12 suites. £105-165. (CC). No restaurant.
The hotel is well located in Knightsbridge, an elegant residential and shopping area (Harrods, Harvey Nichols) near Hyde Park and Park Lane

Portobello AX (❶) – 22 Stanley Gardens, W11 2NG. ☎ 020 7727 2777; Fax 020 7792 9641. No parking. 24 rooms. £140-260 (VAT included). (CC).
The hotel is part of a Victorian terrace near the antique market in trendy Notting Hill; it is decorated in contemporary style and some rooms are quite distinctive.

Pembridge Court AX (❸) – 34 Pembridge Gardens, W2 4DX. ☎ 020 7229 9977; Fax 020 7727 4982. No parking. 20 rooms. £125-195 (service, VAT included). (CC). Dinner (room service only).
A small elegant hotel in a lovely 19C building in a quiet area. It is within walking distance of Portobello market, Hyde Park and Kensington Palace and Gardens. It is famous for its collection of antique clothing.

YOUTH HOSTELS

Holders of an International Youth Hostel Federation card should contact the **International Youth Hostel Federation** ☎ 01707 324 170. Otherwise the **Hostelling International / American Youth Hostel Association** in the US (☎ 202-783-6161) offers a publication *International Hostel Guide for Europe* (US$13.95) – also available to non-members.

Contact the **Youth Hostels Association**, Trevelyan House, 8 St Stephen's Hill, St Albans, Herts AL1 2DY ☎ 01727 855 215; Fax 01727 844 126; www.yha.org.uk for information on youth hostels in the UK.

To book a room in one of the six Youth Hostels in London ☎ 020 7373 3400:

– 14 Noel Street, W1V 3PD,
☎ 020 7734 1618.

– 38 Bolton Gardens, SW5 0AQ,
☎ 020 7373 7083.

– Holland House, Holland Walk,
Kensington, W8 7QU,
☎ 020 7937 0748.

– 4 Wellgarth Road, Hampstead
Heath, NW11 7HR
☎ 020 8458 9054.

– 36 Carter Lane, off St Pauls
Churchyard, EC4V 5AB.
☎ 020 7236 4965.

– Island Yard, 20 Salter Road,
Rotherhithe, SE16 1PP.
☎ 020 7232 2114.

Students should contact the **Central Bureau for Educational Visits and Exchanges**, Seymour Mews House, Seymour Mews, London W1H 9PE, ☎ 020 7486 5101 or try one or other of the following:

International Students House
(ISH), 229 Great Portland Street,
W1N 5HD. ☎ 020 7631 8300 ; Fax
020 7631 8315 – for students
(single, double and dormitory).

YMCA, National Council, 640 Forest
Road, London E17 3DZ,
☎ 020 8520 5599.

YWCA, National HQ, 52 Cornmarket
Street, Oxford OX1 3EJ,
☎ 01865 726 110.

CAMPING

There are several camp sites within reasonable distance of Central London; it is advisable to book in advance; prices vary according to the season:

Abbey Wood, Federation Road,
Abbey Wood, London SE2 0LS.
12mi/19km from Central London.
Open all year. ☎ 020 8311 7708.

Crystal Palace Caravan Club Site,
Crystal Palace Parade, London
SE19 1UF. 8mi/13km from Central
London. Open all year.
☎ 020 8778 7155.

**Eastway Cycle Circuit and
Campsite**, Temple Mills Lane,
Stratford, London E15 2EN. 4mi/6km
from Central London. Open March to
October. ☎ 020 8534 6085.

Tent City, Hackney, Millfields Road,
London E5. 4mi/6km from Central
London. Open mid June to late
August. ☎ 020 8985 7656.

Lea Valley Campsite, Sewardstone,
Sewardstone Road, Chingford, London
E4. 12mi/19km from Central London.
Open Easter to October.
☎ 020 8529 5689.

**Picketts Lock Sport and Leisure
Centre**, Picketts Lock Lane,
Edmonton, London N9 0AS.
10mi/16km from Central London.
Open all year. ☎ 020 8345 6666.

**Riverside Mobile Home and
Touring Park**, Thorney Mill Road,
West Drayton, Middlesex. 14mi/20km
from Central London. Open all year.
☎ 01895 446 520.

Tent City, Old Oak Common Lane,
East Acton, London W3. 6mi/10km
from Central London. Open June to
August. ☎ 020 8749 9074.

ANGUS TAVERNER

Eating out

London has become a haven for gourmets. Restaurants abound specialising in all kinds of cuisine: traditional, nouvelle, continental or ethnic. Refer to the annually revised **Michelin Red Guide to London** for detailed information and prices.

Please note that the addresses listed below are included as representative of a particular establishment specialising in particular types of food; this does however not constitute a recommendation.

A pub lunch in Bayswater

BREAKFAST

Typical English breakfast fry-ups that sustain most of Britain's manual labour force (fried egg, bacon, brownies, fried bread, baked beans, sausage, tomatoes, mushrooms and chips served with milky tea) are to be sought from cafes colloquially known as *'greasy spoons'*. The first to open shop for the day are located by the former wholesale markets like **Smithfield**, just south of the Barbican.

For a slick version try **VingtQuatre** at 333 Fulham Road, W10 (☎ 020 7376 7224) open around the clock serving cereals and fry-ups.

Dining at the Savoy

The Savoy Archive

AFTERNOON TEA

Those who wish to sample the traditional elegance of English afternoon tea should try the Fountain Restaurant in **Fortnum & Mason** or the **Ritz Hotel** in Piccadilly; Brown's Hotel in Dover Street; the Lanesborough Hotel at Hyde Park Corner (home-made lemon curd, jams and marmalades) as well as those other long-established institutions as the **Savoy**, the **Dorchester** (beware of their different dress code conventions), the winter garden of the Landmark London Hotel in Marylebone Road... Order a selection of cucumber sandwiches, scones with clotted cream and jam, hot buttered crumpets and muffins, fruit cake and pastries, accompanied by Indian (Darjeeling) or China (green or flavoured like Lapsang Souchong or Earl Grey) tea.

A SELECTION OF RESTAURANTS

The list below gives restaurants charging an average price of £25 in the "Moderate" category, £28-45 for "Mid-range" and more for "Luxury". These prices will vary depending on the number of courses and the beverages ordered. Wine can be an expensive item and consequently the cost of a meal will be substantially higher.

Depending on what takes the fancy there is a vast choice of restaurants in the metropolis, a left-over perhaps from colonial days when Britain had links with distant lands around the globe. 'Modern British' is served by any of the Conran group of restaurants: Mezzo (seating for 700), Le Pont de la Tour, Quaglino's, Bluebird, Bibendum in the picturesque Michelin building... Otherwise, long crisp white aprons dispense 'designer' food at Kensington Place (Notting Hill Gate), the Fifth Floor restaurant at Harvey Nichols and the OXO Tower, east of Waterloo (*see* Michelin Red Guide).

KENSINGTON AND CHELSEA

This residential area boasts exclusive mansions, elegant specialist shops for clothes, antiques, books and decorative arts along Kensington High Street, Kensington Church Street, Old Brompton Road, King's Road and Fulham Road.

Moderate

Bombay Brasserie – Courtfield Road, SW7 4UH. ☎ 020 7370 4040. Closed 25-27 Dec. (CC)
Indian restaurant with pretty decor and conservatory.

Café Lazeez – First floor. 93-95 Old Brompton Road, SW7 3LD. ☎ 020 7581 9993. (CC).
Specialities from Northern India. Good ambience.

Le Metro (at the Capital Hotel) – 22-24 Basil Street, SW3 1AT. ☎ 020 7589 5171. Closed 25 Dec. (CC)
An informal basement restaurant behind Harrods, perfect for a lunchtime snack.

Wiz – 123A Clarendon Road, W11 4JG. Closed Sun dinner, Monday lunch and 25-26 Dec. ☎ 020 7229 1500. (CC).
A neighbourhood restaurant specialising in organic produce.

Catch – 158 Old Brompton Road, SW5 0BA. ☎ 020 7370 3300. Closed 24 Dec-7Jan. (CC).
A cosy and stylish restaurant specialising in seafood.

Malabar – 27 Uxbridge Street, W8 7TQ. ⊖ Notting Hill Gate. ☎ 020 7727 8800. Closed last week in Aug and four days at Christmas. (CC).
Advance booking advisable. Delicious Indian cuisine. Buffet lunch on Sun.

Mid-range

Belvedere in Holland Park – Holland House, off Abbotsbury Road, W8 6LU. ☎ 020 7602 1238. (CC).
Delightful setting. Garden-orangery in Holland Park.

itsu – 118 Draycott Avenue, SW3 3AE. ☎ 020 7584 5522. (CC).
A modern Japanese restaurant where diners sit around a counter and take dishes going past on a conveyor belt.

Zaika – 257-259 Fulham Road, SW3 6HY. ☎ 020 7351 7823. Closed Sat lunch and bank holidays. (CC).
Modern Indian cuisine in a colourful and stylish setting.

English Garden – 10 Lincoln Street, SW3 2TS. ☎ 020 7584 7272. Closed first two weeks in Aug. (CC)
Set lunch (English menu) £19.50. Located near the Royal Hospital in Chelsea, north of King's Road.

Chutney Mary – 535 King's Road, SW10 0SZ. ☎ 020 7351 3113. Closed 25 Dec. (CC)
Excellent food and good value. Regional Indian and Anglo-Indian cuisine.

Brasserie St Quentin – 243 Brompton Road, SW3 2EP. ☎ 020 7589 8005. (CC).
A busy and bustling brasserie with a strong Gallic flavour.

Luxury

Bibendum – Michelin House, 81 Fulham Road, SW3 6RD. ☎ 020 7581 5817. Closed 25-26 Dec. (CC).

Michelin House, with Harrods Food Hall, is one of the best Art Nouveau buildings in London. Oyster bar on ground floor and gourmet restaurant on first floor.

SOHO – PICCADILLY – STRAND – COVENT GARDEN

Soho is a buzzing entertainment centre famous for China Town, cinemas and theatres, clubs and music venues as well as pubs and cosmopolitan eating places. Strand and Covent Garden are also lively areas in the heart of town while Piccadilly is lined with elegant shops, elegant hotels and prestigious buildings.

Moderate

Alfred – 245 Shaftesbury Avenue, WC2H 8EH. ☎ 020 7240 2566. Closed Sat lunch, Sun and bank holidays. (CC)
North of Soho. Typically British cuisine. Varied menu, good presentation.

Il Forno – 63-64 Frith Street, W1V 5TA. ☎ 020 7734 4545. Closed lunch Sat and Sun, and bank holidays, Christmas and New Year. (CC).
A bright and informal Italian restaurant offering a wide selection.

Fung Shing – 15 Lisle Street,
WC2H 7BE. ☎ 020 7734 0284.
Closed 24-26 Dec and lunchtime bank
holidays. (CC).
*Cantonese restaurant with interesting
dishes.*

Passione – 10 Charlotte Street,
W1P 1HE. ☎ 020 7636 2833.
Closed Sat lunch, Sun, bank holiday
and Christmas. (CC).

Mid-range

Rules – 35 Maiden Lane, WC2E 7LB.
☎ 020 7836 5314. Closed 4 days at
Christmas. (CC).
*The oldest restaurant in London, lavish
décor. Superior English fare.
Traditional ambience.*

The Ivy – 1 West Street, WC2H 9NE.
☎ 020 7836 4751. Closed dinner
24-26, 31 Dec, 1, 3 Jan and August
bank holiday. (CC).
*A well-established restaurant in
theatreland, very popular with actors
and their ilk.*

The Birdcage – 110 Whitfield Street,
W1P 5RU. ☎ 020 7323 9655.
Closed Sat lunch and Sun. (CC).

Luxury

The Restaurant at the Ritz –
150 Piccadilly, W1V 9DG. ☎ 020
7493 8181. (CC).

Soho Soho – First floor. 11-13 Frith
Street, W1V 5TS. Closed Sun, Good
Friday and 25 Dec.
☎ 020 7494 3491. (CC).
A bustling brasserie and bar.

*A small but friendly restaurant with
light modern cooking.*

Simpson's in-the-Strand – 100
Strand, WC2 . ☎ 020 7836 9112
*Traditional British fare in traditional
setting.*

Mon Plaisir – 21 Monmouth Street,
WC2H 9DD. ☎ 020 7836 7243.
Closed Sat lunch, Sun, bank holidays
and 25 Dec. (CC).
*A family-owned, long standing and
proudly French brasserie dating from
the 1940s.*

*An idiosyncratic "fusion" menu in an
eccentrically decorated room full of
artefacts from around the world.*

*London's grandest dining room in an
elegant Louis XIV style, recently
refurbished.*

OXFORD STREET – NEW OXFORD STREET – HOLBORN
Moderate

Union Café – 96 Marylebone Lane,
W1M 5FP. ☎ 020 7486 4860.
Closed Sun, bank holidays, Christmas
and New Year. (CC).
*Not far from Wallace Collection.
First-rate fare, smart decor.*

Mid-range

Villandry – 170 Great Portland
Street, W1N 5TB.
☎ 020 7631 3131. Closed Sun
dinner, 1 Jan, 25 Dec, and bank
holidays. (CC).
*Half shop, half restaurant with
wooden floors and high ceiling.*

RK Stanleys – 6 Little Portland
Street, W1N 5NG.
☎ 020 7462 0099. Closed Sun
lunch. (CC).
*A restaurant specialising in home-made
sausages. Booth seating, diner style.*

St John – 26 St John Street,
EC1M 4AY. ☎ 020 7251 0848.
Closed Sat lunch, Sun, Easter
weekend and Christmas to New Year.
(CC).
Pub style. Robust English cuisine.

CITY OF LONDON
Mid-range

1 Lombard Street – 1 Lombard
Street, EC2V 9AA.
☎ 020 7929 6611. Closed Sat,
Sun, bank holidays and 1 week at
Christmas. (CC).
*A converted bank offering a very
popular and busy bar and brasserie
and a quieter and more formal
restaurant.*

Club Gascon – 57 West Smithfield,
EC1A 9DS. ☎ 020 7796 0600.
Closed Sat lunch, Sun, bank holidays
and 25Dec-7 Jan. (CC).
*Set beside Smithfield market and
specialising in southwest France
cooking, with 'tapas' sized portions.*

MAYFAIR

Mayfair is famous for its grand, luxurious hotels: Grosvenor House, Dorchester,
Claridge's, Connaught, Four Seasons etc... which boast elegant restaurants offering
superior fare at appropriate prices. The following suggestions are indicative:

Mid-range

Tamarind – 20 Queen Street,
W1X 7PJ. ☎ 020 7629 3561. Closed
Sat lunch and bank holidays. (CC).

*Opulent decor. Exceptional Indian
cuisine.*

Luxury

Greenhouse – 27a Hay's Mews, W1X 7RJ. ☏ 020 7499 3331. Closed Sat lunch, bank holidays and Christmas-New Year. (CC).
Georgian mews location. Charming decor, imaginative cuisine.

Grill Room (Dorchester) – Park Lane, W1A 2HJ. ☏ 020 7317 6336. (CC).
Opulent, romantic decor. Set lunch/ dinner £32.50/39.50. The setting, service and exceptional fare make for a memorable occasion.

SOUTH BANK
Mid-range

Brasserie at Cantina Vinopolis – No1 Bank End, SE1 9BU.
☏ 020 7940 8333. Closed Sun dinner and bank holidays. (CC).
Under the railway arch, a brasserie within a large wine museum.

Butlers Wharf Chop House – 36e Shad Thames, SE1 2YE. ☏ 020 7403 3403. Closed Sun dinner, and 1-3 Jan.
Riverside location near renovated docks, view of Tower Bridge. Fine cuisine.

OUTER LONDON
Mid-range

Lawn – Lawn Terrace, Blackheath SE3 9LJ. ☏ 020 7379 0724. Closed Sun dinner, Mon lunch and bank holidays. (CC).
A modern two-level, high-ceilinged restaurant that also serves brunch.

The Glasshouse – 14 Station Parade, Kew TW9 3PZ. ☏ 020 8940 6777. Closed Sun dinner, 1 Jan and 25 Dec. (CC).
A bright and airy restaurant with fixed price menu near Kew Gardens.

POPULAR FARE
Fish and chips

For typical English fare try fresh fish battered and fried in beef dripping (it is quite delicious really):

Sea Shell Fish Restaurant, 49-51 Lisson Grove, NW1. ☏ 020 7723 8703

The Upper Street Fish Shop, 324 Upper Street, Islington, N1. ☏ 020 7359 1401

Geales, 2 Farmer Street, Notting Hill Gate, W8. ☏ 020 7727 6979

Two Brothers, 297-303 Regent's Park Road, N3. ☏ 020 8346 0469

Burgers

Be prepared to queue for a burger or American salad at the most popular establishments:

Hard Rock Café: 150 Old Park Lane, W1. ☏ 020 7629 0382.

Starlight Bar: Hilton Hotel, Park Lane. Extensive views over London's skyline; be warned, it can be expensive!

Planet Hollywood: Trocadero Centre, 13 Coventry Street, W1. ☏ 020 7287 1000.

Sticky Fingers: 1a Phillimore Gardens, W8. ☏ 020 7938 5338.

Specialities

Traditional roast – Be it a loin of pork with crackling and apple sauce, rack of lamb with mint sauce and redcurrant jelly or rib of beef with Yorkshire pudding and horseradish, cut fresh from the bone before you, then go to a famous carvery.

East End delicacies – For 'cheap, cheerful, filling and good value' – seek out **pie 'n' mash, eels and liquor**: a staple dish of minced beef pie served with mash potato, eel and parsley sauce: F Cooke & Son in Dalston, Waterloo, Shepherds Bush, Hoxton and Hackney. For jellied eels: M Manze in Tower Bridge Road, Ada's in Salmon Lane, Clarke's in Clerkenwell.

Pudding – Remember to save room for steamed jam roly-poly or spotted dick; baked bread and butter pudding; Queen of Puddings; fruit pies and crumbles with egg-custard; lemon meringue pie; treacle, jam or custard tart; or that most delectable Summer Pudding, a delicious combination of soft red fruits and bread.

Picnics – Another British institution associated with sunny days at Glyndebourne and Henley, or boating expeditions with Jerome K Jerome *(Three Men in a Boat)* or Ratty *(The Wind and the Willows)*: these can be easily assembled by filling a hamper (from Fortnum and Masons in Piccadilly) with potted shrimps, gentleman's relish and such goodies from Harrods or Selfridges Food Halls (in Knightsbridge and Oxford Street respectively), Partridges (in Sloane Street) or some other delectable delicatessen. Suitable grassy spots where this feast might be enjoyed include Hyde Park, Kensington Gardens, Green Park, St James's Park, Ranelagh Gardens in Chelsea, Holland Park, Kenwood House...

Pubs may be franchised to a brewer or be independent. Cask beers to ask for at brewery pubs are as follows: **Courage** – John Smith's, Ruddles, Directors; **Bass** – Worthingtons; **Fullers** – London Pride; **Sam Smith** – Sovereign. The **Firkin** pubs brew their own brands which vary with region. **Guinness/Beamish/ Murphy's** are famous for their dark Irish stout.

Regular beer-based concoctions include **Shandy** – bitter or lager and ginger beer or lemonade. **Snakebite** – half lager, half cider – a favourite student's tipple as it goes straight to the head... **Black velvet** – a potent mixture of Guinness and Champagne!

Whisky mac – Scotch whisky and ginger wine (produced by Berry Bros). **Pimms** – iced gin or brandy base with lemonade and sliced fresh fruit. **Port and lemon** – a naval concoction from times past. **London Gin and tonic** – speaks for itself.

PUBS AND WINE BARS

A few of the most traditional pubs are shown in red on the maps in the Sights section. Licensing hours run from Mon to Sat, 11am to 11pm, Sun, 12noon to 3pm and 7pm to 10.30pm. London is supplied by her own local breweries while maintaining a major, long-standing tradition of importing fine wines (Ball Brothers in the City and Berry Brothers in St James's). Both at lunchtimes and after the markets have closed in the City, beer and champagne are abundantly available to celebrate the making or to commiserate the loss of millions of pounds on the exchanges.

Beer – The mainstay is a wide selection of draught or bottled beer, served traditionally in half-pint or pint glasses – wine on the other hand is served in metric portions! Each establishment attracts its particular clientele of locals, foreigners in-the-know, social types or trend setters.

'Entire' or Intire Butt beer was first brewed at the Bell Brewhouse in Shoreditch (1722) – a cheap, strong, black hoppy beer made of coarse barley that reacted well with London's soft water, and fermented in large wooden casks over time – its other popular name 'porter' was coined because it was drunk by the manual workers at Smithfield and Billingsgate. A variation of this beer continues to be produced by the principal London Breweries: Fullers, Youngs, Charringtons and Whitbread as are bitter, lager, ale, hock and stout.

Theme bars – These find favour during the football, rugby, formula 1 seasons... The **Sports Café**, in Haymarket, is equipped with banks of TVs for up to date coverage of sporting fixtures while the girlfriend may be shopping. **Shoeless Joe's**, in the King's Road, offers a video wall behind the bar.

Cyber cafés – Send a message home on the Internet, now there is no excuse for not keeping in touch with friends!

Cyberia – 39 Whitfield Street W1, ⊖ Goodge Street is the oldest-running web site: www.cyberiacafe.net

Buzz Bar is situated upstairs at the Portobello Gold, 95-97 Portobello Road, W11 ⊖ Notting Hill Gate; www.buzzbar.co.uk

Global Café is located in Soho and serves delicious hot chocolate – 15 Golden Square ⊖ Piccadilly; www.globalcafe.net

Café Internet which offers vegetarian dishes and a takeaway service is at 22-24 Buckingham Palace Road, SW1. ⊖ Victoria; www.cafeinternet.co.uk.

Atmospheric pubs

The Grenadier in Wilton Row (Belgravia) retains its distinctive stone mounting block outside, a reminder left over from the days when the Officers' Mess of the Duke of Wellington's Regiment was situated here, complete with its cobbled mews behing for the company's horses and carts.

The Guinea in Bruton Place (Mayfair) earned its reputation in the days of the cattle market that was authorised by James II in 1686. Later, as the area was gentrified, the pub must have drawn its regulars from among stable boys and footmen employed locally. A guinea was valued at 21 shillings (one pound and one shilling in old currency).

The Lamb Tavern in Leadenhall (City) overlies a Roman basilica dating from AD 50; in AD 120 this was rebuilt and enlarged to extend from Leadenhall to the far side of Gracechurch Street, the second largest in Europe after Basilica Ulpia in Rome. In the 19C the pub would have provided over-night accommodation to travellers who had booked ocean-passages to distant lands from local shipping companies in Leadenhall Street or East India House.

The French House in Dean Street (Soho). Unofficial home of the Free French during the war and now frequented by a bohemian crowd of writers, actors and artists, with walls covered with photos of the regulars from the past. There is an additional dining room on the first floor.

Entertainment

THEATRE

Today high standards and international reputations are maintained by the Royal Shakespeare Company, the Royal Opera, the Royal Ballet, English National Opera, and the likes of such successful musical writers as Andrew Lloyd Webber and Stephen Sondheim. Experimental theatre starts in the provinces and on London's fringe circuit before moving to the West End for a season. During the summer, open air venues in Holland Park, Regents Park and the Globe Theatre are an unusually historical and informal way to enjoy performances.

Half-Price Ticket Booth, Leicester Square

R. Besse/MICHELIN

Royal National Theatre – *South Bank*. The **National Theatre Company** (founded by Sir Laurence Olivier in 1962), which moved into its new premises designed by Denys Lasdun in 1976, was first nurtured at the Old Vic, a centre for music, opera and drama – especially Shakespeare under Lilian Baylis (d 1937) whose company at some time included almost every British actor of note. The modernist complex boasts three important stage venues the **Olivier** with a large open-platform stage, the **Lyttelton** with its proscenium arch and the **Cottesloe** – a small, flexible studio space. Both restaurants and bars have wonderful views of the river. 40 (Olivier), 40 (Lyttelton), 20 (Cottesloe) tickets daily are retained by the box office for sale on day of performance. Queues start at 8am for most popular shows. Daily backstage tours. ☎ 020 7452 3400; box office ☎ 020 7452 0000.

Tickets for West End theatres and musicals are booked-up by agents who may charge a 10% booking fee on re-sale. To avoid paying a surcharge, seats should be bought via the theatre box office direct, but be prepared for long-term availability. One way to beat the system is to opt for matinée performances, although star casts may be replaced by understudies.

Ticketmaster ☎ 020 7344 4444 and **First Call** ☎ 020 7420 0000/ 0870 333 7770 .

Half-Price Ticket Booth ⊙ – *Leicester Square* ⊖ *Leicester Square*. Run by the Society of London Theatres (SOLT), the ticket booth offers a limited number of half-price tickets to most West End shows on the day of performance. Available on a first-come-first-served basis, cash payment only accepted plus service charge, no returns, maximum four tickets per application. Open Monday to Saturday 1-6.30pm; Sunday and matinée days 12-6.30pm. For more information contact SOLT, Bedford Chambers, The Piazza, Covent Garden WC2. ☎ 020 7836 0971.

Artsline ☎ 020 7388 2227 is a free advice service to assist people with disabilities in accessing arts and entertainment in the capital.

ANGUS TAVERNER

Theatreland

Barbican Arts Centre – *Barbican Centre, Silk Street, EC2.* The **Royal Shakespeare Company** (RSC) performs at two different venues at the Swan Theatre in Stratford-upon-Avon and in London - first at the Aldwych Theatre and since 1982 at the **Barbican** and **The Pit**. The **RSC** has a broad repertoire and a reputation for excellence, notably for interpretations of Shakespeare; it is also a famous training ground for aspiring actors.

The Barbican complex, designed by Chamberlin, Powell and Bon, comprises five floors of facilities including concert halls, a cinema, exhibition areas and refreshment facilities. ☎ 020 7638 8891.

West End Theatre and Musicals – London has always had a strong tradition of popular musical entertainment: in the 19C the musical halls put on variety shows. Although the Savoy operas (1897-99) by Gilbert and Sullivan have lost some of their original huge popularity, musicals continue to be highly successful with many shows transferring to Broadway in New York.

Theatres are listed here alphabetically for ease of reference. In each case it is advisable that facilities available for the disabled are checked prior to booking. Most theatres have induction loops for the hard of hearing.

The Adelphi in the Strand was where Dickens' novels were dramatised almost as soon as they were published (1837-45). Its reputation for popular entertainment is firmly rooted in musicals (Noel Coward's *Words and Music, Me and My Girl, Sunset Boulevard*). ☎ 020 7344 0055.

The Albery, *St Martin's Lane*, boasts a long string of successful productions: Noel Coward's *I'll Leave It To You (1920)*, *St Joan* by G B Shaw, T S Eliot's *The Cocktail Party* and Dylan Thomas' *Under Milk Wood*... ☎ 020 7369 1730.

The Aldwych, *Aldwych*, designed in 1905 by W G R Sprague as a twin to the Strand theatre, was where the **Ben Travers** farces were performed (1925-33). In the 1940s, during the Blitz, the Aldwych hosted the Ballet Rambert. In 1960 Peter Hall secured the Aldwych as a home for his troupe the Royal Shakespeare Memorial Theatre (later the RSC) with Dame Peggy Ashcroft as the Duchess of Malfi. Launch pad for Glenda Jackson. ☎ 020 7416 6003.

The Apollo, *Shaftesbury Avenue*, was home to **The Follies** (1908-12) before securing its reputation for light comedy, farce and revue. ☎ 020 7494 5070.

The Apollo-Victoria, *Wilton Road*, was designed as a cinema (1930) and transformed into a theatre in 1979 for performances by Shirley Bassey, Cliff Richard, Sammy Davis Jnr. Dominated today by Andrew Lloyd Webber's **Starlight Express**. ☎ 020 7416 6070.

The Cambridge, *Earlham Street off Seven Dials*, has hosted opera, dance and theatre. Famous productions starring Albert Finney, Ingrid Bergman, Laurence Olivier, Maggie Smith, Ian McKellen... ☎ 020 7494 5080.

The Comedy, *Panton Street*, has put on performances by Sarah Bernhardt, premieres by Somerset Maugham and productions of *Cat on a Hot Tin Roof, The Rocky Horror Show, Little Shop of Horrors*. ☎ 020 7369 1731.

The Criterion, *Piccadilly Circus*, partly built underground, is one of the most beautiful of the London theatres. ☎ 020 7369 1747.

The Dominion, *Tottenham Court Road,* was designed as a concert venue on a former leper colony and brewery. Reputation for musicals, notably **Grease**. ☎ 020 7656 1888/416 6075.

The Duchess, *Catherine Street,* in the past for plays by J B Priestley, Coward, Pinter is now known for more risqué productions *(Oh Calcutta!).* ☎ 020 7494 5075.

The Duke of York, *St Martin's Lane,* is associated with Shaw, Ibsen, Galsworthy, Coward's interpretation of Slightly in *Peter Pan* (1913); the cradle of the actor's union Equity. ☎ 020 7565 5000.

The Fortune, *Russell Street,* served Flanders and Swann with a packed venue for *At The Drop Of A Hat.* Later taken by storm by Alan Bennett, Peter Cook, Dudley Moore and Jonathan Miller in *Beyond The Fringe.* ☎ 020 7836 2238.

The Garrick, *Charing Cross Road,* is renowned for comedy, farce, and being haunted by the ghost of actor/manager Arthur Bourchier. ☎ 020 7494 5085.

The Gielgud, *Shaftesbury Avenue,* has a lovely oval gallery and Regency staircase; renamed when Sam Wanamaker's vision to recreate Shakespeare's Globe was realised. ☎ 020 7494 5065.

The Lyceum in the Strand, closed in 1939, has recently been reopened as a venue for special shows. ☎ 020 7656 1803.

Lyric, *Shaftesbury Avenue* has staged operetta, light comedy and straight drama. ☎ 020 7494 5045.

Her Majesty's, *Haymarket,* was the cradle of the drama school which latterly has evolved into RADA. Sir John Vanbrugh's original playhouse opened in 1705, its large interior unusually panelled in wood. Today hosts **Phantom of the Opera.** ☎ 020 7494 5400.

The New Ambassadors, *West Street,* designed in 1913 by W G R Sprague, provided Vivien Leigh and Ivor Novello with their West End debuts. In 1952 *The Mousetrap* opened and monopolised the premises for twenty years before moving to St Martin's. Christopher Hampton's RSC *Les Liaisons Dangereuses* enjoyed similar success. ☎ 020 7836 6111.

The New London, *167 Drury Lane,* stands on the site of the Winter Garden Theatre, a place of entertainment since Elizabeth I's reign. Today it stages Andrew Lloyd Webber's long running show **Cats** based on T S Eliot's great classic *Old Possum's Book of Practical Cats* premiered in 1980. ☎ 020 7405 0072 / cc booking 404 4079.

The Palace, *Cambridge Circus,* opened for opera under the ownership of Richard D'Oyly Carte. Grand, ornate and Victorian through and through, it continues to produce musicals *(The Entertainer, Jesus Christ Superstar).* RSC production of Alain Boublil and Claude Michel Schonberg adaptation of Victor Hugo novel **Les Misérables.** ☎ 020 7434 0909.

The sumptuous **London Palladium,** *Argyll Street,* is home to variety shows and musical revivals *(Saturday Night Fever).* ☎ 020 7494 5020.

The Peacock, *Portugal Street.* The Royalty (as it was known until recently), which is associated with Sadlers Wells, provides a venue for small off-beat productions. ☎ 020 7683 8222.

Gilbert Scott's **Phoenix** (1930), *Charing Cross Road,* is decked with a superb Art Deco interior, an appropriate venue for Noel Coward revivals. ☎ 020 7369 1733.

The Piccadilly, *Denman Street,* hosted the early showings of British talkie movies. ☎ 020 7369 1734.

The Playhouse, *South end of Craven Street, Northumberland Avenue,* was extensively refurbished in 1987 thirty-six years after its last live performance; the Franco-Venetian interior resplendent with gilding, plasterwork and murals dates from 1906. ☎ 020 7839 4401.

The Prince Edward, *Old Compton Street,* was launched for musicals and revues, including performances, among others, by Josephine Baker (1933). ☎ 020 7734 8951/447 5400.

The Prince of Wales, *Coventry St,* is famous as a venue hosting musicals. ☎ 020 7839 5972.

The Queen's modernist exterior on Shaftesbury Avenue was designed by Bryan Westwood and Hugh Casson having suffered extensive bomb damage in 1940. Names to tread these boards include Gielgud, Vanessa Redgrave and Nigel Hawthorne. ☎ 020 7494 5040.

St Martin's, *West Street,* was designed as a companion to the Ambassador's next door. For the past twenty years it has produced **The Mousetrap,** based on Agatha Christie's 'who dunnit' of the same name. ☎ 020 7836 1443.

The Savoy on the Strand was built by Richard D'Oyly Carte in 1881 to stage the Gilbert and Sullivan operas (of which 13 appeared between 1875 and 1896). In 1929 it was refurbished with Art Deco fixtures by Frank Tugwell and Basil

The Royal Ballet – *Daphnis and Chloë*

Ionides for Rupert D'Oyly Carte and nicknamed the 'theatre of sunshine' after its daffodil yellow interior; destroyed by fire in 1990, the theatre has been rebuilt. ☎ 020 7836 8888.

The Shaftesbury, *Shaftesbury Avenue*, was designed in 1911. Its huge premises welcomed crowds for Diaghilev's Ballets Russes and Sarah Bernhardt. ☎ 020 7379 5399.

The Strand, *Aldwych*, has hosted one-man shows by Barry Humphries alias Dame Edna Everage, Victoria Wood and Dave Allen. ☎ 020 7930 8800.

The Theatre Royal, Drury Lane *(Covent Garden)* occupies a site that goes back to 1663. The present building was designed by Benjamin Wyatt (1812) for productions starring Nell Gwynne, Mrs Jordan, David Garrick, Edmund Keane and the famous clown Grimaldi. Both George I and George III survived assassination attempts here, although an unknown man, less fortunate, walled up in the upper circle is said to haunt matinees. Home to successful, long-running musicals *(Oklahoma, My Fair Lady, Miss Saigon)*. ☎ 020 7494 5000. Theatre tours daily from foyer. ☎ 020 7240 5357.

The Theatre Royal, Haymarket. The Little Theatre in the Haymarket was where Henry Fielding's satires incurred the wrath of the Lord Chamberlain. Rebuilt in 1821 by John Nash, this theatre is particularly associated with Oscar Wilde *(An Ideal Husband, Woman Of No Importance)*. Back stage tours available; ☎ 020 7930 8800.

The Vaudeville on the Strand opened in 1870. ☎ 020 7836 9987.

Beautiful actresses

Eleanor 'Nell' Gwynne (1650-87) sold oranges outside the Theatre Royal when she was noticed by Charles II. Despite being illiterate, she is reputed to have been good at comedy and reciting prologues and epilogues.

Sarah Siddons (1755-1831) was the eldest of twelve children; she was a tall lady of brilliant beauty with expressive eyes and a dignity of demeanour that heightened the tragedy of the parts she performed, notably that of Lady Macbeth, Desdemona, Rosalind and Ophelia.

Dorothea Jordan (1762-1816) was born in Ireland the daughter of an actress. Dora made her debut at Drury Lane in *A Country Girl* in 1785. In 1790 she became the mistress of the Duke of Clarence, the future King William IV, for whom she bore ten children (the Fitz-Clarences) while continuing to play to packed houses at the Haymarket, Covent Garden, Richmond and touring the Northern Counties; they never married. Dora made her last appearance on the London stage in 1814, three years after separating from the Duke.

The Whitehall, *Whitehall*. This small Art Deco theatre staged farces in the 1950s and 60s under Brian Rix. During the war, the boards were second home to a famed stripper Phyllis Dixey and to Paul Raymond's nudes revue *Pyjama Tops*. ☎ 020 7369 1735.

The Wyndham's, *Charing Cross Road*. Grand late Victorian venue for crime dramas and musicals (*Godspell* with David Essex and Jeremy Irons); one of the most attractive auditoriums in the West End. ☎ 020 7369 1736.

Off the West End Circuit – Many shows start outside the West End at smaller venues with cheaper tickets.

Lyric Studio Theatre – *King Street, Hammersmith*. The theatre, which is incorporated in a modern shopping centre, was reconstructed in 1979 on the site of the original Lyric Opera House or Lyric Hall auditorium built in 1888. ☎ 0208 741 2311.

Mermaid Theatre – *Puddle Dock, Blackfriars*. In 1959 a disused warehouse opened as the Mermaid Theatre, the first theatre in the City for three centuries. In the late 1970s, when the Blackfriars underpass was constructed the road system was entirely redesigned, the tall, inconvenient 19C offices were demolished and the old theatre closed. Some ten years later there appeared on the same site a £4-5 million construction in which offices formed a superstructure to the foyers, exhibition area, bars and, most importantly, the auditorium and modern stage of the new Mermaid Theatre. ☎ 020 7236 2211.

Old Vic – *Waterloo Road*. The cradle of the National Theatre before moving to its new site (1976), was built in 1818 as the Coburg Theatre. In 1880 it was taken by Emma Cons (d 1912), a pioneer of social reform, and run as the Royal Victoria Music Hall and Coffee Tavern with a programme of concerts, temperance meetings and penny lectures, the last proving so popular that in 1889 the Morley Memorial College for Working Men and Women was founded within the theatre. Under **Lilian Baylis** (d 1937), who succeeded her aunt, the theatre, now known as the Old Vic, became a centre for music, opera and drama (especially Shakespeare) and home to a company in which virtually every British actor of note has played at some time. The stage was difficult and draughty; the seats in the pit and the gods were hard and one had to beware of pillars, but prices were low – 4d in the gallery, 5s in the stalls – and the acting was excellent. In 1940 the Vic was bombed and the company moved to the New Theatre, returning after the war in 1976 when, as the National Theatre Company, it moved into the new National Theatre. Now restored to its former Victorian music-hall appearance and refurbished with better facilities, it is once again a thriving repertory theatre. ☎ 020 7928 7616.

Regent's Park Open Air Theatre – *Inner Circle, Regent's Park*. Founded in 1932, the New Shakespeare Company presents a summer season of theatre from May to September. Annual regulars include *Midsummer Night's Dream*. Take something warm, a cushion, an umbrella in case of rain, and a picnic; BBQ and cold buffet available; bar and hot drinks under cover. ☎ 020 7486 2431 / 1933.

Royal Court (English Stage Company) – *Sloane Square SW1*. Farce and 'kitchen sink drama' were both new vogues introduced by the Royal Court Theatre which opened in 1870. Coined as the 'bad boy of West End theatre', this famous institution introduced the Arthur Pinero farces and was the launch pad for G B Shaw (1904-09) and John Osborne (*Look Back in Anger* 1956); famous performers include many of the greatest: Olivier, Gielgud, Richardson. The company also plays at the Duke of York's and at the Ambassadors. ☎ 020 7565 5000.

Sadler's Wells Theatre – *Rosebery Avenue*. From 1934 the Wells specialised in opera and ballet to become the cradle of the future Royal Ballet and English National Opera, which transferred first to Covent Garden (1946) then to the Coliseum (1968). Latterly it has become a major venue for visiting companies from abroad. After extensive refurbishment, the theatre now boasts modern facilities. ☎ 020 7278 8916.

Victoria Palace – *Victoria Street*. Hit musicals have succeeded one another: *Me And My Girl, The Lambeth Walk, Black And White Minstrels' Show, Annie, Charlie Girl, High Society, Buddy*. ☎ 020 7834 1317.

Small Venues and Fringe – Short seasons of experimental theatre are put on in various reliable venues.

Almeida – *Almeida Street, Islington*. Excellent, intimate playhouse for provocative, intelligent, Classical programme. ☎ 020 7359 4404.

Arts – *Great Newport Street*. Premiere of Samuel Beckett's *Waiting for Godot*. Workshops. ☎ 020 7836 2132 / 3334.

Battersea Arts Centre – *Old Town Hall, Lavender Hill*. Three flexible spaces for new writing and mime productions, cabaret, story-telling; Festival for Visual Theatre; Edinburgh Preview Season. ☎ 020 7223 2223.

Bush – *Above the Bush Pub, Goldhawk Road and Shepherd's Bush Green.* Important venue for experimental writing; star performances produced in collaboration with well-established directors. ☎ 0208 743 3388.

Cochrane – *Southampton Row.* One time home for the National Youth Theatre; first black *King Lear.* ☎ 020 7242 7040.

Comedy Store – *Haymarket House, Oxenden Street, SW1.* Stand-up new movement comedy and improvisation on Wednesday and Sunday. Performances at 8pm; midnight Friday and Saturday. Info ☎ 0426 914433; bookings ☎ 020 7344 4444.

Donmar – *Thomas Neal's, Earlham Street.* West End Studio theatre for excellent new productions, often populated by university students. ☎ 020 7369 1732.

Gate – *Prince Albert Pub, Pembridge Road, Notting Hill Gate.* Strong tradition of reviving international Classics: Spanish, Ancient Greek, Latin cycles. ☎ 020 7229 0706.

King's Head – *115 Upper Street, Islington.* Miniature musicals, Classic revivals acted by famous figures (Steven Berkoff, Victoria Wood, Tom Conti). ☎ 020 7226 1916.

Players – *The Arches, Villiers Street.* Victorian music hall, melodrama, pantomime. ☎ 020 7839 1134.

Riverside – *Crisp Road, Hammersmith.* Iron foundry turned film studio, this venue was a major BBC studio from 1954-73. Four spaces for visiting acts; various disciplines (dance, mime, theatre, music, comedy). ☎ 0208 748 3354/ 237 1111.

Young Vic – *The Cut, Waterloo.* Independent from the National Theatre since 1974. ☎ 020 7928 6363.

OPERA AND BALLET

The Royal Opera House, Covent Garden – *Bow Street.* **The Royal Ballet,** which was created in 1956 out of the former Sadler's Wells Ballet, transferred to Covent Garden in 1946, where it was joined by **The Royal Opera** which received a royal charter in 1968. After extensive refurbishment the opera house is due to reopen by the end of 1999..
Around performers (and characters) such as Patti, Melba, Caruso, Elizabeth Schumann, Gigli, Conchita Supervia, Tauber, Flagstad... golden memories abound, legends grow: Patti in 1895 as Violetta wore a white dress studded with 3 700 diamonds and two Bow Street detectives joined the guests on stage in Act 3 of *La Traviata* (Flora's party); Queen Victoria decided that the bearing of Italian choristers appearing in *Fidelio* was unmilitary and that as 'Our soldiers can do better than that' extras to swell processions should be provided from the Brigade of Guards. This practice continued until 1978. ☎ 020 7304 4000.

London Coliseum – *St Martin's Lane.* This large Edwardian theatre was built in 1904 by Sir Oswald Stoll to rival Drury Lane. Retained marble pillars, terracotta front, electrically lit globe winking against the night sky, combined with an interior refurbishing (mosaic ceiling, wood panelling and huge portraits), have transformed it since 1968 into the home of the former Sadler's Wells company, now the **English National Opera.** Stars of the Edwardian Variety hall included Sarah Bernhardt and the Ballet Russe before, briefly, being used as a cinema. The ENO stages operas in English. ☎ 020 7632 8300; Disabled information ☎ 020 7836 7666.

CLASSICAL MUSIC

Royal Albert Hall – *Kensington Gore, SW7.* The Kensington Bowl is home to the **Royal Philharmonic Orchestra** (founded by Thomas Beecham in 1946) and hosts the famous summer season of BBC Henry Wood Promenade Concerts (mid July to mid September). ☎ 020 7589 8212. Between 1997-2003, the Albert Hall is scheduled to have renovation work that will provide underground loading bays for stage scenery etc.

Barbican – *Silk Street, EC1.* Home to the **London Symphony Orchestra** (founded 1904), the Barbican also plays host to visiting orchestras like the Bournemouth Symphony and the City of Birmingham Symphony Orchestra. ☎ 020 7638 8891.

South Bank – *Belvedere Road, SE1.* The **London Philharmonic Orchestra** is based at the **Royal Festival Hall** which was the only permanent building erected in 1951 for the Festival of Britain; the occasion was seized to build a new concert auditorium for London, since the Queen's Hall had been gutted by incendiaries and the Albert Hall's acoustics were still troubled by an echo.
Royal Festival Hall box office ☎ 020 7960 4242; recorded information ☎ 020 7921 0682.
Subsidiary concert venues include the **Queen Elizabeth Hall** and the **Purcell Room.**

The **Promenade Concerts** were initiated by Robert Newman in 1859 and conducted annually by Sir Henry Wood (1869-1944) from the opening night until he died. When the Queen's Hall was destroyed by enemy action in 1941, the concerts transferred without interruption to the Royal Albert Hall. Traditionally, the programme for the second half of the concert on the last night of the season (mid-July to late September) invariably consists of *Fantasia of British Sea Songs* arranged by Wood, followed by *Jerusalem* by Parry and *Land of Hope and Glory* by Elgar to which the promenaders (standing audience in the pit) add their own voice and chanting!

Wigmore Hall – *36 Wigmore Street, W1.* An intimate venue for solo recitals and small chamber orchestras; excellent acoustics, perfect atmosphere. Sunday morning coffee concerts are an institution. ☎ 020 7935 2141.

Churches – Westminster Abbey, Westminster Cathedral and St Paul's Cathedral all boast superb choirs.

St James's Church, *Piccadilly*, hosts the annual Lufthansa Festival of Baroque Music. ☎ 020 7734 4511.

St John's, *Smith Square*, holds frequent Monday lunchtime concerts (1pm); regular evening chamber music and choral pieces starting at 7.30pm. ☎ 020 7222 1061.

St Martin's in the Fields, *Trafalgar Square*, organises lunchtime concerts for young musicians (Monday, Tuesday, Wednesday, Friday at 1.05pm) and evening candle-lit concerts (Thursday, Friday, Saturday) for members of the famous Academy of St Martin in the Fields. ☎ 020 7839 8362/930 0089.

City churches that organise lunchtime concerts include St Bride's, St Anne and St Agnes, St Lawrence Jewry, St Margaret Lothbury, St Martin within Ludgate, St Mary le Bow, St Michael's Cornhill, St Olave Hart Street.

ROCK, ROOTS AND JAZZ

As the scene fluidly changes from acid to funk, hard-core, handbag, Brit-pop, future hop, soul, salsa, techno, garage, it is advised that you check with current fixtures listed in the press **(Time Out** or **Evening Standard Hot Tickets)**.

Academy Brixton – *211 Stockwell Road SW9.* Huge capacity, amazing decor. ☎ 020 7924 9999. ⊖ Brixton.

Africa Centre – *38 King Street, WC2.* Visiting African bands, groovy sound. Friday and Saturday 9.30pm to 3am. Music from 10.30pm. ☎ 020 7836 1973.

Apollo Hammersmith – *Queen Caroline Street, W6.* Big name attractions. ☎ 020 7416 6080. ⊖ Hammersmith.

Astoria – *157 Charing Cross Road, WC2.* Broad range, big venue. Open Monday-Thursday 7pm to 11pm; Friday 11pm to 3.30am; Saturday 10pm to 6am. ☎ 020 7434 0403. ⊖ Tottenham Court Road.

Blue Note – *Hoxton Square, N1.* Jazz, African, Asian, Latin American in small but popular venue. Open daily 8pm to 2am. ☎ 020 7729 2476.

Bull's Head, Barnes – *Lonsdale Road, SW13.* Congenial setting for British jazz scene. Pub opening hours; music 8.30pm daily. ☎ 0208 876 5241.

Cecil Sharp House – *2 Regent's Park Road, NW1.* Folk dancing, singing and music making. Thursday-Saturday 7.30pm to 11pm. Music from 7.30pm. ☎ 020 7485 2206.

100 Club – *100 Oxford Street, W1.* Early haunt of the Sex Pistols, this basement now plays traditional and modern jazz, blues and swing. Monday-Wednesday 8pm to 12midnight; Thursday 8pm to 1am; Friday 8.30 to 3am; Saturday 7.30pm to 1am; Sunday 7.30 to 11.30pm. ☎ 020 7636 0933.

606 Club – *90 Lots Road, SW10.* Tiny basement, good sounds from young musicians. Monday-Saturday 8.30pm to 2.30am; Sunday 8.30pm to 1.30am. ☎ 020 7352 5953.

Forum – *9-17 Highgate Road, NW5.* Best in new music. Monday-Thursday, Sunday 7pm to 11pm; Friday, Saturday 7pm to 2am. ☎ 020 7284 2200. ⊖ Kentish Town.

Jazz Café – *5 Parkway, NW1.* Jazz, soul, Latin American, African rap every night. Monday-Thursday 7pm to 12midnight; Friday, Saturday 12noon to 4pm; Sunday 12noon to 4pm, 7pm to 10.30pm. ☎ 020 7344 0044.

Mean Fiddler – *22-28a High Street, Harlesden, NW10.* Good for sound, beer, and music from the organiser of the big time Folk festivals (Reading). Monday-Thursday 8pm to 2am; Friday, Saturday 8pm to 3am; Sunday 7.30pm to 1am. Music 9.30pm. ☎ 020 7344 0044.

Pizza Express – *10 Dean Street, W1.* Resident band; top visiting bands either here or below; restaurant pizza obligatory. Open daily 8pm to 12.30am. Music Monday-Thursday, Sunday 8.30pm to 12midnight; Friday, Saturday 9pm to 12midnight. ☎ 020 7437 9595.

Pizza on the Park – *11 Knightsbridge, Hyde Park Corner, W1.* Mainstream jazz at the flagship establishment of Pizza Express chain. Open daily 8pm to 12midnight. Music 9.15pm. ☎ 020 7235 5550.

Ronnie Scotts – *47 Frith Street, W1.* Legendary Soho jazz venue; excellent sound and atmosphere; expensive food and drink; booking advisable. Monday-Saturday 8.30pm to 3am. Music 9.30pm. ☎ 020 7439 0747.

Shepherd's Bush Empire – *Shepherd's Bush Green, W12.* West London's big gig scene. ☎ 020 8740 7474. ⊖ Shepherds Bush.

South Bank – Jazz festivals and occasional gigs. Live jazz also played at lunchtimes in the Festival Hall foyer. Check press for details.

Wembley Arena – *Empire Way, Wembley.* The largest indoor venue in London for big bands (see below). ☎ 020 8900 1234. ⊖ Wembley Park or Wembley Central.

Wembley Stadium – *Empire Way, Wembley.* Disastrous acoustics and too large to offer much of a view for anything other than a football match; beware of weather conditions. The stadium is scheduled to close for rebuilding to provide the most up-to-date facilities. ☎ 020 8900 1234. ⊖ Wembley Park or Wembley Central.

CLUBBING

Stringfellows – *16 Upper St Martin's Lane, WC2.* Reputedly glitzy this nightclub attracts star spotters. Open Monday to Saturday 9pm-3.30am.

Carwash – *Le Scandale, 54 Berwick Street.* Velvet sofas and large mirrors 'pinched straight off the set of Starsky and Hutch' *(London Evening Standard)*, standard disco sound. Saturdays 10pm to 2.30am. ☎ 020 7437 6830.

In 1990 all-night clubbing was legalised, however, licensing laws still apply so alcohol runs dry at 3am. Establishments without music-and-dance or club licences are prohibited from selling alcohol after 11pm.

Legends – *29 Old Burlington Street, W1.* Good sound, designer decor, well-stocked bar. Wednesday, Thursday 10pm to 3am; Friday 10pm to 6am; Saturday 10.30pm to 4.30am. ☎ 020 7437 9933.

Cuba – *11-13 Kensington High Street, W8.* Ground floor bar and restaurant; basement club, small and can get crowded. Open daily 6pm to 2am. ☎ 020 7938 4137.

Ministry of Sound – *103 Gaunt Street, SE1.* Rave on a large scale, predominantly garage and house music, immensely successful, big attractions and good atmosphere. Open weekends only: Friday 10.30pm to 6.30am; Saturday 11pm to 9am. ☎ 020 7378 6528.

Le Palais – *242 Shepherds Bush Road, W6.* London's favourite dance hall was opened in 1919. Popular mainstream disco complete with flashing lights and video walls for good bopping. Wednesday 9.30pm to 2.30am; Thursday 9.30pm to 3am; Friday, Saturday 9pm to 3am. ☎ 0208 748 2812.

Rock Garden – *The Piazza, Covent Garden, WC2.* Showcase for aspiring bands; Friday night is club night. Monday-Thursday 8pm to 3am; Saturday 4pm to 10pm; Sunday 12noon to 3pm and 8pm to 12midnight. ☎ 020 7836 4052.

Shopping

The main **shopping centres**, together with large stores like IKEA, Toys R Us, etc are located on the outskirts of London in easy reach of the North (Brent Cross) and South Circulars (Croydon), Lakeside (Thurrock), Bluewater (Dartford). *See also PRACTICAL INFORMATION - General Information.*

DEPARTMENT STORES

For a variety of specialist retail outlets, department stores can be time saving and convenient – especially if you're looking for a bathing costume at Christmas for a winter break!

Harrods – *Knightsbridge SW1.* Harrods boasts that it can supply anything including pedigree pets! Epicurean food halls are especially impressive (fish display, good cheese) with the meat counter claiming to sell steaks of alligator and ostrich, grouse and well-hung game. Other services include hairdressing, beauty salon, travel agency and shipping.

Royal Warrant Holders

Royal Warrants have existed since the Middle Ages when they were granted to craftsmen supplying the King's Wardrobe (the first Royal charter was assigned to the Weavers Company by Henry II in 1155). Today four members of the Royal family are entitled to appoint Royal Warrant holders: HM The Queen, HRH The Duke of Edinburgh, HM The Queen Mother and HRH The Prince of Wales (since 1980). Only tradesmen may qualify (ie no Government Department or professional person like a doctor or dentist) by supplying goods or a service to the Royal Household: specialist craftsmen so honoured have included a whip maker, pin maker, envelope maker, chronometer maker... A Royal Warrant is initially granted for a period of 10 years during which time the business may use the grantor's Royal Coat of Arms on stationery, premises and vehicles. Currently nine firms hold all four – including Harrods, The General Trading Company and the Rover Group. Among those firms who continuously have held Royal Warrants for over 100 years are Cadbury Bros Ltd, Crosse & Blackwell Ltd, Schweppes Ltd, R Twining & Co Ltd, Wilkinson Sword Ltd...

Selfridges – *400 Oxford Street, W1.* Selfridges also has a highly reputable food-hall, is good for domestic necessities (white goods, kitchen appliances, garden equipment), beauty products and stationery.

Liberty – *Regent Street, W1.* Liberty is special. It has a long-standing association with the East: own brand silk and delicate lawn fabrics, ethnic and Art Nouveau jewellery, Indian silks, Chinese ceramics, Arts and Craft furniture, contemporary glassware, cutting edge designer fashion.

Harvey Nichols – *109 Knightsbridge, SW1.* Harvey Nichols aims to be slightly controversial in marketing its image. It very often has eye-catching and unusual window displays and boasts a now famous restaurant on the fifth floor. Designer label fashion, especially small sizes, excellent choice of hats for Ladies Day at Ascot and fine jewellery department (baubles from Christian Lacroix – streamlined modern silversmithing). Since the making of the television series 'Absolutely Fabulous' Harvey Nicks has reinforced its association with aspiring 'Sloanies'.

John Lewis – *Oxford Street, W1.* John Lewis is a purveyor of school uniforms and other functional lines of clothing, home furnishing, household linen, stationery, white goods. A good all-round store for all the practical necessities of life: invisible mending kits, colour-matched lampshades and gloves for Ascot or garden parties! Its sister shop **Peter Jones** is located in Sloane Square.

Other brand names that have franchise stores elsewhere include the **Army and Navy Stores** (in Victoria, Fenwicks off Bond Street, Barkers in Kensington High Street); **Marks and Spencer** has a flagship store at Marble Arch and subsidiary stores throughout the metropolis as do Debenhams, D H Evans...

ART AND ANTIQUES

London has always had a buoyant trade in art and antiques. Fairs are regularly held in London hotels that attract dealers from the provinces: details available from the **Antiques Trade Gazette** which comes out on Tuesdays. For details of the larger, international fairs, contact the **British Antique Dealers Association**, *20 Rutland Gate, SW7.* ☎ 020 7589 4128.

Art dealers – The most established dealers operate from Bond Street and St James's, these include Wildenstein, the Fine Art Society, Colnarghi.

The principal 20C art galleries, meanwhile, are grouped around Cork and Davies Street (Marlborough Fine Art, Waddington, Gimpel Fils). Contemporary art fairs include the Royal Academy Summer Show *(end May and June)* and the Contemporary Arts Fair at the Business Design Centre in Islington.

Auction houses – For details of sales and viewing times either phone the auction house or check the Antiques Trade Gazette.

Bonhams – *Montpelier Street, SW7.* ☎ 020 7393 3900 and at *New Chelsea Galleries, Lots Road SW10.* ☎ 020 7351 7111.

Christies – *8-10 Kings Street, SW1.* ☎ 020 7839 9060 and in *South Kensington* at *85 Brompton Road, SW7.* ☎ 020 7581 7611.

Harmers of London (Stamps) – *91 New Bond Street, W1.* ☎ 020 7629 0218.

Phillips Fine Art – *101 New Bond Street, W1.* ☎ 020 7629 6602 but also at *18 Hayes Place, Lisson Grove, NW1.* ☎ 020 7723 2647 and *10 Salem Road, W2.* ☎ 020 7229 9090.

Sotheby's – *34-35 New Bond Street W1.* ☎ 020 7493 8080.

Spink & Son – (Coins, medals) *5-7 King Street, W1.* ☎ 020 7930 7888.

Stanley Gibbons – (Stamps) *399 Strand WC2.* ☎ 020 7836 8444.

Antique and bric-à-brac markets – Obviously the earlier you get to the markets the greater the choice. Stall-holders are often knowledgeable amateur dealers, but real bargains are rare.

Alfie's – *13-25 Church Street, NW8.* Everything on sale in slightly dingy surroundings, good if you know what to look for. *Tues–Sat 10am–6pm.*

Antiquarius – *131-141 King's Road, SW3.* Art Deco, buttons, textiles, silver, glass, jewellery; fashion stylists' emporium of elegant accessories. 120 dealers. *Mon–Sat 10am–6pm.*

Brick Lane – *North of railway bridge up to Bethnal Green Road.* Big, dirty and disorganised jumble, junk and hardware. Leather and new clothes from local sweatshops at the northern end of Brick Lane. *Sun 6am–1pm.*

Camberwell Antique Market – *159-161 Camberwell Road.* Lesser antiques, frippery and china.

Camden Passage – *Between Essex Road and Upper Street.* Started in 1960s. Antiques: *Wed 7am–2pm (better day), Sat 8am–4pm.* Books *Thur 7am–4pm.*

Charing Cross Collectors Market – *Villiers Street, under Embankment Underground Station.* Coins, medals and badges. *Sat 8.30am to 5pm.*

Saturday morning, Portobello Road

Bermondsey (New Caledonian) Market – *Bermondsey Square, south of Tower Bridge.* Revived on this site in 1950, trade in silverware, copper, Victorian jewellery, furniture and other objets d'art starts early by torch-light for the cognoscenti and business for some is done by 9am, when goods are already on their way to continental destinations. *Fri 5am-1pm.*

Grays Antique Market – *1-7 Davies Mews and 58 Davies Street.* Shelters over 170 permanent stallholders. *Mon–Fri 10am to 6pm.*

Greenwich Antiques Market – *Greenwich High Road. Sat–Sun 9am–5pm.* A flea market operates on *Sun only 8am–4pm.*

Petticoat Lane – *Middlesex and Wentworth Streets.* London's most famous market for general goods and clothes, old and new. *Sun 9am–2pm.* Wentworth Street only *Mon–Fri 10.30am–2.30pm.*

Portobello Road – *Between Chepstow Villas and Lonsdale Road.* Specialist dealers and stall-holders, shops, covered arcades and street vendors selling a huge variety of goods – buttons, china and porcelain, Georgian glass, lace, leather luggage, jewellery, fishing tackle, Victoriana, Oriental antiquities and so much more. *Sat only 8.30am–5.30pm.* Junk and second-hand bits and pieces beyond the Westway between Oxford Gardens and Warrington Road.

Stables Market in Camden *(1 mile northeast of Regent's Park by the canal tow-path. Open Sat–Sun 9am–5pm. ☎ 020 7486 9957)* is a good place to go in search of basic household wares and second-hand bric-à-brac – cutlery, kitchen utensils, salvaged fixtures, 1950s bakelite and lighting; auction house catalogues; 1960s fashion.

Antique collectables – Many dealers are grouped around Islington and Portobello Road but if in search of **porcelain, glass,** chandeliers and furniture, other streets worth exploring are Kensington Church Street ⊖ *Kensington High Street, Notting Hill Gate;* Pimlico Road ⊖ *Sloane Square;* Wandsworth Bridge Road ⊖ *Parsons Green;* White Hart Lane *Overground: Barnes* and Lavender Hill *Overground: Clapham Junction.*

For fine **silver** besides the New Caledonia and Portobello markets, it is well worth exploring the Silver Vaults in the City *(see CHANCERY LANE),* while for **jewellery** the big names line the length of Bond Street and Burlington Arcade.

The most important antique fairs take place in the early summer *(May-June)* at Olympia, Grosvenor House.

Designer furnishings – Areas in which to seek out soft furnishings, design and antique furniture include the north section of Tottenham Court Road (Heal's, Habitat, Sanderson, Maples), Fulham Road and King's Road; the best-stocked department stores for standard fittings are John Lewis and Peter Jones; for wedding lists, glass and china try the GTC (General Trading Company in Sloane Street) or Thomas Goode and Co at 19 South Audley Street.

The other solutions to finding furniture are to visit the auction rooms and large galleries round and about Lots Road or the extensive warehouses down Tower Bridge Road in Bermondsey.

The **Shaker Shop** at 25 Harcourt Street, W1; **Conran Shop** at Michelin House, 81 Fulham Road, SW3; **Habitat/Heals** 196 Tottenham Court Road, W1 and in the King's Road...

FASHION AND CLOTHES

Most of the queen's wardrobe to date has been designed by the late Sir Norman Hartnell – as the display at Kensington Palace will confirm. The late Diana, Princess of Wales, did great things for the British fashion industry, hailing a return to fine tailoring and unconventional glamour to achieve a careful balance of formal elegance and chic. Revivalist culture, pastel colours and Liberty prints are mixed and matched with a taste for the more traditional: hats, gloves, matching shoes and handbags, Eliza Doolittle outfits are flaunted at summer weddings, Ascot, Henley and Royal Garden Parties, while organza and taffeta regale the young bright things at charity and summer balls!

Perhaps the most telling catalogue of British taste in fashion is to be viewed at the Victoria and Albert Museum where the trends set by Punk Rockers, Mods and skinheads, who identify with yet another 'look' have not escaped notice.

Fashion off the peg – Foreign labels line Bond Street and congregate around Knightsbridge (Maud Frizon, Stephan Kélian, Kenzo, Prada, Ungaro, Steiger, Yves St Laurent-Rive Gauche, Chanel, Léo Ferré, Joseph, Dior, Céline, Browns, Cartier, Hermès, Louis Vuitton) at close proximity to the Armani Emporium and **Harvey Nichols.**

Home-grown designers proliferate in Beauchamp Place (Ken Jay, Paddy Campbell, Caroline Charles, Bruce Oldfield) and around Covent Garden (Paul Smith); **Vivienne Westwood** meanwhile, who occasionally draws on the Wallace Collection for inspiration, has her main outlet just off Bond Street at 40-41 Conduit Street.

Offbeat designers fresh from college start business at the London Fashion Week before graduating to **Covent Garden.**

77

British Classics

The Trenchcoat – Back in 1856, Mr Burberry perfected an alternative material to that of the rubberised mackintosh which protected against the wet and windy English climate, this he called gabardine. It was only during the First World War, however that the garment, adapted for trench warfare and issued by the Army, definitively assumed its name. This Burberry and Aquascutum all-time classic was given cult status by Humphrey Bogart during the 1950s. Burberry has branches in the Haymarket and in Regent Street.

The Liberty Print – Arthur Lazenby Liberty inspired by Japanese fabric designs had the brain-wave to westernise oriental floral motifs for the current vogue for Art Nouveau. Several generations later the 'pea-style', a dense repetition of flower sprays, trellised fruit and foliage inspired by the English country garden and printed in delicate colours, defined the fabric that soon became synonymous with the 'English rose', lawn.

Twin sets and pearls – 'To wear the trousers' has a somewhat chauvinist ring to it – however, the kilt, promoted as a fashion item by Prince Albert, loses its masculine associations if worn with cashmere or lambs-wool twin-set and a string of pearls. The short-sleeved sweater and matching cardigan has long been a mainstay of any English lady's wardrobe, forever more or less in vogue. For some it might boldly flatter a cleavage, for others it modestly conceals it.

Markets – **Camden Market,** on the corner of Camden High Street and Buck Street (Thursday-Sunday, 9am to 5pm) proffers endless rails of leather jackets, heavy-duty boots and biking gear. Second-hand clothes from **Covent Garden** (Monday 9am to 4pm), **Greenwich** (Sat–Sun 9am–5pm); grunge from Brick Lane.

Leather – Designer gear available from the King's Road (Harley Davidson) or more cheaply from around the market in Brick Lane.
Dr Martens available from 1-4 King Street, Covent Garden Piazza.

Gentlemen's outfitters – Classic British style and understatement combine elegance, smartness and the 'soigné' look – black tie, smoking or sports jacket, morning suit or blazer and slacks; the image is embodied by James Bond – refined, polished and befitting the occasion. A hire service is available from **Moss Bros Hire Warehouse** at 27 King Street in Covent Garden and 88 Regent Street.

Tailors – Bespoke tailoring survives on either side of Piccadilly in Savile Row and Jermyn Street. Businesses are rooted in generations of experience, moulded by apprenticeship and a rise through the ranks of Moss Bros and the former Simpsons. The product is a comfortable suit that fits, flatters and lasts decades.
Along Savile Row stand Kilgour, French and Stansbury at no 8; Huntsman at no 11; Henry Poole at no 15 (longest established in Savile Row); Anderson & Sheppard at no 30.

Shirtsmiths – For the Jermyn Street shirt, only the finest poplin in two-fold cotton is used and an average 35 components are cut for each, buttons are made of mother of pearl and each side seam is finished by hand. Quality is of the essence: the shirts that grace the cat-walk beneath the Lagerfeld label are those stitched by Hilditch & Key.
Hawes & Curtis at no 23; New & Lingwood at no 53; Turnbull & Asser at no 71-72; Hilditch & Key at no 73; Harvie & Hudson at no 77 and 97; Thomas Pink at no 85; TM Lewin at no 106 Jermyn Street.

Handmade footwear – Boots and shoes are also available, crafted to mould the foot for comfort and durability, especially if one foot is bigger than its mate. Lasts are kept in perpetuity, so orders can be made up long after a visitor has left St James's. Cleverley, 12 Royal Arcade, 28 Old Bond Street. Foster & Son, 83 Jermyn Street. Grenson Bespoke Shoemaking Service, 70 Burlington Arcade. John Lobb, 9 St James's Street. Henry Maxwell & Co, 29 South Audley Street. Poulson & Skone, 53 Jermyn Street. James Taylor & Son, 4 Paddington Street.

Sportswear – The most famous specialists are Lillywhites of Piccadilly Circus (24-36 Lower Regent Street). For hunting, shooting and fishing, try Harrods (87 Brompton Road), Farlow's of Pall Mall (5 Pall Mall), House of Hardy (61 Pall Mall); Orvis Inc (27 Sackville Street) or the gunsmiths Purdey James & Son (57 South Audley Street); Holland & Holland (31-33 Bruton Street).

> **John Galliano,** whose family moved to south London when the boy was six, is the chief designer at the prestigious house of Christian Dior. He served a year in Savile Row acquiring the skills of suit cutter which has underpinned his distinctive ability to cut fabric diagonally on the bias so that it clings to the body without straining.

SPECIALISTS

Perfumers and toiletries – For own brand products: soaps, lotions, gels and creams.
Crabtree & Evelyn *6 Kensington Church Street, W8.* **Neal's Yard Remedies** *15 Neal's Yard, WC2.* **Penhaligon's** *20a Brooke Street, W1 and 41 Wellington Street, WC2.* **Floris** *89 Jermyn Street, SW1.*

Books – Famous antiquarian specialists and dealers in fine manuscripts like Maggs Bros Ltd are to be found in Mayfair and St James's.
For **second-hand** books, browse around Museum Street in Bloomsbury, in Cecil Court off St Martin's Lane, or down Charing Cross Road.
Market stalls regularly open up in Camden Passage *(Thur 7am–4pm)*, Farringdon Road, EC1 *(Mon–Fri 10am–2pm)* and in Greenwich *(weekends)*.
General interest bookshops: Waterstones *121-125 Charing Cross Road, WC2 and 203 Piccadilly, W1.* **Foyles** *113-115 Charing Cross Road, WC2.* **Hatchards** *187 Piccadilly, W1.* **Borders** *Oxford Street, W1* **Dillons** *82 Gower Street, WC1:* situated at the heart of the University area, specialist publications and educational manuals.
Specialists: for art books try the museum bookshops (National Gallery, Courtauld Institute, Wallace Collection, V&A, National Theatre) or Zwemmer 24 Litchfield Street, WC2. **Cookery:** Books for Cooks, *4 Blenheim Crescent, W11.* **Fantasy, horror, science fiction, comics:** Forbidden Planet, *71-73 New Oxford Street, W1.* **Foreign languages** Grant & Cutler, *55-57 Great Marlborough Street, W1.* **Maps:** Stanfords, *12-14 Longacre, Covent Garden.* **Travel:** The Travel Bookshop, *13-15 Blenheim Crescent, W11.*

Handicrafts – **Covent Garden** covered market, **Camden** Canal Market *(Sat–Sun 10am–6pm)*; **Greenwich** Bosuns Yard Market, off the High Street *(Sat–Sun 9am–5pm)*; St James's Church Yard, Piccadilly *(Fri, Sat 10am–5pm)*.

Flowers and plants – If you are bulk-buying for birthdays, weddings, christenings or a large garden, the best value may be had at London's principal wholesale market at Nine Elms. **New Covent Garden** – *Mon–Fri 3.30am–10.30am.* **Columbia Road** – *E2.* To avoid the crush get there early, the best bargains however are to be had towards the end of the morning. *Sun 8am–12.30pm.*
Market-stall florists are to be found outside the Danish Embassy in Sloane Street, outside the Queen's Elm pub in Fulham Road, **Gilding the Lily** outside South Kensington tube, **Wild at Heart** *222 Westbourne Grove...*

Foods – **Korona Delicatessen** *58 Streatham High Road, SW16* (Polish). **The Bagel Bake,** *159 Brick Lane* (24-hour). **O'Hagan's Sausage Shop,** *192 Trafalgar Road, Greenwich, SE10.*
Smoked Salmon – H Forman & Son, *6 Queen's Yard, Whitepost Lane, Hackney Wick, E9.* ☎ 020 8985 0378 – London-smoke is milder flavoured than its Scottish counterpart...

Cheese – **Neal's Yard Dairy** *17 Shorts Gardens, Covent Garden London, WC2.* **Paxton & Whitfield,** *93 Jermyn Street, SW1* (Stilton). **Jeroboams** *24 Bute Street, South Kensington, SW7 or 51 Elizabeth Street SW1.*

Wild at Heart

Fruit and veg – Best from market.

Berwick Street Market – *Between Broadwick and Rupert Streets.* Flowers, fresh produce (organic mushrooms, 'Simply Sausages') *Mon–Sat 9am–5pm.*

Brixton Market – Brixton Station Road, Pope's Road, Electric Avenue. Best fresh produce market south of the river. *Mon–Sat 8am–5.30pm. Wed 8am–1pm.*

Leadenhall Market – *EC3. Mon–Fri 7am–4pm.*

Leather Lane – *Clerkenwell Road and Greville Street. Mon–Fri 10.30am–2pm.*

Portobello Market – Vegetables. *Daily except Thur 9am–5pm.* Organic produce under the Westway flyover *(Thur).*

Spitalfields – *West side of Commercial Street, between Folgate and Brushfield Street.* Special organic produce market *(Sun)* – fruit and vegetables, eggs but also freshly made bread, pastries, jams, chutneys... *Mon–Fri 9am–6pm, Sun 11am–3pm.*

Tea – Twinings are to be found in the Strand; Fortnum and Mason in Piccadilly, Whittards of Chelsea has franchise stores everywhere and there is the Bramah Tea and Coffee Museum in the Cardamon Building on Shad Thames.

Fine wines – Long established vintners are congregated around St James's: Berry Bros, Hugh Johnson, Justerini & Brooks (J & B)...

Fine linen – For sheets and the finest nightwear: **The White House**, *52 Bond Street, W1.*

Music – The Royal Opera House (Covent Garden), the Coliseum *(St Martin's Lane)* and the Royal Festival Hall sell extensive ranges of classical recordings. Otherwise the three big rival names in the business are **HMV** *(150 Oxford Street),* **Virgin** Megastore *(14-30 Oxford Street, Haymarket near Piccadilly Circus)* and **Tower** Records *(1 Piccadilly Circus).* The same three chains of stores stock recordings in the popular, jazz, blues, country and western, rock, funk, reggae, foreign.... categories.

Ray's Jazz Shop *180 Shaftesbury Avenue, WC2.* ☎ 020 7240 3969.

Harold Moore's Records. *12 Berwick Street, W1.* ☎ 020 7494 1081.

Stamps – **Stanley Gibbons** stamp shop and gallery *339 Strand WC2.*

Bespoke stationery – Established in 1889, **Smythsons** at *40 Bond Street, W1* print personalised letterheads, business cards, invitations, announcements, etc.

Toys – Hamleys is a veritable emporium of treasures located halfway down Regents Street. Otherwise, seek out the hand-crafted toys at Covent Garden Market.

Other – **Anything Left Handed** *57 Brewer Street, W1R 3FB.* ☎ 020 7437 3910. **The Survival Shop** (for warm silk long-johns and waterproof outdoor gear) 11-13 West Colonnade, *Euston Station, NW1 1DY.* ☎ 020 7388 8353. **Hi-fi** and computer gizmos from Tottenham Court Road.

Harrods Meat Hall

Faces and flavours of London

London boasts a profusion of diverse ethnic minorities: historically, London has been a haven for refugees from religious persecution on the continent; she has provided employment to thousands of immigrants – goods from all four corners of the British Empire were traded through the Docks, cheap labour was engaged in the East End sweat-shops in manufacturing, and, more recently, a major incentive was launched to attract West Indians to run London's transport services when the native population had been decimated by two world wars. She has been a loyal and generous patron of the arts as kings, guilds and repatriated colonials have employed painters, silversmiths, composers, slaves and servants through the ages.

Addresses given are by no means exclusive: listed restaurants are listed here as suggestions rather than recommendations. For an idea of value and speciality, consult Michelin's gourmet red guide to LONDON Hotels and Restaurants.

AFRICAN AND CARIBBEAN

Food – Strongest influences assimilated into Caribbean traditions come from Nigeria, Ghana and Sierra Leone: yam, goat, chillies, plantain available from daily markets in Brixton, Shepherd's Bush, north end of Portobello Road and Tooting.
Charlie's West African Food Shop *56-58 Esmond Road, NW6.*
Eunice Tropical Food Shop *133 Deptford High Street, SE8.*
Robinson's *50-51 Third Avenue, Granville Arcade, Coldharbour Lane, SW9.*

Restaurants are grouped around the main Afro-Caribbean communities: Brixton; All Saints' Road off Portobello Road. Try **The Calabash** at the Africa Centre in King Street, Covent Garden.

Arts – Rare artefacts on display at the **British Museum** and at the **Horniman Museum** in Dulwich.
Africa Centre, 38 King Street, in Covent Garden provides a concert venue for music, gigs and entertainment. African craft shop.

JEWISH

The origins of London's Jewish community are lost in legend, but it was certainly well established at the time of the Norman conquest (1066). During the Middle Ages, Christians were forbidden to lend money, a practice that was conducted by Jews, who soon became bankers to the Crown – Exchequer receipts were inscribed onto wooden tallies before being split into halves. Numbers dwindled, however in 1290 when Edward I expelled the group from the City. Persecuted in Spain (1492) Sephardi (meaning 'Spanish' in old Hebrew) Jews fled to Portugal and the Low Countries. By 1540, refugees were docking at Bristol and London, impecunious and unable to speak English, they outwardly pretended to be Christian converts. From selling second-hand clothes, hard work and perseverance, Jews aspired to the professional classes, finally being granted freedom to celebrate their faith when Oliver

Notting Hill Carnival

K. Brett

Cromwell readmitted Jews to England in 1656. The second major influx of refugees came from Northern Europe (latter-day Poland, Germany and Austria) establishing an important Ashkenazi professional community including such family names as Goldsmith, Salomon and Rothschild. Traders and brokers specialising in diamonds and bullion, underpinned mercantile business and colonial expansion overseas, while in the East End – Whitechapel, Commercial Road, Spitalfields, Stepney Green and Brick Lane – small workshops propped up the tailoring, cabinetmaking, shoe and boot-making trades satisfying demands from West End retailers.

Today, the principal Jewish communities reside in the north sector of London: Golders Green, Hendon, Brent, Barnet, Harrow and Redbridge. The majority are English-born Orthodox Ashkenasi with smaller pockets of long-established Sephardi Jews.

Synagogues – The oldest (founded in 1701) and perhaps the most atmospheric orthodox **Sephardi** synagogue is the Spanish & Portuguese Synagogue, *Bevis Marks, London EC3.* ☎ 0207 626 1274.

Serving the **Ashkenasi** community: is the United Synagogue, the largest umbrella organisation headed by the Chief Rabbi, formed by an affiliation of three older institutions the Great Synagogue at Mitre Court, Hambro Synagogue (1724) and New Synagogue (1761). Contact address: *Raymond Burton House, 129-131 Albert Road, London NW1 7NB.*

In the City is the Sandys Row Synagogue *at 4 Sandys Row, Artillery Lane, Bishopsgate E1.*

In the West End there are several important centres: the Marble Arch Synagogue (built 1961), *Great Cumberland Place, London W1;* the New West End Synagogue (built 1879) *St Petersburg Place, London W2* and its burial ground in Islington that has been described as the Jewish Westminster Abbey (founder of University College Sir Isaac Goldsmid and his son Frances Henry, the first Jewish barrister).

For followers of the **Liberal and Progressive** (American Reform) and **Reform** (American Conservative) movements, contact the Liberal Jewish Synagogue *28 St John's Wood Road, London NW8* and the Westminster Synagogue, *Rutland Gardens, London SW7.*

Jewish Museum – *Raymond Burton House, 129-131 Albert Road, London NW1.* For a warm welcome and a friendly introduction to the history and culture of London's Jewish community.

For Jewish social history contact the museum's Finchley Road centre at 80 East End Road, London N3. Together, the two centres organise and promote walking tours, the Yiddish theatre and temporary exhibitions.

Jewish Memorial Council (HQ and bookshop) *25 Enford Street, W1.* ☎ 020 7724 7778.

Kosher restaurants – Hendon and Golders Green. For traditional fare visit Blooms, *130 Golders Green Road, NW11.* ☎ 020 8455 1338

The **Rothschild** dynasty dates back to Mayer Anselm (1744-1812) who lived in a Frankfurt Ghetto and who lent money to Prince William. **Nathan Mayer** moved to London in 1798 (*see* CITY – Monument) while his brothers maintained operations in Frankfurt, Vienna, Naples and Paris. **Lionel** (1808-79) was elected a Member of Parliament in 1847, 49, 52 and 57 but was barred from taking his seat as his faith prohibited him from swearing the Christian Oath; eventually a resolution was passed making a variant possible. **Nathan Mayer** (1840-1915) was made a peer by Gladstone – the first Jew to be raised to the peerage. **Lionel Walter** (1868-1937) meanwhile was the naturalist who built up the Tring Park collection, of which some 280 000 skins make up the American Museum of Natural History in New York (1932) – his butterflies and moths now belong to the British Museum.

INDIAN AND PAKISTANI

Ingredients, fashion and crafts from India, Pakistan, Kashmir, Nepal, Bangladesh, Sri Lanka are all available in London.

Supermarkets – Principal communities from the Indian sub-continent are located in the East End of London (Shoreditch and Whitechapel), Shepherd's Bush, Southall and Ealing. Most supermarkets sell cash-and-carry wholesale quantities of rice, dahl, pulses, spices.

Ali Bros *41 Fashion Street, E1.* Tandoori hooks, karais, stainless steel ladles and platters.

Dadu's and **Patel Bros** *190-198* and *187-191 Upper Tooting Road, SW17.* Poppadums, Indian breads.

Dakan & Sons *133-135 The Broadway, Southall, Middx* (largest choice of pickles and spices).

Deepak Cash & Carry Grocers *953 Garrett Lane, SW17.* Large scale catering accoutrements.

Fudgo *184 Ealing Road, Wembley, Middx.* Home ground spices.

Spice Shop *1 Blenheim Crescent, W11.*

Taj Stores *112 Brick Lane, E1.* Halal meat.

Restaurants – The excuse for confusing Indian with Pakistani cuisine perhaps stems from the tradition that most curry houses were set up in the UK by Bangladeshis, a people granted independence from Pakistan in 1971. The area around Brick Lane in the East End is notable for its restaurants.

R. Besse/MICHELIN

Browsing in Southall

Bombay Brasserie: *Courtfield Close, Courtfield Road, SW7.* ☎ 020 7370 4040. *See Eating out.*

Chutney Mary: *535 King's Road.* Cooking school. Authentic family recipes that draw on traditions from Persian, Arab and Turkish cuisine with cassia buds, dried rose-buds, powdered root of vetiver, tamarind and mint. ☎ 020 7351 3113. *See Eating out.*

Vijay: *49 Willesden Lane, NW6.* ☎ 020 8328 1087. Worth the trek for the lemon rice alone!

Khans: *13-15 Westbourne Grove, W2.* ☎ 020 7727 5420. Cheap, cheerful, fast turnover.

> **Technicalities – Vindaloo** is the hottest curry, closely followed by *Madras. Tandoori* is a mild cuisine, slightly dry. *Poppadum* are the crisp pancakes; *Naan* is the soft doughy bread; *Chapati* is drier and lighter.

Neasden Temple – *Sri Swaminarayan Mandir, off the North Circular.* The first traditional Mandir temple erected in Europe opened in 1995. Carved and constructed entirely according to ancient Shilpashastras (no steel, but built of limestone faced with Italian Carrara marble carved in India. English oak structural beams, Burmese teak), thereby reviving traditional crafts and carving methods. Excellent presentation of the Hindu religion, marvellous jewel of a place, welcoming atmosphere.

Arts and crafts – Displays of the most exquisite jewellery and artefacts at the **Victoria and Albert Museum;** exhibition on Hinduism – daily life, sacred places and devotional practices in Southern India at the **Horniman Museum** *(see index).*

FAR EASTERN

Chinese, Thai, Malaysian, Vietnamese, Philippino delicacies come frozen, fresh, pickled, dried, tinned or preserved in **Soho** supermarkets. Chinatown offers cheap utensils, woks, Chinese porcelain, foodstuffs and restaurants for ready-made fare. Home to the annual celebration of Chinese New Year.

Chinese supermarkets – **Cheong-Leen:** *4-10 Tower Street, WC2.* Open daily 10am–6pm. ☎ 0207 836 5378. ⊖ *Leicester Square.*

Loon Fung: *42 Gerrards Street W1.* The biggest supermarket.

Loon Moon: *9 Gerrards Street W1.*

Peking Supermarket: *61 Westbourne Grove, W2.*

Sound of China for contemporary Chinese music: *6 Gerrard Street.*

Chinese Restaurants – Most of London's Chinese population comes from Hong Kong, the cuisine, therefore tends to be Cantonese in style. There are too many establishments in Chinatown and Commercial Road to list them; amongst the most reliable, try: **Poons:** *4 Leicester Street.* ☎ 020 7437 1528.

Soho

Fung Shing: *15 Lisle Street.* ☎ 020 7437 1539. *See Eating out.*
Chuen Cheng Ku: *17 Wardour Street, W1.* ☎ 020 7437 1398. Dim sum daily between 11am and 5.45pm; standard Chinese fare thereafter until 12midnight.
New World: *1 Gerrard Place, W1.* ☎ 020 7734 0396. Dim sum 11am to 6pm daily.
Eat Well: *313-317 King Street, W6.* ☎ 020 8748 6887.
Imperial City: *Royal Exchange, Cornhill, EC3.* ☎ 020 7626 3437 (until 8.30pm only).
Royal China: *11 Queensway, W2.* ☎ 020 7221 2535.

Indonesian specialities – Essential addresses for fresh lime leaves, coriander, palm leaves and lemon grass; noodles, sauces, rice and spices.
Hopewell Emporium: *2F Dyne Road, NW6.*
Maysun Food Market: *869 Finchley Road, NW11.* No fresh fruit or veg.
Talad Thai *320 Upper Richmond Road.*
Towana Oriental Supermarket *18-20 Chepstow Road, W2.* Thai specialities, Burmese pickles; videos, magazines, newspapers...
Restaurants – Try the **Blue Elephant:** *4-6 Fulham Broadway.* ☎ 020 7385 6595.
Tui's: *19 Exhibition Road.* ☎ 020 7584 8359.

Japanese food – Be prepared for limited labelling: dried soups, finely sliced meat and fish, beautiful fruit.
J A Centre: *348-356 Regent's Park Road, N3.*
Ninjin Food Shop: *244 Great Portland Street, W1.*
Teriyaki Japan and Oriental World: *25-26 Newport Court, WC2.* Take-away foods.
Oriental City: *399 Edgware Road, NW9.* 'All Japan under one roof': barracuda, octopus, red snapper, ready prepared sukiyaki meat.

Restaurants – For a quick bite try **Tokyo Diner:** *2 Newport Place, WC2.* ☎ 020 7287 8777 or **Wagamama:** *4 Streatham Street, WC1.* ☎ 020 7323 9223 for a nourishing bowl of noodles in a hip designer ambience. **Hamine:** *84 Brewer Street, W1.* ☎ 020 7439 0785 is a useful address in Covent Garden.

Muji – The Japanese designer store: simple forms, practical raw materials, subdued plain colours; excellent storage systems: *26 Great Marlborough Street.* ☎ 020 7494 1197; *38 Shelton Street* ☎ 020 7379 1331; *157 Kensington High Street.* ☎ 020 7376 2484.

Chinese and Japanese porcelain – The **Percival David Foundation** is dedicated to the promotion, appreciation and study of Chinese art and culture: its collection of porcelain and ceramics rivals only that displayed at the Topkapi Palace in Istanbul. Now administered by SOAS as part of the University of London; situated at 53 Gordon Square. Other important collections at the **British Museum** and the **Victoria and Albert Museum** *(see index).*

Technicalities – *Bento* is served in a compartmentalised lacquered wooden box. *Donburri* is a bowl of rice topped with meat or egg. *Ramen* are Chinese-style noodles. *Sashimi* finest fillets of raw fish. *Sushi* raw fish combined with shellfish, vegetables and glutinous rice, all beautifully presented. *Tempura* consists of fresh fish, shellfish or vegetable dipped in light batter and deep-fried. *Teriyaki* is a sauce that lends its name to meat that has been marinated in it, grilled and served. *Yakitori* is grilled chicken served on skewers.

MEDITERRANEAN

Italian, Greek, Cypriot, Spanish and Portuguese culture is well represented in London.

Italy – **Italian delicatessens:** Lina Stores, *18 Brewer Street, London W1* and Camisa and Son, *Old Compton Street-in Soho.* Luigi Terroni & Sons, *138 Clerkenwell Road, EC1.* Luigi's *349 Fulham Road, SW10.*
Bar Italia: 22 Frith Street, W1 is London's most renowned Italian coffeeshop; open 24 hours and gets especially crowded when Italy plays in World Cup matches.
Italian Trade Centre *37 Sackville Street, W1.*
Italian Bookshop: *7 Cecil Court WC2.* ☎ 020 7240 1634.

Greece – The **Greek Cathedral Aghia Sophia** *Moscow Road, W2,* is modelled on Higha Sophia in Istanbul; the Greek Orthodox church has attracted a number of Greek shopkeepers to the immediate vicinity.
Grecian Foods: *355 Green Lanes, N4.* Halva, olive oil, Cypressa houmus.
Lemonia: *89 Regents Park Road, NW1,* is an atmospheric Greek-Cypriot establishment. Booking essential as well favoured by locals. ☎ 020 7586 7454.

Spain and Portugal – Spaniards and Portuguese have congregated around the top end of Portobello Road: at its heart are a number of grocery stores and the Café Lisboa *(57 Goldborne Road, W10)* which serves endless supplies of scrummy custard tarts throughout the day. R Garcia & Son *248 Portobello Road, W11* is the area's most comprehensive Spanish delicatessen.

Spanish & Portuguese Synagogue – *Bevis Marks, EC3 and 9 Lauderdale Road W9.*

MIDDLE EASTERN

For Turkish, Lebanese, Syrian, Iranian ingredients – delicacies to some, staples to others (Turkish delight, salted nuts, saffron and rose-water) browse through stores in the Edgware Road and the area known as Beirut-on-Thames, Shepherds Market, Kensington High Street and Westbourne Grove.
Fadil: *Catford Bridge, SE6.* Bakery and groceries next door.
Turkish Food Centre: *385-387 Green Lanes, N4.*
Shammiss Abbas: *74 Green Lanes, N4.* Good fresh fruit and veg.
Green Valley: *36 Upper Berkeley Street, W1.* Fabulous Lebanese emporium.
Roushan's Patisserie: *14 Connaught Street, London W2.*
Algerian Coffee Stores: *52 Old Compton Street.* Established in 1887.

Restaurants congregate in similar areas offering sweetmeats and Turkish coffee, fast food (Beirut Express in Edgware Road) or deluxe Lebanese food and belly dancing (Maroush *at 21 Edgware Road.* ☎ 020 7723 0773).
Beit Eddine: *8 Harriet Street, SW1.* ☎ 020 7235 3969.

Islamic Cultural Centre and London Central Mosque – *146 Park Road, NW8.* ☎ 0207 724 3363 ⊖ *Regent's Park.* Modern complex with large spacious prayer hall. Reference library. Friday prayers conducted in Arabic and English, cultural forum and events held weekly on Saturday at 3pm.

Islamic Forum and **East London Mosque** – *94 and 82-92 Whitechapel Road, E1.* ☎ 020 7375 3844 ⊖ *Whitechapel.*

Al Saqi Books – *26 Westbourne Grove, W2.* ☎ 020 7229 8543. Extensive selection of reference, travel, fiction material. Mail order.

Islamic Arts Foundation – *144 Kings Cross Road, WC1.* ☎ 020 7833 3218. Publishers of Arts and The Islamic World.

The fashion for **coffee-houses** was introduced to London during the Commonwealth (1652). Originally they served as meeting places in the City for the exchange of business intelligence. By 1715 there were over 500 not only in the City but also in Covent Garden and the Strand, St James's, Mayfair and Westminster. Customers of like interest would gather regularly, even daily, in the same houses or call at several houses at different times to pick up messages and even letters, to auction a cargo or a ship or to read the news sheets, which at first circulated from one house to another, and the later newspapers (Daily Courant, 1702) which were available to customers for the price of a single cup of hot chocolate or coffee. To raise a loan one went to any of the lounges around the Exchange, to receive shipping news to Lloyd's, to gossip and hold literary talk to Will's, to gather news and write reviews to Button's, to talk of law and art to the Grecian, to discuss Tory politics to the Cocoa Tree in Pall Mall, to embroil in Whig intrigue to the St James's. At the end of the 18C the City coffeehouses reverted to being pubs and the West End houses disappeared, except Boodle's and White's which became clubs.

Sport

Cars – The London to Brighton run was first held on 14 November 1896 to celebrate the repeal of the 'Red Flag Act'. Banger racing at Wimbledon Stadium every Sunday at 6pm (except during June and July).

Indoor Karting tracks have become a popular way to spend an evening with a group of friends: Battersea Kart Raceway, *Hester Road, SW11 4AN*, and Streatham Raceway, *390 Streatham High Road*. ☎ 020 7801 0110. Daytona Raceways, *54 Wood Lane, W12 7RQ*. ☎ 020 8749 2277/8383.

Grand Prix – There is easy access to Brands Hatch in Kent and Silverstone near Towcester in Northamptonshire; although Brooklands, the oldest racing circuit in Britain, alas has been dismantled.

Cricket – This truly ruthless British gentlemen's sport that was exported to the Colonies on the understanding that it might encourage team spirit, discipline and sportsmanship appears to be so well followed there that the 'tourist' sides now seem to have the upper hand: just listen to the mellifluous commentary to appreciate how devoted fans can get carried away. It is strange to think that it was a cricket ball that killed the reviled Prince Frederick.

Lord's Cricket Ground is home to several independent bodies: the ICC (International Cricket Council) which acts as the main comptroller of the sport; the MCC (Marylebone Cricket Club founded in 1787; colours red and yellow) which instituted the TCCB (Test and County Cricket Board) to administer First Class and Professional game issues in the UK; the Middlesex County Cricket Club (founded in 1877). It goes without saying that Lord's is therefore London's principal Test match venue.

The second London ground is south of the river at the **Oval**, Kennington, where Surrey plays.

Dog Racing – Greyhound racing is London's most popular spectator sport after football. Introduced from America in the 1920s, Hackney opened its stadium in 1932. Betting takes two forms: on the tote and with the bookies – for beginners, explanations are provided by staff in the Fleetwood Restaurant.

Howz'at

Cricket is played by two teams of 11 players on a level grass pitch. At the centre is the **wicket**, a strip of ground (22yd long); at each end there is a set of **stumps**, also known as the **wicket**, consisting of three wooden uprights set in the ground, capped and linked by 2 wooden **bales**. A few feet in front of the **stumps** is a parallel white line, the **crease**.

The team which is **fielding** disposes all 11 players on the field at once; one is the **wicket keeper**, positioned behind the wicket and protected by pads and gloves, and those most able take it in turns to bowl. The team which is **batting** sends only two men onto the field at a time to face the bowling. The **bowler** delivers 6 balls, an **over**, and then retires for at least one over. He may bowl fast – up to 100mph – or slow in his effort to knock down the stumps or force the batsman to put up a catch. The **batsman** has to defend his wicket and also try to hit the ball as far as possible in order to score **runs** before the ball is returned to the stumps. A ball hit full toss over the boundary scores **six**; if it bounces first **four**. A **bye** is scored when the batsman has not hit the ball but has time to make a run while the ball is being retrieved. To score a **century** is to make 100 runs; to be out for a **duck** is to make no runs. When the first team has completed its **innings** – all 11 players have been in to bat – the teams change roles.

A match may consist of one or two innings per team and may last for a few hours or several days. One day international matches consist of the best of 55 overs, whereas **test matches** are played over five days. The major national cricketing teams are England, Australia, New Zealand, West Indies, India, Pakistan, South Africa and Sri Lanka. The organising body in England is the MCC, Middlesex County Cricket Club which plays at Lord's, in London; the other famous London ground is the Oval, the home ground of the Surrey team.

What began as a rural game with local rules has evolved into an international sport with its distinctive ceremony and vocabulary. Until recently the players wore white, the ball was red and the applause seemly but the game is still evolving; the modern game has introduced head guards, coloured dress and a livelier response from the spectators.

Wimbledon Stadium: *Plough Lane, SW17 0BL.* ☎ 020 8946 8000. Racing at 7.30pm Tuesday, Friday, Saturday. ⊖ *Wimbledon Park.*

Walthamstow Stadium: *Chingford Road, E4.* ☎ 020 8531 4255. Racing at 7.30pm Tuesday, Thursday, Saturday and 12noon on Sunday. ⊖ *Walthamstow Central* and bus 97, 97A or 215.

Football – The 'soccer' season runs from the end of August to the end of May culminating with the FA Cup Final at Wembley. London boasts a number of Premier League and First Division teams amongst which the most famous are:

Arsenal sport red shirts and white shorts; they are also known as the 'Gunners' after their logo – a cannon. They play at Highbury (⊖ *Highbury & Islington*).

Chelsea attract their fans from the well-heeled Chelsea resident locals and London cab drivers; players wear blue and their emblem is the lion; their home ground is at Stamford Bridge, Fulham Road (⊖ *Fulham Broadway*). The Chelsea hooligans are known as the Chelsea Headhunters.

Tottenham Hotspur or simply 'Spurs' traditionally rallied its team from Jewish North London; they play in white shirts and navy shorts under a symbol of a cockerel; their greatest rival is Arsenal. Home ground at White Hart Lane, *748 High Road, London N17* (Overground: White Hart Lane from Liverpool Street).

Other major London teams include **Brentford, Charlton Athletic, Crystal Palace, Fulham, Leyton Orient, Millwall** (the old dockers' teams now play across the river), **Queen's Park Rangers, West Ham, Wimbledon**...

The main venue matches attracting big crowds are hosted at **Wembley Stadium,** Stadium Way, Wembley (⊖ *Wembley Park*). The stadium is scheduled for redevelopment and is likely to close for a lengthy period.

American Football – A growing interest backs the London Monarchs who borrowed the Fridge from the Chicago Bears at one point. The only other UK based team playing in the European League are the Claymores from Scotland. London bowl played at Wembley in May and August.

Golf – Royal Wimbledon, Datchet, Sunningdale and Wentworth, Richmond Park x 2 (King's and Queens).

Horses – A number of riding stables operate in London usually within easy access of the large parks (Hyde Park and Richmond). Working shires, employed in Richmond Park have recently been reintroduced into Hyde Park. They are stabled with the Royal Parks Constabulary mounts. Stables at Mudchute Farm on the Isle of Dogs is another alternative venue.

Hyde Park Stables: *63 Bathurst Mews, W2 2SB.* ☎ 020 7723 2813.

Flat racing: Betting is organised by the state-run Tote system which gives no odds until all bets have been placed or with bookies who stand by the track rail; these make their own odds, demand a high minimum stake and often pay out only on 'win only' bets. Details of the principal events are advertised in the mainstream broadsheet newspapers.

Sandown Park: *The Racecourse, Esher Station Road, Surrey.* ☎ 01372 470 047. Overground: Esher.

Kempton Park: *Sunbury-on-Thames, Middlesex.* ☎ 01372 470 047. Overground: Kempton Park. Mid-week evening meets during the summer.

Ascot: High Street, Ascot. ☎ 01344 622 211. Overground: Ascot. Race meets throughout the summer.

Windsor: *Maidenhead Road, Windsor.* ☎ 01753 865 234. Overground: Windsor. The evening race course: figure-of-eight track on the banks of the Thames; meets are held on Mondays 6pm to 9pm; dress is smart – ties and cocktail frocks.

Epsom: *Epsom Downs, Surrey.* ☎ 01372 470 047. Overground: Epsom. Home of the Derby (10 June) and the Oaks (also in June).

Polo is played at the Guard's Club in Windsor Great Park, *Smiths Lawn, Englefield Green, Egham.* ☎ 01784 437 797. Matches every Saturday and Sunday at 3pm; Cartier International in July.

The National Women's Polo Tournament is held at Ascot Park (Sunningdale) in early July.

Ice Skating – London's largest ice rink is **Queens Ice Rink** at 17 Queensway, W2 4QP. ☎ 020 7229 0172. Other rinks at Streatham (☎ 020 8769 7771), Lee Valley (☎ 020 8533 3154), Alexandra Palace (☎ 020 8365 2121).

Rugby – Britain's finest sports arena is at Twickenham, home ground of the Rugby Football Union for major international Rugby Union matches, including the Six Nations Trophy – note that the match played between England and Scotland, whether it is played at Murrayfield or at Twickenham is known as the 'Calcutta' Cup match.

Recently refurbished, banks of terraces and wooden stands have been transformed into a futuristic 75 000 seat stadium. The **Twickenham Experience** encompasses access to the 14 themed rooms in the **Museum of Rugby**, a tour through the dressing rooms, past the 50-year-old claw-foot baths retained at the players' request up to the highest point in the north stand. RFU Ground, Whitton Road, Twickenham (Overground: Twickenham from Waterloo). Allow 75min for tours and 75min for museum. ☎ 020 8892 8877.

Club sides include the **Harlequins** who play at the Stoop, near Twickenham; the **Wasps** who play at Sudbury and the **Saracens** at Watford.

Tennis – The original rules for lawn tennis were drawn up by the MCC *(see Cricket at Lord's above)* in 1875, thereafter responsibility for the game and its development was assumed by a croquet club in Wimbledon. The run-up to the famous Lawn Tennis Association Tournament at Wimbledon in June includes the Stella Artois cup played at the Queens' Club. The other main venue for matches is the Hurlingham Club.

Most parks (Hyde, Battersea, Holland Parks, Islington Tennis Centre) have public courts: contact the Lawn Tennis Association for a booklet *Where to Play Tennis in London:* LTA Trust, Queen's Club, W14 9EG.

Real Tennis – The archaic indoor racket game, also known as royal tennis, originated in France: it has been played at Hampton Court since 1530 and at Lord's Cricket Ground since 1838. The layout of the court and its contours echo those of the monastery cloisters where it was first played; rackets are shaped like the palm of a hand; the net sags and serves are delivered only from one end; balls consist of a hard core covered in soft white felt.

Water sports – Useful addresses are given below:
Brockwell Lido: Dulwich Road, SE24. ☎ 020 7274 3088. Huge open-air 1930s pool. Call for opening times.
Docklands Sailing and Watersports Centre: 235a Westferry Road, Millwall Docks, E14 3QS. ☎ 020 7537 2626. Dinghy sailing, dragon boat racing, windsurfing, canoeing. Contact point for details on rowing and fishing in the docks.
Docklands Watersports Club: Gate 14, King George V Dock, Woolwich Manor Way. ☎ 020 7511 5000/7000. DLR: Gallions Reach. Jet skis, wet bikes. Closed Wednesday.
Hampstead and Highgate Swimming Ponds: three ponds for mixed bathing (East Heath Road, NW3. ☎ 020 7485 4491 – May-Sept 10am to 6pm; October-February 7am to 7pm) or single sex bathing (Millfield Lane, N6. ☎ 020 7485 4491 – daily 7am to 9pm or sunset). Open-air, fresh-water and free.

Fishing in Docklands

Doggett's Coat & Badge Race (f 1714) between Freemen of the Water-men's Company recently out of apprenticeship consists of a six single sculls race between London Bridge and Cadogan Pier. The scarlet coat and silver badge are presented at a ceremony to the winner held at Fishmongers' Hall in mid-July.

Public pools include those at the Marshall Street Leisure Centre, 14-16 Marshall Street, W1. ☎ 020 7724 5096 (closed until 2001) and The Oasis, 32 Endell Street, WC2. ☎ 020 7831 1804. Phone for restricted times.

Rowing tends to be organised by private clubs along the river (Chiswick) and in the Docks. For details of dragon racing and competitive events in Docklands, contact **The Royal Albert Dock Trust.** ☎ 020 7474 1111 or the Poplar, Blackwall and District Rowing Club. ☎ 020 7987 3071 for help with getting started.

View of the City by night

© ANGUS TAVERNER

Sights

BAKER STREET

Map p 7 (**CVX**) and area map under MARYLEBONE
⊖ Baker Street

Baker Street, the wide thoroughfare was 100 years old when Conan Doyle invented 221B as the address of his famous detective Sherlock Holmes; 85 was then the highest number as the street was in two sections. Hansom cabs, gas lamps and fog have gone but 221B now exists since the street was renumbered in 1930.

★**Madame Tussaud's Waxworks** ⊙ – Marie Grosholtz (1761-1850) acquired her modelling skills and much of her business through Philippe Curtius (1737-94), a doctor and talented modeller who mixed with the French aristocracy (Louis XV's mistress Mme du Barry is portrayed as *Sleeping Beauty*) and contemporary leading lights including the philosopher Voltaire and American statesman Benjamin Franklin. For nine years she was employed at Versailles supervising the artistic training of the young royal family – for which she was incarcerated and prepared for execution by the guillotine. Released, she was forced to return to work, surviving the terror of the French Revolution by taking death-masks of its victims many of whom she had known personally: Louis XVI, Marie-Antoinette... In 1802, she decided to emigrate with her two children to England: for 33 years the family toured the country before at last she settled on premises in the Baker Street Bazaar. The last figure to be modelled by the old lady is that of a small be-spectacled, but evidently highly alert, person at the age of 81, in fact a self-portrait. The waxworks moved to their present site in 1884.

> An intrinsic fascination in fellow man is somehow stimulated by the visual appeal of the wax figures. It comes as a surprise to take in the short stature of such a powerful personality as Queen Victoria, the remarkable family resemblance of Edward VII and George V, the very human scale of world leaders... This effect is painstakingly achieved by the lengthy procedures involved in creating each scale portrait: wherever possible photographs are taken and studied for attitude and stance, impressions of teeth are made, skin-colour and tone are matched with oil and acrylic paint, ceramic eye-balls are carefully selected, strands of human hair are compared with that of the living model, vital statistics (ears, nose, mouth, chest, waist, hips, etc.) are measured with callipers, clothes are borrowed and replicated (a duplicate of Princess Diana's wedding dress was commissioned from its creators David and Elizabeth Emanuel), some accessories are original possessions (Gandhi's watch, Pavarotti's shoes)... On occasion the displayed clothes and costume are laundered, hair is washed and re-set, waxen faces are cleaned and made-up once more – fresh as a daisy!

Figures are arranged in separate rooms on various floors. **The Garden Party** and **Hollywood Legends and Superstars** exhibitions, which are regularly updated to reflect changing times, allow visitors to mingle and be photographed with contemporary rich and famous personalities drawn from the 'show-biz' worlds of entertainment and sport (music, TV, film, tennis, football, cricket) – the likes of Gazza, Michael Jackson, Madonna, Superman, James Bond, Dame Edna... the list is endless.

Royal, historical and political dignitaries are assembled in the **Grand Hall**: Henry VIII and his wives; the Royal Families of Europe; past and present Prime Ministers and foreign statesmen.

Downstairs, the **Chamber of Horrors** which may be by-passed by the very young and faint-hearted, presents a series of tableaux illustrating various methods of execution (Joan of Arc burning at the stake), famous murderers and serial killers. The **Spirit of London** is a dark ride *(5min)* in a simulated London taxi cab on a whirlwind tour of the history of London: from the reign of Elizabeth I, through the Plague and the Fire, the reign of Queen Victoria, the Second World War to the present day.

★**Planetarium** – Three floors of information – Launch Zone, Planet Zone, Space Zone, and the latest hi-tech Digistar II projector are today accommodated in the old cinema that was bombed during the Blitz. Information panels, complemented by computers, video and interactive displays, intelligibly chart developments in the science of astronomy and elucidate such cosmic phenomena as galaxies, suns, planets, stars, comets, big bang and black holes.

The show 'Cosmic Perceptions' *(30mins)* is projected into the planetarium dome. Dramatic animation effectively transports visitors through time from Stonehenge to the space probe, via observations and discoveries made by Ptolemy, Copernicus, Galileo, Newton, Hubble, Einstein and Hawking...

Sherlock Holmes Museum ⊙ – The interior of the narrow town house, which was built in 1815 and registered as a lodging house from 1860 to 1934, has been arranged as described in the novels by Sir Arthur Conan Doyle. In the study are the familiar pipes and deer-stalker hat, a Persian slipper, a violin and bow, magnifying glass, telescope and binoculars, chemical apparatus and back numbers of *The Times*. Visitors may browse among the photographs, newspapers, literature and paintings of the period exhibited in Dr Watson's room.

★**The Squares** – At the northwest corner of **Portman Square**★ there remain two of the finest houses that ever graced the square. No 20, the former home of the Courtauld Institute by Robert Adam was built and furnished in 1772-77 for Elizabeth, Countess of Hume. No 21 (entrance in Gloucester Place) houses the **Drawings Collection of the British Architectural Library** ⊘ and the **RIBA Heinz Gallery** ⊘ showing changing architectural exhibitions. **Manchester Square** *(see MARYLEBONE)* is to the east of Baker St.

Montagu Square, which dates from the early 19C, is notable for its houses with shallow ground-floor bow windows. At no 39 lived the novelist Anthony Trollope (1873-1880). While the early 19C **Bryanston Square** is graced with long stucco terraces. In **Gloucester Place** there are attractive small doorways, ironwork balconies and railings.

BANKSIDE★

Map p 7 (**FGXY**) and area map under SOUTHWARK
⊖ Blackfriars Bridge

The history of this stretch of riverside is inextricably linked with that of Southwark *(listed separately)*: the western section was leased to the Bishops of Winchester who erected a veritable palace, which they named **Winchester House**, and the notorious prison known as the Clink. Also along the main bank were stews (brothels) whose occupants were known as 'Winchester geese'; the eastern strip belonged to Bermondsey Abbey. At the Dissolution, the site passed first to the Knights Templars and then to the Knights of St John of Jerusalem, remaining private property and therefore outside the jurisdiction of the City.

During the 16C hostelries, brothels (hence the existence of Love Lane), bear-baiting, cock-fighting and other such entertainments were set up in the area stretching westwards between Liberty of the Clink situated by the Clink Prison and Paris Garden, named after Robert de Paris, a 14C nobleman.

In the 16C, permission was accorded by the authorities for two theatres to be set up in the old monastery cloisters north of the river in Blackfriars and the area became known as the playground of London.

The reign of the **Rose** (1587), the **Swan** (1595/6), the **Globe** (1599) and the **Hope** (1613) was however brief: those that had not already reverted or become bull and bear baiting rings were closed finally under the Commonwealth by the Puritans in 1642.

Latterly the area has been redeveloped and one way to explore the area is to walk the Thames Riverside Walkway that extends from Westminster Bridge, beyond Southwark Cathedral to Tower Bridge and Bermondsey *(allow 90 minutes between Bankside and Rotherhithe)*.

★★**Tate Modern** ⊘ – The former **Bankside Power Station**, a massive structure (1957-60), known to some as the 'cathedral of the age of electricity' with its single chimney (325ft) and aztec-inspired stepped brickwork was designed by Giles Gilbert Scott. The oil-fired power station which closed in 1981 has been imaginatively converted with the addition of a glass superstructure and large bay windows to house the Tate Gallery's collections of international **20C art**. *For a review of modern schools see TATE BRITAIN.*

Gigantic sculptures by Louise Bourgeois are set off by the vast spaces of the dramatic turbine hall (500ft/155m long and 115ft/35m high) where overhead cranes recall the building's industrial past; the amazing perspectives can best be appreciated from the upper galleries.

The radical decision to stage themed displays aims to trace the evolution of genres through the 20C to the present day, to explore various aspects of certain works and to place British art in the international context: Landscape, Matter, Environment; Still Life, Object Real Life; Nude Action and Body; History, Memory, Society. Parallels are drawn between works of different periods, historical and stylistic associations are highlighted to challenge the viewer's perceptions of modern art. Artists represented include Monet, Bonnard, Léger, Duchamp, Picabia, Rothko, Picasso, Aeurbach, Beuys, Giacometti, Newmann, Warhol, Spencer, Bacon, Caro, Riley, Gilbert and George, Baumgarten, Mc Queen among others. Schools range from Fauvism, Surrealism, New Realism to Pop Art, Land Art, Fluxus, Russian constructivism and Minimal Art.

Do not miss the panoramic **views**★★★ *(from the top floor)* of the Thames and the city with St Paul as a counterpoint on the north bank which is linked to the museum by the striking **Millenium Bridge**. A remarkable architectural and technical achievement, the suspension bridge (320yds/370m long), built of stainless steel with curving stainless steel balustrades, forms 'a blaze of light' spanning the Thames at night.

Bankside Gallery ⊙ – The gallery, which opened in modern premises by the river in 1980, holds regularly changing exhibitions. It is owned by the Royal Societies of Painters in Water Colours (f 1804) and of Painter-Etchers and Engravers (f 1881) and used by five other clubs.

★**International Shakespeare Globe Centre** ⊙ – *Bear Gardens*. A great aura surrounds England's most famous dramatist as no autographed script survives of his plays, and yet he is considered as the finest exponent of the English Language. The idea for instigating a centre dedicated to encouraging the study and dramatic interpretation of Shakespeare's work came from the late American actor-director Sam Wanamaker. Funding the realisation of such a dream has been arduous – prompting many supporters to sponsor the project by paying for individual bricks.

Globe Theatre – The Wooden O (33ft high, 100ft in diameter and 300ft in circumference) has been modelled on surviving documentary evidence provided by contemporary sketches of the original theatre, pulled down in 1644, and from archeological excavations of the original Globe founded by Cuthbert **Burbage** *(see EAST END – Shoreditch)* around the corner. Wherever possible similar materials (unseasoned oak, reed thatch) and building methods have been used to recreate the half-covered theatre comprising an elevated stage, the open section for groundlings, surrounded on three sides by sheltered tiers of benches. To safeguard authenticity, performances are held during the afternoon much as in Shakespeare's day without the use of artificial stage lighting, and subject to fine weather!

Inigo Jones Theatre – Alongside the main thatched open-air theatre is this small intimate play-house built according to Jones' drawings, adapted today for private concerts, poetry readings and workshop productions all year round.

The Globe Education Centre underpins the spirit of the original enterprise which was to promote the works of Shakespeare by making them more accessible to a larger public, to explore understanding, appreciation and practical interpretation of Elizabethan and Jacobean drama, and most importantly to stress the entertainment value of theatre for actors and audience alike. Other facilities include a permanent undercroft **exhibition** area, a small cinema and lecture hall, audio-visual archive and library.

The Rose Theatre Exhibition ⊙ – *56 Park Street*. An imaginative light and sound brings to life the history of the Rose Theatre, the first theatre on Bankside. Excavations have revealed the remains of the building which are now covered by a pool of water because of lack of funds. It is planned to preserve the remains and put them on show in the future.

Old houses – On either side of **Cardinal Cap Alley** are two 18C private houses. The first (no 49), the oldest house on Bankside,

William Shakespeare (1564-1616)

England's greatest poet and playwright (38 plays) was born the son of a glover; he married Anne Hathaway in Stratford-upon-Avon before coming to London to find success and fame; he had three children, and died on his 52nd birthday. Popularity is rooted in the rich use of colloquial language, humour that sometimes verges on the bawdy, and a timeless portrayal of human nature. A total of 18 plays were printed in his own life time, 36 followed in a folio, the first collected edition, published in 1623. He also wrote 154 sonnets and four long poems.

was built on the site of the Cardinal's Hatte, a 16C stew, some 50 years after the Great Fire (1666). Some doubt therefore surrounds the authenticity of the information on the plaque declaring that it marks the place where 'in 1502 Catherine Infanta of Aragon and Castile and afterwards first Queen of Henry VIII, took shelter on her first landing in London'.
The houses west of the alley, slightly larger and more stylised and now used as the Lodgings of the Provost of Southwark Cathedral, are some 30 years later.

Southwark Bridge – Rennie's bridge (1815-19), referred to by Dickens in *Little Dorrit* as the Cast Iron Bridge, was replaced in 1919 with the present three-arched iron structure by Ernest George.

The Anchor – *1 Bankside*. This tavern was erected in 1770-75 on the site of earlier inns and is associated in its history not only with the river and the prison (truncheons, manacles etc in one bar) but also with Shakespeare, Dr Johnson and his biographer Boswell, through the Thrales who at one time owned it. More importantly Henry Thrale also owned a brewery in Park Street of which Johnson remarked, as executor, 'We are not here to sell a parcel of boilers and vats but the potentiality of growing rich beyond the dreams of avarice'.

Excavations in the Park Street area have revealed traces of a Roman warehouse.

Clink Exhibition ⊘ – *1 Clink Street*. Stairs lead down to a gloomy basement. The exhibition traces the history of imprisonment and torture and of the Bankside brothels.

Winchester Palace – At the heart of a large modern development stands the old ruin comprising the screen wall of the 12C **great hall** pierced by a graceful **rose window** (14C) of Reigate stone; three archways that once would have led to the servery and kitchens; excavation has revealed the cellars below. The existence of the palace is recalled in nearby Winchester Walk and Winchester Square.

The precinct of the Bishop of Winchester's Palace contained a prison for errant clergy and nuns, which lay below the water level at high tide. From the 15C it was known as the **Clink Prison**, from which derives the expression 'to be in clink': between about 1630 until its closure in 1780 it was used for poor debtors.

St Mary Overie Dock – The full-scale galleon replica of Sir Francis Drake's **Golden Hinde** ⊘ is made of African iroko hardwood and caulked with oakum in the traditional way; she was built in Appledore, Devon and launched on 5 April 1973 with a bottle of mead. When not away at sea (she has already undertaken several transatlantic journeys and at least one circumnavigation), the Golden Hinde may be boarded and a tour made with a member of her crew of her cabins and quarters, galley and hold.

> ### The Golden Hinde
>
> Overall length – 120ft (37m)
> Length at waterline – 75ft (23m)
> Hull – 102ft (31m)
> Mean draught – 13.5ft
> Beam – 20ft (6m)
> Mainmast – 92ft (27m)
> Sail (flax) area – 4,150 sqft (386sqm)
> Sailing speed – 6 to 8 knots
> Original crew – 20 officers and gentlemen, 40 to 60 men
> Armament – 4 petera small cannon ; 4 Falcon long range cannon and 14 minion guns.

In 1577 Francis Drake (c 1540-96) set sail on the Pelican into the unknown: he returned three years later from the Pacific having laid claim to Nova Albion (California) and the Port of Sir Francis Drake (San Francisco) on the Golden Hinde, having been renamed as she approached the Straights of Magellan. Drake chose the name after the symbol of a golden passant hind representing the armorial of the expedition's sponsor, Sir Christopher Hatton *(see INTRODUCTION – Elizabethan London)*. On arrival, the vessel was moored at Deptford *(see GREENWICH)* and visited by Queen Elizabeth I who took the opportunity to knight Drake there and then.

A riverside **viewing panel** identifies the buildings on the north bank: the twin pavilions at the north end of **Cannon Street Railway Bridge** were built at the same time as the bridge (1866) by J W Barry and J Hawkshaw, and the (rebuilt) engine shed.

For Southwark Cathedral and Borough High Street see SOUTHWARK: for London Bridge see CITY – Monument.

London Bridge City – ⊖ *London Bridge*. The prime considerations that tailored **No 1 London Bridge**, a highly speculative development of the mid-1980s were speed and economy of construction, hence its description as a prime example of Big Bang Business Building. **St Olaf House** (Hay's Wharf), in contrast with the sleek granite surfaces of its neighbour seems distinctly stylish; here little has been compromised by the musician-turned-architect Goodhart-Rendel (his change of career it is said was prompted by his aversion to Brahms; he later became President of the RIBA). The overall spirit is Art-deco, the material used Portland Stone, fine gilded faience relief panels designed by Frank Dobson provide a central motif on the Thames front, while on Tooley Street the bronze window casements would once have been gold-leafed (the coats of arms are those of the Smith, Humphrey and Magniac families, founders of Hay's Wharf partnership in 1862).

BANKSIDE

Hay's Galleria

Hay's Galleria – The original Hay's Dock has been sealed over: the purpose-built Galleria now boasts a 90ft high glass barrel vault. Pride of place is given to a monumental kinetic sculpture *The Navigators* by David Kemp, a somewhat nostalgic reminder of the clippers that once docked at Hay's Wharf. The buildings converted from warehouses of tea, jute, spices and later adapted into major refrigerated units house shops, bars and restaurants.

HMS Belfast ⊘ – The cruiser saw service with the Arctic convoys and on D-Day. From the flag deck to the hull, it is painted in the original 'Admiralty disruptive camouflage colours'. Seven decks of the ship are on display; the Operations Room is brought to life with a surface action effect and the Forward Steering Position with sound and light displays; appropriate smells identify the bakery, the sick bay and the boiler rooms; the story of the North Atlantic Convoys in the Second World War is told on film; the Falkland War exhibition retraces the campaign to recover the islands after the Argentine invasion in 1982.

HMS Belfast

Launched: 1938
Standard displacement: 11,553 tons
Length: 613 ft (187m)
Beam: 69ft (21m)
Draught: 19ft 9ins (6.1m)
Speed capacity: 32 knots (36mph – 58kph)
Armament: twelve (4 × 3) 6-inch *(firing shells weighing 112lbs, at a velocity of 2,758ft/second with a range of 14 miles on Fo'c'sle and Quarterdeck)*
eight (4 × 2) 4-inch HA/LA *(Boatdeck)*
twelve (6 × 2) 40mm Bofors AA *(antiaircraft guns – Bridge and Bofors Gun Deck)*

London Dungeon ⊘ – *34 Tooley Street*. A gruesome and sombre parade of tableaux, complete with eerie sound effects, relate scenes of death from disease (leprosy and plague), various methods of torture and execution (hanging, guillotine – talking head narrating Anne Boleyn's final demise), and early surgery. Separately narrated story of Jack the Ripper, the East End murderer *(optional)* complete with special effects. The exhibition makes effective use of the space but is unsuitable for the squeamish and very young children.

Winston Churchill's Britain at War ⊘ – *64 Tooley Street*. An old London Underground lift provides Tardis-like time-travel to an underground station fitted with bunks, tables and chairs, a canteen and tea urn, a WVS lending library and a video of scenes from the Second World War, regularly interrupted by the noise of an underground train. The nostalgic exhibition accompanied by rallying music, continues with displays of war-time fashion, mementoes of rationing, air raids, an Anderson shelter and a refuge room, evacuation, women at work in factories and on the land, the life of Sir Winston Churchill and an evocative reconstruction of simulated bomb damage after an air raid.

Archeological excavation of the large site opposite the Tower has identified the precincts of Edward II's 14C Rosary Palace. The site has been selected for a landmark building, in the shape of a 10-storey glass dish, by Sir Norman Foster which will house the office of the Lord Mayor elected in 2000.

If continuing eastwards, turn to TOWER OF LONDON – Tower Bridge and to BERMONDSEY for the Design Museum and Bramagh Tea and Coffee Museum.

BAYSWATER - PADDINGTON

Map p 6 (**BX**)
θ Lancaster Gate; Queensway; Bayswater; Paddington

The name Bayswater is derived from Baynard's Watering, marking the spot where the Uxbridge Road intersected with the Westbourne, a river that runs underground into the Serpentine (now Lancaster Gate); this was where the Bayswater Tea-Gardens were later located. A more gruesome memory is prompted by the Swan Pub where condemned men stopped with their escorts on their way from the Middlesex County Courts to the gallows at Tyburn.

The development of Bayswater as a residential area, north of Hyde Park, between Bayswater Road and Edgware Road, began in 1827 after the gallows had been removed from Tyburn (now Marble Arch). The original layout of crescents, squares and terraces was renewed or restored in the 1960s: period terraced houses survive in Hyde Park Gate, with shallow bow-windows in Gloucester Terrace.

Whiteleys – In 1863 William Whiteley opened a fancy drapery shop at 31 Westbourne Grove, then known as 'Bankruptcy Row', that soon expanded into London's first 'Universal Provider' or department store. Decline in business forced the business to close in 1981, but much of its grandeur has been retained including the fine staircase modelled on that of La Scala in Milan.

Bayswater Road Art Exhibition ⊘ – On Sundays, along the railings on the north side of Hyde Park and Kensington Gardens, runs an open-air exhibition of pictures and crafts offered for sale by aspiring artists.

PADDINGTON

On either side of Praed Street once stood great reservoirs supplying water to Kensington Palace. In 1800 Paddington still numbered fewer than 2 000 souls; by 1900 the population exceeded 125 000. Within a century Paddington had become a canal junction and a railway terminal for the Great Western Railway; a horse-drawn omnibus service had been inaugurated, followed by the Metropolitan and District underground railway.

Paddington Station – The Great Western Railway and its London terminal were built by Isambard Kingdom Brunel *(see index)*. The station (1850) radiated 19C confidence beneath an extensive wrought-iron and glass roof mounted on cast-iron pillars; there were four platforms approached by ten tracks.

The accompanying hotel (1850-52) was designed by Philip Hardwick (the Younger) in a style inspired by French Renaissance and Baroque, and decorated with allegorical sculpture.

St Mary's Hospital – This pioneering hospital, opened in 1851, was where Sir Almoth Wright developed the science of prophylaxis (prevention of disease) and where penicillin was discovered in 1928 – **Sir Alexander Fleming's laboratory** ⊘ has been reconstructed while displays provide an insight into the vital role played by antibiotics in modern day medicine.

Beyond the flyover stands **St Peter's of Paddington Green** where Hogarth secretly married Jane Thornhill (1729); in the churchyard is buried the actress Sarah Siddons *(see index)* who once lived on a farm in Westbourne Green.

Little Venice

LITTLE VENICE

The attractive triangular canal basin, shaded by weeping willows and overlooked by Georgian houses, modern flats and the Canal Office (formerly a toll house) is known as Little Venice, for obvious reasons. *For canal cruises and the Waterbus service see PRACTICAL INFORMATION.*

In 1795 a Cornishman, William Praed, began the canal which was to link the Grand Junction Canal (from Brentford to Uxbridge) to Paddington. By 1801 it was in use carrying produce from the market town to London and taking vast numbers of passengers on outings (half-a-crown to Uxbridge).

The **Regent's Canal** *(tow-path open 9am to dusk)* was begun in 1812 to provide a link with the Thames. It runs for eight miles from Little Venice to Limehouse docks and the Lea Valley *(see DOCKLANDS)*, passing through Maida Tunnel – where the boat crews legged their barges along lying on their sides or backs and pushing against the tunnel roof with their feet, under Macclesfield Bridge – known as 'Blow Up' Bridge after a cargo of gunpowder and petroleum exploded there in 1874, between the animal houses of London Zoo, through **Camden Lock** lined in former times by wharves and stabling for the barge horses, and on to Islington Tunnel. A flight of 12 locks carries the canal down 86ft to the Thames.

BLOOMSBURY ★

Map pp 7-8 **(DEVX)**
⊖ Tottenham Court Road; Goodge St; Russell Square

The once residential area contains many 18C and 19C squares and is dominated by two major learned institutions, London University and the British Museum *(see separate listing).*

The Squares – The development of **Bloomsbury Square** in 1661 introduced a new concept in local planning. The 4th Earl of Southampton, descendant of the Lord Chancellor to whom Henry VIII had granted the feudal manor in 1545, erected houses for the well-to-do around three sides of a square, a mansion for himself on the fourth, northern, side and the innovation of a network of secondary service streets all around, with a market nearby, so ordering, in Evelyn's words, 'a little town'. He was successful: by 1667, when he died, he had a magnificent residence, the focus of fashion had transferred to his estate and he had made a fortune. His only daughter, Lady Rachel, married the future 1st Duke of Bedford, uniting two great estates.

None of the original houses has survived but in the south-west corner of the square are two mid 18C houses; the one with the cherub-decorated plaque was the residence of Isaac and Benjamin Disraeli from 1818-26.

Bedford Square

In his sixties, **Thomas Coram**, a successful sea captain, trader and founder-trustee of the Colony of Georgia, was so distressed on his visits to London by the plight of abandoned infants and small children (the infamous 'Gin Alley' depicted by Hogarth in his engravings would have been inspired by the area around Centre Point) that he determined to better their lot. Campaigns, petitions to George II and determination won a charter of incorporation in 1739; with wide support from the rich, the noble and the prominent, he raised enough money to purchase 56 acres of Lambs Conduit Fields – 20 for buildings and playing fields, the remainder to provide revenue for the hospital by development.

By Coram's death at the age of 83 in 1751, the hospital was soundly established; hundreds of children had been saved. The patronage of artists, begun by Hogarth at the foundation, had already provided outstanding paintings and would continue with gifts and donations by the least and the greatest such as Handel. Coram's tomb is in St Andrew's Church, Holborn.

The other squares, now partly or totally incorporated in the university precinct, followed in the 19C: **Russell** in 1800, **Tavistock** in 1806-26, **Torrington** in 1825, **Woburn** in 1829, **Gordon**, originally by Thomas Cubitt *(see INTRODUCTION – Architecture)* in 1850.

Artistic Tradition – The Bloomsbury district was frequented by artists and writers from the late 18C to the early 20C: Richard Wilson and Constable (no 76) in **Charlotte Street**, which is well known for its restaurants; Madox Brown and Bernard Shaw, Whistler and Sickert in Fitzroy Square; Verlaine and Rimbaud in Howland Street; Wyndham Lewis in Percy Street and David Garnet in Bedford Square.

The most famous residents however, were the **Bloomsbury Group** *(see INTRODUCTION – Painting)* whose members include Virginia Woolf, resident at **29 Fitzroy Square**, Vanessa Bell, Roger Fry the art critic who in 1910 organised the first Post-Impressionist Exhibition to be held in London, Clive Bell, E M Forster, Lytton Strachey – friend and mentor of Dora Carrington, Duncan Grant and Maynard Keynes, resident in Bedford Square. While in the immediate vicinity of Gordon Square resided the likes of Rupert Brooke (war poet), D H Lawrence (novelist), Bertrand Russell (philosopher, social reformer, Nobel Prize for literature, first president of CND) and his mistress Lady Ottoline Morrell (influential patron of the arts). By the early 1930s their ideas and works, literary, critical and artistic, had become widely known and accepted, their influence absorbed into the artistic tradition.

Left over from the Aesthetic movement that thrived as the area was developed are the various furnishing and **interior decoration** businesses: Maples **(no 145)** and **Habitat** and **Heal's (nos 191-196)** are at the northern end of Tottenham Court Road. In Berners Street, Parker Knoll **(no 19)** and Sanderson **(no 53)**, who still use the William Morris blocks for hand-printed wallpapers, have their furniture, wallpapers and fabrics showrooms.

A showcase to the taste of the times is the **Park Plaza Hotel** in Berners Street where the interior décor from 1809 has been carefully preserved, complete with elaborately carved plasterwork, hand-painted glass, marble pillars and staircases.

Medical Expertise – Bloomsbury contains a concentration of medical institutions. The most famous is the **Hospital for Sick Children** (Great Ormond Street) founded some 20 years after the Coram Foundation for Children. Within a small radius of it are ancillary research institutes and clinics: the Homeopathic Hospital and the Italian Hospital (both founded in the 19C) and the National Hospital for Nervous Diseases on the site of another 19C children's hospital. The present **Middlesex Hospital**, rebuilt (1925-36) and extended (1960s), started up in Windmill Street in 1745, before moving to its present site in Mortimer Street in 1754; **University College Hospital**, designed in 1897 by A Waterhouse, stands in Gower Street; the **Eastman Dental Hospital**, the **Royal National Throat, Nose and Ear Hospital** and the **Royal Free Hospital** are scattered in the vicinity, in and around Gray's Inn Road.

Coram's Fields – *Guildford Street*. A park reserved for children extends over part of the area once occupied by the hospital buildings.

In 1926 the children were moved to Berkhamsted, much of the land was sold and most of the buildings subsequently demolished. Some 28 years later (1954) the 2-300 children then in the charity's care were found homes under a new policy of fostering. Meanwhile the Governors had bought back the site of the present museum building and adjoining Coram Children's Centre. The Foundation continues its commitment to childcare and welfare, notably in the fostering and resettlement of children.

The Foundling Museum ⊙ – *40 Brunswick Square*. A bronze statue of Thomas Coram after Hogarth stands before the 1937 neo-Georgian building. The 18C hospital oak staircase (note the cartouches) climbs around an open well, in which stands a jaunty peasant boy, hand on hip.

The Courtroom, exactly rebuilt with dark red walls setting off the moulded ceiling and plaster enrichments, contains the mantelpiece with a relief of Charity Children given by Rysbrack, an oval mirror and eight contemporary views of London hospitals (Charterhouse is by Gainsborough). Other artefacts on display include coins and tokens left by destitute mothers with their children, rare letters and autographs.

The Foundation was supported by many leading lights of the day and became the first place in London where works by contemporary British artists were publicly exhibited together thereby preempting the institution of the Royal Academy by a number of years. The charity therefore has a fine collection of works of art, notably portraits: Hogarth's full-length *Thomas Coram* (1740), a Roubiliac bust of *Handel* (both on landing), the *March of the Guards to Finchley* (1750) by Hogarth (lobby), full-length governors' portraits by Ramsay, Benjamin Wilson, Thomas Hudson, Joshua Reynolds and Millais (picture gallery). Other donations and bequests include part of a cartoon of the *Massacre of the Innocents* from the School of Raphael, the surprising *Worthies of Great Britain* by Northcote, a Georgian silver gilt communion service, pewter porringers, Hogarth's punchbowl of blue and white Lambeth-delft, an organ keyboard presented by Handel and the 1739 royal charter (a fair copy of *Messiah* and other manuscripts are also in the institution's safe keeping).

The Cartoon Art Museum ⊙ – *7 Brunswick Square*. Historic cartoons and caricatures not only chart developments and personalities through the ages but demonstrate a strong and determined sense of humour. The Cartoon Trust and its museum collect and exhibit humorous and satirical artworks, drawings, engravings, illustrations, advertisements, comic strips and animated films from the time of William Hogarth to the present. Evocative names include Mr Punch, Rupert Bear, The Beano, Dan Dare, Andy Capp, Bonzo the Dog, Captain Pugwash, Fred Bassett... Heath Robinson, H M Bateman, Giles, Calman, Garland...

Dickens House ⊙ – *48 Doughty Street*. **Charles Dickens** and his young family moved into the late 18C house, situated then in a private road gated at either end, and attended by burgundy-liveried porters shortly after his marriage to his 'pet mouse' Catherine Hogarth. They were to live there for nearly three years from April 1837 to December 1839, during which time Kate's sister Mary died in Dickens' arms, and he completed *Pickwick Papers,* wrote *Oliver Twist* and *Nicholas Nickleby* besides articles, essays, sketches and letters. The house, which contains portraits and 'knick-knacks', holds an interesting collection of letters and manuscripts,

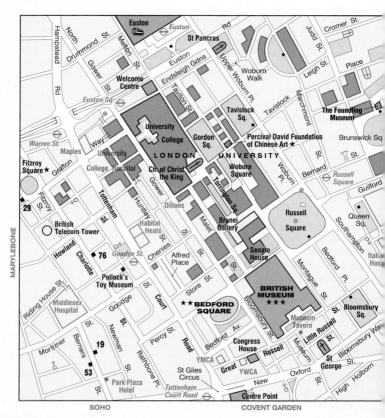

Charles Dickens (1812-70)

Dickens drew generously on his fertile imagination as well as on his own experiences for his serialised novels: characters were modelled on friends, close relations and acquaintances made in connection with the theatre and the amateur dramatics he so enjoyed, and the philanthropic works he undertook. An early, happy childhood in Chatham was brought to an abrupt end when his father was sent to Marshalsea Prison for bad debts and he, aged 12, was put to work blacking shoes. As an office boy he studied shorthand and secured a place on the *Morning Chronicle* reporting on debates in the House of Commons. There he developed his acute sense of observation and sharp humour. Close associates and admirers included Thackeray, Wilkie Collins, Hans Christian Andersen... His wife, Catherine (1815-79) was a promising young journalist when she married the rising novelist (1835). She was to bear him ten children (Dora died in 1851), before being persuaded to accept a deed of separation (1858) — when Dickens was emotionally involved with Ellen Ternan, a beautiful young actress.

the early small paperback parts in which the novels were first issued, the prompt copies he used for his public readings and a large selection of original illustrations to his works.

The cluttered drawing-room, furnished with rosewood furniture and Hogarth engravings has been meticulously decorated as in Dickens' time, while in the basement the washroom and cellar capture a little more atmosphere of Dickensian London. The house is also the headquarters of the Dickens Fellow-ship.

St George's Bloomsbury ⊘ – **Hawksmoor**'s church (1716-31) externally makes the most of a difficult site, with a grand pedimented portico at the top of a flight of steps and a stepped stone tower surmounted by a spire. Topping the steeple, to the contemporary public's derision, is a classical statue of the unpopular George I. Inside the problem of orientation on such a cramped site, resolved by Hawksmoor by hollowing out a small apse in the east wall, has since been settled by the transfer of the high gilded and inlaid reredos (1727) to the north wall. At the centre of the flat rectangular ceiling is a flower 5ft in diameter in richly gilded plaster and in the shell over the east niche another delicate gilded relief, both by the master plasterer, Isaac Mansfield.

Great Russell Street – The west end of the street is marked by the YMCA, built in the 1970s, and the YWCA. The structural mass of **Congress House**, the TUC Headquarters, is lightened by a glass screen at ground level on the east side, giving a view of an inner court and hall, distinguished by a war memorial before a high green marble screen, carved on the spot from a 10 ton block of Roman stone by Jacob Epstein (1958).

Beyond, dominating the southern end of Tottenham Court Road stands **Centre Point** designed by Richard Seifert to comprise 34 storeys of offices, erected in the 1960s.

★**Bedford Square** – The most elegant of the squares was developed in 1775 by Gertrude, widow of the 4th Duke, to designs by Thomas Leverton. It is still complete. The three-storey brick terraces have rounded doorways, delicate fan-lights and first floor balconies; the centre of each is relieved by a pedimented stucco centre-piece.

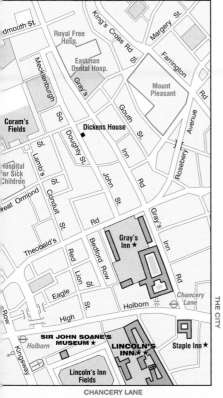

CHANCERY LANE

Contemporary Applied Arts ⊙ – *2 Percy Street*. Exhibitions and information on crafts and applied arts (pottery, studio ceramics, glass, wood, metal, jewellery, textiles and furniture).

Pollock's Toy Museum and Shop ⊙ – *1 Scala Street*. Toy theatres, that 19C delight made from sheets described by Robert Louis Stevenson as 'one penny plain and twopence coloured', can be seen amidst a mass of 19C and 20C toys: wax, tin, porcelain, peg and spoon dolls, teddy bears, carved wooden animals, optical toys, dolls' houses. Live toy theatre performances are given during the school holidays.

British Telecom Tower – The slim landmark, originally known as the Post Office Tower, was erected in 1965 to provide an unimpeded path for the capital's telecommunications system.

Fitzroy Square – This square has changed in character since its inception in 1793 when the east and south sides were completed in Portland Stone to designs by **Robert Adam**; 40 years later the square was completed but with stucco facing rather than stone. Note the giant columned centrepiece on the east side repeated in miniature at either end, and echoed in the centrepiece of the south terrace.

LONDON UNIVERSITY

London University moved to Bloomsbury after the Second World War, although the **Senate House**, a cold Portland stone building with a tall square tower (library) by Charles Holden, had been under construction since 1932. Colleges, faculties and new institutes are now housed throughout the immediate neighbourhood in old 18C-19C houses and in the ever-extending, heterogeneous complex of brick, stone, concrete, steel, mosaic and glass *(in blue on plan)*.

University College – The central range of this, the oldest of the university buildings, designed by William Wilkins, is marked by an imposing pedimented portico, behind which rises a high dome (1827-9); the interior gallery (first floor) is decorated with low-relief panels by John Flaxman. Guarding either side of the University buildings courtyard are a pair of miniature, domed, observatories. The college houses the **Flaxman Sculpture Galleries**, the renowned **Petrie Museum of Egyptian Archaeology** ⊙ and the preserved figure of Jeremy Bentham (1748-1832), inspiration of the college's founders.

Brunei Gallery ⊙ – The School for Oriental and African Studies now boasts a fine venue for temporary exhibitions of fine, decorative and applied arts.

★**Percival David Foundation of Chinese Art** ⊙ – *53 Gordon Square*. The Foundation displays the world famous collection of exquisite Chinese porcelain assembled between the wars by the late Sir Percival David, scholar and connoisseur of great distinction, together with the Elphinstone bequest. This specialist collection of the finest 14 C to 18 C porcelain figures and vessels reflects Chinese imperial taste notably from the Sung dynasty: plain, incised, monochrome, blue and white or bearing polychrome decoration.
Almost all pieces are perfect, selected for their classical shapes or remarkably delicate and refined decoration. Specialist detailed catalogues are available.

Church of Christ the King ⊙ – *Gordon Square*. The neo-Early English Gothic church, built in 1853 to cathedral proportions, the interior is 212ft long and is now the University Church.

Universities

There were only two universities in England, Oxford and Cambridge, both Church of England establishments until 1828 when a group of radicals and dissenters founded University College in London to give education in arts, sciences and medicine in a non-residential and non-sectarian milieu. It was referred to as 'that Godless institution in Gower Street' by supporters of the Anglican Church, who reacted by founding King's College in the Strand in 1829 with a strong theological faculty. Neither college was allowed to grant degrees. The University of London was incorporated by charter as an examining body in 1836 and as a teaching body in 1900. It now comprises many colleges all over London and beyond with internal, external and part-time students.
The City University *(see CLERKENWELL)* was created in 1966 out of the Northampton Polytechnic (founded 1896). It works in association with Gresham College *(see CITY – Guildhall)* and has close links with the City financial institutions; many students undertake sandwich courses sponsored by private business.

Foundation – The final spur to found the British Museum ⊘ was supplied in 1753 when **Sir Hans Sloane**, physician, naturalist, traveller, bequeathed his collection to the nation. Parliament already had stored in vaults in Westminster Sir Robert Cotton's (1570-1631) priceless collection of medieval manuscripts acquired in 1700. Elsewhere there were manuscripts, charters and rolls collected by the Earls of Oxford, Robert Harley (d 1724) and his son Edward (d 1741) which were made available in 1753. In 1756 the old Royal Library of 12 000 volumes, assembled since Tudor times, was officially presented to the museum by George II and deposited in the Westminster vaults in 1823.

A lottery was launched to raise money for a building worthy of such magnificent and extensive collections; £21 000 was spent on the purchase of Montagu House, built in 1675 for the Duke of Montagu, ambassador to the court of Louis XIV, and rebuilt in 1686 after a fire to designs by the French architect, Puget; the building was altered and opened in 1759. At first access was limited to certain weekdays and, until 1810, was by ticket only (always free); attendances soon mounted to 10 000 a year. Engravings show a random display without labels: stuffed giraffes, portraits, fossils and manuscripts, books, dried plants, classical marble statues and coins, pots and Buddhas against a background of heroic frescoes and plasterwork ceilings. Cobbett christened the institution 'the old curiosity shop'.

Collections – Presentations, bequests and special parliamentary purchases swelled the collections and foundations for the present institution were laid. Important acquisitions included: Thomason Tracts, pamphlets published during the Civil War and Commonwealth 1642-60 (presented by George III, 1762); David Garrick Library (1 000 printed plays including First Folios, 1779); Sir William Hamilton collection of antique vases (£8 400; 1772); Cracherode collection of books, fine bindings, great master drawings, Greek and Roman coins (1799); Egyptian antiquities including the Rosetta Stone (under the Treaty of Alexandria, 1802, following Nelson's victory on the Nile); Greek and Roman sculptures, bronzes and terracottas, the Townley Marbles (1804, £20 000); sculptures from the Temple of Apollo at Bassae, 1815; sculptures from the Parthenon, the Elgin Marbles (purchased 1816, £35 000)... Other significant purchases were transacted of manuscripts, minerals (Grenville), libraries (Hargrave, legal), music collections (Burney), natural history collections, French Revolution tracts and ephemera.

In 1823 George IV presented his father's library of 65 000 volumes, 19 000 pamphlets, maps and charts; in 1824 came the Payne-Knight bequest of Classical antiquities, bronzes and drawings; in 1827 the Banks bequest of books, botanical specimens and ethnography.

Accommodation – In 1824 **Robert Smirke** was appointed to produce plans for a more permanent building, which would replace the decayed Montagu House and provide space for the growing number of exhibits. The new building with a Greek-inspired colonnaded façade was completed 20 years later. The Reading Room was

CHANGES FOR THE THIRD MILLENNIUM

The British Museum is presently undergoing major re-organisation and refurbishment: the **British Library** has been transferred to new purpose-built premises at St Pancras and the ethnographic collections formerly at the Museum of Mankind have been reintegrated into temporary, changing, exhibitions.
The Great Court Project, envisaged by Sir Norman Foster, entails the clearance of subsidiary buildings (utilitarian bookstacks) that have encased the central domed Round Reading Room in order to accommodate elliptical mezzanine floors for a sophisticated **Clore Centre for Education** comprising activity areas for the youngest visitors and conference facilities for the most erudite researchers and academics, the Museum bookshop, temporary thematic exhibition areas and restaurants.
Objectives: The Round Reading Room is to be used for research as a high tech Information Centre and for a new public reference library. The Grand Rooms will be restored to their former glorious Regency decorative schemes; the King's Library will provide displays relating to the Age of Enlightenment and connoisseurship; Classical sculpture will be displayed in the Manuscripts Saloon. The North Library will provide an introduction to the **Ethnography Collections** with dependent galleries dedicated to the non-Western cultures of Africa, the Pacific, Asia, Near East and Europe *(completion date 2003)*.
Should you require details on what is displayed the British Museum operates an extremely helpful Information Service ☎ *0171 636 1555. Fax 0171 323 8614.*

added in 1857, the Edward VIII Galleries in 1914, the Duveen Galleries in 1938. In 1978 a fourth extension was opened on the last remaining space on the Bloomsbury site and an additional floor was added to the Duveen Galleries in 1991. Some departments were transferred to other sites: the natural history departments to South Kensington in 1880-83; the newspapers to Colindale in 1905 and the ethnographic collections to the Museum of Mankind (see PICCA-DILLY) in 1970.

Old British Library – In 1973 the museum's library departments were vested in a separate authority and granted funds to have new premises built in St Pancras. The circular **Reading Room** dates from 1857. Antonio Panizzi, a refugee Italian revolutionary, who was appointed Keeper of Printed Books in 1837 and Principal Librarian (Director) in 1856, was determined that the library should be open to 'the poorest student' as well as to the 'men of letters' who had previously been accommodated in rooms in the basement and then on the ground floor. As the King's Library, a splendid room by Smirke, was too small to provide sufficient seating or to house the Grenville Library, bequeathed in 1847, the present Reading Room was designed by Panizzi and the architect Sydney Smirke (Robert's younger brother) to occupy the damp and gloomy courtyard at the centre of the building under a dome (40ft wide). It has accommodated 400 readers and 25 miles of shelving (1 300 000 books). Less spectacular but equally if not more useful was Panizzi's compilation of the catalogue.

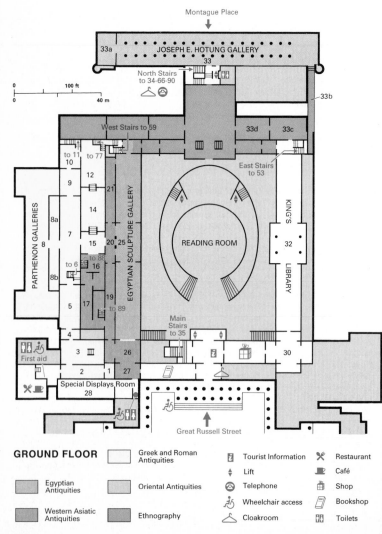

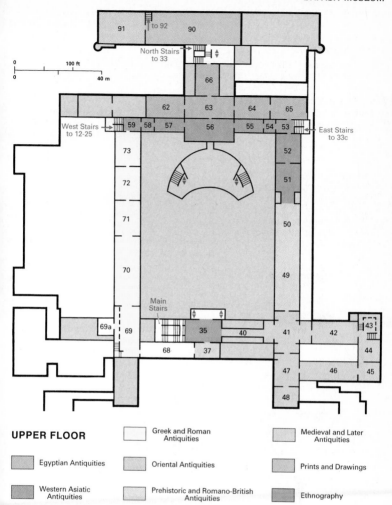

UPPER FLOOR

- Egyptian Antiquities
- Western Asiatic Antiquities
- Greek and Roman Antiquities
- Oriental Antiquities
- Prehistoric and Romano-British Antiquities
- Medieval and Later Antiquities
- Prints and Drawings
- Ethnography

The Classical Collections *Through the bookshop on the ground floor.*

Ancient Greece and Rome – Greek and Roman Antiquities from the dawn of the Bronze Age (3200 BC) to the establishment of Christianity as the official religion of the Holy Roman Empire (Edict of Milan AD 313).

Prehistoric to Archaic Greece – (**1**) **Cycladic** early figurines carved from marble: stylised, simplified nude female forms, excavated in the 1880s. (**2**) **Bronze** then **Iron Age** pottery, jewellery, stonework evolve to (**3**) black-figured pottery in the **Archaic** periods. (**3a**) Early Greek vases display narrative scenes drawn from mythology. (**4**) Andokides Room houses a new type of pottery painted with red figures.

5C BC – (**5**) the **Harpy Tomb** vases, bronzes, terracotta sculpture: Chatsworth head and Strangford Apollo. (**6**) Marble sculpture from the Temple of Apollo at **Bassae**: Centaurs and Lapiths, Greeks and Amazons (c 400 BC). (**7**) Reconstruction of the **Nereid Monument** (c 400) at Xanthos in south-west Turkey: statues of the breezes; lion gate guardians. (**8a, 8b, 8**) The Parthenon Galleries are entirely dedicated to the famous **Parthenon (Elgin) Marbles**, the culmination of Hellenistic art from the 5C BC, which celebrates the Greek victory over Persia: battles of the Lapiths and Centaurs, pediment figures dressed in rippling robes (5C BC); the Horse of Selene; computer-generated imaging of frieze, reconstruction of northwest corner of the Parthenon. (**9**) **Caryatid Room** for sculptures from the Acropolis in Athens; pottery, terracottas, bronzes (430-400 BC).

4C BC – (**10**) Finds from the tomb of **Payava** from Xanthos (400-330 BC): kraters, minute bronzes; clay vessels. (**11**) Red-figure vases from southern Italy, white ground and black-glazed vases (c 440 BC). (**12**) Figurative sculpture from the **Mausoleum at Halicarnassus**, one of the Seven Wonders of the World: battle of Greeks and Amazons.

(14) Excavated **Hellenistic** artefacts from Ephesos, Knidos, Priene; **(15)** Greek and Roman sculpture: Choragic Monument of Thrasyllos 320 BC; Goddess Demeter from Cnidus; bronze head of Sophocles 3C BC; jewelled sceptre.

Follow the stairs down into the basement from Room 16.

Wolfson Galleries – **(82)** Ephesus – Townley Collection. Roman funerary reliefs. **(83)** larger Roman monuments. **(84)** Charles Townley sculpture collection. **(85)** Roman portraiture, heads of deities and heroes.

Continue through Room 82.

(81) Later monuments from Asia Minor: the Mausoleum, temple of Artemis, temple of Athena at Priene; **(80)** earlier Archaic and Classical sculpture from Greece, Asia Minor; **(79)** sculpture from Lycia; **(78)** Latin and Greek inscriptions. **(77)** Greek and Roman architecture.

West stairs up to ground then upper floor.

Greek influences – **(73)**
Greek pottery, terracotta, bronzes found in Southern Italy: cinerary urns, sarcophagi, pottery, bronze figurines, head of athlete with

> **Note:** Room 73 – Bronze horsemen (c 550)

a leather cap (300-200 BC); stone sarcophagus from Tarquinia c 250 BC; bronze horse bit and bridle ornaments early 7C BC.

After photo British Museum

Cypriot Antiquities – **(72)** A G Leventis Gallery: vases with incised and painted decoration c 4500 BC-AD 300; terracotta figurine with earrings 1400-1200 BC; flat limestone statue 575-550 BC.

Italy before the Roman Empire – **(71)** The Etruscans and other contemporary peoples – figures, objets d'art: jewellery from Tomb of Taranto priestess c 350-340 BC; bronze cauldron and red figured cup from Berone tomb 5C BC.

Imperial Rome – **(70)** The Wolfson Gallery of Ancient Roman paintings, jewellery, sealstones, cameos, coins, mosaics, inscriptions, glass. **(69)** Artefacts from daily life: Farming tools, writing materials, weights and measures, games counters; jewellery; sandcore, moulded, carved, blown glass. Quarter of a Roman wooden water wheel.

Coins and Medals *Up main stairs and through galleries 35 and 37.*

Money – The Hong Kong Shanghai Bank Money Gallery **(68)** presents a history of money from a resource of over one million objects: cuneiform tablets from Ancient Mesopotamia, 7C BC coins from Turkey and China, treasure trove,

> **Note:** Room 70 – Portland Vase, rare for its state of preservation and for its considerable influence on Neo-Classical designers (Wedgwood, Flaxman), bronze head of Augustus found in the Sudan.

paper denominations of international currencies, modern-day electronic transfer technology.

Temporary exhibitions may also be mounted in **(69a)**.

> The earliest English gold coin to be struck was the 'penny' minted during the reign of Henry III (1216-72) in 1257.

Prehistoric and Roman Britain *Main stairs to upper level.*

Stone Age to Celtic Britain – **(37, 50)** Iron age implements: flint axes; Bronze Age gold artefacts from Ireland and Cornwall (Second millennium BC); the Celts in Europe from Britain to Romania: **Lindow Man** found in a peat bog in 1984; chalk 'drums' retrieved from a child's tomb in Yorkshire; elegant Celtic bronze wine-flagons c 400 BC found in Basse-Yutz, in France. Celtic armoury, mirrors and torcs: Rillaton cup, Witham and Battersea shields, Welwyn Garden City burial 1C BC.

Roman Britain – **(40)** The Romans invaded Britain in AD 43 with the Emperors Claudius, Nero and Hadrian exerting the greatest influences. Treasures from Mildenhall, Thetford, Lullingstone, Water Newton provide a view of the lavish lifestyle enjoyed by the wealthier classes.

The **Weston Gallery of Roman Britain** (**49**) accommodates the largest permanent display of artefacts relating to Roman Britain, most notably the Mildenhall Treasure. To date the **Hoxne Hoard** which comprises thousands of coins, jewellery and silver plate, acquired in 1994, is one of the finest treasure troves found in Britain (Suffolk). Other important displays include a building façade from Meonstoke in Hampshire and the Vindolanda writing tablets shedding a rare insight on Roman military life in the Border Country along Hadrian's Wall.

Medieval, Renaissance and Modern Collections

Up main stairs, through galleries 35 and 40.

The mid-12C **Lewis Chessmen** are thought to be Scandinavian in origin. The hoard of 80 pieces carved from walrus ivory was found in 1831 buried in a sandbank on the Scottish Island of Lewis, in the Outer Hebrides.

Lewis Chessman

Foreign influences – (**41**) Anglo-Saxon and Romanesque antiquities (4C-11C) found in the British Isles: **Sutton Hoo Ship Burial** shows the rich variety of artefacts retrieved from a royal tomb; Viking hoard found in Lancashire.

(**42**) Religious and secular antiquities (9C-15C) from Western Europe and Byzantium – icons, ivories, enamels, reliquaries, jewellery: Franks Casket, **Lewis Chessmen**, Lycurgus Cup, a rare gittern (c 1300), Paris Royal Gold Cup (c 1380) decorated in *basse-taille* enamel, early 15C Dunstable Swan Jewel, 15C Westminster Sword of State, Savernake horn.

Ceramics (7C-15C) – (**43**) Early English tiles and pottery (13C-16C), Italian maiolica, Venetian glass, Dutch Delft: **Canynges pavement** c 1461.

Horology – (**44**) Clocks, watches, precision regulators (16C-20C): **Strasbourg Clock**, Prague-made Ship Clock (c 1585). (**45**) **Waddesdon Bequest** of Medieval and Renaissance treasures includes a lovely reliquary for a thorn from Christ's crown made for the Duc de Berri (c 1400).

Continental and British applied arts – (**46**) Goldsmithing from the Renaissance to end 18C: **Armada Service**; Wilding Bequest, Lyte Jewel (James I miniature); Limoges enamels; 1554 iron shield, Royal seals; Battersea enamels, Huguenot silver. (**47**) 19C European ceramics (Wedgwood copy of the Portland Vase and Jasperware) and glass: fabulous **Hull Grundy Gift** of jewellery, engraved gems and goldsmithing.

19C and 20C – (**48**) The Modern Gallery is dedicated to European and American decorative arts: examples of work by René Lalique, Christopher Dresser, C R Mackintosh, Henry van der Velde, Bauhaus.

Egyptian Antiquities

Egyptian Sculpture Gallery – *Through the bookshop on ground floor, turn right before the Classical collection galleries.* (**25**) Obelisks, steles, statues of the kings, sarcophagi, colossal red granite statues (1360 BC) – a giant fist, small bronze deities. **The Rosetta Stone**; Lions of Amenophis III; Rameses II (c 1270 BC); King Amenophis III (1400 BC).

West stairs to upper level.

Egyptian tombs – In the Roxie Walker Galleries of **Egyptian Funerary Archaeology**, **mummies** (**62, 63**) bandaged in cases and coffins include the preserved remains of humans, birds and animals, shedding light on the social rituals (amulets, clothing, hairstyles) and scientific advancements (artificial eyes) of the times; the Book of the Dead. Tomb paintings and papyri. Artefacts associated with daily life: furniture,

The **Rosetta Stone** is part of a 6 foot block of black basalt found at Rashid or Rosetta in the Western Egyptian Delta region and retrieved by French soldiers on campaign there during the Napoleonic wars: with the Capitulation of Alexandria in 1801, the French were compelled to surrender the stone to the British: the stone went on show at the British Museum in 1802.

Its significance rests in the parallel transcriptions of a decree passed on 27 March 196 BC in Ancient Greek and two written forms of Egyptian: thereby providing Egyptologists with the wherewithal to decipher pictorial hieroglyphs in use since the third millennium BC and the linguistics of Demotic texts formalised in 643 BC.

farming implements, turned stone vessels, musical instruments, furniture. (**64-65**) **Raymond and Beverly Sackler Galleries** dedicated to Early Egypt up to the Age of the Pyramids, its relationship with neighbouring Africa (Nubia) and the introduction of Coptic Orthodox Christianity: **'Ginger'** – 5 000 year old corpse that predates mummification practices; textiles.

Western Asiatic Antiquities *Through bookshop, squeezed between the Egyptian and the Classical sculpture galleries on the ground floor.*

Assyrian sculpture – Colossal statues and relief carvings (**16-17**) from the entrance of the Palace of Sargon at Khorsabad; bas-reliefs (lion-hunts) from Ashurbanipal's palace at Nineveh. (**19-20**) Nimrud Palace reliefs. (**21**) Nineveh Palace Reliefs: black obelisk
Ancient Palestine: pottery, jewellery, ivories, ossuaries, metalwork. (**26**) Assyrian Sculpture: gateway reconstruction, figures, stelae.
Basement: (**88**) special temporary exhibitions of western Asiatic artefacts.

Assyrian art – (**88a**) Ishtar Temple
(**89**) sculptures of Sennacherib and Ashurbanipal; insight into daily life.

Ancient Iran – *North side of the first floor access from the East or West Staircases.* (**52**) Oxus Treasure (5C-4C BC): Gold Tomb 605 BC, Luristan bronzes (c 1200 BC), Persepolis reliefs (5C-6C BC), Parthian pottery, Achaemenian art, Sassanian vessels.

Ancient Turkey and Iraq – **Raymond and Beverly Sackler Galleries** dedicated to the antiquities (6000-536 BC) of Anatolia: notably the (**53-54**) Hittite and Urartian kingdoms: bronzes from Urartu, Ararat (c 700 BC),

Note: Room 52 – Cyrus cylinder, Sassanian silver from the dawn of Islam (3C-7C AD). Room 56 – enigmatic ram. Room 57 – Syrian king from c 1500 BC

Carchemish (10-8C BC). (**55**) Early Mesopotamia: Babylonian and Assyrian kingdoms between 1600-539 BC: cuneiform tablets from the Royal Library at Nineveh: Flood Tablet. (**56**) Later Mesopotamia: Sumerian and Babylonian antiquities up to 1600 BC: Chaldees treasure including jewellery, 'lyres' and artefacts excavated from the Royal Cemetery at Ur (c 2600 BC).

The Ancient Levant (57-59) – Syrian, Phoenician and Punic antiquities (8000 BC to 6C BC): limestone stelae, pottery, jewellery, seals.

Ethnographic Collections

Museum of Mankind – In 1970 the department of Ethnography was moved to Burlington Gardens because of the lack of space at Bloomsbury. While work is being undertaken to create new galleries for this enormous collection, temporary exhibitions will continue to feature a range of artefacts in the newly refurbished galleries as and when these become available (completion date 2003).

Mexican Gallery – *Ground Floor.* (**33c**) Surveys the art of ancient Mexico before the Spanish Conquest (16C): fabulous Aztec turquoise 14C-16C mosaics; Mayan Temple sculpture (8C AD); Huaxtec figures (10C-15C AD) from the Gulf Coast.

The **Wellcome Gallery of Ethnography**, the centrepiece of the Ethnography Galleries, will introduce cultural themes linking diverse societies to be explored in greater depth in specialised galleries.

The **Sainsbury African Galleries** will explore the interaction of past and present African cultures.

Chase Manhattan Gallery of North America – (**33d**) Dedicated to the life, customs and arts of the Native peoples of North America: New Mexico, Inuit Indians and Eskimos, Cherokee, Iroquois, Navajo, findings of Captain Cook and George Vancouver.

In the east stairs stands a **Canadian Totem pole**, 88 steps high.

Prints and Drawings

National Collection of Western Graphic Art – (**90**) Special exhibitions only are mounted from the extensive collection of drawings, water-colours, etchings, prints, engravings, modern lithographs from the 15C to modern times: works available include those by the likes of Pollaiuolo, Botticelli, Leonardo da Vinci, Bellini, Michelangelo, Tiepolo, Piranesi; Dürer, Hans Holbein, Bosch, Rubens, Rembrandt; Claude, Watteau, Ingres, Rousseau, Corot, Bonnard, Matisse, Picasso; Goya; Gainsborough, Turner, Blake, Henry Moore, Piper, Sutherland...

Easter Island Statue

British Museum

Oriental Antiquities *Ground floor, by the Montague Place entrance.*

Islamic art – (**34**) The **John Addis Gallery** displays antiquities from the Islamic collections: tiles from Isfahan (Iran), Iznik pottery from Turkey, lustreware from Spain, Egyptian enamelled glass mosque lamps.

Korea – *Take the North Stairs to Level 2 and 5.* Korean artefacts are displayed in the north staircase and the north entrance. (**91**) Arts of Korea: gold crown (Silla kingdom 5C-6C), Buddhist art (ceramics) and manuscripts (Amitabha Sutra) dating from 10C to 14C. From 15C onwards Confucianism influenced society: portraits of scholars and high-ranking men.

China, south and south-east Asia – (**33**) **Joseph E Hotung Gallery** accommodates sculptures from the South and South-East Asia: arranged chronologically are Chinese bronzes, exquisite jades (from 3500 BC), ceramics that became mass-produced and diffused throughout Asia to the West. Stylistically, the early pieces show homogeneity from 200 BC when a centralised state had been forged by the first emperor (who built the Great Wall and was buried with the legendary terracotta army). Tang period tomb group (8C AD) complete with representation of horses traded along the Silk Route to Baghdad; silver that may have inspired forms used by potters. Imperial patronage flourished with an ever more sophisticated court culture until the 20C when it was shattered by Communism.
Buddhism, introduced from India, was quickly embraced by the leaders of the Chinese state but followers still incurred brutal persecution. Elsewhere: early Buddhist art from Gandhara (modern Pakistan) reflects the prolific generation of followers from the 5C BC. Pieces in the (**33a**) **Asahi Shimbun Gallery** are from the Great Buddhist Stupa at Amaravati in southeast India. In the main gallery, exquisite interpretations come from Nepal, Tibet and Sri Lanka.
The **Hindu** god Shiva with his consort Parvati are accompanied by followers: Ganesh, Vishnu...
(**33b**) Temporary displays of Oriental ornaments, ceramics, manuscripts and paintings.

Japan – *North stairs to level 5.* Fabulous collection of **netsuke** in lobby outside the (**92**) Urasenke Gallery where the classic **teawares** associated with the famous tea ceremony ritual are on permanent display. (**93**) The main Japanese gallery and the (**94**) Konica Gallery exhibit variable arrangements of objects from the large Japanese collection.

British Museum Study Centre

21-31 New Oxford Street – In the precincts of the former Royal Mail West Central Sorting Office, the British Museum will accommodate facilities to study the reserve collections of anthropological data and important international archeological material: Roman mosaic, Indian rickshaws, Egyptian coffins, Textile centre. This is scheduled to open in 2001.

BUCKINGHAM PALACE ★★

Map pp 7-8 **(DEY)**
⊖ Green Park; St James's Park

Mulberry Garden to Royal Palace – In 1703 a piece of land at the west end of St James's Park, partly planted the previous century by James I as a mulberry garden, was granted by Queen Anne to John Sheffield, newly created Duke of Buckingham, who built a town residence of brick, named Buckingham House. In 1762 the property was purchased for £28 000 by **George III**, presented to his bride, Charlotte and renamed Queen's House. During their occupation the south wing, the octagon library, was added to contain the king's books, which were transferred to the British Museum in 1823 by George IV. The libraries were demolished by Nash and replaced by the Ball Room (1854) built for Queen Victoria.

In 1825 **John Nash**, who had recently completed the Brighton Pavilion for **George IV**, was commissioned to turn the house into a palace. He enclosed the core of the old brick mansion in a cladding of Bath stone, added a grand two-storey entrance portico and a range of rooms along the west front overlooking the garden. The king died however in 1830 before the alterations were complete and, although Nash was technically exonerated from blame for the extravagant expenditure, he was discredited and retired. The work was completed by Edward Blore in 1837, by which time William IV also had died. Three weeks after her accession **Victoria** took up residence and at last the royal standard flew on the Marble Arch which Nash had designed as a state entrance to the open forecourt.

Ten years later a new east range was designed by Edward Blore, enclosing the courtyard and linking the advanced north and south wings; it contains the famous balcony, where members of the Royal Family greet the people massed in the Mall on state occasions. Marble Arch, being superfluous, was removed in 1851 to the north-east corner of Hyde Park. In 1912 under **Sir Aston Webb** the east front was raised in height and refaced in Portland stone to harmonise with the Mall and the new Victoria Memorial. The private apartments of the Royal Family are in the north range.

The palace ⓥ – *Tour: 1 hour.* The interior presents the suite of state rooms designed by John Nash, examples of the later Edwardian taste which replaced the polychrome décor of Victoria's reign, reminders of Britain's imperial past and treasures from the Royal Collection, many of which were originally acquired by George IV for Carlton House: magnificent and rare Sèvres porcelain, ornate 18C French clocks and furniture, royal portraits and chandeliers.

The **Ambassadors' Entrance** is lined with portraits of Hanoverians. The courtyard is dominated by the two-storey **entrance portico**, added by John Nash: carvings of Britannia in her chariot accompanied by tritons and Neptune on the pediment, two relief panels by Richard Westmacott on the attic storey. The **Entrance Hall** is a low room decorated in cream and gold, the scheme introduced in 1902 by C H Bessant who was commissioned to redecorate most of the palace. The **Grand Staircase**, lit by a domed skylight of 80 etched panes, is hung with pictures of the immediate ancestors of Queen Victoria. Scrolling acanthus and acorns surmounted by a laurel rope ornament the balustrade. The four Chinese vases were formerly at Carlton House. 18C Gobelins tapestries and magnificent chandeliers adorn the **Guard Room**. The **Green Drawing Room** contains two 18C cabinets, one by Adam Weisweiler *(far left)* and another by Martin Carlin *(far right)* inlaid with panels of *pietre dure*. The

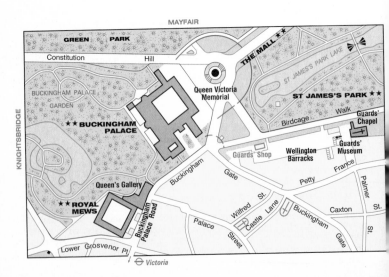

110

coved white and gold plaster ceiling and the gilded frieze of swagged laurels and wreaths are by Nash. Red and gold predominate in the **Throne Room**. The coved part of the ceiling is decorated with shields bearing the coats of arms of England, Scotland, Ireland and Hanover. The two chairs under the canopy were used at the Coronation by the Queen and the Duke of Edinburgh. They are flanked by carved wood and gilt trophies by Henry Holland.

The **Picture Gallery** occupies the centre of the palace under a curved glass roof introduced in 1914. Among the masterpieces from the Royal Collection are two portraits of Charles I on horseback and with his family by Van Dyck; portraits by Rembrandt and Frans Hals; seascapes by Van de Velde; paintings by Vermeer, de Hooch, Rubens, Cuyp, Poussin, Guido Reni. The three adjoining rooms present 18C French clocks, furniture by Weisweiler, silk tapestries and a painting of Queen Victoria's coronation by Benjamin West.

The series of Nash state rooms on the west front begins with the **Dining Room**, resplendent in red and gold with a gilded ceiling by Blore; the walls are hung with royal portraits by Kneller, Van Loo, Allan Ramsay and Lawrence (*George IV* with his hand resting on the Commanders' Table – *see below*, which was commissioned by Napoleon in 1806 and presented to George IV by Louis XVIII in 1817). Chinese celadon vases stand on the mahogany sideboards. In the **Blue Drawing Room** Shakespeare, Milton and Spenser are commemorated in the ceiling arches.

The décor is articulated by 30 columns in imitation onyx topped by gilded Corinthian capitals. Here stands the **Commanders' Table**, decorated with the head of Alexander the Great surrounded by twelve commanders of Antiquity, in hard-paste Sèvres porcelain with gilt-bronze mounts. The four side tables (1823) by Bellange are in marble and gilt. The **Music Room** is dominated by columns coloured to represent lapis lazuli. The vaulted and gilded ceiling contains the rose of England, the thistle of Scotland and the shamrock of Ireland with a border of fleur-de-lys; it is matched by a marquetry floor. The décor of the more intimate **White Drawing Room** dates from 1831. Engaged Corinthian pilasters, embellished with the Star and Garter, alternate with massive pier glasses. Flanking the fireplace is a pair of gilt-bronze candelabra by Thomire. The piano in a gilt case painted with figures is by Erard. The roll-top desk is by Riesener.

Two sculptures by Canova *Mars and Venus* and *A Fountain Nymph* can be seen at the foot of the Ministers' Stairs and in the Marble Hall. The **Bow Room** is named after the Bow porcelain in the display cases rather than the bow window.

From the garden there is a magnificent view of the west front of the palace, much as it was designed by John Nash, although the dome above the central section was replaced by an extra storey in 1832.

The lawns extend to the magnificent herbaceous borders and a lake; the earth produced by its excavation was piled up to conceal the stables.

⋆⋆**Royal Mews** ⊘ – Apart from the earlier Riding House (1764), the mews were built by Nash. A lion and unicorn gate leads to a Classical archway, topped by a small clock tower. The blocks around the square tree-shaded courtyard house stables, harness rooms and coach houses, where the equipages vary in splendour from modest, covered two-wheelers to the open state landau, the Glass Coach in which royal brides and bridegrooms return from their weddings, the Irish Coach in which the Queen rides at the State Opening of Parliament and the gold State Coach (1762) which has been used at every coronation since 1820.

The 129ft long frieze (6 panels) depicts the Coronation procession of William IV and Queen Adelaide in 1831. The very modest predecessor of Queen Victoria was reluctant to have such pomp and circumstance, but he was persuaded otherwise by the Duke of Wellington. The frieze was evidently painted from the golden carriage forwards by Richard Barrett Davis, who seems to have tired of the task by the time he undertook the first and last panel.

Changing the Guard

The ceremony takes place in the forecourt when the sovereign is in residence and the Royal Standard is flying over the palace. The guard is mounted by the five regiments of Foot of the Guards Division. Their uniform of dark blue trousers, scarlet tunic and great bearskin is distinguished by badges, buttons and insignia: the Grenadiers (f 1656) by a white plume and buttons evenly spaced; the Coldstreams (f 1650) by a scarlet plume and buttons in pairs; the Scots (f 1642) by no plume and buttons in threes; the Irish (f 1900) by a blue plume and buttons in fours; the Welsh (f 1915) by a green and white plume and buttons in fives. *Times are given in the Practical Information section.*

In the **Queen's Gallery** ⊙ are mounted small temporary exhibitions of treasures drawn from the Royal collections (Holbein watercolours, Leonardo da Vinci drawings). The gallery is due to close for refurbishment and a new entrance is to be built.

Wellington Barracks – On the south side of the parade ground stand the Wellington Barracks, built in 1833 by Sir Francis Smith and Philip Hardwick.

Guards' Museum ⊙ – The museum presents the history of the Guards Regiments from the Civil War origins to the present day. Dioramas, weapons, trophies, uniforms memorabilia, documents and paintings tell the story of their military campaigns and of their historic role in guarding the sovereign.

Guards' Chapel ⊙ – The chapel dates from 1963. The lofty clean-lined interior is of white marble with clear glass lancet windows opposing brightly lit memorial chapels aligned in a cloister along the south wall. Above hang regimental colours. Note the engraved side chapel windows and the terracotta frieze in the Household Cavalry chapel. The screens in the choir arch and the dark apse, lined with mosaic, are all that remains of the 19C chapel, which was otherwise destroyed by a flying bomb in June 1944 killing over 120 people.

St James's Park – London's oldest park is known today for its brilliant flower borders and for the pelicans and wildfowl on the lake.

From the bridge there are **views** of Buckingham Palace and Whitehall.

> St James's Park pelicans have a long-standing history: the first one, from Astrakhan, was a gift to Charles II given by a Russian ambassador – it promptly flew off and was shot over Norfolk. Peter from Karachi stayed 54 years before emigrating, who knows where. The present pair of *Pelecanus onocrotalus* were acquired from Prague Zoo. Other named birds reside at the Tower of London and the Zoo in Regents' Park.

History – Henry VIII, the inaugurator of London's royal parks, acquired St James's Park in 1532 when he exchanged a building occupied by a community founded before the Conquest as a 'spittle for mayden lepers' for land in Suffolk. According to Stow, the king demolished the hospital and 'built there a goodly manor, annexing thereunto a park, closed about with a wall of brick, now called St James's Park, serving indifferently to the said manor and to the manor or palace of White Hall'.

In Tudor times the park was stocked with deer. James I, a lover of wild life established a menagerie of animals and exotic birds. Charles II aligned aviaries along what came to be called Birdcage Walk. Strongly influenced by the formal gardens of Le Nôtre which he had seen during his exile in France, Charles II had the park laid out according to the standard goosefoot (*patte d'oie*) design. The marshy ponds were systematised into an east-west canal from the west end of which extended two avenues – one along the line of the Mall towards the houses of Charing village.

In the 19C Nash was commissioned to design a project for the park's improvement, with terraces as in Regent's Park; only Carlton House Terrace was built. Nash replaced the high surrounding wall by iron railings and landscaped the park

Buckingham Palace from St James's Park

itself after Repton, planting trees and shrubs and transforming the long water into a lake with islands (on which the duck and wildfowl originally on the 'decoy' have flourished ever since).

★★The Mall – The Mall was first traced at the time of the Stuarts (17C). In 1910 it was transformed into a processional way by **Sir Aston Webb** who designed the **Queen Victoria Memorial**, a white marble monument comprising a seated figure of the Queen facing east and a gilded bronze victory at the summit. George V was the first monarch to ride along the Mall to his coronation.

At the far end, the processional route leads right to Horse Guards *(see WHITEHALL)*, while the thoroughfare stretches straight past a statue of Captain Cook, through Admiralty Arch to Trafalgar Square. The pebble and flint Citadel on the park side of Admiralty Arch served as the operational centre for Churchill, the cabinet and chiefs of staff from 1939 to 1945.

The north side is flanked by Green Park and Carlton Terrace *(see ST JAMES'S)*.

'They're changing the guard at Buckingham Palace –
Christopher Robin went down with Alice.
A face looked out, but it wasn't the King's.
'He's much too busy a-signing things'
Says Alice'

A A Milne – *When We Were Very Young*

CHANCERY LANE ★

Map pp 8-9 **(EFX)**
⊖ Holborn; Chancery Lane

During the Middle Ages, this area depended upon the manors of Holborn around the palace of the Bishop of Ely and surrounded by open fields that have left their name. By the late 16C the four Inns of Court and dependent (now defunct) Inns of Chancery had been established for nearly 300 years as the country's great law societies. Many advocates were employed in the courts in Westminster Hall, in the Court of Star Chamber, in Westminster Palace which heard cases of 'riot, rout and mesdemeanour' until it became a royal instrument in the 17C and was abolished, and in White Hall, the future Lords' Chamber, where there was a Court of Requests for poor equity. Litigation was a serious business; there were endless disputes on land entitlement and inheritance while actions for slurs and insults, real or imagined, were also a fashionable and obsessive pastime indulged in by many. They offered a lucrative field which was also a good stepping stone to high office; from the 16C there were some 2 000 students dining in the halls.

The legal fraternity has always formed a close-knit group, attracting and nurturing many of the most learned men in every age: Thomas More, Thomas Cromwell, Francis Bacon, William Cecil (Lord Burghley), H H Asquith, F E Smith (Lord Birkenhead), Lord Justice Birkett, Lord Denning...

Chancery Lane runs along the border of the City, a mediator between the realms of government and commerce *(see INTRODUCTION)* extending south from Holborn to Fleet Street and the Temple.

HOLBORN

In the Middle Ages this comprised a crossroad for routes to the north, east to the City, and west to Oxford; it was also the site of the Bishop of Ely's palace, alluded to by Richard, Duke of Gloucester: 'My lord of Ely, when I was last in Holborn, I saw good strawberries in your garden there, I do beseech you send for some of them' (*Richard III; 3 iv*) and a number of other manor houses flanked by a market and surrounded by open fields on which beasts grazed, archery was practised, duels were fought and washing laid out to dry. The manors have long been transformed into the Inns of Court, the chapel and site of the episcopal precinct remain in name only, the fields are less in extent but still open, the produce market is a world diamond centre...

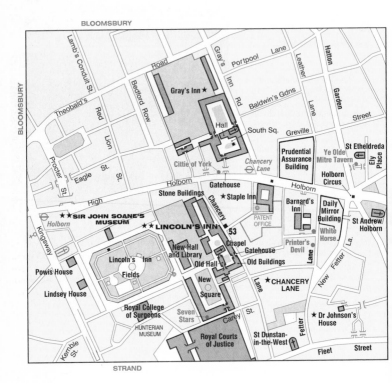

Hatton Garden – Ely Place recalls the Bishop of Ely's town house, which from 1381 when the Savoy Palace was burnt down until his death in 1399, was the residence of John of Gaunt, who converted it into a minor palace, visited over the years by many monarchs.

In 1576 the property, which extended from Holborn to Hatton Wall and from Leather Lane *(daily market)* to Saffron Hill, was given at Queen Elizabeth's command to **Sir Christopher Hatton**, her 'dancing Chancellor' for a yearly rent of ten pounds, a red rose and ten loads of hay. Hatton, whose portion included the famous garden, built a fine house and made such improvements that when he died in 1591 he was in debt to the crown for £40 000. The third Christopher Hatton, who followed Charles II into exile, sold the property to builders who erected slum tenements.

The property deteriorated, except when leased (1620-24) to the Spanish Ambassador as his residence. Under the Commonwealth Ely Place became a prison and a military hospital (1643); a century later the property was purchased through the crown by a Mr Cole who demolished the hall and built the pleasant four-storey brick terrace, with pilastered straight hooded doorways, which still lines the east side of Ely Place.

The Garden, built up in the 1680s, is today the centre of diamond merchants and jewellery craftsmen. Halfway down are the London Diamond Club *(no 87, west side)* – a white stucco house 6 bays wide with a triangular, pedimented door and, on the opposite side, a former church *(no 43)*, attributed to Wren, built in 1666 by Lord Hatton. In 1696 it became a Charity School and figures of 17C charity schoolchildren still flank the pedimented doorway.

Early history is recalled in the name of the **Mitre Tavern** in Ely Court, a narrow alley leading east from Hatton Garden.

St Etheldreda's ⊘ – The church was built as a chapel attached to the Bishop of Ely's house; St Etheldreda was the founder of Ely Cathedral. By the early 17C the crypt had become 'a public cellar to sell drink in'. Mr Cole retained the church for his tenants but stripped it of such medieval furnishings as remained. In 1873 Ely Place again came up for auction and the church became the first pre-Reformation shrine in the country to be transferred to the Roman Catholics. It is owned by the Rosminian Order. Subjected to neglect and wartime bombing, little of the 13C building remains but the outer walls and undercroft. New stained glass windows depict the five English martyrs beneath Tyburn gallows and on the aisles the arms of the pre-Reformation bishops of Ely: note the 4 cardinals' hats. Against the east wall is a carved medieval wood reliquary. The **crypt** has 8ft thick bare masonry walls, modern abstract single colour windows, blackened medieval roof timbers, a floor of London paving stones. The six supporting roof columns were placed down the chamber's centre in the 19C.

The Feast of St Etheldreda is celebrated annually with a street fair, Strawberrie Fayre *(Saturday nearest to 23 June)*.

Holborn Circus is now punctuated by a traffic island with Prince Albert, mounted and with hat aloft.

The **Daily Mirror Building** is marked by a 170ft-high curtain wall of stone, elbowed by yet taller buildings of glass extending south between Fetter and New Fetter Lanes (1957-60). Still within the City boundary, on the site of Furnival's Inn, stands the **Prudential Assurance Building**, an all red building designed by Alfred Waterhouse at the turn of the century for the Pru.

St Andrew Holborn ⊘ – The City church escaped the Fire but was rebuilt nevertheless. Saxon, Norman and 15C churches all stood on the site; by the 17C, however, the medieval church in which Henry Wriothesley, future Earl of Southampton and Shakespeare's patron, had been baptised with Henry VIII as godfather in 1545, had fallen into decay. Wren designed a long basilica of stone with windows in two tiers and a crowning balustrade. Note the stone of the Resurrection *(outside, north wall)* and the figures of two charity schoolchildren above the entrance.

The stout square tower with angle buttresses is ornamented by an overhanging cornice and balustrade decorated at each angle with a great vase.

Gutted by fire in 1941, the church has been restored; its interior is once more panelled complete with pillars which support the gallery and continue as Corinthian columns to the green and gold ceiling, and a stained-glass lunette at the east end. At the west end, in a recess, is the tomb, delightful with its shy child, of **Thomas Coram** (d 1751), sea captain and parishioner, transferred here in 1961 from the Foundling Hospital *(see BLOOMSBURY)*, together with the font (1804), the pulpit (1752), the case and organ presented to Coram by Handel in 1750.

★**Gray's Inn** ⊘ – Gray's Inn dates from the 14C in its foundation and from the 16C in its buildings, many of which, however, have had to be renewed since the war.

The main entrance is from High Holborn through the Gatehouse of 1688, distinguished, above the wide arch, by a bay window flanked by niches; Dryden's publisher kept a bookshop in the house for many years in the late 17C. **South Square**, which, except for no 1 of 1685, has been entirely rebuilt, has at its centre an elegant bronze statue of **Sir Francis Bacon**, the Inn's most illustrious member.

The gardens, delighted in by Pepys and Joseph Addison, were considered by many, besides Charles Lamb, to be 'the best gardens of the Inns of Court'. The very fine wrought-iron garden gateway is early 18C.

The hall, which was burnt out, has been rebuilt in its 16C style with stepped gables at either end and late Perpendicular tracery. Interior panelling sets off the late 16C screen which is said to have been made from the timbers of a wrecked galleon of the Spanish Armada and presented to the Inn by Queen Elizabeth I, and which was saved from the Great Fire.

★**Staple Inn** – Lying just inside the limits of the City, Staple Inn was one of the Inns of Chancery where law students spent their first year studying. Originally the home of wool merchants, it became a dependent of Gray's Inn and now houses the Institute of Actuaries.

For the row of half-timbered houses to have survived on such a site since 1586-96, when they were built, seems incredible: true they have been restored (19C) and the backs rebuilt (1937) but their overall character remains, providing some insight into the appearance of the pre-Fire City. The west house of 2 gables is the taller with two floors overhanging; the east range has 5 gables each marked by an oriel and again two floors overhanging. An arched entrance at the centre leads to the Inn surrounding a central courtyard at the rear. The east and west red brick ranges were erected in 1731-34 and 1757-59. Much of the rest has had to be rebuilt, including parts of the hall which dates from 1581 and possesses an original hammerbeam roof.

Staple Inn, Holborn

Barnard's Inn – Once an Inn of Chancery, it was rebuilt in the 19C; the Great Hall has 16C linen-fold panelling and heraldic stained glass. It is now home to **Gresham College** *(see The CITY – Guildhall)*, an institution that for over 400 years has continued its tradition of free public lectures by the Gresham Professors in Astronomy, Divinity, Geometry, Law, Music, Physic and Rhetoric.

CHANCERY LANE

The lane which takes its name from the grant of land by Henry III to his Lord Chancellor, Bishop of Chichester in 1227 (hence Rolls Passage, Bishop's Court etc) is now commercial as well as legal. At the north end is the Patent Office *(25 Southampton Buildings)*.

London Silver Vaults ⊘ – *No 53 Chancery House.* Some forty rooms, entered through a strong-room door, present an almost blinding array of Georgian, Victorian and modern silver and silverplate.

Further to the south, in the 19C neo-Gothic precincts of the former **Public Record Office** (now removed to Kew) survive traces of the medieval Rolls Chapel built in 1232 for converted Jews, transferred to the Master of the Rolls in 1377 and demolished in 1896.

★★LINCOLN'S INN ⊘

The site belonged to the Dominicans until 1276, when they moved to Blackfriars, before being acquired by the Earl of Lincoln who built himself a large, walled mansion which he bequeathed as a residential college, or inn, for young lawyers.

The buildings – The buildings, mainly of brick with some stone decoration, date from the late 15C. The self-contained collegiate plan of intercommunicating courts is entered through a main gateway and the surroundings enhanced by beautiful gardens with an ornate Gothic toolshed.

The **gatehouse** on Chancery Lane, built of brick with square corner towers and a four-centred arch filled with the original massive oak doors, dates from 1518. Above the arch are the arms of Henry VIII, the Earl of Lincoln and Sir Thomas Lovell.

Once through the arch, the gabled brick buildings immediately south of the court, known as the **Old Buildings**, are Tudor in style (redone in 1609). The stone-faced **Chapel**, which is raised on an open undercroft, was rebuilt in 1619-23 and endowed later in the 19C with pinnacles and extensions at the west end. John Donne laid the first foundation stone and preached at the consecration. In the windows, benchers and treasurers since the Middle Ages are commemorated by their arms and names: Thomas More, Thomas Cromwell, Pitt, Walpole, Newman, Canning, Disraeli, Gladstone, Asquith...

The **Old Hall**, with paired bay windows at either end, dates from 1490. Inside modern linen-fold panelling complements an early 17C oak screen, which is notable especially for the busts carved on the end pilasters; the painting *St Paul before Felix* (1748) is by Hogarth.

Towards Lincoln's Inn Fields is **New Square**, built in 1680 with identical four-storey ranges with broken pediments above the doors and incorporating in the south range an archway to Carey Street, wide and ornate with differing pediments on either side.

The **Stone Buildings** date from 1775-80. The red brick mid 19C **New Hall** and **Library** are diapered in the Tudor manner.

Lincoln's Inn Fields – By 1650 a developer, who had purchased the common fields to the west of Lincoln's Inn twenty years before, had surrounded them on three sides with houses. Of that period, one, **Lindsey House** remains, probably designed by Inigo Jones (since divided, nos 59-60, west side). The brickwork was originally all exposed, giving greater emphasis to the segmental pediment, the accented window and giant, wreathed, pilasters. 18C houses in the square include the Palladian style nos 57-58 dating from 1730, no 66, **Powis House** of 1777 with a pediment marking the centre window. On the north side nos 1-2 are early 18C, 5-9 Georgian, and no 15 with an Ionic columned doorway, frieze and pediment, mid-century.

The Beggar's Opera, a popular musical entertainment written by John Gay opened at the Lincoln's Inn Field Theatre in 1728. As it was a satire of Italian grand opera, topical, recognisable, low-life characters replaced Classical gods and goddesses; only the best tunes were retained. Its huge success was seen by **Hogarth** to reflect the supremacy of Englishness over foreign imported 'art': his six paintings of the scene show the proximity of the high ranking members of the audience to the actors and actresses (a place favoured by dukes and princes enamoured by the likes of Lavinia Fenton and Nell Gwynne) – a practice abolished by **Garrick** in 1763.

The square's south side is occupied by official buildings: the neo-Jacobean Land Registry, neo-Georgian Nuffield College of Surgical Sciences (1956-58), 19C-20C Royal College of Surgeons, housing the **Hunterian Museum** ⊙ dedicated to the study of pathology and anatomy, and the six-storey, 1960s headquarters of the Imperial Cancer Research Fund.

Sir John Soane (1753-1837)

Born the son of a country builder, Soane made his way through his talent: he worked under George Dance Junior and Henry Holland; he won prizes and a travelling scholarship to Italy (1777-80) while at the Royal Academy where, in later years, he was Professor of Architecture. He held the important office of Surveyor to the Bank of England (1788-1833) for which he executed the most original designs ever made for a bank.

★★**Sir John Soane's Museum** ⊙ – *13 Lincoln's Inn Fields*. In 1833 Soane obtained a private Act of Parliament to ensure the perpetuation of the museum after his death. A stipulation was that nothing should be altered in any way, so the house and collections are of interest not only in their own right but as an insight into the particular mind of a British connoisseur and collector of that period.
He acquired as his town house, no 12 Lincoln's Inn Fields in 1792, no 13 in 1805 as his museum and in 1824, built no 14.

Interior – The rooms are small, passages narrow, the stairs not 'grand' (note the wedge shape of the stairs in no 13 following the line of the house site), but recessed and angled mirrors, rooflights and windows on inner courts, ceilings slightly arched and decorated with only a narrow border or, as in the breakfast room of no 12, painted to resemble an arbour, give an illusion of space and perspective. Fragments, casts and models are displayed high and low throughout the galleries, while below ground are the Crypt, the Gothic Monk's Parlour and the Sepulchral Chamber containing the intricately incised sarcophagus of Seti I (c 1392 BC), celebrated on its acquisition in 1824 by Soane with a three day reception.
On the first floor, past the Shakespeare recess on the stairs, in the drawing rooms and former offices are models, prints and architectural drawings (8 000 by Robert and James Adam, 12 000 by Soane), rare books and a collection of Napoleonic medals. The south drawing-room contains original furniture and a painting by Turner hanging in its original position opposite the fireplace.

The ground floor with dining table and chairs, desk, leather chairs, the domed breakfast room, the portrait of Soane at 75 by Lawrence, is highly evocative. His **collection of pictures★★**, mostly assembled on folding planes in the picture room, includes drawings by Piranesi and 12 of **Hogarth**'s minutely observed paintings (from which the engravings were made) of the *Election* and the *Rake's Progress*. Elsewhere are paintings by **Canaletto**, **Reynolds** and **Turner**.

The half timbered building on the corner of Portsmouth Street is said to date back to the late 1500s and may be one of the oldest in London.

The Domesday Book

The famous register of lands of England, named after *Domus dei* – where the volumes were originally preserved in Winchester Cathedral, was commissioned by order of William the Conqueror so that he might ascertain the dues owed to him by his subjects, thereby setting the rules by which the monarch, later the government, might levy tax nationwide. As a result we have a comprehensive idea of how the kingdom was divided in 1085-86 both in terms of land-holding and popular employment. Lords of the manor held the bulk of the land on a freehold basis, which they tenanted or leased to a complex hierarchy of dependents, villeins or freemen. Land was allocated to agricultural functions (meadow, pasture) in proportion to hunting (woodland) and fishing (ponds and rivers)... The **Little Domesday** (384 pages) records estates throughout latter-day Essex, Norfolk and Suffolk, while the **Great Domesday** (450 pages) surveys the rest of the kingdom with the exception of Northumberland, Cumberland, Durham, parts of Lancashire and Westmorland which lay outside the king's jurisdiction. The City of London is also omitted as the conquering king could not have been certain of brokering his rights over the shrewd and powerful business community. A facsimile is displayed at the Public Record Office in Kew.

FLEET STREET ⊖ *Temple.*

Long associated with the printed word, Fleet Street links the City with Westminster – the obvious place between centres of commerce and government for journalists to congregate before modern communications transformed the production of modern newspapers.

St Dunstan-in-the-West ⊘ – Within the City boundary stands this church which was built in 1833 by John Shaw, slightly to the north of a site on which previous churches had stood since 1237 so as not to jut out onto Fleet Street. It was badly bombed in 1944.

The exterior, apart from the neo-Gothic tower which rises from an arched porch to an open-work octagonal lantern, is chiefly remarkable for the additions which associate the church with Fleet Street: the bust of **Lord Northcliffe** (1930), the public **clock** complete with its giant oak jacks (the first with a minute hand was made by Thomas Harrys in 1671 for the handsome sum of £35); the **statues** from the 1586 Lud Gate include that of Queen Elizabeth I modelled during her lifetime (modern inscription) and originally on the gate's west face (this was purchased in 1786 for £15 10s and now stands in a pedimented niche over a doorway), while to the right stand the figures of the mythical King Lud and his two sons (again of 1586 manufacture). Corbels at the main door are carved with the likenesses of Tyndale (west) and John Donne (east) who were both associated with St Dunstan's as were Izaac Walton (the *Compleat Angler* was printed in the churchyard as was Milton's *Paradise Lost*) and the Hoares banking family.

St Dunstan's, dedicated to the patron of goldsmiths, jewellers and locksmiths, is octagonal in plan with a high, star vault. The main altar, oriented to the north, is set in 17C 'choice panelling', Flamboyant Flemish in style.

Since the 1960s, one bay has been closed by an ornate 19C Romanian screen from the Antim Monastery in Bucharest. *(The community hold weekly services)*. The chapel next to the pulpit is used by the Oriental churches (Coptic), while another bay, containing a fine brass (1530), is used by the Old Catholic Churches in the Union of Utrecht.

Fetter Lane – At the north end is the Printer's Devil pub which marks the long-standing association with the printing and publishing world.

Beyond, yet still off the north side of Fleet Street is a series of narrow alleys known collectively as '**the Courts**': alas these have been substantially redeveloped, their names providing the sole vestige of interest: Crane, Red Lion, Johnson's, St Dunstan's, Bolt, Three Kings, Hind, Wine Office, Cheshire and Peterborough.

Samuel Johnson (1709-84)

Johnson was a man of sharp contrasts: in body he was physically very strong but often subject to awkwardness and infirmity; in mind, he was quick-witted and sharp on the uptake but tended also to procrastinate and be slothful; in spirit, he was of kind nature and generous heart but could as easily be possessed of a gloomy disposition and irritable temper. Disabled by scrofula in his youth which left him partially sighted, Johnson spent several years confined to studying in the library of his father, a book dealer; business declined, his father died, the family was destitute. The impecunious Samuel secured a small bursary from a neighbour (1729-31) which allowed him to go to Oxford where he survived humiliating abuse for his wretchedness. He became ever more slovenly and savage which hardly endeared him to London Society, let alone an elderly widow; yet he married in 1735 and became devoted to his 'Tetty' (Mrs Elizabeth Porter: 1688-1752) and soon found work 'reporting' for the Gentleman's Magazine, a periodical with a large circulation, on the speeches and debates delivered in Parliament. His first independent publication to capture an audience was a satire of London society in the style of the Latin poet Juvenal. His eloquent style, humour, diction, observation, satire of manners and morals of the age secured him a more enduring position at the heart of an artistic circle or club that included the likes of Garrick from the realms of the theatre, Goldsmith (light literature), Reynolds (painter), Burke (philosopher), Gibbon (historian), Sir William Jones (eminent linguist), Bennet Langton (Greek scholar), Topham Beauclerk (a great amorist and sarcastic wit who was the great-grandson of Charles II and Nell Gwynne, and married Lady Diana Spencer), the Scot James Boswell (lawyer, Johnson's biographer who persuaded his mentor to visit the Hebrides (1773) and thereafter abandon his scorn for Scotland!)...

★★Dr Johnson's House ⊙ – *17 Gough Square.* This unremarkable house so typical of the late 17C, was home to the great scholar and lexicographer between 1749 and 1759. Modest in size and proportion it was chosen by Johnson (1709-84) almost certainly for its large, well-lit garret, where he worked with his five secretaries to complete his *Dictionary* published in 1755. The small rooms on each floor are sparsely furnished with 18C oak gate-leg tables and chairs, period prints, mementoes and a collection of books on the impecunious essayist's life and times, including his biography by James Boswell.

The work completed, he moved to chambers in the Temple, in 1765 to no 7 Fleet Street (known purely coincidentally as Johnson's Court), and finally to Bolt Court where he died in 1784.

On the south side of Fleet Street stands the **Cock Tavern (Ye Olde Cocke Tavern)** complete with its 17C overmantel, panelled long bar and upstairs restaurant rooms with Dickens and Thackeray associations. At no 17 is **Prince Henry's Room** ⊙: its upstairs tavern room has Tudor panelling with ornate strapwork, a Jacobean ceiling with a centre decoration of Prince of Wales' feathers and the initial PH. It is now overfilled with Samuel Pepys mementoes.

Child & Co – *No 1 Fleet Street.* One of the country's oldest banks (now Royal Bank of Scotland) 'at the sign of the Marigold' *(see OSTERLEY PARK)* has also been known as the Devil Tavern.

Opposite, on the north side of the street are the Royal Courts of Justice *(see STRAND).*

For sights located beyond the Inns of Court, opposite the Temple see The CITY – Cheapside – Ludgate Circus.

Temple Bar has been the City's western barrier since the Middle Ages; the sovereign pauses here to receive and return the Pearl Sword from the Lord Mayor on entering the City. The present memorial pillar with statues of Queen Victoria and the future Edward VII surmounted by the City griffin, dates from 1880. It replaced the 'bars' which had developed from 13C posts and chains and at various times constituted a high, arched building, a prison (thrown down by Wat Tyler in 1381) and finally an arch of Portland stone designed by Wren in 1672 and used in the days of public execution as a spike for heads and quarters. It was dismantled in 1870 and removed to Theobald's Park near Waltham Cross.

★★TEMPLE ⊖ Temple

The Order of the Knights Templars was founded in 1118 to protect pilgrims on the road to the Holy City of Jerusalem, and welcomed to England by Henry I. They settled first at the north end of Chancery Lane before moving to a preferred site by the river where they began building their church in 1185. In 1312 the Templars were suppressed and their property assigned to the Hospitallers who, in turn, were dispossessed by Henry VIII. The church reverted to the crown; the outlying property remained with the lawyers to whom it had previously been leased by the Hospitallers and to whom it was granted, together with the safekeeping of the church, by James I in 1608. The lawyers early formed themselves into three Societies: the **Inner Temple** (being within the City; emblem a Pegasus), the **Middle Temple** (emblem a Pascal lamb) and the **Outer Temple**, which was on the site of Essex Street but has long since disappeared. Today the area is abuzz with lawyers through the week and a haven of peace at weekends; at night, it is lit by gas-light. According to Shakespeare, the origin of the War of the Roses derives from the plucking of a red and white rose from the Temple Gardens in 1430.

Inner Temple – The Tudor **Inner Temple Gateway** *(between nos 16 and 17 Fleet Street)*, gabled, half timbered, 3 storeys high, each advanced on the one below so that the tunnel arch and pilastered stone ground floor are in shadow, dates from 1610 (reconstructed 1906). It leads into the lane, past 19C buildings and the house *(right)* where Dr Johnson lived from 1760 to 1765, to the church.

★★**Temple Church** ⊙ – This special church survived the Great Fire but was badly damaged in the Blitz (1941). 'The two learned and honourable Societies of this House' are the four Inns of Court, the Inner and Middle Temples; it is a private chapel under the jurisdiction of the Sovereign as Head of the Church, who appoints the Master of the Temple (hence the Royal Coat of Arms on the organ case), rather than falling within the diocese of the Bishop of London.

It is largely built of soft-coloured stone, although the northside and tower seem of paler travertine. At the west end, the wall sweeps in a great curve reaching up to a square crenellated roofline. The round-headed west doorway into the round church of 1160-85 is Romanesque, protected from weathering by a rib vaulted porch added later.

The round church is modelled on the Church of the Holy Sepulchre in Jerusalem and dedicated to the Blessed Mary by Heraclius, Patriarch of Jerusalem: six composite piers of Purbeck marble support an arcade of transitional pointed arches that bulge outwards when seen from below, a triforium articulated by interlacing blind arcading and tall round-headed, three-light clerestory windows. Above the door is a Lombard-style radiating window fashioned like a wheel of fortune. Laterally, this open space is ringed first by an ambulatory, then by a continuous stone sill that provides seating before being enclosed by a wall decorated with blind arcading and crisply carved grotesque heads. A sense of clarity and order is further enhanced by the stylised capital decoration and the elegant, polished shafts of Purbeck marble heavily ringed midway, that soar up to the conical roof (dating from 1862 and restored to the original layout after the war). On the stone floor lie ten 10C-13C effigies of knights in armour, Templars and their illustrious supporters (including an Earl of Pembroke and his two sons). The font is a replica, carved with St George and a hunting scene preceded by playing dogs.

Level with the beginning of the hall-church chancel (1220-40) are placed two 16C monuments 'repaired and beautified in 1687' – behind that on the north side (Edmund Plowden d 1584) is the penitential cell dating back to Templar times, a cubicle less than 5ft long (door in chancel).

In the chancel, there is no trace of the transitional phase of Gothic from Romanesque: beautiful, slender Purbeck columns divide the nave from the aisles, rising to form the ribs of the quadripartite vaulting. The oak reredos designed by Wren was carved by **William Emmett** in 1682 for £45. Note in passing the heraldic floor brass (half-way down the nave) with a Latin scroll winding between 29 shields.

In the graveyard (north side) lies Oliver Goldsmith, a contemporary of Dr Johnson. To the northeast of the church stands the **Master's House** rebuilt in 17C style.

The **Inner Temple Hall**, Treasury and Library were all rebuilt after the war.

King's Bench Walk – The northern of the two ranges, in the largest Temple court, dates from 1678 and is by **Wren** (no 1 rebuilt). Below the east gate are two houses of especial note, no 7 of 1685 and no 8 of 1782.

Middle Temple – In **Pump Court** the cloisters (from Church Court) and the south side have been rebuilt (Edward Maufe); the north (except for the 19C Farrar's Building) is late 17C.

★★**Middle Temple Hall** ⊙ – The Elizabethan great hall has ancient oak timbers, panelling and fine carving, heraldic glass, helmets and armour: the roof (1574) is a double hammerbeam, the finest of the period. The small panels in the high wainscot are bright with the arms of readers who instructed the medieval law students who not only ate but attended lectures and even slept in the hall (100ft × 40ft). At the west

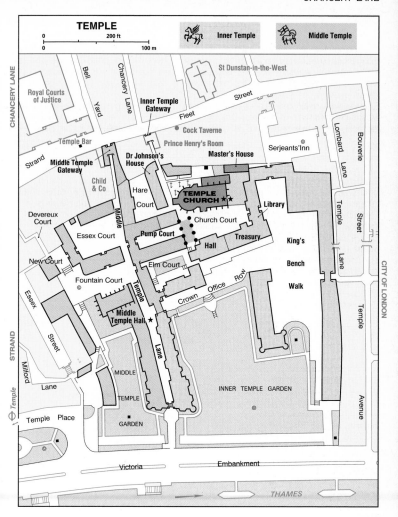

end above the high table are royal portraits (Charles I after Van Dyck, Charles II by Kneller, and Queen Elizabeth). According to tradition, Elizabeth watched the first performance of Shakespeare's *Twelfth Night* (1602) here in the company of the benchers in the hall. When the spectacular 16C carved screen at the hall's east end was shattered by a bomb, the splintered pieces were dug out of the rubble and painstakingly reassembled. The roof, incredibly, remained unharmed.

Up the steps from Fountain Court (immortalised by Dickens in *Martin Chuzzlewit*) is **New Court** with its Wren building of 1676.

Middle Temple Gateway and Lane – The pedimented gateway with giant pilasters was erected only in 1684 although the lane is referred to as early as 1330 since it used to end in stairs on the river, affording a short cut by water to Westminster. Just inside the gate are two houses of 1693, their ground floors overshadowed by jutting timber-faced upper storeys with 17C windows.

★**Victoria Embankment** – The frigate **HMS Wellington** serves as the guildhall of the Honourable Company of Master Mariners.

Victoria Embankment bench

121

CHELSEA ★★

Map pp 6-7 (**BCZ**)
⊖ Sloane Square

The completion of the embankment in 1874 removed for ever the atmosphere of a riverside community: boats drawn up on the mud flats, trees shading the fore-shore, people walking along a country road as painted by Rowlandson in 1789 *(Chelsea Reach)*, watched in his old age at sunset by Turner and luminously captured by Whistler *(Old Battersea Bridge)*.

Chelsea had royal connections but the only royal building to survive is the Royal Hospital. Architectural interest lies in the churches and also in the squares and terraces, attractive houses of all periods and 19C and 20C blocks of flats.

Henry VIII's Palace – The river still served as the main access when the king's riverside palace was built in 1537 near Albert Bridge; it was known as the New Manorhouse as there was an Old Manorhouse, demolished in 1704, on the site of Lawrence Street. The palace was a two-storey Tudor brick mansion including 'three cellars, three halls, three parlours, three kitchens... a large staircase, three drawing rooms, seventeen chambers'; water was brought by conduit from Kensington.

Here resided Prince Edward, Princess Elizabeth and their cousin Lady Jane Grey, followed at the king's death by Catherine Parr (d 1548) and then by Anne of Cleves (d 1557). It was owned by the Cheynes in the 17C and then by **Sir Hans Sloane** *(see index)*, who retired to Chelsea with his two daughters and his collection from 1712 until his death in 1753 when the house was demolished.

Sir Thomas More – Henry VIII's Chancellor bought a parcel of land at the water's edge west of the church (approximately on the site of Beaufort Street). The house he built was large enough to contain his extensive family, portrayed vividly by **Holbein** on his first visit to England. One regular guest in the twelve years More lived in Chelsea, before sailing down river to his execution in 1535, was **Erasmus**; another who came informally, appearing unannounced at the river gate, was Henry VIII himself. Reminders of More, that 'man of marvellous mirth and past-times and sometimes of as sad a gravity, (that) man for all seasons', are to be found at Chelsea Old Church *(see below)*.

SLOANE SQUARE – KING'S ROAD

Chelsea has frequently been the setting for a new or revived fashion: the smart and cosmopolitan crowds in the Ranelagh and Cremorne Gardens, the exclusivity of the Pre-Raphaelites and the individuality of Oscar Wilde's green carnation. The opening of Bazaar in 1955 by the designer **Mary Quant** led to a radical change in dress with the launch of the mini skirt: in the 1960s Chelsea was the 'navel of swinging London' and King's Road, a Mecca of

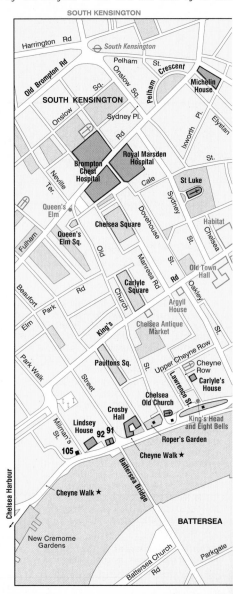

the avant-garde. In 1971 Vivienne Westwood opened her shop at 430 King's Road as an outlet for her clothes; as her partner was Malcolm McLaren, the instigator of the Sex Pistols' pop group, the shop became the centre of Punk fashion. Today, lined with leather shops and trendy boutiques, Marks and Spencer and Waitrose, the King's Road has weathered into a convenient shopping area for local residents...

Sloane Square – The square boasts three very different institutions: Peter Jones, the purveyor of household effects and domestic appliances, has been judged to have one of London's most successful shop exteriors (1936). It was here too that William Willett invented daylight saving or **summer time** (adopted 1916).

The **Royal Court Theatre** has twice, since it opened in 1870, launched a new vogue: in 1904-07 when Harley Granville Barker put on Arthur Pinero farces, and plays by Bernard Shaw and Somerset Maugham and in 1956-58 when the English Stage Co under George Devine presented John Osborne's *Look Back in Anger*.

Holy Trinity ⊘ – *Sloane Street*. The church was rebuilt in 1888 when the Pre-Raphaelites were at their height by a leading exponent of the Arts and Crafts movement, John Dando Sedding (1838-91). **Burne-Jones**, seeing it under construction, proposed the design with flowing tracery of the 48-panel east window with Apostles, Patriarchs, Kings, Prophets and Saints – St Bartholomew by William

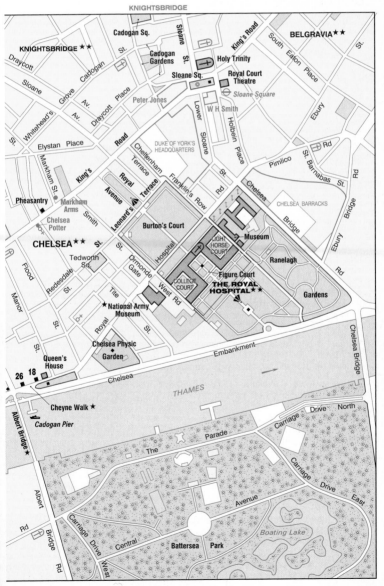

Radical Fashion – The miniskirt 'happened' in 1965 when Mary Quant decided to turn-up the hem of her baggy sweater-dresses. The catalyst that popularised this timeless fashion accessory, however, was the controversy it provoked: miniskirts were blamed for provoking traffic jams in Chelsea; they were banned in Holland but permitted in Poland. Their true moments of glory are probably best immortalised by those bright young things Twiggy and Jean Shrimpton, cult fashion paradigms of the age of Beatle mania *(examples in the V&A fashion collection)*.

In order to protect modesty, Quant commercialised opaque ballet fleshings in white or black under the Ginger Group fashion label as a more streamlined alternative to stockings and suspender belts – later (1968) DIM launched a cheaper product and coined the term *'collant'* from the French verb *coller* – to stick: 'tights' were here to stay!

Morris. All decoration is of the period and harmonises with the High Altar marble crucifix and candlesticks, designed by the architect who had met Morris when he was studying with G E Street. Note also the very fine metalwork inside: bronze panels in the choirstalls, the gilded organ case fashioned like a portcullis, decorative pulpit stair rail, golden lectern; and singular railings outside on Sloane Street.

King's Road – This used to be the route taken by Charles II when calling upon Nell Gwynne at her house in Fulham: between 1719-1830, the King's Road was closed to all but those holding a royal pass owing to its attraction to footpads. It is now famous for its shops selling fashion accessories and antiques, restaurants and pubs, while the small streets around are lined by traditional cottages once built for artisans.

At 173a King's Road were the **Chenil Galleries** built by Charles Chenil in 1905 on the site of the old Chelsea College of Art & Design and the Chelsea Arts Club. Chenil was a prosperous art materials supplier who generously supported and fed a number of needy artists. Turner, Whistler, Sargeant, Augustus John, Eric Gill, Jacob Epstein, Francis Bacon, David Hockney certainly all passed through Chelsea at one time or another. Since 1979, the galleries have accommodated antique dealers.

Between the King's Road and the Royal Hospital lies the playing field **Burton's Court**, flanked by **St Leonard's Terrace** – a most attractive mid 18C Georgian row *(nos 14-31)*. At the centre of the terrace is **Royal Avenue**, planted in 1692-94, which was planned to extend as far as Kensington Palace but was never completed; the houses on either side date from the early and mid 19C. Further down stands what was the **Pheasantry** *(no 152)* which was erected in 1881 by the Jouberts to sell French wallpapers and furniture; alas, only the façade and portico survive. In 1916 the site was occupied by a Russian dance school attended amongst others by Margot Fonteyn. By 1932 it had been converted into a popular meeting-place frequented by Bohemian artists and left-wing politicians. Today it is known as Toad Hall.

St Luke's ⊙ – *Sydney Street.* The Bath stone church of 1820, an early example of the Gothic Revival, is tall and lanky both outside and in. The pinnacled and slimly buttressed west tower (242ft) is pierced at the base to provide a porch which extends the full width of the west front.

Three squares – **Paultons** (1830-40), **Carlyle** (mid 19C) and **Chelsea** (18C-20C) illustrate the evolution of styles in residential development.

THE ROYAL HOSPITAL

★★**The Royal Hospital** ⊙ – Chelsea Pensioners have been colourful members of the local community for about 300 years. The idea for a veterans' hostel would appear to have come to Charles II, who had re-established a standing army in 1661, from reports of the Invalides built by Louis XIV in Paris in 1670. The next ten years are summarised in the Latin inscription in the Figure Court: 'For the support and relief of maimed and superannuated soldiers, founded by Charles II, expanded by James II and completed by King William and Queen Mary 1692.'

The architect Sir Christopher **Wren** provided a quadrangular plan with a main court open on the south to the grounds and the river. He expanded it by abutting courts to east and west always leaving one side open. The long, regular brick ranges are marked at the angles with stone quoins and midway by stone centrepieces pierced at ground level, colossally pilastered and plainly pedimented. The main entrance is beneath the lantern-crowned octagon porch in the north range of the original

Figure Court, so-called after the Classical statue of Charles II by **Grinling Gibbons** at the centre. The porch emerges on the south side beneath a portico of giant Tuscan pillars, which is flanked on either side by a colonnade of small paired Tuscan pillars. Along the entablature runs the historical Latin inscription *(see above).*

Chapel and Great Hall – From the Octagon Porch steps rise on either side to the Chapel and Great Hall, both panelled beneath tall rounded windows. The Chapel has a barrel vault, decorated like the piers and spandrels with delicate plasterwork (Henry Margetts) and, at the end, a domed and painted apse by Ricci. The end wall of the Hall is decorated with an 18C mural of Charles II on horseback before the hospital. Here the Duke of Wellington lay in state in 1852.

Council Chamber – The Chamber *(west wing)* was decorated by both Wren and Robert Adam; Van Dyck painted the portrait of Charles I and his family.

Museum – The exhibits include Wellington mementoes and illustrate the history of the hospital and its members.

Grounds – Since 1913 the Chelsea Flower Show *(see PRACTICAL INFORMATION – Calendar of Events)* displaying flowers, plants and everything imaginable for a garden, has been held in the grounds by the Royal Horticultural Society.

Ranelagh Gardens – In 1805 the Hospital repurchased the land formerly occupied by the celebrated Ranelagh Gardens (1742-1805), which offered patrons *al fresco* meals, concerts and spectacles in the Rotunda, a building (150ft in diameter) containing tiers of boxes.

★**National Army Museum** ⊘ – The museum tells the story of the British Army over 5 centuries from the formation of the Yeomen of the Guard by Henry VII on Bosworth Field in 1485, of the Indian Army and of colonial forces to the rigours of UN peacekeeping today. The Story of the Army illustrates campaigns in every continent, the evolution from armour to khaki and tin helmets, with reconstructions, models, dramatic audio-visual displays (Battle of Waterloo) and dioramas. One gallery celebrates the 'Forgotten Army', another the domestic life of the soldier. A considerable collection of weapons demonstrates the development of hand-held weapons from pikes and swords to revolvers and repeating rifles, pistols and machine guns. The Uniform gallery displays buckskin breeches, helmets, caps and hats. Notable medals, honours and decorations wrought in the finest coloured enamelwork and craftsmanship are also displayed. Other artefacts of interest include portraits by Reynolds, Romney, Gainsborough, Lawrence and others, and the skeleton of Napoleon's horse Marengo.

A varied cavalcade has lived in Chelsea : the famous actresses Nell Gwynne, Dame Ellen Terry, Dame Sybil Thorndyke (who inspired G B Shaw to write *St Joan* for her); Sir Joseph Banks (botanist, explorer and President of the Royal Society); Sir John Fielding (a respected magistrate who was blind from birth), the engineers Sir Marc Isambard Brunel and his son Isambard Kingdom; Charles Kingsley (author of the *Water Babies*); Mrs Elizabeth Gaskell (novelist); the **Pre-Raphaelite** poets and painters Dante Gabriel Rossetti, his sister Christina, Burne-Jones, William and Jane Morris, Holman Hunt, Swinburne, Millais. Other artists include William de Morgan, Wilson Steer, Sargent, Augustus John, Orpen, Sickert. Mark Twain, Henry James, T S Eliot are among Chelsea Americans. Smollett lived in Lawrence Street, **Oscar Wilde** at 34 Tite Street, A A Milne at 13 Mallord Street (1919-42). There were also Hilaire Belloc, the Sitwells, Arnold Bennett...

Chelsea Physic Garden ⊘ – The garden, frequented by such leading lights as Linnaeus who propounded early theories on genetics, was founded in 1673 by the Worshipful Society of Apothecaries of London on land leased from Sir Hans Sloane: in 1722 he granted the lease to the Society in perpetuity.
The record of the garden, overlooked at the centre by a statue of Sir Hans by Rysbrack, is remarkable: Georgia's cotton seeds came from the South Seas via the Physic Garden, India's tea from China, her quinine *(cinchona)* from South America, Malaya's rubber from South America...
The garden of wound medicine shows plants used for medical purposes by the Chinese, North American Indians, Maoris etc.

CHELSEA EMBANKMENT

★**Cheyne Walk** – The terraces of brick houses standing back from the river front are rich with memories of artists, writers and royalty. Corinthian pilasters and an entablature mark the entrance to no 4 where the painter Daniel Maclise lived and George Eliot spent her last weeks. Beautiful railings and fine urns distinguish no 5; no 6 is remarkable for the Chippendale-Chinese gate and railings.

The **Queen's House** *(no 16)* is named after Catherine of Braganza, although it was not built until 1717, twelve years after her death; it was the home of the poet and painter D G Rossetti where the Pre-Raphaelites used to meet. Apart from the bay window, the house is unaltered: central pediment topped with a single urn, segment-headed windows, brick corner pilasters and the finest among several contemporary iron gateways. In the gardens opposite, facing onto the river stands a fountain bearing a portrait bust of Rossetti by Seddon. **No 18**, distinguished by its first floor railed balconies and parapet, was the popular Don Saltero's coffee-house and museum. **Nos 19-26**, built between 1759-65, occupy the site of Henry VIII's riverside palace *(see above)*.

On the southwest corner of Oakley Street is a bronze sculpture of a boy poised high above a dolphin (1975) by David Wynne. The Antarctic explorer, Captain R F Scott, lived at no 56.

Houseboats – Moored on the river are several permanent houseboats: larger and more spacious than a canal barge, these would once have accommodated watermen and river pilots. Today they provide homes for a more Bohemian set of Chelsea residents.

For Albert Bridge see Outer London – BATTERSEA.

Carlyle's House ⊘ – *24 Cheyne Row.* Thomas Carlyle (1795-1881) lived in this modest Queen Anne brick house for 47 years – 'as usual, never healthy, never absolutely ill, - protesting against 'things in general'...'. He had the garret-room at the top of the house sound-proofed by building closets front and back in order to write his biography of Peter the Great. At such times he largely ignored his company-loving, but rather sickly, wife Jafcne Welsh who took to recording her miserable and lonely life in long letters to her family and a journal. On discovering these at her sudden death and the evidence of his wretched behaviour, Carlyle's final years were racked by guilt and shame.

The four-storeyed house is compact, uncluttered and yet filled with portraits of Thomas, his library, his manuscripts, artefacts, relics, Jane's blue and white china and simple furniture that reflect the couple's comfortable but unpretentious lifestyle.

The 'Sage of Chelsea' is commemorated in a statue by Boehm in Cheyne Walk gardens facing onto the river.

In **Lawrence Street** flourished the Chelsea China Works (1745-84) before being transferred to Derby *(see INTRODUCTION – Decorative Arts)*. Among the 18C houses to remain are the early Georgian Duke House and Monmouth House sharing a pedimented porch on carved brackets *(nos 23-24)*.

The 'moral desperado', as he was described by his disciple Ruskin, was born in the Scottish borders into Calvinist peasant stock. **Thomas Carlyle** (1795-1881) was probably destined to become a minister, but being self-taught and blessed with great determination, he embarked upon a career in writing. He despised English parliamentary democracy and detested the social reformers who campaigned for the freedom of slaves, the reform of prisons, or, indeed for the 'universal Abolition of Pain Association'. Greatly inspired by German Romantic mysticism (notably Goethe), he came to worship 'greatness', something which powered his imagination and pushed him to write the important historical works which earned him his reputation and lasting admiration: *The French Revolution, Heroes and Hero Worship, Cromwell's Letters and Speeches.*

Chelsea Embankment continued – The **King's Head and Eight Bells** was undoubtedly frequented by the various artists (including Dylan Thomas) living locally and Charles II in whose reign it was founded and who is reputed to have been a frequent visitor.

Chelsea Old Church ⊘ – The church dates from pre-Norman, possibly Saxon times. By the 20C it consisted of a nave and tower of c 1670, 13C chancel and early 14C chapels of which the south one had been remodelled by Sir Thomas More in 1528. In 1941 all but the More chapel was badly damaged by a bomb; in 1950-58 it was reconstructed on the old foundations, modelled on records provided by old prints and paintings. Inside, the nave divides beneath three arches at the east end into the chancel, the Lawrence and More Chapels. Many monuments were rescued from the rubble; the altar and rails are 17C, the small marble font dates from 1673, the **chained books**, presented by Sir Hans Sloane and the only ones in a London church, consist of a Vinegar Bible (1717), a prayer book (1723), *Homilies* (1683) and two volumes of Foxe's *Book of Martyrs* (1684).

The kneelers, for the most part embroidered 1953-58, bear the coats of arms or symbols of those associated with the church including Elizabeth I, Holman Hunt, Sir Hans Sloane, Sir Thomas More... Among the monuments are the reclining figure of

Lady Jane Cheyne (1699), Sarah Colville with aghast expression and upraised hands (1631; Lawrence Chapel), the massive Stanley monument of 1632 and, near the squint, the small alabaster group of Sir Thomas Lawrence, City goldsmith and merchant adventurer, at prayer with his wife and eight children. More's self-composed inscription stands against the south wall of the sanctuary by the arch with capitals dated 1528, designed by Holbein. The novelist Henry James is also buried here while in the churchyard an urn marks the grave of Sir Hans Sloane and a statue of a seated black-robed figure with gilded face and hands, commemorates Sir Thomas More.

Roper's Garden – This walled garden, once part of More's orchard, is named after William Roper, his son-in-law. An upstanding stone relief of *A Woman walking against the wind* by **Jacob Epstein** commemorates the artist's years in Chelsea (1909-14).

Crosby Hall – The medieval great hall, which was transferred to Chelsea in 1910, was built between 1466 and 1475 in Bishopsgate as part of the residence of the 15C wool merchant, Sir John Crosby; the interior is panelled, has a painted hammerbeam roof and is lit by a three-tier oriel window.

For Battersea Bridge see Outer London – BATTERSEA.

91-94 Cheyne Walk – The first two houses were built in 1771 and have several Venetian windows: no 91 *(entrance in Beaufort St)* has a modest but fine entrance and a first floor conservatory commanding a view of the river, and no 92 is contained between arches serving the front door and former passage. Nos 93 and 94 date from 1777. Whistler resided at no 96.

Lindsey House – The large house with mansard roof-storey, dates from 1752 and served as the London headquarters of the Moravian Brethren (their burial ground to the right of Milman's Street can be seen from the rear of the flats). It was built for the 3rd Earl of Lindsey in 1674 on the site of Sir Thomas More's farm. The 17C Lindsey mansion of brick (since subdivided and painted), is articulated by projecting central and lateral bays.

Marc Brunel and his son, Isambard Kingdom Brunel, the engineers, who lived at no 98, are commemorated in the modern **Brunel House** on the corner *(no 105)*. Note the tall studio south-facing window on the third floor of no 109.

104-120 Cheyne Walk – **Hilaire Belloc** (1873-1953), the Catholic essayist and historian was a versatile writer, author of *Cautionary Tales* and *The Bad Child's Book of Beasts*. **P W Steer** (1860-1942), the son of a portrait painter achieved particular recognition for his landscape paintings. He studied in Paris during the early 1880s but discovered Degas and the Impressionists only towards the end of the decade, after which time his Constable-like style becomes freer and more robust.

J M W Turner (1775-1851) spent his last years in near seclusion at no 119, while taste in his art dwindled and the Pre-Raphaelites found favour.

Sylvia Pankhurst, the second daughter of Emmeline, worked for women's suffrage and participated in organising the Women's Social and Political Union.

Chelsea Wharf – Old and new co-exist as modern developments encroach upon the old warehouses, London Transport Electric Power-substation and gasworks.

Chelsea Harbour – As recently as 1960, this was where barges would unload coal for the London Underground Power Station in Lots Road – a far cry from the luxury, modern riverside development of today, pin-pointed by its Belvedere Tower.

Chelsea Harbour

The **Moravian** Brethren were a sect of a reformed church founded in Bohemia (Czechoslovak Republic) closely associated with the Lutherans. Active missionaries from the start (1722), they were soon preaching in such distant lands as the West Indies (1732) and Greenland (1733). In 1738 Peter Bohler established a religious society in Fetter Lane that was to have great influence on the young John Wesley and the rise of Methodism. The enduring appeal of the sect was its sincere distrust of doctrinal formulae, opting instead for a simple and unworldly form of Christianity which took hold and thrived in rural settlements throughout Britain.

The complex as a whole was developed at break-neck speed: planning permission was granted on 15 April 1986 and a year later, the first residents moved in. Organised around a 75-berth marina, it comprises a series of elegant and exclusive apartments, offices, a hotel, shops and restaurants: those that face onto the river enjoy fine views across the water to St Mary's Church *(see BATTERSEA)* on the south bank.

'Though the philistines might jostle, you would rank as an apostle
In the high aesthetic band
If you swanned down Cheyne Walk with just a sunflower on a stalk
In your medieval hand.'

                       Verse from a popular song.

The City of London, also known as the Square Mile, is a compact area on the north bank of the Thames, now identified with finance and business *(see INTRODUCTION)* and therefore animated by a commuting workforce by weekday and left silent and eerie at night to Barbican residents.

Between and beneath the modern buildings are traces of Celtic and Roman settlements, sections of the city wall, medieval and Wren churches, rare and exiguous gardens, Victorian market and office buildings. Here rather than elsewhere in London, vestiges of the old city, her trades and traditions survive as does the medieval network of narrow courts and alleys, yards and steps steeped in local history by association: Pope's Head Alley, Puddle Dock, Glasshouse Alley, Panyer Alley, Wardrobe Terrace, Seacole Lane, French Ordinary, Ave Maria Lane, Paternoster Row, Amen Court, Turnagain Lane...

Traditions – Of the many practices maintained: the royal carriage still halts at Temple Bar when the sovereign enters the City; annually the Prime Minister makes a major policy speech at the Lord Mayor's Banquet; visitors of state are invited to attend a banquet or ceremony in the City; on 20 June each year the guild of Watermen and Lightermen pays a 'fine' of one red rose to the Lord Mayor imposed on Lady Knollys in 1381 for building a bridge across Seething Lane without permission...

BANK ⊖ *Bank*

Bank of England ⊘ **(CY)** – Seven floors of offices are housed in the Bank, massive, blank and undistinguished, designed and erected by Sir Herbert Baker, an associate of Lutyens (1924-39). It is taller and larger than its immediate, gloriously vaulted, predecessor built by **Sir John Soane** *(see index)*. The façade sculptures representing Britannia served by six bearers and guardians of wealth are by Sir Charles Wheeler.

On the corner of Princes Street and Lothbury stands the Temple, a circular domed pavilion encircled with fluted columns and urns which Soane modelled upon the Temple of the Sibyl at Tivoli, crowned by a statue of Ariel – that ethereal spirit in Shakespeare's *The Tempest*. Masks of Mercury and representations of his caduceus refer to the god's role as patron of bankers.

The Bank, conceived by a Scot, William Paterson, was incorporated under royal charter in 1694 with a capital of £1 200 000 to finance, in the modern way by raising loans and not by royal extortion as heretofore, the continuation of the wars against Louis XIV. It acquired its nickname a century later during the Napoleonic wars during a crisis when the institution was forced to suspend cash payments: Sheridan referred in the House to the 'elderly lady in the City of great credit and long standing', Gillray drew a caricature which he captioned 'The Old Lady of Threadneedle Street in Danger'. The Bank has since weathered other crises, become a bankers' bank and in 1946 was nationalised. It supervises the note issue and national debt and acts as the central reserve. The Governor is appointed by the Crown.

Follow Princes Street to the rear of the building for the museum.

The heart of the City and the national economy is that important institution: the Bank of England **(Bank)** and from here radiate the principal thoroughfares:

Throgmorton Street runs to Broadgate.

Threadneedle Street provides access to **Bishopsgate** and the north beyond the city wall.

Cornhill leads eastwards to Leadenhall Street and Aldgate.

Lombard Street runs east to **Fenchurch Street** and Aldgate.

To the south stands **Monument** and the river.

Mansion House is the official residence of the Lord Mayor.

Queen Victoria Street runs down to Blackfriars Bridge and St Bride's.

Cheapside goes to St Paul's Cathedral.

Due north of Bank sits the **Guildhall**.

Straddling the boundaries of the City of London are the areas **Barbican** and **Smithfield**.

If visiting the area for the first time: start at St Paul's Cathedral *(listed separately)* before popping into St Mary le Bow, walking down past the Bank of England, Mansion House and the Royal Exchange, and on to Leadenhall Market and the Lloyds building. This route will provide an impression of the City's principal institutions and her broad range of architectural styles.

Note: Most of the City institutions do not admit casual visitors off the street for security reasons.

★**Bank of England Museum** ⊙ (CY) – The museum, which traces the history of the bank,
opens with a description of the history of the building in a reconstruction of Sir John
Soane's Bank Stock Office; it continues through a series of chronological displays:
early banking using goldsmiths' notes; the Charter dated 27 July 1694; Letters
Patent under the Great Seal of William and Mary; bank notes; a £1 million note used
for accounting purposes only; display of gold bars (including some dated AD 375
minted in Sirmium, modern-day Bosnia); the Bank Volunteers (1798-1907); paper
money and forgeries; the gold standard; silver vessels; minted coins; interactive
touch screens explain modern banking while a modern dealing desk with telephone
and screen provide an insight into money dealing.

THROGMORTON STREET-BROADGATE

Stock Exchange (CY) – *8 Throgmorton Street.* Trading in stocks and shares
originated in this country, in the 17C: first in the coffeehouses of **Change Alley**
where shopkeepers used to barter for goods, then in the Royal Exchange. The first
stock exchange, as such, was inaugurated in 1773 in Threadneedle Street. In 1801
and 1971 ever larger buildings rose on the site.
In 1986 a change in legislation governing the Exchange abolished any distinction
between jobbers and brokers by introducing electronic dealing systems. Membership is no longer restricted to individuals but is open to outside institutions and to
international share dealers. As transactions are carried out away from the Exchange
the frenetic activity on the trading floor has been stilled.

Dutch Church ⊙ (CY) – The church was founded in 1253 and rebuilt in the 14C;
its Augustinian monastery was dissolved by Henry VIII; in 1550 the surviving nave
was granted to refugees from the Low Countries. The slender lantern crowned by
a spirelet and weathervane was designed by John Skeeping.
The building received a direct hit in 1940 and was entirely rebuilt to a modern
design (1955) by Ansell and Bailey with a hall interior and brilliant windows
beneath a shallow curved roof.

National Westminster Tower (CY) – The headquarters of the National Westminster Bank (52 storeys; 600ft) opened in 1980. Bombed by IRA in 1993, it has
been subjected to major rebuilding.

All Hallows London Wall ⊙ (CX) – The Portland stone tower rises by stages
from a pedimented doorway to an urn-quartered cornice, pilastered lantern cupola
and final cross. The interior, lit by semicircular clerestory windows, has a particularly splendid 'snowflake' patterned barrel vault rising on fluted Ionic pilasters
from a frieze, and a coffered apse. It is now a resource centre for a branch of
Christian Aid; its main focus is on world issues, justice and development.

Finsbury Circus (CX) – Mid 19C-20C buildings surround the only bowling green in
the City.

Broadgate (CDX) – The re-development on a grand scale of the site of Broad
Street Railway Station was begun in 1985 and consists of 39 buildings designed in
a variety of architectural styles, grouped round squares and open spaces enhanced
by fountains and dramatic sculpture. At the centre is a circular Arena for open air
entertainment and an ice rink.

Broadgate Arena

Liverpool Street Station – The station, erected in 1875 on the first site of Bethlehem Hospital (founded 1247, removed 1676) is vast: an iron Gothic cathedral, romantic or impractical according to taste. Adjoining it is the Great Eastern Hotel gabled and mullioned.

Petticoat Lane Market – *Middlesex and Wentworth Streets.* Clothing, household hardware and jellied eels, a traditional East End dish are here on sale. By the 17C the market was well established in the long narrow street, which marks the boundary between Spitalfields and the City. In 1836 the street was renamed Middlesex Street.

For Spitalfields, see Outer London – EAST END.

The Royal Exchange

BISHOPSGATE

★**Royal Exchange** (CY) – The exchange was 'first built with brick at the sole charge of **Sir Thomas Gresham**, merchant, who laid the foundation 7 June 1566... On 27 January (1571) Queen Elizabeth came to view it and caused it to be proclaimed the Royal Exchange. But being consumed by the dreadful Fire in 1666 was rebuilt with Portland Stone by the City and Mercer's Company... King Charles II laying the first stone'. This building, 'esteemed the most beautiful, strong and stately of its kind in Europe' was designed by E Jarman on the same courtyard plan; in 1838 it was again burned down and a third, larger, building constructed. The wide steps, monumental Corinthian portico and pediment with tall (10ft) allegorical figures, provide an impressive entrance to an edifice that was once the very hub of the City. The central courtyard is lined by an arcade at ground and first floor levels, where merchant brokers congregated besides 'walking the central square'; the interior walls are decorated with historical murals (c 1900).

Around and on the outside walls are 19C portrait statues: in front, an equestrian bronze statue of **Wellington** modelled from life and lacking stirrups (Chantrey); against the north wall, Whittington and Myddelton; at the rear, Gresham, whose emblem, a gilded bronze grasshopper, acts as a weathervane (further down Bishopsgate *[no 52]* a beaver weathervane distinguishes the former Hudson Bay House).

> **Prototype** – The original 16C exchange building erected by Flemish masons was modelled on the one at Anvers. Before becoming Financial Councillor to the Crown, Gresham had travelled to Holland to study the cloth trade in order to undermine the hold of the Spanish monopoly in its colony. The building he had constructed comprised an open arcade for galleries of shops at ground level, while above, effigies of the Kings of England nestled in niches.

131

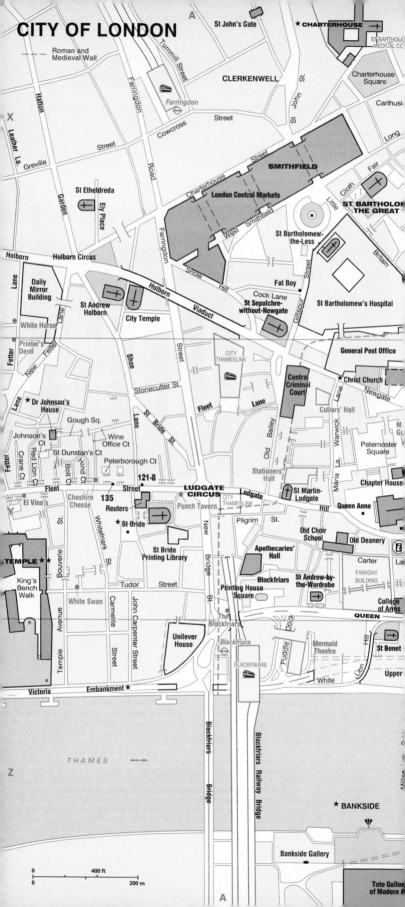

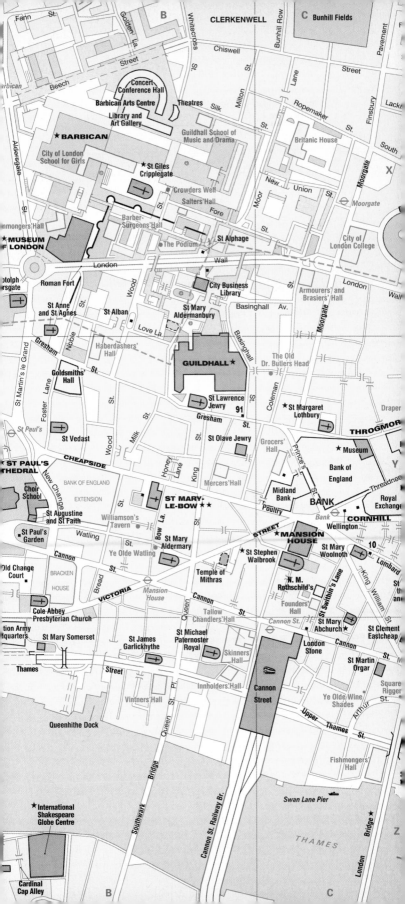

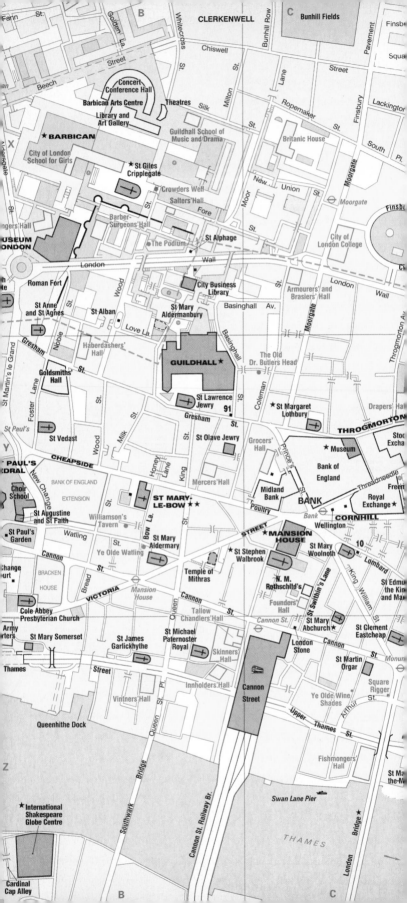

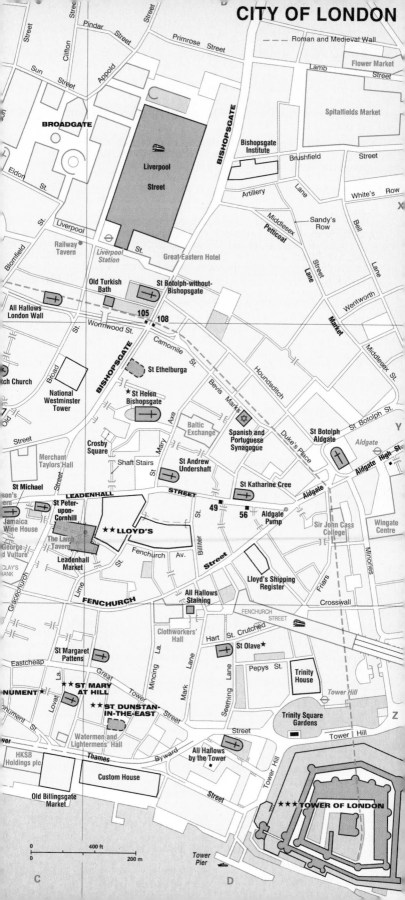

CITY OF LONDON

---- Roman and Medieval Wall

Pindar Street
Clifton Street
Primrose Street
Appold Street
Sun Street
Eldon St.
BROADGATE
Liverpool Street
Flower Market Street
Lamb Street
Spitalfields Market
Bishopsgate Institute
BISHOPSGATE
Brushfield Street
Artillery Lane
White's Row
Blomfield St.
Liverpool St.
Railway Tavern
Liverpool Station
Great Eastern Hotel
St Botolph-without-Bishopsgate
Middlesex Street
Sandy's Row
Bell Lane
Petticoat Lane
Old Turkish Bath
105 108
All Hallows London Wall
Wormwood St.
Camomile St.
Wentworth Street
Market
Middlesex St.
tch Church
National Westminster Tower
Broad St.
BISHOPSGATE
St Ethelburga
St Helen Bishopsgate
Bevis Marks
Houndsditch
St Botolph St.
Aldgate
Baltic Exchange
Spanish and Portuguese Synagogue
Duke's Place
St Botolph Aldgate
Aldgate High St.
Merchant Taylors' Hall
Crosby Square
Shaft Stairs
Mary Axe
St Andrew Undershaft
St Katharine Cree
Aldgate
Wingate Centre
St Michael
LEADENHALL STREET
49 56
Aldgate Pump
Sir John Cass College
son's ern
Jamaica Wine House
St Peter-upon-Cornhill
★★ LLOYD'S
Billiter St.
Minories
George d Vulture
The Lamb Tavern
Leadenhall Market
Fenchurch Av.
FENCHURCH STREET
Lloyd's Shipping Register
Friars
Crosswall
CLAY'S BANK
Gracechurch St.
Lime St.
FENCHURCH
All Hallows Staining
FENCHURCH STREET
St Margaret Pattens
Clothworkers' Hall
Hart Lane
St. Crutched
St Olave ★
Pepys St.
Trinity House
Eastcheap
Mincing La.
Mark Lane
Seething Lane
Tower Hill
NUMENT ★
★★ ST MARY AT HILL
Great Tower St.
Lovat La.
★★ ST DUNSTAN-IN-THE-EAST
Trinity Square Gardens
Tower Hill
onument St.
Watermen and Lightermens' Hall
Byward St.
All Hallows by the Tower
Tower Hill
HKSB Holdings plc
Thames Street
Custom House
Street
★★★ TOWER OF LONDON
Old Billingsgate Market

0   400 ft
0   200 m

Tower Pier

C   D

Freeman's Place – Behind the Exchange is a pedestrian area, with fountains at either end: bronze maiden beneath a pillared red granite canopy; mother and child by Georges Dalou (1879). The seated figure is **George Peabody** *(see index)* the American philanthropist who founded the Peabody Trust to provide housing for the poor.

Crosby Square records the original site of Crosby Hall which now stands on Chelsea Embankment.

★**St Helen Bishopsgate** ⊘ (DY) – Behind a patch of grass and plane trees stands a double-fronted stone façade, beneath embattled gables, surmounted by a small square 17C white belfry turret, lantern, ball and vane.

St Helen's began as a small parish church which by 1150 extended in two equal rectangles from the present east wall to the south entrance (originally Norman arched). In the early 13C a Benedictine nunnery was established in the church grounds and a conventual church was built abutting St Helen's to the north. The nun's chapel was probably wider and considerably longer than the existing parish church which was then extended to give the double front. The arcade between the churches was rebuilt in the late 15C and the dividing screens were removed when the nunnery was dissolved (1538). Restoration following damage inflicted by a terrorist bomb has returned the church to pre-Reformation airiness and lightness.

Furnishings – In the north wall is one of several 13C windows (NW), the **Night Staircase** of c 1500, built from the dormitory to the church for nuns attending night services; the **Processional Entrance**, originally 13C, and, at the east end, the **Nuns' Squint** (since 1525 arranged as a memorial). Note the canopied carved pulpit, the 17C doorcase and font, the grotesque choirstall armrests from the 15C Nuns' Choir and the two sword rests – the one made of wood (1665) being particularly rare. In the south transept are two late 14C piscinas.

★★**Monuments** – In 1874 when St Martin Outwich was demolished, 18 major monuments and brasses were transferred here: the black marble slabbed tomb chest of Sir Thomas **Gresham** (d 1579); the memorial to Sir Julius Caesar Adelmare (d 1636) Privy Counsellor to James I has no effigy but a parchment and seal; railed and canopied is the marble effigy of Sir William Pickering, Elizabeth's Ambassador to Spain (d 1574); others include those of Sir John Crosby (d 1475) and his first wife (d 1460), owner of the great City mansion Crosby Hall *(see CHELSEA)*. There are also 15C-17C **brasses** rich in expression and costume detail.

> ### St Ethelburga
>
> The early 15C church which stood on this site until destroyed by a terrorist bomb on 24 April 1993, was the City's smallest church and one of the few medieval buildings to escape the Great Fire (1666) and survive the Second World War with only slight damage. The church accounts date from 1569. The church will be rebuilt to its original plan as three walls and much of the timber, stone mouldings and fittings have survived; it will serve as a Centre for Reconciliation and Peace.

Windows – There is 15C and 17C glass in the 3rd and 5th north windows and in the Holy Ghost Chapel. Shakespeare (north wall) was assessed for local rates at £5 6s 8d in 1597 but left the parish, according to the record, having paid off only the s and d!

Bishopsgate (DXY) – The gate, said to have been rebuilt slightly west of the Roman gate by Bishop Erkenwald in Saxon times, was renewed several times, once even by the Hanseatic merchants, before being demolished in 1760. Note the gilded mitres from the old Bishop's Gate on the walls of nos 105 and 108 *(first floor, Wormwood and Camomile Street corners)*.

The street, one of the longest in the City, was the principal road to East Anglia in Roman and medieval times.

For the Spanish and Portuguese Bevis Marks Synagogue – listed below under Cornhill – Leadenhall Street, follow Camomile St towards Aldgate.

St Botolph-without-Bishopsgate ⊘ – The church was rebuilt in 1725-29 on a 13C site. The square brick tower, unusually at the east end, rises directly from the Bishopsgate pavement to support a balustrade, clock tower, turret, cupola and crowning urn. The south front, overlooking the former burial ground, is brick trimmed with stone. Inside, giant Corinthian columns support the galleries and wide coffered ceiling; a drum-shaped glass dome was added in 1821; the east window is Victorian and there are 19C box pews. The poet Keats was baptized in the existing font in 1795. The church hall at the west end was built to harmonise with the church in 1861 and restored after the war by the Worshipful Company of Fanmakers. 19C charity school children in Coade stone stand on either side of the doorway.

In the centre of Bishopsgate Churchyard beneath a stained-glass onion dome, stands an exotic one-roomed building faced with decorative glazed tiling and rosewood panelling; this once served as the entrance to an underground **Old Turkish Bath** (1895).

Bishopsgate Institute – This building with its arched entrance, mullioned windows, corner turrets and ornate decoration was designed by Charles Harrison Townsend (1894): it houses a library and a collection of prints and drawings of old London.

The Fire of London as witnessed by Samuel Pepys - 2 September 1666 ... *So near the fire as we could for smoke; and all over the Thames, with one's face in the wind, you were almost burned with a shower of fire-drops... When we could endure it no more upon the water, we to a little ale-house on the Bankside... and there staid till dark almost, and saw the fire grow; and as it grew darker, appeared more and more; and in corners and upon steeples, and between churches and houses, as far as we could see up the hill of the City, in a most horrid, malicious, bloody flame, not like the fine flame of an ordinary fire... The churches, houses, and all on fire, and flaming at once; and a horrid noise the flames made, and the cracking of houses at their ruine. So home with a sad heart, and there to find every body discoursing and lamenting the fire...*

CORNHILL – LEADENHALL STREET ⊖ *Aldgate*

Cornhill (CY) – This is one of the two hills upon which London was first built and is named after a medieval corn market. The junction of Cornhill with Leadenhall Street was once the most central point of London.

St Michael's ⊘ – The tower (1718-24), was designed by Hawksmoor to replace the one that had survived the Fire but which had become unsafe. It rises by four stages to a series of pinnacles, braceleted by a balustrade. The neo-Gothic doorway, framed by small marble columns, and the carved stone covings and tympanum were designed by Giles Gilbert Scott, as part of a later remodelling (1857-60). Inside, Wren's vault rests on tall Tuscan columns (1670-77); the Venetian windows were designed by Scott; the pulpit and lectern by W Gibbs Rogers (19C) as were the carved bench ends in the Wren tradition. The font dates from the 17C; the large wooden pelican from the 18C.

Former Coffeehouses – The **Jamaica Wine House** dates from 1652 when, as the Pasqua Rosee Wine House, it was the first establishment licensed to sell coffee in London. Note the early percolator.
The **George and Vulture**, frequented once by Dickens' Mr Pickwick has been twice destroyed by fire in its 600-year-old history. On the introduction of coffee in 1652 part of the then tavern became a chocolate, tea and coffeehouse. Other Change Alley establishments besides the money-lenders have long gone, including Garraways which was the first to brew and sell tea, and Jonathan's, the haunt of financiers.

St Peter-upon-Cornhill ⊘ – *Entrance from St Peter's Alley.* St Peter's-upon-Cornhill claims to stand on the highest ground and on the oldest church site in the City.
The present building (1677-87) was designed by Wren. The obelisk **spire**, from which flies a vane in the form of a key (9ft long, 2 cwts in weight), is visible only from the churchyard *(south)* and Gracechurch Street *(east)*. It rests on a small green copper dome surmounting a square brick tower. The church is now used as a Christian study centre.
Inside, the basilica is lit by arched windows; square piers rise to tunnel vaulting, the arches articulated by a double plaster fillet that merges with the outline of the rood screen. The upper area is light and minimally decorated; the lower, to sill level, darkly panelled. The pews were all cut down in the 19C save two, retained for church wardens (at the back). The oak **screen★**, one of only two to survive in Wren's churches *(see INTRODUCTION – Architecture)* is said to have been designed by the architect and his young daughter: it has strong central pillars rising high to support a lion and unicorn, the central arch bears the arms of Charles II. The organ gallery which is meant to have accommodated Mendelssohn on at least two occasions is original, as are the door-cases *(west end)*, sounding board with cherubs' heads, pulpit with domed panels and carved drops of fruit and leaves. The font dates from 1681.

Leadenhall Market ⊘ (CDY) – *Gracechurch Street.* Leadenhall, a retail market specialising in game but also selling poultry, meat, fish, fruit, and cheese, is at its most spectacular at the start of the shooting season when the shop fronts are hung

The CITY

with grouse, partridge, pheasant... and at Christmas. In Roman times the area boasted a forum with a basilica for public debate and a central market for trade; then when Whittington purchased and converted the manor there (hence Whittington Avenue), it returned, in part, to being a market under the Corporation (14C). The market takes its name from the house's lead covered roof. Burned down in the Fire the market buildings were re-erected then and again to their present form in 1881

London Metal Exchange ⊙ – *56 Leadenhall Street.* Transposed from Plantation House, the LME trades in non-ferrous metals such as copper and tin.

★★**Lloyd's (DY)** – The trading activities of Lloyds, the biggest insurance corporation in the world, which is said to cover everything except mortality, are conducted in a striking steel and glass building (1986) designed by **Sir Richard Rogers**, one of the architects of the Pompidou Centre in Paris.

The Lloyd's Building

The building is conceived as a great hollow space in which glass-walled galleries of offices are supported by eight colossal internal members. Six towers enclose a central atrium that rises 200ft (90m) to a glass barrel vault. Great long escalators bisect the air linking the storeys with ground level where the business of brokering insurance is transacted in a bustling, noisy open-plan environment between underwriters at old-fashioned benches. More discreet means of accessing higher levels are provided by glass lifts that travel up the exterior of the building. Ventilation shafts, power ducting, water conduits are also streamlined along the outside of the construction.

On the eleventh floor, the Adam or **Captain's Room** is furnished with a 36ft long George III mahogany table, marine paintings and crystal chandeliers from the White Lodge in Richmond Park – the meticulously recreated 1760s decor,

transposed from Bowood House (now demolished), recalls an association with Robert Adam who was commissioned to revamp the 'New' Lloyd's Coffee House at Pope's Head Alley in 1769.

History – In 1691 Edward Lloyd, who owned a coffeehouse near the Tower, took over Pontaq's at 16 Lombard Street (plaque on Coutts' Bank), a French-owned eating house frequented by Pepys, Evelyn, Wren, Dryden, Swift and others. Owing to its situation at the heart of the business world and despite the presence of literally hundreds of competitors, under Lloyd the house became the meeting place favoured by merchants, shippers, bankers, underwriters, agents and newsmen. These he seduced by inaugurating the still current system of posting notices and lists of port agents, transport vessels, cargo shipments agents and other such shipping intelligence. In 1734 began the publication of the daily *Lloyd's List* and in 1760 of the annual *Lloyd's Register*. Edward Lloyd died in 1713 (plaque in St Mary Woolnoth) and in 1769 his successors split; New Lloyd's moved into 5 Pope's Head Alley; the house in Lombard Street closed in 1785.

In 1771 the association became formalised by the institution of a minute book. In 1774, through the good offices of John Julius Angerstein and the Mercers' Company, Lloyd's transferred to more spacious quarters 'over the northwest corner of the Royal Exchange' at Cornhill where it remained until 1928 when the first insurance offices opened in Lime Street (although the offices on the east side of Lime Street date from 1957). In 1871 Lloyd's was incorporated by act of parliament and in 1900 Lloyd's Register of Shipping opened.

The archives include the Nelson Collection and a policy dated 1680 at 4 % on the *Golden Fleece* bound for Venice from Lisbon.

Members of Lloyd's syndicates – Insurance 'cover' is provided by a syndicate of underwriters who are willing to pledge money in case of loss: this policy is then sold by brokers to as many takers as possible. Unless a claim is therefore made, those who have been prepared to risk their money benefit in full. In times past, the so-called Lloyd's 'names' were private individuals: in exchange for the promise of potential gains (and losses) they had to lodge a deposit of £10 000 and be in possession of assets of at least £75 000; they also had to accept unlimited liability for the debts of the syndicates. During the 1970s the insurance business generated large amounts of income; during the late 1980s the tide changed: substantial claims following major disasters at sea has stripped many 'names' of their homes and savings. In 1993 new regulations were introduced to enable companies with limited liability to become members of syndicates at Lloyd's.

The **Lloyd's Register of Shipping** is accommodated in its own premises at 71 Fenchurch Street designed by Sir Thomas Colcutt (the architect of Simpsons in the Strand and Wigmore Hall). This neo-Venetian Baroque columned, turreted building, topped by a gilded ship vane, is decorated with Art Nouveau figures bearing ship-building tools and friezes of marine subjects.

Modern buildings designed by Sir Richard Rogers have recently been erected around these historic offices.

Institute of London Underwriters (DY) – *49 Leadenhall Street.* The institute founded in 1884, only handles marine and aviation insurance and reinsurance worldwide.

St Andrew Undershaft ⊘ (DY) – The present 16C church, the third on the site, is named after the maypole shaft which stood before it until 1517 and, which after being laid up, was finally burnt in 1549. A replica stands further west *(Shaft Stairs)*.

> ### Lloyd's institutions
>
> The **Lutine Bell** was retrieved from *HMS Lutine,* a captured French frigate which was sunk off the Netherlands in 1799 with gold and specie valued at nearly £1.5 million and insured by Lloyd's. Its bullion was partly salved in 1857-61. The bell is struck to mark the end of a crisis involving an overdue vessel: once for a loss, twice for a safe arrival.
>
> A reminder of coffeehouse origins are the **liveried doormen,** resplendent in red frock coats with black velvet collars and gilt buckled top hats.
>
> **Lloyd's Register of Shipping** gives details of ownership, tonnage etc. **Lloyd's Shipping Index** is a daily publication which records the movements of some 20 000 vessels.

A staircase turret breaks the square outline of the ancient stone tower, part of which is probably early 14C; the crenellated top is 19C.

The nave, now bare of pews, is divided from the aisles by five slender shafts and hollow columns which support a plain glass clerestory. Flat wooden roofs cover the aisles and nave, the latter punctuated by 130 carved and gilded 16C oak bosses. The west window (originally at the east end) depicting Tudor and Stuart sovereigns, the Renatus Harris organ, pulpit and font are all late 16C and 17C; the altar rails are by Tijou (1704).

Among St Andrew's **monuments**★ are the Datchelor family *(see index)* memorial and, most famously, in a decorated alcove, Nicholas Stone's half-length carved alabaster ruffed figure of **John Stow** (1525-1605), the antiquarian whose *Survey of London and Westminster,* published in 1598, remains a major source for every guide to London. The quill pen poised to 'write something worth reading about' is renewed annually by the Lord Mayor.

The site of the former Baltic Exchange, irrevocably destroyed by a bomb in 1992, has been redeveloped.

St Katharine Cree ⊘ (DY) – The present compact, light and airy church is thought to be the third on the site which marked the corner boundary of the precincts of the Augustinian Priory of Holy Trinity, Christchurch, founded in 1108 by Matilda, Queen of Henry I, and dissolved in 1539.

The ragstone corner tower, lower section from late 15C and 16C above, rises to a parapet and small white-pillared turret. Note the two tiers of windows in the stone wall on Leadenhall Street, straight headed with centres raised to include 3 lights each. Inside the nave, giant Corinthian columns support a series of decorative round arches below the clerestory. High up, above the plain reredos, is a traceried rose window said to resemble that in Old St Paul's and glazed with 17C glass; the central ridge of the lierne vault is decorated with a row of brightly coloured bosses bearing the badges of 17 City Companies. Note the early 17C alabaster font, 18C pulpit and altar table, and the Throgmorton effigy (1571) in the Laud Chapel.

Since 1960 St Katharine has been the Guild Church for industry, commerce and finance.

Some way north stands another special fragment of Old London tucked away in Heneage Lane, off Bevis Marks.

Spanish and Portuguese Synagogue ⊘ (DY) – The synagogue, a perfectly-preserved vestige of the Old City, is the oldest in England (1701) and the only one in the City of London, succeeding one in Creechurch Lane *(plaque)* which was the first to open after the Jews had been invited to return by Cromwell in 1657 *(see INTRODUCTION – Faces and Flavours of London).*

Set back from the street, this small building is plainly functional. Clear glass windows and dark oak furnishings are set off by the 7 splendid brass chandeliers from Holland which hang down low and which are lit for Yom Kippur, Simhat Torah, weddings and other occasions. It is also notable for other surviving rich appointments: the Ark containing the hand-written Scrolls, the raised Tebah surrounded by twisted balusters. On the Feast of Ab (summer) the Haphtarah is read in medieval Spanish.

Bevis Marks – The street name is a corruption of Buries Marks, an abbreviation for the mark or site of the 12C mansion of the abbots of Bury St Edmunds. In the 16C the mansion was acquired by Thomas Heneage whose name is perpetuated in the nearby lane.

Whitbread

Whitbread was founded by Samuel Whitbread I in 1742 just north of the City of London in Whitecross Street. Eight years later, the business moved to Chiswell Street, selling its porter *(see INTRODUCTION – Eating Out)* through the King's Head at 3d per quart pot, to become London's largest brewery. In 1834 Whitbread began brewing ale, introducing bottled beer in 1869. Breweries were also built in Lambeth and Putney.

Aldgate (DY) – The name derives from the Anglo-Saxon *aelgate* meaning free or open to all. The Romans built a gate here on the road to Colchester. In the 14C Chaucer leased the dwelling over the gate and in the 16C Mary Tudor rode through after being proclaimed queen. The gate was demolished in 1761. The **Aldgate Pump** still stands at the west end of the street.

St Botolph Aldgate ⊘ – The site on the outer side of the gate in the City Wall and beside a bridge spanning the moat (Houndsditch) had been occupied by a church for 1 000 years or more when George Dance the Elder came to rebuild it (1741-44). The stone steeple stands on a four-tier brick tower trimmed with stone quoins. Dance's interior was transfigured in 1889 by J F Bentley who redecorated the church, fronting the galleries with balusters, geometrically re-leading all but the east window, decorating the coved ceiling with a plasterwork frieze of standing angels and shields linked with leafy garlands. The domed font cover, rails and inlaid pulpit are all 19C.

In the forecourt of the Wingate Centre stands a bronze (1980) by K McCarter. The **Hoop and Grapes** pub *(east)* is a 17C brick house with a wooden bay.

FENCHURCH STREET

St Mary Woolnoth of the Nativity ⊘ (CY) – A Saxon church, possibly built on land given by Wulfnoth – hence the name – was rebuilt in stone by William the Conqueror. This medieval church was damaged in the Fire of London and replaced by the present English Baroque structure (1716-27) designed by Nicholas Hawksmoor.

The rusticated stone tower rises to Corinthian columns and twin turrets, linked and crowned by open balustrades. The west façade is surmounted by the unique broad belltower; Hawksmoor's treatment of the blank north wall on Lombard Street is one of the masterpieces of English architecture.

Inside, Hawksmoor planned the nave as a square within a square, with massive fluted Corinthian columns in threes marking each corner and supporting a heavily-ornamented cornice with semi-circular clerestory windows above. Also by Hawksmoor are the reredos with its twisted columns and the inlaid pulpit. William Wilberforce was inspired to work for the abolition of the slave trade through hearing John Newton, youthful slave trader turned priest and hymn writer, preach here. Newton composed the inscription on his monument in the north aisle. On the right wall is a plaque commemorating Edward Lloyd (d 1713).

Lombard Street (CY) – The name derives from the late 13C Italian and Lombard merchants, money-changers and pawn-brokers who settled there. The street, now synonymous with City banking, is lined with 19C and 20C buildings; association dignifies it; the gilt, the brightly painted bank signs, overhanging the pavement, distinguish it. Beginning with Lloyd's horse of 1677 *(left)*, it continues with the 3 crowns of Coutts *(right, no 15)* the grasshopper, 1563, formerly Martins (now Banque Paribas), the crown and anchor of National Westminster *(right)*, the anchor of Williams and Glyn's *(left)*, now the Royal Bank of Scotland, and at the end, a massive Barclays eagle in stone.

The Clearing House – *10 Lombard Street.* This institution has its origins in the 18C and grew out of the daily meeting in the streets of bank clerks, known as 'clearers', to exchange and settle for cheques payable at their respective banks. From a post and one another's backs which they used as desks, the clearers migrated to a bay window, a room and finally a house, always in the same street. The first Clearing House was built on the site in 1833. The present building is post-war.

St Edmund the King and Martyr ⊘ (CY) – The distinctive black (lead-covered) octagonal lantern and stout **spire**★ ending in a bulb and vane, rise from a square stone belfry. The corbelled parapet and inverted brackets at the tower base are decorated with flaming urns. The façade is outlined by quoins and a central pediment.
The interior was altered in the 19C but is remarkable for its woodwork: carved pulpit with drops and swags, urns on choir stalls, balustered railing round the font, panelling in the sanctuary framing the Ten Commandments and paintings of Moses and Aaron attributed to William Etty, RA. The east window was made in Munich c 1880 for St Paul's Cathedral but passed on to this church.
When the church of **All Hallows Staining** (1671) was demolished in 1870, the 15C battlemented ragstone tower was retained; it is now dwarfed by overshadowing office blocks.

★**St Olave's** ⊘ (DZ) – Three parish churches have been built on this site: in wood (c 1050) and stone (c 1200; enlarged to present size c 1450). The church was restored in 1953 after severe bomb damage in 1941. Throughout, associations have been kept alive: the dedication to St Olaf, who in 1013 helped Ethelred against the Danes remains vivid in the new Norwegian flag; a bust (19C) of Samuel **Pepys** appropriately blocks the former south doorway (inscription outside) which used to be the entrance to a gallery where Pepys had the Navy office pew.
The churchyard gateway on Seething Lane, decorated exclusively with skulls is dated 1658; opposite is the site, now a garden, of the Navy office of Pepys' day (burned 1673). The square medieval ragstone tower's upper brick section is 18C; it is crowned with a lantern and weathervane. A round-faced clock projects back over the nave.
The church porch, into which one descends, like the major part of the church, is 15C. The interior is divided into a nave and aisle of three bays by quatrefoil marble pillars, probably from a former, 13C, church; the clerestory and roof are post war, as is the glass, except for the late 19C heraldic panels which had been removed for cleaning in 1939. Furnishings have been presented: the **pulpit**, made reputedly in Grinling Gibbons' workshop for St Benet Gracechurch (by Wren; demolished 1867); Jacobean altar rails; four 18C sword rests. The monuments, which incredibly, survived the fire, include tablets, brasses, natural and polychrome stone effigies: **Elizabeth Pepys** who married at 15 and died aged 29 (17C bust in an oval niche high on the sanctuary north wall), the 17C kneeling Bayninge brothers (below); Sir James Deane (17C kneeling figure with 3 wives and children; south wall over 15C vestry door); Sir Andrew Riccard, Chairman of East India and Turkey Companies (17C standing figure north aisle).
The **crypt** *(steps at west end)* of two chambers with ribbed vaulting, is built over a well and is a survival of the early 13C church.
For Trinity House see TOWER OF LONDON.

MONUMENT ⊖ Bank; Monument

St Swithin's Lane – The street is synonymous with the prestigious merchant bank N M Rothschild's. The clean lined building is post-war; the lane remains old and narrow, and is often blocked from end to end with waiting Rolls-Royces, Bentleys, Jaguars...

★**St Mary Abchurch** ⊘ (CYZ) – The Fire consumed 'a fair church', last of a line dating back to the 12C. The site was minute, some 80ft square, and Wren decided to cover the new church with a painted **dome**★. Approximately 40ft in diameter, it cannot be seen from outside and inside it rises from arches springing directly from the outer walls. There are no buttresses and only one interior column.
Tall carved pews line the north, south and west walls as in the original church – although the kennels reserved for the congregations' dogs have gone.

Receipts in the parish records show that many of the greatest craftsmen of the day worked on the furnishings: the font and stonework, Robert Bird's original gilded copper pelican weathervane (removed as unsafe in 1764) is over the west door, the pulpit with garlands and cherubs' heads, doorcases, font rails and cover, the lion and unicorn and royal arms. Authenticated by bills and a personal letter from **Grinling Gibbons** himself, is the **reredos★★**, massive in size, magnificent in detail and delicacy. Note the many rich monuments and urns.

The **tower and spire★** are on the same small scale as the church: red brick with stone quoins, surmounted by a cupola, lantern and slender lead spire.

N M Rothschild and Sons Ltd

Merchant Banks are private banking firms which do not conduct ordinary banking business as such but confine themselves to loaning or raising money in the commercial sector with share issues. They also broker mergers and acquisitions of businesses thereby maintaining a long tradition of dealing with foreign business transactions and in times past, of currency exchange.

Rothschild's *(see INTRODUCTION – Faces and Flavours of London)* earned its status in this country when in its first years, under its London branch founder, Nathan Mayer Rothschild (1777-1836), it acquired at low cost the drafts issued by Wellington which the government was unable to meet and renewed them; ultimately they were redeemed at par. NMR increased his fortune and the government appointed him chief negotiator of future Allied war loans!

His confidence in victory against Napoleon and in his own intelligence service again increased NMR's wealth, it is said, on the occasion of Waterloo, fought throughout Sunday 18 June: on the Monday, when only rumour was circulating, Nathan bought; the market rose; he sold; the market plunged; he bought again and made a fortune as his personal messenger arrived from the battle scene confirming victory; Wellington's despatches only arrived by messenger the following Wednesday and a report was published in *The Times* on Thursday (22nd). Other business included negotiating lucrative textile deals.

St Clement Eastcheap ⊘ (CZ) – The tower is built of brick with stone quoins and a balustrade.

The former St Clement's was the first City church to burn in the Great Fire; it cost £4 362 3s 4 1/2 d to rebuild to Wren's design (in which there is no right angled corner!) and the architect was presented on its completion by the satisfied parishioners with 'one third of a hogshead of wine' costing £4 2s 0d. The panelled interior is complemented with finely carved 17C door and organ cases (Purcell played on the organ) and a very fine **pulpit★★** surmounted by a massive sounding board, gay with dancing cherubs, flowered garlands and swags of fruit; the font cover bearing the Stuart arms and the sword rest are all contemporary. A gilded oval wreath adorns the flat ceiling while the altarpiece shows the Virgin between St Martin and St Clement.

St Clement claims to be the church of the old *Oranges and Lemons* rhyme: its parish East Cheap dates from the time of the Saxon market on the City's eastern hill, its association with oranges from the Middle Ages, when Spanish barges tied up at London Bridge to sell their oranges on the stone steps all within cry of the church.

Local pubs – Two of the most colourful pubs must be **The Square Rigger** and **Ye Olde Wine Shades**, a double fronted pub (1663) with painted boards outside much like a 17C tavern and kept as authentic as possible inside with dark wooden booths. This claims to be the oldest wine house in London having originally been the bar attached to the Fishmongers' Hall, in whose shadow (immortalised in its name) it was to survive. Presently it is surrounded by the spiky marble and glass buildings of Minster Court.

The square brick and stucco tower (19C) marks the site of the medieval church **St Martin Orgar**.

To remember the dates of the **Great Plague** and the **Great Fire of London** children once were taught:
'In sixteen hundred and sixty five,
scarce a soul was left alive.
In sixteen hundred and sixty six,
London burned like rotten sticks.'

★Monument ⊘ (**CZ**) – The fluted Doric column of Portland stone, surmounted by a square viewing platform and gilded, flaming urn, was erected in 1671-77 in commemoration of the Great Fire. The hollow shaft stands 202ft tall and 202ft from the baker's in Pudding Lane where the Fire began, plumb on the route between London and Southwark until the construction of Blackfriars Bridge (1769). The relief of Charles II before the City under reconstruction (on the west face of the pedestal) is by Caius Cibber. A later inscription blaming the papists for the Fire was finally effaced in 1831.

The **view★** from the platform (up 311 steps) is now largely obscured by the towering office blocks which also mask the column at ground level.

Thames Street (**CDZ**) – Probably in Roman times and certainly in the early Middle Ages, Thames Street ran the length of the river wall; by the 17C, it served as a route between the Wardrobe and the Tower, crossing the furriers' and vintners' quarters: it would have been lined by 8 churches and provided rear access to castles and mansions, quays, warehouses and markets, whose main thoroughfare was the river. Today Upper and Lower Thames Street are separated by London Bridge.

On the west side of London Bridge sits **Fishmongers' Hall**, its fine features best seen from the river. This neo-Greek building (1831-34) enjoys a unique position, light reflected from the water enhances the Hall's rich interior gold leaf decoration (restored post war).

★London Bridge (**CZ**) – London Bridge was the only crossing over the lower Thames until 1750 when Westminster was constructed. The Romans probably built the first bridge on the single gravel spit which exists in the clay; the Saxons certainly erected a wooden structure which had to be repeatedly rebuilt against the ravages of floodwater, ice and fire. Between 1176 and 1209 a stone bridge (905ft long and 40ft wide) was constructed on 19 pointed arches rising from slender piles anchored onto wood and rubble piers. These so obstructed the flow of the river that water gushed through them as if forced through sluices; many refused to shoot the bridge in a boat, the principal transport of the day, so passengers would often disembark on one side only to re-board on the other. In winter, the reduced river flow meant that ice would form so that when at last the river froze over great **Frost**

The Monument: engraving of 1680

Fairs could be held (the most famous being between 1683-84).

The bridge itself was lined with houses, shops, even a chapel – a certain Peter the Bridgemaster is recorded as chaplain to St Mary Colechurch (disappeared); a drawbridge was installed over the seventh arch (southside); at night the gatehouses would be closed thereby securing the City defences; it was here that traitors' heads were exposed Jack Cade (1450), Thomas More (1535).

In 1831, following an act of 1823, John Rennie constructed a robust granite bridge of five wide spans, 60yds upstream. In 1973 it was replaced by the existing sleek crossing, Rennie's bridge was sold for £1 million and removed to Arizona, USA.

St Magnus the Martyr ⊘ (**CZ**) – *Lower Thames Street*. The massive square stone tower★, decorated with a balustrade and urns, rises to an octagonal belfry, a leaded cupola, lantern, and obelisk spire surmounted by a golden vane. A clock (1709) projects over the churchyard.

> The saying '**London Bridge was built upon wool-packs**' alludes to the fact that the new stone bridge was built with money raised from a tax on wool.

From 1176 St Magnus stood a stone sentinel on an ancient Roman wharf at the foot of London Bridge. Wren rebuilt it on the same site. When, c 1760, the houses and shops which lined the bridge were removed, Wren's building was curtailed to leave the tower as a church porch astride the bridge's east foot-path. Its postern situation continued until 1831 when Rennie's bridge was constructed 100ft upstream.

The interior, remodelled in the late 18C, has a barrel-vaulted nave, supported by fluted Ionic columns and punctuated by the deep recesses of the oval clerestory windows. Although much remains from the 17C, inscriptions on the west gallery explain the decoration: the church was 'repaired and beautified' in 1886 and 1924. Note the iron **sword rest★** dated 1708, 16C-17C shrine (right of the altar), altar piece and rails, font (1683) and pulpit.

Between these two elegant period buildings stands a striking blue mirrorglass construction occupied by the **Hong Kong Shanghai Bank Holdings PLC** *(10 Lower Thames St)*.

Old Billingsgate Market (CZ) – There was a market on the site from 1297 to 1982 when the wholesale fish market established as a free fish market in 1699 moved to new premises in the West India Docks on the Isle of Dogs. The market building, designed in 1876 by Sir Howard Jones, with Britannia presiding over two dolphins on its decorative roof, was converted into offices in 1990. At the same time excavation of the lorry park has permitted archaeologists to investigate evidence of a neighbouring Roman quay and Saxon harbour. Although many original features have been retained, the lingering smell of fish has at last subsided!

Custom House (DZ) – The house of rusticated stone and yellow stock brick, nearly 500ft wide, dates from 1813-17; its central river front bay was added later by Robert Smirke (1825). Three storeys high, with five lanterns as sole decoration, it is the sixth to stand on this reach of the Thames.

Across Lower Thames and up St Mary-at-Hill on the left is the small **Watermen and Lightermen's Hall** (1780) which belongs to an ancient City Guild dating back to Tudor times.

★★St Dunstan-in-the-East (DZ) – A magnificent garden flourishes in the ruins of the church, dominated by the elegant Portland stone steeple which rests on a four-tier tower, canted by flying buttresses with pinnacles.

★★St Mary-at-Hill ⊘ (CZ) – *Entrance located between 6 and 7 St Mary-at-Hill.* A church is first mentioned on the site in 1177. The stock-brick tower dates from 1780.

The Wren **plan★** (1670-76), almost square, is divided into 3 x 3 bays beneath a shallow central dome, supported on free standing Corinthian columns; at each corner are plain square ceilings at cornice height.

The interior was damaged by fire in 1988 and not all the **woodwork** for which St Mary's was known was restored: note the font cover (late 17C); great oak reredos, communion table, altar rails (early 18C); organ gallery (musical trophies), lectern and turned balustrade; pulpit garlanded with fruit and flowers beneath a massive sounding board and approached by a beautiful curved staircase by **William Gibbs Rogers** (19C); box pews. Six gilded and enamelled wrought-iron sword rests added to the splendour of the interior.

St Margaret Pattens ⊘ (DZ) – The site at the corner of Rood Lane was possibly already occupied by a wooden church in 1067. A square stone tower, ornamented by a pinnacled balustrade supports a hexagonal lead-covered and therefore black **spire★** which sharpens to a needle point on which balances a gilded vane.

The church, as redesigned by Wren, is a plain oblong with a flat ceiling and round clerestory windows. The carved **woodwork★** is outstanding: to the east, the reredos, 17C, gold lettered and framing a contemporary Italian painting, is carved with fruit, a peapod, flowers; in front, turned balusters support the communion rail; a high boxed beadle's pew and below, a low 'punishment bench' with ferocious devil's head, choir stalls, a finely carved eagle lectern, pulpit with hour glass aloft for all to see the sermon's duration. On the north side, the Lady Chapel has a former door-case as reredos inset with della Robbia roundels and dowel pegs on which to hang wigs on hot days; also in the church are the only two canopied pews in London (the inside of the canopy of the south pew bears a *sgraffito* monogram 'CW 1686', which tradition claims marks it as one occupied by Christopher Wren), 18C monuments and font. 'Pattens' was added to the dedication for distinction and, according to Stow, was after the pattens, iron shod overshoes *(showcase in the south aisle)*, sold in the abutting lane.

Lord Mayor's Show

The show is the Lord Mayor's progress to his swearing-in before the Lord Chief Justice, an observance which dates back to the charter of 1215 which required that the mayor be presented to the monarch or his justices at the Palace of Westminster. The procession was, for centuries, partly undertaken over water when the mayor owned a civic barge (15C). In 1553 full pageantry became the order of the day with men parading their best liveries, trumpets sounding, masques and poems recited along the route. Today with the judges removed from Westminster, the oath is taken at the Royal Courts of Justice in the Strand; the pageantry, after a decline in the 19C, has returned with floats and the new and old mayors progressing in the golden state and other horse-drawn coaches accompanied by outriders.

The spectacular show on the second Saturday in November, is followed on the Monday evening by the Lord Mayor's Banquet in Guildhall which by tradition (although not invariably) begins with turtle soup at which the principal speakers are the new Lord Mayor and the Prime Minister.

MANSION HOUSE ⊖ *Mansion House; Cannon Street; Bank*

★**Mansion House** ⊘ **(CY)** – The house dates only from 1739-52 – previously lord mayors remained in their own residences during the years of their mayoralty. The Lord Mayor is Chief Magistrate of the City and on the ground floor on the east side is a Court of Justice, with cells below, the only such appointments in a private residence in the kingdom.

George Dance the Elder, the architect selected by the Corporation, designed a Palladian style mansion in Portland stone; modest staircases on either side at the front lead to a raised portico of six giant Corinthian columns, surmounted by a pediment – Robert Taylor's allegory of the splendour of London.

The interior, designed as a suite of magnificent state rooms from the portico, leads to the dining or Egyptian Hall (named after an interior Vitruvius described as an Egyptian Hall and favoured by 18C Palladians but having nothing to do with Egypt). In the hall, giant Corinthian columns forming an ambulatory support the cornice on which the decorated ceiling rests; the walled niches are filled with Victorian statuary on subjects taken from English literature from Chaucer to Byron. The Ball Room is on the second floor.

★★**Plate and insignia** – The Corporation plate, rich and varied, dates from the 17C. The insignia includes much older pieces: the Lord Mayor's **chain of office**, c 1535 with later additions, suspends from a collar of SS gold links, knots and enamelled Tudor roses; a pendant known as the Diamond Jewel consists of an onyx piece, carved in 1802 with the City arms, and set in diamonds; the **Pearl Sword**, 16C and according to tradition presented by Queen Elizabeth at the opening of the Royal Exchange in 1571; the 17C **Sword of State** and the 18C **Great Mace** of silver gilt and 5ft 3ins long.

★**St Stephen Walbrook** ⊘ **(CY)** – The **tower and steeple** ★ are square. The ragstone tower rises to a trim balustrade; the later steeple of Portland stone rises through eight similar stages to two balls and a vane. The characteristic dome, green turreted and also vaned can be seen at the rear.

The most striking feature is Wren's **dome** ★ which undoubtedly served as a model for St Paul's which it pre-dates: slightly off centre, the cupola rests on a ring of eight circular arches strategically placed within the asymmetrical square ground plan. The bays are delineated by free standing Corinthian columns grouped to produce unexpected perspectives within the characteristic dark oak panelling and carved lighter wood furnishings.

St Stephen Walbrook

K. Brett

Below the dome and raised on two communion steps sits Henry Moore's monumental altar of golden travertine (1986).
St Stephen's is the birthplace of the Samaritans, an organisation founded in 1953 to befriend the suicidal and despairing and now a major international charity.

Cannon Street (BYCZ) – In the Middle Ages Candelwriteystrete was the home of candle makers and wick chandlers – hence the presence on Dowgate Hill of the **Tallow Chandlers' Hall**, rebuilt in 1670-72 and Italianised in 1880, and **Skinners' Hall**, late 18C building accommodating a fine staircase, aromatic sandalwood panelling dating from 1670, 18C plasterwork and a hall (1850) decorated by Frank Brangwyn (1904-10).

Cannon Street Station (BCZ) – The station stands on the site of two churches and the important medieval steelyard of the Hanseatic merchants. All that remains of the mid-Victorian station building are two monumental towers adorned with gilded weather-vanes flanking the viaduct high above the river bank.

St Michael Paternoster Royal ⊘ (BZ) – The square stone tower rises to a balustrade quartered by urns. The **spire★**, added in 1715, takes the form of three-tier octagonal lantern, marked at each angle by an Ionic column and urn; on high is a vaned spirelet (see St James Garlickhythe). The 'fair parish church', as Stow described it, 'new built by Richard Whittington', in place of the earliest known building of the mid 13C, was destroyed in the Fire; in July 1944 history was repeated.

Set into the wall of 111 Cannon Street (Overseas Chinese Banking Corporation) is the **London Stone**. The block of limestone, 'its origin and purpose are unknown', may have been a milestone or milliary or, according to legend, be a fragment of an altar erected in 800BC by Trojan, the mythical founder of Britain.

The south wall with 6 rounded lights and a balustraded parapet is of stone, the east end of brick, stone trimmed. Above the door and windows are cherubs' head keystones. The pulpit, reredos and lectern are 17C. The red, gold, green windows include (south-west corner) young Whittington with his cat. **Whittington**, who lived in an adjoining house, founded an almshouse, also adjoining, and on his death in 1423, was buried in the church. The last part of the name Paternoster Royal is derived from La Riole, a town near Bordeaux from which the wine long imported by local vintners came. The church is the home of the Missions to Seamen, a society caring from seafarers worldwide.

St James Garlickhythe ⊘ (BZ) – The square stone tower ends in a balustrade quartered by pointed urns. The **spire★**, added in 1713, rises in a square three tiered lantern, quartered by paired and advanced columns, crowned on high by vaned spirelet (see St Michael Paternoster Royal).
Inside the tower, through the door decorated with a scallop shell – the emblem of St James of Compostella to whom the church is dedicated – two tablets summarise the later history of the church which dates back to the 10C-11C. 'This church', the upper plaque states, 'was consumed by the late dreadful conflagration AD 1666; the foundation thereof was laid AD 1676; it was rebuilt and opened AD 1682 and completely finished AD 1683'; the inscription below continues, 'The church was damaged by enemy action in 1940 and 1941; the work of restoration was completed in 1963'.
The church was built to a perfectly symmetrical plan, on an isolated site, and christened 'Wren's Lantern' owing to its many windows. The woodwork is principally 17C: note the dowel peg for the preacher's wig. The marble font carved with cherubs' heads is late 17C. The ceiling is ornamented with gilded plaster-work. **Sword rests★**, complete with unicorn supporters, recall six medieval lord mayors and others.

On the other side of Upper Thames Street stands the **Vintners' Hall**; built in 1671 restored in 1948 and boasting a majestic hall with fine late 17C panelling, staircase with outstanding balusters, a 15C tapestry and 16C funeral pall; its plate includes a double 'milkmaid' cup, the Glass Tun etc. The monarch, the Vintners, and the Dyers own the swans upon the Thames, the company swans being marked on the bill as cygnets at the annual swan upping.
Beyond, an unremarkable inlet is all that remains of **Queenhithe Dock**, once London's most important dock above London Bridge.
After the footbridge but before the tunnel, on the north side of Upper Thames Street stands all that survives of **St Mary Somerset**. The slim, square, white tower (1695), built by Wren and adorned with masks, rises from its garden setting to a parapet, quartered with square finials and obelisk pinnacles.

QUEEN VICTORIA STREET – BLACKFRIARS

⊖ Blackfriars; Mansion House

Queen Victoria Street (BCY) – The street, the first City street to be lit by electricity, was created in 1867-71 by cutting through a maze of alleys and buildings. Stretching from Bank to Blackfriars, it is lined with a number of widely contrasting ancient and modern institutions.

Temple of Mithras (BY) – The stone temple with a double course of red tiles, 60ft long, 20ft wide, was erected on the bank of the Walbrook in the 2C AD when Roman legions were stationed in the City. All traces had long since vanished and even the Walbrook had altered course and level by 1954 when excavations preceding the construction of Bucklersbury House revealed walls laid in the outline of a basilica divided into a narthex, nave and aisles separated by columns and a buttressed apse at the west end.

The head of the god Mithras in a Phrygian cap, those of Minerva and Serapis the Egyptian god of the Underworld with a corn measure on his head, together with other retrieved artefacts are now in the Museum of London *(see Barbican)*. The temple itself, removed to enable the office block to rise as planned, was then reconstructed in the forecourt.

The temple would have stood near the centre of the Roman city: to the south stood the governor's palace on the Thames foreshore, to the northwest was sited the basilica and forum which stretched some 60 acres from Cornhill and Leadenhall Street to Fenchurch Street.

St Mary Aldermary ⊙ (BY) – Corner buttresses, robust pinnacles and gilded finials adorn the Gothic tower of St Mary 'the older Mary Church' older that is than the Norman St Mary-le-Bow. After the Great Fire, a benefactor appeared offering £5 000 to rebuild the church as it had been; Wren, therefore, built a Gothic church for £3 457!

Despite successive remodelling, the interior retains its fan vaulting and central rosettes, a **Grinling Gibbons** pulpit and rich west door-case (with a peapod; from St Antholin), a 1682 font and, against the 3rd south pillar, an oak **sword rest** also of 1682 – one only of four in wood to survive and uniquely carved with fruit and flowers by Grinling Gibbons.

Cole Abbey Presbyterian Church ⊙ (BY) – The small square stone tower, marked by corner urns, supports an octagonal lead **spire★** which rises to **a gilded three-masted ship** weathervane.

The recorded history of the church, formerly known as St Nicolas Cole Abbey, goes back to 1144 but even Stow 'could never learn the cause of the name and therefore let it passe'. The church was burned out in 1666 and again in 1941. The stone exterior is pierced by tall rounded windows beneath corbelled hoods and circled by an open balustrade. Its woodwork is 17C.

On the south side of the broad thoroughfare is the **Salvation Army HQ**, an imposing stone building (1963), its rear dropping down to the level of Upper Thames Street.

College of Arms ⊙ (AY) – The college, overlooking a forecourt behind splendid wrought iron gates, dates from 1671-88 when it was rebuilt after the Fire. Unlike the churches nearby, St Benet's and St Paul's, it was not designed by Wren, but by Francis Sandford, Lancaster Herald of the time, and Morris Emmett, master bricklayer to the Office of Works.

The compact red brick building, formerly pedimented and now parapeted, was truncated when Queen Victoria Street was created. The interior woodwork, staircases, panelling, pilastered and garlanded screen is by William Emmett, a contemporary of Grinling Gibbons. The Earl Marshal's Court, the principal room, is panelled and furnished with a throne and a gallery.

The College is responsible for granting coats of arms and monitoring their application; it also organises State ceremonies and undertakes genealogical research.

St Benet's Welsh Church ⊙ (AZ) – At the time of the Great Fire, the church, which was already some six centuries old, stood directly behind Baynard Castle which fronted the river and, like the church, was totally destroyed. Wren designed a small brick church with a hipped roof, rounded windows with carved stone festoons and a general country, Dutch, air: the castle was not rebuilt. The tower of a dark red brick is defined with white stone quoins and rises only two stages before being crowned by a small lead cupola, lantern and spire.

The interior is lined with galleries, divided at the northwest corner by the tower and supported on panelled Corinthian columns which rise above the base of the galleries. Below all is of wood: the west door-case decked with cherubs and royal arms, a balustered communion rail, ornate table and a high pedimented reredos with surmounting urns.

St Andrew-by-the-Wardrobe ⊙ (AY) – The church was known as St Andrew juxta Baynard Castle until the Great Wardrobe or royal storehouse, previously in the Tower, was erected on a site close by in 1361 *(plaque in Wardrobe Place)*. Church,

Baynard Castle

In c 1100 a fort was built on the river bank, pendant to the Tower downstream, by one 'Baynard that came with the Conqueror' according to Stow. When it burnt down in 1428 it was rebuilt by Duke Humphrey of Gloucester; it was here in 1460 that Richard of Gloucester heard that his plans to seize the crown were progressing (*Richard III*, 3 vii). Henry VII reconstructed a more spacious palace in which Lady Jane Grey received the news that she was to be queen (1553). It finally disappeared in the Fire of 1666.

Wardrobe, Castle and St Ann Blackfriars, were all destroyed in the Fire; only St Andrew was rebuilt. On 29/30 December 1940, fire again gutted the church leaving just the tower and outer walls. It was rebuilt from 1959-61. The galleried church has attractive vaulting and plaster work.

The square red brick tower is decorated with irregular stone quoins and a crowning balustrade.

For the Mermaid Theatre see INTRODUCTION – On the Town.

Blackfriars (AYZ) – The name commemorates Blackfriars Monastery, dissolved in 1538, and abandoned until 1576 when a theatre was founded in the cloisters; here a professional children's company would rehearse before performing at court. Twenty years later **James Burbage** converted another part of the monastery into the Blackfriars Theatre for the performance of Shakespeare's later plays and those of Beaumont and Fletcher. The theatre, demolished in 1655, is commemorated in Playhouse Yard.

Printing House Square (AY) – The square acquired its name after the Fire, when on the site of the Norman Mountfichet Castle and the later Blackfriars Playhouse the King's Printer set up presses and began to publish acts, the King James Bible proclamations and the *London Gazette* (1666 – as *Oxford Gazette* 1665). The name remained after the printer moved, in 1770, nearer to Fleet Street.

In 1784 John Walter purchased a house in the square and the following year began publication of the *Daily Universal Register*, altering its title on 1 January 1788 to *The Times*. In 1964 a new slate and glass building was constructed for the broadsheet's offices with the old square as forecourt; ten years later they moved to Gray's Inn Road before transferring (1986) to Wapping *(see Outer London: DOCKLANDS)*.

The square's history is related in full on a plaque situated on what is now the Continental Bank house.

Up Blackfriars Lane stands **Apothecaries' Hall** (1632, rebuilt c 1670): in the courtyard a pillared lamp stands over the old monastic well; its interior has remarkable oak panelling (1671) and a fine collection of stone jars (one of 1566), apothecary vessels, chandeliers and banners from a former state barge.

The Blackfriars, a wedge-shaped pub (1896), is fronted by a jolly fat friar. Inside the pub is decorated with friezes of monks at work and play in a strange *art nouveau* style.

Blackfriars Bridges (AZ) – James Cubitt's iron and stone road bridge (1899) replaced a previous 18C structure. The iron railway bridge (1896) with high parapet and coats of arms at each end, celebrates the prosperity enjoyed by the railways in the 19C.

A new footbridge will lead directly to the piazza of the Tate Gallery of Modern Art on the south bank *(see Bankside).*

Unilever House (AZ) – The vast stone building (1931) with its rusticated ground floor, pillars, large sculptures and miles of corridors inside, stands on part of the site of **Bridewell Palace**, built by Henry VIII in 1522 and where he received Charles V, who elected to stay in Blackfriars Monastery on what was then the far bank of the Fleet. Edward VI gave the Bridewell to the City which converted it into an orphanage (from where in 1619 two lots of one hundred orphans were sent across the Atlantic to populate the burgeoning State of Virginia) and after the Fire rebuilt it as a prison, soon notorious as one of London's most evil houses (demolished 1864).

CHEAPSIDE – LUDGATE CIRCUS

⊖ *Bank; St Paul's*

Poultry (CY) – The Midland Bank buildings (north side) were designed by Lutyens (1924-39) – high on the corners is a sculpture by Reid Dick of a fat boy driving a goose to the Stocks Market (1282-1737) which was once located nearby, and famous for its herbs and fresh fruit. Rent from the stalls was allocated to the maintenance of London Bridge.

The 1958 **Mercers' Hall** in Ironmonger Lane is situated on the site of the former St Thomas of Acon Hospital.

Cheapside (BY) – Cheapside, a wide commercial street originally known as West Cheap, takes its name from the Anglo-Saxon word *ceap* meaning to barter. The names of the side streets Milk Street, Bread Street, Honey Lane indicate the commodities sold there first from stalls, later in shops, and inhabited by craft and tradesmen.

The street was also the setting for many a medieval tourney with contests being watched from the upper windows by householders and royalty alike; the Lord Mayor and aldermen watched from a balcony in the tower of St Mary-le-Bow which records such scenes in a window. Of the three churches in Cheapside during the Middle Ages, only St Mary-le-Bow was rebuilt after the Fire; an Eleanor Cross *(see TRAFALGAR SQUARE)* erected here in 1290 facing Wood Street was demolished in 1643; three communal fountains served the area: Lesser Conduit at the west end, the Standard before St Mary-le-Bow (a place of public execution) and the Great Conduit, east of Ironmonger Lane.

Bow Lane (BY) – *Runs south off Cheapside to Mansion House underground station.* Stow tells how the area was once occupied by shoemakers and that the narrow and winding Bow Lane was previously known as Hosiers' Lane.

Williamson's Tavern *(Groveland Court)* is accommodated in a 17C house with a contemporary wrought-iron gate which once served as a Lord Mayor's residence (1666-1753).

★★**St Mary-le-Bow** ⊘ (BY) – The tower which advances into Cheapside contains the famous **Bow Bells** and supports Wren's most famous **spire**★★ (1671-80) in which he used all five Classical orders and the bow (the mason's term for a stone arch). The weather **vane,** a winged dragon (8ft 10in long) is poised at the top (239ft) with a rope dancer riding on its back.

Completed in 1673 in Portland stone, the church was Wren's most expensive, costing over £8 000 and the steeple only slightly less. It was based on the Basilica of Constantine in Rome which Wren would have known from engravings by Serlio. The weight of the barrel vault is borne by side piers and diffused through the flat longitudinal arches and smaller transverse arches much as it was in the great Roman Baths – a system Wren may have been experimenting with prior to starting upon the great dome of St Paul's.

> In 1334 the **Great Bell of Bow** called people from bed at 5.45am and rang the curfew at 9pm; the practice continued for over 400 years ceasing only in 1874: this sound came to define the limits of the City, giving rise to the saying that 'a true Londoner, a Cockney, must be born within the sound of Bow Bells'. According to legend it was these bells that chimed out 'Turn again Whittington, Lord Mayor of London'. Wren made room for a peal of 12 although only 8 were hung originally. During the 1939-45 war the 12-bell chime was used as a recognition signal by the BBC and came to mean hope and freedom to millions all over the world thus deserving the title 'the most famous peal in Christendom'.

In May 1941 the church was bombed; only the tower and outer walls remained. The exterior was restored to Wren's design while the interior lay-out was re-designed by Laurence King who also restored the roof. The unique carved rood is a gift from the people of Germany. The bronze sculpture was given by the Norwegians in memory of those who died in the Resistance. The stained glass is by John Hayward. The majestic organ and ornate doorway are adorned with the royal arms. The twin pulpits are used for the famous dialogues where two public figures of opposing views debate moral points.

The Norman **crypt,** built in 1087 with rough ragstone walls on the ruins of a Saxon church, contains the original columns with cushion capitals supporting the bows (arches) from which the church takes its name. Also named after them is the Court of Arches, supreme judicial court of the Archbishop of Canterbury, which has met here since the 12C.

West of the church is a small garden in which stands a statue of Captain John Smith (1580-1631), a pioneer and settler of Jamestown in Virginia. A tablet commemorates the poet Milton.

St Vedast's ⊘ (BY) – *Foster Lane.* The church (1670-73) dedicated to the beatified Bishop of Arras was designed by Wren. The **tower and spire**★ consist of a square stone tower with an overhanging entablature on which Wren later (1697) set a lantern with advanced triple pilaster at the corners through three stages, below the ribbed stone spire surmounted by a ball and vane.

The exterior, with a pre-Fire curving southwest wall which Wren retained when he rebuilt the church for £1 853 15s 6d (the cheapest of all the City churches), is almost unnoticeable from Foster Lane. (The street's name is a corruption of Vedast, 6C Bishop of Arras, to whom the church was dedicated in the 13C.) The interior is entirely new: the floor has been marbled in black and white; pews are aligned collegiate style beneath the **ceiling★**, reinstalled to Wren's design with a central wreath, cornice and end panels in moulded plasterwork, highlighted in gold and silver – St Vedast's is the Goldsmiths' Church. The wooden altarpiece and the ornate octagonal pulpit are also of interest.

Walk around St Paul's – listed separately and on down Ludgate Hill.

Ludgate Hill (AY) – A plaque on the south abutment of the 19C railway states 'In a house near the site was published in 1702 the *Daily Courant* first London daily newspaper'. Above the bridge stood Lud Gate, demolished in 1760: plaque on the wall of St Martin-within-Ludgate *(see below)*. It was the first curfew gate to be closed at night and was named after the legendary King Lud (66BC), who is said to have built the first gate on the site. Statues from the 1586 gate were removed to St Dunstan-in-the-West *(see CHANCERY LANE)*.

St-Martin-within-Ludgate ⊙ (AY) – The church which stood by the medieval Lud Gate and had its west wall just inside the Roman perimeter, is said to have been built first by King Cadwalla in the 7C; it was certainly rebuilt in 1439 before being burnt down in the Fire.

Wren cut off the hill frontage inside by means of stout pillars on which he rested a gallery and thick coffered arches. At ground level beneath the gallery the bays were filled with three doors, their **cases★** richly carved by **Grinling Gibbons**. The remaining area is laid out as a square within a square by means of 4 inner columns on which rest the groined vault formed by the intersection of barrel vaulting above the nave, chancel and transepts. The woodwork is 17C. The churchwardens' double chair dating from 1690 is unique.

From a lead-covered cupola and lantern, ringed by a balcony, rises a black needle **spire★**, the perfect foil to the green dome of St Paul's Cathedral.

Ludgate Circus – The circus, which was built in 1875 on the site of the Fleet Bridge to Ludgate Hill, includes a plaque (northwest angle) to Edgar Wallace (1875-1932), a Greenwich foundling who became a successful writer of crime novels.

St Bride's steeple

★St Bride's ⊙ (AY) – The famous white **spire★★** of St Bride's (dedicated to the 16C Irish Saint Bridget), Wren's tallest and most floating steeple, rises by four open octagonal stages to a final open pedestal and tapering obelisk which terminates in a vane (226ft above ground). When the spire was newly erected a baker used it as a model for wedding cakes; he made a fortune and inaugurated a lasting tradition; his wife's silk dress is in the museum in the crypt.

In 1940 Wren's church, described as 'a madrigal in stone' was gutted by fire leaving only the steeple and calcined outer walls standing. During rebuilding the crypt was opened; it had been used for burials from c 1720 until it was closed after the cholera epidemic of 1853, which killed 10 000 Londoners. Subsequent excavations have revealed a Roman ditch, walls, a pavement and the outlines of church buildings on the site dating to Saxon times at least.

The exterior was restored by Godfrey Allen to Wren's design with tall rounded windows between pedimented doors surmounted by circular windows; above is a line of oval clerestory windows; at the east end a tripartite window beneath a pediment.

The interior has been re-arranged to enclose the nave, now set with collegiate-style pews, and to fill the east end with a massive 17C style reredos against a *trompe-l'œil* painting. Wren's design of a barrel-vaulted nave and groined aisles has been retained. The decoration is 17C.

The nationally famous **St Bride Printing Library** ⊙ and Bridewell Theatre are located nearby as is the **Punch Tavern**, named after the magazine which had premises there.

Fleet Street (AY) – *Runs west from Ludgate Circus.* Named after the River Fleet which flows south from Hampstead to drain into the Thames at Blackfriars, the 'Street of Ink', once synonymous with the press, has changed in character since the age of technology has ousted many of the most famous major newspaper publishers to offices in Docklands *(Daily Mail, Times, Financial Times, Daily Telegraph)* or south of the river *(Financial Times, Daily Express, Observer)*. Yet several names live on: the **Reuters and Press Association** is located at no 85 in premises designed by Lutyens in 1935; the somewhat dilapidated **Express** group building at nos 121-8

Associations

It is St Bride's associations, however, rather than its architecture, that make it unique to many: Thomas Becket was born close by; King John held a parliament in the church in 1210; Henry VIII, advised by Thomas Wolsey, built Bridewell Palace nearby between the church and the river, and received Charles V there in 1522; high ranking churchmen unable to pay for lodgings within the City walls, built town houses in the neighbourhood (Salisbury Square) and since the clergy were the largest literate group in the land it was only natural that when **Wynkyn de Worde** acquired his master's press in 1491, he should remove it from Westminster to St Bride's and Fleet Street (Caxton had been wealthy enough not to have to depend upon the press for his livelihood, unlike his apprentice). By the time Wynkyn died in 1535 (he was buried in St Bride's), the parish boasted several printers, including Richard Grafton who printed the first English Language Bible in 1539. The church was the first to use the Book of Common Prayer, while its neighbouring taverns and coffeehouses were frequented by Chaucer, Shakespeare, Milton, Lovelace, Evelyn, Pepys (born nearby and like all his family christened in the church), Dryden, Izaac Walton, Edmund Waller (poet), Aubrey, Ashmole, John Ogilby (mapmaker), Thomas Tompion (father of English clock and watchmaking), Addison; in the 18C by Johnson and Boswell, Joshua Reynolds, Goldsmith, Garrick, Burke, Pope, Richardson (coffin in the crypt) and Hogarth; in the 19C by Charles Lamb, Hazlitt, Wordsworth, Keats, Hood, Leigh Hunt, Dickens. Today modern pew backs are labelled with the names of contemporaries, for St Bride's remains the printers' church, the Cathedral of Fleet Street where vigils were held for the journalist John McCarthy and Terry Anderson taken hostage by Lebanese Shi'ite militiamen during the 1980s.

remains a landmark, its bold 1931 black and clear glass panels set in chromium, with straight lines throughout except for the corner on Shoe Lane; at no 135 stands the **Daily Telegraph** building (1928) built in a ponderous mixture of styles.

In Wine Office Court is the **Cheshire Cheese** pub and restaurant accommodated in a house that was rebuilt in 1667 complete with small beamed rooms and coal fires on 3 floors.

Nestling between the first floor windows of the gable-fronted Gothic no **143** is a 19C statue of Mary Queen of Scots.

For sites located before the Inns of Court, opposite the Temple see CHANCERY LANE.

GUILDHALL ⊖ *Bank; St Paul's*

★**St Margaret, Lothbury** ⊘ (**CY**) – *From Bank walk up Princes Street.* While the derivations of Lothbury are speculative and various, the church's certain foundation dates back to the 12C. The present building was designed by Wren in 1686-1701. The square stone tower, topped by an iron railing, rises to a lead-covered cupola and a slender obelisk **spire**★ balancing a gilded ball and vane.

The unequal parallelogram inside is divided by Corinthian columns into a nave and chancel and shorter south aisle. The **woodwork**★ is especially remarkable: from a dark base of wall and column panelling and cut-down box pews, rise in clear silhouette, a wonderful oak screen, exquisitely carved pulpit, massive sounding board, gay with dancing cherubs, and a reredos with balustered rails. The **screen**★, made c 1689 for All Hallows, Upper Thames Street, and one of only two to Wren's design, is divided into 4 paired arcs by two strand balusters; at the centre are pierced pilasters and above three broken pediments, the central one supported by a great carved eagle and filled above with a royal coat of arms.

The chapel with a dividing screen made from the altar rails of St Olave Jewry, has a reredos also from St Olave. The **font**★ is attributed to Grinling Gibbons. 18C sword rests and bust of Sir Peter le Maire (d 1631) by H Le Sueur.

Gresham Street (**BCY**) – The street bears the name of Sir Thomas Gresham *(see above: Bishopsgate)*, who in his will founded **Gresham College** as a kind of free university in his mansion in Bishopsgate, Gresham House, which fronted on Old Broad Street. The house was demolished in 1768 and the institution re-established in 1843 at no 91 Gresham Street. The college, an independent institution supported by the corporation of London and the Mercers' Company, now occupies premises at Barnard's Inn *(see CHANCERY LANE).*

Moorgate (**CXY**) – The street is named after a gate cut in the City wall in 1415 (demolished in 1760) to provide access to Moorfields the open common on which people practised archery, dried clothes *(plaque on site of Tenter Street by Tenter House),* flew kites – two and a half centuries later it was one of the main exits for thousands fleeing the Great Plague.

The street is today overlooked by the City of London College which dates from the rebuilding of London Bridge in 1831.

St Olave Jewry (BY) – The two-stage stone tower is topped by a beautiful **weathervane**, a three-master fully rigged, from St Mildred's Church, Bread Street. The church, rebuilt by Wren (1670-76), was destroyed in 1940.

St Lawrence Jewry ⊘ (BY) – The stone tower rises to a balustrade with corner obelisks which enclose a pedimented lantern set in line with Gresham Street but out of alignment with the base, which parallels the west wall. Above is a lead obelisk spire from which flies the original gridiron weathervane, now also incorporating a replica of the incendiary bomb which caused the almost total destruction of the church in 1940.
'St Lawrence, called in the Jury because of old time many Jews inhabited thereabout' was, according to Stow, a 'fair and large' parish church. Built in 1196 and closely surrounded by houses, it perished completely in the Fire. Wren designed a building of modest outward appearance squaring up the interior by varying the thickness of the walls. The restored ceiling, coffered and decorated to Wren's original design with gilded plasterwork, emphasises the rectangular plan. The brilliant windows by Christopher Webb contrast with the plain and unassuming modern woodwork. More ornate are the organ case, modelled on the 17C original, and the screen in the north aisle; the wrought-iron gates, given by the Royal Marines, the Parachute Regiment and Airborne Forces, lead into the Commonwealth Chapel. This modern church by Cecil Brown, which became the church of the City Corporation in 1957, contains pews for the Lord Mayor (sword rest), sheriffs, aldermen, sword and mace bearers; also Sir Thomas Beecham's piano.

★**Guildhall** ⊘ (BY) – 'This Guildhall', Stow quoted in 1598 'was begun to be built new in the year 1411; ... the same was made of a little cottage, a large and great house... towards the charges whereof the (livery) companies gave large benevolences; also offences of men were pardoned for sums of money, extraordinary fees were raised, fines... during 7 years, with a continuation of 3 years more... Executors to Richard Whittington gave towards the paving of this great hall... with hard stone of Purbeck'. All was complete by c 1440. The Great Fire left the outer walls and crypt standing. Rebuilding began immediately and in 1669 Pepys noted 'passed by Guildhall, which is almost finished'.
In 1940, after 18C and 19C restorations and remodelling, history repeated itself. Reconstruction was once more completed in 1954 (west crypt: 1972; new west wing: 1974). In the course of recent building work excavations have revealed the site of a Roman amphitheatre, traces of the medieval Jewish quarter and of the 15C Guildhall chapel.
The City was granted its first charter by William the Conqueror in 1067; the first **Mayor** was installed in a building, of which no trace remains, probably on the present site in 1193; for at least 850 years, therefore, Guildhall has been the seat of civic government.

Dick Whittington

Whittington was four times Lord Mayor; in 1397, 1397-8, 1406-7 and 1419-20; he died in 1423, a man in his early sixties. The 3rd son of a Gloucestershire squire, he came to London, entered the mercers' trade, married well and rose rapidly both in trade, from which he amassed a fortune, and in the Corporation where he progressed from ward member to Lord Mayor. He was not knighted though an important part of his contact with the Crown seems to have been the provision of considerable loans; according to legend he gave a banquet for Henry V at which he burned bonds discharged for the King worth £60 000.
His great wealth continued after his death, as in his lifetime, to be devoted to the public cause: permanent buildings for Leadenhall Market, the construction of Greyfriars Library, half the cost of founding the Guildhall Library, repairs at Bart's, the foundation of a college (dissolved at the Reformation) and almshouses at St Michael Paternoster Royal, the rebuilding of Newgate Prison...
Such great personality, wealth, benefactions, were embroidered into legend until in 1605 licence was granted for performances of a play (now lost), *The History of Richard Whittington, of his lowe byrth, his great fortune;* when an engraver, Renold Elstrack, about the same time portrayed him in classic pose with his hand upon a skull, popular protest was so loud that the engraver altered the plate replacing the skull with a cat which may have given rise to the legend, although an alternative source is a coal barge, known as a catte, since Whittington traded in coal.

Architecture – Guildhall's façade, a mixture of Classical and Gothic motifs, extends across 9 bays, rises to 4 storeys and culminates, on the four buttresses which divide the face into equal parts, in large and peculiar pinnacles. Crowning the central area are the City arms which are composed of the Cross of St George, the sword of the patron saint, St Paul, on a shield supported by winged griffins, probably incorporated in the 16C. All this dates from the restoration of 1788-89 by **George Dance the Younger**. The **porch**, at the centre, however, is still covered by two bays of medieval tierceron vaulting.

Gog and Magog

Guarding the Musicians' Gallery are the post-war replica giants (9ft 3ins tall) carved in limewood by David Evans after the figures set up in Guildhall in 1708, themselves descendants of 15C and 16C midsummer pageant figures who were said to have originated in a legendary conflict between ancient Britons and Trojans in 1000 BC.

Inside, the **hall** also is in part medieval: the walls date back to the 15C and the chamber in which today's banquets are held is the same in dimension (152 x 49 ft) as that in which Lady Jane Grey and others were tried.

A cornice at clerestory level bears the arms of England, the City and the 12 Great Livery Companies whose banners hang in front; below, the bays between the piers contain memorial statues, notably (north wall) a seated bronze of **Churchill** by Oscar Nemon; Nelson; Wellington; Pitt the Elder by John Bacon. East of the entrance porch in the south wall, behind where the lord mayor sits at banquets, is a canopied oak buffet on which are displayed the City sword and mace and plate; to the west beneath the only remaining 15C window are the Imperial Standards of Length (1878) with the Metric measures (1973) on the right.

Crypt ⊙ – The crypt comprises two parts: the western pre-15C section with its four pairs of stone columns was vaulted by Wren after the earlier hall above collapsed in the Fire. The 15C eastern section below the present Guildhall – the largest medieval crypt in London – survived both 17C and 20C fires: it remains notable for its size and the 6 blue Purbeck marble clustered piers supporting the vaulting.

Library ⊙ – The library, founded c 1423, despoiled in the 16C and refounded in 1824, possesses a unique collection of maps, prints, drawings and manuscripts on the history and development of the City and London.

★**Clock Museum** ⊙ – The 700 timepieces which make up the Museum of the Worshipful Company of Clockmakers range in size from long case (grandfather) clocks to minute watches, in date from the 15C to the 20C, in manufacture from all wood composition, in movement from perpetual motion (with a ball that rolls 2 522 miles a year) and in esthetic appeal from a silver skull watch, said to have belonged to Mary Queen of Scots, to jewelled confections, enamelled, decorated, engraved, chased... The collection also includes two Harrison clocks *(see Outer London: GREENWICH – National Maritime Museum)*.

Guildhall Art Gallery ⊙ – In a fine modern building which replaces the original gallery (burned down in 1941) are displayed the art collection owned by the Corporation of London: portraits of dignitaries from 17C to 20C, 18C paintings, works by Victorian painters (Pre-Raphaelites) and other eminent artists.

St Mary Aldermanbury (BX) – The 12C site is now a garden, with only bases of the perimeter walls and pillars outlining the bombed Wren church (1670). The stones were numbered and sent to Fulton, USA where the church has been rebuilt to its 17C plan.

City Business Library ⊙ (BX) – *1 Brewers' Hall Garden*. This is a local authority (Corporation of London) public reference library which provides information on companies, markets, finance, business law, news, the British economy, the regions of the UK and foreign countries.

St Alban (BX) – All that remains of Wren's church (1697-1698) is the pure Gothic tower with slim corner buttresses crowned by a balustrade and crocketed pinnacles, which rises like a white stone needle above the traffic.

Goldsmiths' Hall in Foster Lane dates from 1835. It is endowed by an exceptional collection of gold and silver plate. Its Baroque interior provides a lavish setting for its annual jewellery exhibition.

St Anne and St Agnes ⊙ (BX) – The Lutheran church, which was mentioned c 1200, was rebuilt by Wren (1676-87) to the ancient domed-cross plan within a square, and again after the Second World War. The exterior is of rose-red brick with round-headed windows under central pediments. The small square stuccoed-stone tower is surmounted by an even smaller square domed turret, flaunting a vane in the shape of the letter A.

For St Botolph Aldersgate – see Barbican below.

BEYOND LONDON WALL

★**Barbican** ⊖ *Barbican; Moorgate*

The Barbican project (BX) – A residential neighbourhood incorporating schools, shops, open spaces, a conference and arts centre, to be established in the City on the bombed sites of Cripplegate, was conceived in the aftermath of World War II; construction began in 1962. The first residential phase was completed in 1976 and the arts centre finally opened in 1982.

The rounded arch motif, used vertically in the arcades and on the roofline and horizontally round the stairwells, gives a sense of unity to the various elements: 40-storey tower blocks, crescents and mews linked by high and low level walkways and interspersed with gardens and sports areas. At the heart of this city within a city, beside the lake with its cascades and fountains, stands St Giles' Church *(see below)*, a vestige of Cripplegate and the only tangible link with the past.

Barbican Arts Centre – The complex, of which five out of ten storeys are below ground, contains a concert hall (the permanent home of the London Symphony Orchestra), two theatres (London home of the Royal Shakespeare Company), three cinemas, a library, art gallery, sculpture court (on the roof of the concert hall), exhibition halls, meeting rooms and restaurants. The soaring theatre fly-tower is disguised by a roof-top conservatory harbouring a green jungle of ficus, eucalyptus, ferns and cacti.

Also incorporated into the concrete maze is the Guildhall School of Music and Drama (1977) endowed with a canted façade.

★★**Museum of London** ⊙ (BX) – The museum occupies the best of modern architectural style buildings, designed by Powell and Moya faced with white tiles below and linked by a bridge to a purple brick rotunda set like an advanced bastion in the sea of Aldersgate traffic; in traditional City fashion it makes the best use of an awkward site shaped around Ironmongers' Hall with its 1924 Gothic stone porch.

Barbican

By the main entrance of the museum in Nettleton Court stands a monumental bronze leaf as a memorial to the Methodist **John Wesley** *(see index)*.

The museum operates a team of archeologists specialising in urban excavation; this allows sites to be dug with the cooperation of building developers – work is undertaken to restricted timeframes before great concrete foundations are irrevocably sunk through the layers of history. Over the long term, digs have revealed a broad range of artefacts which, classified and compared to other flora, fauna, bone, wood, ceramic, glass or metal finds provide a reliable record of London and her inhabitants through the ages and ravages of war, fire, flood and plague...

Displays are organised into galleries of bays according to time and theme from pre-history to the present: exhibits include the best Roman wall painting in Britain and the sculptures from the Roman Temple of Mithras, medieval pilgrim badges, a model of the Rose Theatre based on evidence excavated by Museum of London archeologists, the Cheapside Hoard of Jacobean jewellery, a diorama of the Great Fire, the doors from Newgate Gaol, 19C shops and interiors, the Lord Mayor's Coach, souvenirs of the women's suffrage movement, the 1930s lifts from Selfridge's department store and a revealing exposition on the Second World War. The development of domestic life and public utility services – gas, drainage, the Underground – are illustrated as well as political and fashionable London.

Roman Fort ⊙ (**BX**) – This, the west gate of the Romans' north fort, including the outline of the guard turret, lies in a chamber off the west end of the underground carpark.

Aldersgate (**BX**) – The original gate was said to have been built by a Saxon named Aldred. As James I entered the capital at this point on his accession, the gate was rebuilt in 1617 in commemoration of his entry but demolished in 1761.

St Botolph Aldersgate ⊙ (**BX**) – The church (1788-91) built of dark red-brown brick and conventional rounded windows was designed by Nathaniel Wright. Its small square tower is topped by a cupola with a wooden turret and gilded vane. The building was 'improved' in 1829 by the addition of a pedimented east end in stucco. The interior is mainly Georgian with elaborate rosettes in high relief on the white plaster ceiling, coffered apses and 19C glass; in the galleries are two ward rooms where the children sat during the services. One window commemorates John Wesley in Moorfields; the east 'window' transparency depicting the *Agony in the Garden* is a painting on glass by James Pierson (1788). The inlaid pulpit stands on a carved palm tree. Wall monuments are a reminder that the present church is a 3rd rebuilding on the site. The organ (c 1788) is the only playable instrument by Samuel Green.

Given its situation by a gate in the City Wall, the church is dedicated to the 7C Saxon saint and patron of travellers.

★**St Giles Cripplegate** ⊙ (**BX**) – Dwarfed but in no way overpowered by the Barbican, St Giles' tower is built of stone and brick; corner pinnacles guard an open cupola merry-go-round-shaped turret which sports a weathervane. (Peal of 12 bells; chiming clock.)

During its 900 year history since 1090 when a Norman church was first erected on the site outside the City Wall beside the postern gate on to the moor, St Giles has been scarred by regular acts of destruction and re-building – the most recent caused by bombing in 1940. A 15C arcade rises to a clerestory to divide the nave from the aisles. Few memorials, after so many vicissitudes, survive, although signatures recorded in the registers confirm associations with the poet **John Milton** (buried in the chancel, 1674; bust by John Bacon, 1793, south wall), the navigator **Martin Frobisher** (buried in south aisle, 1594), the author of the *Book of Martyrs John Foxe* (buried 1587), the mapmaker **John Speed** (buried 1629 below his monument on the south wall), **Oliver Cromwell** (married 22 August 1620), **Sir Thomas More**, **Ben Jonson**, **Shakespeare** (at the baptism of his nephew), Edward Alleyn, Prince Rupert, Holman Hunt, Sir Ebenezer Howard (pioneer of garden cities). Other notable fixtures include a fine sword rest, lectern and marble font, a display of ecclesiastical and secular silver, and, in the southeast corner of the chancel, a medieval sedilia and piscina.

St Alphage (**BX**) – 14C pointed stone arches in black flint walls mark the west tower of the chapel of Elsing Spital Priory dissolved by Henry VIII. (Revealed by 1940 bombs.)

Smithfield ⊖ *St Paul's; Barbican; Chancery Lane*

Smithfield London Central Markets (**AX**) – Smithfield was opened as a wholesale and retail dead meat, poultry and provision market only in 1868. Previously the stock had come in live, driven into the City through Islington. The name, derived from 'smooth field' is associated with a stock market in Saxon times and from the 12C with the summer Fair of St Bartholomew, held from 1614 all the year round and banned by the Victorians because of the riotous debauchery it provoked. The site was also used for executions until the gallows were moved to

The CITY

Tyburn, and for the burning of martyrs at the stake during Mary Tudor's times. After centuries of overcrowding on the site, chaos and congestion in the narrow streets, the livestock market was transferred in 1855 to the Caledonian Market, Islington. The listed buildings, erected in 1868 and since enlarged, are of red brick and stone with domed towers at either end; they extend over 8 acres, with 15 miles of rails capable of hanging 60 000 sides of beef. An underground railway depot *(car park)* originally linked the market to the national railway network. The market closed in 1998 and the site has been redeveloped.

★★ **St Bartholomew-the-Great** ⊘ (**AX**) – St Bartholomew's was once a great, spacious church of which the present building was only the chancel. It was founded in 1123 by a one-time courtier, Rahere, following a pilgrimage to Rome: on land granted by Henry I he established both the hospital and an Augustinian priory of which he became the first prior. By 1143, when he died, the Norman chancel had been completed; nearly 400 years later the church was 280ft long, the west door being where the gateway on to Little Britain now stands. In 1534 the priory was valued at £693 9s 10 d. In 1539 Henry VIII dissolved the priory, demolished the church nave and ordained that the truncated building be used only as a parish church. The monarch's attorney-general, Sir Richard Rich, paid him £1064 11s 3d for the property which the family retained for 300 years. In that time the church fell into disrepair: the Lady Chapel was 'squatted in', became a printers' workshop (where in 1724 Benjamin Franklin was employed) and later a fringe factory; the north transept was turned into a forge (note the blackened walls) the remains of the cloister became a stable, a thick layer of earth covered the church floor, limewash obscured the walls and murals, a brick receptacle behind the altar, known as Purgatory, was filled with human bones...
Restoration, including the buying out of extraneous occupants, took from 1863 to 1910.

The building – The gateway, a 13C arch and the original entrance to the nave, is surmounted by a late 16C half-timbered gatehouse (restored 1932). The path through the churchyard is at the level of the medieval church. The square brick castellated **tower,** with a small vaned turret, was erected in 1628 off-centre at the west end of the curtailed church. The porch, west front and other exterior flint and stone refacing date from 1839 (restoration by Sir Aston Webb).
The **choir**★ is Norman. An arcade of circular arches spring from massive round piers and plainly scalloped capitals to support a relieving arch and a gallery of arched openings divided into groups of 4 by slender columns. The late Perpendicular style clerestory, rebuilt in 1405, has survived intact save for the insertion of an **oriel** window in the south gallery by Prior Bolton in 1520 stamped with his rebus: a bolt or arrow transfixing a tun or cask and from which, behind the leaded lights, he could follow the service. The Lady Chapel completed in 1336 was all but rebuilt in 1897 so only the end north and south windows are original. 15C oak doors (by the west door) lead to the east walk of the old cloister (c 1405, rebuilt early this century).
Rahere, the founder, lies on a 16C decorated tomb chest beneath a crested canopy, all fashioned some 350 years after his death. The **font,** used at Hogarth's baptism in 1697, dates from the early 15C and as such is one of the oldest in the City.

St Bartholomew's Hospital ⊘ (**AX**) – The hospital, known as Barts, was founded by Rahere in 1123 as part of an Augustinian priory. Modern blocks now supplement the collegiate style buildings (1730-66) designed by James Gibbs. The north wing includes the great staircase decorated with vast murals by **Hogarth** (1734) and the Great Hall *(not open);* displays of items (documents, charters, medical paraphernalia) relate the evolution of this historic institution.
The gatehouse from West Smithfield erected in 1702, contains an 18C statue of Henry VIII who dissolved the priory and gave the hospital to the City of London in 1546.

St Bartholomew-the-Less ⊘ – The 12C hospital church appears on mid 17C maps as a substantial building with a stalwart tower; by the 18C, however, it was so derelict as to need repair first by George Dance the Younger (1789) and again, in 1823, by Philip Hardwick. Monuments date back to the 14C (vestry pavements), while the more modern ones chiefly commemorate hospital personnel. The 15C square tower with a domed corner turret is visible from the market although the church stands within the walls of the hospital.

Fat Boy (**AX**) – The gilded oak figure, said to mark where the Great Fire stopped, stands on a site then known as Pie Corner; hence the saying that the Fire began in Pudding Lane and ended at Pie Corner.

St Sepulchre-without-Newgate ⊘ (**AX**) – The **Church of the Holy Sepulchre** which stands 'without the city wall' was of an earlier foundation, renamed at the time of the Crusades after the Jerusalem church. The square stone tower (restored) surmounted by four heavy crocketed pinnacles dates from 1450 as does the fan vaulted porch decorated with carved bosses. The bright interior is furnished with a

156

contemporary pulpit, font and octagonal cover gay with cherubs' heads, and at the entrance, the beautiful font cover rescued by a postman from Christ Church *(see below)* in 1940. St Sepulchre is 'the Musicians' Church', its choir central to the emergence of the Royal School of Church Music. Along the north side is the Musicians' Chapel which contains the ashes of **Sir Henry Wood** (1869-1944), and windows, chairs, kneelers dedicated to the memory of British musicians. The organ (1670) which has a superb case that includes the monogram of Charles II, is reputed to have been played by Handel and Mendelssohn; it was also where the young Henry Wood aged 14 officiated as assistant organist.

Other mementoes include a stone from the Church of the Holy Sepulchre in Jerusalem; sword rests; the hand bell rung outside condemned men's cells at midnight in the old Newgate Prison; a brass plate to Captain John Smith – sometime Governor of Virginia who died in 1631 and is buried in the church; the colours of the Royal Fusiliers City of London Regiment.

Holborn Viaduct was built in 1863-69 to connect the City and West End; previously all traffic had to descend to the level of Farringdon Street and climb up again. The bridge is an example of Victorian cast iron work: strongly constructed and ornate with uplifting statues and lions.

Alongside the viaduct stands the **City Temple** ⊘ marked by its high square and pillared tower surmounted by a square lantern, lead dome and cross. The history of the City Temple, the only English Free Church in the City, goes back to 1567 although occupation of the site on the viaduct dates only from 1874. The church is famous for its preachers, among whom this century have been Dr Maude Royden, in 1917 the first woman to step into a pulpit, and Dr Leslie Weatherhead. Wartime bombing gutted the sanctuary so that the building now presents the contrast of a Victorian/Palladian exterior and modern interior.

For Holborn see CHANCERY LANE.

Central Criminal Court, the Old Bailey ⊘ **(AY)** – This is the third Criminal Court to occupy this site. The original trial halls, erected in 1539, were built to protect the judges from 'much peril and danger' in the form of sickness and infestation so rife in the gaols – indeed they still carry posies from May to September tradition- ally to ward off gaol fever. The Common Council, therefore, passed a resolution 'that a convenient place be made... upon the common ground of this City in the old bailey of London': the site chosen was located by New Gate, a gate in the wall built by the Romans for the main road west enlarged in the early Middle Ages, near which a City gaol had been constructed (1180) to relieve the ever overcrowded Fleet Prison. Remains of a triumphal arch c AD 200 marking the western entrance to the city have been excavated in Newgate Street.

Fleet Prison, where Mr Pickwick made a brief but not painful stay, is first mentioned in 1197, located by the Fleet River, a putrid and stagnant stream used by local butchers to wash their carcasses. By 1355, choked by sewage and decomposing detritus, the river caused a terrible stench and epidemic that soon raged through the prison. It was demolished in 1844 – having incarcerated John Donne in 1601 (for marrying without his father-in-law's consent). **Newgate Prison,** meanwhile, became notorious for its appalling con- ditions, cruelty and barbarism. In 1381 it was broken open by Wat Tyler and rebuilt in 1423 with a bequest from Richard Whittington; in 1780 it was set alight by the Gordon Rioters and replaced in 1783 to designs by George Dance junior. It was outside the prison that public executions took place, transferred from Tyburn in 1783, until abolished in 1868. The gate was demolished in 1777 and the prison, reserved then for prisoners on trial, was closed in 1902.

The building – The granite structure is dressed in Portland stone, its dramatic entrance emphasised with a broken pediment and allegories of Truth, Justice and the Recording Angel, while the Lady of Justice, a 12ft gold figure holding scales and a sword (3ft 3in) stands high above perched on a green copper dome (1907). This dominant feature of the London skyline is cast in bronze and covered in gold leaf (regilded every 5 years and cleaned every August) – unusually she is neither blind- folded nor blind.

Inside all is marble, a grand staircase sweeping up to halls on two floors decked with painted murals. The four original courts are large, while the annexe, com- pleted in 1972 and faced with Portland stone but otherwise bearing no relation whatsoever to Mountford's building, accommodates small, light-panelled modern courtrooms bringing the number to 18 in all. The complex also has 60 cells to accommodate prisoners brought daily from Brixton and Holloway.

Among those to have been tried at the Old Bailey are **William Penn** and another in 1670 for preaching to an unlawful assembly in Gracechurch Street: a tablet 'commemorates the courage and endurance of the jury who refused to give a verdict against them though they were locked up without food for two nights and were fined for their verdict of 'Not Guilty', since which legislation has ratified the 'Right of Juries to give their Verdict according to their convictions'.

General Post Office (AY) – Plaques on the turn of the century building indicate the site of Greyfriars (f 1225) and Christ's Hospital which occupied the buildings from 1552-1902. Outside the main building stands the statue of Sir Rowland Hill, who in 1840 introduced the penny post, the uniform rate for a letter sent anywhere in the kingdom.

★**Christ Church** (AY) – The slender square stone tower rises by stages alternately solid and colonnaded, adorned by urns, to a slim decorated turret and vane. Christ Church was founded by Henry VIII on the site occupied by the Greyfriars monastery (1225-1538) possibly to serve Christ's Hospital, the second royal foundation nearby, also known as the Bluecoat School (1552-1902). The church, destroyed in the Fire and redesigned by Wren (1667-91) on sufficient scale to accommodate the boys, is now a garden. The tower houses an architect's office.

Nearby stands the **Master Gunner** a pub with Royal Artillery associations.

CLERKENWELL

Map pp 8-9 (**FGV**)

⊖ Barbican; Farringdon

Clerkenwell recalls in name the medieval parish clerks who each year performed plays outside the City at a local well-head *(viewed through a window at 14-16 Farringdon Lane)*. Finsbury is named after the Fiennes family; the owners of the local manor (bury/burh/burg in Old English) who in the 14C gave **Moorfields**, an unprofitable marsh, to the people of London as an open space, the first so designated.

Some open land remains: Finsbury Square, Finsbury Circus, Bunhill Fields and the Honourable Artillery Company Fields *(see below)* but the outflow of artisans and cottage industry workers from the City, particularly after the Plague (1665) and Fire (1666), caused poor quality housing and tenements to be erected right up to the walls of the Charterhouse, St John's Priory, Bethlem *(in what is now City Road)* and the other hospitals in the district – the only one of which now extant is Moorfields Eye Hospital, founded in 1805.

The crowded days of home industry in the early 19C are recalled by the Eagle Pub *(Shepherdess Walk, City Road)* and the old rhyme:

Half a pound of twopenny rice, Half a pound of Treacle,....
Up and down the City Road, In and out the Eagle,
That's the way the money goes, Pop goes the Weasel.

National newspapers in the area are the **Morning Star** *(75 Farringdon Road)* in a plain building of concrete and brick by E Goldfinger (1949) and **The Guardian** *(119 Farringdon Road)*.

★**Charterhouse** ⊙ – At every stage of its history 14C priory, Tudor mansion, 17C hospital and boys' school, 20C residence for aged Brothers. The buildings of the Charterhouse have been replaced or altered in a variety of materials and architectural styles.

Between 1535-37 the Prior and 15 monks of the 170-year-old Charterhouse were executed for refusing to recognise Henry VIII as head of the Church; he dissolved the community and removed treasure, timber, stone and glass for his own use. Within ten years, the house began a new life as a Tudor mansion under the Norths

and then passed to the Norfolks whom Elizabeth visited several times before her host, the 4th Duke of Norfolk, was executed in 1572 for intriguing with Mary Queen of Scots. In 1611 the house was sold to **Thomas Sutton** for £13 000 and letters patent were issued for the founding of a hospital for 80 old men and 40 boys under the name of the Hospital of King James in Charterhouse. Sutton (d 1611) lies in an elaborate tomb by Nicholas Stone in the crypt under the chapel. In 1872 the school moved to Surrey.

The Building – The 15C gateway, with its original massive gates, is built in flint and stone chequer-work like the precinct wall to the east. The superstructure and adjoining house, now the Master's lodging, are dated 1716. The graceful concave pyramidal roof opposite the gate covers the water conduit house of the monastery.

On the north side of Master's Court the Tudor **Great Hall**, with hammerbeam roof and 16C screen and gallery remains intact. The carved stone fireplace was added in 1614. The Elizabethan **Great Chamber**, hung with Flemish tapestries, has a painted and gilded late 16C plaster ceiling, an ornate painted chimney-piece and leaded lights. The ante-room opens on to a terrace built in 1571 by Norfolk above the west walk of the Great Cloister, in which a cell door and hatch have been discovered.

In the tower, to which the belfry and cupola were added in 1614, is the treasury, vaulted in the Tudor period, with a squint looking down on the high altar of the original chapel where the tomb of the founder, Sir Walter Manny (d 1372), was discovered in 1947.

The present **chapel** was created in 1614 out of the monks' Chapter House with the addition of a north aisle and further enlarged to the north in 1824. The 17C screen, organ gallery, pew heads and pulpit are noteworthy.

St John's Gate ⊙ – The Order of the Grand Priory in the British Realm, which developed from the First Crusade as a religious order to look after pilgrims visiting the Holy Land, became a military order during the 12C. It left the Holy Land on the fall of Acre in 1291, establishing itself first in Cyprus, then Rhodes (1310) and finally Malta (1530) where it became a sovereign power. Priories and commanderies were instituted in Europe, the **Grand Priory of England** being in Clerkenwell in 1144; to these were added the Templars' properties on their suppression in 1312. In 1540 Henry VIII dissolved the Hospitallers and in 1546 issued a warrant *(in the museum)* for the buildings to be dismantled (Protector Somerset later took the stone for his house in the Strand) but the gate survived. St John's was re-established as a Protestant Order by Royal Charter in 1888.

Gatehouse and Museum – The 16C gatehouse, flanked by four-storey towers, was the Priory's south entrance. Wide, vaulted, with the lamb of God, the arms of the order and of Prior Thomas Docwra, who built it, on the bosses, it contains the rooms which were occupied in the reigns of Elizabeth and James I by the Master of Revels, licensor of the plays of Shakespeare and Ben Jonson, and in the 18C Edward Cave, publisher and printer of England's first literary periodical; *The Gentleman's Magazine* (1733-81), to which Dr Johnson was a regular contributor.

In the 20C Tudor-style Chapter Hall, where the Maltese banners hang in the lantern, in the Council Chamber and the Library are displayed pharmacy jars from the hospitals in Rhodes and Malta, silver filigree work and a rare collection of beaten silver Maltese glove trays; fine inlay work in wood and marble, two magnificent Chinese tobacco jars and the illuminated Rhodes Missal on which the knights took their vows. A rare 16C spiral staircase with wooden treads leads to a room displaying insignia, portrait medals and the Order's own coinage issued in Rhodes and Malta. The museum illustrates the life of the Order with items from its priories and commanderies and from its hospitals (including the Ophthalmic Hospital in Jerusalem). A new gallery traces the history of the St John Ambulance Brigade from 1887: uniforms, medical instruments, first aid kits, medals...

St John's Church and Crypt – The Grand Priory Church of St John, once extended further west into the square where setts in the road mark the site of the round nave. The 16C and 18C brick walls of the former choir are now hung with the chivalric banners of Commonwealth priories.

The crypt is 12C, the only original Priory building to survive. Beneath the low ribbed vaulting, against the north wall, lie the rich alabaster forms of a Spanish grandee and the cadaverous effigy of the last Prior before the Dissolution.

Clerkenwell Green – The rallying point in 18C and 19C for work people protesting against the social and industrial injustices of the period is an appropriate site for the **Karl Marx Memorial Library**, an 18C house *(no 37a)*. Cheerful pavement cafés strike a more affluent note.

Mount Pleasant – The early 18C landmark, perhaps ironically named as it was the local rubbish dump, is now one of the main Post Office inland mail sorting offices and the centre of the Post Office railway. The line runs 70ft below ground from Paddington to Liverpool Street and Whitechapel, carrying the mail in automatically controlled trucks along 2ft gauge tracks.

New River Head – *Thames Water Authority, Rosebery Avenue.* The neo-Georgian building, now converted into flats, contains a fireplace attributed to Grinling Gibbons and plaster ceilings c 1693.

History – The New River undertaking originated in 1609 when **Sir Hugh Myddelton** (statue on Islington Green), a City goldsmith and jeweller, put up the capital to construct a canal from springs in Hertfordshire to the City. The winding channel some 40 miles long took 4 years to dig and might well have ruined Myddelton but for the personal financial support of James I.

The New River Head was inaugurated in 1613 when water carried down from Clerkenwell to the City in wooden pipes (today it flows into the London Ring Main). Individual subscribers were supplied with water on tap at 5s a quarter; the enterprise was a financial success and was sold for £5 million when taken over by the Metropolitan Water Board (1904-1974) which built its head office on the site of the New River Head so that the river is now only 24 miles long ending at Stoke Newington. The elegant terraces of **Myddelton Square** were built in the late 1700s on part of the New River Company's estate.

Sadler's Wells Theatre – *Rosebery Avenue*. Music house at the centre of late 17C pleasure gardens and medicinal wells, mid 18C theatre, Shakespearean and classical drama centre under **Samuel Phelp** in the 1840s, music hall, derelict ruin: such was the site's history when **Lilian Baylis** took it over and had a new brick theatre built (1931). The theatre is named after a builder, Mr Sadler, whose workmen in 1683 rediscovered the medicinal wells. The well-appointed new building dates from 1998. *See INTRODUCTION – Entertainment.*

City University – *St John Street*. Surrounded by the modern buildings of the City University is the original Northampton Institute (1894-96), designed by E Mountford in an eclectic baroque style.

Companies House ⊘ – *55-71 City Road*. The main archive for the Register of Companies was transferred to Cardiff in 1976. Here, changes in directorships and registered office addresses dating back 7 years are available on microfilm as are the last three annual returns and accounts for over 650 000 companies.

Wesley's House and Chapel ⊘ – *47 City Road*. John Wesley, who is buried in the churchyard, laid the foundation stone of the chapel in 1777. The oblong building of stock brick with a shallow apse, is notable inside for the tribune supported on seven jasper columns, presented by overseas Methodists in replacement of the pine dockyard masts (now in the vestibule) originally given by George III, and the white and gold ceiling by Robert Adam. Wesley's mahogany pulpit, formerly a two decker, 15ft tall, stands at the centre. A **Museum of Methodism** is housed in the crypt.

Next door, the preacher's house is rich in mementoes: his desk, study and conference chairs, clock, clothes, library, furniture and, in the minute prayer room, table desk and kneeler.

Bunhill Fields ⊘ – *City Road*. Long before 1549 when the first wagon load of bones was delivered for burial from the overflowing charnel house in St Paul's Churchyard, the field had been given the name Bone Hill. From 1665, when the City Corporation acquired it, to its closure in 1852, 120 000 were buried there including many non-conformists since the ground was never consecrated.

Among the tombs are those of: William Blake (1757-1827), John Bunyan (1628-88), Daniel Defoe (1661-1731), Susanna Wesley, mother of John and Charles (1669-1742)... In the adjoining Quaker yard is the grave of the founder of the Society of Friends, George Fox (1624-91).

Honourable Artillery Company HQ – *Finsbury Barracks*. The buildings on the historic Artillery Fields, designated for archery practice in Tudor times, date from 1735 and 1857.

John Wesley (1703-91) was born the fifteenth child of Rev Samuel Wesley (1662-1735) and was educated at Charterhouse and Christ Church College, Oxford. Here the group of ardent, scholarly and earnest Christians which soon collected around him was referred to as the Holy Club, the Bible Moths or the Methodists. After being ordained he spent a year in Georgia before returning to London and coming under the influence of Peter Bohler, who inspired him to convert to the Moravian Brotherhood *(see CHELSEA)* and embarking on a life of preaching, travelling up to 8 000 miles a year; in 1747 he went to Ireland, in 1751 to Scotland.

Prompted by his incontestable piety and sense of charity he secured the tenets of Methodism in evangelism and social welfare: in 1760 he sailed for America, where in 1768 he founded the first Chapel in New York. As well as being a man of great courage and tireless persistence he was endowed with an easy sense of leadership and charismatic personality, qualities which ensured that the cult thrived. His younger brother **Charles** (1707-88), the eighteenth child, was educated at Westminster before following John to Christ Church, accompanying him to America, and converting to the Moravian Brotherhood in 1738. In 1771 Charles settled back in London and preached at the City Road Chapel. Less charismatic than his brother, he dedicated his energies to writing hymns (5 500 in all) that might rally spirits and assist missionaries in instructing and inspiring their followers.

COURTAULD INSTITUTE OF ART★★

The narrow Strand façade of Somerset House, inspired by Inigo Jones' Palladian riverside gallery designed for Henrietta Maria, has a triple gateway and giant columns beneath a balustrade decorated with statues and a massive statuary group by Bacon. The Strand block, the most elaborate, has two advanced wings and contains the so-called **Fine Rooms,** notable for their pleasing proportions and handsome plasterwork. This was originally designed for three learned societies: the Royal Society, the Antiquaries and the Royal Academy, now in Burlington House *(see PICCADILLY).*

The foundation of an institute dedicated to art connoisseurship, the teaching of Art History on the lines of the Harvard University – Fogg Museum and the preservation of art was largely initiated by Viscount Lee of Fareham (1868-1947). This extremely fine collection is drawn from several major bequests.

Samuel Courtauld began collecting Impressionist and Post-Impressionist paintings in 1922. His perceptive eye and discerning taste selected some of the most famous expressions of the modern masters.

Count Antoine Seilern (The Princes' Gate Collection – 1978) was Austrian by extraction but British by birth. As he had undertaken research into the Venetian sources of Rubens's ceiling pictures while in Vienna, 32 paintings and over 20 drawings by the master make up the bulk of his important donation which includes works from early Netherlandish (*Entombment* by Master of Flémalle) and Italian Schools (Bernardo Daddi triptych, Tiepolo oil sketches), and several pieces by modern masters Cézanne, Kokoschka, Pissarro, Renoir. There is also a large number of important drawings.

Viscount Lee of Fareham, having given his first collection and Elizabethan manor house 'Chequers' to the Nation in 1917 for use as a country retreat for Prime Ministers in office, began building his second collection in the early 1920s. Italian Renaissance painting (Botticelli *Holy Trinity;* Giovanni Bellini *Assassination of St Peter Martyr;* Paolo Veronese *Baptism of Christ*) complements the Flemish and English portraits (Dobson, Lely, Gainsborough, Romney, Raeburn).

Sir Robert Witt donated his extensive collection of old master drawings collected for their exceptional quality and individual worth (Gainsborough sketchbooks) in the early 1920s. The documentary photographic archive was acquired in 1952. His son, Sir John Witt (1907-1982) also left a number of important British watercolours.

Thomas Gambier-Parry (1816-88) collected 14C Italian Primitives (Bernardo Daddi – Crucifixion polyptych, Lorenzo Monaco – *Coronation of the Virgin,* three Fra Angelico predella panels.

Roger Fry (1866-1934) was an art historian, critic and painter who collected contemporary works by Duncan Grant, Vanessa Bell associated with the **Bloomsbury Group** and the Omega Workshop during the 1930s *(see INTRODUCTION – Painting).* His personal taste was for Bonnard, Derain, Friesz, O'Connor, Rouault, Sickert and Seurat.

Galleries ⊙ – *Allow about 1 1/2 hr.* Paintings are hung chronologically or for contrast and comparison: displays are therefore subject to change. Interior colour-schemes conform where possible, to William Chambers' original specifications.

Gallery 1: Royal Academy Teaching Room – Exquisite examples from the Early Italian and Low Countries Schools have a jewel-like quality that is emphasized by their size, gold background and pious devotional purpose. Rare pieces by the Tuscan Bernardo **Daddi** show the artist tentatively breaking away from Byzantine iconography by animating his figures with emotion – the choir of angels chatter together, the Virgin recoils from the Angel of the Annunciation. Lorenzo **Monaco** endows his elegant figures with weight and volume (*Coronation of the Virgin* – c 1395).

The Northern artists developed a far more detailed style facilitated by oil painting, but drawn from observation: draperies fall into brittle folds and plants are minutely documented. Intense expression pervades the religious subjects, as a tear is wiped away or the angels resigned to Fate bear the symbolic crown of thorns and nails of the cross (**Master of Flémalle** *The Entombment* Triptych – c 1420). In the 16C landscape and architectural features are introduced in sacred painting (*The Madonna with Child and Angels* by Q Massys).

The showcases display English and French ivories carved with religious scenes; Limoges enamels; Venetian and Bohemian glass; Islamic metalwork.

Gallery 2: Royal Academy Ante Room and Library – The main panel depicting the *Theory of Art* by Reynolds has been replaced by a copy. The panels dedicated to Nature, History, Allegory and Fable are by Cipriani.

Botticelli's *Holy Trinity* would probably have been the central panel of an altarpiece commissioned for the Augustinian convent of Sant' Elisabetta delle Convertite, a sanctuary for reformed prostitutes, which would explain the prominence given to John the Baptist (patron saint of Florence) and a penitent Mary Magdalene in the barren landscape. The Archangel Raphael holding the hand of Tobias is often portrayed to represent Redemption – as his name means 'God has healed'.

The culture of the Italian city states in the 15C is exemplified by the combination of secular interests and religious subjects (Perugino). In *The Creation* and *The Fall of Man* by Albertinelli, scenes are shown chronologically in a harmonious composition. The gentle landscape reveals a Flemish influence while the figures are reminiscent of antique statuary.

Gallery 3: Royal Society Meeting Room – The strong colour-scheme is based upon paint samples and surviving original documentation.

The incomplete panel of *The Holy Family* is attributed to **Perino del Vaga**: note how the warm ground pervades the painted figures with a golden hue and the Florentine artist's ability to suggest movement and alertness between the figures. Lorenzo **Lotto**'s *Holy Family with St Anne* is animated by the diagonal emphasis of the composition emphasising the youthful expressions of the fearful Virgin and loving Christ-Child. In *The Virgin and Child* by **Parmigianino** the elegance and poise of the Virgin is characteristic of the artist's refined idea of beauty. The naturalistic treatment of *The Adoration of the Shepherds* by **Tintoretto** reveals the symbolism attached to the Nativity (the Child on a patch of straw, peasant woman offering a basket of eggs). In *The Baptism of Christ* Veronese captures the tension among the protagonists and the play of light on the figures and landscape.

The Morelli marriage chests (*cassoni* - 1472), carved by Zanobi di Domenico and painted by Jacopo del Sellaio and Biagio di Antonio: the front panels depict scenes taken from Books II and V of Livy's *Histories* while the end panels show masculine Virtues, Justice and Fortitude.

Gallery 4: Royal Society and Society of Antiquaries Ante Room – The delicate stucco decoration is French in feeling; wreaths would have framed portrait medallions – now lost: the ceiling grisaille (monochrome) panels show putti playing with objects representing the Four Elements, Earth, Air, Fire and Water; the central panel, by a different hand, shows the head of Apollo surrounded by the signs of the Zodiac. Note also the fine period door handles.

The early tradition of Netherlandish painting is represented by **Bruegel the Elder**: religious subjects set in vast landscapes, balanced composition, bands of colour to emphasise spatial recession *(Landscape with the Flight into Egypt)*, austere composition and monumental figures *(grisaille – Christ and the Woman taken in Adultery)*. *Adam and Eve* (1526) provides Lucas Cranach the Elder, friend and ally of Luther, with an opportunity to represent nude figures, markedly influenced by Italianate prototypes diffused by engravings and woodcuts. Many of the portraits are particularly striking (*Sir John Luttrell* by H Eworth). A rare double-sided panel depicting *The Annunciation* and *Christ bearing the Cross* by Pieter Aerlsen is set in an exquisite early 16C Italian frame.

Gallery 5: Society of Antiquaries Meeting Room – Several works by **Rubens** demonstrate the master's ability to treat historical and religious subjects, portraits and landscape with equal adeptness. Strong contrasts of light and texture, gesture and emotion characterise the colourful and restless compositions, exaggerated to some extent in the *modelli* or oil sketches produced for a large altarpiece commissioned for Antwerp Cathedral. The portrait of Baladassare Castiglione is copied from an original painting by Raphael in the Louvre. The intimate scene *The Family of Jan Bruegel* has great impact. The *Landscape by Moonlight*, painted late in the painter's life is more contemplative in nature; the first documented owner of this painting was Reynolds, its possible influence upon subsequent generations of English painters, Gainsborough and Constable included, therefore is worthy of note.

Gallery 6: Royal Academy Council and Assembly Rooms – The ceiling panels painted by Benjamin West and Angelica Kauffman were moved to Burlington House when the Royal Academy moved there in 1837.

Portraiture became an important genre in the 17C. **William Dobson** and **Sir Peter Lely** emerge as masters of a style pioneered by Van Dyck and providing modern viewers with a strong idea of contemporary dress and attitude.

Van Dyck also contributed to developments in English painting: his portraits are dignified yet informal, the eye of the sitter is often engaged by that of the onlooker. Rich painterly effects of fabric, fur, hair and skin are all detailed with energy and skill.

Brilliant terracotta bust of Charles I painted to look like bronze, by Roubiliac.

Gallery 7: Antique Academy – As with landscape painting, portraiture emerges in the 18C as uncontroversial subject matter in which English artists achieved new heights: **Gainsborough, Reynolds, Raeburn, Ramsay** preserve natural likenesses of the leading thinkers, intellectuals, leaders and gentry of the Age of Enlightenment.

Sketches for altarpieces and ceiling frescoes in luminous colours reveal G B **Tiepolo**'s (1696-1770) technical mastery and deep, religious feeling.

The collection of silver was made by three generations of the Courtauld family, Huguenot refugees from western France; their work moved from the elegant Queen Anne style, through mid-century Rococo to the neo-Classical style in the late 1760s.

Important figures of 18C Italian painting include the Venetians Tiepolo, Canaletto and Guardi. All three excelled at capturing on canvas the sparkle of light and a suggestion of atmosphere in landscape. **Tiepolo** seems to allow his figures to float in space while **Canaletto** and **Guardi** specialised rather in topographical views favoured by Englishmen on the Grand Tour.

Galleries 8 and 9: Ante Room and Royal Academy Great Room – Light is the main preoccupation of the 19C French landscape painters at Barbizon and their followers the Impressionists. Bonnard, Boudin, Cézanne, Pissarro, Sisley, Seurat, Monet and Renoir all explored landscapes with stretches of water *(Deauville, Autumn Effect at Argenteuil, Boats on the Seine, Le Lac d'Annecy, The Bridge at Courbevoie)*.

Informality seems to pervade the early 20C collection. **Fry**'s collection of French pictures included **Bonnard**'s *Young woman in an interior*, a portrait of the artist's mistress and subsequent wife Marthe Boursin. Another key influence is **Derain** who painted simplified forms with bold colour.

E. Manet: *A Bar at the Folies-Bergère*

Courtauld Gallery

Manet's *A Bar at the Folies-Bergère* is a late work presented as a bold portrait of a young working woman; the wealthier members of the audience reflected in the mirror behind her seem oblivious of the trapeze artist wearing green pumps suspended in the top left corner. The sketch for *Le Déjeuner sur l'Herbe* (final version in Musée d'Orsay – Galerie du Jeu de Paume) was intentionally controversial, while being 'modern' Manet desperately hoped to earn respect from the Salon establishment; his figures, dressed in contemporary fashion, echo pictures from the Renaissance (Titian's *Concert champêtre* in the Louvre and Raimondi engraving after Raphael's *Judgement of Paris*). **Degas** was a close ally of Manet. He was particularly influenced by Japanese prints and photography, experimenting with viewpoints – down and across the stage in *Two dancers on stage* thereby leaving a large section of the picture plain empty. In *Woman at a window*, the light source is behind the sitter thereby obscuring her features completely.

Toulouse-Lautrec uses paint as if it were pastel, faces are lit and even distorted by artificial light *(Tête-a-tête Supper)* and volumes are flattened: in *Jane Avril at the entrance to the Moulin Rouge* Jane's fur-collared coat is defined as economically as the hat and coat hanging on a peg behind. **Cézanne**, considered as the 'father of modern art' builds a suggestion of space and depth into still-life *(Still-life with plaster Cupid)* and landscape *(Montagne Ste Victoire)* by means of colour (blues and greens give depth whereas reds and oranges give relief) and form arranged in the foreground, middleground and background. His figures *(The Card-players)* meanwhile are strong and direct studies of personality.

In *Nevermore* and *Te Reriora*, painted at the height of **Gauguin**'s Tahitian period, naturally posed figures are shown in the intimacy of the home, in harmony with a more primitive way of life. **Van Gogh** also developed his own individual style: *Peach blossom in the Crau* working in the mainstream Impressionist manner where fractured light is boldly captured by strong brushstrokes of thick paint. In his

Self-portrait with bandaged ear the artist is dressed in a greeny-blue coat which gives his eyes a haunting look; behind, Van Gogh acknowledges the inspiration he derived from Japanese prints, here apparent in the blue doorframe and easel used to suggest the features of the picture space. Just as Van Gogh, Degas and Monet use strokes of contrasting strong colour together, **Seurat** mechanically painted in dots of colour which if seen from a particular distance merge into tonal values. Comparative examples of Pointillism are the dusty interior scene *Young woman powdering herself* and the misty outdoor landscape *Bridge at Courbevoie*.

Galleries 10, 11: Private rooms – These rooms are now used for thematic displays drawn from the Institute's collection of Impressionist and Post-Impressionist works. Domestic interiors provide recurrent subjects for Walter Sickert, Roger Fry and Vanessa Bell, members of the Omega Workshops, an artistic faction of the **Bloomsbury Group** (*Lily Pond* four-fold screen by Duncan Grant). This collection of works by British artists should be considered as a selection made by discerning individuals for their own personal pleasure rather than for a major public museum, and as such modern art is presented as highly approachable.

Gallery 12: Royal Academy School of Painting – The room where the Royal Academy once presented its exhibitions is now used for special displays.

COVENT GARDEN★★

Map p 9 **(EX)**
⊖ Covent Garden

In the Middle Ages, St Giles consisted of a leper colony established outside the town limits by Queen Matilda in 1117 (dissolved 16C) and Covent Garden was a 40 acre walled property belonging to the Benedictines of Westminster. Henry's dissolution of the monastery at Westminster and confiscation of the garden was followed in 1552 by the first of the royal warrants which were to shape the area to its present form, thereby establishing several important traditions and much of its character.

Edward VI granted the land to the long-serving Tudor diplomat and soldier, John Russell, later 1st Earl of Bedford. The 4th Earl, on payment of £2 000 – Charles I was ever impecunious – obtained a licence in 1631 to erect buildings 'fitt for the habitacions of Gentlemen and men of ability' subject only to the approval of the King's Surveyor, Inigo Jones.

When the theatres, hitherto principally in Southwark, which had been closed during the Commonwealth, reopened after the Restoration (1660), Charles II – a lover of the theatre and its actresses – permitted women to tread the boards (perform on stage) for the first time and granted two royal warrants for theatres. The first resulted in the **Theatre Royal, Drury Lane** (1663), the second in the **Theatre Royal, Covent Garden** (1732) which opened with Congreve's *Way of the World*. The theatrical tradition of Covent Garden was so well established that, when the monopoly of the two royal theatres was broken by the Theatre Regulation Act in 1843, some 40 new theatres mushroomed within as many years; in 1987 the Theatre Museum opened.

Street entertainment in Covent Garden

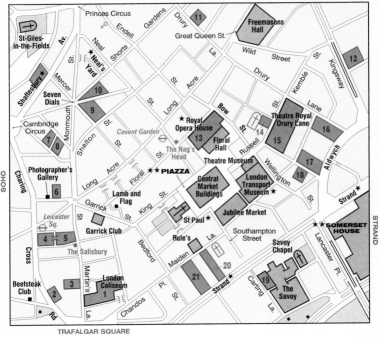

Today, a general air of prosperity and success pervades Covent Garden: old warehouses have carefully been adapted to accommodate enticing small shops and boutiques selling off-the-peg designer clothing to young people (Nicole Farhi, Calvin Klein, Paul Smith...), while long-established businesses continue to thrive (*The Lady Magazine*, Moss Bros, the map specialists Stamfords). Street cafés cater to the browsers by day and smart restaurants to the theatre goers by night.

★★The Piazza – The 1631 licence gave Inigo Jones the opportunity to design London's first square which he modelled after those he had seen in Italy: approach roads bisected the north and east sides interrupting the terraces of three-storey brick houses rising tall above a stone colonnade; behind the covered walkway nestled shops and coffee-houses. On the south side, meanwhile, ran the garden wall of the earl's new town house which fronted on the more fashionable Strand. By 1681, the area was populated with brothels, so when fashion departed, Bedford House was demolished (1700) and the area was developed.

★St Paul's Church – *Entrance from Bedford Street or down alley off King's Street.* A church was planned for the west side of the Piazza but the Earl was unwilling to afford anything 'much better than a barn' so Jones, declaring he should have 'the handsomest barn in England', designed the church with classical simplicity in red brick (the easterly stone facing was a later addition) covered with a pitched roof. Almost ever since the church was completed (1633) it has been closely associated with the world of entertainment: actors, artists, musicians and craftsmen – a wreath of limewood, carved by Grinling Gibbons for St Paul's Cathedral, now decorates the west screen (beside the door).

Overlooking the square is the famous Tuscan portico from which on 9 May 1662 Pepys watched the first ever **Punch and Judy** show in England; much later Shaw set the opening scene of *Pygmalion* there. Today, it provides a dramatic backdrop to jousting acrobats, mime artists and colourful clowns happy to perform to the passing public.

Covent Garden Market – The market was set up by the monks before the Reformation and persisted throughout the development of the Piazza; it was regularised by Letters Patent in 1670 and reconstituted in 1830 when royal permission was granted for special buildings to be erected. The **Central Market Buildings,** consisting of three parallel units running off a north-south colonnade, were designed by Charles Fowler (1832) and linked by glass canopies in 1872.

165

By the turn of the 20C, the market not only filled the Piazza but spilled into the neighbouring streets. Throughout the day, from midnight to noon, the district was brilliant with flowers and fruit, crowded with vendors, porters and buyers who frequented the area's open pubs and blocked the thoroughfares with lorries. In November 1974 the market and its characteristic reek of old cabbage moved to Nine Elms *(see Outer London: BATTERSEA)*, leaving Eliza Doolittle's flower market to franchised shops, canopied cafes, vaulted pubs and wine bars.

Jubilee Market is let out to stall holders selling antiques (Monday), general goods (Tuesday to Friday), hand-made crafts (Saturday, Sunday). The Jubilee Hall (1904) nearby is now a leisure centre.

★**London Transport Museum** ⊙ – The Transport Museum documents 200 years of history and technology. Formed in the 1920s and 30s by the London General Omnibus Company, the collection was moved from Syon Park in 1980 into part of the old flower market. Extensive refurbishment has provided 2 additional floors of steel and glass that complement the fabric of the original cast iron structure, which in its own time predated the building of St Pancras and Waterloo railway terminals. 14 permanent displays show the development of one of the world's earliest and largest networks, and its impact on London from trams and trolleybuses, the advent of the motor bus and its extended use into the suburbs, the first under ground – its design, form and function and finally the development of driver-less LRT (Light Rapid Transit) used by the Docklands Light Railway.

Real vehicles and fixtures withdrawn from service include the Shillibeer Horse Omnibus (1829-34), Type B Bus (1910-27), Metropolitan Railway Class A Loco motive (1866), ticket machines, signalling equipment, power generator control panels, etc. Technical information, such as manufacturing specifications, is available from touchscreen terminals; historical data is presented by video projections of newsreel, documentary and archive photographs. Interactive learning is encouraged for all ages with bus interiors and driver's cabs to be explored, scale models of steam/electric engines to be activated.

The **Harry Beck Gallery** – named after the engineer draftsman who adapted geograph ical conventions to design the first schematic map of the underground (1931) based on an electrical circuit diagram – displays London Transport maps. The **Ashfield Gallery,** named after the American pioneer of reliable cheap transport for the working middle classes, holds temporary exhibitions on secondary issues associated with the service (immigrant workforce, town-planning consequences, patron of Poster art and Poetry).

The **Frank Pick Gallery** exhibits selections by theme or series, of posters commissioned by London Transport from an archive of 5 000 or more, reflecting changes in fashion and taste, commemorating great events or achievements, sport or general interest. Works by important British artists include Graham Sutherland and Paul Nash. Pick (1878-1941) joined London Underground Electric Railway in 1906 and rose to become vice-chairman (1933-40). His vision transformed London Transport into a modern system, instigating a Corporate Image that has endured – fanatical about design, he advocated the universal application of particular typefaces for all printed documentation and station signage.

Theatre Museum ⊙ – The Theatre Museum of the Victoria and Albert Museum opened in April 1987 in the old flower market. On the ground floor a large mural a golden angel blowing a horn, ornate theatre boxes and an old box office set the theatrical theme. Its rich collections relate to all aspects of the performing arts opera, ballet, Edwardian melodrama, pantomimes, circus, toy theatre and plays popular music, music hall and puppetry, and include designs, archives, portraits, drawings, photographs and a wealth of other material. A gallery houses a semi-permanent display of the story of the performing arts. Two other galleries are devoted to temporary exhibitions. There are also a Paintings Gallery and a theatre for special events.

Theatre Royal, Drury Lane – The present Georgian theatre is the fourth on the site, one of London's largest (2 283 seats) and beautiful inside with symmetrical staircases, rising beneath the domed entrance to a circular balcony.

Killigrew's company, known as the King's Servants, opened in 1663 in the first theatre which was frequently patronised by the monarch who met 'pretty witty Nell' there in 1665. After being burnt down the theatre was replaced in 1674 by one designed by **Wren** which knew a golden age under **Garrick** (who was manager from 1747 to 1776 and lived at 27 Southampton Street), the Kembles and Sarah Siddons and was replaced in 1794 by a third building which opened under **Sheridan's** management with his new play *The School for Scandal*. Fire again destroyed the theatre and the present house, to designs by **Wyatt**, was erected in 1812. Kean Macready, Phelps, Irving, Ellen Terry, Forbes Robertson played there; Ivor Novello's dancing operettas filled the stage; *My Fair Lady* entranced there...

The **Baddeley Cake** is a Lane tradition even older than the ghost; it is provided from money left by an 18C actor, Robert Baddeley, and is cut on stage after the performance on *Twelfth Night*. The ghost emerges from the left circle wall (where a corpse and dagger were found bricked up in the 19C) to cross the auditorium and disappear.

Bow Street – 'So called as running in the shape of Bent Bow' according to John Strype, the early 18C mapmaker. By the mid 18C, when **Henry Fielding**, novelist, dramatist and magistrate and his half brother, John, the **Blind Beak**, moved into a house opposite the Opera House the street had become the haunt of footpads. At once the Fieldings began their crusade for penal and police reform which included the organisation in 1753 of the **Bow Street Runners**. The present building on the site of their house dates from 1881; it was the only police station in the country to be identified by white lights instead of the customary blue, because the blue reminded Queen Victoria of the death of her husband, the Prince Consort. In 1992 the Police moved to new premises at Charing Cross.

Bobbies and Coppers

Until the mid 18C thieves, miscreants and the innocent, footpads and murderers alike were seized by paid informers, thief-takers and hired strong men and brought before so-called 'trading justices'. If convicted malefactors were thrown into one of the infamous jails or, if convicted of any one of the then 156 capital offences, were hanged. Between 1170 and 1783 when the gallows were removed to Newgate, there were 50 000 hangings at Tyburn – an average of 12 public hangings a month.

Reform began in Bow Street under the honest magistracy of the Fieldings: Henry, the novelist, and his younger half-brother, John, the Blind Beak who recruited the first band of 6 honest men, the Bow Street Runners, to apprehend villains.

So great was the fear of a national police body that it was not until 1829 that Sir Robert Peel's bill was passed, founding the Metropolitan Police Force. The River Police were formed in 1800. When the 'Peelers' or 'Bobbies' first appeared on the streets they wore navy serge frock coats and top hats to attract as little attention as possible and, as now, were unarmed, except for a discreetly concealed truncheon.

The Metropolitan Police are under the jurisdiction of the Home Secretary; the City Police, founded in the same decade, are a separate body under the Corporation of the City of London.

★Royal Opera House – Charles II's patent was eventually secured by John Rich whose earlier presentation in 1728 of John Gay's *The Beggar's Opera* 'had the effect, as was ludicrously said, of making Gay rich and Rich gay' (Samuel Johnson). He leased a site, erected a playhouse and in December 1732 opened his Theatre Royal, Covent Garden, with Congreve's *Way of the World* which he followed with a revival of *The Beggar's Opera*. A second theatre, designed by Robert Smirke, after the first had burned down, opened in 1809 with a double bill lasting nearly 4 hours, presenting Kemble and Mrs Siddons in *Macbeth* plus a musical entertainment. The public not caring that rebuilding had cost £187 888 and convinced that price increases were due to exorbitant fees paid to foreign artists, drowned the stage in what came to be known as the OP or **Old Prices Riots**. Two months later prices were reduced (pit: 3s 6d). After a second fire in 1856 the present house was built, with a first floor portico and Classical pediment facing Bow Street, thus leaving room to the south for E M Barry's green-painted glass and iron structure, known as the **Floral Hall** which was used for promenade concerts and balls. When the theatre fell into financial straits the hall was leased to the market in 1887 and for nearly 100 years served as an annexe to the fruit and vegetable, not the flower, market. Inside the theatre, decoration has always been white and gold with deep crimson and rose hangings; the blue dome is also a dominant feature. From the first there was a Crush Room.

Extensions to the west (in the 1858 style) house new dressing rooms and rehearsal facilities. A second phase of improvements provides the opera house with an exquisitely restored auditorium with raised seating, improved sightlines and air conditioning, modern facilities for storing and shifting scenery and for staging big productions. The iron and glass Floral Hall is used to great effect as the main foyer with escalators rising to the mezzanine galleries which accommodate bars and restaurant – panoramic views of the piazza from the loggias. There are also airy rehearsal studios for the ballet company and ample space for the costume departments under the eaves.

The Sadler's Wells Ballet transferred to the house in 1946 and in 1956 it was granted a charter by the Queen to become **The Royal Ballet**.

COVENT GARDEN

The area's long standing theatrical association attracted builders of new theatre when the passage of the Theatre Regulation Act in 1843 broke the Covent Garden and Drury Lane monopoly and some 40 new playhouses were licensed and erected in as many years.

Royal Masonic Institution – *Great Queen Street*. The Masons occupy the greater part of the street which includes 18C houses *(nos 27-29)* and the **Freemasons Hall** (1927-33).

★**Neal's Yard** – The picturesque yard, complete with period hoists, dovecote, trees in tubs and geranium-filled window-boxes has attracted eco-friendly shopkeepers: vegetarian food bars, organic produce and essential remedies; other specialist shops are to be found in Neal Street.

St Giles-in-the-Fields ⊘ – The church was rebuilt in 1734 by Flitcroft after the styles of Wren and James Gibbs; the steeple rising directly from the façade echoes St Martin-in-the-Fields. The pulpit in the north aisle was used for almost 50 years by John and Charles Wesley when it was in their 'West Street Chapel'.

Seven Dials – Seven Dials derives its name from a 40ft Doric column, adorned with a sundial on each face, erected at the centre of seven radiating streets when the area, a notorious slum, was rehabilitated in the early 1690s by Thomas Neale. It was pulled down by a mob in 1773 on a rumour that treasure was buried underneath it. Crime was rife in the area in the 18C-19C. A replica of the pillar has been erected on the original site.

Pubs, Clubs and Coffee-houses – The quarter's oldest tavern is the **Lamb and Flag (Rose Street):** it opened in 1623 as the Cooper's Arms and became known unofficially as the Bucket of Blood from 1679, after an incident involving John Dryden who was attacked outside while on his way home to Long Acre.
Two traditional clubs still flourish: the **Garrick** (founded in 1831) has since 1864 occupied its purpose-built premises in the new street which the club requested should be named after the actor *(no 15)*; on the walls hang an unrivalled collection of theatrical portraits that may be glimpsed from the street on a summer evening; the **Beefsteak** *(9 Irving Street)* is a dining club that dates from 1876 and which has always drawn its members from the worlds of politics, the theatre and literature.
Of the 17C and 18C coffee-houses for which Covent Garden was as famous as the City, none remain: **Will's**, frequented by 'all the wits in town' according to Pepys used to stand at no 1 Bow Street, **Button's** in Russell Street, the **Bedford**, the **Piazza**.

Rule's – *34-35 Maiden Lane*. Caricatures and prints recall the law, theatre and artists, in London's oldest restaurant and oyster bar, established in 1798 by Benjamin Rule and his sons, 'who rush wildly about with dozens of oysters and pewters of stout'.

The fashion for coffee-houses was introduced to London during the Commonwealth (1652). Originally they served as meeting places in the City for the exchange of business intelligence. By 1715 there were over 500 not only in the City but also in Covent Garden and the Strand, St James's, Mayfair and Westminster. Customers of like interests would gather regularly, even daily, in the same houses or call at several houses at different times to pick up messages and even letters or to read the news sheets, which at first circulated from one house to another, and the later newspapers (*Daily Courant*, 1702) which were available to customers for the price of a single cup of hot chocolate or coffee. At the end of the 18C the City coffee-houses reverted to being pubs and the West End houses disappeared, except Boodle's and White's which became clubs.

A new concept in travel planning.
When you want to calculate a trip distance or visualise a detailed itinerary; when you need information on hotels,
restaurants or campsites, consult Michelin on the Internet.
Visit our Web site to discover our full range of services for travellers:
www.michelin-travel.com.

HYDE PARK - KENSINGTON GARDENS ★★

Map pp 6-7 (**A-DXY**)

⊖ Hyde Park Corner; Marble Arch; Lancaster Gate; Queensway

n Saxon times the acres were part of the Manor of Eia which, until 'resumed by the King' in 1536, belonged to Westminster Abbey. Henry VIII enclosed the area and having stocked it with deer kept it as a royal chase. In the 16C and later the park was used for military manoeuvres and encampments. In 1637 it was opened as a public park and the crowds came to watch horse-racing and other sports only to be debarred when it was sold by the Commonwealth to a private buyer who, to Pepys' indignation, charged for admission. At the Restoration the contract of sale was cancelled and the park again became public although access was restricted, since it was surrounded by a high wall, replaced by railings only in 1825.

The activities of those who frequented and made use of the park were even more diverse in the 18C and 19C than now: the last formal royal hunt was held in 1768; pits were dug along the east and north boundaries to supply clay for bricks to build the new houses of Marylebone and Mayfair; gunpowder magazines and arms depots were sited in isolated parts; there was a large reservoir on the eastern boundary; soldiers were executed against the wall in the northeast corner; at the same time it was a fashionable carriage and riding promenade first round the road known as the Tour and then **the Ring** (originally a small inner circle) or along the Row **(Rotten Row)**. It was a convenient place for duels and a common spot for footpads (Horace Walpole wrote to all his friends about being robbed in the park in 1749).

Great Exhibition –

The most extraordinary event to take place in the park was the Great Exhibition, the first in the international field, which was conceived and planned by Prince Albert and opened in less than two years despite initial bitter and often spiteful opposition in parliament. The huge exhibition was housed in the **Crystal Palace**, a vast iron and glass structure, designed by Joseph Paxton, the Duke of Devonshire's gardener at Chatsworth. The palace was capable of rapid erection owing to the use of prefabricated unit parts and tall enough to enclose the giant elms on the site; it was the problem posed by sparrows roosting in the trees which caused Wellington's celebrated retort 'Try sparrow-hawks, Ma'am'.

Crystal Palace in 1851

The products of 13 937 exhibitors, displayed inside, demonstrating man's inventiveness and 19C British achievement in particular, attracted huge interest. Queen Victoria, Wellington and some 6 030 195 others visited the exhibition and it made a net profit of just under £200 000. The profit was used to establish the museums in South Kensington *(listed separately)*. The Crystal Palace *(see Outer London: DULWICH)* was dismantled and re-erected at Sydenham where it was destroyed by fire in 1936.

HYDE PARK

It was Pitt the Elder in the 17C who aptly called the former deer park 'the lungs of London' and still today, the extensive green acres are put to many uses. It is a place of relaxation and free speech, a rallying ground for parades and royal salutes, since 1800 a burial ground for pet dogs (at the Victoria Gate). Every day, people flock to the park to walk their dogs, jog, ride, go boating, swim (even if it means breaking the ice on Christmas morning), roller blade, sail model boats, feed the pigeons, play bicycle polo, rounders, tennis or bowls...

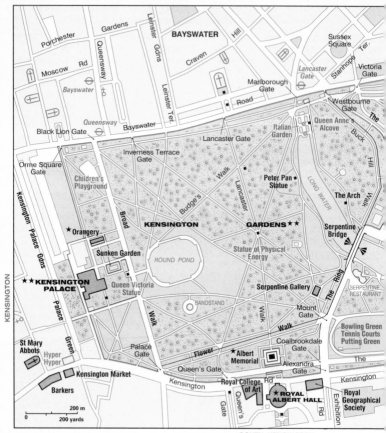

SOUTH KENSINGTON

Marble Arch – At the northeast corner stands a fine triumphal arch of Italian (Seravezza) white marble with three closely patterned bronze gates. Modelled on the Arch of Constantine in Rome by **John Nash** (1827) it was intended to stand before Buckingham Palace, a monument to celebrate the end of the Napoleonic wars but the central archway was not wide enough to accommodate the Gold State Coach: when Queen Victoria needed to enlarge the palace to accommodate her expanding family of nine children, the arch was dismantled (1837) and in 1851 was rebuilt where the **Tyburn gallows** had stood until 1783 when hangings were removed to Newgate. For many years it accommodated a Police reporting centre for bobbies on the beat. Two narrow spiral staircases at either end access a broad central room with in-built furniture.

Speakers' Corner is a relatively modern feature of the park; not until 1872 did the government recognise the need for a place of public assembly and free speech. Anyone may mount their soap box and address the crowds irrespective of creed (Darwinians or Hebrew scholars), colour or persuasion (Communists or Nationalists) as long as the speaker does not blaspheme or incite a breach of the peace.

At the bottom end of Park Lane stands the **Queen Elizabeth Gate**, erected in 1993 in celebration of Queen Elizabeth, the Queen Mother's 93rd birthday. The two sets of gates, designed by Giuseppe Lund, provide a cast-iron screen for the central lion and unicorn panels sculpted by David Wynne.

Inside the park is Richard Westmacott's so-called **Achilles** statue (18ft), cast from captured cannon and modelled on an antique horse tamer on the Quirinal Hill in Rome – it is said to have embarrassed the women who presented it to Wellington by its nakedness. Opposite is Byron meditating on a rock, in his own words '... worst bust'.

Hyde Park Corner – The southeast corner of the park was transformed in 1825-28 by the erection of a triple arched **screen**, crowned by a sculptured frieze and a **triumphal arch** surmounted by a colossal equestrian statue of the Duke of Wellington, intended by Decimus Burton to mark the royal route from the palace to the park. In 1883 the arch was moved to its present position, the statue was transferred to Aldershot and replaced by a quadriga (1912). The present **Wellington Monument**, placed before the entrance to Apsley House *(see PICCADILLY)*, is by

170

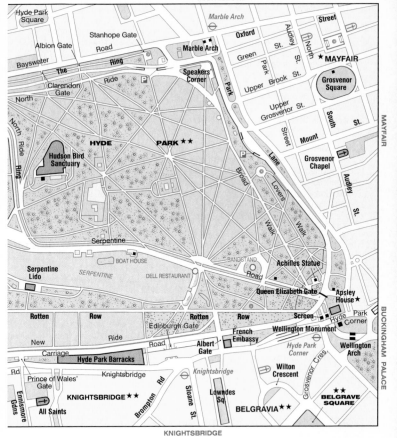

MARYLEBONE

KNIGHTSBRIDGE

Boehm (1834-90); cast from captured guns, it shows the duke mounted on his horse Copenhagen, guarded by a Grenadier, a Royal Highlander, a Welsh Fusilier and an Inniskilling Dragoon. With his back to Park Lane stands *David leaning on Goliath's sword* (1925; Derwent Wood), while facing the Lanesborough Hotel *(see KNIGHTSBRIDGE- BELGRAVIA)* stands the memorial of the Machine Gun Corps and the Royal Artillery War Memorial.

On Carriage Road (south side) the angular dark red brick building is Sir Basil Spence's **Hyde Park Barracks** and stables (1970-71). From here the Guardsmen ride down to Horse Guards' when the Queen returns to London.

At the centre of the park is the **Hudson Bird Sanctuary**, marked by the Jacob Epstein sculpture *Rima* (1925), where over 90 species have been recorded.

The **Serpentine Bridge** (1826-28), designed by John Rennie, spans the Long Water and the Serpentine. It also links Hyde Park to Kensington Gardens.

KENSINGTON GARDENS

The gardens, originally 20 acres and extended finally to 275, were at their prime under Queen Mary, Queen Anne and Queen Caroline, consort of George II and the Royal Gardeners, Henry Wise (portrait in Kensington Palace) and his successor in 1728, Charles Bridgman. The original style of geometric and formal wilderness was transformed in the 18C when an octagonal basin, the **Round Pond**, was constructed facing the State Apartments of Kensington Palace *(see below)*. With the pond as focal point, borders were planted around it with flowers and small trees and avenues radiating north and southeast and due east to the New River, now the Serpentine and the Long Water terminating in the Italian Garden and Queen Anne's Alcove. Other features of the period which persist are the **Broad Walk**, recently re-planted, and the **Orangery★** with a massive stone centrepiece by Hawksmoor (1705). Later additions are the Edwardian **sunken garden** in which pleached limes surround brilliant flower beds and a long canal, the statue of **Peter Pan** (1912) to the west and **The Arch** sculpted by Henry Moore in 1979 from Roman Travertine *(removed for restoration 1996)* to the east by the Long Water and the **Flower Walk** north of the Albert Memorial.

Tyburn gallows – The gallows, first a tree, then a gibbet, was finally replaced by an iron triangle for multiple executions. From the Tower or Newgate the condemned were drawn through the streets on hurdles to be hanged (and sometimes drawn and quartered too) before the great crowds who gathered to hear the last words, see the spectacle and enjoy the side shows. Popular victims were toasted in gin or beer as they passed. A stone in the park railings in the Bayswater Road marks the site.

Serpentine Gallery ⊙ – This small compact pavilion, shaded by great trees holds exhibitions of modern art. *Check press for details.*

★**Albert Memorial** – Proverbial as the epitome of mid-Victorian taste and sentiment, the memorial which stands at the summit of 4 wide flights of granite steps, was designed by Sir George Gilbert Scott (1872) as a neo-Gothic spire (175ft), ornamented with mosaics, pinnacles and a cross. A gilded figure (14ft) of the Prince Consort sits at the centre surrounded by allegorical statues. Around the podium runs a frieze of 169 named architects, artists, composers, poets. *For details of Royal Albert Hall and surrounding buildings across Kensington Road, turn to SOUTH KENSINGTON.*

★★**Kensington Palace** ⊙ – 'The house is very noble, tho not greate, the Gardens about it very delicious'. Since its purchase in 1689 by William III, Kensington Palace has passed through three phases: under the House of Orange it was the monarch's private residence with **Wren** as principal architect; under the early Hanoverians it was designated as a royal palace with **William Kent** in charge of alterations; since 1760 it has been a residence for members of the royal family notably the late Diana, Princess of Wales.

'Kensington is ready' wrote Queen Mary to her husband, William, in July 1690 and, disliking Whitehall, she moved in. The house was not to be free of builders and carpenters until 1702 when it had grown from an early 17C Jacobean house, rebuilt in 1661, to a rambling mansion around three courts. Throughout Wren kept to a style befitting a modest house – it was known as Kensington House in the 17C and 18C – in red brick beneath slate roofs.

Boating on the Serpentine

Kensington Palace

Crown copyright HRP - Andrew Holt

Decoration was limited to the finely carved William and Mary monogram in the hood above the entrance to the Queen's Staircase and the royal arms on the pediment of the turreted clock tower. When Hawksmoor, working for Wren in 1695-96, designed the south front, the only embellishment was a central attic screen topped by Portland stone vases. Subsequent external modifications were of a minor character: a Georgian doorway acceding to the Queen's Staircase, a portico on the west front.

The **State Apartments** are approached up the Queens' Staircase designed by Wren (1691).

The Queen's Apartments: Gallery, Closet, Dining and Drawing Rooms, Bedroom – The 84ft gallery is rich in carving, with cornice and door-heads by **William Emmett** and sumptuous surrounds to the gilt Vauxhall mirrors above the fireplace in the gallery by Grinling Gibbons in 1691. Portraits in the rooms are personal: *Peter the Great* in armour by Kneller in commemoration of his visit in 1698, *William III* as King and Prince of Orange, Queen Mary by Wissing, *Anne Hyde* by Lely and in the adjoining closet where the final quarrel (1710) took place between 'Mrs Freeman' and 'Mrs Morley', *Queen Anne* and *William, Duke of Gloucester* by Kneller. In the Dining Room there is a painting of Katherine Elliot who was James II's nurse; in the Drawing Room Kneller painted *Queen Anne* in profile and the first Royal Gardener, *Henry Wise*. The furniture includes an 18C mahogany cabinet (gallery), a late 17C inlaid cabinet, 17C-18C Oriental porcelain and a fine Thomas Tompion barometer of c 1695, one of many possessed by William III who was a chronic asthmatic (drawing room). In the bedroom are a state bed of James II and an ornate, mid 17C, Boulle writing cabinet with gilt mounts, marquetry and semi-precious stone inlays.

Privy and Presence Chambers, King's Staircase and Gallery – The lofty rooms designed by Colen Campbell in 1718-20 for George I, bear William Kent's strong decorative imprint. The **Privy Chamber**, above busts of distinguished 17C-18C scientists and David Garrick, blue and white Oriental porcelain and Mortlake tapestries of the months, has an allegorical ceiling of George I as Mars; the **Presence Chamber**, a red and blue on white ceiling with arabesque decoration in the Pompeian manner by Kent in 1724 (the earliest in England and later popularised by Adam). Remaining from the 17C are the cornice and the Grinling Gibbons pearwood overmantel.

The **King's Grand Staircase**, built by Wren in 1689, was altered first in 1692-93 when the Tijou iron balustrade was incorporated and again in 1696 for George I by Kent who covered walls and ceiling with *trompe l'œil* paintings including a dome and gallery of contemporary courtiers.

The King's Gallery – The gallery was intended as the setting for the greatest pictures in the royal collection and decoration was, therefore, limited to an elaborately carved cornice, enriched window surrounds and the practical and ornamental wind-dial (1624) connected from its position over the fireplace to a vane on the roof. The ceiling by Kent depicts scenes from the story of Ulysses. The gallery is hung with 17C paintings from the Royal collection.

Although the 19C **Victorian Rooms** were redecorated by Queen Mary, all else belonged to and epitomises Queen Victoria and her family: furniture, wallpaper, ornaments, portraits, photographs, toys and dollshouse, dried flowers under glass domes, beading, tasselling, commemorative china... The **Council Chamber** at the far end of the east front, contains mementoes of the 1851 Exhibition, including the famous picture of the opening crowds in the Crystal Palace, a garish jewel casket with inlaid portraits of the royal family and a massive carved Indian ivory throne and footstool. Only the ceiling of arabesques, figures and medallions remains of Kent's Baroque decoration in the **King's Drawing Room.** The musical clock (1730) depicts four famous figures (Alexander, Cyrus, Ninos, Augustus). In the **Cupola Room,** high and square with a vault patterned in blue and gold, where Queen Victoria was baptised, are trophies and gilded Classical statues and busts divided by fluted pilasters and a colossal marble chimneypiece.

The Red Saloon in which Queen Victoria held her Accession Privy Council in 1837 and the room in which she is said to have been born in 1819 are also on view.

The **Court Dress Collection** traces the evolution of court dress from the 18C to the 20C. Dictated by protocol, elegant dresses and accessories (Orders of Chivalry), court suits and ceremonial uniforms resplendent with gold and silver, lace and embroidery, worn at levées and at court are presented in contemporary settings. More contemporary exhibits include pieces from the Queen's wardrobe, largely designed by the late Sir Norman Hartnell to suit the sovereign's various State functions.

Kensington Palace Gardens and Green – The private avenue, guarded at either end, is now almost exclusively the preserve of ambassadorial residences and embassies of which the most remarkable is the modern Czechoslovak complex at the north end. The original houses were built in the mid 19C when the palace kitchen gardens were sold for development. More or less Italianate in style their opulence earned the avenue the sobriquet, Millionaires' Row.

To the northwest of Kensington Gardens is **Notting Hill Gate**, a fashionable residential area that boasts London's oldest working cinema; separating the gardens from the Bayswater Road are the railings where artists exhibit their works on Sunday *(see BAYSWATER – PADDINGTON).*

★**Portobello Road** – The winding road, once a cart-track through the fields from the Notting Hill turnpike, comes unhurriedly to life on Saturdays as a motley crowd arrives to search the stalls and shop tables for Victoriana, later silver, chinaware, stamps, small items *(see INTRODUCTION – Shopping).*

The last weekend in August, the area is thronged with revellers attending the Notting Hill Carnival.

KENSINGTON★★

Map p 4 (**ABXY**)
High Street Kensington; South Kensington

The village of Kensington was for centuries manorial, with a few large houses at the centre of fields. It increased slowly from small houses lining the main road to squares and tributary streets as estates and separate parcels of land were sold.

Among the famous mansions were Nottingham House – later Kensington Palace, Campden House, Notting Hill House later Aubrey House, Holland Park House and, on the site of the Albert Hall, Gore House, the home of William Wilberforce until 1823 and for 12 years from 1836 the residence of 'the gorgeous' Lady Blessington whose circle included Wellington, Brougham, Landseer, Tom Moore, Bulwer Lytton, Thackeray, Dickens, Louis Napoleon and other such poets, novelists, artists, journalists, French exiles...

Kensington High Street – In 1846 when Thackeray and his daughters moved into a house in Young Street, the eldest described Kensington High Street as 'a noble highway, skirted by beautiful old houses with scrolled iron gates', while Thackeray himself noted that there were 'omnibuses every two minutes'. Within a few years the population was to multiply from 70 to 120 000; shops spread along both sides of the High Street.

Down Young Street is **Kensington Square,** one of the oldest in London with houses dating from the 17C-19C, as varied in design as the people who have lived in it: Sir Hubert Parry *(no 17),* John Stuart Mill *(no 18),* Mrs Patrick Campbell *(no 33).* The two oldest houses are nos 11 and 12 in the southeast corner; a cartouche over the door mentions previous owners: the Duchess Mazarin (Henrietta Mancini, niece of the Cardinal) 1692-98, Archbishop Herring 1737 and Talleyrand 1792-94.

Over British Home Stores (BHS) is the **Roof Garden** ⊙ *(no 99 Kensington High Street; entrance in Derry Street),* laid out in the 1930s in three sections: Spanish, Tudor and a water garden whose fountain is fed by an Artesian well.

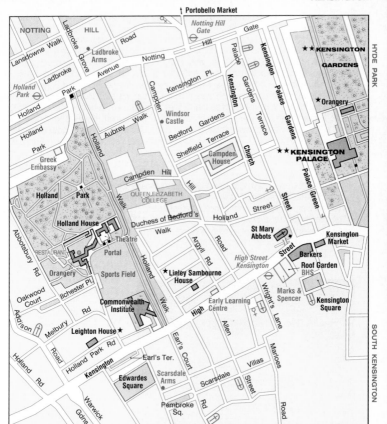

Kensington Church Street – Commercial and residential developments stretch right across the Campden House estate. On the corner with the High Street an unusual vaulted cloister leads to the parish church of **St Mary Abbots**, built in 19C Early English style, with a towering spire (278ft high), although the dedication goes back to the 11C.

In the churchyard sits the tomb of Elizabeth Johnston, modelled by John Soane in 1784 on the oval sarcophagus of Cecilia Metella.

★ **Linley Sambourne House** ⊘ – *18 Stafford Terrace*. Edward Linley Sambourne, a leading *Punch* cartoonist and book illustrator, moved into this later Victorian town house on its completion in 1874. The original wall decoration by William Morris *(see index)* and the furniture, listed in an inventory dated 1877, have survived largely unaltered.

Cartoons by Sambourne and his contemporaries line the stairs; pictures occupy every inch of spare wall space in the crowded rooms. The fan *(principal bedroom)* signed by Millais, Frith, Alma-Tadema and Watts testifies to the family's artistic connections; the back bedroom typifies Edwardian bachelorhood. The stained glass panels were designed by Sambourne.

Note the enclosed window boxes like mini greenhouses, the aquarium on the landing, the ventilators incorporated in the ceiling roses, the bell pulls and speaking tubes complete with whistles.

Commonwealth Institute – *Kensington High Street*. The unique tent-shaped building, with its 4 peaked, green copper roofs supported on glass curtain walls, was opened by the Queen in 1962 to replace the former Imperial Institute, opened in 1893 by Queen Victoria, of which only the imposing Queen's Tower *(see below)* survives.

This modern complex equipped with three floors of gallery space and an area for live theatrical, dance performances is dedicated to celebrating the different cultures of the 50 commonwealth countries.

Holland Park ⊘ – It is 100-200 years since Holland House was in its heyday and approaching 400 since the City merchant and courtier Sir Walter Cope built the first large house in the scattered village of Kensington. The mansion, characterised by Dutch gables, and known until 1624 as Cope's Castle, was lavishly furnished, equipped with a library and soon became a place of entertainment for king and court. Advanced wings on either side of the central range were added by Cope's daughter whose husband, in 1624 was made Earl Holland in recognition of soldierly and other such services. The tradition of hospitality was maintained in the 2nd Earl's time and extended when his widow married **Joseph Addison.**

In the mid 18C Holland House was acquired by the politician Henry Fox, who was also created Baron Holland. He was rich, a spendthrift and corrupt; he knew everyone, entertained lavishly and fathered a second son, **Charles James Fox** who continued to frequent the house when it passed to his nephew, 3rd Baron Holland, politician, writer, literary patron and the last great host of Holland House. Among those who dined and visited frequently were the Prince Regent, Sheridan, Wilberforce, William Lamb – the future Lord Melbourne, Byron, Talleyrand, Louis Napoleon, Macaulay (whose own house, Holly Lodge, stood on the site now occupied by Queen Elizabeth College), William IV, and almost the last visitor, Prince Albert; little wonder that Sydney Smith in a bread and butter letter to his hostess had once written 'I do not believe all Europe can produce as much knowledge, wit and worth as passes in and out of your door'.

Today, the restored east wing and George VI Hostel by Sir Hugh Casson serve as a youth hostel. In summer the forecourt is canopied to accommodate open-air performances of opera and dance. A restaurant occupies part of the 17C stable block converted to a conservatory in the early 19C; the Ice House and Orangery, meanwhile are used for private functions and exhibitions.

The woodland has been re-established and the gardens replanted after long neglect; peacocks flaunt their plumages in the gardens and water tinkles through the Japanese garden.

Arab Hall, Leighton House

★ **Leighton House** ⊙ – *12 Holland Park Road.* The Orientalist **Lord Leighton** (1830-96), President of the Royal Academy, Victorian painter supreme, 'high priest of the cult of eclectic beauty' as he has been described, remains most originally reflected in the house which he built for himself in 1866. True to High Victorian fashions in art the house is furnished and appointed to the highest standards: domestic rooms upstairs contrast with the entertaining rooms on the ground floor. The **Arab Hall** is covered with exotic panels of glazed tiles imported from the Middle East (13C, 16C and 17C tiles from Rhodes, Damascus and Cairo), some bearing formal floral arrangements, others Arab inscriptions from the Koran set below an elaborate frieze of fabulous animals, mythological birds and stylised flora designed by **William de Morgan** *(see BATTER-SEA – De Morgan Foundation).* A mosaic floor spreads around a bubbling, cool fountain inspired by Leighton's own travels and those of such friends as the flamboyant Sir Richard Burton (Translator of *The Arabian Nights, The Kama Sutra, The Perfumed Garden*). The dining room painted in deep red is particularly stunning in the early spring, its interior contrasting brilliantly with the view of new green grass and fresh bluebells...

Upstairs, the walls are hung with pictures by Leighton, Burne-Jones, Millais and their contemporaries.

Edwardes Square – Tucked away behind the Odeon Cinema, and the uniform brick range of large houses known as Earl's Terrace (1800-10) is this elegant square. The east and west ranges are composed of more modest 3-storey houses (1811-20) complete with balcony, garden and square ironwork, built as a single undertaking. In the southeast corner stands the **Scarsdale Arms**, a flowered Victorian pub 'established in 1837'.

To the south is **Pembroke Square**, lined on three sides with Georgian ranges, matching iron balconies and, in the southeast corner, its pub.

KNIGHTSBRIDGE – BELGRAVIA★★

Map p 7 (**CDY**)
⊖ South Kensington, Knightsbridge

Until the end of the 18C **Knightsbridge** was an unkempt village beside a stone bridge across the Westbourne River (marked by Albert Gate). As it lay outside London and a major highway it soon accommodated spitals, cattle markets and slaughterhouses, taverns, footpads and highway robbers, and pleasure gardens.
In 1813 Benjamin **Harvey** opened a linen draper's (Harvey Nichols), in 1849 Henry **Harrod** took over a small grocer's shop; today Knightsbridge is the shopping ground of the elegant and wealthy residents of Belgravia and Chelsea.

Brompton Road – The triangle between Kensington Road and Brompton Road developed as a residential district in typical Georgian fashion around a series of squares: **Trevor Square** (1818), **Brompton Square** (1826), **Montpelier Square★** (1837); the houses have trim stucco ground floors and basements with trick upper storeys, neat windows and doors and slender balconies. Linking the squares are narrow streets, mews and closes lined by one-up one-down colour-washed cottages with handkerchief-sized front gardens (Rutland Street). **Ennismore Gardens**, although only slightly later in date, is mid-Victorian in style, its stucco ranges having square pillared porches; **All Saints**, also built at that time in the Early English style, is now a Russian Orthodox Church.

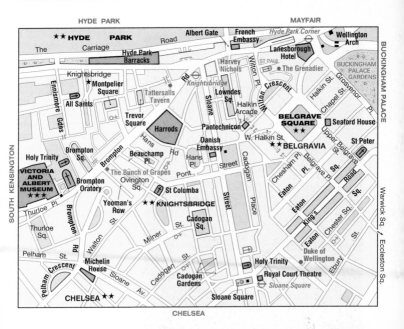

Oratory of St Philip Neri (Brompton Oratory) ☉ – The main body of the church was designed (1881) by Herbert Gribble in the Italian Baroque style in Portland stone, the dome and lantern, meanwhile, was planned by George Sherrin (1895-96) so as to span the exceptionally wide and lofty nave. The 18C Italian Baroque statues of the Twelve Apostles by Giuseppe Mazzuoli (1644-1725) used to stand in Siena Cathedral. The Baroque pulpit and much of the mosaic decoration are by Commendatore Formilli. The inlaid wooden floor and carved choirstalls inlaid with ivory date from the previous church. In St Wilfrid's Chapel is a photographic replica of the original triptych by Rex Whistler depicting Thomas More and John Fisher; the altar is early 18C Flemish Baroque.
A monument by Chavalliaud to Cardinal Newman, who preached at the official opening in 1884, stands in the forecourt.
Hidden behind Brompton Parish Church is the attractive **Holy Trinity Church** garden; the building dates from 1827 and the chancel by Blomfield from 1879.

Harrods – Since 1905 the shop, which claims to sell everything, has been housed in the familiar terracotta building with towers and cupolas; the lofty **food halls** are decorated with *Art Nouveau* wall tiles *(see INTRODUCTION).*

Sloane Street – The street, first developed in 1773 to link Knightsbridge to Chelsea and the river, has been rebuilt piecemeal. The **Danish Embassy** (1976-77) was designed by Ove Arup. The area west of Sloane Street was developed late in the 18C and is known as **Hans Town**. The tall red brick building, purpose-built to provide London lodgings, belong for the most part to the Cadogan Estate.

177

St Columba's ⊘ – *Pont Street.* The London Church of Scotland (1950-55) was designed by Edward Maufe; its square stone tower capped by a green cupola stands on the axis of Pont Street.

In the late 19C the area around **Cadogan Square** and Cadogan Gardens was rebuilt in unfading red brick, nicknamed 'Pont Street Dutch'.

★★BELGRAVIA

It was probably George IV's decision to transform Buckingham House into Buckingham Palace which provided the impetus for the development of Belgravia (150 acres), part of the Grosvenor estate. Until 1821 it consisted of the Five Fields and market gardens, bordered along Upper Grosvenor Place by houses and stables and St George's Hospital *(see below)*. The site was prepared with soil excavated from St Katharine Docks *(see Outer London: DOCKLANDS)*. It was developed to the basic terrace design of the architect, **George Basevi**, varied by the addition of combinations of a restricted number of related forms of ornament to afford a strong overall family resemblance. The builder was **Thomas Cubitt** *(see index)*. By 1827 **Wilton Crescent, Belgrave Square** *(see below)*, Eaton Place and **Eaton Square** had been erected. Cubitt and Basevi were probably responsible for the adjoining square and streets extending far south into Pimlico: Eccleston (formerly New) Square, Warwick Square, Upper Belgrave Street, Belgrave Place and Chester Square.

Homage to Leonardo, Belgrave Square

K. Brett

★★Belgrave Square – The square (10 acres) is bordered by twinned, but not identical, ranges consisting of a uniform three storeys, cornice and upper floor, all in white stucco. The centres and ends are in the Corinthian style with urns and balustrades, pillared porches and an attic screen decorated with statues. Three of the corners are canted allowing two roads to enter on either side of a detached house also facing the square. The ironwork matches the fence enclosing the central garden; a bronze statue of Simon Bolivar stands in a bay at the southeast corner. Seaford House *(opposite)* was the residence from 1841 to 1870 of the statesman, Lord John Russell.

Wilton Crescent – The diameter and inner perimeter are lined by stucco terraces. The 17C brick terraces of Wilton Place predate by a century St Paul's Church, which was erected in Perpendicular style by Thomas Cundy in 1843 on the site of a guards' barracks, still recalled in local street and pub names.

Lowndes Square – The square is not part of the Grosvenor estate; it was developed separately and largely rebuilt in the 20C.

Pantechnicon – The august Doric columned warehouse dates from 1830. On either side and in West Halkin Street and Halkin Arcade are a number of small shops dealing in luxury goods.

St Peter's – The church was erected in 1827 in the Classical style, as part of the original development project; owing to its position parallel with Eaton Square there is no vista of the elegant portico. The interior was refurbished after a fire in 1988.

Lanesborough Hotel – *Hyde Park Corner.* The handsome building (1827-29) has a central porch with square columns facing east, flanked by two wings. It was designed by William Wilkins to house St George's Hospital, which was founded in 1719 in Lanesborough House in Westminster and moved to Tooting in 1980.

For Apsley House see PICCADILLY.

LAMBETH

Map pp 6-7 (EFY)
⊖ Lambeth North

In the Middle Ages the public horse-ferry from Westminster landed at Lambeth and it was here, close but not too close to the crown, that the Archbishop of Canterbury obtained a parcel of land on which he built himself a London seat, first known as Lambeth House, then **Lambeth Palace.** From outside the high crenellated wall one can glimpse the mellow red brick building, begun in the early 13C, the Lollards' Tower (1434-35) and the Great Hall with hammerbeam roof. The magnificent gateway dates from 1490.

Museum of Garden History ⊘ – The Museum was founded by the Tradescant Trust (1977) in the redundant church of St Mary-at-Lambeth, which contains the graves of the two John Tradescants, father and son, who planted the first physic garden in 1628 at their house in Lambeth and were gardeners to the first Lord Salisbury and Charles I.

The centrepiece in the churchyard is a garden, including a knot garden, created with 17C plants. There is an exhibition of historic garden tools. Lawrence Lee designed the window depicting Adam and Eve and the Tradescants.

At their house they also exhibited a collection of 'all things strange and rare' which later, under their neighbour, Elias Ashmole, formed the nucleus of the Ashmolean Museum in Oxford. Admiral Bligh of the *Bounty*, who lived at 100 Lambeth Road, is buried in the churchyard and commemorated in the church.

St Thomas's Hospital – The red and white buildings have scarcely changed in outward appearance since being built in 1868-71. In the 1970s some of the eastern blocks were replaced by buildings of 7-14 storeys containing treatment centres, clinics, medical school...

From 13C infirmary to 20C teaching hospital – The hospital, at first dedicated to St Thomas Becket, originated in an infirmary set up early in the 13C in Southwark by the Augustinians of St Mary Overie Church, possibly immediately after the great fire of 1212. By 1228 the priory quarters were too small and a hospital was built opposite on a site which eventually extended the length of St Thomas Street. It was endowed by Dick Whittington *(see index)* with a laying-in ward for unmarried mothers. In the 16C, although St Thomas's was caring for the sick, the orphaned and the indigent, it was forfeited, as a conventual establishment, to Henry VIII and closed, only to be rescued in 1552 by the City which purchased it for £647 4s, and rededicated it to Thomas the Apostle (Thomas Becket having been decanonised).

The story since is one of expansion, of removal to Lambeth in the 19C, of research and development, of the foundation of the Nightingale Fund Training School for Nurses, of ten aerial attacks between September 1940 and July 1944 when at least one operating theatre was always open...

Florence Nightingale Museum ⊘ – *2 Lambeth Palace Road.* The work of Florence Nightingale (1820-1910), nicknamed the 'Lady of the Lamp' by the British soldiers she nursed during the Crimean War (1854-56) has become legendary in pioneering healthcare. Photographs and written panels are supplemented by various personal exhibits: souvenirs of her girlhood and family; case notes, a prescription book, her medicine chest; a Scutari lamp and relics from the battlefields; Crimean medals and commemorative pottery; copies of her many publications on nursing and the organisation and design of hospitals; a nurse's uniform (1880); honours and gifts she received.

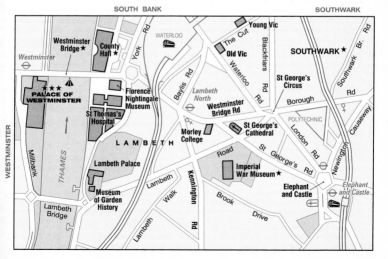

Waterloo International Terminal – Almost in honour of the great Victorian engineer Isambard Kingdom Brunel, the new 'Gateway to Europe' was conceived by **Nicholas Grimshaw** primarily as a simple, functional train shed spanning five new railway tracks laid by British Rail for the high-speed Eurostar trains. Below ground level, built over the Underground tunnels, sits a great carpark which in turn provides support for a two-storey viaduct bearing the unusually long platforms. A glass canopy, comprising standard-size glass sheets sealed with concertina-designed joints, slinkily snakes its way over the curving tracks.

Westminster Bridge Road – The road which was developed in 1750 when the bridge was built, has a distinctive landmark in the white spire encircled by red brick bands of Christchurch, built in 1874 with funds from the USA. Further along is **Morley College** *(no 61)*, erected in 1920 when the college removed from the Old Vic, and rebuilt in 1958 to designs by Edward Maufe, with interior murals by John Piper and Edward Bawden. It has a strong musical tradition.

> ### St George's Circus
>
> The circus, now a forlorn roundabout, was laid out in 1769 by act of parliament as London's first designed traffic junction with an obelisk to Brass Crosbymarking the central island. Five, now six, roads converged at the centre of St George's Fields, long an open area crossed by rough roads where rebels had assembled (the Gordon Rioters), cattle had grazed, a windmill turned, preachers roused crowds.

St George's Roman Catholic Cathedral ⊙ – *Lambeth Road; SW of St George's Circus.* St George's, one of the first major Roman Catholic churches to be built in England after the Reformation, was opened in 1848. It was designed by **A W Pugin** (1812-52), the impassioned advocate of the Gothic Revival (of the late 13C and early 14C English architectural style), who ended his days in the Bedlam hospital opposite, now the Imperial War Museum. The cathedral, destroyed by incendiary bombs during the War, was rebuilt to the design of Romilly Bernard Craze and reopened in 1958. Pugin's vision was never realised, so the stock brick exterior is characterised by a massive stump, the foundation of what was to have been a soaring spire.

Interior – The new cathedral with an added clerestory is much lighter than the old: fluted columns of white Painswick stone support high pointed arches; plain glass lights the aisles, the only elaborate windows being those at the east and west ends which form jewelled pendants with rich red and deep blue glass. The new building's sole ornate feature is the high altar with its carved and gilded reredos. Statues are modern in uncoloured stone, memorials few but include the canopied figure of Cardinal Manning.

★**Imperial War Museum** ⊙ – The museum covers all aspects of warfare, military and civil, allied and enemy, involving Britain and the Commonwealth since 1914.

History – The museum of what Churchill termed the Age of Violence stands on the site of a 19C madhouse. It was founded in 1917, opened in 1920 at the Crystal Palace, transferred in 1924 to South Kensington and in 1936 to the present building. This, to which the dome and giant columned portico were added by Sydney Smirke in 1846, originally comprised the present 900ft wide central area and extensive patients' wings since it was designed in 1812-15 to serve as the new Bethlem Royal Hospital or Bedlam, as it was known, which dated back to the founding of the Priory of St Mary of Bethlehem in Bishopsgate in 1247. In 1547 this had been seized by Henry VIII but then handed over to the City Corporation as a hospital for lunatics. It was transferred in 1676 to Moorfields where the inmates afforded a public spectacle. A century and a half later came the move to Southwark and in 1930 the final remove to Beckenham.

The white obelisk milestone, originally at St George's Circus, commemorates Brass Crosby, Lord Mayor of London in 1771 who refused to convict a printer for publishing parliamentary debates. The authorities thereupon imprisoned the mayor in the Tower but he was freed by the populace and press reporting of Commons proceedings was inaugurated.

The exhibits – The museum in no sense glorifies war but honours those who served Two British 15" naval guns command the main gate. A wide range of weapons and equipment is on display: armoured vehicles, field guns and small arms, together with models, decorations and uniforms. Among the more notable exhibits are a Mark V Tank, 'Ole Bill' (most famous of the London 'B' type buses which carried troops to the Western Front in the First World War); a Spitfire; the smallest craft used in the Dunkirk evacuation in May 1940; Churchill Mark VIII infantry tank; the M3A3 Gran tank used by Montgomery during the Battle of El Alamein; the Trench Experience the Blitz Experience *(10min)*; the Jericho Operation simulating an RAF flight over France in 1944 to release captured Resistance fighters; the VC and GC Room

Imperial War Museum

Historic documents include the typewritten sheet of foolscap which was the Instrument of Surrender of German armed forces in northwest Europe signed, complete with the corrected date, 4 May 1945. There are numerous mementoes of famous men and women, many unknown until all too often a final act of bravery or skill brought posthumous award. The **Holocaust Exhibition** is a sober testimony to this sombre page of history: original artefacts, documents and moving audio-visual presentations.

Paintings and sculptures from the museum's collection of 10 000 works of art reflect particularly the individual's lot in war: Orpen, Augustus John, Paul Nash, Piper, Moore, Stanley Spencer, Sutherland, Topolski painted food queues, people sleeping in tube shelters, the wounded, service life, boredom...

Elephant and Castle – The crossroads, where the Roman Stane Street from Sussex was joined on its way to London Bridge by Watling Street from Kent and local roads from such villages as Lambeth, remained unnamed until the middle of the 18C, when the corner smithy became a tavern and took as its sign the elephant and castle of the Cutler's Co which, like so many other City companies, has associations with the area. Roads proliferated with the construction of bridges over the Thames in the 18C and 19C until congestion at the junction became notorious. Aerial devastation produced a new opportunity and in the 1950-60s, the 40 acre site was entirely redesigned and rebuilt except for the Metropolitan Tabernacle (1861) with its pillared portico rising majestically near the circus.

MARYLEBONE ★

Map p 7 (**CDVX**)
⊖ Regent's Park, Bond Street

The only remaining traces of St Marylebone village are Marylebone High Street and its continuation south, Marylebone Lane, which followed the winding course of the Tyburn River. The land belonged to Barking Abbey until the Reformation when it was confiscated by Henry VIII, who enclosed the land which lay northeast of the village, to form a royal park. He built a hunting lodge, the Manor House (demolished 1791), which he and Elizabeth I used for entertaining important guests.

In 1611 the southern part of the royal lands was sold off by James I. In 1650 part was laid out as the **Marylebone Gardens** where patrons could wander under the trees or take tea and bread and butter in pleasant arbours; the gardens closed in 1778.

18C Development – Early in the 18C Edward Harley, 2nd Earl of Oxford, who had inherited the land sold by James I, began to develop Cavendish Square. By the end of the century St Marylebone village and the surrounding waste land was covered by the most complete grid layout of streets in any area of London; each street is named after

181

MARYLEBONE

a member of the Earl's family or their titles or estates. Between Oxford Street and Regent's Park the only streets not to conform to the rectangular theme, are Marylebone Lane and Marylebone High Street.
In 1756 Marylebone Road and its eastward extension then known as the New Road was created to link the City directly to Paddington and west London.

Marylebone Road – The road is now a six-lane highway, bordered by several buildings of interest.

St Marylebone ⊘ – The church by Thomas Hardwick was completed in 1817, a large balustraded building with a three-stage tower ending in gilded caryatids upholding the cupola. The pedimented Corinthian portico was added by Nash to provide an appropriate close to the view from Regent's Park down the axis of York Gate. It was here that Robert Browning illicitly married the poet Elizabeth Barrett (1846).
A sculptured panel showing characters from the six principal works written by Charles Dickens commemorates the novelist who lived in a house on the site.
On the north side of Marylebone Road is the **Royal Academy of Music** accommodated by an attractive building (1911) in red brick and stone, ornamented with reclining figures in the large segmental pediment.

Manchester Square – The last of the three principal squares dates from 1776 when the 4th Duke of Manchester acquired the land after the death of Queen Anne brought an abrupt end to plans for an elegant square to be completed in her honour. Manchester Square, which is attractive with late Georgian houses,

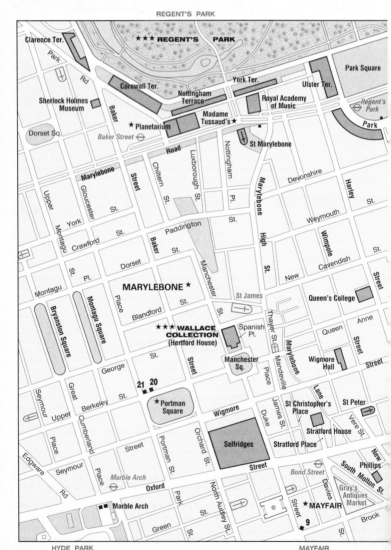

developed to the south of the house during the next 12 years. The house served as residence to the Spanish ambassador, who built the Roman Catholic Chapel of St James's in the adjoining street, henceforth known as Spanish Place, and then his French counterparts (Talleyrand and Guizot amongst others). In 1872 the house was bought by Richard Wallace, Marquess of Hertford, who renamed it **Hertford House** and entirely remodelled it to display the **Wallace Collection** *(listed separately)*.

St Christopher's Place – The narrow pedestrian passage is well known for its cafés and its shops.

Stratford Place – This quiet cul-de-sac recalls the early 18C; the north end is closed by **Stratford House** (also known as Derby House and now the Oriental Club), designed in 1773 by R Edwin in the Palladian style.

St Peter's ⓥ – *Vere Street.* Originally designed as a chapel of ease to serve the residents of Cavendish Square, this attractive small dark brick building (1721-24) has quoins emphasising the angles, square turret and open belfry.

The unexpectedly spacious interior includes galleries supported on giant Corinthian columns with massive entablatures. Designed by the architect James Gibbs, St Peter's may have been an experimental model for St Martin-in-the-Fields *(see TRAFALGAR SQUARE)*. Having collaborated with Gibbs in the painting of *'The Pool of Bethesda* and *The Good Samaritan* in Bart's Great Hall, Hogarth used St Peter's to set the marriage scene in *The Rake's Progress*. The quite lovely stained-glass windows were designed by Edward Coley Burne-Jones and made by William Morris & Co at their Queen's Square premises.

It is now the home of the London Institute for Contemporary Christianity.

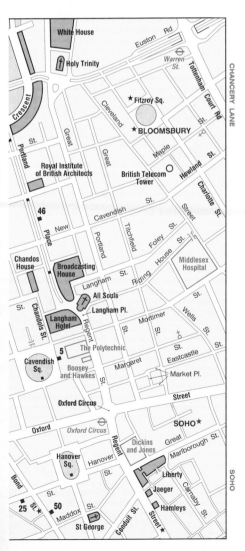

Wigmore Hall – The concert hall, famed for its intimate atmosphere conducive to chamber music and solo recitals borrows its name from the street.

Wimpole Street – No 64 is the home of the **British Dental Association**. Before her marriage to Robert Browning in the Church of St Marylebone in 1876, **Elizabeth Barrett** lived at no 50, which was demolished when the street was largely rebuilt at the turn of the century. At no 80, died the novelist Wilkie Collins (1889).

Cavendish Square – On the north side of the square (1717) stands a pair of stone-faced Palladian houses of the 1770s *(opposite John Lewis)*: these are now linked by a bridge designed by Louis Osman (1914-96) against which stands a moving composition of the *Madonna and Child* by Jacob Epstein (1950) cast in lead to prevent staining. There are late 18C and 19C houses, much altered, along the east side; no 5 was the home of Nelson in 1787 and of Quintin Hogg (d 1903), founder of the Regent Street Polytechnic.

The square was designed as a focal point north of Oxford Street with dependent residential and service streets and a local market; Market Place still exists on the east side of Oxford Circus. Where John Lewis, the department store now stands used to be the house where Lord Byron was born (1788).

Harley Street – It seems that every door, three steps up from the pavement, is emblazoned

---

'Modern' Medicine

In the 1700s, the population of London was 670 000; by 1820 it had doubled to 1 274 000 owing, in no small measure, to a sudden advance in medical knowledge. In the 18C the number of apothecaries and barber-surgeons declined; the Royal College separated from the City guild in 1745. In addition to the two medieval foundations of St Bartholomew's (Bart's) and St Thomas's (Tommies), five new hospitals were established between 1720 and 1745: Guys, the Westminster, St George's, the London and the Middlesex as well as Thomas Coram's Foundling Hospital and the Lying-in Hospital. Anatomy schools existed in the universities but those who wished to practise came to London to acquire their knowledge from hospitals, private laboratories or dissecting rooms often set up for research by men of science in their own houses – an example set by Thomas Linacre, physician to Henry VII and VIII, who founded the Royal College of Physicians in his house in 1518. A century later, William Harvey gave his early lectures on the circulation of the blood to members of the college.

In the 18C, after studies in Glasgow and Edinburgh where there had been advanced medical schools since 1505, William Hunter came south to become the first great teacher of anatomy and later of obstetrics. He was joined in 1748 by his younger brother, the anatomist and physiologist, John Hunter, who was elected surgeon at St George's in 1758. Other pioneers include Jenner (first vaccination against smallpox made 1796), Gray (*Gray's Anatomy* 1858), Fleming (discovery of penicillin)...

---

with the brass plates of medical consultants. The street is an architectural mixture, dating from the original Georgian, through the terracotta, brick and stone of the mid 19C to the present. Florence Nightingale lived at no 47. The Tuscan pillared stucco portico *(nos 43-49)* is the entrance to **Queen's College**, the oldest English school for girls, which was founded in 1848 initially to provide a proper training for governesses and counted Miss Beale and Miss Buss among its early pupils.

Before it was monopolised by the medical profession operating their private surgeries, Harley Street was home to many eminent figures, notably Wellington *(11)*, Turner *(64)*, Gladstone and Allan Ramsay.

MAYFAIR ★

Map p 7 **(DXY)**
⊖ Bond Street; Green Park;
also Piccadilly Circus; Oxford Circus; Marble Arch; Hyde Park Corner

The name Mayfair, immortalised by Waddington's board-game Monopoly, is derived from the cattle and general fair which was held annually in May; this became so unruly and the neighbourhood so notorious that it was officially closed in 1706. In 1735 the architect, Edward Shepherd took a 999 year lease on the site and opened a food market for the sale of fish, fowl, herbs and vegetables. Around the square and dependant streets he erected small houses, a practice renewed by his heirs, so creating Shepherd Market. Development elsewhere arose as a rich over-spill from the City.

Today, Mayfair is synonymous with elegance and luxury. It is enclosed by four important thoroughfares: Oxford Street to the north, Regent Street to the east, Piccadilly to the south and Park Lane to the west: through the middle runs **Bond Street** agleaming with handsome shop-windows full of rare and exquisite goods.

Park Lane – Once a winding road on the edge of Hyde Park, Park Lane is now an eight-lane highway. At the north end a few individual houses with graceful curved balconies have survived; elsewhere the town residences of local estate owners have been replaced by hotels: **Grosvenor House** (1930) replaced the early 19C mansion of the Duke of Westminster; the **Dorchester** (1930) replaced the mid 19C Dorchester House; the **London Hilton** (1960s) replaced a short terrace; the Londonderry stands on the site of Londonderry House (1765); the **Inn on the Park** and the **Intercontinental** *(Hamilton Place)* occupy the site of the Earl of Northbrook's residence.

Grosvenor Square – The square (1725), one of London's largest (6 acres), might be said to have been effectively redesigned in the 20C. Even the garden, originally circular with a central statue of George I, is now square with a memorial to Franklin Roosevelt on the north side and a monument to the RAF American squadrons. The first American resident *(at no 9)* was **John Adams**, the first Minister to Britain and later President. Today the neo-Georgian buildings to north, east and south are almost all US State Department offices while the entire west side, since 1961, has been filled with the embassy designed by **Eero Saarinen**.

South Audley Street – Purdeys, the gun and riflemakers at **no 57** established in 1881, bears the richly-coloured royal coat of arms above the door.

The **Grosvenor Chapel** ⊙ (1739) has a distinctive Tuscan portico, square quoined tower and octagonal turret. The garden was part of Berkeley Wood before becoming the burial ground for St George's Hanover Square *(see below)*.

Down South Street and beyond in Farm Street stands the **Church of the Immaculate Conception** ⊙, the 1844-49 church of the Jesuit community with a particularly fine high altar designed by Pugin.

Curzon Street – This street is different again, being part residential and part commercial. There are 18C houses along the south side at the Park Lane end. Disraeli died in 1881 at **no 19**, MI5 occupied premises at no 1 until 1995 when they moved to Vauxhall Cross.

Crewe House – *No 15.* The house standing back behind gates and lawns is the only surviving example of a type familiar in engravings as an 18C gentleman's London mansion. Sometime residence of the Marquess of Crewe (d 1945), the house was built in 1730 by **Edward Shepherd** and subsequently enlarged and altered to its present seven bays with large bow fronted wings at either end. The entirely white stucco is relieved and ornamented by the curves of Venetian windows, a pillared, square porch and above, a triangular pediment.

★**Shepherd Market** – A maze of streets and paved courts linked by archways forms the market which contains Victorian and Edwardian pubs and houses with small, inserted shop fronts which serve as pavement cafés and antique (brass) shops.

Charles Street – The street contains several 18C houses, some refaced or remodelled in the 19C, such as the English Speaking Union (no **37**); it ends in a confusion of backs and fronts and a small 19C-20C pub in a cobbled yard.

Berkeley Square – Berkeley Wood is recalled by the plane trees which date from 1789. Berkeley House, erected in 1664 overlooking Piccadilly, was replaced in 1733 by Devonshire House which was demolished this century. The square was laid out in 1737. On its west side survive a few 18C houses with ironwork balconies, lamp holders at the steps to each house and torch snuffers: the façade to no **52** is in Charles Street; no **50**, a four-floor brick and stucco house is occupied by Maggs, the antiquarian book and map specialists; no **47** was rebuilt in 1891; stone-faced and pedimented nos **46** and **45** have balustraded balconies at the first floor windows; Clive of India lived at no 45.

Mount Street – A leisurely air pervades this street which veers round to the right from the northwest corner of Berkeley Square past the **Connaught** (that epitome of late 19C luxury hotel building) to Park Lane. It is lined by tall, irregularly gabled terracotta brick houses of 1888, 1893... At street level, window after window displays choice objects: antique furniture, Lalique glass, porcelain, pictures, Oriental screens... and then comes a butcher's shop faced internally with turn of the century tiles.

During the Civil War the parliamentarians raised defensive earthworks here; hence the name and the topography.

Davies Street – Davies Street runs north from Berkeley Square to Oxford Street. At no 2 stands **Bourdon House**, a small square brick house (now Mallett's antique dealers) which was built in 1723-25 as a manorhouse amidst fields and orchards. It boasts a fine 18C interior.

For **Gray's Antiques Market** *see INTRODUCTION – Shopping.*

Handel in Mayfair

George Frederick Handel (1685-1759) came to England in 1711 in the wake of George IV *(see INTRODUCTION – Music)*; his Italian operas were received with great acclaim. Over a period of 18 years he wrote nearly 30 such operas and, as popularity for this genre waned, he turned to composing oratorios with as much success, setting works by Milton and Congreve – adapted by Pope and Dryden.

Handel lived at **25 Brook Street** for 36 years, over which time he came to love England and seek naturalisation (1726). It was here that he composed *Messiah,* and as his sight gradually failed and he became increasingly crippled by arthritis, he continued to dictate compositions to his amanuensis John Christopher Smith. He was a practising Christian and a regular attender at St George's as his contemporary, Sir John Hawkins recorded 'For the last two or three years of his life he was used to attend divine service in his own parish church of St George, Hanover Square... expressing by his looks and gesticulations the utmost fervour of devotion'. Handel House Trust ☎ 0171 495 1685.

Grouped around **South Molton Street**, an attractive pedestrian precinct, are pavement cafés, restaurants and small fashion boutiques.

* **Bond Street** – Bisecting Mayfair from north to south is Bond Street which existed in Tudor times as a lane named after Sir Thomas Bond who was treasurer to Henrietta Maria. Having given £20 000 to the impecunious Duke of Albemarle, he demolished the mansion and began redeveloping the area around Old Bond Street, Dover Street, Stafford Street and Albemarle Street *(see PICCADILLY)*.

New Bond Street was constructed in 1720 and soon boasted such residents as (Lord) Nelson and Emma Hamilton, Byron, Boswell and Beau Brummell – the *Beau Monde* that were happy to employ local bespoke tailors, haberdashers and perfumers. Bond Street therefore predates Sloane Avenue as the street that retails elegance, the unique and the luxurious. It is lined with specialist shops offering handmade leather goods and luggage (Hermes, Louis Vuitton, Loewe, Gucci), stationery (Smythsons), perfume and toiletries (Fenwick), antique furniture and fine art (Bond Street Antique Centre, Wildenstein, Partridge, Fine Art Society, Mallett ...). From the

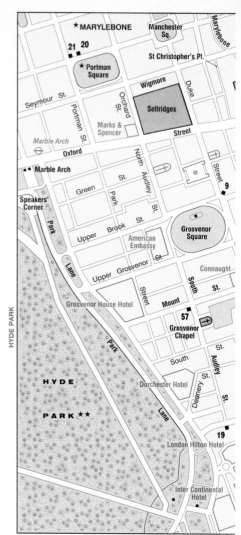

Churchill and Roosevelt in Bond Street

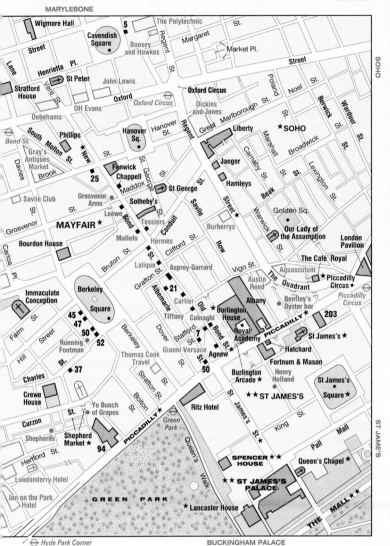

MARYLEBONE

Wigmore Hall

Cavendish Square

5

The Polytechnic

Regent

Margaret

Market Pl.

Street

Street

Henrietta Pl.

Boosey and Hawkes

St Peter

John Lewis

Vere St.

Stratford House

Oxford

Oxford Circus

DH Evans

Oxford Circus

Dickins and Jones

Marlborough

Great

Poland

Noel

Berwick

Wardour

SOHO

Debehams

South Molton

Phillips

New

St.

Hanover St.

Hanover Sq.

Regent

Liberty

★SOHO

Broadwick

Lexington

St.

Bond St.

Gray's Antiques Market

Davies

Brook

St.

George

Maddox

St George

Jaeger

Carnaby

Marshall

Broadwick

Beak

St.

25

Fenwick Chappell

Sotheby's

Loewe

Tessiers

Conduit

Hamleys

Warwick

Golden Sq.

Savile Club

Grosvenor Arms

Savile

St.

Our Lady of the Assumption

London Pavilion

MAYFAIR ★

Mallets

Hermès

Burberrys

Row

Grosvenor

Bourdon House

Bruton St.

Clifford

St.

The Café Royal

Carlos Pl.

Lalique

Asprey-Garrard

Vigo St.

Aquascutum

The Quadrant

Piccadilly Circus ★

Grafton St.

Albemarle

21

Austin Reed

Albany

Piccadilly Circus

Immaculate Conception

Berkeley Square

Cartier

Old

Bond St.

Colnaghi

Burlington House

Bentley's Oyster bar

203

Farm

45

47

50

Dover

Tiffany

Stafford St.

7

Royal Academy

PICCADILLY

St James's ★

Street

Running Footman

52

Berkeley

Gianni Versace

Agnew

Hatchard

Hill

St.

Thomas Cook Travel

Stratton St.

50

Fortnum & Mason

St.

◆ **37**

Burlington Arcade ★

Henry Holland

St James's Square

Charles

Bolton

★★ ST JAMES'S

Crewe House

Ye Bunch of Grapes

Ritz Hotel

James's

St.

King

St.

Pall

Mall

Curzon

St.

Green Park

Shepherds

Shepherd Market ★

PICCADILLY

94

SPENCER HOUSE ★★

Queen's Chapel ★

Hertford St.

Queen's

Londonderry Hotel

Walk

★★ ST JAMES'S PALACE

Inn on the Park Hotel

GREEN PARK

Lancaster House

THE MALL ★★

↙ ⊖ Hyde Park Corner

BUCKINGHAM PALACE

realms of haute couture the register lists such international names as Betty Barclay, Cerruti, Louis Féraud, Guy Laroche, Lanvin, Ballantyne, Max Mara, Valentino, Céline, Yves St Laurent, Salvatore Ferragamo...

At no 63 is the department store **Fenwick**; no 50, the musical store **Chappell's**, no 35, **Sotheby's** who began in 1744 as book auctioneers produced a turnover of £826 in the first year and are now the biggest firm of art auctioneers in the world – their notable rivals, **Phillips' (7 Blenheim Street)** are also located nearby – their first big sale on 9 February 1798 consisted in auctioning Marie Antoinette's pictures; no 143 has an early 19C chemist's shop-front and interior; the fine art dealers Partridge (no **144**), Mallett's (no **141**), the Fine Art Society (no **148**).
For Old Bond Street (see PICCADILLY).

St George's ⊙ – The church (1721-24) is a distinctive landmark with its tower with a lantern after St James' Garlickhythe *(see CITY – Mansion House)* and its portico projecting across the pavement flanked by two cast-iron game dogs. Inside all is white with the detail picked out in gold.

Hanover Square – North of the church the street widens as it approaches the square, which was laid out in about 1715.

The key on page 4 explains the abbreviations and symbols used in the text or on the maps.

NATIONAL GALLERY ★★★

Map p 8 (**EX**) and area map under TRAFALGAR SQUARE
⊖ Charing Cross

Origin and habitat ⊘ – The collection was founded, after more than a century of discussion, by parliamentary purchase in 1824. The nucleus was not the spoils of monarchy as so many of the older European collections were, but 38 pictures assembled by **John Julius Angerstein** (1735-1823), City merchant, banker, owner of a mansion in Greenwich, a town house at 100 Pall Mall and friend of Sir Thomas Lawrence whose portrait of him can be seen in the main vestibule. £57 000 was given for the pictures: Titian's *Venus and Adonis*, Rubens' *Rape of the Sabine Women*, Rembrandt's *Woman taken in Adultery* and *Adoration of the Shepherds*, five paintings by Claude, Hogarth's *Marriage à la Mode* series and Reynolds' *Lord Heathfield* which remained in Pall Mall, where 24 000 people came to view them in the first seven months.

Move to Trafalgar Square – Only in 1838, fifteen years after Angerstein's death was the new gallery completed in Trafalgar Square on the site of the Royal Mews. At first it was shared with the Royal Academy before the latter's removal to Burlington House. The gallery was intended to provide an architectural climax to the square; it succeeded better, however, in its internal arrangement than in its monumentality of which the most spectacular feature in the long, disproportionately low and subdivided front relieved by a small dome and turrets, is the great pedimented portico composed of Corinthian columns, similar to those of the recently demolished Carlton House. The Carlton House columns had been frugally preserved by the authorities who, however, had not noticed their friable condition so that no economy was effected since, the design having been approved, more solid ones had to be made.

In subsequent years various alterations and extensions were made to William Wilkins' original building to afford additional space not only for the permanent collection but also for occasional special exhibitions based on the gallery's pictures supplemented by private and international loans, complemented by furniture, sculpture and fine art from other museums.

During the Second World War the collection was evacuated to Wales but every month one painting was brought to London and exhibited to long queues of art lovers.

Sainsbury Wing – After much public discussion of content and architectural style during the 1980s, the Sainsbury Wing, designed by R Venturi to complement the existing building, was opened in 1991. Its five floors provide additional permanent and temporary exhibition galleries, a theatre and cinema, a computer information room, shop, restaurant and cloakroom facilities. With the improved design of lighting and ventilation systems, the Sainsbury Wing accommodates the earliest and most fragile paintings of the collection, although the numbering of the galleries continues that already in use in the main building.

The pictures – There are now more than 2 000 paintings in the collection hung in chronological order; they represent the jewels in the public domain from early to High Renaissance Italian paintings, early Netherlandish, German, Flemish, Dutch, French, Spanish pictures and the masterpieces of the English 18C. A fuller representation of the British School of Painting, together with 20C art is in the Tate Gallery.

Painting from 1260 to 1510 –
Sainsbury Wing

Giotto and Leonardo – (**51**) The earliest identifiable master, Giotto is considered as the fore-father of Renaissance painting.

Leonardo's fragile preparatory 'cartoon' of *The Virgin and Child with St Anne and John the Baptist* is spectacular, representing two ageless allegories of motherhood with their young sons. *The Virgin on the Rocks* is similarly enigmatic and engaging: *sfumato* light picks out the figures from the dark background of craggy rocks and identifiable plants.

NATIONAL GALLERY

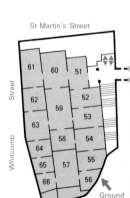

St Martin's Street

Pall Mall East

SAINSBURY WING

PAINTING FROM 1260 TO 1510

🄳 Tourist Information

Cloakroom

188

Italian School before 1400 – (**52**) Three-panelled triptych; gold backgrounds, Byzantine features, graceful lines, incised patterns heighten the jewel quality of these small devotional pieces. **Duccio**'s green underpainting that once would have given the Virgin an ivory glow now strangely tinges the fleshtones. Slowly perspective is used to suggest space, figures are given bulk and volume with shadows and enveloping draperies.

Italian School after 1400, Wilton Diptych – (**53**) Narrative is introduced: a figure is painted several times embarked on a journey or enacting several consecutive incidents on the same journey. The *Wilton Diptych* (*c*1395) could be French or English.

Masaccio, Sassetta – (**54**) The Florentine Masaccio explores space and volume, using light to cast shadows and mould three-dimensional form: *Virgin and Child*. Realism is infused into the work of the Sienese Sassetta, but an air of gentleness still animates his figures and colours are delicately subdued: *Story of St Francis*.

Uccello, Pisanello – (**55**) Uccello exploits strong lines and colour to define perspective: *The Battle of San Romano*. Pisanello is a master of detail: armour is carefully drawn, animals and plants are sensitively arranged in a pictorial world where visions and miracles are completely credible: *Vision of St Eustace*.

Campin, Van Eyck, Van der Weyden – (**56**) Haunting realism and solemn stillness pervade these works, painstakingly painted in some cases as a document, witnessed by the artist: *Virgin and Child before a Firescreen, Arnolfini Portrait, The Magdalene Reading*.

Crivelli, Tura – (**57**) Brittle textures, complex imagery and restlessness are characteristic of the Master of Ferrara: *The Annunciation with St Emidius, St Jerome*.

Botticelli – (**58**) Florentine artist of the early Renaissance, supreme master of line: *Portrait of a Young Man, Venus and Mars, Mystic Nativity*.

Pollaiuolo, Piero di Cosimo – (**59**) Note Pollaiuolo's complementary arrangement of nude figures in *Martyrdom of St Sebastian*.

Raphael, Perugino – (**60**) Master of the Umbrian School, Perugino learned the art of colour from Piero and taught Raphael to endow his figures with grace and poise: *The Virgin and Child with Saints*. Raphael's style radically altered when he went to Rome, evolving into what is considered as the epitome of the High Renaissance: strong portrait of his patron *Pope Julius II*.

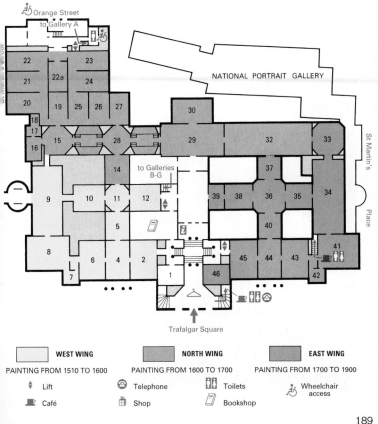

PLANNING YOUR VISIT

Rambling through a large museum is both exhilarating and exhausting. If you are pressed for time, choose a favourite period in history, locate it on the gallery floor plan and explore the art of the times. Because individual pieces in the collection are occasionally rehung it is impossible to pin-point special master-pieces. Browsing, however, will allow you to discover unfamiliar images and perhaps provide you with new 'favourites'.

Gallery floorplans – Free of charge, these are available from the entrance foyers.

Books – The NG has an extensive bookshop selling general and specialist publications on the fine arts, cards, slides and posters.

Gallery Soundtrack – Soundtrack is a random-access audio CD Rom guide to the NG main collection providing pertinent information to over 1 000 paintings. A shorter tour of 30 highlights is also available in several languages.

Micro Gallery – This is a computerised information system containing background information on every painting in the NG Collection: 12 workstations access this visual encyclopedia free of charge.

Popular exhibitions – For the important temporary exhibitions in the Sainsbury Wing Basement, it is sometimes necessary to control the number of visitors with timed tickets.

Special note – Be aware that the NG stays open until 8pm on Wednesday evenings.
NG Information ☎ 020 7747 2885.

Bellini, Mantegna – (**61**) Mantegna studied the arts of Antiquity; strong use of line and uncompromising realism: *Agony in the Garden*. Bellini perfected the use of oil paint, using it to capture rich tones of colour and contrasted light: *Madonna and Child*.

Northern Schools – Development of landscape painting, as imaginary or topographical views stretch beyond the reality of a religious figure or portrait. In France, patronage from noble courts betrays an early interest in fashion. Introduction of oil painting into Italy. Netherlands and France (**62**); Germany (**63**): Dürer. Netherlands and Italy (**64**).

Antonello, Bellini – (**65**) Glorious portraiture influenced by the unforgiving realism of Northern painting; early use of oil painting in Italy: *Doge Leonardo Loredan*.

Hans Holbein: *Lady with a Squirrel*

Piero della Francesca (**66**) Perfect balance achieved with calculated symmetry and perspective pervade *The Baptism of Christ*. *St Michael*, *The Nativity*.

Painting from 1510 to 1600
West Wing

Temporary displays – (**1**)

Correggio, Parmigianino – (**2**) The formality of the High Renaissance is gone; playful gestures and softness hint at the advent of Mannerism, which eventually degenerates into elongated forms and contorted positions.

Shop – (**3**).

Holbein, Cranach, Altdorfer – (**4**) As Humanism reached the north which was already troubled by the Reformation, different genres develop: piercing realism fashions portraiture; fervent spirituality pervades religious subjects; mysticism shapes landscape and idealised mannerism figurative subjects: *The Ambassadors, Cupid complaining to Venus, Christ taking leave of His Mother.*

Dosso, Garolfalo; Lotto, Moretto, Moroni – (**5; 6**) Accomplished artists demonstrating their even abilities in portraiture, religious and mythological subjects in an age of relative ease in Italy.

Tintoretto, El Greco – (**7**) Grand gesture and bold use of paint from the Venetian: *St George and the Dragon.* Obvious influences absorbed by El Greco who was born in Crete, trained in Venice and settled in Spain: *Agony in the Garden.*

Michelangelo, Sebastiano, Bronzino – (**8**) Powerfully distinctive styles reflecting the current tastes in Rome. Michelangelo's monumental yet uncompleted *Entombment;* Sebastiano's crowded *Raising of Lazarus* echoing gestures from other works; Bronzino's enigmatic, almost awesome *Allegory with Venus and Cupid.*

Titian; Veronese; Tintoretto – (**9**) The transfer of patronage to Venice following the Sack of Rome (1507). Bold compositions, luminous use of colour on a grand scale, celebration of texture: *Bacchus and Ariadne, The Vendramin Family.*

Venetian School – (**10**) Large decorative pieces often painted as panels for a sumptuous palace or dimly-lit church. Perceptive informal portraiture; important allegorical iconography relevant to patron, with complex perspective arranged to suit a particular context and which may appear odd in a picture seen at close quarters.

Veronese – (**11**) This highly accomplished artist was prolific. His decorative schemes are often conceived as theatrical backdrops to the celebration of mass in church, the welcome of dignitaries to a palace entrance hall or an exuberant banquet in a sumptuous dining room: *Allegory of Love, The Family of Darius before Alexander.*

Gossaert, Brueghel – (**12**) Portraiture verging on the caricature as these perceptive portrayers of personality exaggerate features and facial expression: *An Elderly Couple, Christ Mocked.*

Domenichino frescoes – (**13**) Sensitive and decorative rendering of landscape, contrived by the artists as an organised series of elements. Apparent subdued colour appropriate to the medium which involves paint being applied to and absorbed by wet plaster: *Apollo pursuing Daphne.*

Painting from 1600 to 1700 North Wing

Ter Brugghen, Hals – (**14**) Ter Bruggen visited Rome from whence he brought back a style resembling that of Caravaggio, heightened by candlelight: *The Concert.* Hals revels in painting formal portraits and happy lowly people or 'genre' subjects; fabulous technique animates the surface of his paintings: *A Boy with a Skull.*

Claude and Turner – (**15**) This unusual association is a special concession made for Turner who bequeathed many paintings to the Nation with the specification that his *Sun Rising through Vapour or Fishermen cleaning and selling fish* and *Dido building Carthage or The Rise of the Carthaginian Empire* should be hung with *Seaport with the Embarkation of the Queen of Sheba* and *The Mill: Landscape with the Marriage of Isaac and Rebekah* by Claude. Turner greatly admired Claude and his audacious depiction of the sun (as the source of pure light had hitherto not been painted as a ball of colour).

Vermeer, De Hooch – (**16**) Tranquil domestic scenes bathed in a balmy winter light: *A Young Woman at a Virginal, A Woman and her Maid in a Courtyard.*

Dou, Van Mieris, Hoogstraten Peepshow – (**17, 18**) Dou collaborated with Rembrandt *(Tobit),* specialising later in elaborately wrought small scenes from everyday life.

Claude – (**19**) Pastoral landscapes and peaceful coastal scenes at sunset are given mythological subjects almost in order to raise the status of landscape to History painting so sought after by wealthy patrons in and around Rome for their country villas and *castelli.*

Poussin – (**20**) Poussin spent many years in Rome. In 1629-30 he suffered from a grave illness which radically altered his style: he abandoned the showy Baroque in favour of a more intellectual, Classical style inspired by the poets of Antiquity (Tasso). He constructed his compositions with the help of a miniature stage set in which wax figures could be placed. Notable patrons secured in France included Cardinal Richelieu: *The Adoration of the Golden Calf, Cephalus and Aurora.* The gallery is also hung with works by Champaigne, an early colleague of Poussin, who was an accomplished portraitist: *Cardinal Richelieu.*

French School and Painting in Paris – (**21, 22**) The climate of the Age of Reason in France allowed for a broad range of subject-matter and styles that would appeal to the Crown, the Church and the wealthy nobility.

Dutch School – (**23, 24**) The main patrons of painting in Holland were wealthy merchants and traders: for them the landscape of their homeland bathed in different light and subject to seasonal changes in the weather was enough material for paintings. Avercamp, Van Goyen and **Ruysdael** depict various aspects of the landscape.

Cuyp, Both – (**25**) Luminosity is perhaps the characteristic quality of the landscape painted by these artists; incidental scenes full of warm light, shaded by feathery foliage.

Hals, Rembrandt – (**26, 27**) People are the main subject of Rembrandt's paintings: *Belshazzar's Feast, Saskia, A Woman bathing in a Stream, Margaretha de Geer, Self-portrait.*

Rubens – (**28**) Whereas Rembrandt is Dutch, Rubens is Flemish: the alliance of the Low Countries with Spain and therefore with the Court of Naples and Venice permitted the diplomat to live at, travel to and visit other Royal courts, assimilating influences and inspiration for his painting along the way. Rubens demonstrates his skill in all genres: *Portrait of Susanna Lunden* ('Le Chapeau de Paille'), *Peace and War, Judgement of Paris, Autumn Landscape.*

Velazquez, Murillo, Zurbaran – (**29**) The political climate in Spain, however, was far from exuberant or liberal: only the most uncontroversial subjects were permitted. Velazquez evolves a strong portrait style under Royal patronage: *Kitchen Scene with Christ in the House of Martha and Mary, The Toilet of Venus (The Rokeby Venus), Philip IV of Spain in Brown and Silver.* Murillo uses delicate colours in his gentle, religious, devotional pieces: *The Two Trinities (The Pedroso Murillo).* Zurbaran's pictures are edged with realism.

Van Dyck – (**30**) Glorious portraiture in a grand confident style: *Equestrian Portrait of Charles I, The Balbi Children.*

Carracci, Caravaggio, Guercino – (**32**) Intense drama animates these pictures painted at the height of the action, often with intense emotion. Caravaggio intensifies the theatricality with the use of strong highlights and dark shadows known as *chiaroscuro: The Dead Christ Mourned, The Supper at Emmaus, The dead Christ mourned by Two Angels.*

Painting from 1700 to 1900 *East Wing*

Chardin, Fragonard – (**33**) Small pictures for more intimate interiors. Chardin's paintings stand out as simple domestic scenes often with a moralising overtone: *The House of Cards.* Fragonard caters to the contemporary taste for the Rococo: delicate, flouncy, pretty pictures, beautifully painted, as did Boucher and Lancret.

Reynolds, Gainsborough, Turner, Constable – (**34**) Two mainstays of the British School at its height: portraiture and landscape - *see INTRODUCTION* – Painting. *Anne, Countess of Albemarle; The Morning Walk; The Fighting Temeraire; Rain, Steam and Speed; The Haywain.*

Hogarth, Gainsborough, Stubbs – (**35**) Small scale 'Fancy' pictures of a more lowly artform: Hogarth's narrative cycles, sporting and animal pictures and picturesque landscapes of the highest quality. *The Marriage Contract; Wooded Landscapes; The Melbourne and Milbanke Families.*

18C British portraiture – (**36**) The extensive Royal family, successful naval and military leaders, statesmen, members of the Royal Society commission formal portraits of themselves and their consorts from the likes of Sir Thomas Lawrence, Allan Ramsay.

Solimena, Giaquinto – (**37**) Solimena was described in 1733 as 'by universal consent the greatest painter in the world'; he forged his style from that of several Baroque artists (Luca Giordano) to paint gentle figures in soft colours, often in religious subjects.

Canaletto – (**38**) The Venetian master of sparkling topographical landscape painting was especially popular with English travellers on the Grand Tour of Italy.

Guardi, Goya – (**39**) Two quite distinctive masters responding to the different types of patronage available in Spain and Venice.

Tiepolo – (**40**) Gloriously bright decorative painting on a large scale.

David, Ingres, Delacroix – (**41**) Neo-Classicism came into favour with the rise of Napoleon as a counter-reaction to the Rococo of the Ancien Régime. David is a master of draughtsmanship; Ingres follows closely, producing clear and penetrating portraiture: *Mme Moitessier.* Delacroix, together with Gericault, was sparked rather by colour and atmosphere, the glories of Napoleon's campaigns in North Africa, the relationship of a man over his horse. Beautiful flower paintings by Fantin-Latour.

Corot, Friedrich – (**42**) The Barbizon School practised landscape painting out of doors. Corot captures the different tonality of sunlight on the landscape; figures are usually incidental.

In Germany, the power and magic of Wagner's Romanticism is transposed into paint.

Impressionism – (**43**) Topographical views of landscape and informal figure compositions are the trademarks of this new and exciting movement in art. The transient quality of light is carefully explored and captured in intimate family scenes (*Boating on the Seine*) by the likes of Pissarro, Renoir, Monet and Manet, or in a celebration of modern industrialisation – street lighting in *The Boulevard Montmartre at Night*, trains in *The Gare St Lazare*...

Van Gogh, Cézanne, Seurat – (**44**) Three highly individual artistic styles: different subject-matter, different techniques are used to apply the paint, different reactions to the social climate of the age. *Van Gogh's Chair; Sunflowers; Bathers; Bathers at Asnières*. Another distinctive figure is **Henri Rousseau** (*Tiger in a Tropical Storm*).

Cézanne, Picasso – (**45, 46**) Together with **Matisse**, these three masters stand as the heroes of modern painting. Not only do they explore colour, form, space and composition, they experiment with the relationship between the two-dimensional picture plain and the three-dimensional space within.

NATIONAL PORTRAIT GALLERY ★★

Map p 6 (**EX**) and area map under TRAFALGAR SQUARE
Leicester Square

Portraiture forms an important part of the British School of painting having evolved as a genre to satisfy different patrons through the ages. Sitters are portrayed as active within or aspiring to various social classes and provide a colourful insight into the spirit of each historical period. The key to this collection is therefore as a social history of each age.

The National Collection – Founded in 1856, the collection moved to its present late 19C Italian-Renaissance gallery behind the National Gallery in 1896. Today, the policy of commissioning and collecting works by contemporary artists continues with over 5 000 personalities portrayed in various media representing the young and the old, the rich and poor, the famous and the unknown, from times past and present.

The permanent collection is presented in chronological order. With the redisplay of the Tudor Gallery the portraits illustrate the 16C in a fresh perspective. The Balcony Gallery presents distinguished contemporary figures and the IT Gallery makes the gallery's collections accessible and offers state-of-the-art facilities.

After extensive redevelopment, the gallery now boasts an imposing entrance hall with escalators rising to the upper levels. A roof-top restaurant gives a panoramic view. Some of the works listed below may have been moved to a different location.

Level 4

As in architecture (*see INTRODUCTION*) the king and his court were the most obvious patrons of portraiture, eager to define their status as handsome, powerful and wealthy monarchs: **Edward IV; Richard III; Henry VII** (1457-1509) is painted four years before his death by the Flemish artist Michel Sittow; Holbein's fragment of a larger sketch, intended as a mural for Whitehall Palace, shows **Henry VIII** (1491-1547) and his wives: Catherine of Aragon (first); Anne Boleyn (second); Catherine Parr (sixth and last); **Edward VI** was painted by William Scrots (1546) (*stand on the extreme right*).

Level 5

16C – *Room 1a, b and c.* **Sir Thomas More** (1478-1535) is portrayed with his family by Rowland Lockey: the author and statesman's most lasting work is *Utopia*, a description of an ideal state that conforms to Humanist ideals; he was executed for opposing Henry VIII's self-appointment as Head of the Church. Famous Tudor personalities include **Thomas Cranmer** (1489-1556), the author of the English Bible and Book of Common Prayer and ardent supporter of the Reformation, he served as archbishop of Canterbury both under Henry VIII and **Edward VI**; he was burnt at the stake unable to recant his Protestant faith. Roman Catholic **Mary Tudor**, Mary I (1516-58) reversed the religious changes instituted by her father Henry VIII and brother Edward VI and sent 300 Protestants to death – including her half sister Lady Jane Grey (1537-54), before marrying Philip of Spain.

Elizabeth I (1533-1603) is painted aged 42 at her coronation and in old age (1592) by Gheeraerts, who came to London with his Protestant family to escape religious persecution. Although capricious and vain, she was a stable and intelligent monarch who saw the Spanish defeated, the New World revealed, the Church of England established and a flowering of literature and liked to be portrayed as such as in the 'Ditchley' portrait. **Mary Stuart** – Queen of Scots (1542-87) was the daughter of James V of Scotland and married to the Dauphin of France; deemed to be a threat in her claim to the throne, she was imprisoned and executed by Elizabeth I.

Sir Walter Raleigh (1552-1618), pictured with his son Walter, was an adventurer and favourite at the court of Elizabeth I – he helped to quell the Irish Rebellion, initiated the colonisation of Virginia (introducing potatoes and tobacco to England in 1584); under James I he was sent to the Tower of London, where he wrote his *History of the World*; he was executed when the expedition to conquer the Orinoco failed. In a rare painting attributed to John Taylor, **William Shakespeare** (1564-1616) appears at the apogee of his career. A showcase of **miniatures★** illustrates the exquisite art of Hans Eworth, Nicholas Hilliard and Isaac Oliver, designed as powerful tokens of love and political loyalty – Elizabeth I (1572) and her favourites, Robert Dudley (1576), Sir Francis Drake (1581) and Sir Walter Raleigh (c 1585), Robert Devereux (1596) and Anne of Denmark (1589), wife of James I and their son Henry, Prince of Wales.

Room 2 – The son of Mary Stuart, **James I** (1566-1625) acceded to the throne of Scotland in 1567 before being crowned King of England in 1603 following the death of Elizabeth I; known as 'the wisest fool in Christendom', James was considered more of a scholar than a leader, notably when dealing with Puritan restlessness – his portrait is by Daniel Mytens (1621), that of his wife Anne of Denmark, is attributed to Marcus Gheeraerts the Younger (c 1612); their children Elizabeth and Frederick of Bohemia are painted by Honthorst (1653).

During the Civil Wars **Oliver Cromwell** (1599-1658) fought against the king under the Earl of Essex; he promoted the king's trial and subsequent execution (1649), and was appointed Protector of the Commonwealth of England, Scotland and Ireland in 1653.

An electrotype metal statue commemorates the philosopher **Francis Bacon** (1561-1626) who contradicted Aristotle's deduction logic (presupposing certain basic truths) with inductive reasoning based on observation; he also upheld the practice of debate and his writings underpin the objectives behind the foundation of the Royal Society *(see index)*.

Charles I (1600-49), King of England, Scotland and Ireland attracted to his court the diplomat and painter P P Rubens (*Thomas Howard, Earl of Arundel* – 1629) and Sir Anthony van Dyck (*Henrietta-Maria*, painted in 1635, was the daughter of Henri IV and Marie de Medici of France and wife of Charles I).

Room 3 17C Arts and Sciences: the London-born poet **John Milton** (1608-74) was a supporter of Cromwell and ardent advocator for a free press. This is also the age of John Donne, Ben Jonson, the philosopher Thomas Hobbes and the diarist John Evelyn (note his effeminate hands).

The showcase of delicate miniatures demonstrates the continued prestige of the genre: Cromwell (1649) is painted by Samuel Cooper who painted his subjects by candlelight to accentuate the contours; Charles I (1628) is portrayed by Honthorst and (1631) by Daniel Mytens; his children Charles II aged 9, James II aged 6 and Mary in a blue dress are by Cornelius Johnson.

Room 4 Charles II and James II: Charles II (1630-85) is portrayed by Thomas Hawker in old age with mace and garter at his knee – although the hands are those of a younger man. After the Civil War Charles fled to France where he resided until 1660, consolidating his sympathy for the Roman Catholics; he was amorous by disposition but a shrewd and realistic ruler, notably in settling delicate issues with Parliament. It was during his reign that the skyline of London was irrevocably changed as plague, then fire devastated the City – witnessed by **Samuel Pepys** and transcribed in cypher in his diaries; Nell Gwynne; **Robert Boyle** (1627-91) who established the law of physics which states that the volume of a gas varies inversely as the pressure put on it, provided temperatures are constant; **John Locke** (1632-1704) the liberal philosopher and founder of empiricism, the doctrine that all knowledge is derived from experience; **Henry Purcell** (1659-95); **John Dryden** (1631-1700), a prolific poet and dramatist.

Charles' younger brother **James II** (1633-1701) – James VII of Scotland (1685-8) was an honest and capable admiral; unable, however, to achieve reforms for his Catholic supporters, he was forced to flee in 1688.

Room 5 William and Mary, Queen Anne: William III(1650-1702), the grandson of Charles I, and Mary II (1662-94), daughter of the Duke of York and future James II acceded to the throne in 1688. Their joint rule brought tolerance to the kingdom, although the king was preoccupied with the threat of war from France. He is painted by Lely and she by Wissing. The portrait of **Queen Anne** (1665-1714), the second daughter of James II who succeeded her brother-in-law William in 1702, is from the studio of John Closterman.

The ivory medallion bearing the profile of Sir Christopher Wren (in the showcase) was sculpted by David le Marchand from Dieppe (1723); others pictured include **Isaac Newton** (1642-1727) who learnt how to split the spectrum, invented the calculus (separately from Leibniz) and established the concept of gravitation; **Grinling Gibbons**.

Room 6a The Jacobites: *In the hall.* The last of the Jacobites are represented by the

> **Sir Peter Lely (1618-80)** — Pieter van der Fies was born in Germany of Dutch parentage. He served his apprenticeship in Haarlem and moved to London in the 1640s. He produced uncontroversial history pictures during the Commonwealth, tailoring his grand and influential manner for the Restoration, succeeding Van Dyck as Principal Painter to Charles II in 1661. Ladies of the Court were endowed with languid beauty (Nell Gwynne, the actress and king's favourite): victorious military leaders with masculine dignity.

Old Pretender, **James Edward** (the son of James II by his second marriage – *see above*) and his sons **Charles Edward** (the Young Pretender) and Henry Benedict. The throne, meanwhile, passed to the Hanoverian **George I** (1660-1727), Elector of Hanover and James I's grandson, who was elected king by Act of Parliament: he is here represented by a fine terracotta bust (1720-35) by Rysbrack.

Room 6 Early 18C Arts and Sciences: **Sir Godfrey Kneller** was Court Painter (self-portrait); **Sir Christopher Wren** was professor of mathematics and astronomy, but achieved fame as Surveyor of the Royal Works charged with rebuilding St Paul's Cathedral; **Nicholas Hawksmoor** was Wren's successor; **James Thornhill**, the decorator of St Paul's dome; **Edmond Halley** (1656-1742) predicted the return of the comets, furthered the studies of Newton on gravitation and published a map charting the winds around the globe; **Sir Hans Sloane** (1660-1756) left his huge personal library to the nation providing a foundation for the British Museum; **Jonathan Swift** (1667-1745) wrote *Gulliver's Travels* – not to mention Addison; Steele; Congreve; Vanbrugh; Pope...

Room 7 Kit-Cat Club: The Kit-Cat Club attracted its distinguished members from political and literary circles. They used to meet for dinner in a tavern run by Christopher Cat and sup upon delicious mutton pies called 'Kit-Cats', while proposing toasts to the ladies. For over 20 years Kneller, himself a member, painted the faces of the members while his assistants filled-in the rest; these were collectively nicknamed the 'Whigs in wigs'.

Room 8 George I and George II: *End room.* George II (1727-60) by Thomas Hudson; The Court of Chancery picture is interesting with the dogs in attendance; *A Conversation of Virtuosi* (1735) shows leading artists and architects of the 1730s by Gawen Hamilton; bust of the actor and dramatist Colley Cibber (1671-1757); **Horace Walpole** (1717-97); the Roman Catholic poet and author of *The Rape of the Lock* Alexander Pope (1688-1744); the beautiful Catherine Hyde 'who died from a surfeit of cherries'. Terracotta bust (1741) of Hogarth; marble bust of John Wesley.

Room 9 18C Arts: Portraits by Sir Joshua Reynolds of himself; the writer Laurence Sterne (1713-68), author of *Tristram Shandy* and *A Sentimental Journey;* the compiler of the first English dictionary **Samuel Johnson** (1709-84) and his biographer James Boswell (1740-95), **David Garrick** and Eva, his wife; the Irish author of *She Stoops to Conquer* and *The Vicar of Wakefield* **Oliver Goldsmith** (1728-74); the musician and composer Handel (1685-1759); J C Bach; the musicologist and renowned organist Dr Charles Burney; Sir Lancelot (Capability) Brown (1769) by Nathaniel Dance; self-portrait of Hogarth, George Stubbs; Gainsborough.

Room 10 Struggle for America: General James Wolfe (cast c 1760) who captured Quebec; portraits of George Washington (1732-99) by G Stuart and of George III (1738-1820) in gold and ermine by A Ramsay.

Room 11 Britain becomes a World Power: Masterpiece by Reynolds (1768) of Hastings, who went to India in 1750 and became Governor General (1774-85); **Captain James Cook** (1728-79) at the Cape of Good Hope on his third voyage; Robert Clive of India (1725-74) who laid the foundations of English power in India. Chinese portrait of Joseph Collet (1673-1725), administrator of the East India Co.

Room 12 Britain at War (1793-1815): Two political rivals William Pitt (1759-1806) and Charles James Fox (1749-1806); Edmund Burke (1729-97), the Whig writer and political philosopher; Admiral Lord Nelson (1758-1805) and his beautiful mistress Emma, Lady Hamilton (c 1765-1815); the Duke of Wellington (1769-1852).

Room 13 The Romantics: The Neo-Classical sculptor John Flaxman who worked for J Wedgwood (c 1796); John Opie (self-portrait 1785); the essayist Charles Lamb (1775-1834); Mary Shelley, author of *Frankenstein;* the visionary poet and illustrator **William Blake** (1757-1827); **J M W Turner** (1775-1851); the good-looking Constable, Girtin, Bonnington *(see WALLACE COLLECTION);* the poets John Keats (1795-1821), John Clare (1793-1864), Wordsworth (1770-1850), **Coleridge** (1772-1837), P B Shelley (1792-1822), Robert Burns (1759-96), **Byron** (1788-1824) in his Greco-Albanian costume. Deathmasks of Keats and Wordsworth.

Room 14 Science and the Industrial Revolution: Portraits of inventors: John McAdam (roa surfacing material), James Watt (steam engines), George Stephenson (railways) John Wilkinson (first iron ship), the Duke of Bridgewater (first canal); Josia Wedgwood (famous potter); Humphrey Davy (miners' lamps in the *SCIENC MUSEUM*): civil and mechanical engineers: I K Brunel, Telford, Sir Richard Ark wright, Robert Owen, Samuel Crompton.

Room 15 The Regency: The House of Commons (1833) by Sir George Hayter. A serie of portraits by Sir Thomas Lawrence: the **Prince Regent** (c 1814); his wife Caroline c Brunswick; Lord Castlereagh (1809-10); William Wilberforce(1828); Georg Canning.
Portrait (1788) by Reynolds of Maria Fitzherbert who secretly married the Princ of Wales in 1795; William IV (1800) by Sir Martin Archer Shee; two portraits b Henry Perronet Briggs: Charles Kemble, actor, and Rev Sydney Smith (1840) portrait by Sir William Beechey of Sarah Siddons (1793), actress; Jane Auste (c 1810) by her sister Cassandra.

Level 3

Victorian and Edwardian eras – Statue (landing) of Victoria and Albert as ancien Saxons by William Theed (1868).

Science and Technology:
Michael Faraday (1841-42); I K Brunel (1857); Charles Darwin (1881); Thomas Huxley (1883).

Exploration and Empire: Sir Richard Burton (1875), the African explorer, by Sir Frederic Leighton; Rudyard Kipling (1899) by Sir Philip

> **Note:** The 19C and 20C part of the National Portrait Gallery collection is so large that displays are regularly altered. Listed below are a selection of works available that may or may not be on show.

Burne-Jones; portraits by Sir Hubert von Herkomer of 1st Earl Kitchener c Khartoum (1890) and Robert Baden-Powell (1903); Queen Victoria presenting Bible (c 1861) by Jones Barker.

Victorian Drawings and Photographs: Drawings by Sydney Prior Hall of the Parne Commission. Portrait photographs by Barraud and Walery of W G Grace; Cardin. Newman; Ellen Terry; Alma Tadema; Robert Browning; Charles Kingsley; Anthon Trollope; Oscar Wilde; Wilkie Collins; Frederic Leighton. Portrait drawings by Danie Maclise. Victorian portrait photography.

Politics and Public Life: Queen Victoria by Sir George Hayter; Prince Albert by Franz Xave Winterhalter; 7th Earl of Shaftesbury (1862) by G F Watts; portraits by J E Millais c Gladstone (1879) and Disraeli (1881); caricatures drawn for *Vanity Fair*.

Artists, Writers and Performers: Sir Edwin Landseer (1852) by Sir Francis Grant; por traits (1858) by Michele Gordigiani of Elizabeth Barrett Browning and Rober Browning; Alfred Lord Tennyson (1840) by Samuel Lawrence; Charles Dicker (1839) by Daniel Maclise; the Brontë sisters (1834) by Patrick Branwell Brontë.

G F Watts – Self-portrait; portraits by and of G F Watts: Ellen Terry (c 1864), futur actress; her marriage at 16 to Watts, thirty years her senior, lasted barely a year.

Later Victorian Arts – W S Gilbert; Sir Arthur Sullivan; Sir John Tenniel; William Holmar Hunt; William Morris; James Abbott McNeil Whistler; Walter Sickert; J K Jerome; S Henry Irving; Thomas Hardy; R L Stevenson (bust 1893) by Allen Hutchinson.

The Edwardians – Edward VII (1907); Queen Alexandra, replica by Sir Luke Fildes their three daughters Victoria, Mau and Louise (1883); Joseph Conra (bust 1924) by Sir Jacob Epstein Rupert Brooke (1911); Henr James, an American who took Brit ish nationality (1913), by his frien John Singer Sargent.

The National Portrait Gallery, London

Sam Walsh: Paul McCartney

Level 2

20C – *Landing* Portraits of the Roy Family.

Early 20C – Several General Officers c the Great War (1922) by John Sing er Sargent; Sir John Alcock (1919 by Ambrose McEvoy; Sir Willian Orpen (self-portrait 1910); Si Oswald Moseley (1925) by Glyn Phi pot; **Sir Winston Churchill** (1927) by S Walter Sickert; Viscount Montgon ery (1945) by Frank Salisbury.

Members of the **Bloomsbury Group** (Virginia Woolf by George Beresford and Vanessa Bell); Augustus John (bust 1916) by Sir Jacob Epstein; Laurence Stephen Lowry (self-portrait in pencil c 1920); E M Forster (1920s) by Dora Carrington; Dame Edith Sitwell (1927) by Pavel Tchelitchew, and (c 1923) by Maurice Lambert; D H Lawrence (1923) by Edmond Xavier Kapp; Evelyn Waugh (1943) by Felix H Man; Bertrand Russell (c 1923) by Roger Fry; Laurence Olivier (bust 1950) by Peter Lambda.

Level 1

20C from 1945 – Sir Alec Guinness (bronze 1984) by Elisabeth Frink; Christopher Fry (bronze 1951) by Peter Lambda; Mervyn Peake (self-portrait 1932); Sir Michael Tippett (bronze 1966) by Gertrude Hermes; Richard Rogers (bronze 1988) by Eduardo Paolozzi; Henry Moore (bronze 1962) by Marino Marini; The Beatles (1963) by Norman Parkinson; Peter Sellers by Bill Brandt (1963); Sir Winston Churchill (sketch 1954) by Graham Sutherland; Elizabeth Taylor by Andy Warhol (1967); Harold Wilson (1974) by Ruskin Spear; two bronzes by Angela Connor of Harold Macmillan (1973) and Sir John Betjeman (1973). HRH The Princess of Wales by David Bailey (1988).

Peter Blake by Clive Barker; Dirk Bogarde by David Tindle; Paul McCartney by Humphrey Ocean; Margaret Thatcher; HRH The Prince of Wales; Dame Iris Murdoch; Philip Larkin; Julian Bream; George Melly by Maggie Hamblyn...

NATURAL HISTORY MUSEUM★★

Map p 6 (**BY**) and area map under SOUTH KENSINGTON
⊖ South Kensington

The main building ⊘ (1873-80) expresses the solemn reverence and sense of mission in public education in the 19C. Alfred Waterhouse, the architect, took as his model 11C to 12C Rhineland Romanesque cathedral architecture, producing a vast symmetrical building (657ft from end pavilion to end pavilion) with central twin towers (190ft high) above a rounded, recessed entrance, ornate with decorated covings and pillars. The fabric is buff and pale slate-blue terracotta blocks. The decoration includes lifelike mouldings of animals, birds, fishes: living organisms in the western half of the building; extinct specimens in the eastern half. A new east wing was opened in 1975 to house the Paleontology Department. Since 1989 the museum has incorporated the **Geological Museum**, which was established in an adjoining building in 1935 to display the specimens accumulated in 1835 as a result of the Geological Survey of Great Britain. The museum has accumulated about 68 million specimens; the collections continue to grow by some 350 000 specimens a year of which 250 000 are insects. Such increase would not have surprised **Hans Sloane** *(see index)* whose own collection, begun with plant specimens from Jamaica, had outgrown his house, the house next door and the accommodation at Chelsea Manor, when he bequeathed it to the nation.

It formed the nucleus of the British Museum, founded in 1753, which almost immediately trebled in size and continued to expand so that by 1860, despite new wings and annexes, the galleries were chaotic and quantities of objects were unable to be shown. The decision was therefore taken to move natural history to South Kensington, where the present museum opened to the public in 1881.

The **Walter Rothschild Zoological Museum, Tring**, which was bequeathed to the nation in 1938 by Baron Rothschild *(see index)*, also houses mammals, insects and the major bird collections.

Note: numbers in italics given here refer to gallery numbers.

Life Galleries *Ground Floor*

The display in the **dinosaur gallery** *(21)* traces the development and extinction of these creatures: an elevated walkway provides a close view of skeletons suspended from the ceiling; tableau of three smaller reptiles killing and eating a larger (blood and sound effects). In **Human Biology** *(22)* the displays explain the working of the human brain, hormones, reproduction, the development of a baby, memory, vision, colours and language. The gallery on **marine invertebrates** *(23)* displays corals, urchins, crabs, starfish, sponges, molluscs, squid and shells. A blue whale suspended from the ceiling dominates the gallery on **mammals** *(24)*; the relationship between four-footed mammals and their environment is explained through audio-visual programmes *(3min)*, films, sounds, written panels, illustrations and stuffed originals; whales and their relatives are described in the gallery (upstairs). **Creepy Crawlies** *(33)* illustrates the nature and diversity of anthropods, how and where they live and their relationships with man. **Fish, amphibians and Reptiles** *(12)* includes snakes, tortoises, terrapins, turtles, lizards, crocodilians, coral reef fish etc. The **Ecology Gallery** *(32)* traces the impact of man's activities on our living planet through spectator participation. The **Bird Gallery** *(40)* displays birds from all over the world.

The **Ecology Gallery** has been carefully designed to complement the nature of the displays therein. Opti-white glass is illuminated by coloured lights to suggest fire, water and sheer ice. Clear strips seem to have been rubbed as if from a frosted window. Raised walkways are made from different materials to illustrate earth's different elements.

First Floor – The **Origin of Species** *(105)*, Darwin's theory of evolution by natural selection, is elucidated in the west gallery; the adjoining balcony is devoted to primates. The east balcony traces **our place in evolution** *(101)*. The east gallery displays **minerals, rocks and meteorites** *(102 and 103)* in show cases.

Second Floor – At the top of the stairs is a slice through the trunk of a Giant Sequoia *(201)* felled in 1892 in San Francisco.

Natural History Museum

K. Brett

Earth Galleries

Enter into the secret of the planet: a gallery of gods stands for the timeless mysteries associated with our world. **Visions of Earth** feature displays of gleaming gems, minerals and fossils set against etched slate walls; an escalator lends a sense of journeying from the molten magma core to the tallest mountains, up to the first floor where, with sound effects, flashing lights and vibrations, **the power within** is outlined in terms of earthquakes and dramatic volcanic activity. Video footage relates the experiences of eye witnesses.
The restless surface, meanwhile, comprises an excellent explanation on erosion. The various changes in the earth's surface caused by water (tidal waves, flood, avalanche, landslide) and wind (hurricanes, tornadoes, sandblasting) are provocatively presented. **From the beginning** traces the history of the earth from the Big Bang through rocks and fossils of extinct species and predicts its future. A glittering array of precious stones is the highlight of **Earth treasury** presenting rock and mineral specimens. Exploration and sustainable use of mineral and energy resources, man's demands on the environment are the themes explored in **Earth today and tomorrow**. The diversity of British geology is featured in **Earth lab** where visitors can identify their own fossils, rocks and minerals by comparison with the exhibits, and using museum database and electronic imaging techniques.

The chapter on Practical Information at the end of the guide lists:
local or national organisations providing additional information,
recreational sports,
thematic tours,
suggested reading,
events of interest to the tourist,
admission times and charges.

PICCADILLY ★

Map pp 7-8 (**DEXY**) and area map under MAYFAIR
⊖ Piccadilly Circus, Green Park, Hyde Park Corner

In the early 16C, the area was owned by Eton College and the Mercers' Company. The name Piccadilly is derived from Pickadill Hall (c 1612), an imposing family mansion built on a plot of land adjoining Great Windmill Street, by a Somerset tailor who had made a fortune manufacturing frilled lace borders known as 'pickadills' which fashionable Elizabethans attached to their ruffs and cuffs.

★**Piccadilly Circus** – The circus, once considered the hub of the Empire, still draws the crowds. It was created by John Nash as part of his new road from Carlton House in St James's to Regent's Park. The statue of **Eros**, officially the Angel of Christian Charity, is a memorial (drinking) fountain erected in 1892 to the philanthropist, Lord Shaftesbury.

The south side of the circus, built on the site of the 17C St James's market, is occupied by the **Criterion**, a Victorian building from the 1870s with pavilion roofs containing a hotel and restaurant. The 19C mosaic ceiling is still visible in the Criterion Brasserie; 19C decorative tiles line the foyer of the **Criterion Theatre**, which was incorporated in the building largely underground in 1874 and was one of the first theatres to be lit by electricity.

On the southeast corner *(at the top end of Haymarket)* stands a four horse fountain by Rudy Weller: high above, three divers reach for the sky.

The north side is taken up by the **London Pavilion**, crowned by 13 sculptures of Victorian maidens, which was redeveloped in the 1980s to contain shops and restaurants. The **Rock Circus** ⊘ *(second floor)* is owned by Madame Tussaud's *(see BAKER STREET)* and presents the history of rock and roll.

Trocadero ⊘ – A place of gentle entertainment throughout the Victorian and Edwardian eras when waltzing to Strauss was all the rage, has been lavishly redeveloped to accommodate a futuractive theme park-cum-computer-age emporium of sound, virtual reality and special effects spread over seven storeys. Be prepared for launch up 100m with the Rocket Escalator (biggest and best of its kind) to access the ever-changing interactive rides (Mad Bazooka, Beast in Darkness, Aqua Planet, Ghost Hunt, Space Mission, James Bond 007): £45 million has been invested by the Japanese games giant Sega Enterprises on a scale that supersedes Joypolis in Yokohama.

★**Piccadilly north side** – **The Albany** is named after Frederick, second son of George III, Duke of York and Albany – who is perched on his column overlooking the Mall *(see BUCKINGHAM PALACE)*. Compelled by substantial debts, the prince sold the 18C house designed by **Sir William Chambers** to a builder who converted it into 'sets' or 'chambers for bachelors and widowers' which remain, increased in number to 69, to this day. The building, as altered by **Henry Holland** in 1804, is in the shape of an H, the front, with a forecourt on Piccadilly, is of brick with a central pediment and porch, while at the rear it forms a stuccoed court on Vigo Street enclosed by two lodges between neighbouring 18C houses. Distinction has always come to Albany through its residents which have included Gladstone, Macaulay, Byron, J B Priestley, Malcolm Muggeridge, Graham Greene, Sir Isaiah Berlin, Alan Clark (and Raffles the fictitious jewel thief)... To preserve the peace, trustees rule that occupants are not allowed to whistle, keep cats, dogs or children under the age of 13!

★**Burlington House** – In 1664 the 1st Earl of Burlington bought a plot on which to build a town house on the edge of courtly St James's; the 3rd Earl, an architect in his own right, together with **Colen Campbell** remodelled and refaced the house in the Palladian style (1715-16). In the 19C the house was altered again, the second time in 1867-73 to its present neo-Italian Renaissance appearance.

The rear of Burlington House was remodelled in 1869 in ornate Italian style with towers, an upper portico of giant columns and a colossal porch, and suitably decorated with more than 20 magisterial statues. On completion the building became for many years the headquarters of London University *(see BLOOMSBURY)*. This section now houses the Royal Academy Schools that provide training in drawing, painting and sculpture.

Royal Academy ⊘ – The Academy, founded in 1768, was first accommodated in Somerset House *(see STRAND)*. When it moved to Burlington House the interior was drastically modified to provide a grand central staircase and exhibition galleries. The light and versatile Sackler Galleries, designed by Sir Norman Foster RA were opened in 1991 by the Queen. The academy's treasures, usually exhibited in the Private Rooms, include paintings by members (Reynolds, Gainsborough, Constable, Turner), 18C furniture, Queen Victoria's paintbox, **Michelangelo**'s unfinished marble tondo of the *Madonna and Child (in the sculpture section outside the entrance of the Sackler Galleries)*, and the famous copy of **Leonardo da Vinci**'s *Last Supper.*

Today, besides the Royal Academy of Arts, the adjacent wings of the complex accommodate the Geological Society, Royal Astronomical Society and the Society of Antiquaries.

Burlington Arcade, before Ascot

At the back of Burlingto House is located the Roy. Academy School of Fin Art. At no 6, the origin. headquarters of Londo University were built. Fo lowing the transfer of th Museum of Mankind to th British Museum, thes premises may be absorbe by the Royal Academy. the north stretch: Cor Street, where a clutch c spacious galleries concei trate on selling the best i modern art, Old Burlingto Street which was laid ou by Colen Campbell an **Savile Row**, the one-tim home of William Ker (no 1) and of several tailoi ing businesses since th 19C.

★ **Burlington Arcade** ⊙ – Th arcade along the west sid of Burlington House, delectable with tradition. purveyors of luxury good. table-linen, fine antiqu jewellery, cashmere kni wear, leather and shoes ai enticingly presented i bright shopwindows. It w. built in 1819 and is patrolled by beadles; the gates are closed at night and c Sundays.

★ **Old Bond Street** – This street is lined with well-established institutions specialising i fine porcelain, jewellery and watches (**Cartier, Tiffany, Boucheron – no _180_**, Bentley & Co no _8_, George Jensen, **Asprey & Garrard** – nos _43_, _165_...), Antiques and fine art (Agne – no _43_, Marlborough Fine Art – no _39_, Colnarghi – no _14_). Beyond the bronz group of Churchill and Roosevelt extends New Bond Street _(see MAYFAIR)_.

Albemarle Street – Several 18C houses survive here: no 7 and no 21 are occupied b the Royal Institution (f 1799) and the **Michael Faraday Laboratory and Museum** ⊙ respectively. No 50 is home to the veteran publisher, John Murray.

Michael Faraday (1791-1867)

Faraday was apprenticed to Sir Humphry Davy at the Royal Institution, succeeding him as professor of chemistry. It is in the field of electromagnetism, however, that he is particularly revered, having set himself the objective of ascertaining the links between the forces of light, heat, electricity and magnetism: theories that were to lead to the advent of the electric motor, the transformer and the dynamo, so crucial to the development of physics and electronics. Other areas of research include the properties of fuel, notably the isolation of benzene.

He was also responsible for inaugurating the tradition of Christmas Lectures held at the Royal Institution for young audiences.

Piccadilly south side – The stretch of Piccadilly that includes Wren's churcl Fortnum and Mason, Hatchard's is commonly associated with St James's _(liste separately)_.

Ritz Hotel – The 130-bedroom hotel was opened on 24 May 1906 by César Ritz, Swiss waiter turned entrepreneur, at the height of the Edwardian era. It was a immediate success, bordering on the decorous and the decadent with single roon costing 10s 6d a night (521/2p)! Externally, the early frame structure was fashione by Mewès and Davis to the French Classical style, while inside all was gilde Louis XVI decoration and marble. Regular patrons have included royalty (the futui Edward VII, the Duke of Windsor and Wallis Simpson, Queen Elizabeth the Quee Mother) the rich (the late Aga Khan, Aristotle Onassis), the glamorous (Rit

Hayworth) and the plain famous (Noel Coward, Charlie Chaplin, Winston Churchill)... During the 1970s and 1980s a selection of spare jackets and ties was supplied so that 'pop' stars might conform with the strict dress code.

The ornamental gates on the north side of Green Park *(see ST JAMES'S)* were designed by Robert Bakewell of Derby to grace the entrance to Devonshire House.

Barclays Bank – *No 160.* A fabulous branch of the bank 'Big Bow-Wow style of Corinth USA' on the outside and inside, decked in the most sumptuous red, black and gold exotic decoration. Designed for Wolseley Motors as car showroom (1922), William Curtis-Green (1875-1960) was asked by Barclays to transform his interior into a banking hall.

Piccadilly north side – The west end of Piccadilly is lined by late Georgian houses occupied by a growing number of hotels, at the demise of the gentleman's clubs. No **94** was the home of the Naval and Military (f 1862), which is known as the 'In and Out Club' after the words on the piers at the entrance. The modest townhouse of 1756-60, two storeys high, with a Venetian window beneath the central pediment, was formerly the residence of George IV's son, the Duke of Cambridge (1829-50), and from 1854-65 of Lord Palmerston. No 128 harbours the **Royal Air Force Club.**

★**Apsley House** – Apsley House stands on the former site of a public house, and later, the old lodge of Hyde Park. As the first house beyond the turnpike, it became known in the 19C as No 1, London.

The present house was

> On the south side of Piccadilly, by the Hyde Park Corner underpass stands a **porters' rest**, a solid plank of wood at shoulder height on which porters could rest their back-packs without unloading them.

purchased by Wellington in 1817, having been designed nearly 40 years before by Robert Adam for Baron Apsley: topographical views painted on porcelain in the Plate and China Room show Adam's house as being small, square and built of brick. It was subsequently altered by the duke and his architect Benjamin S Wyatt: the exterior was given a pedimented portico and refaced entirely in golden Bath stone; the interior, meanwhile was rearranged (save the Portico and Piccadilly Drawing Room) and in 1812, extended. The transformation was such as to befit the town residence of the victorious general and national hero (later prime minister). On the ground floor it provided for the Muniment or Plate and China Room to house a priceless collection of treasures and on the floor above, the splendid Waterloo Gallery.

In 1947 the 7th Duke presented the house to the nation.

★**Wellington Museum** ⊘ – Most of the objects displayed have significant associations with Wellington himself: orders and decorations include the silver Waterloo Medal, the first ever campaign medal, 85 tricolours paraded on 1 June 1815 in Paris. This includes his highly personal collection of objects selected as supreme examples of quality and artistry: porcelain and silver, beautiful jewellery, orders of chivalry, field marshal's batons and snuffboxes. Of the paintings by English, Spanish, Dutch and Flemish masters, more than 100 had been appropriated from the Spanish royal collection by Joseph Bonaparte and acquired from him in 1813 following the Battle of Vitoria. The chandeliers are 19C English.

Plate and China – Exquisitely painted Meissen porcelain complements contemporary taste in the exotic and the topographical that was promoted by Napoleon following his major military campaigns in North Africa and Northern Europe. The opulent splendour of the Egyptian (Sèvres: 1810-12), Prussian (Berlin: 1819), Saxon and Austrian porcelain services compares well with the glorious gold and silver plate (Wellington Shield, solid silver candelabra), silver and gilt services (most of several hundred pieces) that would be used for lavish celebratory banquets. Meanwhile, the rich gold, enamelled and jewelled snuffboxes evidently reflect a more personal appreciation for quality.

In the basement are displayed the **Duke's death mask,** his uniforms and garter robes, his and Napoleon's swords from Waterloo, a panorama and a programme, printed on silk, of his remarkable funeral and a commentary on his political career by newspaper cartoonists of the day (1852).

Standing in the staircase vestibule is a Carrara marble (11ft 4in) likeness of the Emperor Napoleon Bonaparte, posed like the god Apollo, sculpted by **Canova** – not something that Wellington could very easily hide away! Other portraits of *Napoleon* by Lefèvre and Dabos, of the *Empress Josephine* and *Pauline Bonaparte* by Lefèvre hang upstairs.

On the first floor, formal portraits line the walls – notable works include those by Wilkie (William IV), Reynolds and Lawrence. In the Piccadilly Drawing Room and Portico Room are beautiful examples of interior Adam decoration. The most striking room, however, is the **Waterloo Gallery**. The early Waterloo Day (18 June) reunion dinners, with only the generals present, used to be held in the dining

PICCADILLY

room: but by 1829, with Wellington now premier, the guest list had grown to su
an extent that he added the 90ft gallery. This he had decorated in 18C French st
which set a fashion favoured until the end of the Edwardian era: on the ceiling
Wellington arms are combined with the George within the Garter collar.
windows that once would have had a rural view, are fitted with sliding mirr
which enhanced still further the already glittering gold decoration, flicker
candles, glistening chandelier, silver centre-piece and plate, the blue and
uniforms with gold buttons and braid...

The **paintings** are dominated by the p
traits of Charles I after Van Dyck, a
the Goya portrait of the duke himself
the standard Spanish heroic pose
horseback – recent x-rays have revea
that it was painted somewhat prem
turely and the head of Joseph Bo
parte had to be overpainted with that
the ultimate victor. Other major mast
pieces hung here include works
Murillo, Rubens, Reynolds, Ribera, Men
Brueghel, **Velasquez,** notably *The Wa
Seller of Seville* and *A Spanish Gen
man* and the Duke's favourite, *
Agony in the Garden* by Corregg
Many of these were seized from Jose
Bonaparte in 1813, who had in tu
stolen them from the King of Spain.
The Yellow Drawing Room is hung w
yellow damask resembling that origin
in the Waterloo Gallery, while t
striped drawing room is devoted to *
Battle of Waterloo* by Sir William A
(about which the Duke comment
'Good; very good; not too mu
smoke').

Dining Room – The amazing portrait of George IV in Highland dress by Wi
overlooks the banquet table set with the silver centre-piece (26ft) from
Portuguese service.

REGENT'S PARK ★★★

Map p 7 (**CDV**)
⊖ Regent's Park

The proposal – It was a superb plan: the government needed something done w
Marylebone Fields (which had been enclosed by Henry VIII and divided under
Commonwealth into manor farms of which the leases reverted to the crown in 18
and a direct route from north central London to Westminster. **Nash** devised a t
landscaped park with a serpentine lake bounded by a road along which, on all exc
the north side, which was to be left open for the view of Primrose Hill and the heig
of Hampstead and Highgate, there would be a series of terrace-palaces, provid
three-bay town houses for the noble and fashionable. Within the park would be
circus, ringed by houses facing both in and outwards and, surmounting the uprais
centre, a valhalla; elsewhere there would be a *guinguette* or summer pavilion for
Prince of Wales, which would be approached along a wide avenue (the Broad Walk)
an axis with Portland Place. Numerous other villas were planned to nestle, half-hidd
amongst the trees, while the central feature would be the proposed Regent's Canal.
in all, the park would become the most exquisite garden suburb.

The constraints – Portland Place, a most successful speculation begun by the Ad
brothers in 1774 consisted of a private road lined by substantial mansions and clos
at the south end by Foley House, whose owner insisted on an uninterrupted vi
thereby dictating the street's 125ft width. Between the place and park ran New R
(Marylebone Road), a psychological barrier that bisected the area into two –
junction would be transformed into a circus around St Marylebone Church (not th
built). Portland Place, which Nash greatly admired should be extended due so
across Oxford Street and Piccadilly by means of circuses, to arrive at Carlton Hou
The section south of Oxford Circus would be lined with a continuous arcade of she
sheltered by colonnades with balconied houses above; below would be excavated
much needed new sewer system for central London.

The realisation – In essence the plan survived considering that it was subject
government commissions and the hazards of land purchase. The *guinguette*, all
seven villas and the would-be double Bath Crescent did not materialise but an In

rcle was laid out as a botanic garden, now transformed into **Queen Mary's Gardens.** The pproach from Portland Place was modified to the open armed Park Crescent and ark Square. The extension south from Portland Place was given a pivoted turn by the nstruction of the circular porch of All Souls, and the angle at the south beautifully vept round by means of the Quadrant. The project took eight years to achieve 817-25): New Street, as it was called at first, was a fashionable and glittering uccess clinched by the social promenaders and followers of Beau Brummel; the houses ong the park were snapped up; meanwhile, the Prince, by now George IV, had nfortunately tired of Carlton House but it remained a worthy focal climax until 1829 'hen it was demolished and replaced by Waterloo Place and Carlton House Terrace ee ST JAMES'S).

ash himself probably designed only a few of the **terraces**★★, houses and shops, but he et the style sufficiently explicitly for different architects, among them Decimus Bur- on, to draw up plans, which subject to approval by Nash to ensure homogeneity could e executed. Giant columns, generally Ionic or Corinthian, are used throughout to rticulate the centre and ends of the long façades which, in addition, were usually dvanced and sometimes pedimented or given an attic screen decorated with statuary. olumns, of a different order, formed arcades or were implemented to frame doors or round floor windows; balustrades and continuous first floor balconies of iron or tucco ran the length of the long fronts uniting them into single compositions. 1828 London Zoo opened on the north side of the Park beside the canal.

Park Crescent – The crescent was designed by Nash to link Portland Place to Regent's Park. Just beyond Park Crescent stands a statue of **John Fitzgerald Kennedy.**

Holy Trinity ⊙ – *North side of Euston Road.* The church, designed by **Soane** in 1826, is surmounted by a thin egg-shaped cupola which rises from a square pillared base above a balustrade and Classical pedimented portico. The outside pulpit dates from 1891. The sanctuary is still used for services; the rest of the building was converted in 1955 to house the offices and bookshop of the Society for Promoting Christian Knowledge (SPCK).

White House – *Albany Street.* The nine-storey apartment-hotel block (1936), faced overall in white ceramic tiles was designed to a star-shaped plan by R Atkinson.

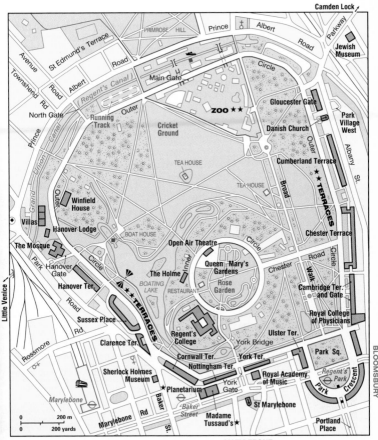

MARYLEBONE

★★THE PARK

The terraces, named after the titles of some of George III's 15 children, and oth principal buildings are described in order starting from Park Crescent and circl the park clockwise, with a detour south from Winfield House to the Inner Cir and open-air theatre returning north via the Broad Walk and the Zoo.

Inner Circle – Regent's College is on the site of South Villa and St John's Lod rebuilt and enlarged this century in red brick; formerly it was occupied by Bedfc College, which was founded in 1849 in Bedford Square and later amalgamat with Royal Holloway College at Staines.

The Holme is one of the 18C villas.

Queen Mary's Gardens were created out of the original Botanic Garden.

The **Open Air Theatre** presents a summer season of open-air performances of plays Shakespeare and other playwrights.

The **Broad Walk** crosses the park on a north – south axis, linking Primrose H Regent's Canal and the park with Portland Place and Regent's Street.

★★**The Terraces – Park Crescent** (1821): paired Ionic columns in a continuous porc and a balustrade and balcony emphasise the classical curve. The Doric Lodges or flanked iron gates closing off the crescent and the square from the main road. Pa **Square, East and West** (1823-24): single Ionic columns.

Ulster Terrace (1824): the idiosyncrasy appears in two closely positioned pairs of b windows at either end.

York Terrace (1821; west end now named **Nottingham Terrace**): 360yds long or nea half the width of the park, the terrace comprises two symmetrical blocks, Yo Gate in the axis of St Marylebone Church *(see MARYLEBONE)* and some detach houses. The sequence of column orders is giant Corinthian in the mansions either end, Ionic above Doric colonnades in the pedimented main blocks and Ionic the houses at York Gate.

Cornwall Terrace (1822): the 187yd front, marked at either end and the centre Corinthian columns, is divided into a number of receding planes. Note through t trees the modest 18C brick houses and old pub on the far side of Baker Stree Park Road, also the lodge with rounded windows and pitched slate roof.

Clarence Terrace (1823): heavily accented Corinthian centre and angles above an lo arcade.

Sussex Place (1822; **London Graduate School of Business Studies**): the most surprisir finialled, slim, octagonal cupolas, in pairs, crown the ends and frame the pe mented centre of the curved terrace; below the domes are canted bays ar between, a continuous line of Corinthian columns (the far side from the park w rebuilt in a modern buttressed style in brick in 1972).

Royal College of Obstetricians and Gynaecologists (1960): the four-storey brick buildi has a stone wing at right angles encompassing the low recessed entrance and ov it, the hall.

Cumberland Terrace, Regent's Park

Hanover Terrace (1822-23): pediments coloured bright blue as a background to plasterwork and serving as pedestals for statuary silhouetted against the sky, mark the terrace. Hanover Gate has a small, octagonal lodge with heavy inverted corbel decoration and niches with statues beneath a pitched slate roof and central octagonal chimney.

The **Mosque** (1977), marked by its 140ft minaret, white with a small gold coloured dome and finial crescent, stands on the site of one of Nash's villas (Albany Cottage) and was designed by Sir Frederick Gibberd. The mosque itself has a pale grey façade pierced by tall arched windows of five lights arranged in groups of four; blind arcades support the drum which rises to a huge, gilded copper dome. Other new buildings accommodate a school and the Islamic Cultural Centre.

Hanover Lodge, one of the 18C villas, has a large modern brick addition. The row of three modern villas alongside (1989) are named **Ionic Villa**, **Veneto Villa** and **Gothick Villa**.

The neo-Georgian house of 1936, **Winfield House**, now the residence of the US ambassador, was built on the site of St Dunstan's Lodge where the organisation for blinded ex-servicemen was founded in 1915. The lodge was designed by Decimus Burton in 1825 for the 3rd Marquess of Hertford *(see index)* who, it is said, used it as a harem. The southern section is flanked by the **Avenue Gardens**, which are being relaid according to the designs prepared by William Andrews Nesfield in 1862.

Park Village West – *Albany Street.* This is the most attractive of the two dependent streets to the terraces. The small houses and modest terraces are in Nash's country cottage style, although not designed by him.

Gloucester Gate (1827): angle pediments with plasterwork against red painted tympana and surmounting statues, mark the main terrace.

Danish Church ⊙ (1829): neo-Gothic church in stock brick. It was built for the St Katharine Royal Hospital Community *(see Outer London: DOCKLANDS)* but was taken over in 1950 by the Danish community whose own building in Limehouse had been bombed. Inside are a coffered ceiling, below the windows shields of English queens from Eleanor to Mary, and beside the modern fittings, John the Baptist and Moses, two of the four figures carved in wood by the 17C Danish sculptor **Caius Cibber** for Limehouse. Outside to the right is a replica of the Jelling Stone.

Cumberland Terrace (1826): the Ionic pillars of the 267yd long façade recur in the intervening arches. Britannia, the arts and science are represented in the central pediment behind squat vases.

Chester Terrace (1825): the longest unbroken façade (313yds) has Corinthian columns rising from ground level to emphasise the ends, centre and mid points between; at either end triumphal, named, arches lead to the access road to the rear.

Cambridge Terrace (1825): The terrace and neighbouring buildings have been restored.

Cambridge Gate (1875): the totally Victorian, stone faced block with pavilion roofs, stands on the site of the Coliseum, a large circular building with a portico and glazed roof used for exhibitions and panoramas (or dioramas).

Royal College of Physicians (1964): tesserae-faced building by Denys Lasdun which extends squarely forward to afford a recessed entrance encased in glass contrasting with a long polygonal construction of black brick to one side covering a hall.

★★**London Zoo** ⊙ – The foundation of a Zoological Society of London was spearheaded by Sir Stamford Raffles (of Singapore fame) and Sir Humphry Davy (1826) for 'the advancement of Zoology and Animal Physiology and the introduction of new and curious subjects of the Animal Kingdom'.

Jumbo has given his name to cuddly toys, chocolate bars and airplanes: the African bull came to London zoo from the Jardin des Plantes in Paris as a sickly (4ft) calf in 1865; when he grew too tall (11ft) and big to offer joy rides to the public, he was sold to the American Circus owner P T Barnum (1882) – his departure attracted such crowds that enough money was raised to fund a new Reptile House (now the Bird House). **Winnie the Pooh** (d 1934) was an American black bear from Winnipeg who was left at the zoo when her owner, Canadian Lieutenant Colebourne, went to the front in 1914; she was so tame that children were allowed to feed her condensed milk and golden syrup in her den – as did Christopher (Robin) Milne. **Guy** the Gorilla **Fawkes** (d 1978) arrived on 5 November 1947 – hence his name. Goldie the Golden Eagle found fame when she escaped (1965) and eluded her captors for a whole fortnight, hovering above the aviary as if in contempt. More contemporary personalities include Chi Chi and Chia Chia the pandas from China, **Josephine** the elderly Great Indian Hornbill spinster (b 1945), who came from Cheshire!

The first part of the original concept has been realised by a collaboration between the Zoological Society and the zoo staff who research into systematic anatomy – the Wellcome Institute of Comparative Physiology (f 1962) and the Nuffield Institute of Comparative Medicine (f 1964) have streamlined studies in reproductive physiology (including human fertility), biochemistry and disease which affect diet, health and husbandry.

The second part of Sir Stamford's proposal to introduce 'curious subjects to the animal kingdom', was realised in 1828 when the Society opened on a site (5 acres) in Regent's Park with a small collection of animals looked after by a keeper in a top hat, bottle green coat and striped waistcoat. The first big cat came from the menagerie at the Tower of London (closed by William IV); the first giraffes, unloaded in the Docklands, had to be led all the way through the City to Regent's Park (May 1836). During the Second World War, the most dangerous animals were destroyed in case the zoo were bombed with devastating consequences.

Today, the major objective of the zoo is to conserve and breed endangered species and to pursue research into the biology of rare animals. A large proportion of the animals are bred in Regent's Park or at Whipsnade Wild Animal Park: two **pandas** are in residence on loan for breeding – Ming Ming from China and Bao Bao from Germany. Domestic animals are presented at close quarters in the **children's zoo.**

Housing – The zoo gardens were originally laid out by **Decimus Burton** who also designed several buildings of which there remain the Ravens' Cage on the Members' Lawn, the Clock Tower, the Giraffe House and the East Tunnel.

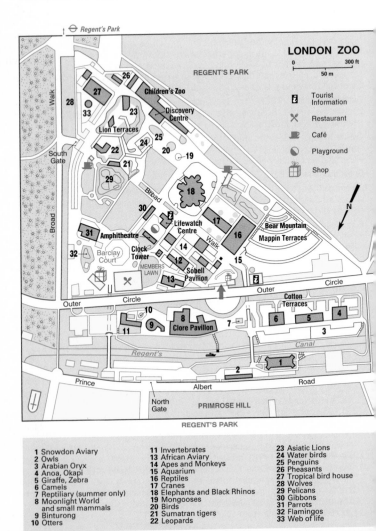

LONDON ZOO

| Tourist Information |
| Restaurant |
| Café |
| Playground |
| Shop |

1 Snowdon Aviary
2 Owls
3 Arabian Oryx
4 Anoa, Okapi
5 Giraffe, Zebra
6 Camels
7 Reptiliary (summer only)
8 Moonlight World and small mammals
9 Binturong
10 Otters
11 Invertebrates
13 African Aviary
14 Apes and Monkeys
15 Aquarium
16 Reptiles
17 Cranes
18 Elephants and Black Rhinos
19 Mongooses
20 Birds
21 Sumatran tigers
22 Leopards
23 Asiatic Lions
24 Water birds
25 Pheasants
26 Pheasants
27 Tropical bird house
28 Wolves
29 Pelicans
30 Gibbons
31 Parrots
32 Flamingos
33 Web of life

Activities

The programme of **daily events** includes animal **feeding times**, bath time for the elephants, animals in the **Amphitheatre** and **animal encounters** in which the keepers introduce the animals in their charge. The Society's latest conservation, scientific and veterinary work is presented in the **Lifewatch Centre**, where the **London Zoo Experience** brings the history of the zoo to life. The **Discovery Centre** enables visitors 'to walk like a camel, hear like an elephant, fly like a bird and see like a giraffe'.

The **Reptile House** (1902) displays crocodiles, snakes, lizards, constrictors, tortoises and alligators behind glass. A cluster of locusts attracts attention in the **Insect House** (1912). Houses for all animals from tropical climates used to be kept heated and closed until the end of the 19C when **Carl Hagenbeck** of Hamburg Zoo revolutionised contemporary practice by providing paddocks for tropical animals and surrounding enclosures not with bars but moats and ditches. His example led to the construction of the **Mappin Terraces** (1914) in London and to the creation of Whipsnade (1931) on derelict farmland (480 acres) in Bedfordshire.

The Zoo has commissioned some highly innovative architecture. Berthold Lubetkin designed the **Great Apes Breeding Colony** (1933) and the **Penguin Pool** (1934) with its intersecting spiral ramps for the penguins to parade 'like arctic supermodels', the first example of such use of pre-stressed concrete, now in standard use. The **Cotton Terraces** (1963) present giraffes and zebras, camels and llamas, horses and cattle, antelope and deer (Père David herd) in new pavilions and Burton's altered Giraffe House. The distinctively roofed **Elephant and Rhino Pavilion** (1965) is by Sir Hugh Casson. Lord Snowdon designed the **Snowdon Aviary** (1965) (150ft by 80ft high) which in summer contains as many as 150 birds in natural surroundings and through which the visitor passes on an elevated walkway. The **Charles Clore Pavilion** for Small Mammals (1967) contains the **Moonlight World**, where one sees animals active only at night.

In 1972 the **Michael Sobell Pavilion** for Apes and Monkeys was built. The **Lion Terraces**, several enclosures planted with trees and bushes from which the big cats survey all lesser mortals, date from 1976. The design for an energy-saving glass building housing the **Web of Life**, which opened in 1999, draws inspiration from a termite nest. The exhibits are devoted to biodiversity and conservation: invertebrates, evolution and extinction of species.

REGENT STREET

Map p 7 (**DX**)
⊖ Oxford Circus

Nothing remains of Nash's colonnades, conceived to run from Oxford Circus to Carlton House *(see REGENT'S PARK)*; all that survives of his scheme is the graceful curve of the **Quadrant**. The New Street, as it was then called, contained chapels and a theatre but the shops (butcher's, greengrocer's and public houses were prohibited) had no room to expand so that from the turn of the century the Classical style fronts were demolished and replaced by the large, dignified buildings of today with plate glass windows and upper sales floors.

On old maps **Oxford Street** appears variously as Tyburn Road, Uxbridge Road and Oxford Road. By the mid 18C it was almost entirely built up on the south side and Cavendish Square *(see MARYLEBONE)* had been laid out on the Harley Estate (north side). A turnpike just before the junction with Park Lane marked the western limit of what soon became London's prime shopping street.

Portland Place – In the 18C the street was a fashionable promenade; the north end was closed by gates; both sides were lined by houses designed by Robert and James Adam; its width was dictated by the façade of Foley House at the south end. At either end are statues of Lord Lister (1827-1912) – the founder of antiseptic surgery who lived in Park Crescent, and Quintin Hogg – who founded the Regent Street Polytechnic in 1882. Only one *(no 46)* of the Adam houses has survived. The tall stone corner building *(no 66)*, adorned with reliefs on the façade and on the pillars, was erected in 1934 to celebrate the centenary of the **Royal Institute of British Architects** (RIBA). In 1864 Foley House was replaced by the **Langham Hotel**, a high Victorian building with a pavilion roof. The distinctive curved front of **Broadcasting House**, home to BBC Radio, was designed by G Val Myer in 1931.

The BBC Experience ⊘ *(timed tickets, 90mins)* celebrates a few of the most classic radio programmes like *The Archers*, *Desert Island Discs* and *Hancock's Half Hour* and provides a rare insight into the workings of a great British institution.

All Souls ⊘ – The church was designed by John Nash as a pivot between Portland Place and Regent Street. Its unique feature, a circular portico of tall Ionic pillars, surmounted by a ring of columns supporting a fluted spire, was designed to look the same from whatever angle et was approached. The church, Nash's only important church, is a traditional, galleried hall church, built of Bath stone. The unusual inverted arches of the foundations were revealed in 1976, when the undercroft was excavated and the floor raised 18ins. The BBC morning service usually comes live from All Souls.

Chandos Street – The street is named after the Duke of Chandos, who proposed to build a palatial residence but was hard hit when the South Sea Bubble burst in 1720. At the north end, facing south, is the perfectly proportioned **Chandos House** (1771), now occupied by the Royal Society of Medicine, designed by the Scotsman Robert Adam and resembling one of his own immaculate drawings. It is built of Portland stone, is four bays wide and three floors high; the only embellishments are a narrow frieze above the second floor, the square porch and the 18C iron railings, complete with lamp holders and snuffers.

Oxford Circus – Oxford Street stretches west to Marble Arch and Hyde Park beyond. Its status as a shopping street was confirmed when Gordon Selfridge erected his vast and imposing shop in 1908; colossal Ionic columns soared up through three floors to an attic and

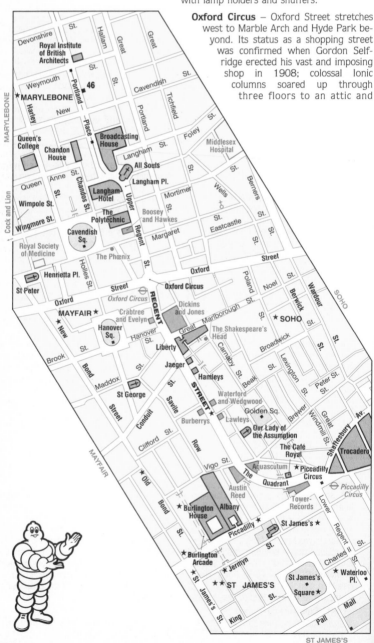

ST JAMES'S

balustrade; a canopy protected the entrance and the windows displayed goods in a new way. The other major shops are John Lewis, D H Evans, Debenhams and Marks and Spencer.

Eastwards this major thoroughfare becomes New Oxford Street and stretches to the TUC building.

* **Regent Street** – Dickins and Jones, Liberty's, Jaeger, Hamley's Toyshop, Aquascutum, the Café Royal, Austin Reed all line this elegant street sweeping southwards to Piccadilly Circus and the heart of the West End.

Regent Street Polytechnic

On 20 February 1896 the first public demonstration of the Lumière Brothers' Cinématographe was made at the Regent St Poly at 9 Regent's Street, now part of the University of Westminster. Due to the apparent lack of interest, the showing of the most popular films, *The Arrival of a Train* and *Baby's Breakfast Time*, were soon moved from the Great Hall to the Marlborough Hall. On 9 March screenings were transferred to the Empire in Leicester Square – which continues to this day to premiere films.

Liberty & Co – was founded by Arthur Liberty, the son of a draper, in 1875 with a loan of £1 500 from his future father-in-law: it soon acquired the dignified title of 'Emporium' stocking broad ranges of exotic silks imported from the East, Japanese porcelain – wallpapers and fans followed, and when it introduced a 'costume department... to establish the craft of dressmaking upon some hygienic, intelligible and progressive basis, uninfluenced by the ateliers of Paris' under the direction of the architect-designer E W Godwin it was quick to become associated with the Aesthetic Movement. Furniture, made in workshops in Soho supplemented the imported ranges. Own brand fabrics were made to different weights (from lawn to furnishing and upholstery materials) after traditional Indian prints so familiar already to colonials and from designs commissioned from C F A Voysey, Butterfield, Arthur Silver – sympathetic to the Aesthetic and Arts and Crafts Movements. The Liberty jewellery resulted from dealings with the Continent where Art Nouveau was flourishing and from where furniture was imported. An affiliation with a Birmingham firm of goldsmiths (W H Haseler) was consolidated in the Cymric range of silver and enamel pieces, the pewter Tudric range followed. The distinctive spirit of the Liberty Style was modelled on Celtic entrelacs and flowing organic asymmetrical designs. Emphasis was placed upon craftsmanship and applied to contemporary ceramics from factories in Germany and Hungary as well as at home: Wedgwood, Poole, Royal Doulton and glassware. The success of the Art Nouveau Style lasted until the outbreak of war in 1914, after which furniture manufacture reverted to Queen Anne and Tudor styles. Liberty fabrics and jewellery, however continue much in the same traditional vein.

Note the splendid pediment on the Regent Street facade, dominated by the great figure of Britannia, with three stone ladies behind overlooking the parapet! The **Tudor Building** (1922-24) in Great Marlborough Street, was designed by Edwin T and Stanley Hall, and built from oak and teak timbers taken from the Royal Navy's last two sailing ships.

The **Café Royal**, now a multi-floored restaurant with a hall where the National Sporting Club meets, a Masonic Temple and banqueting rooms, began as a tiny eating house opened in 1863 in Glasshouse Street by a Burgundian and his wife. Daniel Nichols, as he anglicised his name, built up a reputation for good wine and good food, prospered and moved to the fashionable site in the Quadrant. In France the Second Empire was at its height; in Regent Street the Café Royal adopted a new name and as house emblem a crowned N wreathed in laurel leaves! In the 1890s the café became the meeting place of writers and artists Oscar Wilde, Lord Alfred Douglas, Aubrey Beardsley, Whistler, George Moore, Max Beerbohm, Augustus John, Orpen...

On the south side of the Quadrant several small streets lead through to Piccadilly.

For Piccadilly Circus, see PICCADILLY.

The Importance of Being Earnest, a 'Trivial Comedy for Serious People', opened at the St James' Theatre in 1895. The play in four acts was cut by George Alexander for production, during the rehearsals attended by Oscar Wilde, he is reported as having commented 'Yes, it is quite a good play. I remember I wrote one very like it myself, but it was even more brilliant than this.'

ST JAMES'S ★★

St James's earned its name from a hospital for 'maidens that were leprous' founded, it is thought at the time of the Norman Conquest, and dedicated to St James the Less, Bishop of Jerusalem. The buildings were acquired by Henry VIII who subsequently built a palace there. The domain was later given by Charles II at the Restoration to his loyal courtier, Henry Jermyn, later Earl of St Albans, who speedily developed the empty fields into an elegant suburb for members of the re-established court.

The founder of the West End, as he has since been described, laid out his estate around a square from which roads led from the centre of each side (not, as became the custom, from the corners): to the east was a large market bordered by the Haymarket, to the north lay Jermyn Street, the local shopping street and, in the axis of Duke of York Street stood the church. The community was self-contained; within a railed enclosure in the square the fashionable residents could take a promenade.

At the end of the Stuart monarchy, vacated private houses were taken over by the clubs. The latter had originated in taverns, coffee and chocolate houses where men of similar calling or like interest, who enjoyed congenial company, made a practice of meeting regularly. Their gatherings developed into subscription groups with reserved quarters and finally they took over the houses in which they met, employing the owner or publican as manager and enhancing the amenities, particularly the food for which many became famous. In the period of Beau Brummell (1778-1840) and the Prince Regent, the clubs were known as the resort of the wealthy and the fashionable and as infamous gambling centres. Numbers grew until by the turn of the 19C-20C there were nearly 200 in the West End; now there are fewer than 30. Their character has also changed from 18C flamboyance, to 19C silence and reserve and now to a modified social function or gaming.

St James's has remained a masculine world of bespoke boot and shoemakers, shirt-makers and hatters, sword, gun and rod makers, antique and 18C picture dealers, wine merchants, cheese vendors, jewellers traditional and modern, fine art auctioneers. Although banking and property companies have invaded St James's Street it is still the address of eight of London's principal clubs, Pall Mall of five.

★**Piccadilly south side** – The shops here parade their merchandise with flair: silk, leather, cashmere, tweed; wines and spirits, fruit and preserves; books; china, glass and kitchenware; military memorabilia; umbrellas and walking sticks; hairbrushes; rifles and guns...

Of the most traditional establishments, it is worth noting no **203** (formerly Simpson's, now Waterstone's) for its fine, elegantly proportioned, simple yet sophisticated building (1935); **Hatchard's** *(no 187)* established by John Hatchard in 1797 with a capital of £5 and still trading from its original 18C building with small-panelled windows on either side of the entrance. In **Fortnum and Mason's** (founded 1707) the tail coats of the assistants once added to the sense of luxury; when the clock (1964) above the Piccadilly entrance chimes the hour Mr Fortnum and Mr Mason emerge and bow to one another.

★**St James's Church** ⊙ – Wren, the automatic choice of architect in 1676 for the new parish church, built a plain basilica of brick with Portland stone dressings and balustrade and a square tower. Plain glass windows, segmental below and tall and rounded above, line the north and south walls and a tripartite and superimposing Venetian window fills the east end. The original entrance was placed in the south wall looking down Duke of York Street to the square; in the 19C the local emphasis had changed and new entrances were made on both sides of the tower.

The galleried interior is roofed with a barrel vault and entablature, richly decorated with plasterwork, fashioned from mouldings made from bomb damaged fragments. The organ came from the Roman Catholic Whitehall Chapel, donated by Queen Mary, the daughter of James II; its case, surmounted by figures, is original as is the altarpiece of gilded wood with garlands of flowers and fruit, the pelican with her young all carved by **Grinling Gibbons**, and the marble font in the form of a tree of life with Adam and Ève on either side. Several artists including the two van der Veldes are buried here (plaque in vestibule) in what is the parish church of the Royal Academy. The outdoor pulpit against the north wall dates from 1902.

★**Piccadilly Arcade** – This arcade, bright with bow fronted shops, links Piccadilly to Jermyn Street.

★**Jermyn Street** – The narrow street boasts shirtmakers, pipemakers, antique dealers, antiquarian booksellers, the original Walls sausage shop (no 113), a chemist with real sponges, a provision merchant *(Paxton and Whitfield, no 93)* selling countless varieties of cheese over a wooden counter, a perfumer *(Floris, no 89)* modern jewels *(Andrew Grima, no 80)*, restaurants (including Wall's original shop), bars, chambers and the Cavendish, a luxury hotel, on the site of the famous Edwardian rendezvous.

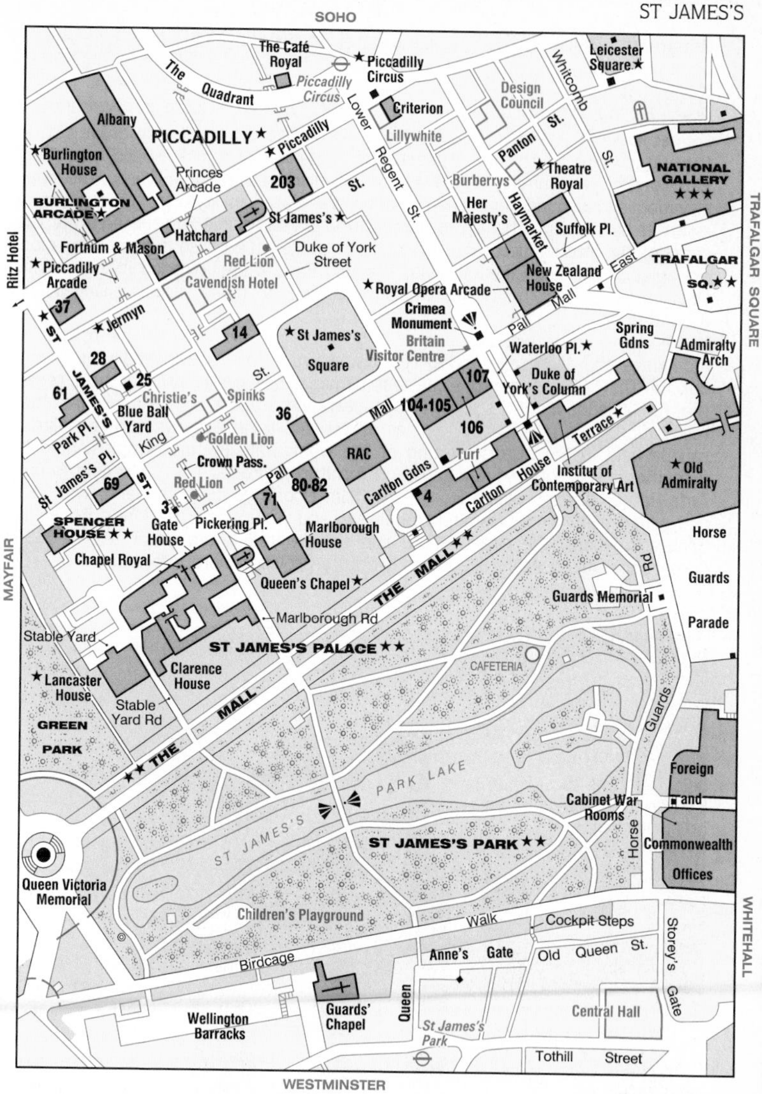

★**St James's Street** – The wide street, unnamed but clearly marked in early 17C maps as the approach from Piccadilly to St James's Palace, developed as part of the district and by the end of the century was lined on either side by town houses including those of merchants who fled the City after the Great Plague and Fire of 1665 and 1666. It retains an atmosphere of quiet elegance with individual shops, restaurants and clubs. The most famous buildings (from north to south) include:

White's Club (*no 37*) established in 1693 from a coffee-house of the same name. This club, the oldest and Tory in character, occupies a house of 1788 to which the famous bow window was added in 1811. The façade was renewed in 1852.

Boodle's Club (*no 28*) dates from 1762 and the building from 1765. Between identical porches is a bay window (1821) below a rounded Venetian style window.

The Economist (*no 25*) complex consists of three canted glass towers around a courtyard (1966-68) and provides the periodical with editorial offices as well as a space for exhibitions of contemporary art.

Brooks's Club (*no 60 – opposite The Economist*) was founded as the rival Whig club to White's in 1764 by the politician Charles James Fox and the Duke of Portland. The club occupies a house built of yellow brick and stone designed by **Henry Holland**, Robert Adam's rival, in 1778 in which year it took over the famous Almack's of Pall Mall.

Park Place – The narrow street is almost filled with the buildings and annexes of the **Royal Overseas League** (f 1910; 50 000 members). No 14 was formerly Pratt's.

Blue Ball Yard – The far end of the gaslit yard is lined by stables of 1742, now garages, but still with round niches in the walls where iron hay baskets once hung. Above are the old tiled cottage quarters and, in the corner, the Stafford Hotel.

ST JAMES'S

St James's Place – The L shaped street is lined by 18C houses, some with decorative fanlights and continuous iron balconies. Castlemaine House (1959-60), a block of flats, strongly horizontal in line, was designed by **Denys Lasdun**. The Royal Ocean Racing Club *(no 20 – around the corner)* is a neat Georgian town house.

★★**Spencer House** ⊘ – *No 27.* Spencer House is, today, the city's only great 18C aristocratic town house to survive intact. The house was built in 1756-66 for John, 1st Earl Spencer who initially employed the Palladian architect John Vardy; the external elevation and ground floor rooms reflect the Palladian style. In 1758 Vardy was replaced by James 'Athenian' Stuart who was responsible for the accurate Greek detail of the interior decoration (first floor rooms); the house is one of the pioneer examples of the neo-Classical style. The 2nd Earl, who succeeded in 1783, invited Henry Holland, son-in-law of 'Capability' Brown, to make various changes to the ground floor.

In 1942 the house was stripped of original fixtures with chimneypieces, panelling mouldings and architraves being removed to Althorp – providentially as it turned out for the house suffered some war damage. Spencer House has now regained the full splendour of its late 18C appearance after a ten-year programme of restoration. It is now partly used as offices and as a place where entertainments can be held in the historic setting of the eight State Rooms complemented by a magnificent collection of paintings and furniture: *(ground floor)* Morning Room or Ante Room; Library; Dining Room; the Palm Room, designed by Vardy with carved and gilded palm trees, framing the alcove; and *(first floor)* the Music Room, Lady Spencer's Room, the Great Room and the Painted Room decorated in Stuart's Greek style. An excellent illustrated brochure provides more information.

St James's Palace

The **Carlton Club** *(69 St James's St)*, which originated as 'Arthur's', was formed in 1832 by the Duke of Wellington. It is now in an early 19C Palladian stone building which incorporates rooms once part of White's Chocolate and Gaming House. No **74**, formerly the Conservative Club, was designed by **George Basevi** and **Sydney Smirke** in the mid 19C, in modified Palladian style including a canted bay window.

The Constitutional Club (1883), the Savage (1857), the National and the Flyfishers were formerly located at no 86 in a magnificent Victorian golden ochre stone building (1862).

On the opposite side of the street stands **Byron House** *(nos 7-9)*, built in the 1960s on the site of the house in which Byron awoke to find himself famous after the publication of his *Childe Harold* (1811). Long-established businesses in the vicinity include **Lobb's** the bespoke bootmaker *(no 9)*; **Lock's** the firm of hatters *(no 6)* since 1700 – the topper in the window is 19C and **Berry Bros & Rudd** *(no 3)*, the wine merchants 'established in the XVII century'. The half timbered passage beside the shop (note the wall plaque recording the stay of the Republic of Texas legation in an upstairs room 1842-45) leads to **Pickering Place**, a gaslit court of 18C houses, reputed to be the site of the last duel to be fought in London.

At the south end, echoing the corner opposite, are two buildings by **Norman Shaw** in terracotta brick and stone, with asymmetric gables, friezes and an angle tower.

Pickering's, later known as **Berry Brothers & Rudd Ltd,** has occupied this site, identified as Henry VIII's tennis court, since 1731. The sign of the coffee-mill hanging outside no 3 was put there by the Widow Bourne to mark her grocer's shop (1690s). As the shop was handed down through the generations, business, which had included 'arms painting and heraldic furnishings', moved into spices, smoking tobacco, snuff, fine teas and coffee, maybe claret and port, to become one of the best and most comprehensive grocer's of the day, judiciously placed for the 18C Beau Monde by St James's Palace. The variously fashionable commodities were carefully weighed from the great brass weighing beams, as were the more notable customers: indeed, a Register of Weights has been kept since 1765. The last remaining stocks of groceries were sold in 1896. The original dark panelling, oval table and Windsor chairs all date from the 18C.

★★**St James's Palace** – In 1532 the 'goodly manor' built by Henry VIII was converted into a crenellated and turreted palace entered through the **Gate House** at the bottom of St James's Street, even then a regular thoroughfare. The original and early palace buildings, considerably more extensive before the fire of 1809, which destroyed the east wing, are of the traditional 16C Tudor red brick with a diaper pattern and stone trim along the line of the crenellations. With later additions they now surround only four courts: Colour, Friary, Ambassadors' and Engine which are lit at night by crowned wall standards.

St James's Palace was the last royal palace to be built as such in the capital. Many kings and queens have been born or died in the palace. Charles I spent his last night in the guardroom, before walking across the park to his execution at the Banqueting House on 30 January 1649. After Whitehall Palace had burned down in 1698, St James's became the chief royal residence and, although no longer so, it remains the statutory seat – proclamations are made from the balcony in Friary Court and ambassadors are accredited to the Court of St James. The interior of the palace bears the imprint of successive architects and designers: Wren, Grinling Gibbons, Hawksmoor, Kent and William Morris. The splendid State Apartments are hung with full length portraits of Stuart and Hanoverian monarchs. Today the palace serves as the official residence of the Prince of Wales, the Duke and Duchess of Kent and Princess Alexandra.

Chapel Royal ⊙ – *Ambassadors Court.* The huge Tudor Gothic window, visible from the exterior to the right of the palace gateway, lights the Chapel Royal and its so-called Holbein ceiling. The choir is famous for its long tradition since the medieval period and the choristers wear scarlet and gold state coats at services. Besides several royal marriages conducted here including that of Queen Victoria to Prince Albert (1840), was the wedding of Sir Christopher Wren to his second wife Jane Fitzwilliam (1676).

For security reasons, access to this area is severely restricted: the buildings may be clearly seen however from Green Park, accessible at the far end of Cleveland Row, and the Mall.

Clarence House – *Stable Yard.* The distinctive white stucco home of Queen Elizabeth, the Queen Mother, was built in 1825 by John Nash for the Duke of Clarence, the future William IV. It is best seen from the Mall.

Lancaster House – *Stable Yard.* The golden Bath stone mansion, designed by Benjamin Wyatt in 1825 for the Duke of York, who died in 1827, then became the town house of the Marquesses of Stafford and the Dukes of Sutherland. For many years in the 19C it was the setting for balls and soirées; today it maintains that function as the Government's hospitality centre.

Inside reigns an opulent Baroque magnificence – not for nothing did Queen Victoria on a visit declare to her hostess 'I have come from my house to your palace'. Painted plaster ceilings, vast pictures, gilding and chandeliers deck the state apartments.

Green Park – The acres now known as Green Park were added to St James's Park in 1667 by Charles II, who in the early morning would regularly walk up a path to what is now Hyde Park Corner – hence 'Constitution Hill'. From the east side of the park there is a fine view of Spencer House.

Follow left towards the Mall for a good view of Buckingham Palace, and continue round to Marlborough Road. Note in passing the gaslight lanterns crested with gilded crowns.

★**Queen's Chapel** ⊙ – Past a large *art nouveau* bronze group in memory of Queen Alexandra (1926) is the entrance to the Queen's Chapel, intended for the Infanta Maria of Spain but completed for Charles I's eventual queen, Henrietta Maria, in 1625 by **Inigo Jones**. It was the first church in England to be designed completely outside the Perpendicular Gothic tradition. As a Roman Catholic foundation it was at first served by a friary of Capuchins and originally formed part of the palace; the road separating it from Friary Court dates from 1809.

The pedimented exterior of rendered cement with Portland stone dressings has three principal windows at the west end, of which the central one is arched above the unobtrusive, straight-headed door; at the east end is a broad Venetian window. The curved white coffered ceiling, framed by a richly detailed cornice, is picked out in gold above the chancel. The greyish-green walls are the original colour, the royal and other galleries, lower panelling, stalls and lectern are mid 17C; the organ loft is by Grinling Gibbons. The beauty of the small edifice lies in its perfect proportions (a double cube) and the simplicity of the interior decoration.

On the corner overlooking the Mall note the life-like relief by Reid-Dick of Queen Mary.

Marlborough House – While John Churchill, **Duke of Marlborough**, was winning the final victories in the seemingly endless War of the Spanish Succession (Blenheim 1704, Ramillies 1706, Oudenaarde 1708) and the Duchess was appointed one of the Ladies of the Bedchamber to Queen Anne and supervising the construction by Vanbrugh of Blenheim Palace (1705-24), Wren, in two years (1709-1711), designed and completed Marlborough House. It was altered in 1771 by William Chambers and enlarged in the 19C.

Diana, Princess of Wales (1961-97)

Following the tragic death of Diana, Princess of Wales in a car accident in Paris, her body was brought to the Chapel Royal, St James's Palace. On Friday 5 September the coffin was transferred to her private apartments at Kensington Palace before being carried in procession through Hyde Park, down Constitution Hill, along The Mall, through Horse Guards and Whitehall to Westminster Abbey for the funeral service, and thereafter north by road to her final resting place in Althorp Park, the Spencer family seat.

Pall Mall – The ancient way from the City to St James's Palace is named after an avenue planted to its north which served as an alley for the game brought over from France early in the 17C and much favoured by the Stuarts. When St James's was developed, the avenue was cut down, the road lined with houses and renamed after the old alley.

Crown Passage *(opposite Marlborough House, under 59-60)* is a narrow alley leading past the 19C **Red Lion** pub and the back entrances to Locks' the hatters. The far end opens out into King Street where the two world-famous establishments: **Christie's** *(no 8)*, fine art auctioneers, founded in 1766 at the height of the fashion for doing the Grand Tour, and **Spinks** *(no 5)*, specialists in coins, medals and orders, as well as antiques of all kinds, have their headquarters.

Angel Court leads back past the **Golden Lion**, a Victorian pub, gleaming with cut mirror glass and mahogany, to Pall Mall.

The **Oxford and Cambridge Club** *(no 71)* was founded in 1830 by Lord Palmerston at the British Coffee-house in Cockspur Street.

The dark red brick exterior of **Schomberg House** *(no 80-82)* dates from 1698; Nell Gwynne lived next door *(no 79)*, still the only freehold property on the south side of the street.

The **Army and Navy Club (no 36)** (founded 1839) was rebuilt in 1963 – not to be confused with the Naval and Military in St James's Square.

The **RAC** (Royal Automobile Club) is a vast building (1911) constructed by the builders of the Ritz.

★**St James's Square** – The square, with a Classical equestrian statue of William III (1807) beneath very tall plane trees, is encircled by modern offices and 19C residences except on the north and west sides where there are still Georgian town houses. Of them the most notable are no 4 of 1676, remodelled in 1725 – Ionic porch, rich cornice and continuous iron balcony – and now the home of the Naval and Military Club; no 5 of 1748-51 with 18C and 19C additions; no 13 of 1740 with faked mortar uprights to give an all-header effect to the blackened brick wall; no 15, **Lichfield House**, of 1764-65 James 'Athenian' Stuart's perfect Classical stone façade with its continuous iron balcony; fluted columns mark the doorway and embrace the upper floors beneath a pediment (the first house on the site was built in 1673 and occupied by Frances, Duchess of Richmond, a famed beauty in her day known as 'La Belle Stewart' who modelled as the Britannia featured on the old penny coin); and no 20 built by Adam in 1775 with no 21 its 20C mirror image. No 32 was the town residence of the Bishops of London from 1771 to 1919. No 31, Norfolk House, where George III was born, served as General Eisenhower's headquarters in 1942 and 1944.

No 14 (of 1896) is the **London Library**, no 12 with a stucco front and Tuscan pillared porch is possibly by Cubitt (1836) and nos 9-10, Chatham House, the Royal Institute of International Affairs (f 1920). The houses date from 1736 and no 10, in its time, has been residence of three Prime Ministers: William Pitt 1757-61, Edward Stanley 1837-54 and William Gladstone, 1890.

The **Reform Club (104-105 Pall Mall)**, which was established in opposition to the Carlton by Whig supporters at the time of the Reform Bill in 1832, is housed in a 19C Italian palazzo building, on the renumbered site of the house where John Julius Angerstein lived.

The **Travellers' Club (106 Pall Mall)**, also an Italian palazzo building (19C), was founded in 1819 with a rule that members must have travelled a minimum of 500 miles (now 1 000) outside the British Isles in a straight line from London.

★**Waterloo Place** – Pall Mall is intersected by Waterloo Place designed by John Nash as a broad approach to Carlton House, the southern end of his grand route linking the royal residence to Regent's Park; it lost its climax when the house was demolished in 1829 but gained a vista across St James's Park *(see BUCKINGHAM PALACE)*. In the northern half stands the **Crimea Monument**. The beginning of the southern half is marked by two clubs, planned by Nash, which face each other across the place. The **Athenaeum** *(no 107 Pall Mall)*, designed by Decimus Burton, is a square stucco block (1829-30) with Classical touches: torches, Roman Doric pillars supporting the porch, the gilded figure of Pallas Athene and the important Classical frieze in deference to the membership of the club which was founded as a meeting place for artists, men of letters and connoisseurs. South of the entrance is the Duke of Wellington's mounting block. Opposite *(no 116)* stands a building of similar size and style, designed by Nash but remodelled by Burton in 1842; formerly the United Services Club, it now houses the Institute of Directors.

Carlton Gardens is a small grass plot shaded by plane trees and surrounded by four grand houses. Kitchener lived at no 2 and Palmerston at no 4 (demolished and rebuilt in 1933): between 1940-45 it served as the headquarters of the Free French Forces. A tablet is inscribed with General de Gaulle's famous call to arms to the French people broadcast on 18 June 1940. The statue (1993) of the general is by Angela Conner.

At the west end of the Carlton House terrace, overlooking the Mall is a slim bronze statue of **George VI** by William McMillan.

★**Carlton House Terrace** – In 1732 Frederick, Prince of Wales purchased **Carlton House** (1709) which stood on the south side of Pall Mall backing on to St James's Park. The house had been refaced in stone when it was taken over in 1772 by the Prince Regent, who commissioned Henry Holland to make further alterations. At a cost of £800 000, it was transformed into the most gorgeous mansion in the land. In 1825, however, five years after his accession to the throne, George IV grew tired of the house and transferred his attention to Buckingham Palace.

Carlton House was demolished in 1829 and the government commissioned Nash, who had just completed the development of Regent's Park, to design similar terraces for St James's Park; only two were built.

The entrances, on the north side, have porches, sometimes in pairs, flanked by Tuscan or Ionic pillars and capped by balconies; Lord Curzon once lived at no 1. Between the two terraces, at the top of the steps leading down to the Mall is the **Duke of York's Column**, a pink granite column just tall enough, according to his contemporaries to place the Duke out of reach of his creditors; this is the same 'Grand Old Duke of York, who had ten thousand men; he marched them up to the top of the hill and marched them down again'.

The south side of the terrace, facing onto St James's Park is more majestic: each block is 31 bays wide with central pediments and angle pavilions, giant Corinthian columns and balconies, resting on squat, white-painted fluted cast-iron columns.

Turn back up to Pall Mall.

★**Royal Opera Arcade** – The delightful row of bow-fronted shops was designed by **Nash** and Repton in 1817 as one of three arcades surrounding the then Royal Opera House to harmonise with other buildings opposite in the Haymarket and Suffolk Place. It presently accommodates a number of branches of Farlow's who specialise in equipment for hunting, fishing, shooting and other country pursuits.

New Zealand House – *Haymarket.* Since 1963, the 15-storey tower above a 4 storey podium, 225ft in all, has stood sentinel at the bottom of the street. It is glazed overall, banded in stone, recessed at ground level to provide a canopy. The bronze statue of George III on horseback in Cockspur Street completes the scene – the future king was born in St James's Square.

Her Majesty's (The King's) – Opposite, on the corner of Charles II Street, is the fourth theatre on the site, a Victorian, French pavilioned, building with an ornate but efficient interior plan, constructed by Beerbohm Tree as his own in 1895-97. Originally home to the Italian Opera in London, the theatre now stages major musicals.

★**Theatre Royal, Haymarket** – When **John Nash** designed the theatre in 1821 with a great pedimented portico, he resited it to stand, unlike its predecessor of 1720, in the axis of Charles II Street and so enjoy a double aspect. The interior (remodelled) is most elegantly decorated in deep blue, gold and white.

Panton Street recalls Colonel Panton, a notorious card-player and gambler, who of an evening in 1664 won enough money to purchase 'a parcel of ground at Piccadilly'.

For Leicester Square turn to SOHO.

ST PANCRAS

Map p 7 (**EV**)
⊖ King's Cross-St Pancras

The area contains three of London's six mainline railway terminals situated as near the city centre as was permitted in the 19C. To the east stands **King's Cross** (1852), the Great Northern terminus, built by Lewis Cubitt; the clock in the tower was displayed at the 1851 Exhibition *(see SOUTH KENSINGTON)*; the front is largely masked by an advanced single-storey hall providing covered access to the platforms at the rear. **St Pancras** (1864), the Midland terminus, medieval Gothic in brick with Italian terracotta, was designed by Sir George Gilbert Scott. **Euston** (1837), the London and North Western terminus, was rebuilt in 1968; exposed plain black piers support glass panels; the interior is recessed west of the centre to provide a colonnade; a statue of Robert Stephenson, chief engineer of the London Birmingham line (1838) stands in the forecourt.

London Canal Museum ⊙ – *12-13 New Wharf Road.* The museum is housed in an old ice house beside the Battlebridge basin on the Regent's Canal which once supplied Carlo Gatti, Victorian London's leading ice-cream maker with natural ice from Norway. An old film, *Barging through London,* illustrates canal life in 1924.

St Pancras' Station building

The display records the building of canals in England, the construction of the Regent's Canal, the various methods of towing or propelling the barges (horse-power, legging, poling, steam tug, towpath tractors), 20C decline and conversion to leisure use: towpath walk (1970); boating, canoeing, fishing.

Camley Street Natural Park – Overlooked by the Victorian gas-holders at King's Cross, a wild life haven has been created in a 2 acre park on the banks of the Regent's Canal including ponds, a marsh and reed beds with the aim of attracting insects, butterflies, birds and wild fowl.

British Library ⊙ – *96 Euston Road.* Eight years behind schedule and three-times over budget, the new red brick premises have earned few compliments, described by the Prince of Wales as 'a dim collection of sheds groping for some symbolic significance'. In the forecourt stands a powerful statue of Sir Isaac Newton by the British sculptor Edouardo Paolozzi.

In contrast the entrance hall in light Portland stone rises the full height of the building and the eye is drawn to the stacks of the King George III Library. The reading rooms which boast computerized catalogues are quiet havens. Three exhibition galleries present the library's treasures – advanced technology enables visitors to turn the pages of rare books at the touch of a finger; the story of book production from the Middle Ages to the present time and temporary exhibitions on related themes.

The British Library collections include rare manuscripts, Books of Hours, examples of early printing (Caxton and Wynkyn de Worde's books), famous works (Lindisfarne Gospel, Codex Sinaiticus, Gutenberg Bible), handmade books, children's books, postage stamps, George III's library, Henry Davis' Gift (fine bindings). Among the broad range of historical documents (early maps, musical scores, modern calligraphy) are copies of the Magna Carta, Essex's death warrant, Nelson's last letter, Shakespeare's signature and first folio (1623). The core collection is stored on site while books less in demand are kept at different locations.

The new precincts now also accommodate the **National Sound Archive** for discs and tape recordings of music, oral history, documentary material, spoken literature, language and dialect.

St Pancras Parish Church ⊙ – *Upper Woburn Place, Euston Road.* The church was built in 1819-22 at the time of the Greek Revival and William Inwood's design, selected from 30 submitted in response to an advertisement, echoes the Erechteon in the caryatids supporting the roofs of the square vestries, north and south. The columned two-stage elevation of the octagonal steeple and front Classical colonnade are modelled on Pericles' Temple of the Winds.

Too tall to fit, the caryatid figures had to have their trunks shortened – hence their air of malaise.

Wellcome Building – *183 Euston Road.* The Institute houses **Science for Life** ⊙, an exhibition about medical research and bio-medicine. Changing thematic exhibitions based on the Henry Wellcome collection show how instruments and technology are used in medical treatment and interventions. The Trust also runs an **Information Service** for members of the public wishing to research any aspect of the human sciences: medical treatments, different surgical interventions and current published findings into genetic disorders and such diseases as cancers, AIDS, schizophrenia, etc.

CAMDEN TOWN ⊖ *Camden Town*

Roundhouse – *Chalk Farm.* Ambitious plans to turn the 1840s former locomotive shed, a listed building, into television, radio and recording studios and to create large and small theatre spaces, a glass-covered restaurant and landscaped garden are in hand.

Jewish Museum ⊙ – *129/131 Albert Street, near Parkway, Camden Town.* The museum at Raymond Burton House provides an introduction to the history of London's Jewish community with coins, silver and artefacts acquired. Portraits of worthies (17C-19C) record the faces of successful individuals while painted porcelain figures (Bow, Minton, Derby and Rockingham) illustrate the more familiar sight and character of the rag trader. The Alfred Rubens Ceremonial Art Gallery *(upstairs)* displays a fabulous collection of ritual objects including a 16C Venetian Ark of the Law, Torah scroll holders of beaten silver and mantles of embroidered silk; exquisitely crafted silver receptacles from the Continent. Prayer books and intricately painted parchment marriage contracts emphasise the importance of ceremony and devotional tradition in Jewish culture.

In stark contrast to the local terraced houses, the Post-modernist **TV-AM building**, in Hawley Crescent, was designed by T Farrell.

Camden Market – *Corner of Camden High Street and Buck Street.* Endless rails of leather jackets, heavy boots and biking gear *(see INTRODUCTION: Shopping).*

Camden Lock Market – *Chalk Farm Road to Camden Town.* Facing onto the canal, the former timber wharf was renovated in the late 1980s and offered at low rents to young artisans for use as workshops. At weekends, endless ethnic food stalls open up to cater to the crowds of browsers. The **Regent's Canal Information Centre** presents historical displays relating to the canal development.

The Stables Antique Market – The Stables, as their name suggests were built in the 1840s to accommodate the horses that hauled the barges along the Regent's canal. The present buildings put up in the 1950s provide spacious premises for a large market for dealers in collectables (Art-Deco

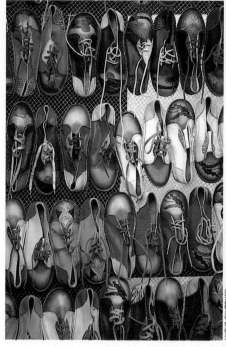

Footwear from Camden Lock Market

artefacts, 50s and 60s clothing, period fixtures and fittings) and antiques. Outside, the cobbled yard has more stalls and dealers.

ST PAUL'S CATHEDRAL★★★

Map pp 8-9 (**FX**) and area map under CITY.
⊖ St Paul's

St Paul's Cathedral is the mother-church of the Diocese of London which embraces some 500 parishes north of the Thames. It was here on 19 July 1981, that the mariage of HRH Prince Charles to Lady Diana Spencer was celebrated with pomp and glory.

Ever since the dome of St Paul's first rose out of the ashes of the Great Fire (1666) amongst a host of elegant church spires it came to be a talisman for Londoners. In December 1940 when the whole City and docks were set ablaze, the dome soared above the smoke and flames, a symbol of hope appearing each morning serene against the pale dawn sky (specific orders for its protection were given by Churchill).

After nearly three centuries this glorious dome has lost none of its majesty although it is now surrounded by towering office blocks.

For the sights outside the immediate vicinity, turn to the section entitled The CITY.

Old St Paul's – The present cathedral of St Paul is probably the fifth or even the sixth to stand on the site. Records document a church founded here in AD 604. A second edifice may have been built under the aegis of St Erkenwald, Bishop of London (675-685); it or its successor was burnt down by the Danes in 962. A subsequent building was then devastated by fire in 1087.

The next cathedral was planned on a grand scale with a nave of 12 bays, far-flung transepts and a shallow, apsed chancel; in 1221 the massive tower above the central crossing was embellished with a lead-covered 514ft steeple (in 1561 this was struck by lightning and caught fire – despite the evidence of some contemporary engravings, it was never replaced); work lasted until 1240. In 1258-1314 the chancel was replaced by a longer decorated choir so that the building measured 620ft from east to west.

During the 14C the building was allowed to suffer neglect and even desecration: the west towers were used as prisons, relics and shrines were looted, according to a Bishop of Durham of the time 'the south aisle'was used 'for popery and usury and the north for Simony, and the horse fair in the midst for all kinds of bargains, meetings, brawlings, murders, conspiracies and the font for ordinary payments of money'.

Royal commissions under the first two Stuarts on the 'decayed fabric' resulted in repairs to the choir screen, the refacing of the nave and west transept walls and in the addition at the west end of an outstanding Classical portico with columns (50ft high) designed by **Inigo Jones.**

The Civil War brought, in Carlyle's words, 'horses stamping in the canons' stalls' and mean shops squatting in the portico. A new commission (1663) was selected and included **Christopher Wren**, then 31 and untried as an architect though reputed as a geometer, astronomer and Fellow of the Royal Society (FRS). On 27 August 1666 his fellow commissioner John Evelyn noted in his diary 'I went to St Paul's church with Dr Wren... to survey the general decays of that ancient and venerable church; ... we had a mind to build it with a noble cupola'. Ten days later, the Fire was over, he wrote 'St Paul's is now a sad ruin and that beautiful portico now rent in pieces...'.

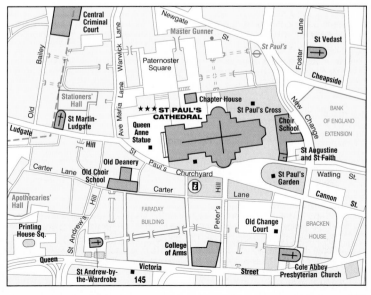

Wren's cathedral ⊙ – Within 6 days of the end of the Fire, Wren had submitted a plan for rebuilding the City; it was not accepted. For two years the authorities dallied with the idea, opposed by Wren of patching up the cathedral fabric. At last in 1668 they invited him to submit designs for a new building; he produced the First Model, the Great Model and the Warrant Design but each, in turn, was rejected by the church authorities. Having been appointed Surveyor General to the King's Works in 1669, Wren resolved to submit no more plans but to go ahead 'as ordered by his Majesty'.

The foundation stone was laid without ceremony on 21 June 1675. In 1708, after 32 years of unceasing work, Wren saw the final stone, the topmost in the lantern, set in place by his son; Wren was 75. 15 years later (1723) he died and was buried within the cathedral walls.

Exterior – The building is dominated by its **dome**, which rises from a drum to a stone lantern crowned by a golden ball and cross. The lantern, 21ft across, has detached columns projecting on all four sides and a small cupola serving as plinth to the golden ball (6 1/2ft diameter).

The exterior of the drum is divided into two tiers; the lower storey is crowned by a balustrade and encircled by columns which are punctuated (for structural reasons) at 8 points by a radiating wall containing a decorative niche; the upper tier is recessed behind the balustrade so as to provide a circular viewing gallery, the **Stone Gallery.**

Unlike the dome of St Peter's Basilica in Rome which so fascinated and influenced Wren, the dome of St Paul's is not a true hemisphere. In fact it consists of three structures *(see illustration):* the outer lead covered timber superstructure designed to satisfy purely esthetic considerations, an invisible inner brick cone which supports the weight of the lantern (850 tons) and the inner brick dome which opens at the apex (20ft diameter) into the space beneath the lantern.

At the **west end,** beyond a statue of Queen Anne, in whose reign the cathedral was completed, a broad flight of steps sweeps up in two stages to a two-tier portico of coupled Corinthian and composite columns supporting a decorated pediment surmounted by the figure of St Paul by Francis Bird. On either side rise the west towers, Wren's most Baroque spires, designed as foils to the dome.

The shallow **transepts** terminate in semicircular, columned porticoes surmounted by triangular pediments crowned by statues.

The **north and south sides and the east end** are enclosed within a two-storey wall articulated by coupled pilasters against the rusticated stone. The lower storey beneath the cornice frieze is pierced by round-headed windows with segmental hoods, garlanded and decorated with cherubs. The upper storey (111ft) is punctuated by blind windows, designed as niches; except at the east end and the south and north end of the transept, the upper storey forms an advanced screen, enclosing the structural buttressing and supporting the dome.

The carving and texture of many features are particularly emphasised if floodlit, animating the statues, reliefs, figures by Caius Cibber and Francis Bird; garlands, swags, panels, cherub heads in stone by Grinling Gibbons.

Interior – The greatest impact is the size and scale of the building, its almost luminescent stone flattered by gold and mosaic. Wren's church was designed to have no extraneous monuments but in 1790 the figures of four national benefactors Joshua Reynolds, the penal reformer John Howard, Dr Johnson and the orientalist Sir William Jones were placed by the dome piers. Since then marble statuary has proliferated.

Nave – At the west end of the aisles are the chapels of St Dunstan *(left)* and St Michael and St George *(right),* each preceded by a finely-carved wooden screen (17C to 18C) rising to a crest incorporating broken pediments and coats of arms.

Facts and figures

The cost of the cathedral, recorded as £736 752 3s 3 1/4d, was met, together with the cost of rebuilding the City Churches, by a tax levied on all sea coal imported into the Port of London. Wren was paid £200 a year during the construction of the cathedral.

The cathedral's overall length is 500ft; height to the summit of the cross 365ft; height of the portico columns 40ft; height of the statue on the apex of the pediment 12ft; length of the nave 180ft, width of the nave, including the aisles, 121ft; width across the transept 242ft; internal diameter of the dome 110ft; height of the nave 92 1/2ft; height to the Whispering Gallery 100ft; height to the apex of the internal dome 218ft; total surface area approximately 78 000 sq ft.

St Paul's Cathedral

The square pillars dividing the nave and aisles are faced (on the nave side) with fluted, Corinthian pilasters which sweep up to the entablature, wrought-iron gallery railing, clerestory and garlanded-saucer domes.

The Wellington monument (1), which occupies the entire space between two piers in the north aisle and ascends from a recumbent bronze effigy at the base to a full-size equestrian statue of the duke at the apex, was the lifework of Alfred Stevens and completed only in 1912 long after the sculptor's death in 1875.

The bronze gasoliers date from the late 19C. In the pavement are the Night Watch memorial stone (cathedral guardians 193945) and the inscription commemorating the resting of Sir Winston Churchill's coffin in the cathedral during the state funeral on 30 January 1965. Beneath the dome is Wren's own epitaph in Latin: 'Reader, if you seek his monument, look around you'.

Crossing and transepts – The space beneath the dome is emphasised by the giant supporting piers which flank the entrances to the shallow transepts. The north transept serves as a baptistry and contains a dish-shaped font carved in 1727 by Francis Bird. The south transept includes the exceptional portrait statue of **Nelson** by Flaxman (3) and another by reynolds (4) and the beautiful wooden door-case with fluted columns made up in the 19C from a wood screen designed by Wren and decked with garlands carved by Grinling Gibbons.

The Light of the World

'Behold I stand at the door and knock: if any man hear my voice, and open the door, I will come into him, and will sup with him, and he with me.'
Revelations (3:20)

Holman Hunt's best known religious painting (2) hangs in the north transept. This large Pre-Raphaelite Brotherhood painting is one of three versions of the same subject (Keble College, Oxford and Manchester City Art Gallery) for which Hunt built an outdoor straw hut where he might settle to study and paint the light of a full moon between the hours of 9pm and 5am. It was described by Ruskin as *'one of the very noblest works of sacred art ever produced in this or any other age'*.

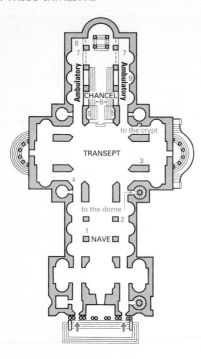

Dome – *Entrance in the south transept*. From the **Whispering Gallery** *(259 steps)* there is an impressive, unusual perspective of the choir, arches and clerestory far below, and a closer view of the dome frescoes painted by **Thornhill**. A hushed word uttered next to the wall can be heard quite clearly by a person standing diametrically opposite.

The **Stone Gallery** *(530 steps)* provides a good but less extensive view★★★ than that perceived from the **Golden Gallery** at the top of the dome over the present day City rooftops.

Choir and Ambulatory – The east end is filled by the marble high altar set below a massive post-war *baldachino*, which was carved and gilded according to drawings by Wren. Gilding also offsets the glass mosaics (19C-20C) above which continue in the chancel aisle vaulting (note the Christ in Majesty in the domed apse).

In the foreground, warm in the light of red-shaded candle lights, pillared beneath a crested canopy, are the dark oak **choir stalls**★★ (6), the exquisite work of **Grinling Gibbons** and his craftsmen. Each stall is different from the next – see how the cherubs' expressions vary as do the flowers, leaves and fruits that make up the wreaths and garlands; even the stall backs are carved forming a screen between the choir and the chancel aisles.

The organ, a late 17C Smith instrument, together with its Gibbons case (5), have been divided and now towers on either side of the choir opening.

The iron railing adapted from the original altar rail, the gates to the chancel aisles and the great gilded screens (7) enclosing the sanctuary, are the work of **Jean Tijou**, wrought-iron smith extraordinary.

In the north aisle, before the Chapel of modern martyrs, a 14C Graduale, a "Breeches" Bible (16C) and mementoes of thanksgiving services from Queen Anne to Elizabeth II are on display. The graceful marble sculpture of the Virgin and Child (8) is by **Henry Moore** (1984).

In the south chancel aisle, against the first outer west pillar, is a statue of **John Donne** (9) carved by Nicholas Stone: the metaphysical poet and Dean of St Paul's (1621-31) is shown wrapped in his shroud, standing on an urn in the up-ended coffin (which he kept in his house), but, from his expression, very much alive.

Crypt – *Entrance in the south transept*. At the east end, simply decorated with royal banners, is the Chapel of the Order of the British Empire (OBE). Grouped in bays, formed by the massive piers which support the low-groined and tunnel vaulting, are the tombs, memorials and busts of men and women of all the talents, of the 18C, 19C and 20C, of British, Commonwealth or foreign origin, who contributed to the national life; not all those commemorated are buried in the crypt.

– In south aisle, east of the staircase, is **Artists' Corner** honouring John Rennie *(2nd recess)*; Sir Max Beerbohm and Walter de la Mare *(north and west faces of pillar)*; Christopher Wren, beneath a plain black marble stone with above him the inscription: *Si monumentum requiris circumspice*. There are also monuments to George Dance the Younger, William Blake, Ivor Novello,

St Paul's dome (cross section)

Sir Edwin Lutyens, Sir Edwin Landseer, Sir Thomas Lawrence, Benjamin West, Lord Leighton, Sir John Everett Millais, J M W Turner, Sir Joshua Reynolds and Holman Hunt.

– In the north aisle are commemorations of Sir Arthur Sullivan, Parry, William Boyce *(on the floor)*, John Singer Sargent – beneath a relief by himself *(choir face of dividing wall)*, Wilson Steer, Sir Alfred Munnings, John Constable, Sir Alexander Fleming and Sir Stafford Cripps – bronze bust by Jacob Epstein (1953).

– Down the steps: **Wellington** occupies the Cornish porphyry sarcophagus; memorials to ten of the great soldiers of the Second World War are a more recent addition; beyond, to the south, is a plaque to Florence Nightingale.

Below the dome: at the centre of a circle of Tuscan columns lies **Nelson** beneath a curving black marble sarcophagus (originally intended for Cardinal Wolsey and subsequently proposed but rejected for Henry VIII). Beneath the arches to the south are Admirals Beatty, Jellicoe and Cunningham, and a bronze bust of W E Henley by Rodin (1903). Opposite on the north side are more military figures including T E Lawrence by Epstein. Only a handful of effigies were rescued from Old St Paul's in which were buried John of Gaunt, Thomas Linacre (c 1460-1524), founder of the Royal College of Physicians, teacher of Greek to Thomas More and Erasmus, Sir Philip Sidney and Sir Anthony van Dyck *(modern plaque)*.

North transept: the **Treasury** displays plate and vestments belonging to the Cathedral and on loan from parishes in the London Diocese.

West end: models showing the construction of the Cathedral and dome.

Environs

Chapter House – This perfectly proportioned red brick building, with a crowning parapet and stone quoins marking the angles and centre, was built by Wren (1710-14). The iron hand pump *(west)* was erected in 1819 by the parishioners of St Faith's *(see below)*.

St Paul's Cross – The cross *(site marked on the pavement north of the apse)*, which is known to have been in existence as a preaching cross in 1256, became the centre and symbol of free speech and so was removed by the Long Parliament in 1643. The monument in the garden with St Paul at the top dates from 1910.

Choir School – The modern buildings of the choir school abut the tower of the church of **St Augustine and St Faith** (1680-87) which was built by Wren and destroyed during the Second World War. The square tower of newly-hewn stone ends in a pierced parapet quartered by obelisk pinnacles; above rise an almost black, tulip-shaped dome and lead spire, rebuilt since the war to Wren's original design.

St Paul's Garden – The garden is complemented by a sculpture *The Young Lovers* by George Ehrlich and basin of water.

Old Change Court – The modern piazza is adorned by a statue *Icarus* (1973) by Michael Ayrton. In the northwest corner is the circular City Information Centre.

Old Deanery – *Deans Court*. The house (1672-73) was built by Wren.

Old Choir School – *Corner of Carter Lane*. The building (now a youth hostel) was built in 1873 and is decorated with *sgraffito* ornamentation in the spandrels and a terracotta inscription from Galatians IV, 13.

SCIENCE MUSEUM★★★

Map p 6 (BY) and area map under SOUTH KENSINGTON
⊖ South Kensington

The spirit of the **Science Museum** ⊘ is to encourage initiative and reception in learning and education by presentation, exploration and explanation. There are an innumerabl number of objects displayed and constantly up-dated relevant and topical 'Scienc Boxes'.

This factory-laboratory of man's continuing invention extends over 7 acres on seven floors – with an annexe at the rear for a Wellcome Wing devoted to innovativ displays on contemporary science, technology and medicine entitled **Making of the Moder World**. Some of the exhibits listed below may have been moved to a different location There are innumerable working models and interactive computer terminals with han dles to turn and buttons to press, while assistants are on hand throughout th galleries to advise and inform.

PLANNING YOUR VISIT

Highlights – For a quick tour consider visiting the sections entitled Power; Space Exploration; Land Transport; Optics; The Science and Art of Medicine (Sir Henry Wellcome collection); Flight; Chemical Industry; Food for Thought.

Children – For the very young, recommended sections include those entitled Launch Pad *(basement)*, Pattern Pod, Fire Fighting, Land Transport and The Exploration of Space *(Ground floor)*; Food for Thought *(First floor)*; Flight and Flight Lab *(Third floor)*; Glimpses of Medical History *(Fourth floor)*.

Interactive learning – Demonstrations are given in Food for Thought, Launch Pad and Flight Lab sections: enquire at the information desk for times.

Overcrowding – To save popular galleries from becoming over-run with parties of school children, a system of timed-ticketing has been implemented. Ask at the information desk for details.

Science Museum Library – A reference library is available for study and research, located within the precincts of Imperial College; enquire at the Visitor Information Desk or call ☎ 020 7938 8234.

Books – The museum boasts a large and well-stocked bookshop with technical manuals, documentation, teaching packs and souvenirs.
General information ☎ 020 7938 8080 or 8008; Educational group visits ☎ 020 7938 8222.

Floor	Galleries	Individual exhibits
Basement	Launch Pad	Hands-on models, experiments an Puzzles demonstrating the principles o technology; Grain pit exhibit.
Ground floor	Synopsis Gallery *(stairs up to mezzanine)*	Review of the contents of the museum Arkwright's water frame; Davy's Safet lamps.
	Power - water, turbines, steam	Boulton and Watt engine; Trevithic engine and boiler; Mill engine (1903).
	hot air, gas, oil and electricity	Foucault's pendulum demonstrates th rotation of the earth.
	Rockets	Gunpowder; WWII V2 rocket.
	Exploration of Space	Apollo 10 command module; Ander: space suit; Mir space station.
	Land Transport-Roads, bridges and tunnels (balcony)	*Puffing Billy* (1813); 1905 Rolls Royce Stephenson's *Rocket* (1829); Rove safety cycle
	Fire Fighting	Fire engines.
First floor	Glass	10C to 12C distillation apparatus.
	Iron and Steel	Model of an open-hearth furnace; Louth erbourg's *Coalbrookdale by Night*.
	Telecommunications	Marconi beam transmitter; electric tele graph (1846); ship's radio cabin (1910)
	Plastics	Lotus Excel car.
	Agriculture	Bells' reaper (1826).
	Gas	Off-shore gas drilling rig (1970s).
	Surveying	Ramsden's theodolite.
	Meteorology	Barographs; anemometers.
	Time Measurement	Wells Cathedral clock; Coster cloc (c 1658).
	Food for Thought	Nutrition, diet, additives, energy bike weight/height chart; 1920s Sainsbury store.

Second floor	**Chemistry**	Cells; Crick and Watson's DNA model; radio carbon dating.
	Weighing & Measuring	National standard measures bearing royal ciphers.
	Lighting	Lacemakers' condenser.
	Printing & Papermaking	18C printing shop.
	Nuclear Physics & Power	Thomson's electron tube.
	Chemical Industry	Man-made dyes.
	Petroleum	Making polythene, 1933.
	Picture Gallery Computing Then and Now	Babbage's Difference Engine; Pilot Ace computer (1950).
	Shipping & Navigation	Gyro compasses; radars; airliner cockpit.
	Marine Engineering	Turbines, paddlewheels; steerage.
	Ships	Ship models; *HMS Prince*.
	Docks and Diving	Diving bell; aqualung; suits.
Third floor	**Optics**	Holograms; colour mixing.
	Heat & Temperature	Joule's apparatus.
	Science in the 18C	Hauksbee's air pump; Adam's silver microscope.
	Photography & Cinematography	Inventions of Daguerre, Fox Talbot, Muybridge, Marey, Edison.
	Health Matters	20C Western medicine practices.
	Flight Lab	Interactive hands-on exhibits testing the principles of flight.
	Flight	Balloons; Wright brothers' plane; Hawker P1127 jump jet; Whittle's jet engine; air traffic control.
Fourth floor	**The Wellcome Museum of the History of Medicine: Glimpses of History**	Dental treatment (1930s); 1905 pharmacy; childbirth (1860s); open heart surgery (1980); eradication of smallpox; Lister's ward (1868).
Fifth floor	**The Science and Art of Medicine**	17C Chinese acupuncture figure; leper's rattle; drug jar (1641); Genoese medicine chest (c 1565); Jenner memorabilia; Laennec stethoscope; Pasteur's equipment; 19C strait-jacket.
	Veterinary History	Anatomical model of a horse.

SOHO ★

Map pp 7-8 (**DEX**)
⊖ Piccadilly Circus; Leicester Square

Soho, which lies to the north of Piccadilly Circus and Leicester Square, is at the hub of London's advertising and film industry during the day, while at night the place takes on new life as lights flicker in the windows of the various clubs, bars, restaurants (French, Italian, Greek and Chinese), jazz venues, nightclubs, cinemas and theatres thronging with night owls.

In the Middle Ages Soho was a chase, named after the cry of the medieval hunt which was often found in the vicinity of St Giles'-in-the-Fields *(see COVENT GARDEN)*.

Early maps show a windmill marking Great Windmill Street, two breweries in Brewer Street, a bottle glass factory in Glasshouse Street and several big houses of which only their names survive: Newport House (built c 1634, demolished 1682), Monmouth House (the residence of the Duke of Monmouth from 1682 until his execution on Tower Hill in 1685), Karnaby House corrupted to becoming Carnaby Street.

By the mid 19C, through piecemeal development, Soho included the worst slums in the capital. The building of Regent Street divided the West End from its disreputable neighbour and three new streets were built to penetrate the foetid tangle: Charing Cross Road (1880), Shaftesbury Avenue (1886) and Kingsway (1905).

People of all nations – The indigenous Londoners of Soho have always been artisans (tapestry weavers, furniture and violin makers), cottage industry workers, and, until planning regulations eliminated local factories, craftsmen in labour-intensive manufacture. Refugees began to arrive in the 17C, settling where their skills and labour would find a market: Greeks fleeing the Ottoman Turks; persecuted Huguenots after the revocation of the Edict of Nantes (1685); Frenchmen hounded by the Revolution and later by political changes – these established French restaurants and cafés (Wheeler's at **19 Old Compton Street** was founded by Napoleon III's chef; the York Minster pub at 49 Dean Street, run by two generations of French landlords became known as the French Pub). Waves of Swiss, Italian, Spanish immigrants followed. Then came the Chinese from Hong Kong, Singapore and the docks to transform Gerrard Street into a Chinatown with exotic street furniture and great festivities at Chinese New Year (a moveable feast in January or February) celebrated in traditional fashion.

Commerce – Today Soho survives on the various trades associated with entertainment. The southern end of Shaftesbury Avenue is known for its theatres; the are
around Golden Square is dominated by the film industry, television productio
companies, cinema advertisers, photographers; sleazy parts boast peep-shows ar
sexshops below lurid neon signs and blackened windows; this is also the home
London's mainstream jazz – instruments, specialist music shops and clubs pepp
Shaftesbury Avenue, Charing Cross Road, and Denmark Street.

★**Leicester Square** – The square is now a pedestrian precinct surrounded b
cinemas and eating houses. At the centre stands the Shakespeare Memorial Four
tain (1874) facing a statue of **Charlie Chaplin** *(north side)* by John Doubleday (1980
On the circumference of the inner paving are plaques identifying the direction ar
distance of the capital cities of the Commonwealth countries, while around th
railings sit busts of famous local residents – Reynolds, Newton, Hunter, Hogart
panels tell the history of the square from Leicester Fields, common ground whe
people dried their washing, to the building of the Alhambra (1854), Daly's Theat
and the **Empire**, which established the reputation of the square as a centre for lig
entertainment.

On the south side of the central garden is the **Half-Price Ticket Booth** *(see INTRODU
TION – Entertainment)*, while in the northeast corner of the square stands th
Swiss Centre and its **Glockenspiel** ⊙.

Notre Dame de France ⊙ – *Leicester Place.* The circular Roman Catholic church wa
erected from the ashes of a 19C predecessor. Inside, an Aubusson tapestry hang
above the altar, mosaic ornaments a side altar and paintings by **Jean Cocteau** adorn th
walls.

William Blake was born in Soho (1757), Hazlitt died there (1830); Edmund
Burke, Sarah Siddons, Dryden, Sheraton lived there; Marx, Engels, Canaletto, Haydn lodged there; Mendelssohn and Chopin gave recitals at the 18C
house in Meard Street of Vincent Novello, father of Ivor and founder of the
music publishers. J L Baird first demonstrated television in Frith Street in
1926...

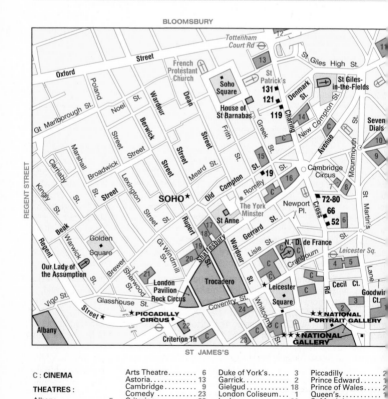

The Empire, Leicester Square

Wardour Street – The street and its immediate vicinity (Beak Street, Dean Street and Soho Square) conjure up the **film industry** from the creators of blockbuster movies and catchy commercials.

St Anne's, consecrated in honour of Anne, Princess of Denmark as Soho's Parish Church (1686) was bombed in the war. The tower, now occupied by the Soho Society, was restored, together with the clock, in 1979. Beneath it are buried the ashes of Dorothy L Sayers, churchwarden and detective-story writer, while Hazlitt and the legendary 18C Theodore, King of Corsica, lie in the churchyard.

The **Berwick Street Market** dates from 1778.

Tucked away in Warwick Street off Regent Street, stands **Our Lady of the Assumption**, a plain church, originally the chapel of the Portuguese, rebuilt in 1788 after the Gordon Riots with only a pediment as decoration.

House of St Barnabas ⊙ – *Greek Street*. The House of Charity, a temporary home for women in need, was built c 1750. The exterior is plain except for two obelisks at the entrance; the interior, one of the finest in Soho, has beautiful plasterwork ceilings and walls, and an unusual crinoline staircase. The proportions of the small chapel, built in 1863 in 13C French Gothic, are unique.

Charing Cross Road – Foyle's (no **119**), Zwemmer's (nos **72, 80**), Collet's (nos **52, 66, 131**), Waterstone's (no **121**) are just a few of the bookshops to line Charing Cross Road, immortalised in Helene Hanff's novel *84 Charing Cross Road*.

'Of all quarters in the queer adventurous amalgam called London, Soho is ... untidy, full of Greeks, Ishmaelites, cats, Italians, tomatoes, restaurants, organs, coloured stuffs, queer names, people looking out of upper windows, it dwells remote from the British Body Politic'.

John Galsworthy

SOUTH BANK★

Map pp 6-7 (EFY)
⊖ Waterloo

The area on the south bank remained rural until the construction of Westminster and Blackfriars Bridges and their approach roads in the mid 18C. The evolution of public transport developed the area from village to town and spa, where the modestly wealthy such as Henry Thrale built out-of-town residences. Finally the area became a suburb where squares and terraces were erected by Thomas Cubitt and lesser men, which agglomerated in a network of small streets between the major roads.

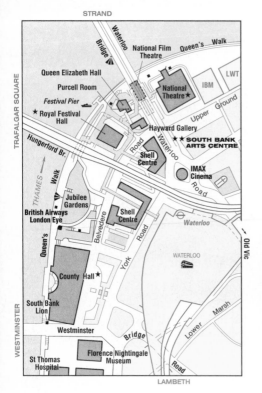

Victorian industrial works

Benefiting from an ample workforce and easy transport by river, and later by railway, this area has boasted a long list of works and plants: an ordnance factory (Charles II reign), the Vauxhall Plate Glass Works (1665-1780), the Coade Stone Factory (late 18C), Doultons, lead-shot foundries (a shot tower stood at the centre of the 1951 Festival), Price's candle works (Battersea), vinegar, basket, brush factories, boatyards, breweries, distillers, specialist workshops and potteries included one producing Lambeth delft. Bombing during the war devastated acres of Victorian streets, slums, the Lambeth Walk and factories making it possible for the authorities to rebuild on a vast scale.

Today the area may be explored by means of the **Riverside Walk** or Queen's Walk so named to mark the Queen's Silver Jubilee in 1977 – which extends from County Hall downstream to Southwark and Tower Bridge *(listed separately)*.

★**County Hall** – *Belvedere Road*. County Hall was the headquarters of the London County Council and its successor, the Greater London Council until 1986.

The hall, a colonnaded arc 700ft in diameter and still, amidst all the new constructions, one of London's most distinctive buildings, was designed in 1908 by 29-year-old architect, Ralph Knott. The stone pile with Renaissance-inspired steeply pitched, dark tile roof with a multitude of dormers, only completed in 1922, has since been trebled in size but always in compatible style. 'A fish cathedral', a monumental **aquarium** ⊘ has been built in the basement, reaching two floors below the Thames water level. Highlights include moon jellyfish and friendly flatfish. Other attractions include the **FA Premier League Hall of Fame** tracing the story of English football and a Dali exhibition.

South Bank Lion – The lion, 13ft long, 12ft high, carved out of Coade stone gazes speculatively from a plinth at the foot of Westminster Bridge. Painted red, it was the mascot in the 19C of the Lion Brewery until poised at the bridgefoot in 1952.

Jubilee Gardens – The gardens, on the site of the 1951 Festival and incorporating the flagpole from British Columbia, were opened in 1977 to celebrate the 25th anniversary of the Queen's accession. A bronze sculpture by I Walters (1985) dedicated to the International Brigade (1936-39). Nearby is the Jubilee Oracle, smooth bronze by Alexander (1980).

The **British Airways London Eye** ⊘, which is a triumph of engineering, is a new spectacular landmark on the Thames. Sightseers (trip 30min) accommodated in closed pods, enjoy unparalleled views of London extending 20km in all directions as the wheel rotates to its apex.

Coade Stone

Cheap forms of external building ornamentation were made possible during the 18C with the invention of **Coade stone**, a durable non-porous terracotta material. As it was fired very slowly, there was little shrinkage or distortion. It was shaped in hollow moulds which permitted the creation of large sculptures as well as small architectural ornaments. The formula, discovered early in the 18C by Mrs Eleanor Coade, was a secret for many years until County Hall was built on the site of the Coade factory and some pieces of Coade stone were analysed. The Coade factory in Lambeth flourished from 1769-1830.

Shell Centre – The Shell Centre, built between 1957-1962, comprises three blocks beside the Thames: the Upstream and Downstream (the latter now turned into flats), stone-faced, 10-storey buildings, and a 26-storey tower, 351ft high. As one of the biggest office blocks in the kingdom it has 43 acres of floor space, 7 000 windows, 88 lifts, 12 escalators, 240 telephone lines and 4 500 extensions.

*★**South Bank Arts Centre** – After the war, the LCC, under Herbert Morrison, cleared bomb-damage debris from the riverside to make way for the 1951 Festival of Britain and a future arts centre.

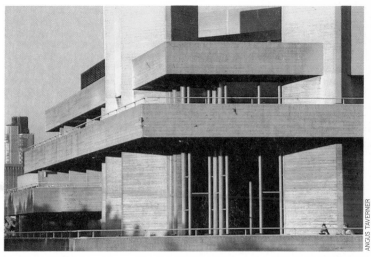

South Bank Centre, detail

The arts complex, connected by elevated walkways (shown in grey on plan) has been described as 'a sterile concrete wasteland disastrously out of character and contact with the rest of London' – in an attempt to rectify this, plans for extensive redevelopment of the entire riverside precinct have been approved.

★**Royal Festival Hall** – The building was planned by Sir Leslie Martin and Sir Robert Matthew, LCC architects, who worked, it was said, from the inside. Design began with the hall: its acoustics, the visibility of the stage capable of holding a choir of 250, comfortable seating for an audience of 3 000 – in that order. They succeeded both aesthetically and practically in the design of foyers, staircases, concourses, bars and restaurants, managing the space to avoid crowding, afford views of the river and inner perspectives of the building itself; finally the whole edifice was insulated against noise from nearby Waterloo Station. In 1954 an organ was installed. In 1962-65 the river frontage was redesigned to include the main entrance, and faced with Portland stone.

Queen Elizabeth Hall and Purcell Room – In 1967 a second smaller concert venue with seating for 1 100 was opened with a third, the Purcell Room providing a recital room for 370 planned in the second phase of building. The exterior is in unfaced concrete; the interior acoustics are superb.

Hayward Gallery ⊙ – The gallery, purpose-built to house temporary exhibitions of painting and sculpture was opened in 1968. The building, a terrace-like structure of unfaced concrete, in fact 'works' successfully to provide on two levels five large gallery spaces and three open air sculpture courts.

South Bank skyline, detail

National Film Theatre – The NFT, which opened in 1951, was rebuilt in 1957 ar
enlarged in 1970 so that it now comprises two cinemas (seating 466 and 162). Th
NFT, one of the world's leading cinematheques, organises the London Film Festival
November each year.

IMAX Cinema – Rising at a busy roundabout at the southern end of Waterloo Bridg
the circular structure houses a state-of-the-art cinema screening 2D and 3D film
The auditorium has 482 seats. Be prepared for exciting adventures as the came
explores distant horizons and new worlds!

★**National Theatre** ⊘ – The theatre opens the third phase in the South Bank schem
both by its position downstream from Waterloo Bridge and, more importantly, by i
design. The architect, **Denys Lasdun**, has incorporated three theatres: the Lyttelto
with proscenium stage and seating for 890; the Olivier, with large open stage ar
audience capacity of 1 100 and the Cottesloe, a studio theatre with a maximum
400 seats; workshops, bookshops, bars and buffets, within a spacious constructi
in which the external height is bisected by strata-like cantilevered terraces whi
parallel the course of the river outside and 'release' the beautiful view of Somers
House and St Paul's beyond.

In front of the theatre stand a pleasing stone sculpture, *Arena*, by J Maine (198
84) and a bronze of *London Pride* by F Dobson, a sculpture commissioned for t
1951 Festival.

Waterloo Bridge – The sleek five-arched concrete structure faced in Portla
stone was designed by G G Scott in 1945; it replaced the original by Rennie th
was opened on the second anniversary of the Battle of Waterloo (18 June 181
From the bridge is a fine view: east of the National Theatre stands the IB
building, faced in concrete and granite and designed by Sir Denys Lasdun (1983)
harmonise in scale and structure with the National Theatre. Next in line is t
London Weekend Television building dominated by the IPC towers (magazine pu
lishing group). On the waterfront is the lively **Gabriel's Wharf** ⊘, a workplace f
craftspeople which has evolved alongside the gardens and low-cost housing of t
Coin Street development.

Stamford Wharf is marked by the OXO tower, a former beef-extract factory and now
restaurant, with the distinctive river façade of Sea Containers House beyond.
continuing eastwards, turn to *BANKSIDE*.

Plan ahead!
To plan your route, the sights to see, to select a hotel or a restaurant, Internet users c
log in at www.michelin-travel.com.
In France, consult the French videotex service Minitel 36 15 MICHELIN.

SOUTH KENSINGTON ★★

Map pp 6-7 (**BCY**)
⊖ South Kensington

When the Great Exhibition held in 1851 in Hyde Park was over, Prince Albert, its initiator, proposed that the financial profit, nearly £200 000, be spent in establishing a great educational centre in South Kensington by buying land on which have become established the world famous museums and colleges to be found there today. In the event 86 acres were bought and there began a sequence of construction.

1856: William Cubitt erects a utilitarian glass and iron building the "Brompton Boilers" in Cromwell Road to house former 1851 exhibits and various art collections.

1861-1863: Commemorative Exhibition statue erected (now sited behind Albert Hall).

1861: Prince Albert dies; the Albert Memorial (1864-72) erected. 1876 unveiled.

1862: International Exhibition held on site now occupied by Natural History Museum.

1867-1871: Albert Hall built on site of Gore House as national memorial to Prince Consort.

1867-1871: Huxley Building erected, Exhibition Road (originally as the Science Schools).

1873-1880: Natural History Museum.

1875: National School of Music later (1883) Royal College of Music founded in building; since 1903 the Royal College of Organists.

1881-1884: City and Guilds College; rebuilt 1962 as Imperial College extensions.

1883: Royal College of Music (transferred from previous building).

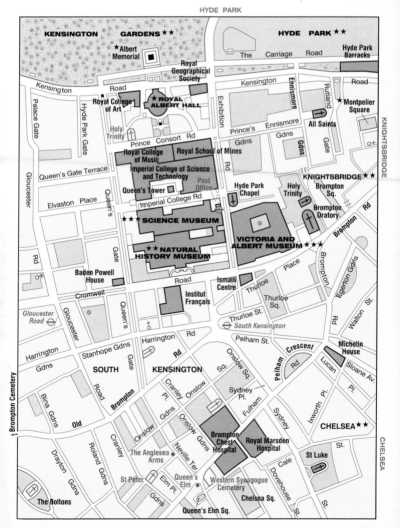

Royal Albert Hall, detail

1887-1893: Imperial Institute. Buildings demolished 1957-65, save for existing central tower, to assist expansion of Imperial College.

1899-1909: Victoria and Albert Museum.

1909-1913: Royal School of Mines (now part of Imperial College).

1914: Science Museum.

1933-1935: Geological Museum.

1960-1964: Royal College of Art beside Albert Hall, first stage of a development to centralise College buildings scattered in South Kensington.

★**Royal Albert Hall** – The round hall was designed by Captain Fowke, a Royal Engineer: almost mile in circumference, built of red brick with a shallow glass and iron dome, it is the foil in shape and ornament to the memorial since its only decoration is an upper frieze of figures illustrating the Arts and Sciences. Reunions, pop and jazz sessions, exhibitions, boxing, political meetings, conferences and concerts, particularly the eight week summer series of **Promenade Concerts**, fill the hall with up to 7 000 people at a time.

Behind the Albert Hall stands a monument to Prince Albert, a driving force behind the 1851 Great Exhibition; the square chimney is a ventilation shaft for an electricity substation.

Royal College of Art – The Darwin Building, designed by Cadbury-Brown, with eight floors of studios and workshops is built of purple brown brick, dark concrete and glass. It dates from 1961 and, uniquely in such a district, is without applied adornment.

The Royal College evolved from a fusion of the Government School of Design and the National Art Training School (1896). In its time it has nurtured many eminent artists, architects, sculptors, craftsmen, industrial and fashion designers.

In sharp contrast, the small building alongside is the former home of the **Royal College of Organists**. 4 floors tall, 3 bays wide and designed by another RE, Lt H H Cole (1875), it is almost obscured by its ornate decoration (F W Moody) of chocolate brown panels patterned in cream, a frieze of putti carrying musical instruments, garlands incorporating the VR monogram around the door.

Royal Geographical Society ⊘ – The society was founded in 1830. The Map Room contains 30 000 old and historic maps beside the largest modern private collection in Europe. Statues of Shackleton and Livingstone adorn the outer wall of the many-gabled house which was designed in 1874 by Richard Norman Shaw.

Royal College of Music – The college is an architect's building of 1893, as opposed to an RE's; Sir Arthur Blumfield designed in dark red brick and grey slate stepped and decorated gables between pavilion roofed towers and finally quartered his construction with pepper pot turrets after the French style. Inside are the **Department of Portraits** and the highly prized **Museum of Instruments** ⊘, including the Donaldson, Tagore, Hipkins, Ridley and Hartley Collections, Handel spinet and Haydn clavichord.

Imperial College of Science and Technology – The schools which go to make up Imperial College extend from either side of the Royal College of Music in Prince Consort Road south to the Science Museum, apart from the small enclaves occupied by Holy Trinity Church (1909 replacement of a chapel of 1609, itself a rebuilding of the chapel of a former leper hospital), the Edwardian Post Office Building and the Underground exit. With the exception of the neo-Georgian 1909-13 **Royal School of Mines** of stone with an apsed entrance flanked by giant sculptures, the buildings date from the mid 50s. They are vast but homogeneous in proportion and human in scale, clean lined, in single, right-angled and hollow square ranges, surrounding interconnected quadrangles. From one of the quadrangles, guarded at its foot by a pair of lions, rises the old **Queen's Tower** (280ft high), brick and stone below, green copper and gold turreted at the summit, last relic of Colcutt's Imperial Institute (1887-93), erected following the Colonial Exhibition of 1886; history has been imaginatively preserved in the midst of the present. Opposite, the glass-fronted Sir Alexander Fleming building with a stepped double-glazed roof designed by Sir Norman Foster combines architectural flair and high technology.

Hyde Park Chapel – *Exhibition Road.* The stylish Mormon chapel dates from 1960 and is surmounted by a needle spire of gilded bricks.

The SCIENCE MUSEUM, NATURAL HISTORY MUSEUM and VICTORIA AND ALBERT MUSEUM are listed separately.

Ismaili Centre – This distinctive modern building faced in grey-blue marble and adorned with slim windows, designed by the Casson-Conder Partnership, serves as a religious and cultural centre for Ismailis.

Institut Français – The institute buildings, although in *art nouveau* style, date only from 1938. It is a cultural and educational centre founded in 1910. Many of the students enrolled in the Institut and the nearby Lycée are English.

Baden-Powell House ⊘ – The house built in 1961, signalled outside by a bare-headed statue of B-P, is the headquarters of the Scout movement and a hostel for visiting scouts. There is a memorial exhibition to the founder inside.

Michelin House – The 1910 purpose-built building, the first in Britain to be constructed with a rein-forced-concrete frame, is the former UK headquarters of the Michelin Tyre PLC. Its original *art nouveau* decoration has been lovingly restored and the tiled tyre-fitting bays preserved despite considerable internal restructuring (sixty steel pillars have been inserted from the open ground floor to support a fourth floor).

K. Brett

Michelin House

South of the **Old Brompton Road**, graceful Pelham Crescent (mid 19C) is probably by Basevi, while the fine white-stuccoed houses in **The Boltons**, laid out in a mandorla crescent, are by Cubitt. In between are Onslow Gardens, a typical mid 19C development of tall cream stuccoed houses with advanced pillared porches, and 19C artisan cottages in Elm Place and its immediate vicinity, still surrounded by small gardens brilliant with flowers throughout the summer. The Tudor style architecture of **Queen's Elm Square** reflects the tradition that Elizabeth I sheltered here under an elm tree during a storm.

Royal Marsden and Brompton Chest Hospitals – The Royal Marsden Hospital was built in 1859, the Brompton in 1844-54. Attached to the second is the Cardiothoracic Institute and to the first the Institute of Cancer Research (including the Chester Beatty Research Institute), both part of London University.

Brompton Cemetery – The vast necropolis, founded in the mid 19C, contains hundreds of neo-Gothic, Egyptian, Baroque style, tombs.

Michelin Green Guides are regularly revised.
Use the most recent edition to ensure a successful holiday.

SOUTHWARK ★

Southwark, which extends south from the Thames to Crystal Palace includes the Borough and Walworth, Bermondsey, Rotherhithe, Camberwell and Peckham and Dulwich *(see separate listings).*

The Roman invasion to the Dissolution of the Monasteries – The construction by the Romans of a bridge and the convergence at the bridgehead of roads from the south of England attracted settlers to the fishing village already established on one of the few sites relatively free from flooding on the low-lying marshlands of the Thames' south bank. By Anglo-Saxon times the bridge had become a defence against ship-borne invaders and the village, the *sud werk* or south work, against attacking land forces: **Olaf of Norway**'s rescue of Ethelred from the Danes is commemorated locally in Tooley Street (a corruption of St Olave's Street); the Conqueror fired Southwark before he took London by encirclement. In the *Domesday Book,* Southwark was described as having a strand where ships could tie up, a street, a herring fishery and a minster or priory. In 1540, at the Dissolution, the priory reverted to the crown; Henry acquired from Archbishop Cranmer the Great Liberty Manor, granted to Canterbury in the 12C (which extended from the Old Kent Road to the High Street). Among its tenants were the Bishops of Winchester and the Knights Templar whose 100 acres had by the 15C become the famous Paris Garden *(see BANKSIDE).*

There were also two hospitals, St Thomas's, originally at the priory gate and subsequently across the road, and the Lock or Leper Hospital in Kent Street (Old Kent Road) beyond the Bar or bounds of the medieval town (closed 1760).

Borough Market – The people of Walworth, Newington, Camberwell, grew and sold produce at the market first held on London Bridge, later in the High Street and finally on the present site; the Borough Market, London's oldest (13C), was formally established in 1756 and the profits go to rates relief. Southwark people were also fishermen and boatmen. Industries developed such as plaster and mortar making (pollution from the lime burners was being complained of to the King in 1283), weaving, brewing (by refugees from the Low Countries), glassmaking and leather tanning (note the windows in Christchurch, *see below*).

For entertainment there were the midsummer Southwark Fair, the occasional frost fairs when the Thames froze over, the Elizabethan theatres, the brothels and taverns. Not all inns were licentious; many prospered as staging posts for the coaches going south and to the ports and as hostelries for travellers awaiting the morning opening of the bridge to enter the City.

The Dissolution to the 20C – Henry VIII rapidly sold off the monastery estates. The City increased its interests in Southwark but it never acquired jurisdiction over the Clink prison or Paris Garden which was therefore a popular location for theatres.

The area close to the river, largely owned by the City and known as the Borough of Southwark, which time has shortened to the **Borough**, became heavily industrialised following the building of the bridges, the 19C expansion of the docks and the coming of the railway. It also attracted alms houses and charities founded by the City livery companies: the **Hopton Almshouses** *(Hopton Street)* consist of two-storey brick and tile cottages, the main wing pedimented, built round three sides of a garden in 1752; a terrace in **Nelson Square** survives from 1799 – now adjoined to post-war municipal accommodation, and the **Drapers' Almshouses**, two-storey cottages with neo-Gothic windows from 1820.

By the end of the 19C the last of the prisons had been demolished: the **Clink**, instituted for miscreants within the liberty, in 1780; the **Marshalsea**, where for three months in 1824 Dickens' father had been locked up for debt, in 1842; King's Bench in 1860 and Horsemonger Lane Jail in 1879.

In 1939-1945 came widespread devastation. Southwark is now after extensive rebuilding, an amalgam of the very old and the hi-tec, each area with its particular characteristic even to street furniture such as the bollards made from sawn-off cannon with a cannon ball in the mouth, inscribed Wardens of St Saviour's 1827, and Clink 1812.

★★**Southwark Cathedral** ⊘ **(St Saviour and St Mary Overie)** – The history of the site records a progress from Roman building to Saxon minster, from Augustinian priory (1106) to parish Church of St Saviour (1540) in the Winchester diocese and finally, to Cathedral (1905). The name, according to Stow, derived from the convent being endowed with 'the profits of a cross-ferry' from which the church came to be known as "over the river" or St Mary Overie. The first sight of the present building, which lies below the level of London Bridge and Borough High Street and is screened from its parish by a railway viaduct is of a solid square central tower, 14C below, early 15C above, with paired lancets surmounted by a chequer pattern and pinnacles. It is proposed to remove the modern chapter house and other buildings at the base of the building to give a clear view of the cathedral from the river.

Interior – Immediately to the left is the Gothic arcading of the church rebuilt after a fire in 1206, for in addition to the succession of "owners" who altered, embellished, restored or neglected the church, it suffered disastrous fires. Against the west wall at the end of the north aisle are 12 ceiling **bosses** rescued from the 15C wooden roof when it collapsed in 1830: the pelican, heraldic sunflowers and roses, malice, gluttony, falsehood, Judas being swallowed by the devil... Nearby stands a black marble stoup with a gilt cover set in a frame. The **nave** was rebuilt in neo-Gothic style in 1890-97 to harmonize with the 13C chancel. There are fragments of a Norman arch in the north wall. More vestiges of the Norman church have been discovered behind a doorway near the north transept, also a holy water stoup of great antiquity. John Gower (1330-1408), poet and friend of Chaucer, with "small forked beard, on his head a chaplet of four roses, a collar of Essex gold about his neck" lies, pillowed on his own works, beneath a canopy of red, green and gold. The **north transept**, with 13C Purbeck marble shafts set against 12C base walls, includes the allegorical Austin monument of 1633 showing a standing figure, Agriculture, between girls in large sun hats, fallen asleep in the harvest field; also the reclining figure, with gaunt face framed by a full wig, of the quack doctor, Lionel Lockyer (1672). Note also the Jacobean communion table with turned legs in groups of four in front and three behind, pulpit (1702) and wooden sword rest *(north transept end wall)*.

From the nave near the transept crossing where the great brass candelabrum of 1680 is suspended between the massive 13C piers which support the central tower, there is an uninterrupted view of the intimately proportioned, 13C chancel in true Early English style.

The **altar screen** appears in sumptuous Gothic glory, framed by the virtually un-adorned arches to the chancel aisles, triforium and clerestory. The screen, which was presented by Bishop Fox in 1520, remained empty until 1905 when statues were carved to people the niches; the lower register was gilded in the thirties. Funeral pavement stones commemorate the burial in the church of Edmund (d 1607), brother of William Shakespeare, and the Jacobean dramatists, John Fletcher (d 1625) and Philip Massinger (d 1640).

Adjoining the asymmetrical, stilted arch which opens the north chancel aisle is the **Harvard Chapel**, dedicated to, the founder of the Harvard University of America, John Harvard who was born in Borough High Street and baptised in the church in 1607 (emigrated 1638). Mementoes include the American made window and a tablet to the Pilgrim Trust.

The wall monument with the colourful three-quarter figure is to John Trehearne (d 1618), "Gentleman porter to James I" (note the epitaph). Next to it lies a 15C stone effigy of a corpse in a shroud. Beyond, against the wall, is a rare figure of a knight, possibly a Templar, meticulously carved in oak (1280-1300). To the right is the free standing monument to Richard Humble and his wives in full 17C finery. The sparsely adorned retrochoir, 13C and square ended, is divided into four equal chapels by elementarily shaped piers; from 1540-1617 it served as tribunal, prison, billet, sty and bakery. Note the Nonesuch Chest (1588) of inlaid wood.

In the **south chancel aisle** near the altar is the free standing tomb of Lancelot Andrewes (d 1626), Bishop of Winchester, member of the commission which produced the Authorised Version of the Bible, a figure in shallow ruff and ample deep blue robes, beneath a modern canopy, gilded and crested. Nearby is displayed a statue of a Roman Hunter God (c 2C-3C AD) found in excavations beneath the cathedral. In the **south transept** mainly 14C and early 15C, with early Perpendicular tracery (renewed) in the three light windows, the large window ornately 19C are, to the left, the red painted arms and hat of Cardinal Beaufort, 15C Bishop of Winchester, and on the right, a miniature recumbent effigy of William Emerson (d 1575), high above, a colourful half figure in gown and ruff, John Bingham (d 1625), saddler to Queen Elizabeth. Note the tessellated paving from a Roman villa at the chancel step.

Against the wall of the south aisle is the memorial to Shakespeare: a 1911 alabaster figure, reclining beneath a modern Shakespearean window.

Borough High Street – The Borough, kernel not only of Southwark but of London south of the Thames, rings with historic street and inn names though many of the old buildings have now gone. The street is slowly drawing a fashionable crowd as new attractions and restaurants open in the area.

Old Operating Theatre, Museum and Herb Garret ⊙ – The attic of St Thomas's Parish Church was already in use as a herb garret when, in 1821, it was converted into a women's operating theatre for St Thomas's Hospital *(see LAMBETH)* which moved to its present site near Westminster Bridge in 1871. The theatre predates the advent of anaesthetics and antiseptic surgery, the only one of the period to be preserved in London, last used in 1862. It is semicircular, about 40ft across with a 14ft amphi-theatre ringed by 5 rows of 'standings' for students. The operating table is a sturdy wooden structure with upraised headpiece; below on the floor was a wooden box of sawdust which could 'be kicked by the surgeon's foot to any place where most blood was running'. In the corner was a small wash-basin about the size of a large soup plate, in which surgeons washed their hands after – sometimes even before – operating.

In the 19C the church attic adjoined the Dorcas women's ward in one of the two front blocks of St Thomas's Hospital, which extended east from the High Street in three quadrangles.

One wing of the old buildings, now occupied by the Post Office, still exists set back off Borough High Street, just north of St Thomas Street, which was lined from halfway along by officials' houses of which the late 18C terrace remains (the wide gateway served as a hospital side entrance).

Guy's Hospital – The vast, 1 000 bed unit, which includes one of London's tallest towers among its new buildings, retains the iron railings, gateway and square forecourt of its foundation construction of 1725. The court is flanked by the original tile-roofed brick wings which lead back to the slightly later, Palladian style, centre range with a stone frontispiece decorated with allegorical figures by Bacon.

In the court stands a bronze statue by Scheemakers of Thomas Guy (1644-1724), son of a Southwark lighterman and coal dealer, who began as a bookseller (Bibles), gambled successfully on the South Sea Bubble and other enterprises and then, like his 20C successor at Guy's, Lord Nuffield, who also rose from humble stock, became a munificent patron of medical institutions. In the chapel (centre of the right wing) is a full size memorial in high relief by John Bacon of Guy, portrayed before the 18C hospital into which a stretcher case is being borne. In the quad-rangles to the rear are a statue of Lord Nuffield and a mid 18C alcove from old London Bridge.

The Yards and the Inns of Southwark – Several narrow streets and yards off Borough High Street, south of St Thomas Street, mark the entrances to the old inns which were the overnight stop of people arriving too late at night to cross the bridge into the capital. These inns were also the starting point for coach services to the southern counties and the ports.

King's Head Yard [1]: the King's Head, known as the Pope's Head before the Reforma-tion, now a 19C building, sports a robust, somewhat supercilious, coloured effigy of Henry VIII.

White Hart Yard [2]: the pub (no longer in existence) was the headquarters of Jack Cade in 1450 and where Mr Pickwick first met Sam Weller.

★**George Inn** ⊙ **[3]** – The **George Inn**, when rebuilt in 1676 after a fire, had galleries on three sides, only part of the south range remains but this still possesses two upper galleries outside and panelled rooms inside. Shakespeare is played in the cobbled yard in summer and open fires and traditional fare warm customers in winter. Note the Act of Parliament clock constructed in 1797 when a tax of 5s made people sell their timepieces and rely on clocks in public places; the act was repealed within the year.

Talbot Yard [4]: recalled by Chaucer in the Prologue: "In Southwark at the Tabbard as I lay, At night was come into that hostelrie Wel nyne and twenty in a compagnye of sondrye folk... and pilgrims were they alle That toward Canterbury wolden ryde".

Queen's Head Yard [5]: site of the Queen's Head (demolished: 1900) sold by John Harvard before he set out for America; Newcomen Street: the King's Arms (1890) takes its name from the brightly painted lion and unicorn supporting the arms of George II (not George III as inscribed), a massive emblem which originally decorated the south gatehouse of old London Bridge.
A plaque at no 163 indicates the first site of **Marshalsea Prison** (1376 to 1811), the notorious penitentiary of which only one high wall remains on the later site *(no 211)*. No 116 marks the location of the 16C palace of the Duke of Suffolk who married a daughter of Henry VII.

St George the Martyr ⊙ – The stone spire and square tower of the 1736 church on a 12C site mark the end of the first section of the High Street. Dickens features the church in *Little Dorrit*, who is commemorated in the east window. The alms chest is a converted lead water cistern (1738), the pulpit the highest in London, the chandelier Georgian and the Te Deum ceiling unique, a replica of the late 19C Italian-style original, destroyed in the war, with cherubs breaking through a clouded sky accompanied by rays of glory.

★**Trinity Church Square** – The early 19C square with its distinctive lamp standards is an unbroken quadrilateral of three-storey houses, punctuated by round-arched doorways and united above by a narrow white course and coping. The statue in the central garden is more than lifesize and is known as **King Alfred**; it is believed to have been brought in 1822 from Westminster Hall where it had stood in a niche for 450 years so making it the oldest statue in London. The church (1824), which has a portico of colossal, fluted columns and a small open-work tower, was converted in 1975 into a studio for use by major orchestras.

★**Merrick Square** – The early 19C square with elegant lamp standards and modest houses is named after the merchant who left the property in 1661 to the Corporation of Trinity House.

Other attractions

Christchurch ⊙ – *No 27 Blackfriars Road.* The South London Industrial Mission, rebuilt in brick, stands in a shady garden; the interior is lit by modern windows illustrating all the local trades including that of the Mrs Mops who in delighted return keep the church clean and polished.

London Fire Brigade Museum ⊙ – *94a Southwark Bridge Road.* The brave history of the fire fighting services is illustrated by fire marks, uniforms, medals, paintings, old fire engines as well as modern appliances.

Fire service

Frequent fires, a 'London inconvenience' as Fitzstephen termed them in the 12C, raged unchecked until the Great Fire (1666) stimulated invention. Engines were built which forced a jet of water on burning buildings and fire insurance increased so much that insurance companies organised private brigades; they issued their own firemarks, made of tin, copper and cast-iron, to advertise and identify the properties they covered. Among the 150 companies which issued firemarks were the Sun Fire Office (f 1710), Hand-in-Hand (f 1696) and Royal Exchange Assurance (f 1720).
By 1833 ten major companies had combined to form the London Fire Brigade but even it was powerless to prevent the burning of the Houses of Parliament in 1834, the Royal Exchange in 1838, the Tower armoury in 1841 and three acres of warehouses, worth £2 million, in Tooley Street. In 1866 the government recommended that a Fire Brigade should be established at public expense by the Metropolitan Board of Works.
The London Fire Brigade now operates under the London Fire and Civil Defence Authority.

STRAND ★

Map pp 6-7 **(EFX)**
⊖ Temple, Charing Cross

The Strand was an ancient track, midway between the Thames, London's main thoroughfare, and the highway leading west out of the City. Only the churches have survived from the medieval period. From Plantagenet to Hanoverian times it was a street of great mansions and law students' hostels (inns). The south side was particularly favoured by provincial bishops for their town houses. After the Dissolution of the monasteries, the palaces and mansions were purchased by the nobility. Several of these are recorded for posterity in local street names: Essex Street and Devereux Court record the site of Essex House owned by Robert Devereux and later by another Elizabethan favourite, Robert Dudley, Earl of Leicester. Arundel Street recalls the great house of the Howards.

In 1624 James I presented York House, one-time palace of the Archbishop, to George Villiers, Duke of Buckingham; Of Alley has been renamed York Place but the rest of the Duke's name is perpetuated in the streets east of Charing Cross railway station. Hungerford Lane recalls the 15C house of a notorious family who replaced it with a market to pay off gambling debts and even built a footbridge (1854) to attract customers, before selling the site for the construction of the railway station.

Between the big houses and down the side lanes were hundreds of small houses, ale houses, bordels, coffee-houses and shops. The **New Exchange** (1609 to 1737) was an arcade of shops of which 76 of the 150 were milliners and mercers, patronised by James I and his queen, by Charles I and later by Pepys who recounts how he bought gloves, linen, lace, garters, stockings and even books there. The Grecian, later the Devereux public house and a favourite with Addison, is now the Edgar Wallace with an Edwardian decoration and interesting mementoes.

In the late Victorian and Edwardian era the Strand was known for its restaurants and hotels — the Cecil (now Shell-Mex) had 1 000 bedrooms, the Metropole, the Victoria and the Grand, and for its theatres: a popular 19C music hall song was *Let's all go down the Strand*.

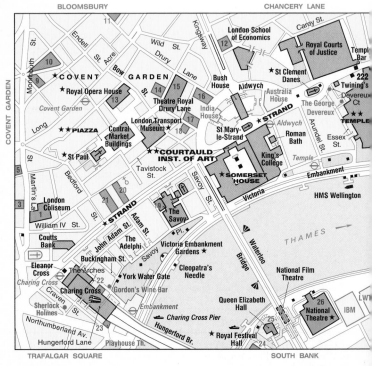

THEATRES:			
Adelphi 21	Donmar	New London 11	Royal Festival Hall .. 24
Albery 5	Warehouse....... 10	Players 22	Royalty 13
Aldwych 16	Duchess 18	Playhouse.......... 23	Savoy 19
Cambridge 9	Duke of York's 3	Queen	Strand 17
London Coliseum... 1	Fortune 14	Elizabeth Hall.... 25	Theatre Royal
	National	Royal Opera,	Drury Lane 15
	Theatre 26	Covent Garden ... 13	Vaudeville 20

238

Charing Cross Station Viaduct – The modern station buildings conceived by Terry Farrell (1990) as part of a larger all-encompassing design project spanning both banks of the Thames, feature a great white arch over and beyond the station viaduct. This giant glazed railway 'hangar' lodged between four granite-faced corner service towers, boldly occupies its strategic position in the riverside panoramic profile; a differently clad street frontage, meanwhile, is scaled to more human and less intimidating proportions appropriate to the Strand site, alongside E M Barry's neo-Gothic **Charing Cross Station Hotel** (1863-64).

In the station forecourt stands a reproduction, designed by E M Barry, of the original **Eleanor Cross** which stood in Trafalgar Square.

Down by the river, beneath the viaduct is held the **Charing Cross Collectors Market** ⊘ coins, medals, stamps, Victoriana.

Hungerford Bridge – A footbridge runs parallel to the east side of the plain lattice girder structure (1862) which carries the railway. It replaced a suspension bridge (1845) by Brunel which was later incorporated into Clifton Suspension Bridge. It is due for a face-lift as part of the redevelopment of the South Bank.

Strand – Today the Strand links Trafalgar Square to Fleet Street and the City and is in the process of re-development. The elegant open glazed building of **Coutts Bank** *(no 440)* was designed by Sir Frederick Gibberd to be sympathetic to its 19C neighbours in the style of John Nash. The bank was transferred to this address in 1904 by Thomas Coutts.

Buckingham Street – *(River side).* 17C and 18C brick houses with pilastered, hooded and corbelled doorways still line both sides (nos 12, 17, 18, 20 date from the 1670s) down to Victoria Embankment Gardens. Pepys lived at no 12 from 1679-88. At the south end stands **York Water Gate**, a triple arch of rusticated stone, decorated with the Villiers arms and a scallop shell, built in 1626 at the water's edge by Nicholas Stone, master mason to George Villiers, 1st Duke of Buckingham.

★**Victoria Embankment Gardens** – The gardens, complete with their bandstand for summer concerts, were created in 1864. Opposite the gardens on the river front, flanked by great bronze lions stands **Cleopatra's Needle**, erected after a long saga in 1878: one of two needles uncovered at Heliopolis (c 1450 BC), it was first offered to George IV by Mehemet Ali of Egypt.

The 68ft monolith sits on a pedestal enclosing two earthenware jars which contain various momentous objects (standard foot and pound, a full set of British Empire coinage, Bibles in different languages, *Bradshaw's Railway Guide, Whitaker's Almanack*, copies of contemporary newspapers and journals...). Similar obelisks stand in Paris (Place de la Concorde) and New York.

The dolphin lamp standards and decorated bench ends are appropriate to their riparian location.

The Adelphi – The river front retains the name although the massively ungraceful stone and brick block with cumbersome angle statues could scarcely be more remote from the Royal Adelphi Terrace erected by Robert Adam in 1768-72 (demolished 1937). The Adam brothers – *adelphi* is the Greek word for brothers – purchased the site on a 99 year lease and transformed the area by the construction along the foreshore of a towering embankment arcade, the Adelphi Arches, supporting a terrace of eleven houses. The row was framed by John (now John Adam) Street, Robert Street and Adam Street, the end houses in the two latter, which overlooked the river, pedimented and decorated to form advanced wings to the terrace. It was the first and possibly finest of Thames-side concepts but the expense was exorbitant and doomed to be a financial failure; now only a few houses remain to give an idea of how the quarter must have looked in the 18C. Famous figures to have treasured the views over the Thames, but endured the stench at low tide include the actor Garrick, Thomas Hardy and the members of the Savage Club and Dr Munro, patron of the young Turner and Girtin. At no 10A lived George Bernard Shaw (1896-1927).

Adam Street: the east side has a run of houses beginning with no 10, Adam House, neat and compact with a rounded corner and curved ironwork; 9 and 8 are the street's standard with attractive pilastered doors; no 7, in the axis of John Adam Street, is a typical example of the Adam decorative style including his favourite acanthus leaf motif applied to pilasters, cornice and ironwork.

John Adam Street: no 8 was built for the **Royal Society of Arts** in 1772-74 by Adam with a projecting porch surmounted by a giant order of fluted columns framing a Serlian window and graces with refined and delicate ornamentation. The RSA, founded in 1754 'to embolden enterprise, to enlarge science, to refine art, to improve our manufacture and extend our commerce' was responsible for organising the Great Exhibition of 1851, and re-structuring the Learned Institutions (Royal Academies); it continues to resolve issues affecting commerce, manufacturing, patenting and copyright, education and the environment.

The **Royal Society,** founded as the Philosophical Society in 1645, was granted a royal charter at the Restoration (1660) and incorporated in 1662. It took as its province the whole field of human knowledge. Founder members were drawn from all walks of life: **Robert Boyle** – a natural philosopher and chemist; **Abraham Cowley** and **Dryden** – poets; **John Aubrey** – antiquarian; **John Evelyn** – diarist and the society's first secretary... Meetings were held in Gresham College, the City institution founded in 1597 under the will of the Elizabethan financier, Sir Thomas Gresham, to which **Christopher Wren** was appointed Professor of Astronomy in 1657. Since its earliest days, members have been men of wide experience and interest; these include **Pepys** – Naval officer and diarist (president from 1684-85); **Sir Hans Sloane** – connoisseur (president 1727-40); **Newton** – physicist; Humphrey Davy, T H Huxley, Lister, Rutherford and Florey, all of whom presented original papers to the Society. Other societies formed at the time, or later in the same spirit, include the Society of Antiquaries (1717), the Linnaean Society (1778), the Geological Society (1807), the Royal Geographical Society (1830) and the British Association for the Advancement of Science (1831).

The Savoy – The Savoy is now a precinct which comprises a chapel, a **theatre,** the first public building in the world to be lit throughout by electricity and a **hotel** built by D'Oyly Carte in 1889 . Its many famous satisfied guests (the hotel's motto being 'For excellence we strive') include the Impressionist painter Monet, who was well placed there to study the changing light over the Thames, and Arnold Bennett who subsequently wrote *Imperial Palace.*

The name dates from 1246, when Henry III granted the manor beside the Thames to his queen's uncle, Peter of Savoy. On the acres extending from the Temple to the Adelphi he built a palace which by the 14C had passed to the Dukes of Lancaster and as "the fairest manor in England" became until his death, the "lodging" of King John of France, captured by the Black Prince at Poitiers (1356). The last owner was John of Gaunt who, however was forced to flee to Ely Place *(see CITY – Holborn)* in 1381 when the palace was sacked by Wat Tyler's Kentish rebels. The manor was annexed in 1399 by Henry IV.

The Queen's Chapel of the Savoy ⊙ **(Chapel of the Royal Victorian Order)** – *Savoy Hill.* The chapel, largely rebuilt after the war, dates back to a bequest by Henry VII for the construction of a hospital for 100 "pouer, needie people" and the erection of dependent place of worship in 1510-16. The hospital was dissolved in 1702 but the chapel and burial yard survived to be made into the Chapel of the Royal Victoria Order in 1937.

Savoy Hill is famous as the site of the BBC's first studios and offices: 1923-32 (plaque on the Embankment façade of no 2 Savoy Place).

The ever burning light in Carting Lane is fuelled by sewer gas.

The restaurant **Simpson's in the Strand** replaces a coffee house – The Grand Cigar Divan founded by Samuel Reiss in 1828. The association with John Simpson came some twenty years later, and Simpson's became 'the' place at which to dine on traditional 'joints from the wagon'.

★★Somerset House – The present building, foretaste in size of future ministries, was erected enduringly in Portland stone in 1776-86 to the designs of **Sir William Chambers** and modelled on the grand style prevalent in pre-Revolution France; it housed the Navy and Navy Pay Offices, the, then small, Tax and Excise offices and three learned societies: the Royal Academy, which Chambers was instrumental in founding and of which he was treasurer, the Antiquaries and the Royal Society.

The 18C building stands on the site of the palace begun by Protector Somerset in 1547 and still incomplete when he was executed in 1552. He had an obsession for building; to acquire additional land he demolished the 13C Mary-le-Strand, bishops' palaces and an Inn of Chancery; he collected stone from buildings forfeited under the Reformation. He achieved a palace of entirely new appearance, which extended from the Strand to the river and which, on his execution, passed to the crown and was given by each Stuart to his queen: Anne of Denmark (when it was known as Denmark House), Henrietta Maria, who returned to it at the Restoration, and Catherine of Braganza.

The building – Through the arch is a vast courtyard (nearly 120yds long by over 100yds across) surrounded by ranges of buildings treated like rows of terrace houses round a square. A continuous balustrade, punctuated by vases (supplied by Mrs Coade at 6 guineas each!) unites the fronts. The riverside front, which is 800ft long including the later extensions, stands on a continuous line of massive arches which in the 18C were at the water's edge.

Located in Somerset House today are the **Courtauld Institute of Art** *(listed separately)*, the dazzling **Gilbert Collection**★★ ⊘ (South and Embankment Buildings) donated to Britain in 1996 by Sir Arthur Gilbert, a discerning collector, and The **Hermitage Rooms** ⊘ which present rotating exhibitions from the prestigious State Hermitage Museum in St Petersburg offering a unique insight into Russian art and history. Fountains adorn the piazza which is used for public entertainment and fine **views**★★ of the Thames may be enjoyed from the riverside façade.

★★**The Gilbert Collection** – From the main entrance (Embankment) pass into the splendid vaulted rooms displaying richly ornamented mosaic cabinets, tables and decorative panels with at the far end superb gilded and silver gates. The magnificent array of **tableware** (mezzanine) in silver and silvergilt includes large platters and ewers made by De Lamerie and Storr among others from stately homes such as Althorp, Belton, Stowe and Powderham Castle and some solid gold vessels. Among the outstanding collection of gold boxes are six jewelled snuff boxes which belonged to Frederick II of Prussia. The micromosaics are remarkable. An 18C barge in the King's Barge House recalls a past era when the Thames was a busy waterway.

St Mary-le-Strand ⊘ – Until the Reformation, a market cross would have identified the spot where the Itinerant Magistrates of Middlesex once held their Assizes, at a time when the Strand was lined with town houses for bishops. This compact, Baroque miniature (1714-24) was the first commission to be undertaken by **James Gibbs** on his return from Rome where he had studied architecture under Carlo Fontana. It is sober and ordered: a simple apsed space that is light and harmoniously proportioned.

The tower rises in four tiers over the rounded porch and first floor pediment to a gilded weather vane – a singularly English arrangement of Classical features *(see Wren's St Clement Danes and Gibbs' St Martin-in-the-Fields)*. Two superimposed orders, Ionic and Corinthian on the outside and Corinthian and Composite inside, articulate the walls of the single storeyed interior: solid at ground level and the large windows above – intended to lessen the constant noise of traffic over the cobbles. Fine carvings decorate the exterior, but it is perhaps the Italianate plasterwork ceiling which is particularly worthy of note: executed by English craftsmen, the stylised flower heads are especially delicate.

In 1984 the church, which has been known as the Cabby's church since Captain Bailey set up the first hackney carriage rank on the north side in 1634, has become the official church of the Women's Royal Naval Service, the Women's Royal Naval Reserve with the Association of Wrens.

Much of the church plate has been entrusted to the Victoria and Albert Museum and the Treasury of St Paul's Cathedral.

King's College – King's College, founded in 1829 and since 1898 a part of London University, was housed from its earliest days in the east extension of Somerset House, built in accordance with Chambers' designs; in the 1970s the Strand front was renewed in an unrelated, modern style. The courtyard, long and narrow, is terminated by the colonnaded pavilion which completes the Somerset House river front.

Down Surrey steps and to the right may be seen the **Roman Bath** ⊘ *(5 Strand Lane)*, fed by a nearby spring, visible through a window *(timed light switch)*; although possibly Tudor, more likely 17C, it is certainly not Roman. Note the 17C traditional delft Dutch tiles, bearing figures and tulip designs.

At 1 Maltravers Street (Smith & Nephew) stands **Temple Place**, one-time residence and office of William Waldorf Astor, the wealthy American politician, diplomat and newspaper baron, who emigrated to Britain in 1890. The unprepossessing house dressed in Portland stone is decked inside with English oak, Spanish mahogany, cedar, ebony, marble, jasper, porphyry, onyx...

Aldwych – The sweeping semicircle was laid out in 1905. The huge half-moon island on the Strand is occupied by massive buildings: Australia House, India House (reliefs) and, in the centre, the 1925-35 **Bush House**, base of the BBC External Services.

For details of the twin theatres, the **Aldwych** and the **Strand**, turn to the Entertainment Section of the Introduction.

London School of Economics – *Houghton Street*. The school which numbers 3 700 full-time students and 500 part-time students (40 % postgraduates), was founded in 1895 under the auspices of Sidney Webb and has been part of London University since 1900. The British Library of Political and Economic Science, which contains some 2 750 000 items, including pamphlets and tracts, is also housed in the building.

★St Clement Danes ⊘ – St Clement's, designed by **Wren** in 1682, with the
open spire in three diminishing pillared stages – the steeple was added by
James Gibbs (1719), was burnt out on 10 May 1941 and rebuilt as the RAF
church in 1955-58. The dark oak panelling, first floor galleries beneath a
richly decorated vault and plasterwork Stuart coat of arms conforms to
Wren's original design, now embellished with Air Force mementoes that
include 800 squadron and unit badges carved in Welsh slate and inlaid in the
pavement, floor memorials of the badges of the Commonwealth air forces
and the Polish squadrons, a USAAF and other shrines, and a series of
Memorial Books listing over 125 000 names. The grand pulpit is the original
one by Grinling Gibbons, carefully restored after the war. In the crypt, a
burial place until 1853, are the Norwegian Air Force font and the Netherlands Air Force altar. The memorial to Bomber Command (outside) by Faith
Winter was erected amid much controversy in 1992.

Tradition has it that the original 9C church of St Clement Danes was built
by Danish merchants married to Englishwomen, allowed to reside between
Westminster and Ludgate; St Clement, Bishop of Rome and patron of seafarers, was martyred under Trajan by being tied to an anchor and thrown
into the sea. 'Oranges and lemons say the bells of St Clement's' refers to
the boats that came up the Thames to land fruit for sale in Clare Market
(on the site of Kingsway, Drury Lane) and paid a tithe in kind to the
church and although the association is disputed with St Clement Eastcheap
(see CITY - Monument), the carillon rings out the **nursery rhyme.**

At the east end stands a statue of Dr Samuel Johnson, a worshipper at the church
who lived near by.

Twinings – *No 216.* Two Chinamen flanking the Twining lion over the door
identify the very narrow shop, which sells tea and contains a small museum; it
opened in 1706 as Tom's Coffee House. Several generations have witnessed
changes in tea trading: the Commutation Act almost cancelled the hefty tax
imposed by the Treasury (1784); in 1839 the clipper *Calcutta* landed Indian tea
from Assam thereby breaching the Chinese monopoly; new supplies were imported
from Ceylon in 1879. Today Twinings manufacture over 150 blends of tea, herb
and fruit infusions.

Lloyd's Law Courts Branch – *No 222.* The **Palsgrave Tavern**, as frequented by the
dramatist Ben Jonson, was named after Frederick Palsgrave, later King of Bohemia, who married Elizabeth, daughter of James I. All three figures are commemorated in the singular glazed earthenware decoration supplied by Royal Doulton. In
1883, the premises were refurbished and renamed the Royal Courts of Justice
Restaurant complete with electric lighting generated by steam engines and dyna-
mos, an elaborate ventilation system modelled on that used in ships' holds and its

The Savoy Hotel

The guest list has included many a *diva* (Lily Langtry, Melba for whom
Escoffier invented the famous peach *entremets*, Sarah Bernhardt, Gigli who
when performing at Covent Garden got his wife in Rome to send him his
favourite dishes), the artists Monet and Whistler, and famous millionaires
(the Duc d'Orléans and his three pet lion cubs)...

The idea was born from extensive travel to America and the realisation that
whereas Englishmen had their clubs in which to dine, comfortable facilities
for foreign visitors were sparse in London. The seven storey, steel-framed
concrete building (among the first in London) was completed in five years: it
boasted its own electric generators and private water supply (vital to its
survival during the Blitz), seventy bathrooms (compared to the Hotel Victoria, its rival in Northumberland Avenue, which had four bathrooms to serve
500 guests), continual 'shaded electric light' and 'luxurious ascending rooms
running all night' (lifts), speaking tubes with the explanation 'Please command anything from a cup of tea to a cocktail, and it will come up in the
twinkling of an Embankment light'. Its early success must in part be credited
to César Ritz and his famous retinue that included that 'Emperor of Cooks'
August Escoffier, whose short stature forced him to wear high-heels so that
he might reach over his open ranges, and Echenard, 'one of the world's
supreme judges of wine'; at one time Johann Strauss and his orchestra were
hired to play waltzes in the restaurant. Together they made dining at the
Savoy the 'done thing' be it at a large public banquet or for a private
intimate dinner...

own Artesian well to provide elaborate fountains, but the business failed. Inside, the building, a branch of Lloyds bank since 1895, is panelled with American walnut and sequoia, inset with tiles designed by John McLennan from his Lambeth studio (other commissions were undertaken for the Great Ormond St Hospital, Birkbeck Bank, the Tsar of Russia and the King of Siam).

Wig and Pen Club ⊘– *229/230 Strand.* The building, which survived the Great Fire (1666), dates from 1625. The club, which is the home of the London Press Club, draws its members from journalism, business and the law. Among the memorabilia is the official press wire announcing the death of Adolf Hitler.

Royal Courts of Justice ⊘– The Law Courts date from 1874-82 when the Perpendicular design of G E Street was constructed to replace the ranges erected around the courts' original seat in Westminster Hall. The centre-piece inside is the Great Hall, a vaulted arcade, 230ft long, 82ft high, decorated with foliated doorways, blind arcades, diapering and a seated statue of the architect. The early courtrooms and the majority (still there are more than 20) depend from the hall which is marked outside by a needle spire, counterpoint to the long arched façade, the heavy tower and polygonal west end. There is a small exhibition of legal costumes.

At this point, the Strand gives way to Fleet Street enclosed within the confines of the City of London: the boundary is marked by the Temple Bar *(see CHANCERY LANE).*

TATE BRITAIN★★★

Map p 8 **(EZ)**
⊖ Pimlico

Tate Britian ⊘ is the national gallery of British Art (16C to the present day) and the national gallery of international modern art. It is also entrusted with the Archive of Twentieth Century British Art for art-work, artist's writings, film, video, sound recordings and associated printed ephemera.

National gallery of British art – 50 years after the purchase of the Angerstein Collection and the founding of the National Gallery (1824), the nation had acquired a large number of works that were shuffled between the National Gallery, the Victoria and Albert Museum and Marlborough House: the **Chantrey Bequest** provided for the purchase of works by living artists; the **Vernon** and **Sheepshanks** Collections; the Turner Bequest (1856) included 300 oil paintings and 20 000 water colours and drawings from the artist's personal estate.

In 1889 the initiative was taken by the sugar broker Henry Tate who was an astute collector of British art; he offered his collection of 67 paintings (including J E Millais's *Ophelia*) to the nation together with £80 000 for a purpose-built gallery dedicated to British art post 1790 on condition that the government provide a site for it. The Tate opened in 1897 on the site of the former Millbank Prison.

National collection of modern foreign art – In 1915, Sir Hugh Lane died when the *Lusitania* was torpedoed off the south coast of Ireland leaving 39 paintings, including some superb Impressionists, 'to found a collection of Modern Continental Art in London' *(see NATIONAL GALLERY).* Extensions to the original building were endowed by the son of Sir Joseph Duveen in 1926 and in 1937 to accommodate sculpture; further building was completed in 1979; the Tate then took over the former Queen Alexandra Hospital, before the Clore Wing was designed by James Stirling (1987) to accommodate the Turner collection.

In 1954 the Tate Gallery became legally independent of the National Gallery.

Further to the opening of Tate Modern in 2000 *(see BANKSIDE)* which is devoted to international 20C art with British art presented in the international context and the upgrading of the present site as part of the Centenary Development scheme *(completion 2001)* to provide more display space and better access and facilities, a new focus has been defined for Tate Britain. The museum is devoted exclusively to **British art from 1500 to the present day** illustrating the quality, diversity, character, originality and influence of British art over five centuries.

The imaginative thematic displays – Private & Public, Literature & Fantasy, Roast Beef and Liberty, Home and Abroad, Artists & Models – stress continuity through the ages but add an element of surprise which, although sometimes controversial, fosters greater awareness and appreciation of works by British-born artists, by artists from abroad working in Britain or with themes related to Britain.

Special displays feature major figures such as Hogarth, Blake, Gainsborough and Hockney. New acquisitions are also on view and major exhibitions proclaim the Tate's commitment to promote British art.

Practicalities – It is advisable to obtain a gallery plan from the information desks as the galleries are regularly re-hung.

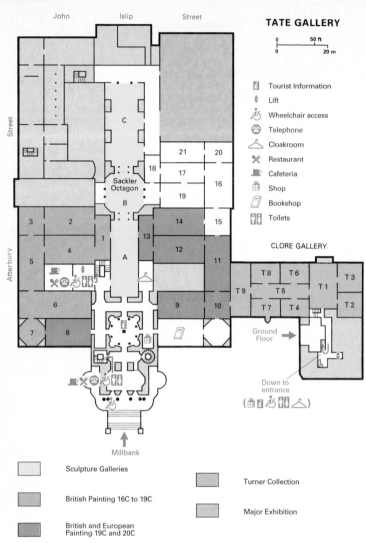

TATE GALLERY

0 ___ 50 ft
0 ___ 20 m

🛈 Tourist Information
↕ Lift
♿ Wheelchair access
☎ Telephone
⌂ Cloakroom
✗ Restaurant
🍴 Cafeteria
🏬 Shop
📖 Bookshop
🚻 Toilets

CLORE GALLERY

Ground Floor →

Down to entrance
(🏬🛈♿🚻⌂)

Millbank

Sculpture Galleries

British Painting 16C to 19C

British and European Painting 19C and 20C

Turner Collection

Major Exhibition

The vulnerability of many works on paper to exposure to light means that they ar displayed for short periods only (and then in subdued light) – while endeavours t represent paintings by each artist are made, it is impossible to ensure that a particula watercolour is on view; if you intend to visit the collection so as to see a particula work of art it is advisable to contact the Gallery first to check whether it is on displa This also applies to pieces from the Modern Art Collection which may be temporari at premises in St Ives in Cornwall or Liverpool.

Duveen Sculpture Galleries – A, B and C on floorplan. The lofty spaces of th central galleries, particularly the Sackler Octagon, make a superb setting f displays of modern sculpture taken from the gallery's collection (Rodin, Reno Henri Gaudier-Brzeska, Eric Gill, Henry Moore, Jacob Epstein, Dame Barba Hepworth) or on temporary show.

Painting in Britain 16C – 19C

For more information on the evolution of the British School, see INTRODUCTION Painting.

Image and Allegory: Tudor and Stuart Painting – John Bettes is the earlie English work in the collection: his *Man in a Black Cap* betrays the influence of Holbei highlighting the face against a background of mottled brown wall and fur collar, blac cap and robe. **Hans Eworth** demonstrates a similar talent at rendering the exquisi details of an embroidered dress and a chalcedony cameo set in gold.

244

Nicholas Hilliard, the most famous Elizabethan miniaturist encapsulates an idealised vision of his gracious queen: flat, stylised, linear, exquisite, fragile... Elizabeth is shown holding a rose, a Tudor emblem, red for the House of Lancaster, thornless like that borne by the Virgin Mary, 'the rose without thorn': a powerful image full of political allegory.

Other continental painters (Geerhardt, Mytens) attracted by royal patronage gently chart a change in climate from simple austerity to a celebration of status: the prolific **Van Dyck** paints his figures standing comfortably in space, poised in movement or gesture.

William Dobson's portrait of *Endymion Porter (see INTRODUCTION – Painting)*, executed during Charles I exile in Oxford during the Civil War, shows the artist's concern for capturing the personality of his sitters.

Peter Lely adapted to the delicate political climate: his sitters are shown with elegant informality in uncontroversial poses. His biblical and mythological subjects *(Susannah and the Elders)* meanwhile, verge on the erotic, hitherto unprecedented in the Puritan age.

Hogarth and his Contemporaries

Hogarth and his Contemporaries – Hogarth was a perceptive portraitist *(Captain Coram)* and versatile painter, the patriotic author of 'modern moral subjects' and humorous satires that make him the first great commentator of his era *(O The Roast Beef of Old*

> The unsigned portrait of *The Cholmondeley Sisters* is highly stylised but is nevertheless quite striking; it naively records in the bottom left corner that it depicts two ladies of the family who were born, married and gave birth on the same day.

England or *Calais Gate; Scene from the Beggars Opera VI; The Dance* or *The Happy Marriage)*. In *The Painter and his Pug,* the oval self-portrait rests upon three volumes labelled Shakespeare (comic and tragic theatre), Swift (acutely observed social and political comment in fictional novels) and Milton (epic poetry) – as if to confirm the complementary objectives of painting and literature; Trump, his pet pug, represents the private side of the sitter.

The fashion for 'conversation pieces', usually representing a domestic interior, were popular with his successors **Francis Hayman** and Joseph Highmore, who exploited the illustrative quality of the genre. Hayman was amongst the first to draw inspiration from Shakespeare *(As You Like It)* and the novels of Richardson *(Pamela);* alas, little remains of the series of panels he produced for the supperboxes or pavilions at the Vauxhall Pleasure Gardens, other than engravings which betray the influence of French Rococo painting (especially Watteau who visited London for medical reasons 1719-20) with its accent on playfulness set in pretty, idyllic landscapes.

Eighteenth Century: Age of Confidence and Grand Manner – During the Age of Confidence the term 'Grand Style' alluded to art in the manner of the great Italian Renaissance masters (Michelangelo, Raphael, Titian): subjects were usually drawn from the Bible, Classical Mythology or Literature and thus qualified as 'high art'. The taste for this kind of painting was given a further stamp of approval when the Royal Academy was founded in 1768. **Reynolds**, its first president, was quick to recognise that English 'history' pictures found little favour with English patrons, and therefore fashioned his own style of portraiture: sitters were flattered and posed as Classical gods *(Three Ladies Adorning a Term of Hymen – The Montgomery Sisters)*, actresses were painted in costume. In contrast, **Gainsborough**'s portraits are full of movement and gesture, colour, light and space. His patrons were largely country gentry (Sudbury, Suffolk; Bath; London) and his sitters often are depicted in Arcadian (imaginary) landscapes.

Landscape Painting: Aspects of Naturalism, Sporting Art and Genre Painting – The man who most successfully painted landscape in the Grand Manner was **Richard Wilson**, having travelled in Italy for seven years. His topographical landscapes suggest admiration for Claude and the Venetians (Canaletto), and were popular amongst London-based merchants and businessmen *(Westminster Bridge Under Construction; On Hounslow Heath)*.

Benjamin West, an American-born artist who settled in London in 1763, succeeded Reynolds as President of the RA.

George **Stubbs** adapts the Grand Manner to sporting pictures, Joseph **Wright of Derby** to modern genre painting and portraiture, often celebrating scientific invention. *Sir Brooke Boothby* is shown inspired by his friend Jean Jacques Rousseau, the 'Noble Savage' author and philosopher.

Subsequent developments in landscape painting overlap with its treatment in literature: Burke outlines a new kind of Beauty between the Sublime and the Beautiful, Jane Austen satirises **The Picturesque** in *Sense and Sensibility* (1811) and *Northanger*

Abbey (1818), while Wordsworth composes pastoral poetry and Blake the words to *Jerusalem* (1804-20). Watercolour becomes the favourite medium of travellers to the continent for recording impressions of lofty mountains, avalanches, sun-baked plains and erupting volcanoes.

This drama is perpetuated, meanwhile by **Loutherbourg** who settled in London in 1771: as scenery painter at Drury Lane, he conceived his pictures rather as a theatrical set, like Hogarth had before him, but now introducing dramatic natural phenomena like lightning and thunderbolts; one of his principal followers was Francis Danby.

Works on Paper: Watercolours and prints 1680-1900 – **William Blake** and his followers include his patron John Linnell and the visionary painters Samuel Palmer, Edward Calvert, George Richmond, known as the 'Ancients'. Blake (1757-1827) pioneered monotype printing methods for his limited edition illustrations of the Creation: pigment was applied to a hard board upon which sheets of paper were laid, each taking a different impression before the colour dried; this image was then worked up separately with pen, ink and watercolour. Romantic subjects were chosen from great literature (The Bible, Dante's *Divine Comedy*, Virgil's *Eclogues*) as his poetry explored the themes of Youth, Wisdom, Innocence, Guilt... Blake never tasted success in his own lifetime despite the exhibitions of his 'tempera' pictures.

Palmer (1805-1881) was profoundly impressed by Blake, not only in the use of woodcut and tempera on a relatively small-scale (oil paint was identified with Rubens and Rembrandt and regarded as too sensuous and unctuous for the spiritual honesty of their work) but also in his mystical view of the English landscape, in Palmer's case around Shoreham in Kent. He was followed by **Richard Dadd** (1817-86) who produced highly individual illustrations (Shakespeare's *Midsummer Night's Dream*): in 1843, Dadd murdered his father and was condemned to Bethlem Hospital and Broadmoor Prison where he was able to explore his hallucinatory world of fantasy, visions, fairies and hobgoblins.

Realism and Idealism – The British interest in topographical drawings, coloured with ink or wash, is rooted in the 17C Dutch tradition. During the 1750s artists were employed by gentlemen-travellers on the Grand Tour to record sights, ruins, monuments much as we might today use photography; draughtsmen were charged with making meticulous studies that might allow their patrons to have facsimiles made on their return home. In the 19C, Ruskin, Leighton and Lear were all supreme draughtsmen.

Girtin's *The White house in Chelsea* marks a new departure in watercolour painting: from the stained, monochrome drawings of 18C to the luminous, atmospheric 'impressions' of the 19C. Great swathes of delicate wash are applied to the absorbent white paper which he favoured, the low horizon a homage to the watercolours and etchings of Rembrandt.

John Constable: *Flatford Mill; The Lock; The Opening of Waterloo Bridge; Chain Pier Brighton; Cloud Study;* David Cox: *A Windy Day.*

Victorian Romanticism – The Royal Academy School taught technique, its gallery displayed current artistic trends: Wilkie (1785-1841), Frith (1819-1909), Landseer (1802-73), Queen Victoria's favourite painter who had been an infant prodigy exhibiting his work at the RA from the age of 12 and who learnt to endow his animal subjects with human-like expressions.

Pre-Raphaelites and Symbolists – **J E Millais** encapsulated the ethic of the PRB in his painting *Christ in the House of His Parents (The Carpenter's Shop),* exhibited in 1849, and full of meticulous realism and elaborate iconography: the carpenter's shop was based on premises in Oxford Street, Joseph's figure and hands are modelled upon those of a real carpenter, his head is a portrait of Millais father, the sheep were drawn from two heads obtained by the painter from a local butcher's, the still life on the back wall is charged with the symbolism of the Crucifixion (Dove of the Holy Spirit, the triangle of the Trinity, the tools that represent the Passion)... The overall effect was new and precipitated controversy: to quote part of Dickens' diatribe

'Wherever it is possible to express ugliness of feature, limb or attitude, you have it expressed. Such men as the carpenters might be undressed in any hospital where dirty drunkards, in a high state of varicose veins, are received. Their very toes have walked out of St Giles's'.

Rossetti was the son of an Italian political refugee, living in London. He learnt to paint from Cotman and Hunt; from an early age he showed a fascination for Dante and the dreamy world of Romance, legend, pure love and chivalry that were also to inspire him to write poetry. In 1850 he met Elizabeth Siddal, she became his muse and eventually his wife (1860), only to die two years later from an overdose of laudanum, a derivative of opium. In the posthumous portrait *Beata Beatrix*, Rossetti includes two ephemeral but complementary (red and green) figures – these may be allegories of life and death or allude to the ideal couple Eve and Adam, Beatrix the Muse and Dante the artist joined by an arched bridge based on the Ponte Vecchio in Florence; the bird is the messenger of death; the white opium poppy the instrument; the sundial marks time. He later courted William Morris's wife Jane (1871), but bereft of his muse, Rossetti became a virtual recluse and eventually died a chloral addict.

The delicate moral question of infidelity and prostitution was topical at a time when abandoned mistresses and high-society prostitutes used to flaunt themselves on horseback in Hyde Park: in literature the subject once treated by Abbé Prévost *(Manon Lescaut)*, Marquis de Sade *(Justine, ou les Malheurs de la Vertu)*, Laclos *(Liaisons Dangereuses)*, Dumas *(La Dame aux Camélias)*, Flaubert *(Madame Bovary)* was worked in music by Mozart *(Don Giovanni)* Verdi *(La Traviata)*, Rossini and Massenet... In painting, the cause was publicised with realism by Frith, Millais, Tissot or condoned by the Aesthetes and Decadents with idealisations of exotic beauty (Leighton, Alma Tadema, Russell Flint).

Holman Hunt's *The Awakening Conscience* is set in St John's Wood and shows a 'maison de convenance' where lovers have illicitly met (a wedding ring is missing from her bejewelled hand, the cat plays with a bird under the table).

William Frith's *Derby Day* was much admired when it was exhibited in 1858. It is a prize piece of Victorian genre complete with accurate portraits of recognisable people (young and old, rich and poor), realistic vignettes of such an occasion (the gambling, the entertainment, the social scene, lavish picnics and ragged beggary) all set against a meticulously rendered view of Epsom Racecourse, painted from specially commissioned photographs.

Edward Burne-Jones (1833-98) is closely associated with William Morris. His idealised young subjects are bathed in a dreamy soft light; profiles and textures are carefully contrasted one with another (flesh tones, stone carving, embroidered fabric, metal armour, flora and foliage). A preference for tall compositions may reflect the contemporary use of paintings as decorative panels integrated into more complex interior schemes.

Aestheticism – The movement's call for 'art for art's sake' evolved during the 1870s and found its manifesto in Walter Hamilton's *The Aesthetic Movement in England*, published in 1882. Whistler and Albert Moore imported their own ideas from Paris; at home, the handsome, intellectual, well-travelled and charismatic **Lord Leighton**, elected President of the Royal Academy in 1879, assumed the mantle. Alma-Tadema, Watts and Poynter, otherwise known as the Olympians, drew inspiration from Hellenistic Greece and the images evoked by the Elgin Marbles. Composition is simplified, colour is carefully blended into harmonious arrangements, form is precisely outlined and defined by texture or surface decoration, the fall of drapery, the perspective of a tiled floor...

'Just the other day a young American artist, J M Whistler, was showing a set of etchings, as subtle and lively as improvisation and inspiration, representing the banks of the Thames; wonderful tangles of rigging, yardarms and rope; farragoes of fog, furnaces and corkscrews of smoke; the profound and intricate poetry of a vast capital...'
Baudelaire *Painters and Etchers*, 14 September 1862

Foreign influences – The most original painter to digest the current influence and instigate continental modernism was **Whistler** (1834-1903). Receptive to all the prevailing artistic movements in Paris, Whistler assimilated influences from the Impressionists (overall composition), imported Japanese prints (unusual perspective and muted colour), the writings of established art critics like the Romantic poets Baudelaire and Gautier as well as the spirit of his middle-class Parisian contemporaries Gustave Moreau, Marcel Proust, George Sand, Chopin, Gounod, Berlioz... In London, he painted *Nocturne in Blue and Gold: Old Battersea Bridge* which, in spirit, betrays all these influences: the scene was sketched from life and the impression transposed from memory; perspective has been distorted for the sake of the composition, realism has been forsaken to evoke atmosphere.

John Singer Sargent (1856-1925), an American painter who had worked outdoors with Claude Monet and Camille Pissarro moved to London in 1885.

Monet *Poplars on the Epte*; Pissarro *A Corner of the Meadow at Eragny*; Degas: *Two figures of dancers*; Renoir: *Dancing Girl with Castanets; Dancing Girl with Tambourine*; Sargent *Carnation, Lily, Lily, Rose*.

20C: The International Context

NB: collections have been transferred to Tate Modern *(opened in 2000)*, Bankside

France – Primitive Art inspired the amateur 'Sunday' painters Douanier **Rousseau** (1844-1910) and **Gauguin** (1848-1903) who stylised form, and used patches of flat colour for space within a composition, pattern to provide texture and relief. **The Nabis** (1889-1899) – from the Hebrew word for prophet – included Edouard Vuillard, Bonnard, Maurice Denis and Maillol, rejected realism: 'Remember that a picture .... is essentially a flat surface covered with colours assembled in a certain order'.

Out of Impressionism was precipitated **Van Gogh** (1853-90) who used pure colour, painted out of doors and produced informal portraits of friends; his strong brush stroke and impasto technique betray a searing malaise with life. Only his early flower pieces show sensitivity to transient, ephemeral light.

The Neo-Impressionist **Georges Seurat** (1859-91) was fascinated by optics: as white light might refract the spectrum, so he might suggest luminosity by juxtaposing coloured dashes. His Divisionism or pointillist technique is applied with scientific precision and application.

Henri Matisse (1869-1954) had a traditional artistic training first with Bouguereau and later with the Symbolist Gustave Moreau. Matisse was extremely versatile and prolific: he collaborated with the **Nabis** (Bonnard and Vuillard), the **Fauves** (Derain *Port of London* and Vlaminck), Cézanne, Signac, and Picasso. He travelled extensively and secured patronage from several collectors within his own lifetime.

Paul Cézanne (1881-1973) conceived landscape in terms of basic geometric volumes (cube, sphere, pyramid) existing in space in which perspective is determined by colour: green and blue for depth of field, warm golds and earthy ochres for foreground. His portraiture *(The Gardener)* and still lives are also conceived as studies of mass, textured by pattern, moulded by shadow.

Pablo Picasso (1881-1973) draws on the Symbolist use of colour to suggest mood. Gouache, drawings and etchings dominate his Blue and Pink periods, echoing a transition from a desolate, poor and sad life to one shared with Fernande Olivier at the Bateau-Lavoir.

Picasso, Braque, Modigliani and Brancusi were all greatly impressed by stylised Iberian sculpture and Oceanic carvings then displayed at the ethnological museum in Paris *(see Green Guide PARIS)*. From this powerful primitive artform, each explored the realms of eroticism or abstraction.

Cubism (1906-1914) was the first truly abstract movement that evolved as a counter-reaction to the visual appeal of Impressionism and Fauvism: instead of flattening a three dimensional object to a two-dimensional picture, Cubism attempted to capture the volume or essence of the subject (form, shape, texture, purpose) as a series of fractured details: as Picasso stated 'A face consists of eyes, nose, ears, etc. You can put them anywhere in the picture, the face remains a face'. In a *Clarinet and Bottle of Rum on a Mantlepiece*, **Braque** presents the instrument as something associated with music (represented by the word VALSE and symbols for the treble and bass clefs); later compositions evolve into collages. Fernand **Léger** meanwhile, forged his own interpretation of the movement by integrating fragmented form, which he highlights with colour, with bits of black and white geometric patterning.

Dada and Surrealism – Dada (1915-22) came from Zurich: a deliberately nihilistic anti-artform that was intended to shock and scandalise. Breton, Tzara, Duchamp *(Large Glass)*, Arp and Picabia explored the fundamental nature of art by contradicting any established classification or justification with sharp wit and clever humour. Later, a more intellectual approach – prompted in part by the publication of Freud's theories – was pioneered by the Surrealist writers Apollinaire and Eluard who experimented with language, the realms of the subconscious, drug-induced dreams. They were joined in Paris by a second wave of foreign artists: Ernst *(Celebes)*, de Chirico, Magritte *(The Reckless Sleeper)*, Dali *(Metamorphosis of Narcissus, Lobster, Telephone)*, Miro, Penrose ...

Futurism – 'A new art for a new century' was formulated by a group of Italians (Balla *Abstract Speed – the car has passed*, Boccioni *Unique Forms of Continuity in Space*, Carra, Severini *Suburban Train arriving in Paris*) to celebrate modern civilisation: the advent of electricity, mechanisation, the invention of the motor car, the glory of war... Tragically, several of the main protagonists died during the First World War, by which time the essence of the movement had fired the **Vorticists**.

German Expressionism –

In sympathy with ideas expressed by Gauguin, the Expressionists were happy to compromise naturalism by exaggerating form and colour if the end result had a more powerful impact (something Grunewald was doing in the first quarter of

> The wealth of the Tate Gallery Collection is largely due to the bequests made by Sir Roland Penrose, the one-time friend of Picasso and Ernst, and that of Edward James, a patron of Dali and Magritte.

the 16C). **Die Brucke** (1905-13) meaning 'The Bridge' united Kirchner *(Bathers at Moritzburg)*, Heckel, Schmidt-Rotluff *(Dr Rosa Shapire)* and Bleyl in Dresden; soon it included Nolde *(The Sea B)* and Pechstein, the Norwegian Edvard Munch *(The Sick Child)* and **Der Blaue Reiter** (The Blue Rider), a group which was started in 1911 in Munich by Marc, Kandinski, Macke, Campendonk and Klee.

Major movements and artists of the 20C

Shaded off colours indicate the origin and/or influence of a movement.

Timeline axis: 1900 · 10 · 20 · 30 · 33 · 40 · 50 · 60 · 70 · 80

NEO-EXPRESSIONISM — FETTING LUPERTZ MIDDENDORF

TRANSAVANTGARDE — CLEMENTE PALADINO

GRAFFITI ART — HARING COMBAS — ERRO BASQUIAT RICHTER GAROUSTE

NEW FIGURATIVE PAINTING — KIEFER BASELITZ CHIA GUSTON SCHNABEL

HOCKNEY

POP-ART — ROSENQUIST OLDENBURG WARHOL — BLAKE LICHTENSTEIN

PAOLOZZI

FREUD

HYPERREALISME — ESTES CLOSE — RAYNAUD SPOERRI

NOUVEAU REALISM — ARMAN CÉSAR

NEW DADA — JOHNS RAUSCHENBERG ROTELLA DEL PEZZO — KLEIN

LAND ART — CHRISTO LONG DE MARIA

SUPPORT-SURFACE GROUP — VIALLAT DEZEUZE CANE BUREN MOSSET

KINETIC ART — TINGUELY SOTO BURY

OP-ART — VASARELY — LOUIS NOLAND KELLY

MINIMAL ART — STELLA ANDRÉ JUDD LEWITT SERRA — COX SCULLY

HALLEY TAAFE

PRINCE LEVINE GRAHAM DURHAM — BOLTANSKI LEROY CRAIG-MARTIN VENET

COBRA — APPEL ALECHINSKY CONSTANT

BACON SUTHERLAND

MAFAI

RICHIER

DE STAËL BAZAINE ESTÈVE

TANGUY

ABSTRACT EXPRESSIONISM — NEWMAN REINHART POLLOCK DE KOONING MOTHERWELL HOFMANN ROTHKO KLINE STILL

CARO COHEN

HAACKE BEUYS HESSE

NEW EUROPEAN SCULPTURE — PENONE FABRO DEACON CRAGG

ART AND LANGUAGE — FLANAGAN DYE HILLIARD

ARTE POVERA — KOUNELLIS MERZ

CONCEPTUAL ART — MORRIS KOSUTH GILBERT & GEORGE BROODTHAERS

ART INFORMEL — WOLS FAUTRIER RIOPELLE — SOULAGES BURRI

ART BRUT — DUBUFFET — BAERTLING PASMORE TAPIES

NEO-CONSTRUCTIVISM — MARTIN HILL

2nd wave of emigration to the USA

CORRENTE — BIROLLI SASSU

EXPRESSIONISM — BARLACH MARCKS SCHMIDT-ROTTLUFF BECKMANN HECKEL PERMEKE KOKOSCHKA

BRÜCKE — KIRCHNER BLAUE NOLDE REITER MARC MACKE LEHMBRUCK SCHIELE

FAUVISM — MATISSE DERAIN VLAMINCK VAN DONGEN DUFY

KUBIN ROUAULT

NEW OBJECTIVITY — DIX HUBBUCH GROSZ SCHAD SOLANA CHAGALL SOUTINE

BOMBERG

VORTICISM — LEWIS EPSTEIN

MODIGLIANI

CALDER

CUBISM — PICASSO BRAQUE DELAUNAY GRIS

LÉGER ARCHIPENKO ZADKINE BRANCUSI LAURENS LIPCHITZ GONZALEZ MARINI

LE FAUCONNIER GLEIZES

GIACOMETTI

SURREALISM — ARP PICABIA ERNST MAN RAY MIRÓ DALI MATTA DE CHIRICO MAGRITTE DE PISIS DOTTORI FILLIA MAGNELLI DEPERO

DADA — DUCHAMP

FUTURISM — CARRA SEVERINI BOCCIONI BALLA RUSSELL

KUPKA

UNIT ONE — MOORE HEPWORTH NASH

FONTANA

ABSTRACTION-CREATION — VANTONGERLOO HÉLION HERBIN

NEO-PLASTICISM — VAN DOESBURG MONDRIAN

BIRTH OF ABSTRACT ART — KANDINSKY

BAUHAUS — ITTEN KLEE MOHOLY-NAGY SCHLEMMER BRAUNER ALBERS

MURAL PAINTING

BILL NICHOLSON

1st wave of emigration to the USA

SYMBOLISM — PUVIS DE CHAVANNES MOREAU REDON KLIMT KHNOPFF

ENSOR HODLER MUNCH

GAUGUIN

NABIS — DENIS VUILLARD BONNARD MAILLOL

NEO- AND POST-IMPRESSIONISM — CÉZANNE ROUSSEAU RENOIR MONET SIGNAC DEGAS

RODIN BOURDELLE

SUPREMATISM — MALEVITCH LISSITZKY

CONSTRUCTIVISM — GABO PEVSNER LARIONOV TATLINE

SOCIAL REALISM

Legend:
- Movement originating in Europe
- Movement originating in the USA

VAN GOGH · PRIMITIVE ART · IMPRESSIONNISM

249

George Grosz *(Suicide)* admitted his 'profound disgust for life' before the outbreak of war, and his contempt was intensified by experience: familiar themes include prostitutes and bloated businessmen, death, an isolated church bathed in golden light. **Max Beckmann** was scarred by the war; having served as a hospital orderly on the Belgian Front, he was discharged in 1915 and evolved a new style of unnerving realism *(Carnival)*.

Abstraction – If form is whittled to its purest outline and most perfect surface, then the subject has forsaken its personality and become abstract. In the pursuing abstraction, an artist must necessarily pare away his character to explore his inner spirituality or religion: Theosophy is the mystical rationale contained in Kandinsky's *Uber das Geistige in der Kunst* (Concerning the Spiritual in Art). **Suprematism** was pioneered by Malevitch who rejected the 'weight of the real world' in favour of a simple black square, suspended in a void. **Constructivism** originated in Russia out of collages via reliefs and mobiles into abstract compositions of diverse materials (wire, glass, metal, perspex in space). By 1921 the movement was dead, its exponents Taitlin, Pevsner and Gabo (who moved to England in 1935-46) dispersed, its concepts transposed to architecture and furniture design.

De Stijl was a Dutch magazine that promoted **Mondrian** (who was in London 1938-40) and Neo-Platonism. Born from a graphic medium, the greatest impact was delivered to poster art, packaging and commercial art, however, it also left its mark on Gropius and the Bauhaus ideals.

British Abstraction – In Britain, an interest in abstraction can be dated to the organisation of the conservative Seven and Five Society in 1919, which soon attracted **Ben Nicholson** (1924), **Barbara Hepworth** and **Henry Moore** (1932); it reformed in 1926 as the Seven and Five Abstract Group and enlisted John Piper. **Paul Nash**, meanwhile, started Unit One which also included Hepworth, Moore and Nicholson.

Realism and traditional values returned after the War, when it was recognised that art had splintered into fractured groups. **Stanley Spencer** excelled at figurative painting, **Lucian Freud** evolved his own searching realism from painting from life, the **Kitchen Sink** school emerged from the Royal College in the 1950s. More violent and brash is the style fashioned by Dubuffet and Giacometti who preceded the trio **Francis Bacon**, **Graham Sutherland** and **Henry Moore**, who each individually reworked traditional subjects (Crucifixion; landscape at sunset; Mother and Child, reclining nude).

Repercussions – The **Euston Road School** was founded in 1937 as a counter reaction to the avant-garde, its prospectus stated 'In teaching, particular emphasis will be laid on training the observation... No attempt, however, will be made to impose a style and students will be left with maximum freedom of expression'. London provided a fertile source of subject-matter in which Coldstream, Graham Bell, Rogers, Pasmore sensed the advent of the Depression. **Piper** and his wife Myfanwy Evans became exponents of a neo-Romanticism. A new look was cast at the English landscape, its profiles, colours, heritage.

The Four Seasons Series

In 1958/9 Mark Rothko was commissioned to paint several mural panels for the exclusive and stylish Four Seasons Restaurant in the famous Seagram Building designed by Mies van der Rohe and Philip Johnson on Park Avenue in New York. As he worked, his palette was progressively reduced to black and dark red, his composition to black or dark red on maroon. Inspiration, he said, came subconsciously from his admiration of Michelangelo's blind windows in the ante-room of the Laurentian Library in Florence. The impact is sombre, solemn, powerfully conducive to contemplation or meditation, and as such inappropriate for a restaurant. Inspired by the idea that these works might hang below the same roof as others by Turner, Rothko suggested selecting four panels and presenting them to the Tate on condition they were housed in a gallery of their own. The gift was agreed in 1969, the crates arrived in 1970 and as the paintings were unpacked, a telegram from New York announced that the artist had been found dead in his studio.

Abstract Expressionism (1942-52) originated in New York, where Ernst, Masson, Matta, Mondrian sought refuge during the war, with de Kooning (b 1904), Barnett Newman (1905-70), Pollock (1912-56), Rothko (1903-70) all exploring similar concepts in different media and styles, often on a large scale: 'The familiar identity of things has to be pulverised in order to destroy the finite associations with which our society increasingly enshrouds every aspect of our environment' (Rothko, 1947). A common sense of the collective unconscious was given in the ideas propounded by Jung, reinforced by examples from primitive (American Indian, Mexican, Eskimo) art, Surrealism, mythology, mysticism, the occult even...

Op and Kinetic Art, which explores the distinction between reality, appearance and the nature of illusion, was developed largely by the Hungarian Vasarely and Bridget Riley.

Pop Art and New Realism is drawn as its title suggests from popular culture and graphic art. In the 1950s at the ICA, the likes of Paolozzi and Hamilton used collages of mundane objects to capture the spirit of the period. The second phase (1961) emerged from the Royal College with Hockney, Peter Blake, Jones, Boshier, Phillips, Caulfield: in America the movement was taken up by Lichtenstein, Oldenburg, Warhol, Jasper Johns...

J M W Turner: *Burning of the Houses of Parliament*

Contemporary Figurative Art – Frank Auerback, Francis Bacon, Lucian Freud, David Hockney, Howard Hodgkin, R B Kitaj, Leon Kossof, Uglow today continue a historic British preoccupation for portraiture and the representation of contemporary figures in their social context.

Clore Gallery: Turner Collection

Turner bequeathed a large proportion (100) of his finished paintings to the nation, with the request that they be hung in their own separate gallery. The will was subsequently challenged by his heirs and after much tribulation, the Tate received some 300 oil paintings together with 19 000 watercolours and drawings. The Turner Bequest is presently displayed in its purpose-built three temporary and six permanent galleries.

Much research has been undertaken to analyse Turner's genius: influences have been traced to Poussin, Claude, Vernet, 17C Dutch masters, Salvator Rosa, Wilson, Lambert as he switches from Historical subjects *(Hannibal and his army crossing the Alps)* to Classical *(The Decline of the Carthaginian Empire)* and topographical ones *(London from Greenwich)*. Perhaps it is sufficient to admire them for their suggestive evocation of wind and sunshine *(Shipwreck)*, reality or imagination *(Norham Castle, Sunrise; Childe Harold's Pilgrimmage)*, artistic talent and technique, and enjoy them for their colour, light, movement and poetic spirit.

Studies and Projects: *self-portrait* (1800). Works produced during visits to Petworth and East Cowes: *Chain Pier, Brighton.* The Classical Ideal: works produced in admiration of Claude before Turner's first visit to Italy in 1819. Italy and Venice: *Bridge of Sighs, Ducal Palace and Custom House.* Later works: seascapes and whaling *(Shipwreck).*

TOWER OF LONDON★★★

Map pp 9-10 (**HJXY**)
⊖ Tower Hill

Over the centuries **Tower Hill** has preserved its traditional role as a place of free speech and rallying point from which marchers set out, nowadays, usually to Westminster. In 1380 Wat Tyler and the Kentish rebels summarily executed the Lord Chancellor and others outside the Tower.

Trinity Square Gardens – The gardens include the site *(railed area)* of the permanent **scaffold and gallows** erected in 1455; the last execution took place in 1747.

On the north side stands **Trinity House**, the seat of the Corporation of Trinity House (1514), guarded by twin cannon. The principal business of the Corporation is the safety of shipping and the welfare of seafarers. Founded (13C) perhaps as a benevolent semi-religious guild of shipmen and mariners, and once managed by Samuel Pepys, diarist and founder of the modern Navy, its main responsibilities include the maintenance of automatic lighthouses, lightships, navigation buoys and beacons. The elegant two-storey building relieved by plain Ionic pillars and capped by a fine weather-vane, was rebuilt after the war.

On the south side are the **Mercantile Marine Memorials** (1914-18) designed by Edwin Lutyens and (1939-45) by Edward Maufe.

Further east are a section (50ft) of the **City Wall**, part medieval and part Roman, a monumental Roman inscription (original in the British Museum) to the procurator who saved London from Roman vengeance after the City had been sacked by Boadicea in AD 61, a statue presumed to be of Emperor Trajan (AD 98-117) and the remains of a 13C gate tower.

★★★**Tower of London** ⊘ – This royal residence was established by William I primarily to deter Londoners from revolt; additionally its vantage point beside the river gave immediate sighting of any hostile force approaching up the Thames. The first fortress of wood (1067) was replaced by a stone building (c 1077-97) within the

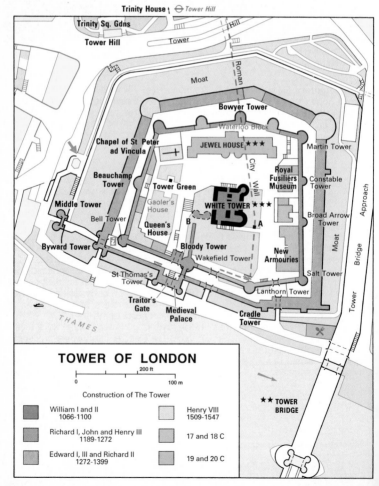

252

Roman City Wall, of which a piece still stands (**A**). Norman, Plantagenet and Tudor monarchs extended the fortress until it occupied 18 acres. Excavations have revealed part of a 13C perimeter wall and the Coldharbour Gate (**B**); St Peter's Church was incorporated within the Tower, a second fortified perimeter wall was built, the moat was excavated, barracks were erected; the royal residence was transferred to new (now demolished) palatial buildings against the south wall, where Anne Boleyn stood trial in the 16C. The last sovereign in residence was James I. The Tower was opened to the public in Victorian times, drawing large crowds intrigued by lurid tales of Romantic literature.

Royal Stronghold – The reputation of the Tower rests mainly on its role as a prison and place of execution for traitors rather than a centre of torture. 600 Jews accused of adulterating the coin of the realm were confined within its walls in 1282. Among later unwilling inmates were individuals captured in battle or suspected of intrigue: David, King of the Scots (1346); King John of France (1356-60) captured at Poitiers; Richard II (1399); Charles Duke of Orleans (1415-37) captured at Agincourt; Henry VI (1465-71); the Duke of Clarence, drowned in a butt of Malmsey (1478); the Little Princes (1483-85), Edward V and Richard of York, who according to legend, were murdered in the Bloody Tower and may have been buried in the White Tower where children's bones were discovered beneath an old staircase in the 17C, now in Westminster Abbey; Perkin Warbeck (1499); Thomas More (1534-35); Anne Boleyn (1536); Thomas Cromwell (1540); Protector Somerset (1552); Lady Jane Grey (1554); Robert Devereux, Earl of Essex (1601); Sir Walter Raleigh (1603-16); Guy Fawkes (1605); James, Duke of Monmouth (1685); Lord Lovat (1745-47); Roger Casement (1916) and Rudolf Hess (1941).

Officer in the Tower

The last prisoner of the Tower was Norman Baillie-Stewart, by all accounts an extremely charming and handsome lieutenant with the Seaforth Highlanders, who was charged with treason for selling information to the Germans in 1933. He became a notorious tourist attraction when he was forced to take exercise under the public gaze in full Highland dress, accompanied by a Coldstream Guards officer. He was released in 1937 and went to live in Germany. He was later re-arrested in Austria (1945) for having made the original *Germany calling* broadcasts during the war under the pseudonym 'Lord Haw-Haw' (William Joyce who subsequently continued the programme was hanged as a traitor in 1945). Baillie-Stewart was forced to serve another five years in prison before moving to Ireland where he died in 1966.

Following the restoration of the monarchy in 1660 when Charles II returned from exile, the Tower underwent major re-modelling and a permanent garrison was posted within the precincts equipped with a full battery of weaponry.

From 1300 to 1812 the Tower housed the **Royal Mint** and, for a brief period, the Royal Observatory. Because of its impregnability it became the **Royal Jewel House** and it was used for a period as a bank by City merchants until 1640 when Charles I 'borrowed' the commoners' deposits amounting to £130 000. From the 13C the **Royal Menagerie** was kept in the Lion Tower (demolished); it was closed in 1834 by the Duke of Wellington.

For centuries the Tower served as an arsenal for small arms. The **Royal Armouries** collection was started by Henry VIII and augmented under Charles II when suits and accoutrements from Greenwich, Westminster and Hampton Court were redistributed between Windsor Castle and the Tower. A considerable part is now housed in the purpose-built Royal Armoury Museum in Leeds – *see Green Guide to GREAT BRITAIN*.

Ceremony and Tradition – The 40 **Yeoman Warders** (including Gaoler and Chief Warder) originally consisted of a detachment of the Royal Bodyguard founded by Henry VII on Bosworth Field (1485); it is now made up of former long-serving non-commissioned officers from the Army, Royal Marines or Royal Air Force holding the Long Service or Good Conduct Medal. It is unclear where the misnomer 'Beefeater' comes from. They wear Tudor uniform (dark blue and red 'undress' for every day – introduced in 1858, scarlet for ceremony), embroidered with the sovereign's monogram and may be seen on parade in the Inner Ward *(daily at 11am)*.

The **Ceremony of the Keys**, the ceremonial closing of the Main Gates, takes place every night *(at 10pm; admission on written application only)*. After the curfew a password, which is changed daily, is required to gain admission.

Every third year at Rogationtide the 31 boundary stones of the Tower Liberty are beaten by the choirboys of St Peter ad Vincula, armed with long white wands, the Governor and Warders in procession (1999, 2002, 2005...).

Royal Salutes are fired by the Honourable Artillery Company from 4 guns on the wharf *(at 1pm)*, 62 guns for the Sovereign's birthday, accession, coronation; 41 guns for the State Opening of Parliament, birth of a royal child...
Tours are conducted by Warders, for a full visit allow 3 hours.

Landward Entrance – The first element used to be the Lion Tower (demolished; position marked by stones in the pavement) which took its name from the Royal Menagerie introduced by Henry III (1216-72) which included an elephant donated by Louis IX of France in 1255, three leopards given by the German Emperor and a polar bear from the King of Norway. The **Middle Tower** (13C; rebuilt in the 18C) stood between the 2nd and 3rd drawbridges and was originally preceded by a causeway. The moat was drained and grassed over in the 19C.
Pass through the **Byward Tower** (13C) where the portcullis and lifting machinery are still in position even if not visible; continue straight on before turning left through the Bloody Tower *(see below)* uphill into the main enclave.

Queen's House – Elizabeth I, among others, was confined in the **Bell Tower**, and took exercise on the ramparts beyond.

Beauchamp Tower – The three-storey tower, which served from the 14C as a place of confinement large enough to accommodate a nobleman's household, is probably named after Thomas Beauchamp, 3rd Earl of Warwick (imprisoned 1397-99). On the ground floor is displayed a fine crossbow; the main chamber *(first floor)* contains many graffiti carved by the prisoners.

Tower Green – The square was the site of the scaffold where executions took place; a new block was made for each victim (the last was in 1601 for the Earl of Devereux). A plaque bears the names of the seven most famous victims who were privileged to be beheaded within the Tower; all were beheaded with an axe except Anne Boleyn, who was executed by the sword.
Beneath the lawn were interred the bodies not only of those executed on the green but also of many of those executed on Tower Hill where public executions took place; their heads were placed on pikes and displayed for all to see at the southern gateway to London Bridge.

Chapel Royal of St Peter ad Vincula – The chapel takes its name from the day of its consecration in the 12C: the feast of St Peter in Chains. It was rebuilt in the 13C and the 16C. It is the burial place of "two dukes between the queens, to wit, the Duke of Somerset and the Duke of Northumberland between Queen Anne and Queen Catherine, all four beheaded", to whom Stow might have added Lady Jane Grey, Guildford Dudley her husband, Monmouth and hundreds more. Note the Tudor font and the carvings by Grinling Gibbons.

★★★**Jewel House** – The antechamber, bearing the armorials of every ruling monarch from William the Conqueror to Queen Elizabeth II serves as a rightful reminder of the long tradition associated with the Crown jewels. Yes, for the most part, the priceless gems are real, and yes, the coronation regalia is still used for formal occasions such as the opening of Parliament.
The jewels are presented in the order in which they come in the coronation procession representing each individual stage: the bejewelled **Procession Sword** set with diamonds, emeralds and rubies in the form of roses, thistles and shamrocks, the emblems of England, Scotland and Ireland, and **St Edward Staff** are followed by the anointing objects (the engraved **Anointing Spoon** is the oldest piece of regalia having been made for Henry II or Richard I; the eagle **Ampulla** holds the holy oil with which the monarch is anointed). The **coronation ornaments** include robes, armills and spurs: the 22 carat Elizabeth II armills, made by the Royal jewellers Garrard & Co in 1953, were offered by the Commonwealth countries Australia, Canada, Ceylon, New Zealand, Pakistan, South Africa and Southern Rhodesia.
Most of the **Crown Jewels**, which consist of crowns, orbs and rings, date in fact from the Restoration (1660) as the earlier regalia was sold or melted down on the orders of Cromwell.

St Edward's Crown, so named because it may have belonged to Edward the Confessor, was remodelled for the coronation of Charles II; it weighs nearly 5lbs and is worn only at a coronation. The **Imperial State Crown** was made for Queen Victoria in 1838 and is worn on state occasions such as the Opening of Parliament *(see illustration in INTRODUCTION – Government)*. It contains a total of 3 733 precious jewels: the balas-ruby is the one said to have been given to the Black Prince by Pedro the Cruel after the

It must be noted, however, that in days of yore, it was common practice for stones to be 'rented' at a proportion of their real value for the singular occasion of a coronation: George IV's coronation crown was endowed with jewels worth £62 250 for the ceremony, the frames were then filled with paste for display purposes (Mary of Modena crown) or melted down.

Battle of Najera in 1367 and to have been worn by Henry V at Agincourt; the diamond (incorporated centuries later) is the second largest of the Stars of Africa cut from the **Cullinan diamond**, mined in 1905 and presented to Edward VII in 1907. The **Koh-i-Noor diamond**, the stone found in 1655 and presented by the East India Company to Queen Victoria, is incorporated in the crown made for Queen Elizabeth the Queen Mother for the coronation in 1937. The **Royal Sceptre** contains the **Star of Africa**, the biggest diamond (530 carats) in the world.

On a more modest scale note Queen Victoria's small crown familiar to every stamp collector.

Of the large gold and silver vessels that fill the subsequent cases (banqueting plate, altar plate and christening fonts) the **punchbowl and ladle** are perhaps the most impressive: the main vessel was supplied to George IV in 1829 – it weighs over a quarter of a tonne (257kg) and will hold up to 144 bottles of claret; the ladle came later.

Crowns and diamonds – In the Martin Tower is arranged a display of additional royal crown frames that would have been temporarily fitted with cut diamonds and precious stones – these include the Imperial State Crown of George I (1715) and the Coronation Crowns of George IV (1821) and Queen Adelaide (1831).

★★**White Tower** – The White Tower, one of the earliest fortifications on such a scale in western Europe, was begun by William I in 1078 and completed 20 years later by William Rufus. The high walls (100ft) of Kentish rag stone (Blue stone) dressed with Portland stone, form an uneven quadrilateral, defended at the corners by one circular and three square towers. It became known as the White Tower in 1241 when Henry III had the royal apartments and exterior white-washed. In the 17C repairs were made and the windows were enlarged on all but the south side. The interior is divided on every floor by a wall into two unequal chambers.

White Tower

Ph. Gajic/MICHELIN

Henry VIII had one suit of armour made in 1520, when the Tudor king was 29, and weighed 49lbs; a larger suit was made in 1540, silvered and engraved for the king and his horse. Some suits were made in Greenwich including examples tailored to Robert Dudley (c 1575) and for Worcester (110lbs). Note also the armour made in France in 1598 for the Earl of Southampton (1573-1624), the only acknowledged patron of William Shakespeare; a 3/4 gilt suit with helmet and cuirass, probably made for Charles I as a boy (c 1610); the ornate Stuart royal armours (c 1625-30).

★★ Chapel of St John the Evangelist – *Entrance from south side*

The second floor Caen stone chapel (55 1/2ft long and rising through 2 storeys) has changed little since its completion in 1080 although the interior painted decoration and rood screen have gone. The nave is divided from the aisles and ambulatory by an arcade of 12 great round piers (known as the 12 Apostles) with simply carved capitals rising to typical Norman round-headed arches, a tribune gallery and tunnel vault. Medieval monarchs, accompanied by their chosen Knights of the Bath passed the night in vigil in this chapel before riding to their coronation at Westminster; some also lay in state there – Henry VI in 1471, while Mary Tudor was betrothed there by proxy to Philip II in 1553.

The Royal Armouries Collection – The history of the White Tower is inextricably linked with the Royal Armouries Collection (formerly managed by the Office of Armoury) for it has served as a depository of arms for centuries. Displays explore its role as a medieval castle – and later as a menagerie. The early organisation of a Royal Armoury begins with Henry VIII, his personal armours, his private arsenal and surviving pieces associated with the Stuart dynasty. Between the 15C and 19C, the nation's arsenal depended upon the Office of Ordnance which supervised the design, manufacture and trial of arms for service on land and sea, while maintaining fortifications of the realm and its garrisons. Besides arms and armour, a large number of paintings, engravings and documentation are used to complete the exhibitions.

The collection also includes a large selection of smaller arms, several more gruesome weapons allegedly captured from the Armada (1588), larger trophies retrieved from various battle fields such as cannon and mortar, wooden carvings and miscellaneous artefacts, along with instruments of torture of foreign manufacture imported to the Tower for display purposes in the 19C, and an executioner's axe and block.

The **Line of Kings** (which originally was displayed in the New Armouries building) reunites a series of 17C life-size portraits of the kings of England dressed in personal attire or suits of armour.

Royal Fusiliers Regimental Museum ⊙ (**F**) – *Separate entrance charge.* The history of the regiment is presented from its formation in 1685 to the present day. Banners, documents, paintings, medals and paraphernalia.

Bloody Tower – The former Garden Tower acquired its lurid name only in the 16C, probably because the Little Princes were last seen alive there or after the suicide of Henry Percy, 8th Earl of Northumberland. It was once the main water gate and the portcullis can be seen in the lower storey. The study, which is paved with the original tiles (protected by matting), is furnished as in the time of **Sir Walter Raleigh**, the longest and most famous 'resident' who wrote his *History of the World* while imprisoned there (1603-16).

Traitors' Gate – The gateway (13C) served as the main entrance to the Tower when the Thames was London's principal thoroughfare. Only later, when the river was used as a less vulnerable and more secret means of access than the road, did the entrance acquire its chilling name.

The Medieval Palace (**C**) – St Thomas' Tower contains the Great Chamber where King Edward I would have slept. Meticulous archeological research has allowed this Magna Camera to be

The Ravenmaster

re-created. **Edward I** ruled as an absolute monarch from here, subduing the Welsh Tribes (nominating his son the Prince of Wales – a title conceded traditionally thereafter to the Monarch's eldest son) and extended English power across to France. Modifications to the 13C building were made by Henry VIII. The end room or Aula was where the king would have played chess and taken his meals.

The octagonal Throne Room in the **Wakefield Tower** (1240) would have served as the main official government chamber: it is furnished with reproductions of a throne based upon the Coronation Chair in Westminster Abbey, a German corona, candelabra, French oak chests and a chapel screen appropriate to the period; the corner turret accommodates a small oratory where Henry VI is thought to have been murdered while at prayer on the orders of Edward IV.

The walk passes through the **Lanthorn Tower** (13C, demolished in 1776 and rebuilt in 1883), which contains a display of rare objects from the domestic life in the age of Edward I, accompanied by 13C music.

The Ravens

Ravens are usually regarded as birds of ill-omen, feeding as they do on carrion and dead flesh: it is their absence from the Tower, however, that is feared, as legend has it that this would portend disaster. The practice of having six ravens at all times was decreed by Charles II, two extra are kept in reserve. To prevent them from flying away, they have one wing clipped by the Raven Master: this is a painless operation and by imbalancing their flight, the birds do not stray far. Each is identified by a coloured leg ring. The oldest resident, Jim Crow lived to the great age of 44, and occasionally ravens have been dismissed for 'unbecoming behaviour' – Raven George was sent to the Welsh Mountain Zoo for consistently perching up on TV aerials. Since 1987 several clutches have successfully been reared.

Henry III's Watergate – A private entrance for royalty arriving by river was built east of the Wakefield Tower in the 13C.

East Wall Walk – The walk starts in the **Salt Tower** (1240), passes through the **Broad Arrow Tower** (1240) furnished as a knight's lodging in the 13C, through the **Constable Tower** (1240, rebuilt in the 19C) and ends in the **Martin Tower** which at one time was used as a Jewel Tower.

Cradle Tower – A watergate was created here (1348-55) as a private entrance for the king.

ENVIRONS

Old Royal Mint – *Tower Hill.* The Classical stone building, converted into offices, was the home of the Royal Mint from 1811 to 1968 when the operation was transferred to Llantrisant near Cardiff. The Master Worker and Warden of the Mint is the Chancellor of the Exchequer. The first mint in London was set up by the Romans; by the 11C there were 70 in various parts of the country; by the 14C there were only two, which under Henry VIII amalgamated into one; in the mid 16C it was located in the Tower of London.

Excavations on the site have revealed the remains of St Mary Graces Abbey, a Cistercian convent (c 1350).

★★**Tower Bridge** ⊙ – The bridge was designed by Sir John Wolfe Barry and Horace Jones to harmonise with the Tower of London. The familiar Gothic towers are linked by high level footbridges, encased in steel lattice-work, which provide **panoramic views**★★★ of London and a comprehensive display entitled the Tower Bridge Experience; the changing skyline is demonstrated by compact disc interactive terminals. Visitors pass from the Northwest to the Southeast Tower guided by an animatronic figure called Harry, who, aided by films and models, explains the construction of the bridge (1886 to 1894); the design had to allow for the passage of road traffic without impeding the river traffic in the Port of London, hence the bascules (1 100 tons) which lift to allow the passage of a ship; in 1952 a bus failed to heed the lights and signals and was caught on the bridge as it opened but successfully 'leaped' the gap of several feet.

In the Power House beneath the southern approach to the bridge are the original steam engines, now operated by electricity, which until 1976 drove the hydraulic pumps which raised the bascules. The royal opening of the bridge by Edward, Prince of Wales, is recreated using traditional 19C theatre techniques in a reconstruction of a small Victorian theatre.

If continuing south over the river, turn to BERMONDSEY for the Design Museum and the Bramah Tea and Coffee Museum.

Tower Bridge, detail

All Hallows-by-the-Tower ⊙ – The square brick tower dates from the 17C. The lantern, encircled by a balustrade and supporting a tapering green copper spire, was added after the war making it the only shaped spire to be added to a City Church since Wren. The tower is the one climbed by Pepys on 5 September 1666 when he "saw the saddest sight of desolation that I ever saw".

The church, that time, was saved by Sir William Penn, whose son William, founder of Pennsylvania, had been baptised there on 23 October 1644. Four churches have stood on the site: in the late 7C, a chapel erected soon after its parent house, Barking Abbey; 12C and 14C churches and finally 20C rebuilding. Inside, the south wall of the tower is pierced by the only Anglo-Saxon arch (AD 675) still standing in the City; modern sculpture has been grouped in the south aisle; in the baptistry is an exquisite wooden **font cover**★★, attributed to Grinling Gibbons for whom, obviously, no cherub was anonymous, 18 exceptional **brasses**★ dating from 1389-1591 (of which 8 may be rubbed – *by appointment only*), wall tablets, sword rests, model ships in the Mariners' Chapel; the **Toc H** association chapel and lamp, give the church a distinctive atmosphere despite its inevitable 'newness'.

In the undercroft are tessellated Roman pavement fragments, pottery, 11C Saxon stone crosses, memorials of Archbishop Laud, William Penn's baptism record and the marriage lines of John Quincy Adams (1794), Sixth President of the USA who was married here.

Use the key at the beginning of this guide to get the most out of your Michelin guide.

TRAFALGAR SQUARE★★

Map p 8 (**EX**)
⊖ Charing Cross

The square celebrates Britain's naval prowess following Nelson's victory at Trafalgar (20 October 1805), and the full glory of her Colonial Empire. It is here that people congregate in times of strife or celebration: for political rallies, at Christmas around the Norwegian Christmas tree, or on New Year's eve pending the chimes of Big Ben... To the north stretches the length of that glorious institution, the **National Gallery** *(listed separately)*; to the east stands **South Africa House** designed by Herbert Baker in 1933 where pickets rallied for the release of Nelson Mandela and an end to apartheid; opposite sits **Canada House**, a classical building of golden Bath stone (1824-27) conceived by Sir Robert Smirke in fact for the Royal College of Physicians. While in the immediate vicinity of the square stand a myriad of other Commonwealth High Commissions (Australia House in the Strand, New Zealand House in Haymarket, Nigeria in Northumberland Avenue...).

Another celebration of British power is embodied by **Admiralty Arch**, built across the Mall (the central gateway being the Sovereign's Gate) on the site of the Spring Gardens frequented in the 17C by Pepys. This massive curved structure by Sir Aston Webb in 1906-11 takes its name from the admiralty buildings on the south side of the square.

Creation – The square was laid out by Nash in 1820 as part of a proposed north-south route linking Bloomsbury to Westminster across open space on the edge of Char-ing Village (*ceirring* from the Anglo-Saxon word for a bend): here the Strand, running west from the City, turned south to meet King Street (Whitehall). Pall Mall East was built, St Martin's Lane was straightened and Charing Cross Road was laid out in the 1880s. Twenty years later, the square was completed by Sir Charles Barry who also constructed the north terrace in front of the National Gallery – formerly the Royal Mews.

In the southeast corner was the early 17C Northumberland House (demolished in the 19C to make way for Northumberland Avenue), identified by the magnificent Northumberland lion, now at Syon *(Outer London: SYON HOUSE)*, which stood above the gate.

Monuments – **Hubert Le Sueur**'s statue of **Charles I** *(south side)* was cast in Covent Garden in 1633 (date and signature on the left forefoot); in 1655 it was discovered in the crypt of St Paul's by Cromwell's men who sold it 'for the rate of old brass, by the pound rate' to a brazier who made a fortune from its supposed 'relics'. Eventually it was purchased for £1 600 by Charles II and set up in 1675 overlooking the execution site (wreath-laying 30 January at 11am by the Royal Stuart Society). From this point are measured mileages from London *(plaque in pavement behind statue)*.

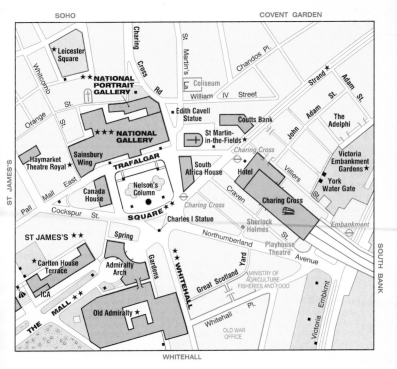

Nelson, a small man in life, is here three times lifesize in a sculpture 17ft 4 ins tall. The monument rises from a pedestal – decorated with bronze reliefs commemorating the Battles of St Vincent, Aboukir, Copenhagen and Trafalgar cast from French cannon, via a fluted granite column (98ft), to a bronze Corinthian capital supporting the admiral – a full 185ft overall.

Horatio Nelson, 1st Viscount (1758-1805) was the son of a Norfolk clergyman. He went to sea aged 12 and rose through the ranks to become captain in 1793. During various French revolutionary actions, he lost his right eye (1794) and his right arm (1797) before defeating them at Aboukir Bay (1798), and destroying the fleet at Trafalgar. It was during this final campaign that he died from a musket wound to the shoulder (ball conserved at National Maritime Museum in Greenwich, as are many letters, personal possessions and memorabilia).

Landseer Lion, Trafalgar Square

Landseer's bronze lions (20ft long, 11ft high) were mounted in 1867, twenty five years after the column was erected.

Against the north terrace wall are Imperial Standards of Length and busts of 20C admirals; the northeast pedestal is occupied by a bronze equestrian figure of **George IV**, originally commissioned by the king for Marble Arch and installed here in 1843 on the south corner plinths are mounted two 19C generals (the two lamps are from or modelled after those on the *Victory*, the east one on a police observation post).

On the outside of the square, before and behind the National Gallery are figures of **James II** by Grinling Gibbons, **George Washington** after Houdon (marble in Richmond, Virginia) and Henry Irving. On the island (NE) is Nurse **Edith Cavell**.

Eleanor Cross

In 1290 Edward I erected 12 crosses to mark the route taken by the funeral cortege of his queen on its journey to Westminster. It was here, in Trafalgar Square that the last of the solid-looking octagonal structures of marble and Caen stone was placed; it was destroyed by the Puritans but a 19C reproduction now stands in the forecourt of Charing Cross Station. A mural in the underground station (Northern Line) shows the medieval cross being built.

★**St Martin-in-the-Fields** ⊙ – The church is famous not only for its architecture – particularly its elegant spire – nor, since the 1930s, as a shelter for the homeless but also for giving its name to the world-famous chamber orchestra the **Academy of St Martin-in-the-Fields**, which maintains the church's long standing tradition for classical music with recitals and concerts. Records confirm the existence of a church on the site in 1222 and its rebuilding in 1544 before the present edifice was designed by Gibbs in 1722-26. The steeple, which then towered above the surrounding slums, rises in five stages to a pillared octagonal lantern and concave obelisk spire. Before the west door is an outstanding Corinthian portico crowned by a triangular pediment bearing the royal arms justified by the fact that Buckingham Palace stands within the parish boundary. The spacious galleried interior is barrel vaulted, the stucco work by the Italian pair Artari and Bagutti; the pulpit is by Grinling Gibbons.

In the vaulted crypt is accommodated a shop, an inexpensive canteen/cafeteria and the **London Brass Rubbing Centre** ⊙ which has replicas of brasses from churches in all parts of the country and from abroad, including some Celtic engravings.

In the courtyard flanking the northern side of the church is a lively arts and craft market, while beyond the Post Office stands the striking Edwardian **Coliseum**, home to the English National Opera *(see INTRODUCTION - Entertainment)*. In the alley behind the market, a bronze head with flowing locks crowning a granite slab in the shape of a sarcophagus commemorating **Oscar Wilde** is by Maggie Hamblyn (1998).

For the NATIONAL GALLERY and NATIONAL PORTRAIT GALLERY see separate listings.

Tourists should refrain from visiting churches during services.

VICTORIA AND ALBERT MUSEUM ★★★

Map p 7 (CY) and area map under SOUTH KENSINGTON
⊖ South Kensington

Museum of Manufactures ⓥ – The Victoria and Albert Museum, Britain's National Museum of Art and Design, was created to accommodate the contemporary works manufactured for the 1851 Exhibition *(see SOUTH KENSINGTON)*. In 1857 the collection was moved from Marlborough House to the South Kensington Museum housed in a building known as the Brompton Boilers; later (1899) the museum was renamed in honour of the Queen, who laid the foundation stone of the present idiosyncratic brick-fronted building, and Prince Albert, the museum's instigator. The original disparate collection was soon extended to include various items accumulated by the Government School of Design in Ornamental Art at Somerset House; subsequent gifts, bequests and purchases have since transformed the collections through time (4 million objects; 7 miles of galleries) to encompass 'the fine and applied arts of all countries, all styles, all periods'. The **Henry Cole Wing** (1867-71) on Exhibition Road which commemorates the eminent civil servant who conceived the Great Exhibition comprises the former Huxley Building designed by General Henry Scott as lecture halls for a variety of scientific educational institutions. Besides the premises in South Kensington, the V & A is also curator to the Wellington Museum at Apsley House, the Museum of Childhood at Bethnal Green and the Theatre Museum in Covent Garden.

A proposed extension, an amazing cubist-inspired structure of inclined planes forming a self-supporting spiral clad in ivory coloured tiles, designed by Daniel Libeskind, is scheduled to be completed by 2004.

Note – This vast establishment maintains its prime educational and didactic purposes by providing important study collections for specialists, historians, artists, collectors and connoisseurs. Its conservation department was set up in 1960. For the one-time visitor its sheer size may at first be overwhelming: it is advisable therefore to make for the departments that might be of personal interest and then to meander back through the other sections. For this reason, the departments have been presented here to echo the central organisation of the museum and allow the visitor to seek advice or assistance relative to their interest from the appropriate curators.

The British Galleries are closed for major reorganisation and are due to reopen in 2001. Other galleries are likely to close temporarily as work progresses.

WESTERN WORKS OF ART

Sculpture – The National Collection of European post-Classical sculpture spans the ages from Early Christian times to 1914 – pieces thereafter are displayed at the Tate Gallery *(see separate listing)*.

Ivories – *Level A: 43; Lower level B: 62.* An early artform that provided precious, portable images and mascots during times when people undertook long, arduous and hazardous journeys, ivories might be carved from the tusk of an elephant, walrus or moose, hippopotamus, or rhino horn. Amulets, early Christian religious icons, Carolingian caskets and pyxes, decorative panels set into manuscript bindings were followed in the 13C by exquisite Gothic figures. The art of ivory carving in France reached great heights in the 1300s (secular toilet articles), before declining in the mid 15C, it enjoyed a brief revival in the 17C notably for portraits, only to revert to incidental detailing inlaid or adorning furniture.

Renaissance sculpture – *Level A: 12-20; Lower level B: 63-64.* Many important Italian masters are represented using different media (wax, terracotta, bronze, marble): Giovanni Pisano (*Crucified Christ* c 1300), **Donatello** (*The Chellini Madonna* 1456; *The Ascension of Christ with the Giving of the Keys to St Peter* c 1430 – Gallery 16) Ghiberti, Rossellino, della Robbia (*Adoration of the Magi* early 16C), Sansovino, **Cellini**, Torrigiano, Lombardo, Riccio *(Shouting Horseman,)* Giambologna (*Samson and the Philistine* c 1562), **Bernini** *(Neptune and a Triton)*... Perhaps the most highly prized is **Michelangelo**'s *Slave*, a wax preparatory model for a figure intended for the tomb of Pope Julius II.

It is interesting to compare the stylistic differences in modelling, gesture, expression, texture, perspective, scale, and canons of beauty between the Italian, French, Flemish, German and Spanish Schools. This is particularly pertinent in religious compositions and portraiture (De Fries, Bernini, Le Sueur, Roubillac). Later works include those by Canova, Barye, Flaxman *(Level A: 50);* Rodin *(Henry Cole Wing 419)*...

Medals also form part of this large department with notable examples by the eminent Renaissance medallist Pisanello.

Cast Courts – *Level A: 46a (Italy) and 46b (Northern Europe).* The architecture of the courts (1868-73) is typically Victorian. The casts were made (1860-80) for the benefit of art students who could not afford to travel abroad; they still serve a useful purpose as the originals have in many cases suffered from the damaging effects of pollution: *Trajan's Column* (AD 113); bronze doors of the Baptistery in Florence by Ghiberti; statue of St George by Donatello; *David* and *Moses* and *Dying Slave* by Michelangelo.

Major Galleries

Supplementary Galleries

Temporary exhibitions

Closed to the public

LEVEL B

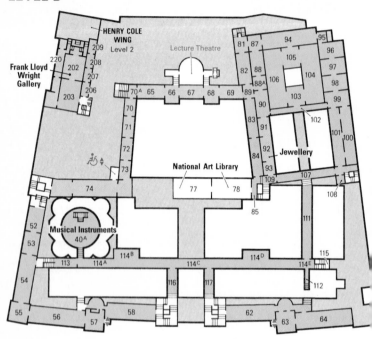

LEVEL A

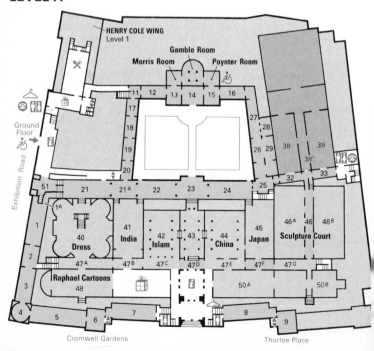

ALBERT   MUSEUM

ⓘ Tourist Information		⇕ Lift		♿ Wheelchair access		☏ Telephone
Cloakroom		✕ Restaurant		☕ Café		🏠 Shop
Library		Toilets				

```
0          100         200 ft
0          50          100 m
```

LEVEL D

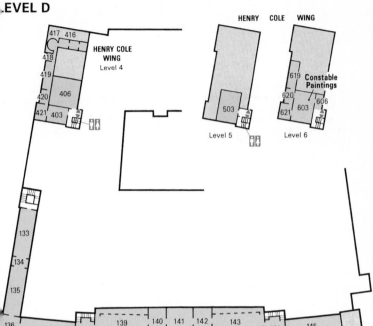

LEVEL C

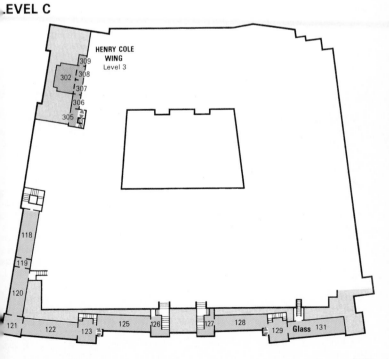

British collection

Art and Design 1500-1750 *Lower level B: 52-58*
Art and Design 1750-1900 *Level C: 118-126*
Art and Design 20C *Level B: 70-74*

European collection

Italian Art 1400-1500 *Level A: 11-20*
European Art and Design 1500-1600 *Level A: 21*
Northern Europe: Art and Design 1100-1450 *Level A: 22-24*
Spanish Art *Level A: 25*
Northern Europe: Art and Design 1450-1550 *Level A: 26-29*
European and American Art and Design 1800-1900 *Lower level A: 8-9*
20C Study Collection *Level B: 103-106*
European Dress *Level A: 40; Lower level B: 52*
European Folk Dress *Level B: 96 and 99*
European Ornament Gallery *Henry Cole Wing: 217-221*
European Painting *Henry Cole Wing 403, 417-421*
European Prints *Henry Cole Wing 207-209*
Fakes and Forgeries *Level A: 46*
National Art Library *Level B: 77-78*

Eastern collection

Chinese Art *Level A: 44*
Indian Art Nehru Gallery *Level A: 41*
Islamic World 700-1800 *Level A: 42*
Japanese Art Toshiba Gallery *Level A: 45*
Korean Art Samsung Gallery *Level A: 47g*

★★★**Highlights** – German amber altarpiece; Henry VII bust by Torrigiano; Michelangelo's *Slave*, Donatello's *Ascension with Christ giving the keys to St Peter;* Bernini's *Neptune;* Houdon busts (Voltaire); Roubillac's *G F Handel* from Vauxhall Gardens.

Prints, drawings and paintings – Besides the well-established media of printmaking and watercolour, this collection includes other commercial graphic material drawings, wallpaper samples, fashion plates, posters, photographs, packaging; caskets, painted furniture and banners decorated or designed by the likes of Botticelli Crivelli, Tintoretto, Becafumi...

Prints – *Henry Cole Wing 207-209 and 503.* The print collection includes narrative illustrations (woodcuts, engravings, etchings, linocut, lithography, silkscreen) and design pattern book plates for all the decorative arts (armour, ceramics, furniture silver, jewellery). Artists range from Rembrandt *(Virgin and Child with Cat and Snake)* to the post-Impressionist Kitaj.

National Collection of Watercolours – *403, 417-421.* Topographical, architectural studies and drawings (Sir John Vanbrugh, Frith, Henry Fuseli, Landseer, C F A Voysey, Henry Moore, Paul Nash, Stanley Spencer, the Bauhaus teacher Joseph Albers, Helen Chadwick).

National Collection of Portrait Miniatures – Since the foundation of the Tate Gallery for British Art, the V & A has limited itself to acquiring miniatures: Hans Holbein *(Anne of Cleves),* Nicholas Hilliard, Isaac Oliver *(Girl aged four holding an apple; Girl aged five holding a carnation).*

Bequests – The **Sheepshank Gift★★** (Henry Cole Wing: 419), one of the earliest bequests of paintings (1857) comprised contemporary works in oil and watercolour – Turner, Blake, Palmer, Waterhouse. These attracted great crowds to the museum when on Monday evenings the galleries were gas-lit. Later, the bequest of Constable paintings and drawings (1888) was made by the same benefactor's children *(see below).*

Pieces in the collection by continental artists are largely due to the bequests of such collectors as **John Jones** *(Lower level A: 1-7)* – 18C French Rococo: Boucher's portrait of *Madame de Pompadour,* Rev C H Townsend – mid 19C Swiss, **C A Ionides** – 18C-19C French: Ingres, Delacroix, Courbet, Daumier, Barbizon School, Degas... *(Henry Cole Wing 403, 417-421).*

Raphael Cartoons – *Level A: 48a.* These were commissioned in 1515 by Pope Leo X for the Sistine Chapel and illustrate incidents from the lives of the Apostles St Peter and St Paul. Since 1864, the seven tapestry patterns from a series designed by Raphael were purchased by Charles I in 1623 and used at Mortlake Tapestry workshops; in 1699 they were framed by Sir Christopher Wren and hung at Hampton Court; they are presently owned by HM the Queen who has entrusted them to the V & A.

John Constable Collection – *(Henry Cole Wing: 603, 606, 620, 621.)* The largest collection in the world of works by Constable, presented in 1888 by the artist's daughter, Isabel, includes paintings exhibited at the Royal Academy summer exhibitions and demonstrates the artist's technique through sketches in pencil, watercolour and oil from which the finished oil paintings were created: *Dedham Lock, Salisbury Cathedral, Boat-building.*

Hierarchy of artistic subjects – The Great Staircase in the Henry Cole Wing is hung with 300 paintings arranged according to the hierarchy of artistic subjects defined by Sir Joshua Reynolds, first President of the Royal Academy, beginning at the bottom with life studies and copies of Old Masters, the basis of academic art training and therefore the least important, and mounting through landscape and genre painting to historical and religious subjects at the top.

★**Highlights** – Raphael Tapestry Cartoons; John Constable Collection of paintings and watercolours; Boucher's portrait of *Madame de Pompadour.*

Furniture and Woodwork

– The collection ranges from the Middle Ages to the present day and is drawn from an area that embraces Europe, the Middle East and America. Many fabulous items from the collection are loaned to other museums and country houses where they

> **Note** – Temporary exhibitions are mounted in the Print Room *(Henry Cole Wing: 503):* check on arrival what is on display from the information desk before deciding whether to include a visit to this section of the museum.

might be seen in their original period interiors (Apsley House – *see PICCADILLY*).

British Furniture 1500-1900 – *Lower level B: 52-58; Level C: 118-126.* Little pre-16C furniture survives other than chests and odd chairs. Perhaps the most remarkable single piece from this period is the **Great Bed of Ware** of carved oak: mentioned by Shakespeare, the bed has become legendary since it was made as a tourist-attraction for the White Hart Inn, a popular hostelry on the way from London to Cambridge.

Of particular interest is the **18C Collection,** as pieces by the great furniture designers **Chippendale, Sheraton,** Hepplewhite *(see INTRODUCTION – Furniture)* and the architects-cum-interior designers and decorators **William Kent, Robert Adam** *(Kimbolton Cabinet),* **William Chambers** may be compared and contrasted to appreciate the variety and craftsmanship prevalent at that time. Important recreated interiors include the Clifford's Inn Room (c 1687); Henrietta Place Room (c 1725) by James Gibbs; Hatton Garden Room (c 1730); Norfolk House Music Room (1756); Wotton-under-Edge Room (provincial Rococo); Croome Court Library (1760) and Glass Drawing Room from Northumberland House (1700s); Lee Priory Room (1785, Gothic Revival).

The 19C section is one of the strongest of the furniture collection as it shows the various styles presented and exhibited at the different European International Exhibitions (London: 1851; Paris: 1867, 1900); many of these pieces were made specially for show and as such, were not intended for everyday use, however, they demonstrate the eclectic tastes of the Victorians and the high quality of cabinet-making prevalent at that time. Notable pieces include **Pugin**'s armoire; a Medieval revival painted cabinet by **Burgess;** a cabinet by Ernest **Gimson;** a painted screen by **Vanessa Bell** reflecting the influence of Matisse; a very fine rectilinear Japanese-inspired ebonised mahogany sideboard signed **E W Godwin;** Art Nouveau oak chair designed by the architect **C F A Voysey.**

European Furniture – This collection is divided into two sections spanning the years 1400-1600 *(Level A: 12-27)* and 1600-1800 *(Lower level A: 1-7).* Room 21 is dedicated to remarkable 16C Italian pieces including a series of very fine carved and painted chests. Fabulous bone-inlaid portable German writing desk c 1600; fine ebony cabinet with silver mounts from Augsburg c 1600; a cabinet made by one of Napoleon's favourite cabinet makers Jacob.

American and European 1800-1900 – *Lower level A: 8-9.* The 19C Collection items displayed here were all bought new by the museum. These include the **Hoffmeister** throne; Louis Majorelle Art Nouveau walnut armchair; striking pre-Art Deco marquetry desk and chair... The Art Nouveau objects were for the most part purchased from the Paris Exhibition of 1900.

Morris, Gamble and Poynter Rooms – *Level A: off 13-15.* Three refreshment rooms (in use as such until 1939) added from 1866 onwards with tile panels and an iron brass grill by Sir Edward Poynter, stained glass and ceramics by Gamble, wallpaper and stained glass by William Morris and Burne-Jones, furniture by Philip Webb. Other Morris & Co furnishings are displayed in Level C: 118-119.

Frank Lloyd Wright Gallery – *Henry Cole Wing: 202.* F L Wright (1867-1959) has been described as 'the greatest American architect to date' by Pevsner. Responsible for the conception of his Prairie House and the Larkin Building, complete with correspondingly appropriate furnishings, his importance as an interior designe stems from his association with the Chicago Arts and Crafts society (f 1897), whic closely echoed the ideas and objectives of the British Arts and Crafts movement.

The gallery displays examples of furniture, metalwork, stained glass, prints, book and graphic designs; the office interior he tailored for the Pittsburg departmen store chief Edgar J Kaufman (25ft x 22ft) in 1936-37, a great admirer and patro of Wright in the last years of his long career.

20C Study Collection – *Level B: 70-74; 103-106.* Pre-1960 British furniture is on view in Room 74. A changing display of furniture from the period 1960-1991 is per manently housed in galleries 103-106. This might include pieces designed b Le Corbusier, Koloman Moser, Eileen Gray and Frank Lloyd Wright.

William Morris (1834-96) epitomises the Victorian age as a well educated, middle class, talented and successful designer, craftsman, poet, conservator (founder of the Society for the Protection of Ancient Buildings) and political (Liberal then Socialist) theorist, endowed with enormous vision, imagination and energy. Morris went to Oxford to study theology; there he came across the teachings of Ruskin and met members of the Pre-Raphaelite Brother-hood (D G Rossetti, Burne-Jones, Ford Madox Brown); he joined the architectural practice of G E Street who worked in the neo-Gothic style; in 1859 he married Jane Burden and commissioned his friend Philip Webb to design a house in Bexleyheath; when trying to furnish The Red House, Morris discovered how 'all the minor arts were in a state of complete degradation' (1860) and set about improving the situation. **Morris, Marshall, Faulkner & Co** quickly proved successful specialising in church fixtures – two stands in the Medieval court of the 1862 International Exhibition earned them good publicity and forced a move to larger workshops (1865); major projects included reception rooms at St James's Palace and a new refreshment room for the South Kensington Museum (V & A); in 1875 the company was reformed as **Morris & Co,** a shop was opened in Oxford Street (1877). Manufacturing was moved to Merton Abbey in 1881 where production continued until 1940. He employed the services of other like-minded talented technicians and draughtsmen: Webb, Burne-Jones (figurative tapestries and stained glass), George Jack (furniture including the famous Morris chair, **William de Morgan** (ceramics including lustreware); from embroideries he moved on to wallpapers, stained glass, printed and woven textiles, carpets (Hammersmith factory making hand-knotted carpets opened in 1880), rugs, tapestries, furniture, light fittings, ceramics... In 1890 he founded the **Kelmscott Press** for the specialist production of exquisitely printed books modelled on Medieval manuscripts including Morris's own translation of Icelandic myths. Morris upheld the importance of good craftsmanship in the face of mechanisation and industrial processes, the use of the most appropriate materials for functional objects, and the need for good design in even the most lowly, domestic things; his lasting reputation and example has inspired the ethic of 20C industrial design.

Musical Instruments – *Level B: 40a; Lower level B: 52.* It is to be noted that the larg range of Western instruments has been collected here for their applied decoratio rather than their value as musical instruments, for this reason some may b displayed with other contemporary furniture as part of an interior display.

★★★**Highlights** – Great Bed of Ware; Musical Instruments; Queen Elizabeth's virginals Grinling Gibbons' reliefs *(Crucifixion, Stoning of St Stephen);* Jones Collection: 18(French commode, secretaire, bed; Mme de Serilly's boudoir (Marie-Antoinette' music stand and work-table); Taskin harpsichord, Riesener jewel casket; 18C Italia Cabinet of Mirrors; Italian oval room (c 1780); 5 lapis lazuli columns illustrating th five orders of architecture made for Marie Antoinette; William Morris Room; Fran Lloyd Wright study.

Textiles and Dress – This is one of the world's most extensive collections c textiles spanning 5 000 years from Europe, the Near, Middle East and Central Asia The Dress Collection (late 1500s-1990) consists of trend-setting European designs The models also show the underwear and foundation garments and the influence c new technology.

Woven Fabrics – *Level B: 100.* The earliest samples are Pharaonic linens retrieved fron excavated Egyptian tombs; later examples include Classical, early Christian, Copti styles, silk from Byzantium and the dawn of the Islamic Near East. Woven silks fron Italy (13C-15C) show developments in patterns; sumptuous vestments from the Renaissance in silk and velvet; ravishing 17C furnishing fabrics echo paintings c Titian and Veronese. France begins her own silk-weaving industry in Lyon (1650s).

> **Spitalfields silk factories** were established by Huguenot weavers in the East End
> of London after the revocation of the Edict of Nantes (1685). Early produc-
> tion consisted of plain materials, but this was soon supplemented with
> velvets, damasks and figured brocades with gold and silver threadwork for
> articles of dress. The industry was further sustained by legislation that
> banned the import of Indian calico (1701), levied heavy duty on printed
> cotton (1712-1714) and banned its manufacture in England (1720-74).
> Exports soared while war disrupted the competition in France and Spain.
> Designs are taken from French originals: fantastical asymmetrical Bizarre
> patterns (1700), naturalistic floral designs (1730s), delicate Rococo sprigs
> and ribbons (1740s). The industry eventually declined in the 1770s.

The principal factories in England were located at Spitalfields, Manchester, Maccles-
field and Norwich – *Lower level B: 57; Level B: 100, Level C: 125*.
The 19C is well documented with important items from the 1851 Great Exhibition
(William Morris fabrics and hangings; shawls from Paris, Norwich, Paisley).

Embroidery – *Level B: 101*. English Medieval ecclesiastical embroidery was so
renowned (13C-14C) as to have its own name **'opus anglicanum'** (Clare chasuble; Syon
cope); it earned particular recognition in 1246 when Pope Innocent IV noticed the
vestments of visiting English bishops and commissioned some for himself. The
ground is usually silk or satin; couched gold thread is used for background; figures
are worked in silk in fine split-stitch; designs are drawn from contemporary manuscript illustration. In the mid 14C decoration begins to dominate the figures,
pre-empting a subsequent decline in standards of craftsmanship; elements become
increasingly stylised; production dwindles at the Reformation.
Of the later post-1500 embroideries from Western Europe, English examples still
dominate – the most popular being the **Oxburgh hangings** with its exotic animals and
birds, flowers and beasts worked by the likes of Mary Queen of Scots, Bess of
Hardwick and their entourage (linen canvas embroidered in silk cross-stitch) and
the **Bradford table carpet** with its fabulous border illustrating contemporary late 16C
life (linen canvas embroidered in silk canvas-stitch).

Lace – *Level B: 96*. The art of lace-making from Italy and Flanders (late 15C) is well
represented as lace was applied to vestments, collars and ruffs, church and domestic
linen. Lacemaking machinery was invented by John Heathcote (1808-9), but it was
unable to rival the best hand-made designs.

Tapestries – *Level B: 94; Level A: 22-24*. The Dukes of Devonshire 15C **Gothic Hunting
tapestries** are among the masterpieces of the collection, woven probably at Arras in
wool (c 1430). Examples from the London factories at Mortlake *(see Outer London:
BARNES – Mortlake)*, Soho, Lambeth and Fulham – set up by an ex-employee of the
Savonnerie Factory (1750-55) and purchased by Claude Passavant, an associate of
Thomas Whitby of the Axminster carpet factory fame. Works also include pieces
from the continent like the Gobelins and Aubusson factories (Alexander Calder:
Autumn leaves 1971).

Carpets – *Level A: 42 and 33 stairs*. The highlight of this section is undoubtedly the
Ardabil mosque carpet, the largest Persian carpet in the world (1540; 30 million
knots, woollen pile on silk weft, called after its weaver Maqsud of Hashan – *Level A:
42)*; other pieces (9C-20C) illustrate styles from Iran, Turkey, Turkestan, India,
North Africa, America and Europe (English Turkey work).

Printed fabrics – *Level B: 100-101*. Cotton was imported from India in the 16C in the
form of chintz (five-colour, block-printed) and calico (painted, printed or stencilled)
but subjected to taxes in order to protect the native wool and silk industries. Early
wood-block printing with madder dyes (black, reds, purple and brown) evolved with
the use of indigo (blue) and weld (yellow) in the 1750s. Naturalistic organic designs
were introduced in the mid 1750s. In 1752 copper-plates began to be used in
Ireland, with use spreading to England in 1756 and to France in 1770 (with
Oberkampf at Jouy); this facilitated complicated designs in monochrome (reds, sepia
and indigo) on white. In 1783, a Scotsman patented metal roller-printing which
simplified production still further; garish modern colours and designs were checked
by William Morris and the Arts and Crafts movement which prescribed good design
and craftsmanship in industrial textile production.
Patchwork is displayed in Level B: 102.

Dress – *Level A: 40*. This wonderful collection charts developments in men's, ladies'
and children's wear from the 16C. Displays start with a rare linen shirt from the
1540s. Items from the 17C include the most expensive outfits: heavy cloaks, jackets,
bodices... The 18C includes items familiar from contemporary portraiture: hooped
skirts, embroidered silk or velvet court suits; Neo-Classical gowns with the most
complicated trimmings and contrivances deemed fashionable in this age of eclectic
taste (1740s court mantua, 1770s polonaise, 1790s shawl-dress).

The late 19C and early 20C is predominantly represented by Miss Heather Firbank's collection (1905-20) and that accumulated by the famous fashion photographer Sir Cecil Beaton (post 1920s). More recent designs (1960-90) have been donated or acquired by a special committee at one time headed by Jean Muir. From the gorgeous to the weird, designers represented include Fortuny (Delphos dress) Worth, Poiret, Schiaparelli, Dior, Chanel, Norman Hartnell, Balenciaga, Balmain, Saint-Laurent, Galliano, Versace, Mary Quant, Karl Lagerfeld, Zandra Rhodes, Caroline Charles, Vivienne Westwood, Issey Miyake, Rifat Ozbek and accessories: Shilling (millinery), Vuitton (luggage), Ferragamo (shoes), Montblanc pens, Sony Walkman, Filofax organisers, besides the gloves, fans, umbrellas and parasols, canes and sticks, socks and stockings, bags and pouches, handkerchiefs and ties, haircombs and hatpins...

★★★ **Highlights** – For general interest, the Fashion Galleries will provoke a smile on the face of anyone remotely interested in the tides of fashion; the Textile Study Collection is a haven for embroiderers, sewers and design professionals.

Chelsea factory: The Music Lesson

Ceramics and Glass – The foundations of the collection were laid in the 19C with objects selected for the improvement of contemporary British design: examples from the rest of Europe, China and Islam have been acquired since.

The Ceramic Galleries chart the evolution of pottery and porcelain world-wide. Greek and Roman pottery; pieces from the Near East, the discovery of tin-glaze; Moorish Spain; Renaissance Italy maiolica; Germany; Turkish, Persian. Chinese and Japanese pottery and porcelain prompted the Europeans to copy not only the elegant shapes of these exotic wares but also to replicate the delicate white texture of porcelain into their soft and hard-paste equivalents.

Porcelain – *Level D: 139-145.* Gallery 139 displays a fabulous bequest made by Lady Charlotte **Schreiber** (1884) including pieces from the Chelsea, Bow, Derby, Worcester porcelain factories and Staffordshire pottery. British porcelain is displayed in Level D:139-140; European porcelain in Level D: 142, French factories Lower level A: 4; Far Eastern ceramics in Level D: 143-145.

Soft-paste *(pâte tendre)* porcelain was invented first by the Persians (12C), then by the Italians in Florence and Venice (1575-87) before the secrets of 'true' porcelain were discovered: early examples consist of white clay mixed with ground glass and fired at 1250°C; a second firing fused the white tin glaze; enamel colours required a third firing: a lengthy process which levied high casualties. Factories include Rouen, Saint-Cloud, Bow, Capodimonte, Chantilly, Chelsea, Derby, Mennecy, Vincennes.

Hard paste *(pâte dure)* is made from a kaolin or white china clay that is found naturally. Its chemical make up (potassium silicate and aluminium) allows it to be fired at very high temperatures (1250-1350°C) producing a glass-like translucent compound with a fine ring when sounded; unglazed this is called biscuit porcelain; colour (manganese and cobalt only until the 1800s) could be applied under the glaze at the first firing; enamel colour required a second firing. Factories include Meissen, Vienna, Venice, Sèvres, Plymouth.

Bone China is a third type of porcelain where bone ash is added to the clay compound: the practice came into wide use after 1748 when Thomas Frye of Bow registered a patent for it – Sèvres (1754/5), Lowestoft, Chelsea, Derby. An alternative comprising kaolin and stone was developed in the late 18C by Spode in Stoke on Trent and Barr at Worcester; this is still used today as a softer alternative to hard paste but a cheaper and more durable one to soft paste.

Pottery – *Level D: 134-138.* **Tin glazed earthenware:** the application of a white glaze to biscuit-fired pottery was inspired by Chinese porcelain and perfected in the 9C in Baghdad from where its use spread to Spain and Italy (13C). Once dipped in glaze (tin and lead oxide mixed with silicate of potash) high temperature resistant colours may be applied as decoration, additional gloss may then be achieved by applying a lead glaze. Variations include maiolica from Italy, faience from France, Delft from Holland and England.

Stoneware: this very hard, dense, resonant, opaque grey or red, non-porous material is contrived from clay and fusible stone (feldspar) fired at very high temperatures (1200-1400°C). Pioneered in China, the technique developed in Europe in the Rhineland. Early types of salt glaze were achieved by throwing salt onto the kiln fire during firing: the heat breaks the chemical compound releasing the chlorine as a gas while the sodium combines with the silicates in the pottery to provide a thin glaze. Perhaps the most important English potter before Wedgwood was **John Dwight** (c 1635-1703) who established his pottery in Fulham and perfected the use of stoneware for figures (very fine portraits of his dead daughter and Prince Rupert) and practical vessels (bottles, teapots). **Josiah Wedgwood** (1730-95) produced broad ranges of vessels in response to changing tastes and demand from the rising middle classes; he pioneered the mass-production of Neo-Classical shapes and decoration (Etruria ware, jasper ware and black basalt ware aped Roman designs excavated in Italy; cream coloured earthenware was called Queen's ware once royal approval had been secured – *Level C: 121, 123*), his first factory (1759) was soon supplemented with others, thereby establishing the famous Staffordshire potteries for all time.

Art pottery evolved at the end of the 19C at the tail end of the Arts and Crafts movement; exploiting various techniques were William de Morgan and the Martin Brothers. From this developed the English **Studio Pottery** *(Level D: 137)* epitomised by Bernard Leach and Lucie Rie, which spread to Scandinavia (Stig Lindberg), America (Rudy Autio) and into the industrial mainstream of today.

All the **tiles** save the Spanish and Islamic collection, are displayed in drawers for convenient comparison *(Level D: 141).*

Faience and French porcelain are displayed on the floor below in galleries 127 and 128.

Pottery

Iznik, in Turkey, produced the finest quality pottery of the Islamic world.

Hispano-Moresque was made in Islamic Spain (8C-1492): colours include green, yellow, white, black and manganese; shapes include albarello drug or water jars.

Delftware or Dutch tin-glazed earthenware was inspired by Italian maiolica (Antwerp c 1584). The commonplace use of underglaze blue was a direct response to Chinese wares imported through the Dutch East India Company founded in 1609.

Lustre is the name given to the iridescent metallic finish: silver oxide provides a brassy yellow colour, copper for a rich red. Pioneered in Baghdad, developed in Spain (Malaga, Valencia) and Italy (Deruta, Gubbio), revived by William de Morgan (19C). Other, less durable gilding methods adopted by Wedgwood included the use of platinum salts for silver, gold for pink, purple lustre.

Cream ware consists of lead glazed stoneware with a cream-coloured body containing flint (silica). Cheap to produce, hard wearing and a lighter alternative to porcelain, it also facilitated intricate open basket work. Its colour was ideally suited to transfer printing.

Slipware suggests the use of diluted clay (slip) for trailed or dripped decoration, sealed with clear glaze.

Enamels – *(Level A: 43; Level B: 89)* from Limoges are cased alongside the French collection.

Glass – *Level C: 131.* Just as artists copied one and another, so did craftsmen: the impact of Venetian blown glass reached the Low Countries and England, generating an important lead glass industry at Nailsea, Newcastle-upon-Tyne, that culminated with George Ravenscroft (1632-83), the most famous of the English glass-makers and inventor of flint glass as an indigenous alternative to Venetian glass.

European glass remained essentially functional until the mid 19C which then encompassed cameo cutting, acid etching, moulding, iridescent and lustre texturing (Lalique, Tiffany, Dale Chihuly). More recently, the Gallery has acquired a number of contemporary studio pieces from home and abroad.

The Story of Glass, a history combining information from the Corning Museum of Glass in New York is available on computer in the gallery.

Stained Glass – *Level B: 111 and 117.* English and European stained glass, medieval to 19C, notable display of 15C-16C German stained glass. A rare panel designed by Frank Lloyd Wright is displayed in the Henry Cole Wing.

★★★**Highlights** – Meissen goat modelled by Kaendler for the Japanese Palace at Dresden; supreme and rare pieces commissioned by the Medici Grand Duke of Tuscany (1570s). Delftware charger made by Christian Wilhelm, the founder of the Pickle-herring pottery in Southwark. Palissy and St Porchaire pottery. Examples of glass by the Venetian Verzelini active in London in the 16C.

Metalwork and Jewellery – This is perhaps the most diverse and eclectic national collection ranging from 2C BC to the 20C AD and encompassing a broad selection of items (jewellery, watches, cutlery, plate, ormolu, mortars, British biscuit tins) made of different materials: platinum, gold, silver, copper, brass, bronze, iron, tin, lead, alloy and plastic. Only items since the 9C are now actively acquired.

Medieval Treasury and Church Plate – *Level A: 43; Level B: 83-84.* From the earliest times, supreme craftsmanship has been dedicated to liturgical objects (12C Gloucester candlestick, Eltenberg reliquary, Ramsey Abbey censer, Studley bowl, Swinburne pyx); many pieces disappeared at the Reformation when a market developed for domestic objects (Valence casket).

Silver – *Level B: 65-69.* England boasts an important silver tradition, sustained in London by the Worshipful Company of Goldsmiths *(see CITY).* Note the intricate workmanship of the **Howard Grace cup** (also known as the Thomas-a-Becket cup) set with pearls and garnets and the Vyvyan salt with its panels of *verre eglomisé.* In the national collection designs by Paul de Lamerie (sumptuous Newdigate centre-piece), Robert Adam (elegant sauce boats), A W N Pugin, William Burgess, Christopher Dresser, C R Ashbee, Harold Stabler mark high points in patronage and aesthetic movements. The development of Sheffield plate as an alternative to solid silver achieved high standards of quality of its own *(Level B: 82).*

Important 15C-17C European secular pieces (German and Spanish) come from the bequest made by Dr Hildburgh. Rare examples of French silver include the 14C Rouen treasure and 1528 Burghley nef showing Tristan and Iseult playing chess on their journey from Ireland to Cornwall: designed to carry salt, its position on the high table at a banquet would mark the guests of honour 'above the salt'. The Bergamo cross is perhaps the most exceptional Italian piece (c 1390). Russian enamelled silver.

The art of goldsmithing is explored and celebrated in Lower level A: 7; Level B: 91-93.

Iron – *Level B: 113-114.* Fine range of locks, wrought-iron grilles, railings, firebacks and shopsigns illustrate the rich variety and skill of the blacksmith through the ages. Other items in the collection list clocks (displayed in the Musical Instruments Gallery), pewter receptacles and cutlery *(Level B: 81)* arms and armour *(Level B 88a and 90).*

Jewellery Gallery – *Level B: 91-93.* Beyond the Saxon brooches, gold and silver set with enamels and gemstones are sets of exquisite Prussian iron jewellery and psychedelic modernist plastic costume pieces. Note the particularly fine Armada jewel of enamelled gold, set with diamonds and rubies enclosing a miniature painting of Elizabeth on vellum.

Simon Costin's fishhead brooch (1988) is made from a real red bream head dried and preserved in formaldehyde, lined in 18ct gold and decorated with a taxidermist's glass (puma) eye, Venetian glass beads, enamel paint and watercolour and glazed with polyurethane varnish; the original was eaten by rats in the artist's studio – this therefore, strictly speaking is a replica! *(Level B: 102).*

Oriental jewellery is exhibited with other indigenous artefacts – *see below.*

★★★**Highlights** – Jewellery galleries; Burghley nef; Nuremberg beaker; Collection of clocks, sundials, watches displayed with the Musical Instruments *(Level B: 40a).*

National Art Library – *Level B: 77-78.* The reference collection comprises some 300 000 publications on architecture, sculpture, topography, theatre, fashion, heraldry, printing, binding, manuscripts and autographs.

EASTERN WORKS OF ART

Far Eastern – Sixty thousand artefacts from China, Korea and Japan make up this collection.

T T Tsui Gallery of Chinese Art – *Level A: 44.* The oldest artefacts (5000-1700BC) have been retrieved from burial sites: these include ritual items, seals, cylinders and jade discs bearing the most intricate designs given the basic technology and tools available at the time. The first historic culture of China is associated with the Bronze Age **Shang** state (1700BC) when metal signified the greatest wealth and luxury.

The **Han** dynasty (206BC-AD220) was evidently a period of sophistication celebrated in naturalistic tomb paintings and extensive reliefs; funeral items include pottery and carved jade. The ensuing period was marred by war and strife.

The **Tang** dynasty (618-906) enjoyed another flowering of the arts: lavish objects found in tombs include beautifully carved animals (camels and horses), elegant silver and gold receptacles, incense burners, funerary jars, head rests, early examples of white porcelain.

Between 960 and 1278 the **Song** period witnessed the development of new forms of ceramic including the Ru and Guan imperial wares, and specific styles of embroidered ritual robes. Then followed the **Yuan** dynasty of the Mongols (1279-1368); political ambition is echoed in bolder technique and style in painting and ceramics; this is when underglazed blue was perfected. The **Ming** dynasty (1368-1644) is remembered for the building of the Forbidden City in Peking furnished with plain but 'designer' furniture (canopied bed 1650), ornaments, writing and painting materials, fabulous silk textiles and intricate tapestries embroidered with exotic birds and beasts, dragons and flowers.

Chinese items of 20C urban and rural dress from the Valery Garrett Collection are shown in Level B: 98.

Gallery of Chinese Export Art – *Level A: 47e and 47f.* Under the Qing dynasty (1644-1911), trade with the west flourished and goods were manufactured specially for the European market: topographical views of coastal towns, lacquered furniture, exquisite fancy goods of carved ivory, porcelain objects (barber's shaving bowl), painted silk cloth and decorative fans.

Samsung Gallery of Korean Art – The main collection dates from the Koryo dynasty (918-1392) when the arts were already highly developed (bronze vase inlaid with silver wire; gold and colour depiction of the Buddha Samantabadhra on silk). The greatest sense of perfection probably emanates from the ceramics: simple pure forms, restrained decoration, harmonious colours and delicate glazes. After the devastation wrought by the Mongol invasions (13C) the new **Choson** dynasty (1392-1910) emerged and the arts flourished once more, almost in defiance of the Chinese threat.

Toshiba Gallery of Japanese Art – *Level A: 45.* The most important single factor in the development of Japanese art was the introduction of Buddhism to the Asuka court (552-645) from Korea. The following **Nara** dynasty (645-794) maintained relations with China, assimilating Tang influences into ceramic designs and metalwork. The **Heian** court (794-1185), based in Kyoto, patronised the arts and culture; this was continued by the **Kamakura** rule (1185-1333) during which time paintings and sculptures of Buddha become increasingly more refined.

The famous rituals enacted at tea ceremonies crystalised during the 16C and 17C, just as Japan evolved her own porcelain factories and the art of 'japanning' furniture for the export markets in Europe **(Van Diemen Box** and the **Mazarin cabinet).** Supreme levels of craftsmanship were attained during the Edo period (1615-1868) in the production of porcelain and wood-block printing (collected during the 1860s by the likes of Monet, Degas and Whistler), lacquerware for domestic use (picnic set, incense ceremony utensils, writing utensils); folk craft; textiles; dress and accessories. The museum's present policy is to boost its historic collection with important contemporary works selected from the various modern Japanese studio crafts.

Note: the Momoyama period six-fold screen depicting the arrival of European traders in Japan.

Indian and South East Asian
– Artefacts from India, Pakistan, Bangladesh, Sri Lanka, Tibet, Nepal, Bhutan and the Himalayas, Burma, Thailand, Cambodia, Vietnam, Malaysia and Indonesia are all collected together in an overview of the South East Asian continent.

Nehru Gallery of Indian Art 1550-1900
– The Indian subcontinent, as large and culturally diverse as Europe, has produced an immense range of folkloric, religious, imperial art through the ages. The V & A collection is the largest and most complete, assembled from the

Tipu's Tiger

M. Kitcatt

end of the 18C when Indian decorative arts became appreciated by Europeans. Sculpture in terracotta (most ancient female figurines), stone (*yakshan* nature spirits), bronze, wood, stucco and ivory has been crafted to the glory of Hindu, Buddhist and Jain deities, eclipsed at times by Islam from the north and Deccan (13C).

In the 16C the Mughal established their court and fostered a great flowering of the finest arts. As their empire crumbled, regional kingdoms were subjugated by European trading companies like the English East India Company. In 1857 British power transferred to government with the institution of the Raj until independence was granted in 1947.

The exhibits are presented in seven sections, pre and post Mughal: **Hindu, Buddhist and Jain India.** Highlights include stylised figurative works: an exceptionally refined 11C-12C gilt bronze Buddha from the heart of Buddhism introduced into Southern India in the 3C BC; his handsome head crowned like a monarch or conforming to a strict iconography (forehead *urna*, elongated earlobes, high hair knot); a smiling *yakshi* tree spirit; Siva's sacred bull Nandi, ascetics, dancers.

Tipu's painted wood tiger represents an Indian tiger mauling a British officer. The tiger's body contains a miniature (possibly French) organ which ingeniously simulates its roar as well as the groans of its victim. Captured in 1799 at the fall of Seringapatam, during which Tipu the ruler of Mysore was killed, it became a favourite exhibit in the East India Company's London museum; it is also mentioned in Keats' satirical poem *The Cap and Bells*.

Mughal, Rajput and British India (Mughal Age, Sultanates of the Deccan, Rajput Courts, India and Europe, Regional Courts, Britain and India 1850-1900). Northern India was dominated by Moslem sultans from the 13C. In 1526 Prince Babur invaded Delhi and founded the Mughal empire; successive generations nurtured peace, extended their territories and patronised the fine, decorative and applied arts (fabulous illuminated manuscripts: *The Akbarnma*, Jahangir's *Memoirs, Bhagavata Purana, Harivamsa*, wonderful carvings, introduced carpet weaving from eastern Persia), their naturalism prompted by European influences (Jesuit missionaries, Portuguese, Dutch, English traders). Exhibits range from arms and armour to garments, carved screens, Bidri ware, cotton chintz and muslin, carpets, embroideries in gold and silver thread and exquisite jewellery set with enamel, gems and semi-precious stones.

★★★**Highlights** include the Sri Lankan Robinson Casket, a Gujurati travelling box set with mother of pearl, Tipu Sultan's Tiger, the golden throne of Maharaja Ranjit Singh (1780-1839) who reputedly united the Sikh community until war forced the British to annexe the Punjab after his death.

Nepal and Tibet – The Himalayan regions boast a long and vital link with Buddhism: Buddha is alleged to have been born in Lumbini (southern Nepal) and the religion was nurtured in Tibet with influences from India (8C-13C) alongside a complicated indigenous animistic religion (Bön) which it slowly assimilated. The arts of the region, meanwhile, blended Indian and Chinese, Kashmiri, Nepalese and Central Asian designs.

Nepal was sustained more directly by eastern India (Gupta, post Gupta and Pala Styles span 4C-12C AD). The finest artists and craftsmen seem to have come from the Newar community which served Hindu and Buddhist patrons alike. This duality is transcribed into a distinctive artform where imagery and iconography are synchronised.

South-East Asia – The area described by Ptolemy (2C AD) as 'India beyond the Ganges' was united by a Sanskrit Brahman culture promoted by the educated priesthood and ruling class. Regional traditions were evolved from Indian practices. The artistic legacy is that of Angkor in Cambodia, Pagan in Burma, Sukhothai in Thailand and the complex temple communities of central and east Java. Religious tolerance prompts a variety of styles: Indian cults of Siva, Vishnu and Harihara; Mahayana Buddhism; Hinduism. The revival of Hinayana Buddhism, as practised today, was prompted by Sri Lankan monks who regarded themselves as the guardians of the true cult and worked as missionaries. Iconography is embellished and complicated by influences brought by the trade routes between China and Persia.

Islamic Collection – The faith of Islam is rooted in the 7C teachings of the Arab Prophet Mohammed (d 632), later recorded in the Koran. From Mecca and Medina, where it united various tribal factions, the Islamic armies undertook to conquer Syria, Egypt, sections of the Byzantine and Sasanian empires that included Iraq and Iran; from Spain to Central Asia lands were united under Islam, their arts subjugated to rigorous rules (the mosque's orientation towards Mecca, the prohibition of human or animal representations, the emphasis on the word of God) that encouraged alternative embellishment in the form of superlative calligraphy, painted tiles, carpets, lamps, carved and inlaid wooden furniture: in more secular contexts, the rules are less formally abided. Objects, however, are always functional (lustre and slip ware pottery, carved boxes and writing sets, carpets and hangings, brass furnishings or receptacles).

★★★**Highlight**: the **Egyptian Rock crystal ewer** (c 1000) carved from a single block of stone, must surely be the most supreme example of craftsmanship. The **Luck of Edenhall**, a Syrian glass goblet with enamelled decoration would have come to Europe with the Crusaders; the **Ardabil carpet** *(see* Carpets *above)*, and the elaborate, classical Persian **Chelsea carpet**.

WALLACE COLLECTION ★★★

Map p 5 **(DX)** and area map under MARYLEBONE
⊖ Bond Street

On the north side of Manchester Square at the heart of Marylebone, stands **Hertford House** ⊙, formerly Manchester House, which was built (1776-88) by the 4th Duke of Manchester. The house was let to the Spanish Embassy (1791-95) and later to the French Embassy (1834-51). From 1872 to 1875 the house was remodelled by the architect Thomas Ambler to house Richard Wallace's collection. The east and west wings of the main façade were raised and three sides of an inner quadrangle added at the back of the house. An ingenious remodelling of the courtyard (1999-2000) creating a glass-roofed Sculpture Court, galleries exhibiting the reserve collection and better facilities, further enhances the appeal of this charming museum.

Noble patronage – The Marquesses of Hertford are descended from Edward Seymour, Duke of Somerset and Lord Protector, brother of Queen Jane Seymour. The family art collection was started by the 1st Marquess (1719-94) Ambassador in Paris and Lord Lieutenant in Ireland, increased by the 2nd Marquess (1743-1822) Ambassador to Berlin and Vienna and further enlarged by the 3rd Marquess (1777-1842) who provided a model for Thackeray's sinister Marquis of Steyne in *Vanity Fair* and Disraeli's Lord Monmouth in *Coningsby*; he purchased 17C Dutch paintings, 18C French furniture and Sèvres porcelain while acting as a saleroom agent for the Prince of Wales.

Wallace Collection

18C French Cabinet by A C Boulle

THE COLLECTION

For a full tour allow about 4 hours. For those with less time available most Medieval and Renaissance pieces, and the armouries collection are displayed on the ground floor; Old Master pictures are hung in Gallery 22; finest 18C French furniture, porcelain and paintings in Galleries 4, 16, 24 and 25.

It was transformed into one of the world's finest collections of 18C French art by the reclusive 4th Marquess of Hertford (1800-70) who lived most of his life in Paris at his small château, Bagatelle, in the Bois de Boulogne and at no 2 rue Laffitte *(demolished – see Michelin Green Guide PARIS)*. His taste was traditional; he collected old masters, tapestries, accumulating the most comprehensive collection of Sèvres porcelain (1752-94) and the finest French furniture of the 17C and 18C from the workshops of the master cabinet makers: **Boulle** (1642-1732), **Cressent** (1685-1768) and **Riesener** (1734-1806). He declared 'I only like pleasing paintings' and bought extensively the 18C French painters, Watteau, Boucher and Fragonard.

Richard Wallace, the 4th Marquess' natural son (1818-90), founder of the Hertford British Hospital in Paris and provider of the drinking fountains still known by his name (one in the forecourt), moved the collection to Britain for safety from the Commune uprisings and added the European armoury, the substantial collection of majolica, 15C and 16C Limoges enamels (plaques after Dürer of the Passion; portraits), medieval and Renaissance bronzes and goldsmiths' work. The collection was bequeathed to the nation by his widow Lady Wallace (1897) on condition that the government provide premises in central London for the collection and that objects never be loaned or sold. Hertford House was therefore purchased from the Wallace family heir and transformed into a museum (1900).

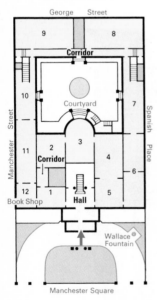

GROUND FLOOR

Entrance Hall – *The Arab Tent* (1866) by Landseer is the collection's most expensive work, having been purchased from Edward VII for £7 800.

Gallery 1 and adjoining corridor – The former Breakfast room now accommodates the book and card shop.

Gallery 2 – The Billiard Room is presently furnished with Louis XIV (1643-1715) and Régence (1715-23) period furniture: Portrait of Louis XIV and his Bourbon family; animated portrait busts by Coysevox, the *sculpteur du Roi* from 1666; reduced copies of the Marly horses after Coustou; inlaid coffers on stands (c 1820); wardrobe and inkstand by Boulle.

Gallery 3 – The former dining room displays the fine and applied arts of the **Louis XV** (1723-74) and **Louis XVI** (1774-92) periods: fabulous crystal chandelier and period wall-sconces; paintings by the master of still-life **Oudry** *(The Dead Wolf* and *The Dead Roe)* and the portraitist of elegant society **Nattier** *(Mlle de Clermont en sultane);* lovely **Carlin secretaire** (1776) and *table à pupitre* (1783) with drawers, candlestands and bookrest concealed within, veneered in tulip wood with inset porcelain plaques made by Sèvres painted with exquisite floral arrangements of roses and convolvulus by Bouillat.

Gallery 4 – The Back State Room is decorated in the Louis XV Rococo style: Georges Jacob chairs, the most eminent chair-maker of the age, covered in Beauvais tapestry; fine Caffieri chandelier; magnificent Sèvres porcelain produced by their chief designer Duplessis *père* (c 1695-1774) and painter Dodin; four overdoor animal pictures by Oudry.

The elaborate astronomical clock has several dials: the top one is set with Greenwich mean time (blue steel hand) and tells apparent solar time (gilt hand); the central face shows the passage of the sun through the Zodiac constellations, the age, longitude and phases of the moon and the time anywhere in the northern hemisphere (map engraved on circular plate); the two lower faces show the rising and setting of the sun (left) and moon (right).

André-Charles Boulle (1642-1723) was the most eminent and celebrated cabinet-maker of his age who perfected the technique of inlaying wood with the style of brass and tortoiseshell marquetry named after him. Particularly admired by Colbert, Boulle was lodged at the Louvre where he enjoyed royal patronage at home, notably for Versailles, and abroad. Some of his finest designs include casements for barometers, bracket and long-case pendulum clocks (mechanisms mostly made in England). He is also associated with a new style of elaborate, sumptuous gilt bronze mounts, often modelled on figures from classical mythology (Ceres the god of corn and plenty, Bacchus of wine and revelry). He demonstrates his supreme skill as a craftsman in 'first' and 'counter' part pieces where the 'positive' panels of marquetry in one are reversed as a 'negative' in its pair or companion piece.
He was succeeded by his sons André-Charles 'Boulle-de-Sève' (1685-1745) and Charles Joseph (1688-1751).

Gallery 5 – The Front State Room is hung with English 18C and 19C portraits by Reynolds, Hoppner *(George IV as Prince of Wales)*, Lawrence *(Countess of Blessington)*, enamels by Henry Bone, furnished with glorious red curtains and Caffieri chandelier; pair of corner cupboards (1773) by Joubert; striking *bleu céleste* Sèvres wine and ice-cream coolers from an 800-piece dinner service (1778-79) made for Empress Catherine II (the Great) of Russia.

Galleries 6 and 7 – The Canaletto and Sixteenth Century room contains Medieval, Renaissance and Baroque works of art and curiosities, mostly from the collections of Napoleon III's Director of Fine Arts, the Comte de Nieuerkerke and Vicomte de Tauzia purchased by Sir Richard Wallace: *Eleonora di Toledo* after Bronzino (1503-72); 15C and 16C Italian and Northern School sculpted figures (bronze, boxwood, ivory); wax miniatures *(case 2);* fragments of 14C and 15C illuminated manuscripts *(case 3);* Limoges enamels; chased silver plate; Venetian glass and Syrian Mosque lamp (c 1350); fragments of paintings by Vicenzo Foppa *(Young Cicero reading)*, Memlinc and Crivelli.

The former Smoking Room was, until 1937, decorated throughout with Iznick-style Minton tiles. Cases enclose rare medals of Gianfrancesco Gonzaga **(Pisanello)**, Sigismondo Malatesta, Desiderius Erasmus **(Massys)** and Emperor Charles V **(Dürer)**; Renaissance jewellery including early pieces set with faceted gems and pendant Baroque pearls; a lovely French girdle enamelled with hunting scenes and fable illustrations; earthenware and stoneware ceramics by Bernard **Palissy** (1510-90), **Hispano-Moresque**, Italian **maiolica** and lustreware from Urbino, Gubbio, Faenza, Deruta and Castel Durante which over-flow into the corridor beyond. Note also the fabulous horse trophy and elegant silver ewer.

Galleries 8, 9, 10 – European weapons and arms fabulous for capturing the spirit of a lost age were largely from the collection of Sir Samuel Meyrick. Displays are arranged chronologically – *Gallery 10: Medieval and Renaissance; Gallery 9: Renaissance; Gallery 8: 16C-19C*. Remarkable items include rapiers, daggers, fighting, 'dress' and ceremonial cast and decorated swords; firearms, inlaid crossbows, pistols; powder flasks; chased steel armour and shields, engraved helmets, chain-mail, horse armour and red velvet trappings. Detailed catalogues available for consultation.

Gallery 11 – Oriental arms with hilts carved of jade and set with gemstones, armour and works of art; 19C French Orientalist paintings echoing a taste for North Africa and the Middle East prompted by Napoleonic campaigns there.

Gallery 12 – The former Housekeeper's Room is dedicated to English and French paintings 1820s and 1830s, notably by **Richard Parkes Bonnington** (1801/2-28) who at one time shared a studio with Delacroix: shimmering landscapes, Romantic history pictures.

Stairs – The Louis XV wrought-iron and brass **balustrade** is chased and decorated with interlaced Ls and sunflowers, made (1719-20) for the proposed Banque Royale in Paris; it was sold for scrap-iron in 1868, rescued by the 4th Marquess and adapted by Wallace to the present marble staircase.

The walls are hung with large decorative canvases by Boucher: *The Rising* and *The Setting of the Sun* – Mythological subjects that once ornamented Mme de Pompadour's château of Bellevue, and *An Autumn* and *A Summer Pastoral* illustrating theatrical scenes after pantomimes by Favart.

Madame de Pompadour, besides being the king's mistress was a great patron of the arts: under her influence the royal (soft-paste) porcelain works moved from Vincennes to Sèvres (1756) and was bought by the king in 1759. During the 1760s the factory acquired the wherewithal to make hard paste *(see VICTORIA & ALBERT MUSEUM – Ceramics)* in the manner of highly-prized imported Chinese wares and Meissen factory pieces.

Gallery 13 – In Lady Wallace's boudoir hang paintings reflecting the 18C cult of sensibility coinciding with the writing of Rousseau and Richardson: post-Revolution sentimental genre pictures by **Greuze** (*The Inconsolable Widow, The Broken Mirror* and *Innocence*, the most expensive 18C French picture in the 4th Marquess's collection) and fancy pictures by **Reynolds** (*Miss Jane Bowles* and *The Strawberry Girl* of which he was particularly proud). Empress Josephine's work-table by Weisweiler, inset with Wedgwood plaques.

Corridor – Collection of exquisite gold **snuff-boxes★** painted with enamels or lacquered, and set with precious stones, Sèvres porcelain, mother-of-pearl and tortoiseshell.
Louis XV perpetual almanack in four sections (1741-2) to record days of the week, phases of the moon, various feast and saint's days, signs of the zodiac. The extravagant 55-piece silver writing, breakfast and toilet service dates from 1757-73.

Gallery 14 – Sir Richard Wallace's study accommodates marquetry furniture by **Boulle** (wardrobe with ormolu groups of *Apollo and Daphne* (left) and *The Flaying of Marsyas* (right); toilet mirror and writing table; pedestal clock mounted with four figures representing the four continents) and paintings attributed to Drost, a follower of Rembrandt *(The Unmerciful Servant)* and the Dutch society portraitist Van der Helst.

> **Jean Henri Reisener** (1734-1806), a versatile designer who commanded large prices for his workmanship, epitomises the Louis XVI style. He achieved recognition for the completion (initiated by Oeben) of earliest *Bureau du Roi* or roll-top desk (original at Versailles, the 19C copy here commissioned by the 4th Marquess has Wedgwood-style Sèvres plaques: note that the roll-top marquetry bearing the royal cyphers were replaced at the Revolution with attributes of the Arts) earned the royal favour of Marie Antoinette for whom he made pieces for her Fontainebleau and Saint-Cloud apartments. Characteristic features include the use of superb *ormolu* (gilt bronze) mounts and supreme craftsmanship in his easy interpretations of the feminine, serpentine and curvacious Rococo or more masculine, rectilinear, austere pre-Revolution and Directoire styles.

Gallery 15 – The Oval Drawing Room is the only room of the house that retains its original fireplace. Besides the 18C paintings (a history piece by Greuze, Mme Vigée-Lebrun's *The Comte d'Espagnac or Boy in a red coat*, Fragonard's charming *A Boy as Pierrot* – maybe the painter's son), it is ornamented with two marble busts by **Houdon** from the height of his career and furnished with a roll-top desk by **Reisener**, elegant upholstered ladies' chairs by **Boulard**, very fine wall-lights of a kind made for Versailles and Marie Antoinette's apartments at Saint-Cloud.

Galleries 16 and 17 – The Large and Small Drawing Rooms are hung with sparkling views of Venice by **Guardi** and **Canaletto**. Sèvres soft-paste porcelain (rare inkstand with terrestrial and celestial globes and toilet service) ornament the Louis XV furniture. Note in Gallery 16 the pier-glass and in Gallery 17 the magnificent cartel (spring-driven) wall-clock by Charles **Cressent** (1685-1768), a contemporary of Watteau, with Love triumphing over Time.

Gallery 18 – Small 17C Dutch and Flemish easel pictures deck the walls of the East Drawing Room: the most striking being the floral piece painted from life by Van Huysun over several months so as to include the different varieties; Drost, Ter Bol. Note the intricate workmanship at the back of the Boulle toilet mirror.

Rooms 19, 20, 21 – A Boulle knee-hole desk complements the pair of Boulle side tables in the first of these galleries built to accommodate Richard Wallace's oriental armoury. The 17C Dutch paintings include wooded landscapes by **Ruisdael**, his pupils **Hobbema**, Wijnants, and Everdingen, a follower of Rembrandt; the idyllic marine and waterside scenes by Willem **van de Velde** the younger and **Cuyp**; oil sketches by Rubens; genre scenes by **Steen** (*Celebrating the Birth* satirises the foolishness of man – the real father signals as he leaves, an expectant mother drinks, broken eggs suggest a sterile marriage), Metsu, De Hooch.

Gallery 22 – The large purpose-built Gallery is hung with the larger 17C pictures and Old Master paintings in the collection: **Titian**'s *Perseus and Andromeda* (painted in 1554 for Philip II of Spain and subsequently owned by Van Dyck); *The Holy Family, The Rainbow Landscape* and *Christ's Charge to Peter* (note the interplay of block colour and facial types contrasting youth with age) by **Rubens**; Philippe de Champaigne's *Annunciation, Adoration of the Shepherds, Marriage of the Virgin* and a fine portrait of *An Echevin of Paris*; several religious paintings by **Murillo**; *A Dance to the Music of Time* by Poussin is a dramatic landscape inspired by Ovid – a literary source that was also to provide subjects for Salvator Rosa, Claude and Dughet; portraits by **Velazquez** *(A Lady with a Fan, Don Balthasar Carlos)*, Rembrandt *(The artist's son*

Titus), Van Dyck (formal portraits of his friend *Philippe le Roy* and his wife *Marie de Raet* with their respective dogs), **Gainsborough** (*Miss Haverfield* a small girl in a large ribboned hat and red slippers; *Mrs Robinson Perdita*, (1781) an actress who as Perdita in *A Winter's Tale* by Shakespeare enchanted the Prince Regent); **Lawrence** (*George IV* portrayed full-length by a Boulle table and ormolu inkstand); **Reynolds** (*Nelly O'Brien*, a well-known courtesan; *Perdita, Mrs Carnac*): the most popular being a portrait of an unknown sitter, **The Laughing Cavalier** by Frans Hals.

A Dance to the Music of Time was painted for Giulio Rospigliosi, a learned patron of Poussin who later was elected Pope Clement X. It represents the perpetual cycle of the human condition: Poverty (crowned with leaves) holds hands with Labour who rises to Riches and Pleasure, only to indulge in excess and luxury that will lead back to Poverty. Seated putti watch bubbles and an hour glass that allude to the brevity of life as the winged figure of Father Time plays upon his harp. In the heavens, Apollo represents the inevitable change of day into night, while the two-faced stone term of Janus on the right looks perpetually back to youth and forwards to old age.

Gallery 23 – 19C French painting and miniatures: Romantic history pictures by Scheffer, Delacroix *(Execution of the Doge Marino Faliero)*, Delaroche, Couture, Prud'hon, Decamps; genre scenes from recent history by Meissonier, Vernet, Augustin and Isabey who specialised in portrait miniatures of Napoleon, his Empress Josephine, the Empire court and the Bourbon monarchy (in the central cases).

Jean François Oeben (c 1721-63), who joined the Boulle workshop in 1751, won favour from Mme de Pompadour and rose to become *ébéniste du Roi* (1754) and represent the transitional period between Louis XV and Louis XVI. A skilled mechanic and metalworker he specialised in *meubles à secrets* and *meubles à surprises* which were often compact, elaborately fitted pieces of furniture with hidden compartments and concealed accessories, decorated with naturalistic floral or stunningly intricate geometric marquetry (boudoir pieces and cylinder or roll-top desk often known as a *bureau*). His widow subsequently married Jean Henri Riesener in 1768.

Gallery 24 – The former dressing room of Sir Richard and Lady Wallace is furnished with fine 18C French furniture: combined toilet and writing table with four drawers, a stamped leather writing surface and toilet mirror by **Oeben**; chest of drawers by Gaudreaus with superb dragon mounts; two drop-front secretaire by **Reisener** made for Marie Antoinette (at Versailles and the Petit Trianon).
Rococo landscapes painted by **Watteau** include *A Lady at her Toilet, The Music Party, Fête in a Park, Halt during the Chase, The Music Lesson, Gilles and his family* (a portrait in fact of glass-dealer friend Pierre Sirois); Lancret: *La Belle Grecque; Mlle Camargo dancing* (a famous Spanish dancer who made her début in Paris in 1726); by **Fragonard**: *Souvenir, The Swing*. **Miniatures** include a portrait of **Holbein** by Lucas Horenbout.

Jean Antoine Watteau (1684-1721) was Flemish in origin; he arrived in Paris in 1702 and went to work first with a theatre painter, then with the Keeper of the Luxembourg Palace who gave him access to the Marie de Medici cycle by Rubens, this together with works by the Venetian painter Veronese was assimilated by Watteau to form his own 'Rubénisme' style. His magical, sometimes melancholic, landscapes are populated with characters from the Commedia dell'Arte or with young figures engaged in music-making and light entertainment or *fêtes galantes*.
At an early age, Watteau contracted tuberculosis for which he came to London in 1720 in search of a cure; his closest followers were Lancret and Pater.

Gallery 25 – Lady Wallace's Bedroom is appropriately decorated in a feminine 18C style with elegant perfume burners by Gouthière (note the free-falling snakes and smiling satyr masks), the glorious Avignon clock and delicate paintings by Mme de Pompadour's favourite painter François **Boucher** (1703-70): *Mme de Pompadour; The Judgement of Paris*.

WESTMINSTER★★★

Westminster embodies two important institutions of state: Westminster Abbey *(listed separately)*, where coronations and royal weddings are held, and the Palace of Westminster, the seat of both Houses of Parliament.

The district acquired its name meaning the minster in the west, as opposed to St Paul's Cathedral, the minster in the east, when Edward the Confessor rebuilt the abbey church on Thorney Island; he also built a royal palace and the parish church of St Margaret next to the abbey precincts.

★★★PALACE OF WESTMINSTER

Royal Palace – 'King William I built much at his palace, for' according to Stow, he found the residence of Edward the Confessor 'far inferior to the building of princely palaces in France'. Unlike the Tower, William's palace at Westminster was never strongly fortified but remained intact for centuries. It was never deliberately demolished but gradually disappeared beneath frequent rebuilding occasioned by fires, the most devastating occurring in 1298, 1512 and 1834. Hemming in the palace on all sides were houses for members of the court, knights and burgesses, who, as representatives of local communities or commons, began from 1332 to meet apart as the House of Commons.

Early Parliaments – The opening ceremony of Parliament took place then, as it does now, in the presence of the monarch but in those days it was held in a richly ornamented hall known as the Painted Chamber. The Lords then adjourned to the White Hall, while the Commons remained or adjourned to the Westminster Abbey Chapter House *(see WESTMINSTER ABBEY)* or to the monks' refectory. After the fire of 1512 the old palace was not rebuilt and Henry VIII had no royal residence in Westminster, until he confiscated York House from Wolsey in 1529.

In 1547 St Stephen's Chapel, the king's domestic chapel, was granted by Edward VI to the Commons as their chamber. It was while they were in St Stephen's Chapel that King Charles came to arrest and impeach Hampden, Pym and three others (1642) and it was there that they continued to sit until the 19C. The Lords, so nearly blown up in the **Gunpowder Plot** (1605), continued to meet in the White Hall until the night of 16 October 1834 when cartloads of notched tally sticks (old Exchequer forms of account) were put into the underground furnace which overheated. In hours the buildings had burnt almost to the ground; the only ones to survive were Westminster Hall, St Stephen's Crypt, the two-storey St Stephen's cloister (1526-29) and the Jewel Tower.

Houses of Parliament – In 1835 a competition was held for new Parliament buildings, which, it was decided should conform to an English style, preferably Tudor or Gothic. The winners were both Gothicists **Charles Barry** by necessity and **Augustus Pugin** by innermost fervour.

Barry's ground plan is outstandingly simple: two chambers are disposed on a single, processional north-south axis so that the throne, the woolsack, the bars of the two chambers and the Speaker's chair are all in line. At the centre is a large common lobby, which the public enter through St Stephen's Hall. Libraries, committee rooms and dining rooms, parallel to the main axis, overlook the river. Above the central lobby rises a lantern and slender spire (originally part of the ventilation system); each end is marked by a tower: the Victoria Tower over the royal entrance, the other housing a clock. The external design is equally remarkable – symmetrical and yet asymmetrical: the ends of the complex are marked by two quite dissimilar towers, the St Stephen's turrets do not match; the long waterfront is entirely regular, articulated from end to end with Gothic pinnacles and windows and decorated with medieval tracery, carving, niches and figures, individually designed by Pugin in Perpendicular Gothic. The stone used was Yorkshire limestone (badly quarried and in constant need of repair). Hundreds of painters, sculptors and craftsmen combined in the realisation of Barry's plan and Pugin's décor. The foundation stone was laid in 1840, the Victoria Tower completed by 1860; there were over 1 000 rooms, 100 staircases and 2 miles of corridors spread over 8 acres.

In 1852 Barry was knighted and Pugin died in Bedlam, the asylum for the insane.

Exterior

★**Big Ben's Clock Tower** – St Stephen's 316ft clock-tower was completed by 1858-59, thereby replacing another that stood close to the site of the old palace clock tower (1288-1707), which at one time had the staple or wool market at its foot. Inside is a luxurious prison cell in which the leader of the militant movement for women's suffrage Emmeline Pankhurst was detained in 1902.

The name **Big Ben**, probably after Sir Benjamin Hall, First Commissioner of Works and a man of vast girth, applied originally only to the bell which was cast at the Whitechapel Foundry. The clock with an electrically wound mechanism has proved reliable, except for minor stoppages, for 117 years until it succumbed to metal fatigue in 1976 which required major repairs. Big Ben was first broadcast on New Year's Eve in 1923. The Ayrton light above the clock is lit while the Commons is sitting.

> Measuring 9ft in diameter and 7ft in height, **Big Ben** weighs in at 13tons 10cwts 3qtrs 15lbs, it also has a 4ft crack which developed soon after being installed.
> The **clock** mechanism weighs about 5 tons. The dials of cast-iron tracery (diameter 23ft) are glazed with pot opal glass; the figures are 2ft long; the minute spaces are 1ft square; the 14ft long minute hands are made of copper, weigh 2 cwts and travel 120 miles per year.

New and Old Palace Yards – In New Palace Yard is the Jubilee Fountain of heraldic beasts, sculpted in iron and inaugurated by the Queen in May 1977.

Further south a plinth supports the telling statue by Hamo Thorneycroft of **Oliver Cromwell**; opposite, above the small northeast door of St Margaret's Church *(see below)* is a small head of Charles I. **Richard the Lionheart** meanwhile, patiently sits astride his horse in Old Palace Yard.

★**Victoria Tower** – The Victoria Tower (336ft), taller than the clock tower, was designed as the archive for parliamentary documents, previously kept in the Jewel Tower *(see below)* and therefore saved from the fire in 1834. The **House of Lords Record Office** ⊙ now contains 3 million papers including master copies of acts from 1497, journals of the House of Lords from 1510 and of the Commons from 1547, records of the Gunpowder Plot, Charles I's attempted arrest of Hampden, Patents of Nobility, the Articles of Union of 1706 etc.

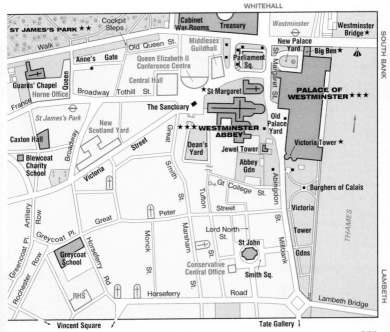

279

Victoria Tower Gardens – The statuary in the gardens includes a cast of the great bronze group by Rodin, **The Burghers of Calais**, who ransomed themselves to Edward III in 1347, a slim statue of the suffragette Emmeline Pankhurst and a bronze medallion of her daughter, Christabel.

Jewel Tower ⊘ – The L-shaped tower with a corner staircase turret, dates from 1365 when it was built as the king's personal jewel house and treasury and surrounded by a moat. There is a brick vaulted strong-room on the first floor with a later iron door (1612). When Westminster ceased to be a royal palace, the tower, with window renewed in 1718, became the archive for parliamentary papers *(see below)* and subsequently the weights and measures office Standards of Weight and Length are displayed in the top chamber. In the vaulted lower chamber are the tower's rediscovered ancient wooden foundations, bosses from Westminster Hall and capitals.

Adjoining the Jewel Tower in Abingdon Garden stands the sculpture *Knife Edge to Edge* by Henry Moore (1964).

Interior *Guided tour on application to a Member of Parliament only*

★**Westminster Hall** – The hall was added to William I's palace by his son, William Rufus, in 1097. Throughout the Middle Ages it was used for royal Christmas feasts, jousts, ceremonial and congregation. It was repaired by Thomas Becket, flooded in the 13C "when men did row wherries in (its) midst" and re-roofed by command of Richard II in 1394. In 1401, however, before the work was complete, the King was arraigned there before parliament and deposed. Sir Thomas More (1535), Somerset (1551), Northumberland (1553), Essex (1601), Guy Fawkes (1606) and Charles I all stood trial in the hall.

When peripatetic courts following the king were abandoned, Westminster Hall was appointed the permanent seat of justice until the Royal Courts of Justice *(see STRAND)* moved to the Strand in the 1870s; the floor space was divided between courts of Common Pleas, Chancery and King's Bench, bookstalls and shops. This century monarchs and Churchill have lain in state there.

The superb **hammerbeam roof★★★**, probably the finest timber roof of all time, was constructed by Henry Yevele, master mason, and Hugh Herland, carpenter, at the command of Richard II in 1394. The upper walls were rebuilt and buttresses added to the exterior to support the weight (over 600 tons). The roof rises to 90ft at the crest and depends on projecting hammerbeams (21ft long x 3ft 3in x 2ft 1in thick), supported on curving wooden braces resting on carved stone corbels. The beams, now reinforced with steel, which support the vertical posts on which the superstructure rests, are carved with great flying angels.

Palace of Westminster

The hall (240ft x 70ft) is lit by 9-light Perpendicular windows at each end. The south window was removed to its present position in the 19C by Barry; beneath the resulting arch, now flanked by six 14C statues of early English kings, Barry inserted a dramatic flight of steps rising from the hall to **St Stephen's Porch**.

St Stephen's Crypt (St Mary's Chapel) – The domestic chapel built (1292-97) by Edward I was on two levels, the upper being reserved for the royal family. After St Stephen's had been granted to the Commons, the lower chapel was used for secular purposes until the 19C when the medieval chamber was redecorated as a chapel.

Nancy Astor (1879-1964) was born in the United States. She came to London in 1904 and married Waldorf, second Viscount Astor. She was an untiring campaigner for social, moral and religious causes; in 1914 she converted to Christian Science; when Waldorf inherited his father's peerage (1919), he was forced to abandon a promising career in the House of Commons, at the ensuing by-election his wife succeeded him – the first woman to take her seat. As a complementary foil to her rather upright husband, Nancy was impulsive, extrovert, an inspired and charismatic hostess; together they instigated legendary parties at Cliveden, given to them as a wedding present by his father William Waldorf Astor, resident at Temple Place (see STRAND).

St Stephen's Hall – The long narrow hall, the public entrance to the Central Lobby, was constructed by Barry with ribbed vaulting springing from clustered piers to look like the 14C St Stephen's Chapel, where the Commons had met. At the end are two superimposed arches, the upper filled with a mosaic of St Stephen between King Stephen and Edward the Confessor. The brasses on the floor mark the limit of the old Commons chamber (60ft x 30ft).

★**Central Lobby** – The octagonal lobby (75ft high) is the hub of the building, where constituents waiting to see their MP may spot many well-known political figures. Every element of the design is by Pugin: Perpendicular arches framing the windows and entrances, decorated with English sovereigns, life-size 19C statesmen, mosaics over the doors, gilded and patterned roof ribs and the chandelier.

Commons Lobby – When the lobby, destroyed in an air raid in 1941, was reconstructed, stones from the original fabric were incorporated in the **Churchill Arch**; it is flanked by his statue in bronze by Oscar Nemon and a statue of Lloyd George.

★**House of Commons** – The chamber, also destroyed in the 1941 raid, was rebuilt simply, without decoration. The roof is a plain Gothic timber structure. The parallel benches in the traditional green hide provide seating for 437 of the 651 elected

ANGUS TAVERNER

members. At the end is the canopied Speaker's chair; before it are the seats of the Clerks and the table of the house bearing the mace and the bronze-mounted despatch boxes. The red stripes on either side of the green carpet mark the limit to which a member may advance when addressing the house; the distance between the stripes is reputedly that of two drawn swords. The government sits on the Speaker's right, the Prime Minister opposite the despatch box. When a division is called, members leave for the tellers' lobbies past the Speaker's right for Aye and through the far end for No.

Libraries – The libraries, overlooking the river, are oases of silence. The Lords' library, which is the more remarkable owing to the decoration by Pugin, contains the warrant for the execution of Charles I signed by Cromwell and the council.

Terrace – The terrace is reserved for Members of Parliament and their guests, a very special place to take tea.

★★House of Lords – The 'magnificent and gravely gorgeous' chamber is the summit of Pugin's achievement; a symphony of

PALACE OF WESTMINSTER

Bridge St.

Westminster ⊖

BIG BEN ★

New Palace Yard

St. Margaret St.

WESTMINSTER

HOUSE OF COMMONS ★

HALL ★

Commons Lobby

Commons Library

Cromwell

St Stephen's Porch

CENTRAL LOBBY ★

WESTMINSTER ABBEY

St Stephen's Hall

Richard Lionheart

Peers' Lobby

Terrace

Old Palace Yard

HOUSE OF LORDS ★★

Peers Library

Prince's Chamber

Royal Gallery

Norman Porch

Jewel Tower

Royal Entrance

Robing Room ★

Victoria Tower ★

Abingdon St.

Victoria Tower Gardens

design and workmanship in scarlet, gilding and encrusted gold. At one end of the chamber on a stepped dais stands the throne beneath a Gothic canopy, decorated with niches and finials, mounted on a wide screen, all in gold. The ceiling is divided by ribs and gold patterning. The woolsack, symbol of England's medieval wealth is said to be 'most uncomfortable'. The benches are covered in red buttoned leather; the one with arms is for the bishops (possibly to retain those who have dined too well). The cross benches are between the clerk's table and the bar of the house, behind which the members of the House of Commons stand when summoned by Black Rod to hear the speech from the throne at the State Opening of Parliament in November. Between the windows are statues of 18 barons who witnessed King John's assent to the *Magna Carta*. When the Lords divide on an issue they vote Content or Not Content.

Royal Gallery – The gallery (110ft), the sovereign's processional way, is decorated with frescoes by Daniel Maclise, gilt bronze statues of monarchs from Alfred to Queen Anne and portraits of all the sovereigns and their escorts since George I. In the following **Prince's Chamber** are representations of the Tudor monarchs and their consorts, including all six wives of Henry VIII.

★Robing Room – Here the sovereign assumes the Imperial State Crown and crimson parliamentary robe. The room, like the Lords' Chamber, presents Pugin's most remarkable concentration of decorative invention; the panelled ceiling is ornamented with sovereigns' badges, patterned and gilded, coloured, carved; the walls are hung with flocked paper and pictures or decorated with frescoes depicting the legend of King Arthur.

Royal entrance and staircase – On ceremonial occasions, such as the Opening of Parliament, the sovereign is met by high officers of state at the entrance to the Victoria Tower; members of the Household Cavalry line the flight of stairs leading up to the **Norman Porch,** which is square in shape and Perpendicular in style with gilded vaulting.

Other sights

★St Margaret's Church ⊘ – The Parish and Parliamentary Church was built by Edward the Confessor to serve local parishioners. In the mid 14C the wool staple (market) was established at Westminster, close to the site of the clock tower; the subsequent increase in prosperity enabled the church, by then dilapidated, to be rebuilt. A third reconstruction (1488-1523), scarcely completed at the time of the Reformation, would have been demolished and the stone used to build Protector Somerset's palace in the Strand had not the parishioners 'with bows and arrows, staves and clubs and other such offensive weapons... so terrified the workmen that they ran away in great amazement'. Much of the church's present late Perpendicular appearance derives from the radical restoration undertaken by Sir Gilbert Scott in the mid 19C.

St Margaret's is the church of the House of Commons not only because the Palace of Westminster lies within the parish but by a tradition inaugurated on Palm Sunday 1614 when the Commons met for the first time for corporate communion and, being mostly Puritans, preferred the church to the abbey.

Each year in November a **Garden of Remembrance**, composed of commemorative Flanders poppies, blossoms in the churchyard.

Interior – The interior presents a rich assemblage of Tudor monuments: sympathetic old Blanche Parry, Chief Gentlewoman of Queen Elizabeth's privy chamber (to the right side of the porch on entering), the figures of Thomas Arnway (d 1603) and his wife, who left money to be loaned to the young to set up in business, a Yeoman of the Guard (d 1577 at 94), Richard Montpesson, kneeling by his wife's tomb. There are two plaques *(by the east door)* and fragments of a window *(north aisle)* as memorials to **Caxton**, buried in the old churchyard; Walter Raleigh executed in Old Palace Yard on 29th October 1618 and buried beneath the high altar is commemorated in a tablet near the east door and in the west window, presented in the late 19C by citizens of the USA. The carved limewood reredos (1753) is based on Titian's *Supper at Emmaus*. The east window is special having been made in Flanders in 1501 at the behest of Ferdinand and Isabella of Spain to celebrate the marriage of their daughter Catherine to Prince Arthur; by the time it arrived Arthur was dead and the princess affianced to the future Henry VIII. The window was despatched outside London and retrieved only in 1758 when the House of Commons purchased it for 400 guineas and presented it to the church.

★Westminster Bridge – The stone bridge (1750), where Wordsworth composed his sonnet (1807), was the first to be built after London Bridge. It was replaced in 1862 by a flat stone structure by Thomas Page comprising seven low arches. From the bridge there is a fine view of the terrace and river front of the Houses of Parliament. At the bridgefoot is a sculpture of **Boadicea** heroically riding in her chariot in her campaign against the Romans.

Parliament Square – The square and Parliament Street, which were laid out in 1750 at the time of the building of the first Westminster Bridge, were redesigned in 1951. The bronze statues are of **Churchill** by Ivor Roberts Jones, **Smuts** by Jacob Epstein, **Lord Palmerston**, Lord Derby (note the pedestal reliefs of the old Commons in 1833), **Benjamin Disraeli, Robert Peel, George Canning** and Abraham Lincoln.

On the west side stands **Middlesex Guildhall** (1905), described as *art nouveau Gothic*, richly embossed with figures beneath a turreted tower.

The Sanctuary – In the monastery's day the right of sanctuary extended over a considerable area. The quarter became so overbuilt with squalid houses and the right was so abused by vagabonds, thieves and murderers that it was first restricted and finally abolished in all but name, under James I.

The Gatehouse in which Sir Walter Raleigh spent the last night before his execution and Richard Lovelace penned the line 'stone walls do not a prison make nor iron bars a cage' was demolished in 1776; on the site stands a red granite column erected in memory of former pupils of Westminster School *(see below)* who died in the Indian Mutiny and the Crimean War. Nearby, on the opposite side of Great Smith Street, stood the almonry where the well-to-do cloth merchant **William Caxton** set up his press in 1476 using as his imprint William Caxton in the Abbey of Westminster (publishing Chaucer's *Canterbury Tales*, Malory's *Le Morte d'Arthur* and Aesop's *Fables*).

Opposite the Sanctuary buildings, designed by Sir Gilbert Scott with an archway through to the Dean's Yard *(see WESTMINSTER ABBEY)*, are in marked contrast with the 1970s **Queen Elizabeth II Conference Centre** and **Central Hall**, designed as a Wesleyan church with the third largest dome in London by Rickards and Lanchester in 1912 and now used as an examination hall or hired out for public events.

Behind, flanked by the Home Office buildings on the left, is **Queen Anne's Gate**, an L-shaped street of substantial three-storey terrace houses built of now darkened brown brick that date from the reign of Queen Anne (1704) – a statue of the queen as a very young woman stands between blind windows in an end wall *(no 15, south side)*. The sash windows are square beneath continuous eaves and wide stone courses; in several instances, the pilastered doorways are protected by flat wooden hoods, decorated with rich carving and hanging pendants. The street's hall-mark is the white satyr's mask set in place of a tablet stone above the ground and first floor windows of every house.

Cockpit Steps now lead to Birdcage Walk and St James's Park *(see BUCKINGHAM PALACE)* but in the days of Whitehall Palace they led down to a cockfighting pit.

Old Queen Street is incomplete but contains several 18C houses, one *(no 28)* with a rounded hood on corbels.

Ben Jonson (1572-1637) seems to have been an exuberant fellow, outspoken and honest. The ingenious characterisation of his plays must have been drawn from his eventful life. Born, it is thought, and partly educated in Westminster, Jonson was apprenticed as a bricklayer before serving as a soldier in the Low Countries. By 1598 when he directed his first play *Every man in his Humour* with the participation of Shakespeare, Jonson had been married, been imprisoned for killing a man in a duel, converted to Catholicism, been released for good behaviour, relinquished his worldly goods and had his left thumb tattooed! He rose quickly to the post of King's Entertainment Steward producing masques for James I; he went to France as governor over the eldest son of Sir Walter Raleigh; when in 1618 he decided he needed a holiday from writing plays for the Mermaid Theatre, he set off for Scotland on foot; a year later he was back in London and Master of Revels at Court, but refused the knighthood that the king intended to bestow upon him.

Unfortunately many of his works perished in a fire that destroyed his personal library: *Everyman* (set in Florence) and *Volpone* (set in Venice) show his genius at indirectly attacking the morals of contemporary London. In his own life time he was described as 'never a good actor, but an excellent instructor' (Aubrey).

Victoria

Victoria Street – The street was cut through the Georgian slums to link Parliament to Victoria Station in 1862. It is now lined with 20C buildings – tower blocks in steel and brown glass, faced with marble, stone and concrete, providing offices for government ministries and international companies.

On the north side in an old churchyard, shaded by plane trees, is a monument to the suffragette movement by E Russell (1974). Among the neighbouring buildings are: **New Scotland Yard** (1967); London Transport's headquarters (1927-29) by Charles Holden with decorative statuary groups by Jacob Epstein and reliefs by Eric Gill, Henry Moore and others; **Caxton Hall** (1878), once famous for registry office weddings; the old **Blewcoat Charity School** *(Buckingham Street)*, a delightful square red brick building erected in 1709 to house the school which was founded in 1688 and now the property of the National Trust *(shop)*. At the west end of the street stands **Little Ben**, a model (30ft high) of Big Ben. **Victoria Railway Station** was built in the 1870s on the site of the Grosvenor Canal; the present buildings date from the turn of the century. The Grosvenor Hotel (1860-61) was designed by J T Knowles. In Stag Place, a great bronze stag marks the site of the Stag Brewery (closed 1959).

★**Westminster Cathedral** ⊙ – Set back from Victoria Street and graced by a modern piazza, **Ashley Place**, towers the remarkable neo-Byzantine Roman Catholic cathedral. In 1884 when Cardinal Manning purchased the site, the land was in disuse: early records show it as a marsh before the Benedictines of Westminster Abbey established a market and fairground there; following the Reformation it was occupied by a maze, a garden, a bullring, a house of correction and then a prison which during the Commonwealth detained 1 500 Scots taken prisoner at the Battle of Worcester (1651), pending their deportation.

Despite the fashion for neo-Gothic, Cardinal Manning and his successor Cardinal Vaughan, determined on early Christian inspiration for the architecture of the new cathedral, in part perhaps because they had no wish to emulate the style of Westminster Abbey. The architect **J F Bentley**, travelled widely in Italy before producing (1894) plans for an **Italianate-Byzantine** building; construction started promptly in 1895 and was completed so far as the fabric was concerned by 1903. The building (360ft long x 156ft wide) is composed of 12.5 million bricks and distinguished by a domed **campanile** (273ft high).

Interior – The initial impression is of vastness and fine proportions. The nave, the widest in England, is roofed by three domes. The decoration is incomplete; above the lower surfaces and piers, which are faced with coloured marble and granite, rise unpointed bare brick walls, awaiting mosaics. The eye follows the successively raised levels of the nave, chancel and apse. The altar, beneath its baldachino supported on yellow marble columns, is dominated by a suspended crucifix. On the main piers are the 14 Stations of the Cross, distinctive low reliefs over beautifully incised lettering by Eric Gill, sculptor and type-face designer.

The body of the English martyr, John Southworth, hanged, drawn and quartered at Tyburn in 1654, lies in the second chapel in the north aisle. The south transept contains an early 15C alabaster statue of the Virgin and Child, carved by the Nottingham school, which originally stood in Westminster Abbey but was removed to France in the 15C and returned in 1955; there is also a bronze of St Teresa of Lisieux by Giacomo Manzù and a Chi-Rho, executed in flat-headed nails, by David Partridge.

The cathedral has its own choir school and is known for its music.

Greycoat School – *Greycoat Place.* The grey uniform of this Westminster Charity school, founded in 1698, can be seen on the small wooden figures in niches contrasting puritanically with the brilliantly coloured royal coat of arms set between them on the pedimented stucco; it is now a girls' school. There was a green liveried school (1633) nearby in Greencoat Place.

Vincent Square – The large square was laid out in 1810 on part of the old Tothill Fields to provide playing fields for Westminster School *(see WESTMINSTER ABBEY).* On the northeast side is the **Royal Horticultural Society** (f 1804), a square brick building with the New Horticultural Hall (1923-28) at the back where monthly flower shows are held *(open to non-members).* Its library, the Lindley Library was founded in 1886 and boasts some 50 000 volumes dating back to 1514 and rare botanical drawings.

Smith Square – The square itself, the four streets which enter midway along each side and the streets to the north include many of the original Georgian houses: nos 6-9 Smith Square, all Lord North Street except at the northern end and at the south end of Cowley Street (occasional date stones 1722, 1726).

Today, the square is associated with politics; in the southwest corner is **Conservative Central Office** whilst many properties all around accommodate MPs' offices or lodgings.

At the centre stands **St John's, Smith Square,** a tall Baroque church which now serves as a concert hall. The church (1714-28), designed by Thomas Archer, is lit by Venetian windows (east and west) and has great porticoes (north and south) composed of colossal pillars beneath open pediments. Its four ornate corner towers having been compared by the queen to an up-turned footstool gave rise to its nickname 'Queen Anne's Footstool'. It was badly bombed during the Second World War but the interior has been restored with giant Corinthian columns beneath a deep cornice and an 18C chandelier.

Michelin Route Planning on Internet **www.michelin-travel.com.**

Michelin, your companion on the road, invites you to visit our Web site and discover European route planning on the Internet.

Whether you just want to know the distance between two points, or need a detailed itinerary, for a holiday or on business, we provide all the information necessary for accurate travel planning.

WESTMINSTER ABBEY★★★

Map p 8 (EY)
⊖ Westminster

Westminster Abbey ⊘ was a royal mausoleum for many centuries and became national shrine owing to its situation next to the Palace of Westminster, once th sovereign's residence and now the seat of Parliament. Since the coronation of William in 1066, all but two of the kings and queens of England have been crowned in th Abbey. In more recent times, it has hosted the marriage of the future George IV Elizabeth Lyons (1923), Prince Andrew to Sarah Ferguson (1986) and the funeral Winston Churchill (1965) and Diana, Princess of Wales (1997).

Monastery Church – Sebert, 6C King of the East Saxons is credited with building th first church and monastery on Thorney Island, a triangle of land formed by the tw outflows (700 yds apart) of the Tyburn into the Thames.

Intending to make the church his sepulchre, **Edward the Confessor** 'built it of new' in th Norman style and indeed died and was buried in it within a week of the dedication c 28 December 1065. It was in this abbey church that William I was crowned c Christmas Day in 1066.

In 1220, inspired by the Gothic style of Amiens and Reims, the Plantagenet king **Henry III**, began to rebuild the church, starting with the Lady Chapel to provide a nob shrine for **Edward the Confessor** who had been canonised in 1163. By the late 13C, th east end, transept, choir, the first bay of the nave and the chapter house wer complete; work then came to a halt and another two centuries passed before the nav was finished.

When **Henry VII** constructed his chapel (1503-19), Perpendicular Gothic was the fash ionable ecclesiastical style; Henry VII's Chapel is the jewel of its age, more delicate with finer niches and pinnacles than any other part of the abbey.

Later additions, notably the upper parts of the west towers (1722-45) by **Wren** an **Hawksmoor**, and repairs by Sir Gilbert Scott and others have echoed the Gothic theme heavenward vaulting, soaring windows between slender buttressed walls, flying but tresses, gabled transepts surmounting rose windows with delicate tracery and door with enriched coffering. Recent additions (1998) on the west front are limeston statues of modern Christian martyrs (Grand Duchess Elizabeth of Russia, Maximilia Kolbe, Martin Luther King, Oscar Romero among others) placed in niches abov figures depicting truth, justice, mercy and peace.

Royal Peculiar – When Henry VIII ordered the Dissolution of the monasteries 1540, the abbey's treasures were confiscated and its property forfeited but th buildings were not destroyed. The 600-year-old Benedictine community of som 50 monks was disbanded; the abbot, who enjoyed both temporal and spiritual powe and his own lavish household, was dismissed; so too were those who supervised th widespread property or served on missions abroad. In 1560 Elizabeth I granted charter establishing the Collegiate Church of St Peter, with a royally appointed dea and chapter of 12 prebendaries (canons), and also the College of St Peter, general known as Westminster School, which replaced the monastic school.

> **Bells** – There are 12 bells which ring out, generally between 12noon and 1pm, o great occasions and on some 25 days of festival and commemoration including 25 26 and 28 December, 1 January, Easter and Whit Sundays and the Queen's offici birthday.

> **Interior** – The **monuments** to national figures, which crowd the abbey, date fror the early Middle Ages. The older monuments, the figures on the ancient tombs, ar mostly in the chapels east of the high altar; some are derived from death mask and are revealing in expression; others make no pretence of portraying the living In the 18C it became the practice, when a famous man was interred in the abbey to erect memorials to others of equal standing in his field. This resulted in a surfe of monuments in the 18C and 19C sculpted by the great artists of the day Roubiliac, the Bacons, Flaxman, Le Sueur, Westmacott, Chantrey. Permission to b buried in the abbey or for a memorial to be erected is granted by the Dean.

Nave – The soaring vaulting retains the beauty of its original conception; the carvin is delicate, often beautiful, sometimes humorous.

At the west end of the nave is the memorial to the **Unknown Warrior** (1), set in th pavement and surrounded by Flanders poppies.

Statistics

The abbey dimensions are: internal length from west door to east window 511ft 6in; length of nave 166ft; length of Henry VII's Chapel 104ft 6in; width of the nave including the aisles 72ft; height of the nave 102ft; overall external height to the top of the pinnacles on the west towers 225ft; height to the top of the lantern 151ft. The fabric is Caen and Reigate stone.

Against the first south pier is the **painting of Richard II** (**2**), the earliest known painting of an English sovereign. In the north aisle, low down, is the small stone which covered the upright figure of the playwright "O rare Ben Johnson" (**3**) (misspelt).

Musicians' Aisle – The graves and memorials of famous musicians include Orlando Gibbons, John Blow and Henry Purcell, all organists of the Abbey.

North Transept – The transept is also known as the Statesmen's Aisle as it contains many graves and memorials of famous national figures.

Choir – The choirscreen, which faces the west door, is a 13C structure of stone, with lierne vaulting under the arch; it was richly re-designed with gabled niches in the 19C when the choir was re-embellished.

Sanctuary – This is where the monarch is crowned and receives the peers' homage in the **coronation** ceremony. The area is approached by a low flight of steps, flanked (left) by a gilded and blackwood 17C pulpit. The floor is laid with a 13C Italian pavement of porphyry and mosaic. Behind the altar is the gilded blaze of the 19C high altar screen. To the right hangs a 16C tapestry behind a large 15C altarpiece of rare beauty. Beyond is an

WESTMINSTER ABBEY

Battle of Britain Memorial Window

30 ft
0 — 10 m

HENRY VII'S CHAPEL

Queen Elizabeth

St Paul
St John the Baptist
Chapel of our Lady of the Pew
Islip

St Nicholas
St Edmund
St Benedict

Edward the Confessor

Ambulatory

Sanctuary

Poets' Corner

St Michael
St Andrew   St John

Statesmen's Aisle

TRANSEPT

Choir

Musicians' Aisle

GREAT

CLOISTERS

NAVE

← N —

Deanery

Jericho Parlour

Jerusalem Chamber

ancient 13C sedilia painted with full length royal figures (Henry II, Edward I and a bishop). On the left are three tombs, each a recumbent figure on a chest beneath a gabled canopy: Aveline of Lancaster (**4**; d 1274), a great heiress of renowned beauty; Aymer de Valence, Earl of Pembroke (**5**; d 1324), cousin to Edward I; Edmund Crouchback (**6**; d 1296), youngest son of Henry III, husband of Aveline.

North ambulatory – On the right are visible the small gilded kings and queens on the tomb of Edmund Crouchback (**6**). Opposite is the chantry chapel of Abbot Islip, known for its rebus – an eye and a slip or branch of a tree clasped by a hand, also a man slipping from a tree.

The **Chapel of Our Lady of the Pew**, in the thickness of the wall, contains a modern alabaster Madonna and Child, modelled on the original which is now in Westminster RC Cathedral. The chapels of St John the Baptist and St Paul contain elaborate gilded wall memorials crested with helms and medieval tombs with highly coloured effigies in decorated recesses or beneath ornate canopies.

Queen Elizabeth Chapel – In the north aisle of Henry VII's Chapel is the tomb of **Queen Elizabeth I** (**7**) in white marble, ruffed and austere, the only colour being the regalia, lions and the overhead canopy; beneath is the coffin of Mary Tudor without any

Henry VII's Chapel

monument. At the east end are memorials to two young daughters of James Princess Sophia and Princess Mary (8) and in a small sarcophagus, the bones foun in the Tower of London presumed to be those of the Little Princes (9).

***Henry VII's Chapel** – The eye is directed first to the superb fan-vaulted roof, then to th banners of the Knights Grand Cross of the Order of the Bath, hanging still an brilliant above the stalls, which are crowned with pinnacles, helmets and coifs, an ornamented with the heraldic plates of former occupants and their esquires; th witty and inventive misericords date from the 16C to 18C. The chapel was first use for the knights' installations in 1725 when George I reconstructed the order.

At the east end is the tomb of Henry VII and Elizabeth of York (10). Beyond, in th RAF Chapel, is the **Battle of Britain Memorial Window** (1947), a many-faceted, brightl coloured screen containing the badges of the 68 Fighter Squadrons which took par The great double gates at the entrance are made with wooden frames in which ar mounted pierced bronze panels of the royal emblems of Henry Tudor and hi antecedents: the roses of Lancaster and York, the leopards of England, the fleur de-lys of France, the falcon of Edward IV, father of Elizabeth, Henry's queen.

Chapel of Edward the Confessor – The chapel, also known as the Chapel of the Kings contains the tombs of five kings and three queens around the **Confessor's Shrine** (11). The shrine itself is in two parts; the lower, prepared by Henry III is Purbec marble, the upper is a stepped wooden construction made to replace the origina which had been looted at the Dissolution. Against the north wall are **Queen Eleanor c Castille** (12; d 1290), in whose memory the Eleanor crosses were erected *(se TRAFALGAR SQUARE)*, slender and serene, in gilded bronze by the master gold smith William Torel; Henry III (13; d 1272), in gilded effigy, builder of the chape who spent more than all the money he possessed in constructing the abbey

Edward I, Longshanks (**14**; d 1307), the first king to be crowned in the present abbey (1272) and the Hammer of the Scots, who brought south the Scottish regalia and the stone of Scone in 1297.

The carved **stone screen**, which closes the west end of the chapel, was completed in 1441. At the centre stands the **Coronation Chair** (**15**) made of oak and once brightly painted and gilded with the Stone of Scone beneath the seat (now removed to Scotland); for coronations the chair is moved into the sanctuary.

Against the south wall are Richard II (**16**) who married Anne of Bohemia in the abbey in 1382 and raised her tomb there in 1394; the gilt bronze figure of Edward III (**17**; d 1377) on an altar tomb of Purbeck marble, surrounded in niches at the base by the bronze representations of his children, of whom six remain (facing the ambulatory) including the Black Prince; carved in white marble, once painted and gilded, his queen, Philippa of Hainault (**18**; d 1369) who interceded for the Burghers of Calais. At the east end on a Purbeck marble tomb is the oak figure, once silverplated, of the young Henry V (**19**; d 1422); above is the king's chantry chapel in which Katherine de Valois is now buried.

South Aisle of Henry VII's Chapel – Here are buried, without sculptured memorials, in a royal vault (**20**), Charles II, William III and Mary, Queen Anne and her consort, George of Denmark. Three grand tombs occupy the centre, all effigies upon tomb chests: Lady Margaret Beaufort (**21**; d 1509), mother of Henry Tudor, in widow's hood and mantle, her wrinkled hands raised in prayer, her face serene in old age, a masterpiece by **Torrigiano** in gilt bronze; **Mary Queen of Scots** (**22**) in white marble like Elizabeth I but beneath a much grander canopy and with a crowned Scottish lion in colour at her feet; Margaret Douglas, Countess of Lennox (**23**; d 1578), niece of Henry VIII, mother of Darnley and grandmother of James I, a beautiful woman carved in alabaster.

South Ambulatory – St Nicholas' Chapel contains the tomb of Philippa, Duchess of York (**24**; d 1431) with wimple and veil about her expressive head; the vault of the Percys (**25**); the tomb of Anne, Duchess of Somerset (**26**; d 1587), widow of the Protector. In St Edmund's Chapel are the tomb of William de Valence (**27**; d 1296), half brother of Henry III, the figure remarkably carved with clothes and accoutrements powdered with crests, and the marble effigy of John of Eltham (**28**; d 1337), second son of Edward II. In the centre, on a low altar tomb, is the abbey's finest **brass** of Eleanor, Duchess of Gloucester (**29**; d 1399) beneath a triple canopy. On the north side of the ambulatory are Sebert's tomb (**30**) and the sedilia painting of the Confessor.

★**Poets' Corner** – This famous corner of the abbey in the south transept contains the tomb of Chaucer (**31**), who as Clerk of Works was associated with the abbey and the palace; statues of the court poets Dryden (**32**) and Ben Jonson (**33**), William Shakespeare (**34**) (a 'preposterous monument' in Horace Walpole's opinion), John Milton (**35**), William Blake (**36**) (bust by Epstein, 1957), Robert Burns (**37**), Longfellow (**38**), Joseph Addison (**39**) who observed at the time (18C) 'In the poetical quarter I found there were poets who had no monuments and monuments which had no poets'. Plaques and stones are now more the order of the day: W H Auden, Thomas Hardy, Gerard Manley Hopkins, Dylan Thomas and Lewis Carroll (**40**). Oscar Wilde, who died in Paris is honoured with a window.

Great Cloisters – Preserved in the abbey's precincts are a number of historical buildings.

Chapter House ⊙ – The octagonal chamber (1248-53), used at one time as a royal treasury, measures 60ft in diameter, its fine vault supported by an elegant central pier braced with shafts of Purbeck marble. On the outside, eight marble columns diffuse the weight borne by the lierne ribs to the tiled floor (1255). In between, set back from the ledge, marble shafts crowned with trefoiled blind arcading encircle the house. The walls are further decorated in parts with medieval paintings of the Last Judgment and the Apocalypse. The large windows date from the transitional period not followed in the body of the church as it would have spoilt the architectural unity: each bay rising (nearly 40ft) to quatrefoils and cusped circles.

In 1257 the King's Great Council, under Henry III, met in the chapter house indicating that it was intended from the first to accommodate secular assemblies as well as the 60-80 monks of the abbey. Under Edward I it became the **Parlement House of the Commons** and continued after the Dissolution, when the hall passed into the direct ownership of the Crown. By the 19C it had become an archive for the state papers; the floor had been boarded over and a second storey inserted. In 1865 the building's condition necessitated complete restoration. A century later, when the damage caused during the Second World War was repaired the windows were reglazed with clear glass, decorated with the coats of arms of sovereigns and abbots and the devices of the two medieval master masons, Henry de Reyns, who designed Henry III's abbey, and Henry Yevele, who built the nave (southwest and southeast windows).

Westminster Abbey Library ⊙ – The Library is housed in part of the former monks' dormitory which has a fine late 15C to early 16C hammerbeam roof. The collections include manuscripts, incunabula, printed books and bibles. On display are the Litlyngton Missal, a 13C bestiary, the Charter of Offa, King of Mercia AD 785, the oldest document among the muniments.

Chapel of the Pyx ☉ – The chamber built between 1055 and 1090 as a monastery chapel and retaining the only stone altar in its original position, was converted into the monastery treasury in the 13C to 14C. At the Dissolution it passed to the Crown and was used as the strong-room in which gold and silver coins were tried against standard specimens kept there in a box or pyx. Today it is used to display church plate from the abbey and from St Margaret's Church *(see WESTMINSTER)*, notably a 17C cloth of gold cope and a late medieval oak cope chest.

Westminster Abbey Museum ☉ – The museum is housed in the low Norman undercroft; two of the several pillars in its length (110ft) are still decorated with 11C carving. It contains historical documents, gold plate, reproductions of the coronation regalia, a number of unique wax and wood funeral effigies. Edward III and Katherine de Valois, both full length, are of wood. Of the 11 wax effigies, the contemporary figure of **Charles II** in his Garter robes is unforgettable though not carried at his near clandestine funeral. Among the women are Catherine, Duchess of Buckingham, natural daughter of James II and wife of John Sheffield, builder of Buckingham House, who had her effigy made during her lifetime, and Frances, Duchess of Richmond and Lennox who was the model for Britannia on the old penny piece.
Nelson, of whom it was said by a contemporary 'it is as if he was standing there', was purchased by the abbey in 1806 in an attempt to attract the crowds away from his tomb in St Paul's Cathedral.

Abbey Garden ☉ – The garden, 900 years old, is an oasis of quiet at the heart of Westminster, surrounded by the buildings of Westminster School.

Jericho and Jerusalem Chambers – *Closed to the public*. Both are in the lodgings, formerly of the abbot, now of the Dean. The Jericho Parlour has early 16C linen-fold panelling on the walls and is 150 years older than the Jerusalem Chamber where Henry IV died in 1413 *(Henry IV, Part II: 4 iv)*.

Dean's Yard – The yard, once the heart of the Abbey precinct, is now a tree-shaded lawn. The eastern range of buildings, some medieval, some Georgian, contains a low arch, the entrance to **Westminster School** *(private)*, which extends eastwards from Little Dean's Yard to the Palladian College, the mid 17C brick Ashburnham House, incorporating part of the Prior's Lodging (12C to 13C), and the Great Hall (known as School), which is part of the monastic dormitory (late 11C) and until 1884 was the school's only classroom, now rebuilt and again emblazoned with the arms of former headmasters and pupils; College hall, formerly the abbot's state dining hall, serves as the school refectory.
The south side of Dean's Yard is filled by **Church House** (1940), containing the large circular Convocation Hall, where the General Synod of the Church of England meets, and the Hoare Memorial Hall, where the Commons sat during the war.
On the west side are parliamentary offices and Westminster Abbey Choir School.
The North Gate is flanked by the Sanctuary buildings, designed by Sir Gilbert Scott, and leads into the Sanctuary.

WHITEHALL ★★

Map p 8 **(EY)**
⊖ Westminster; Charing Cross

Whitehall, formerly known as King Street, and Parliament Street are lined by government offices. Whitehall is synonymous with the executive as Westminster is a synonym for the legislature *(see INTRODUCTION)*.

Palace of Whitehall – Henry VIII's confiscation of Wolsey's London palace in 1529 was a matter of convenience as well as concupiscence. The property dated back to the mid 13C when it had passed by bequest to the See of York; in 1514 Wolsey made it his, personally rebuilding, enlarging and enriching it, adding to the grounds until they occupied 23 acres. Henry VIII continued building and increased the royal precinct until it extended from Charing Cross to Westminster Hall, from the river to St James's Park. In 1996 archeologists confirmed their finding a sophisticated type of Turkish bath fitted with a 12ft stove and lined with British-made tiles located below the Ministry of Defence.
The early owners of Whitehall had shown respect for a parcel of land known as Scotland, which until the 16C had been the site of a Scottish royal palace. When it was eventually built over, the streets were named Little, Great **Scotland Yard** etc. The newly formed Metropolitan Police, given an office there in 1829, became known by their address and retained it when they moved in the 1890s along the Embankment and later, in 1967, to Victoria Street.
Tudors and Stuarts continued after Henry to live in and alter Whitehall Palace but William and Mary disliked it and bought Kensington and, after a disastrous fire in 1698, did nothing to restore it. All that remains are Tudor walls and windows behind the Old Treasury *(visible from Downing Street)*, the end of Queen Mary's Terrace, a riverside quay and steps built in 1661 by Wren *(NE corner of the Ministry of Defence)* and the highly decorative Banqueting House *(see below)*.

Old Home Office, Foreign and Commonwealth Offices and Treasury – The two Victorian-Italian palazzo style buildings of 1868-73 and 1898-1912 are best known for the Treasury door on Gt George Street, from which the chancellor goes to the House on Budget Day, and the former Home Office balcony, from which members of the Royal Family watch the Remembrance Day service.

Cabinet War Rooms ⓥ – *Clive Steps, King Charles Street.* The underground emergency accommodation provided to protect Winston Churchill, his War Cabinet and the Chiefs of Staff of the armed forces from air attacks was the nerve centre of the war effort from 1939 to 1945. The nineteen rooms on view include the Cabinet Room prepared for in-camera discussions on national security and action; the Transatlantic Telephone Room – a secretive alcove for one-to-one strategic discussions,

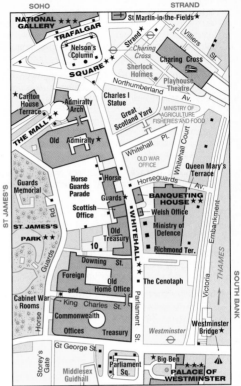

for direct communication with the White House; the Map Room decked with original maps from a pre-computer age marked with pins and coloured strings, and a bar chart of sticky paper, three distinctive figures represent the different armed forces (Navy, Air Force and Army); the Prime Minister's Room, and the room from which Churchill made direct broadcasts to the nation. Other paraphernalia so typical of the contemporary bureaucratic civil services includes 'the beauty chorus' of coloured telephones, functional knee-hole desks and iron beds, detailed notices and printed instructions. Also in situ are the wedged wooden supports which were installed by the Naval team assigned to reinforce the premises against collapse during shelling and the tunnel to the map room annexe which had to be drilled through concrete poured into the Camp Commandant's cramped quarters located below a staircase in the main building.

Sir Winston Leonard Spencer Churchill (1874-1965)

Churchill was perhaps Britain's most charismatic leader: his speeches – broadcast worldwide by the BBC, rallied military troops in action, civilians at home and in occupied Europe, prisoners, spies, friends and foes... He is still remembered for his bursts of anger and impatience by those who knew him, but is respected rather for his brilliance, staunch patriotism and remarkable use of the English language. His school report (aged nine) describes him as 'very bad... a constant trouble to everybody and is always in some scrape or other' – a far cry from the man who was to rise through Harrow, soldiering, to the war premiership, and become an elder statesman through the Cold War crisis.

He was a creature of habit: on the whole, he would wake at 8.30am, hold court from his bed throughout the morning until it was time for his bath (mid/late morning); he would then lunch, take a nap and maybe another soak before going out to dinner and dealing with business late into the night; meals were preferably accompanied by champagne, and punctuated by a dozen or so cigars smoked throughout the day. His presence lives on in the Cabinet War Rooms while his distinctive silhouette holds guard over the House of Commons from Parliament Square.

The Cenotaph – The slim white monument by Lutyens (1919) is without any effigy; the horizontal lines are very shallowly arced, the verticals converge 1 000ft up in the sky; flags stir in the wind on either side.

On Remembrance Sunday *(November)* a service is held at which those who died in battle are remembered.

Downing Street – No 10 has been the residence of the Prime Minister since 1731 when Sir Robert Walpole accepted it *ex-officio* from George II. The 'four or five very large and well built houses, fit for persons of honour and quality, each having a pleasant prospect of St James's Park', were erected in the 1680s by Sir George Downing, diplomat, courtier and general opportunist of the Commonwealth and Restoration. The speculation was successful. The row was rebuilt in the 1720s. No 10 contains the **Cabinet Room** and staircase, on which hang portraits of each successive resident.

Richmond Terrace – The terrace was designed by Thomas Chawner in 1822. The façade has been restored to its original design and the Fine Rooms reinstated.

Ministry of Defence – In front of the monolithic building stands the small, jaunty, bronze of **Sir Walter Raleigh**, who was beheaded nearby. Next to him stands '**Monty**', a 10ft solid bronze statue of Field Marshal Lord Montgomery of Alamein by Oscar Nemon, unveiled in 1980.

Old Treasury – Treasuries have stood on the site since the 16C. The present one of 1845 by Barry, using the columns from the previous building by Soane, was the first of the phase of government building which has continued to the 20C.

Scottish Office and Welsh Office – The 18C **Dover** and **Gwydyr Houses**, both named after 19C owners are, in the latter case, open to the street, the only ornament a Venetian window above a tripartite door and in the former, a tall screen with an advanced porch designed by Henry Holland for the then owner, Frederick, Duke of York, in 1787.

★★**Banqueting House** ⊘ – The hall, the third on the site, has been called a memorial to the Stuarts: it was commissioned by James I (1619-1622); Charles I had the sumptuous ceiling paintings painted by the Flemish diplomat P P Rubens in 1629 and stepped on to the scaffold in Whitehall through one of its windows on 30 January 1649; Charles II received the Lords and Commons in the hall on the eve of his restoration on 29 May 1660; after James II's flight in 1689, William and Mary received within it the formal offer of the crown.

The Banqueting House laid for a function dinner

Banqueting houses served many purposes: as a setting for court ceremonial and revelry, for the reception of royalty and embassies, state banquets, the distribution of Royal Maundy, touching for the King's Evil, for dancing, music-making and courtly masques.

Inigo Jones, King's Surveyor and famous masque designer, constructed for James I at the centre of the Tudor palace, a Palladian-inspired building. It was conceived as a double cube but made the exterior appear as a two-storey palazzo. The use of pedimented windows, swags and delicate rustication are borrowed directly from Palladio. Although the exterior has been refaced in Portland stone (1829 by Soane) and a new north entrance and staircase were added by Wyatt in 1809 (lead bust of Charles I over the door and bronze of James I by **Le Sueur** inside) and although the interior was used as a chapel and a museum from the 18C-20C, it now looks as splendid as it might have done in the 17C and still serves superbly beneath the chandeliers for occasional official functions.

Exterior – The building stands two storeys high above a rusticated basement with an open balustrade at the crest. Note how the windows are alternately pedimented and, above, straight hooded; four columns with projecting entablatures give the side elevation a central feature, while pilasters articulate the side bays.

Interior – Inside it is a single empty space, a gilded stage awaiting players. It has the distinction of being a double cube 110ft × 55ft × 55ft with a delicate balcony, supported on gilded corbels on three sides; above, richly decorated beams quarter the ceiling decorated with Rubens' flamboyant **paintings** in praise of James I. In Stuart times the lower walls would have been hung with Mortlake and other tapestries.

★Horse Guards ⊘ – The low 18C stonefaced edifice designed symmetrically by **William Kent** around three sides of a shallow forecourt is pierced by a central arch and marked above, like its mid 17C predecessor on the same site, by a clock tower. The plain building acts as the official entrance to Buckingham Palace and as such is where all dignitaries on State visits to London are greeted – only holders of an 'ivory' pass may use the entrance. To this end it is guarded by mounted sentries: when the Queen is in London this comprises an officer, a corporal major to bear the standard, two non-commissioned officers, a trumpeter and ten troopers (Long Guard); otherwise there are two non-commissioned officers and ten troopers only (short guard). Sentry duty by statue-still members of the Household Cavalry Mounted Regiment alternate between the Life Guards

in scarlet tunics and white plumed helmets, and the Blues and Royals in blue with red plumes. The west front *(through the arch)* overlooks the parade ground where the Colour is Trooped in June.

Among the statues and memorials is a huge French mortar from Cadiz (1812) mounted on the back of a winged and scaly dragon *(against the west front),* and the **Guards' Memorial** (1926) *(on the far side)* backed by St James's Park *(see BUCKINGHAM PALACE).*

★Old Admiralty – The Old Admiralty of 1722-26 was, in Horace Walpole's phrase 'deservedly veiled by **Mr Adam's** handsome screen' in 1759-61, a single storey, blind porticoed wall with angle pavilions and a central arch crowned by a low balustrade between winged seahorses. In the 1890s vast terracotta brick additions were made to the rear.

Ph. Gajic/MICHELIN

Sentry duty at Horse Guards

Pagoda, Kew Gardens

Outer London

OUTER LONDON

WHIPSNADE PARK ZOO, WATFORD \ BIRMINGHAM ↑ BEDFORD

0   3 km
0   2 miles

BARNET

FINCHLEY

★★ RAF MUSEUM

HARROW

A 409

A 410

A 5

A 41

M 1

A 406

A 1000

HENDON

Hampstead
Garden Suburb

★★ Harrow Museum
and Heritage Centre

A 4006

A 502

A 404

★★ KENWOOD

St Mary ★   HARROW
    Harrow School

BRENT

★ Fenton House

HAMPSTEAD ★

A 312

A 4005

A 4088

CAMDEN

Wembley

WEMBLEY

A 404

Swiss
Cottage

A 5

WILLESDEN

Grand Union Canal

GREENFORD

A 312

A 40

A 4127

A 4005

A 40

EALING

Y

A 4020

ACTON

A 4020

M 41

EALING

HAMMERSMITH
AND FULHAM

★★ HYDE PA

A 4127

B 454

A 403

KENSINGTON

M 4

CHISWICK ★★

HAMMERSMITH

WINDSOR / LONDON AIRPORT

★★ OSTERLEY PARK

A 4

Chiswick House ★

★★ CHELS

A 315

A 316

Fulham
Palace

A 308

HOUNSLOW

★★ SYON PARK

KEW ★★★

BARNES

FULHAM

West
Heli

BASINGSTOKE

A 20

A 315

MORTLAKE

PUTNEY

A 3

Rugby Ground

Crane

A 305

A 205

RICHMOND ★★

WANDSWO

ROEHAMPTON

A 3

A 219

Marble Hill House ★

A 316

WANDSWORTH

TWICKENHAM

Richmond
Park
★★

HAM HOUSE ★★

A 308

WIMBLEDON

Wandle

★ Strawberry Hill

A 313

A 311

RICHMOND
UPON THAMES

A 310

A 307

A 219

M 3

SOUTHAMPTON

A 308

THAMES

A 238

A 238

MERT

A 24

A 29

Mole

★ HAMPTON COURT ★★★

KINGSTON
UPON THAMES

A 3

Beverley Brook

MERTON

A 243

↙ EPSOM, PORTSMOUTH   ↙ WORTHING

Sightseeing suggestions

Day 1: Start at **Westminster** with the Houses of Parliament and Big Ben, Westminster Bridge (**view** of the Thames and the Houses of Parliament), **Westminster Abbey**, Parliament Square – walk up **Whitehall** to **Trafalgar Square** *(lunch at St Martin's in the Fields or in the National Gallery)*. Visit the **National Gallery** and **National Portrait Gallery** or continue up to **Leicester Square** and **Covent Garden** for tea, window shopping and an evening drink.

Day 2: Aim to start at the **Tower of London** as early as possible to avoid the crowds attracted by the Crown Jewels. From here it is easy to wander into the **City** *(see below)*, past Monument to the Bank of England and **St Paul's Cathedral**. Otherwise on a sunny day, walk under Tower Bridge and saunter around St Katharine Docks (marina with bars and restaurants) crossing to the south side of the River Thames to explore **Bermondsey** (Design Museum, Bramah Tea and Coffee Museum) and **Bankside** (HMS Belfast, London Dungeon, Golden Hinde, Shakespeare's Globe).

Day 3: Begin at **St Paul's Cathedral** before exploring the **City**: the Bank of England Museum, Leadenhall Market at lunchtime before continuing to marvel at Richard Rogers' Lloyds' Building; the Guildhall; the Barbican and Museum of London.

Day 4: A day may easily be spent in the museums around **South Kensington (Science Museum, Victoria & Albert Museum, Natural History Museum)** with time for browsing around the shops in **Knightsbridge.**

Day 5: Treasures from around the world are collected together at the **British Museum** which is located in **Bloomsbury,** once the heart of the literary set. An afternoon in **Regent's Park** may include a visit to the zoo or a short break from sightseeing in the rose garden. If the weather is unkind, the **Wallace Collection** is a safe distraction from shopping in Oxford Street.

Day 6: A round trip down river from Westminster to **Greenwich** (National Maritime Museum and Queen's House, Old Observatory, Cutty Sark) may be combined with a return through **Docklands** (Canary Wharf) by Docklands Light Railway to Tower Gateway *(see PRACTICAL INFORMATION)* and the West End.

Day 7: Beyond the confines of Inner London there is **Kew** and **Hampton Court:** having visited the palace and gardens, consider returning down river by boat *(see PRACTICAL INFORMATION).*

BARNES – ROEHAMPTON

Map p 296 (TY)
Overground: from Waterloo Station

Arranged around its tree-planted village green, Barnes remains remarkably countrified in character. Besides its pond, weatherboarded early 19C Sun Inn and former village school, there are a number of 18C houses; the oldest being **Rose House** in the High Street *(no 70)*, others congregate by the church. Milbourne House in Station Road was where Henry Fielding lived in the 1750s.

St Mary's ⊘ – The Parish church, said to have been consecrated in 1215 by Archbishop Langton after the signing of Magna Carta *(see INTRODUCTION: History)*, was burnt out in 1978 but reopened in 1984 after sensitive rebuilding to Edward Cullinan's designs around existing elements from former structures. The medieval tower, nave and chancel, with its triple lancet windows and frieze, form the narthex of the much enlarged new church. The nave extends northwards to a high wall containing a delicate neo-Gothic east window (1852) and rose window and to the east and west to the round turret and old vestry.

Barnes Common *(east of the Green)* – Some of the open heath is laid out as cricket and football pitches. Further north downstream from Hammersmith Bridge a **wildlife reserve** around lagoons, marshes and water meadows has been created at the north end of the Barnes Elms reservoirs site.

MORTLAKE

Upriver from Barnes towards Kew comes Mortlake, reputed in the 16C for its salt glaze pottery and in the 17C for its **tapestry works** producing hangings that were highly prized for their fine weaving and elaborate borders. Examples survive in the Victoria & Albert Museum collections, at Hampton Court, Kensington Palace and in the House of Lords (arms of Charles II). These days, Mortlake is known rather for its brewery and as the finishing point of the Boat Race *(see Outer London: PUTNEY – WANDSWORTH)*.

The **Mortlake Tapestry Factory** was the most important in England founded in 1619 by Flemish weavers: in 1623 Prince, later King Charles I specially acquired Raphael's cartoons of *The Acts of the Apostles* for reproduction by the works. Quality declined as royal patronage dwindled with the approach of the Civil War; under the Protectorate a series based on Mantegna's panels *The Triumph of Caesar* was made; during the 1670s the workers dispersed, several going to Soho to ply their trade under the directorship of John Vanderbank (chief Arras worker of the Royal Wardrobe). Francis Poyntz went to serve at the Royal Wardrobe as well as maintaining his own workshops in Clerkenwell and Hatton Garden. The Mortlake factory, marked by a white shield with a red cross, closed in 1703.

Mortlake High Street – The north (river) side of the street is bordered by short ranges of old cottages and several 18C houses: Acacia House *(no 115)*; Afon House *(no 117)* with its off-centre door and unusual peaked roof; a brick L-shaped house *(no 119)*. The splendid dull red brick, two-storey **house** *(no 123)* was built c 1720 and subsequently extended. The pedimented porch on Tuscan columns is repeated at the top of a short flight of steps at the rear where it overlooks the garden and river. When Turner was painting his Mortlake Terrace pictures *Early Morning* and *Summer Evening*, he stayed in this house, then known as *The Limes*.

St Mary the Virgin Church ⊘ – The greater part of the church dates from the 19C-20C, of the 17C fabric only the brick vestry with its corner door shaded by a square hood on carved corbels survives together with the west tower which was built on foundations laid by order of Henry VIII. It is here that Dr John Dee, philosopher, mathematician and astrologer to Elizabeth I lies buried. (A collection of salt glaze pottery may be seen on application.)

In the churchyard of St Mary Magdalen *(North Worple Way)* is the tomb of the explorer **Sir Richard Burton**, marked by a Bedouin tent in stone erected by his widow in 1890.

ROEHAMPTON

The railway has never come to Roehampton and so its transformation to a residential suburb from a Surrey village, ringed by Georgian family mansions among magnificent Lebanese cedars, came about only this century through the combustion engine.

The narrow **High Street** contains a few small 19C houses with shops on the ground floor (an ironmonger dated 1885, in a tall weatherboarded corner house) and three pubs: The Angel, rebuilt this century on a traditional site, the 18C brick Montague Arms, and at the junction with Roehampton Lane, the rambling white weatherboarded 17C-18C, King's Head.

Of the Georgian mansions to survive, most now house educational establishments:
Battersea College of Education (*Holybourne Avenue*) occupies the Classical **Manresa House**, a plain four-storey brick house with a slate roof built in 1750 by Sir William Chambers for Lord Bessborough.

Garnett College (*Roehampton Lane*) is accommodated in Downshire House – a two-storey, square, parapeted house of red brick (1770). Note the garden and contemporary Cedar Cottages.

Queen Mary's Hospital (1915), set behind tall iron gates, occupies Roehampton House, a wide, parapeted brick mansion of seven bays, four storeys high, built by Thomas Archer in 1712 and extended in 1910 by Lutyens with curving arcades on either side of the forecourt to new wings and pavilions. Adjoining are the Roehampton Artificial Limb Fitting Centre and related factories.

The white, Palladian style of 1772, **Mount Clare** (*Minstead Gardens*) with twin curving staircases and a balustraded portico added in 1780, is superbly sited on the crest of a hill. The great cedar beside it was planted in 1773 by Capability Brown.

The **Froebel Institute** occupies three properties: Grove House (*corner of Roehampton and Clarence Lanes*), a low white stone and stucco mansion of nine bays built by James Wyatt in 1777 to which an Italian wing was added in 1850; Ibstock Place (*Clarence Lane*), an early 18C mellow brick house with dormers in the tiled roof and an attractively irregular front; Templeton (*Priory Lane*) a tall, late Georgian, plain brick house with a rear terrace extending the width of the house and overlooking a garden enclosed by yew hedges and shaded by two massive cedars.

Two strange houses mark Roehampton's north end: a deeply thatched white cottage of irregular shape (*by Rosslyn Park RFC, at the junction of Roehampton Lane, Rocks Lane and Upper Richmond Road*) and the Coach House (*1 Fitzgerald Avenue, Upper Richmond Road West*), a 19C Gothic folly with disordered gables, pepperpot roof turrets, phoney Latin plaque, wall sundial: an Arthur Rackham illustration in a suburban street!

BATTERSEA

Map p 7 (**CDZ**)
Overground: Battersea Park from Victoria; Queenstown Road from Waterloo

Battersea's transformation from a rural town into an industrial town took just 100 years. In 1782, 2 160 souls were engaged in cultivating strawberries and asparagus, herbs (Lavender Hill) and vegetables for seed; they sent their produce to Westminster; by 1845 the railway had extended to Clapham (originally Battersea) Junction and the population explosion had begun.
Local street names recall the St John Bolingbroke family and their successor, Earl Spencer, Lord of the Manor since 1763.

Battersea Old Church, St Mary's ⊙ – Since Saxon times there has been a church well forward at the river bend. The current building with a conical green copper spire dates from 1775 (portico 1823); the 14C east window encloses 17C tracery and painted heraldic glass. The aisle windows commemorate famous people with local connections: the 18C botanist William Curtis who is buried here, William Blake who married here and Turner who sketched the river from the vestry window and whose chair now stands in the chancel. Amusing epitaphs and memorial busts of the St John Bolingbroke family, lords of the manor in the 17C to 18C.

De Morgan Foundation ⊙ – Old Battersea House, a 2-storey brick mansion with a hipped roof and pedimented doorway, built by Sir Walter St John in 1699, now houses the De Morgan Foundation Collection of ceramics by William de Morgan who was associated with the Arts and Crafts movement, and paintings and drawings by Evelyn de Morgan Spencer Stanhope, J M Strudwick and Cadogan Cowper.

Vicarage Crescent – Devonshire House is an early 18C stucco house of three storeys with a Doric porch, small curved iron balconies and a contemporary wrought-iron gate. St Mary's House is a late 17C mansion.

High Street – The Raven, with curving Dutch gables, has dominated the crossroads since the 17C. Sir Walter St John School, founded in 1700, was rebuilt in the 19C-20C on the original site in Tudor Gothic style. Note the St John motto surmounted by helm and falcon at the entrance.

★Albert Bridge – The cantilever suspension bridge, which is most attractive when lit up at night, was designed by R W Ordish in 1873; it was modified by Joseph Bazalgette and reinforced with a central support in the 1970s; spare bulbs are stored in the twin tollmen's huts at either end.

Battersea Bridge – Battersea Railway Bridge (1863) was for many years the only bridge which carried a railway line directly connecting north and south England. The present construction was designed by Joseph Bazalgette in 1890. Its predecessor, a wooden bridge (1771) lit first by oil lamps (1799) and then by gas (1824), was the inspiration for Whistler's painting entitled *Nocturne*.

Battersea Park – The marshy waste of Battersea Fields was popular in the 16C for pigeon shooting, fairs, donkey racing and duels; by 1828, however, when Wellington and Lord Winchelsea exchanged shots over the Catholic Emancipation Bill, they had become ill famed. In 1843 **Thomas Cubitt** *(see index)* proposed that a park be laid out; a bill was passed in 1846 and 360 acres purchased. The site was built up with land from the excavation of the Victoria Docks.

The park includes a boating lake, a garden for the handicapped, sculptures by H Moore and B Hepworth and sports facilities.

The Japanese Peace Pagoda (1985) complete with gilded windbells and seated Buddhas is one of several instituted by the organisation dedicated to World peace.

Marco Polo House – The bold building on Queenstown Road to the east of the park, has been compared to something resembling from a packet of liquorice allsorts or from Legoland: clad in hi-tech Japanese panels of Neo-Paries, a synthetic-looking light and finely finished material, and Pilkington glass, the building's simplified classical lines make it somehow endearing. It presently accommodates the *Observer* newspaper editorial offices.

Battersea Power Station – The completion of this familiar landmark, largely built in 1932-34, was overseen by Giles Gilbert Scott after the Second World War. He extended the chimneys to 337ft and endowed the colossus with surface detailing – fluting and ridging to lessen its bulk. The power station shut down in 1983; plans to convert the massive structure and its 31 acre site into a shopping and entertainment, while retaining the fine Art Deco interiors of the two turbine halls and control room, are still under review.

Battersea Dogs' Home ⊘ – *4 Battersea Park Road*. The home, established in 1860, moved to its present site in 1871. The number of dogs and cats brought in annually runs into thousands.

Chelsea Bridge – The 1934 suspension bridge by Forest and Wheeler, replaces an earlier one from 1858.

Battersea Power Station

BERMONDSEY – ROTHERHITHE

Map pp 10-11 (**HJKY**)
⊖ London Bridge; Tower Hill

Until the Reformation Bermondsey was known for its famous Cluniac monastery. Bermondsey Abbey, founded in 1082, was located between Abbey Street, Tower Bridge Road, and Grange Road. At Bermondsey Priory in Rotherhithe, the monks brewed beer. In the 18C the area became fashionable as a spa famous rather for its spring water. Several street names – Leathermarket, Tanner, Morocco – recall the activities of Elizabethan tradesmen working the calf-skins and hides landed there from Southern Ireland.

Situated on the south bank of the Thames extending east of Tower Bridge, the area has been subjected to redevelopment, sponsored in part by private investment.

For details of the famous Friday Bermondsey or New Caledonian Market, see INTRODUCTION – Shopping.

Butlers Wharf – Presently listed as a conservation area, this part of London is slowly developing its own resident population and commercial interests; for the moment epicure restaurants and designer bars line the waterfront.

Design Museum ⊘ – *Shad Thames*. The museum opened in 1989 to popular-ise, explain, analyse and criticise design of the past and present and speculate about design in the future. True to the ethic of the Conran empire, the complex has been summed up as 'modest, clean, spacious and white'. The **Review Gallery** on the first floor displays a se-lection of state-of-the-art products from around the world. The main space is dedicated to temporary (six monthly) exhibitions of product or graphic design and architecture: early designs and manufacture are compared and con-trasted with current fads and fashions produced by different industrial proc-esses. Experimental projects are presented with concept foam or painted MDF pro-totype and test models, and visuals.

New Concordia and China Wharves

The airy top floor space is reserved for the museum collection of household appliances, television sets, cameras, spectacles, furni-ture, office equipment, cars, bicycles... VDUs are available for access to a database.

★**Bramah Tea and Coffee Museum** ⊘ – *The Clove Building, Maguire Street*. The museum is appropriately situated among the historic warehouses that once handled consign-ments of tea, coffee and spices from the East. The museum traces the fashion for tea and coffee drinking in England, the establishment of coffee houses and tea gardens in the 17C, the levy of taxes and the origins of the Boston Tea Party, smuggling and adulteration. A vast and varied collection of tea pots includes Chinese and Japanese ceramic pots, European designs made of metal, ceramic and plastic. Ones shaped like the monkeys which were trained to pick tea, a tilting teapot for idle addicts, the Simple Yet Perfect pot, samovars, many fantasy designs and the largest teapot ever made.

The display of coffee pots illustrates the persistent search for the perfect way to brew good coffee.

Church of St Mary Magdalen ⊘ – The parish church founded in 1290 was rebuilt in 1691 and twice restored in the 19C. It retains 12C carved capitals (from Ber-mondsey Abbey, once on the same site), 17C woodwork, boards inscribed with 18C charity donations, three hatchments vividly painted with armorial bearings and tombstones in the aisle pavements giving a sad insight into 18C infant mortality.

China Wharf

Beyond the Design Museum, Cinnamon Wharf (the first residential ware-house conversion on Butler's Wharf) and St Saviour's Wharf stands China Wharf facing conspicuously onto the river. Completed in 1988, this striking, orange-red, scalloped building sitting in the river has won its architects CZWG several awards (RIBA Urban Design 1986, Civic Trust 1989). The unit consists of 17 two-bedroom apartments designed to fill a gap between the existing New Concordia and Reed Wharves. Note the front entrance balcony named The Great Harry.

Other inventive warehouse conversions include: the glazed design-studio-cum-residential **David Mellor Building** *(22-24 Shad Thames)*, the modernist **Saffron Wharf** *(18)* and the untreated Iroko timber-clad **Camera Press** *(21/23 Queen Elizabeth St)*. The four gently curved blocks that make up **The Circle** *(Queen Elizabeth St)*, faced with glazed cobalt-blue tiles, replace the Courage Brewery stables, its balconies swirl in a great spiralling sweep – a far cry from Jacob's Island, the inspiration for Bill Sykes' abject den of vice and poverty described in Charles Dickens' *Oliver Twist*.

ROTHERHITHE ⊖ *Rotherhithe*

The name may be a corruption of 'red reed' or 'red riff' (Redriff being the fictional home of Jonathan Swift's hero Gulliver). In 1013 the village served as a mooring to Olaf, King of Norway when he supported King Ethelred the Unready against the invading Danes (c1012). In the reign of Henry VIII it became a Tudor dockyard and it was to a berth in Rotherhithe that the *Mayflower* returned after her historic voyage in 1621. Later, the *Temeraire*, a fighting ship that survived the Battle of Trafalgar and immortalised in Turner's painting was towed here to be broken up in 1838.

The Angel Inn – *24 Rotherhithe St*. An 18C partly weatherboarded inn painted white, overlooking the river, mentioned by Pepys.

St Mary's ⊙ – *St Marychurch St*. Churches have stood on this site for at least 1 000 years. The present building, which dates from 1715, has a stone trim and is crowned by an octagonal obelisk spire, collared by thin columns (rebuilt 1861), which is visible from the river. The interior is ceiled by a wooden-framed barrel roof resting on four massive piers consisting of tree trunks, fashioned as ships' masts and encased in plaster. The communion table and two Bishop's chairs are of wood from the *Temeraire*; the altarpiece includes rich garlands by **Grinling Gibbons** 'signed' with open peapods. The church's associations with the Royal Navy are so numerous that it flies the White Ensign. The captain of the *Mayflower* is buried in the churchyard.

Opposite the church is an 18C **Charity School**, 3-storeyed, 3-bayed, with coloured figures of a contemporary schoolboy and girl above the door. Next stands the **Watch House** (1821) matched by the **Engine House** (façade only); between them is the churchyard with the **Old Mortuary** on the south side.

Mayflower Inn – *117 Rotherhithe Street*. The pub takes its name from the ship that briefly moored here prior to setting sail for the Americas with the Pilgrim Fathers in 1620. It claims an ancient licence to sell British and American postage stamps.

Brunel Engine House ⊙ – Thames Tunnels, the first under water tunnel in the world, was constructed by Marc Brunel between 1824-43 during which time work was suspended seven years after excavations caved in twice, and caused sickness and death among the labourers. Its completion was celebrated by an underground banquet and a knighthood for the engineer. Although the twin tunnels were designed for wheeled traffic, the spiral approaches were never built and the tunnels were used by pedestrians until 1869 when they became part of the underground train network. Interestingly, the same systems of excavation have been used to dig the Channel Tunnel (1990s).

The engine house (1842, restored), which contained the machinery for keeping the tunnels drained, recounts the history of the project and the technique of soft-ground tunnelling using a shield, which was pioneered by Brunel; it also contains a J & G Rennie compound horizontal V steam pumping engine (1882).

Scandinavian seamen's mission churches – The 1926 red brick Norwegian mission at 1 Albion St, **St Olave Kirk**, stands at the entrance to the Rotherhithe Tunnel. The hospital and the attractively spare **Swedish Church** (rebuilt 1966) are in Lower Road. The 1957 **Finnish Mission** *(33 Albion St)* is distinguished by a spectacular belfry and an interior east wall of dark stone, decorated to resemble the swell of the sea.

Surrey Commercial Docks – Howland Great Wet Dock was the first dock on the south bank. Dug in 1693, it held up to 120 ships. It was renamed Greenland Dock in 1763 having become the principal whaling base; as whaling declined in the 1840s Canadian produce (cheese, cured bacon) was imported here. The Grand Surrey Docks and the Commercial Dock opened in 1807. Other docks followed: Baltic Dock (1809), East Country Dock (1811), Albion Dock (1860), Canada (1876), Quebec (1926). They all amalgamated in 1864.

The demise of Mulberry Quay, however, is more recent having been used to build the artificial Mulberry harbours that were floated to Normandy for the D Day landings.

Lavender Pond – Part of the old Surrey Docks has been transformed into a nature reserve (2 acres). Lavender Pond was once used to store timber brought from Canada and Scandinavia. The pumproom has been converted into classrooms.

BLACKHEATH★

Map p 297 (**UY**)
Overground: Blackheath from Cannon Street or London Bridge

he heath has always been an open space bisected by major roads; the course of the Roman Watling Street between the south coast and London is marked by Blackheath Road, Blackheath Hill and Shooters' Hill, which were notorious for highwaymen in the 8C.

Rebel forces have used the heath as a rallying ground: Wat Tyler (1381), the Kentishmen under Jack Cade (1450), the Cornishmen under Audley (1497). In more joyful mood in 1415 the people greeted Henry V on his victorious return from Agincourt; in 1660 Charles II was welcomed by the Restoration Army and in 1608, so it is said, while in residence at Greenwich, James I taught the English to play golf on Blackheath. Today, it provides an ideal site for a traditional fairground during Bank Holiday weekends.

★**Blackheath** – The heath is ringed by stately **terraces** and **houses**★ mostly built of brick relieved by dressings of stone or of sparkling white painted stucco. They date in the main from the 18C and early 19C when merchants, newly rich from the expanding docks, began to build in the vicinity.

On the south side stands All Saints Church, a neo-Gothic oddity by Furley, built of Kentish ragstone, with the tower unusually placed on the south side.

Overlooking the heath from the **south side** is an almost unbroken line of buildings: **Colonnade House** *(South Row)* is a large early 19C house with a Tuscan portico extending the full width of the front; **The Paragon**, a late 18C shallow crescent by Michael Searles, consists of fourteen semi-detached brick villas linked by Tuscan colonnades; Lindsey House *(Lloyds Place)* is in brick with white trims; Grotes' Buildings is a mid 18C terrace; Heathfield House, a stucco building, with a Tuscan-columned, paired bow window, dates from the early 19C.

On the **west side** in Dartmouth Row are the early 18C Spencer House and Perceval House with eleven bays, several Georgian houses and a few of the original houses (1680-90).

Blackheath Village – The main street and Tranquil Vale, which despite its name is full of noisy traffic, lead off the heath southwards to modern estates by Span and other architects.

Morden College, St German's Place

The college *(closed to the public)*, founded as a 'refuge for discrete merchants' who had fallen on hard times, stands in an 18C landscaped park. The attractive low, two-storey building in mellow brick with stone dressings, was designed by Sir Christopher Wren in 1695. The figures of the founder, Sir John Morden, a city merchant, and his wife, stand in a double niche above the central stone gateway which leads to an inner quadrangle.

Michelin Maps and Guides:
Keep them in your car when you travel.

CAMBERWELL - PECKHAM

Map p 297 (UY)

Until the 18C the district south of Southwark was covered by market garden supplying the City of London with fresh produce. In the 18C and 19C merchants an businessmen began to build out-of-town houses in Camberwell, the village which gav its name to the Camberwell Beauty when that butterfly was first seen in England. Th fields, where Robert Browning had once walked, were soon covered by dense urba development when the penny workmen's return fare to London Bridge was intro duced.

In the 20C two pioneer ventures were launched in the district. **Clubland** *(56 Camberwe Road)* was an educational and social youth centre, founded by James Butterworth, Methodist, in the 1920s; the chapel designed by Edward Maufe was destroyed in th Second World War and rebuilt in 1962. The **Peckham Experiment** *(St Mary's Roac* was conducted from 1935 to 1945 as a social and recreational centre, concerne with preventive as well as curative medicine for an all-income, cross-section of th community.

Camberwell Road – Cambridge House *(no 131)*, composed of early 19C houses is now the University Settlement; Camberwell Antique Market *(nos 159-161)* i filled with lesser antiques, frippery and china.

Denmark Hill – On either side of the road are **King's College** and **Maudsley Hospital** Beyond, in Champion Park, behind the bronze statues of the General and his wife Evelina, stands the **William Booth Memorial Salvation Army Training College** (1932).

Camberwell Grove *(off Camberwell Church Street)* – The wide avenue rise between closely planted trees and late 18C and early 19C Georgian town house and terraces, Victorian cottages and villas. At the end for many years stood Mar Datchelor Girls' School. The school, which closed in 1981, was founded from monies left in 1726 in charity by Mary Datchelor who had inherited a Cit coffeehouse from her father. In 1863 the coffeehouse was sold for £30 000 an the school established in Camberwell where from the late 19C it was endowed an administered by the Clothworkers' City Company.

Grove Chapel (1819) stands near the top of the avenue opposite a small crescen of attractive stuccoed houses (1830).

PECKHAM

Strung along **Peckam Road** is the neo-Gothic Church of **St Giles** with a towering spire the exterior is decorated with remarkable gargoyles of Gladstone and other states men; the interior is adorned with brasses dating from 1497 (Mighell Skinner) 1532 or later.

Georgian Terraces line both sides *(nos 29, 30-34)*. The northerly of the two ranges once known as Camberwell House, was at one time a school attended by Thoma Hood; the southern asymmetrical terrace, east of Lucas Gardens, is preceded by cobbled forecourt furnished with a contemporary gas lamp, iron gateway etc Camberwell School of Arts and Crafts and the South London Art Gallery combin massive elongated new buildings with the old school (1903) where caryatids guar the entrance and the even older gallery (1897).

St John's Church *(Meeting House Lane)*, designed by David Bush in 1964, has a high asymmetrical brick end wall; the interior roof lines and curving organ pipes lea the eye to the bronze Christ, rescued from the bombed parish church and posi tioned high on the brick wall behind the altar; colour is provided by the window a ground level, a glowing abstract of blues, greens, yellows, and from a joyou *Mother and Child* by Ron Hinton (1966).

In Asylum Road *(left)*, set back round three sides of a forecourt, is a long two-storey brick range with a central, pedimented portico, the Licensed Victualler Benevolent Institution of 1827 (now Caroline Gardens).

Nunhead Green – *Southeast*. The green is marked by the rebuilt tavern, the Ol Nun's Head, which claims a licence dating back to Henry VIII's reign and th **Beeston's Gift Almshouses** *(Consort Road)*, erected in 1834 by the Girdlers' Compan on land left them in the 16C by Cuthbert Beeston.

hiswick retains something of the country village which it was until the 1860s; by the
880s the population had increased from 6 500 to 15 600; in the 20C the motorway
M4) and its feeder flyover divided the riverside from the rest.

eorgian houses survive, however, in Church Street and other parallel roads to the
ver and in Chiswick Mall overlooking the river and the Eyot.

★**Chiswick House** ⊙ – *Burlington Lane.* In 1682 the first Earl of Burlington purchased a Jacobean mansion set in extensive acres at Chiswick. During the 18C the
house was altered and extended by Richard Boyle, the 3rd **Earl of Burlington** (1695-
1753), connoisseur and generous host and patron to Kent, Rysbrack, Campbell,
Pope, Swift, Gay, Thompson, Handel... Burlington acquired his understanding and
appreciation of Palladian Architecture first hand having visited Italy on the Grand
Tour (1714) and subsequently specifically to study the villas around Vicenza
(1719). In accordance with the change in fashion from Wren's ebullient Baroque to
the Classically inspired, Burlington designed a Palladian villa (1725-29) in which to
display his works of art and entertain his friends. In plan, it strictly adheres to
Palladio's principles: main front, garden façade, two identical lateral elevations;
symmetrical arrangement of rooms along the main axis: he justified having a
variety of shaped rooms by saying they were modelled upon study of Roman Baths
detailed in Palladio's *Four Books on Architecture*.

Much of the interior decoration and the gardens – complete with temples and a
canal – were the work of his protégé **William Kent** (1686-1748) 'the history painter
from Hull' (Peter Murray). The villa still stands but nothing remains of the
Jacobean mansion nor of additions made in the 18C and 19C by Georgiana,
Duchess of Devonshire and queen of society, and her successors, who entertained
Charles James Fox, George Canning, Edward VII and the tsars.

Exterior – An avenue of terms approaches the villa endowed with all the grace of
Classical proportion. Paired dog-leg staircases overlooked by statues of Palladio *(left)*
and Inigo Jones *(right)* lead up to a portico; behind the pediment is a raised
octagonal dome, flanked by obelisks, which contain the chimney flues.

Interior – The lower floor octagon hall (with wine cellar below), lobbies and library
now displays drawings and other material about the design and restoration of the
house and garden. From the library the pillared link building leads to the Summer
Parlour (1717) originally connected to the Jacobean mansion. The grisaille paintings
are by Kneller (1719).

Chiswick House Interior

On the first floor or 'piano nobile' *(staircase to the left of the library)* publi function rooms follow a square plan of intercommunicating rooms arrange around a central octagon. The central **Dome Saloon** has eight walls punctuate alternately by Classical busts and pedimented doors with gold highlights; th coffered cupola rises from an ochre coloured entablature to a windowed drum The Red, Green and Blue Velvet Rooms have richly gilded coffered ceiling: Venetian windows and pedimented door casings, carvings, chimneypieces. Th roundels in the Blue Room are of Inigo Jones (by Dobson) and Pope (by Kent) Along the west front runs the **gallery** which consists of three rooms: the apse oblong central room communicates through arches to circular and octagonal en rooms, their space and sparkle exaggerated by being reflected and refracted b mirrors. From the octagonal room a passage leads north into the upper store of the link building which is adorned with Corinthian columns.

Gardens – The gardens were landscaped mostly by Kent who planted the giant cedar and modified Burlington's earlier geometrical plan of avenues and formal vistas; th canal was adapted into a series of serpentine curves, while temples, obelisks an statues were strategically placed so as to catch the stroller unawares. Georgian made the design even less formal and commissioned Wyatt to build a bridge acros the water. The greenhouse was probably the work of Joseph Paxton from Chats worth. Italian formal gardens were laid out providing a brilliant pattern of colou The Inigo Jones Gateway *(northeast of the house)* was erected in 1621 outsid Beaufort House in Chelsea and presented to the 3rd Earl of Burlington by Sir Han Sloane in 1736.

Around the corner stands Hogarth's House, the very antithesis of William Kent' Italianate taste.

★Hogarth's House ⊙ – *Immediately on the left down the west carriageway of th Great West Road after the Hogarth Roundabout.* William Hogarth was 52 and we established when he acquired the 3-storey brick house which he called his 'littl country box by the Thames', and to which he added a hanging bay window abov the front door. The mulberry tree in the small garden was alive in his day. H spent not only the summer but ever longer periods at Chiswick, entertaining suc contemporaries as David Garrick.

Hogarth found fame as a commentator on 18C London life and the house display several 'Conversation pieces' collected by contemporaries who recognised in then personalities of the day: *The Election, London Scenes, The Harlot's Progress Marriage à la Mode* and many more.

Across the Hogarth roundabout stands the **Fuller, Smith and Turner Griffin Brewery** ⊙ which was relocated from Bedford House in Chiswick Mall.

William Hogarth (1697-1764)

Born the son of a bankrupted author near Bart's Hospital, Hogarth started work apprenticed as an engraver to a silversmith while living in Leicester Fields (now Leicester Square). Recognising the need for a formal training he enrolled at St Martin's Lane Academy but failed to grapple academic figur- ative painting in the grand manner. Instead, he developed the 'conversation piece' (1729), a more informal type of portraiture representing his middle- class sitters in domestic interiors – a reflection perhaps of his own happy marriage to Sarah Thornhill, daughter of Sir James, the great English decorator of St Paul's Cathedral (Greenwich Hospital and Hampton Court). For these uncontroversial representations of contemporary life, depicted in literature by Daniel Defoe *(Moll Flanders)* and Samuel Richardson *(Clarissa)*, Hogarth must have drawn inspiration from the theatre of John Gay *(The Beggar's Opera)*: in describing his 'moralities' – *Rake's Progress* (1735), *Marriage à la Mode* (1743-5) – he writes: 'I therefore wished to compose pictures on canvas, similar to representations on the stage; and farther hope, that they will be tried by the same test, and criticised by the same criterion... I have endeavoured to treat my subjects as a dramatic writer; my picture is my stage, and men and women my players, who by means of certain actions and gestures, are to exhibit a *dumb show.*' His acute powers of observation, innate humour and sharp wit animate his narrative pictures which found a large audience when copied and reproduced as engravings. Admirers recognised their contemporaries lampooned by caricatures and sympathised with the artist's patriotism as a defender of things 'English'. Aware and sensitive to the hardship of life in London as portrayed in his prints (child mortality, alcoholism, prostitution and corruption, cruelty to animals), Hogarth was appointed governor of Captain Coram's charitable institution, the Foundling Hospital in Bloomsbury.

St Nicholas Parish Church ⊘ – The site was mentioned in 1181 and the list of vicars traces incumbents, with a few gaps, by name from 1225. This deceptively broad church has a buttressed and battlemented west tower (1436); the rest dates from the 1880s as do the highly decorative windows; the chancel ceiling has been blackened by fire. The ring of eight bells includes five hung in 1656, reputedly because of the intervention of the parishioner Lady Mary Fauconberg, daughter of Oliver Cromwell: in the family vault below the chancel are three coffins, the shortest possibly holding the headless body of Cromwell, exhumed from Westminster Abbey and rescued from Tyburn in 1661. In the churchyard lie **Hogarth** (enclosed with railings) – under David Garrick's epitaph 'Farewell, Great Painter of Mankind'; Lord Burlington; William Kent; **J M Whistler**; Philippe de Loutherbourg; the Italian poet Ugo Foscolo (disinterred and re-buried in Florence).

Chiswick Square – *Burlington Lane*. Low two-storey houses (1680) flank a forecourt in front of the three-storey Boston House (1740) where, in the novel *Vanity Fair* by Thackeray, Becky Sharp threw away her dictionary.

★★**Chiswick Mall** – Elegant 18C-19C houses, with bow windows and balconies, overlook the river: **Morton House** (1730) is built of brick with red brick surrounds to the windows of its three storeys; **Strawberry House** (1735) has six bays, two floors surmounted by attic dormers, a wide central balcony supported on iron pillars and slender fluted pillars outlining the porch; **Walpole House**, begun in the 16C and enlarged in the 17C, presents an irregular advanced brick face preceded by a fine iron gate and railings; in the 18C it was the residence of Barbara Villiers, Duchess of Cleveland, in her latter days (d 1709); in the 19C it became a school with Thackeray among its pupils.

CLAPHAM

Map p 297 (**UY**)
⊖ Clapham Common

Clapham village expanded into a fashionable residential area in the 17C and 18C as citizens moved out of London to avoid epidemics and frequent City fires, notably the Great Fire (1666) which destroyed so many City merchants' houses. Around the common rose mansions and terraces for the prosperous, houses in dependent streets for the more modest and, in the 19C, terrace houses and shops along the High Street. The original inhabitants, others of low income and the very poor congregated round the railway, particularly Clapham Junction (known first as Battersea), built in 1845. By the late 19C it had become and has remained Britain's busiest junction handling some 2 000 trains daily.

Public transport began modestly enough in the early 18C with a single stage coach making the journey daily from Clapham village to Gracechurch Street. A century later (1827) the service had expanded into 'short stage' coaches travelling several times a day to the City, Westminster, Piccadilly Circus and Holborn. By 1839 there were horse-drawn omnibuses operated by twelve rival companies. 1870 saw the tube (Clapham Common station), 1903 the first electric tram and 1912 the first motor omnibus. Gone were the days of highwaymen on the common (the last hold-up was in 1801), of roads being so poor that it took several hours to reach the capital: Clapham, the site of a Roman battle, a medieval village, 'pretty suburb' in the words of William Thackeray, had become a part of the great metropolis.

Among Clapham's famous men are the social reformer William Wilberforce (1759-1833); Lord Macaulay (1800-59) who grew up in a house on the Pavement; Thomas Hood (1799-1845) who went to school on North Side; Lytton Strachey (1880-1932) born at Stower House; Henry Cavendish (1731-1810), who retired to a house in the road now named after him; Cardinal Bourne (1861-1935), Archbishop of Westminster, born at Larkhall Rise and ordained at St Mary's, Clapham.

Holy Trinity – The church at the northeast corner of the common was erected in 1776 to replace the parish church which had fallen into ruin. The rectangular stone quoined building with two tiers of plain, round-headed windows, was embellished, in keeping with growing local prosperity, by the addition of the giant columned portico and clock tower turret in 1872.

North Side – The long mellow brick terrace with an archway in the west end houses dates from 1720. Many of the doorways, windows, iron gates and arches are original *(nos 14, 16, 21)*. **Clarence House** is credited with being the home of Captain Cook (1728-79), Chase Lodge on the corner of The Chase, as the oldest house in Clapham. No 29 opposite is a grand Georgian mansion which was for years the home of Sir Charles Barry, architect of the Houses of Parliament (now Clapham Trinity Hospice). **Cedar** and **Thornton Terraces** (flanking Cedars Road) epitomise hybrid Victorian French Renaissance revivalism: round and flat topped windows with coarse iron infillings, cornices, balconies, are crowned by high pavilion slate roofs coronetted with ironwork.

Old Town – *Northeast end of North Side*. This road which leads into Rectory Grove and St Paul's Church beyond, is graced with a few modest Georgian houses and short terraces: nos 39-43 is a group of mellow red brick with uniform windows and dormers; no 4, proudly sports two royal warrants, an unusual façade with a projecting upraised and pillared porch and two half moon windows. No 23, St Peter's Vicarage, has round-headed ground floor windows and an early iron gateway with an overhead arch. No 52 Rectory Grove is unique in its Coade stone decoration including a false arch on the side wall.

St Paul's Church – By 1232, and probably long before, there was a parish church by the name of Holy Trinity in Clapham; by 1774-76 it had fallen into ruin and had been superseded by the new Holy Trinity; in 1814 a plain Georgian brick building was erected in which there are several interesting monuments *(southeast end)* to past residents (1401, 1589, 1647, 1689 Sir Richard Atkins in full armour, his wife and three children, lords of the manor from 1590; 1715 Richard Hewer, naval administrator and friend of Samuel Pepys; 1849 a tablet records the death of John Hatchard, who with a capital of £5 in his pocket founded the bookshop in Piccadilly in 1797).

Crescent Grove – *Off Clapham Common South Side*. Only the grove, a wide ar and terrace of identical tall stucco houses, remains entire of the extensive Clapham Park Estate laid out by **Thomas Cubitt** *(see index)* as a series of squares and crescents in the 1870s.

DOCKLANDS ★

Map pp 10-11 **(HJKL-XYZ)**

'Docklands' stretches across a great swathe of land south of the East End between the Tower of London and Woolwich. Under the Docklands Joint Committee established in the 1970s, and its successor the London Docklands Development Corporation (LDDC) established in 1981, the redundant London docks have been transformed into a modern annexe to the City, thus regenerating the riverside communities: Wapping, Isle of Dogs and Silvertown – some 5 000 acres extending 8 miles east of Tower Bridge on the north bank and Bermondsey and Rotherhithe on the south bank.

The area is accessed by an efficient automated overground light transport facility, the **Docklands Light Railway** (1987), and the Jubilee Line of the underground network.

WAPPING

⊖ *Tower Hill, Wapping, Shadwell; DLR: Tower Gateway, Shadwell*

The Romans built a signal station at Wapping, which was just a village beside the Thames until the 16C when a continuous riverside sprawl began to develop; in 1598 Stow was describing the riverside, east from St Katharine, as a 'continual street... or filthy strait passage, with alleys of small tenements or cottages inhabited by sailors, victuallers almost to Radcliffe and Radcliffe itself hath been also increased in building eastward (to) Limehouse'.

Radcliffe was well known for ship building and repairs; Samuel Pepys took the boat at Radcliffe Stairs to cross to Deptford. In the past there were many stairs (landing places) along the densely populated waterfront cut by alleys, steps, stages and docks, where Charles Dickens set several of his novels.

Commercial Docks – The first docks to be built in Wapping were the **London Docks** (1805) which handled imports of tobacco, rice, wine and brandy; they consisted of the West Basin, the East Basin and the Shadwell Basin. The **St Katharine Docks**, built in 1828, consisted of two basins surrounded by warehouses (25 acres) designed by **Thomas Telford**. The two enterprises eventually amalgamated; they were damaged by bombing during the war and finally closed in 1969. The London Docks were in-filled and redeveloped as the offices of News International (1986) responsible for publishing *The Times* and *Sunday Times*. The radical move into using computers for newspaper production and distribution irrevocably emancipated the industry from Fleet Street working practices.

St John's Wharf and Gun Wharf warehouses on the waterfront have been converted into luxury flats.

★ **St Katharine Dock** – The dock take its name from the **Hospital of St Katharine by the Tower** a medieval community founded in 1148 by Queen Matilda, the first of an unbroken succession of royal patrons, which traded from its own wharves. Located as it was outside the City, within which no immigrant might live, it soon had its own hospital travellers' hostel and refugee settlement. Among the first to be sheltered were the

St Katharine Dock

English, forced to quit Calais in 1558: Flemings, Huguenots and others soon followed. By the 18C the overcrowded settlement numbered nearly 3 000. When the site was sold in the 19C, the Community moved to Regent's Park but returned to Wapping in the 1920s.

In 1968 the 19C dock basins were converted into a **yacht marina**; Telford's Italianate building, renamed **Ivory house**, was transformed into residential units and arcades of shops; part of a pre-1820 timber brewery built of European redwood and discovered within the brick cladding of one of the old cooperage and sugar-crushing house, was re-sited and converted into a three-storey restaurant and pub, the **Dickens Inn**; other warehouses were demolished; the **Coronarium Chapel** ⊘ which was consecrated in June 1977 to commemorate the medieval hospice, consists of seven Doric metal columns from a former warehouse arranged in a circle around a plastic sculpture of an irradiated crown.

New buildings on the dockside accommodate the **World Trade Centre** *(east side)*, the **London Commodity Exchange** ⊘ *(north side)* which trades in commodity futures (cocoa, coffee, sugar, pork bellies, etc.) and the **International Petrol Exchange**.

★**Tobacco Dock** ⊘ – *The Highway*. The beautiful brick vaults and cast-iron superstructure of the Skin Floor (1811-13) of the London Docks, have been converted into a shopping and entertainments complex.

At the rear on the canal are moored the *Sea Lark*, an American-built schooner which ran the blockade from 1810 to 1814, ceased trading in 1885, and now tells the classic adventure of *Kidnapped* by R L Stevenson. The *Three Sisters*, a replica of the original which traded from 1788 to 1854, traces the history of piracy, on three decks.

St George-in-the-East ⊘ – *Cannon Street Road or Cable Street*. The church, which was designed by Hawksmoor and consecrated in 1729, was severely damaged in 1941; after the war a modern church (1964) was built within the 18C shell. The **tower** comprising a two-tier octagonal lantern squarely buttressed and crowned with a balustrade and flat-topped sculptured drums, is the most distinctive in the East End.

St Paul's Church ⊘ – In the 17C and 18C it was known as the Church of the Sea Captains, one of whom was Captain Cook.

Old Pumping Station – The attractive old building, which was originally a pumping station providing hydraulic power (1892-1977), is used as a rehearsal hall and recording studio by the Academy of St-Martin-in-the-Fields *(see TRAFALGAR SQUARE)*.

Wapping Pier – The two parallel terraces of 18C houses, which originally flanked the entrance to the London Docks were built for dock officials.

River Police Boat Yard – The modern building houses the 33 craft of the **Metropolitan Special Constabulary** (Thames Division), which patrols the last 54 miles of the River Thames. The original River Police were established in 1798.

Waterfront Pubs – A few of the once numerous riverside pubs have survived. **The Town of Ramsgate**, named after the fishermen who unloaded their catches here, sits by Execution Dock where the bodies of pirates and thieves condemned to death by hanging (Captain Kidd in 1701) were left for the tide to wash over them three times. **The Prospect of Whitby** (1520), possibly the oldest riverside public house in London, was once called the Devil's Tavern, frequented by muggers and thieves. It was later patronised by the likes of Turner, Whistler, Gustave Doré and a particular local market-gardener who in 1780 persuaded a young sailor, newly returned from the West Indies, to part with a cutting of some hitherto unknown plant, later called a fuchsia, in exchange for a noggin of rum. The **Barleymow** was formerly the Dockmaster's House. **The Grapes** dates back to the 18C appearing as *The Six Jolly Fellowship Porters* in *Our Mutual Friend* by Charles Dickens.

St Katharine – *Butcher Row*. In the 1920s the St Katharine Community *(see above)* returned from Regent's Park to the Thames and settled in new buildings in Limehouse next to St James's Park.

Captain Kidd was dispatched by William III (1700) to curtail increased pirate activity on the high seas. Bored by long periods off-shore his crew began rioting on board; the captain ended up murdering a man, for which he would have to face the death penalty. He therefore decided to turn his own hand at piracy and raised the Jolly Roger. Captured and repatriated, he was tried on 3 May 1701 and hanged at Execution Dock; the first time the rope stretched and broke, the second time he was less lucky.

LIMEHOUSE *DLR Limehouse*

Limehouse Basin – From Dunbar Wharf, Pale India Ale, brewed locally, was shipped to India and Australia. **Regent's Canal Dock**, built in 1820 and enlarged in 1836, 1852 and 1865, used to acccommodate barges coming down the Regent's Canal to the Thames, or into the Lea Navigation canal system via the Limehouse Cut (1 miles long).

St Anne's Limehouse ⊘ – A distinctive square tower marks Hawksmoor's first church in the East End of London (1712-24).

★ISLE OF DOGS
DLR: West India Quay, Canary Wharf, Crossharbour, Island Gardens

The Isle of Dogs is a tongue of land round which the Thames makes a huge loop south from Limehouse to Blackwall, dominated today by the slick outline of Canary Wharf tower. Some say the Island acquired its name from the loud howling and baying of hounds kennelled on the north bank when 'the Queen' or 'her Dad', alluding to Elizabeth I and Henry VIII, were in residence at Greenwich. For centuries the marshy pastures were used to fatten cattle for the City; a single track led south to the Greenwich ferry. In the 19C the Island developed into a densely-populated industrial district with three dock systems. In the fifty years from 1850 to 1900 the population grew from 5 000 to 21 000. Since the docks were closed to shipping in 1980, the area, a designated 'Enterprise Zone' has been transformed under the auspices of the LDDC into a hi-tech commercial alternative to the City.

West India Docks –
Extensive development of
the Island began early in
the 19C when the **West India
Docks** (Import Dock 1802
and Export Dock 1806)
were built to receive rum

Mystery still surrounds the **Limehouse Porcelain Factory** (1747-48) which according to
some would have been the first to make
soft paste porcelain in England.

and sugar from the West Indies. They were the first commercial wet docks built in
London, enclosed by a high brick wall and patrolled by their own police force;
warehouses and other buildings were designed by George Gwilt. The **City Canal**
(1805), built to provide a direct passage for ships from Blackwall to the London
Docks in Wapping, was transformed into a dock in 1870.

★★**Canary Wharf** – The overseer of this ambitious project, sponsored entirely by
private funding, fell to Skidmore, Owings and Merrill. Development was managed
in phases, initiated with the construction of the seven buildings suspended in part
over water, enclosing **Cabot Square**. As intended, these buildings conceived to exude
corporate power are dominated by Cesar Pelli's tower block **1 Canada Square**
(800ft-50 floors), which he described as 'a square prism with pyramidal top in the
traditional form of the obelisk, which is the most archetypal way of creating a
vertical architectural sign... this is the essence of the skyscraper.' Critics have
alluded to it as a monument to the age of Margaret Thatcher, which also witnessed
the demise of the property developers Olympia & York (1992) and Paul Reichman,
the entrepreneur behind Battery Park in New York. However, in 1995 an investor
group headed by Reichman has regained ownership of Canary Wharf which has
been floated on the stock market in 1999.

The tallest towerblock in London, it is also the first to be clad in stainless steel, a
reminder perhaps of its hi-tech purpose and to reflect light like a beacon visible for
many miles across the flat riverside landscape.

Ships belonging to the **Maritime Trust** are sometimes moored in the docks. The
development also houses a concert hall, restaurants, pubs and shops and open
spaces.

Canary Wharf

311

The blue-glass South Quay Plaza shimmers with reflections from the still waters. It is remarkable for having been constructed in record-breaking times: Peterborough House, the **Daily Telegraph** editorial offices were erected in a mere 74 weeks. In January 1996, this area was severely damaged by an IRA bomb. By 1999 eleven buildings in the scheme have been completed with seven under construction and Canary Wharf has attracted many prestigious firms including investment banks.

Old West India Dock Buildings – At the west end of the old import (north) dock stand the **Cannon Workshops**, so called because a cannon once stood at the entrance, now occupied by a number of small businesses; they were formerly the Quadrangle Buildings (1824), built to provide offices, stores, a cooperage and engineering shops. To the north stands the old **Dockmaster's House**. The north quay of the dock is lined by two **warehouses** (1802), designed by George Gwilt, the earliest multi-storey warehouses surviving in London.

New Billingsgate Market – The wholesale fish market moved from Old Billingsgate *(see CITY – Monument)* in the City to its new tentlike building in 1982.

Millwall Docks – The name Millwall recalls the windmills which once lined the west bank of the peninsula. The **Millwall Docks** (1868) were built on the site of earlier shipyards: Napier's Yard where Brunel's *Great Eastern* was launched in 1858 and Yarrows which moved to the Clyde in 1904. Their 9 metre draft was required in order to accommodate the larger ships bringing cargoes of grain and timber.

Mudchute Park ⊘ – The open space by the banks of a stream supports a riding stables and small urban farm. Earlier in the 20C the park was divided into allotments. The name Mudchute recalls how silt dredged from the Millwall docks was deposited here by a special machine.

Island Gardens – The riverside garden, which was opened in 1895 by the Commissioners of the Royal Naval Hospital at Greenwich, provides a famous **view**★★★ south to Greenwich and the Royal Naval College which laid out the garden to improve its own view north.

Footway Tunnel – *Open daily.* In the round domed building beside the river a lift (or 100 steps) leads down to a foot tunnel beneath the Thames *(10min)* to Greenwich.

Cubitt Town – Little remains of the community developments financed by the property speculator Sir William Cubitt in 1843 for Irish labourers, save **Christ Church (Manchester Road)**, a Victorian Gothic church (1857).

Island History Trust ⊘ – *Island House, Roserton Street.* The Trust, which is mainly of interest to people with a local connection, maintains an extensive archive of photographs about living on the Island and organises open days and bi-annual festivals of local history, recollection and reunion.

Glengall Bridge – The blue Dutch-design lifting bridge (1969) marks the eastern entrance to the City Canal *(see above)*.

The Gun pub dates from the 15C and from time to time Lady Hamilton stayed in the upper room. It is rumoured that her ghost haunts the building, which people say is connected by a passage to a house occupied by Nelson.

BLACKWALL *DLR: All Saints*

When in 1600 Queen Elizabeth granted a charter to the **East India Company**, it established a shipbuilding and repair yard at **Blackwall** where it landed its cargoes – although excavations have since found traces of far earlier ships, notably of Roman and Viking origins. Its offices were in the city on the site now occupied by Lloyd's *(see CITY)*. Houses and inns developed on either side of Poplar High Street, an important thoroughfare busy with traffic between the City and Blackwall, where some passengers would disembark to complete their journey to London more quickly by coach. In 1776 the company built St Mathias Church (now a nursery) with seven mighty masts to support the roof. Brunswick Dock was built by the company in 1789 and equipped with a mast house, seven storeys high, which was an important landmark until it was demolished in 1862; in 1806 this dock was incorporated into the new **East India Docks**.

> The statue by W Wyon (1865) on East India Dock Road shows **Richard Green** seated with his dog and scenes of 19C shipbuilding on the west side of the base. The Green family owned the Blackwall shipyard and were local benefactors.

Whitebait Dinners

Blackwall was associated with the 19C political whitebait dinners. The Bruns-wick Hotel and Tavern, built in 1835 by the East India Company at Black-wall, was patronised by the Fox Club, adherents of Charles James Fox *(see index);* their political opponents, Sir William Pitt, Gladstone and their Whig followers dined at Greenwich where the tradition of whitebait dinners still thrives (Trafalgar Tavern).

Early 17C emigrants to America and later mid 19C emigrants to Australia and New Zealand sailed from Blackwall. In 1812 the congestion in Poplar High Street was so great that the East India Dock Road and Commercial Road were created.
The Blackwall yard made its name with fast clipper ships and later with iron ships; in 1943 the East India Import Dock was used for the construction of the Phoenix units of the floating Mulberry harbour used in the D-day Normandy landings in 1944. Today, just above the Blackwall Tunnel, impressive modern buildings along-side the *Financial Times* printworks accommodate the Town Hall.

Blackwall Tunnel – The Old Tunnel (1897) was built for vehicles and pedestrians; it has carried only northbound traffic since the New Tunnel (1963) was built for vehicles travelling south.

Financial Times Printworks – *240 East India Dock Road.* The award-winning building (1988) was designed by Nicholas Grimshaw for housing offices, plate-making rooms and printing presses, visible through the Pilkington Planar glass front.
Alongside stands **Telehouse,** a blind stronghold for communication technology.

Reuters Docklands Centre – *Blackwall Yard.* In this building designed by Richard Rogers, function dominates aesthetic considerations: black glass preserves anonym-ity and ensures security. As with the Lloyds Building, the austerity of the architec-ture is relieved by coloured service-ducts.

Bow Creek – This is the name given to the estuary of the River Lea. In the 18C it was the site of the famous Thames Ironworks which was also a shipbuilding yard from 1846 to 1912.
For details of the Royal Docks and the Thames Barrier, see Outer London: SILVER-TOWN – NORTH WOOLWICH and WOOLWICH – CHARLTON.

DULWICH ★

Map p 11 **(UYZ)**
Overground: West Dulwich from Blackfriars

King Edgar bestowed the manor of Dilwihs on one of his thanes in AD 967. It was then owned by Bermondsey Abbey until the Reformation and in the 17C was acquired by Edward Alleyn *(see below).*
Dulwich's glory lies in its trees. The houses reflect the transition from 17C manorial village to small country town where 18C-19C city merchants and gentlemen chose to reside (a low triangular milestone on Red Post Hill *(north of railway station)* indicates that it is 4 miles to the Standard in Cornhill or the Treasury in Whitehall).
Commuter trains and cars have transformed it into a south London suburb; yet it remains rural in character, the main street, known as Dulwich Village, dividing at the green where Alleyn built his school.

DULWICH

★**Dulwich College** – **Edward Alleyn: man of the Theatre, founder of God's Gift,** born in 1566 the son of a City innkeeper, was by common consent one of the greatest actors of his day although Shakespeare disagreed and voiced his dislike in Hamlet's counsel to the Player King. His marriage in 1592 to the step-daughter of Philip Henslowe, theatrical businessman, leaser of plays, costumes and theatres, builder of the Rose Playhouse (1587), extended Alleyn's interests so that by 1605 he had virtually retired from the theatre and for £5 000 bought Dulwich manor. Having no heir, he established in 1613 a charity for 'six poor men and six poor women and the education of twelfe poor children', which he named the Chapel and College of God's Gift (1619).

Old College and Chapel – The buildings on the triangular site, where the main street divides, are entered through 18C iron gates surmounted by the Alleyn crest. Be-tween the much altered two-storeyed white building which still serves as alm-shouses, stands the central wing including the clock tower and door to the chapel where Alleyn is buried.

Dulwich Picture Gallery

★Dulwich Picture Gallery ⊙ – Dulwich Gallery, which opened in 1814, is the oldest public picture gallery in the country. Edward Alleyn bought pictures as a man of substance rather than a connoisseur: in 1618 he paid £2 for six royal portraits and later £2 13s 4d for a further eight crowned heads! His final collection of 39 pictures, including his own full length portrait, probably painted from a death mask, was later increased by 80 likenesses of contemporary authors and players: Michael Drayton, Richard Lovelace, **Burbage**, Nat Field (now mostly in the East Room).

In 1811 a double legacy of 400 pictures necessitated the construction of a special gallery. This gift originated with a Frenchman, **Noel Joseph Desenfans**, unsuccessful language teacher, who changed his profession to become the richest picture dealer of his day. Among his patrons was King Stanislaus of Poland who commissioned a gallery but abdicated in 1795 before paying for the paintings which Desenfans incorporated in his own collection and left to his widow and his friend, **Sir Francis Bourgeois**, who chose Dulwich as the gallery site. Mrs Desenfans contributed £6 000, suggested Sir John Soane as architect and presented the furniture still on display.

The building – Sir John Soane was given a free hand in 1811 and three years later the gallery, much as it is today, was opened. The plain exterior belies the skilful inside plan: facing the central entrance, on the far side of two adjoining square galleries is the small domed mausoleum of the founders, Sir Francis Bourgeois, Noel Desenfans and his wife: symmetrically dependent on this central suite are oblong and final square galleries of subtly varied dimensions. The rooms are ingeniously lit by skylights, and the walls have been restored to their original red colour. An extension (1999) comprises an elegant cloister in glass and bronze linking the gallery to a new wing which provides more display space and better facilities.

The pictures – Several landscapes by **Aelbert Cuyp**, three superb **Rembrandts** including *The Girl at a Window* and *Titus*, 17C and 18C landscapes and pastorals by **Poussin**, Claude, Watteau and Lancret; **Gainsborough** portraits of the Linley family, a **Reynolds** self portrait and portrait of *Mrs Siddons* are among the highlights of the collection which also includes works by Van Dyck, Teniers the Younger, Raphael, Tiepolo, Canaletto, Rubens, Murillo (peasant boys and *Flower Girl*), Reni, Rosa, Lebrun, Guercino and Veronese – although some may be on temporary loan to other galleries. Secondary pictures hang high above the Old, or modern (Francis Bacon) Masters.

Dulwich Village – Pond House, Village Way, at the opening of the Village, is a three storey house with spanking white trims, a delicate balustrade edging the roof at the rear and a round headed door complemented by the curving lines of the porch, steps and balustrades.

Nos 60, 62 – **The Laurels, The Hollies** – date from 1767. In the 18C the ironwork canopy on iron pillars over the pavement shaded the fare of the village butcher. Nos 93 and 95 – North and South – Houses are of a later date. Nos 97-105 is an 18C terrace, the last two houses mid 1700s.

College Road – On the pair, nos 13 and 15 built c 1765, note the early Sun Insurance fireplate. The small house at no 31, Pickwick Cottage, is said to be where Dickens envisaged Mr Pickwick retiring. Bell Cottage *(no 23)* is a rare example of the once common small white weatherboarded local cottages; by contrast the brick-built Bell House dates from 1767.

Dulwich College, now nearly 1 400 strong, is housed in buildings of 1866-70 designed by Charles Barry in Italian Renaissance style, complete with a stout campanile. Great crested iron gates mark the entrance in College Road.

Pond Cottages (beyond the main road, Dulwich Common) is an 18C group over-looking the Mill Pond, several wholly or partly weatherboarded. The **Toll Gate** is the last in use in the London area: charges at one time were registered as 6d or 10d for 'a score of beasts'...

Kingswood House – *Seeley Drive*. The castellated house built of ragstone in 19C baronial style, was known, when the owner was the founder of the meat extract firm, as Bovril Castle! The Jacobean style interior now serves as a library and community centre.

ENVIRONS

★**Horniman Museum and Gardens** ⊘ – *London Road, Forest Hill*. Tribal masks, Buddhas, lutes and bagpipes line one's path until suddenly there is the walrus. This museum is one of great variety, re-arranged and displayed in modern manner but continuing the enquiring tradition of its founder, Frederick John Horniman (1836-1906), tea merchant and MP. Successful private views decided Horniman to con-struct a museum, which was designed by Harrison Townsend (1901) in *art nouveau* style; Horniman then presented it 'as a gift to the people of London'. A mosaic by Anning Bell decorates the façade. The founder's conservatory and some beautiful gardens are to be found in the park (16 acres).

Church of the Resurrection (RC) – *Kirkdale, Upper Sydenham*. The low fortress building of yellow brick is lancet windowed and buttressed (D A Reid: 1973-74). Surmounting the plain wooden door is a bronze and lead relief of Christ showing his wounds as the shroud drops away (Stephen Sykes).

St Antholin Spire, Roundhill – *Dartmouth Road, Forest Hill*. The slender stone spire by Wren with dragon's head weathervane, purchased in 1874 on the church's demolition by a City master printer to adorn his estate, now stands beside a cedar, at the centre of a modern housing estate.

★**Crystal Palace Park** ⊘ – The park is now the site of the **National Sports Centre**, a sports complex, built to Olympic standards. It also contains a variety of entertain-ments for all ages: a farmyard, 29 life-size dinosaur models, a funfair, a lake *(boating, summer concerts)*.

The Crystal Palace, an enormous cast-iron and glass structure, was designed by Joseph Paxton to house the Great Exhibition *(see SOUTH KENSINGTON)* held in Hyde Park in 1851. When the exhibition closed, the palace was re-erected on Sydenham Hill, where it served as a place of public entertainment until 1936, when it was destroyed by fire. Its successful new role led to imitations: Alexandra Palace *(see Outer London HAMPSTEAD – HIGHGATE)* in north London and Albert Palace *(demol-ished)* in Battersea. The twin water towers (290ft high) designed by Brunel survived the fire but were demolished five years later for fear that they would serve as land-marks to enemy bombers. A familiar modern landmark is the TV relay mast.

EALING

Map p 296 (TY)
⊖ Ealing Broadway, South Ealing, Acton Town

With the arrival of the railway in 1838 Ealing grew from a small village into a residential town with a dignified Town Hall (1888), attractive Georgian cottages and 19C houses surrounded by parks. The old parish church of St Mary (1739, rebuilt 866) contains 17C and 18C tablets and memorials.

Ealing Abbey, St Benedict's RC Church – *Charlbury Grove*. This once powerful community founded in the Middle Ages grew from the small number of Benedictines sent by Pope Gregory to England in the 6C; it was dissolved in the 16C by Henry VIII. The re-established community has erected a new neo-Gothic abbey (1897-1935).

Pitshanger Manor Museum ⊘ – *Mattock Lane*. The south wing and central range only remain of the house built by **George Dance junior** in 1770, and bought by **John Soane** as a country villa in 1800. Soane retained the south wing containing an upper and a lower room, both of modest proportions with finely moulded plaster decorations and added, besides other rooms, an entrance of four colossal Ionic columns surmounted by standing figures before a high, ornamental screen. Many features reappear in the house in Lincoln's Inn Fields *(see CHANCERY LANE)*. Today the house displays a rare collection of **Martinware** (Doulton-style stoneware produced by the Martin brothers in Fulham (1873-77) and later at Norwood Green, Southall until 1914).

Katyn Memorial – *Kensington Cemetery*. The polished black granite obelisk crowned with a gold eagle was erected in 1976 in memory of the Polish officers massacred at Katyn during the Second World War.

EAST END

The East End of London includes the riverside communities on the north bank (see *Outer London: DOCKLANDS)* and the districts to the north, into which the population spread in the 17C, 18C and 19C as commercial and industrial activity increased Spitalfields, Whitechapel, Stepney, Mile End and Bethnal Green, names which became synonymous with overcrowding and poverty.

Urbanisation – The odd manor was recorded in the Domesday Book; by the 12C the population east of the City, grouped in small communities, had grown to 800, and the area east as far as the River Lea and north to Hackney Downs was entrusted to the constable and named Tower Hamlets (a name revived under the 1965 Local Government Act).

In the first instance, the population was swelled by the arrival of English craftsmen woodworkers, boat-builders and masons, then 10 000 freed slaves who fled to the waterside to work as dockers. In the 16C Dutch traders and craftsmen began to settle: leatherworkers, nail and locksmiths. The overcrowding was further exacerbated by many waves of refugees: Dutch and French Huguenots (13 000 French arrived in 1687), Irish, Jews, Chinese – the latter settled near Limehouse Causeway.

From the 16C to the 19C houses were used as workshops, factories and dwellings families moved on as soon as they had the means to leave the appalling conditions which were starkly described by Mayhew in his *Survey of the London Poor* (1850). In the 20C many of the slums were demolished and replaced by more modern low-cost housing, inhabited by immigrants from the West Indies, India, Pakistan and Bangladesh...

Institutions – Several national or famous philanthropic institutions were born in the East End of London. These include **Dr Barnardo's** first children's home (1874) in Stepney; Toynbee Hall *(Commercial Street),* the first **university settlement**, instituted in 1884; the **Salvation Army** began on Trinity Green in the Mile End Road.

The **Salvation Army**, founded in 1765, was organised strictly on a military basis requiring 'unquestionable obedience' and complete self-denial from its members. It rejects all sacraments and stresses the moral side of Christianity; aggressive and direct in its recruiting methods, the Salvation Army rallies its forces at open-air meetings with brass bands and banners. Its aspirations, however, are dedicated to major social activities and rescue work; the army cares for animals, runs soup kitchens, workers' hostels, night shelters, hospitals and schools.

The **London Hospital**, which now operates on three sites, was founded in 1740 by John Harrison, a young surgeon, with six others in a tavern in Cheapside; it started as the London Infirmary in a house near Bunhill Fields *(see CLERKENWELL),* soon removed to Prescot Street in Wapping and thence to Whitechapel in 1757. A display of archive material is accommodated in the crypt of the former hospital church St Augustine with St Philip.

Queen Mary College, which was incorporated in the University of London in 1905 originated in the mid 19C as the Philosophical Institute in a grand building and library, it was taken over by the Drapers' Company which reconceived it as a People's Palace combining education with gymnastics, swimming, music, etc., taking its present name in 1934 upon receiving a Royal Charter. Later it merged with the Bromley and Bow Institute to form the **East London College** and become part of London University. The College is housed in a terracotta brick and stone building (1885), fronted by a wide forecourt on the Mile End Road, and in additional buildings of glass, brick and concrete (1950s).

Jewish Community – The Jewish community in the East End, which in 1850 consisted of a ghetto round Petticoat Lane, grew rapidly in the 1880s with the influx of 100 000 Russian and Polish Jews and about 20 000 German, Austrian, Dutch and Romanian Jews (Baptist meeting house converted to Synagogue at 48-50 Artillery Lane in 1896). By 1914 the East End of London contained the largest Jewish community in England.

As they became more affluent, they moved away to the outer suburbs of London or abroad; as numbers dwindled their synagogues disappeared as did the Jew's Free School (founded about 1821) and Jewish Care, the successor to the Jewish Board of Guardians *(plaque: 129 Middlesex Street)* founded in 1859 to help the poorer immigrants by offering evening classes in English, sewing classes, apprenticeships and interest-free loans. Among the few landmarks that have survived is the **Brady Street Cemetery** (1761-1858) where **Nathan Mayer Rothschild** *(see INTRODUCTION)* is buried.

SHOREDITCH ⊖ *Old Street*

In the reign of Elizabeth I, when theatrical performances were disapproved of and frequently banned by the City authorities, many theatre folk lived in and around Shoreditch. The first English playhouse, **The Theatre**, was founded within the precincts of the former Holywell Priory in Shoreditch in 1576 by **James Burbage** (d 1597) a joiner by trade who became head of Lord Leicester's players; he also founded the **Little Curtain** named after the curtain wall of the enclosure. In 1597 The Theatre in Shoreditch was pulled down, on the orders of the Privy Council, and the materials were used by James' son Cuthbert (d 1635) to build the **Globe** (*see BANKSIDE*) on the South Bank in 1599; his other son **Richard Burbage** (d 1619) was the first actor to play *Richard III* and *Hamlet* – all three lie buried in St Leonard's Church.

St Leonard's Church ⊙ – *119 Shoreditch High Street*. The mid 18C building with its 192ft spire replaces another earlier church. Within its precincts were buried one of Henry VIII's court jesters William Somers (d 1560); one of Queen Elizabeth's players, Richard Tarleton (d 1588); James **Burbage** (d 1597) and his sons Cuthbert and Richard; Gabriel Spencer (d 1598), a player at the Rose Theatre who was killed by Ben Jonson (*see WESTMINSTER*); William Sly (d 1608) and Richard Cowley (d 1619), players at the Globe on Bankside.

Housing – From the late Middle Ages the City Companies and a few endowed charities provided almshouses for a small number of old employees; working citizens lodged in their own houses or rented what they could – a room or part of a room in the case of the very poor; many lived on the streets, especially orphan children.
The first major housing scheme was financed by the American philanthropist **George Peabody**, who in 1864 constructed in Commercial Street in Spitalfields a massive 5-storey building of 3-room flats with running water, sanitation and laundry facilities available at 5s a week.

★Geffrye Museum ⊙ – *Kingsland Road*. The almshouses and chapel were erected around three sides of an open court planted with plane trees (1712-19) by the Ironmongers' Company with a bequest left by Sir Robert Geffrye, Lord Mayor. The two-storey brick buildings are decorated with continuous modilioned eaves; at the centre, marking the chapel, is a pediment and niche in which stands the periwigged figure of the founder.
Inside a series of rooms displays furniture and furnishings from Tudor times to the 1950s: including John Evelyn's Closet of Curiosities, several Georgian shopfronts and a woodworker's shop with bench and tools and, at the back, an open hearth kitchen. A distinctive horseshoe extension comprising two brick warehouses with pitched roofs and simple gable ends curves around a central light stairwell, an inspired architectural device. In the upper gallery, the new rooms take the collection to the present day and include a minimalist loft. In the grounds there is a large walled herb garden and other historic gardens.
For HACKNEY see separate listing.

SPITALFIELDS ⊖ *Aldgate East, Shoreditch*

The market (fruit, vegetables and flowers) was granted a royal charter by Charles II in 1682 and acquired by the City Corporation in 1902; in 1991 London's largest wholesale depot was moved to Leyton. Food shops abound, but the best market is held on Sundays. Look out for the mechanical railway sculpture...

Christ Church ⊙ – Hawksmoor's spire still dominates the area almost as it did when built in 1714-30, although now more starkly having been rebuilt in the 19C without the original dormers on each face, corner crockets and stone finial. It rises above a Classical west portico through an interplay of ascending circular bays and arches, dramatically cut by the horizontal lines of the entablature and cornice. At the east end a Venetian window is framed by paired niches beneath a pediment.
Fournier Street contains a series of handsome Georgian houses (1718-28), which were once occupied by silk weavers and merchants when Spitalfields silk was famous in the late 17C to mid 19C (*see VICTORIA & ALBERT MUSEUM*).

Brick Lane – The history of the **mosque**, which was built as a Christian chapel in 1743 and later became a synagogue, reflects the successive waves of immigrants who have lived in the district. On Sunday mornings, a bric-a-brac and second-hand clothes **market** spreads through the district around Bethnal Green Road, Cheshire Street.
The spacious glass-fronted reception area of **Truman's Brewery**, founded 1666, reveals older buildings round a cobbled yard.

WHITECHAPEL ⊖ Aldgate East

The gleaming white **Sedgwick** Centre (1986) houses a conference centre, sports complex and the Chaucer Theatre.

Whitechapel Art Gallery ⊘ – The gallery provides exhibition facilities for modern and contemporary art by non-established artists; Barbara **Hepworth** and David **Hockney** first showed their work here. The building (1901) was designed by C H Townsend; it is decorated with contemporary Arts and Crafts reliefs and surmounted by twin-angle turrets.

Passmore Edwards Library – The library was built in the Arts and Crafts style. In the entrance is a panel composed of decorated tiles depicting the Whitechapel Hay Market which flourished for over three hundred years until it was abolished in 1928 as an obstruction.

Whitechapel Bell Foundry – The foundry has been on its present site since 1738; its records go back to 1570 but it may be 150 years older. It has cast and recast, owing to fire in 1666 and the Second World War, the bells of St Mary-le-Bow, St Clement Dane's and Big Ben.

East London Mosque – The mosque was built in 1985 by the most recent immigrants who came from the Indian sub-continent.

BETHNAL GREEN ⊖ Shoreditch, Bethnal Green

St Matthew – The parish church of Bethnal Green was built (1743-46) by George Dance the Elder and the interior remodelled (1859-61) by Knightly. The **Watch House** (1826) stands in the southwest corner of the churchyard.
The west tower of Sir John Soane's **St John's Church** ⊘ (1825-28) though not high, is an easily distinguished landmark as it rises from a square clock stage, through a drum with blind arches to a vaned cupola.

Bethnal Green Museum of Childhood ⊘ – *Cambridge Heath Road.* The museum houses the Victoria & Albert Museum's collection of toys, dolls, dolls' houses, games, puppets, toy theatres and toy soldiers, as well as a collection of children's clothing, furniture, paintings, prints, photographs, books and other artefacts of childhood.
The building, the oldest surviving example of the type of pre-fabricated iron and glass construction utilised by Paxton (now with a brick encasement) was originally erected to contain items from the 1851 Exhibition *(see VICTORIA & ALBERT MUSEUM)*; it was re-erected and opened on the present site in 1872.

Mile End Road – ⊖ *Whitechapel.* The **Trinity Almshouses**, built by the Corporation of Trinity House in 1695 for '28 decay'd Masters and Comanders of ships' or their widows, form a terrace of basement and ground floor cottages around three sides of a tree-planted quadrangle.
On Trinity Green stands a statue (1979) of General William Booth erected on the 150th anniversary of his birthday to mark the site where he began the work of the Salvation Army.

STEPNEY ⊖ Stepney Green; DLR: Limehouse

St Dunstan and All Saints ⊘ – The church stands on an early Christian site; the later additional dedication to Dunstan the great divine, Bishop of London in the 10C, was made when Dunstan was canonized. The building dates from the 13C as do some of the memorials inside; the church registers go back to the early 16C. St Dunstan's is also known as the Church of the High Seas as the birth of anyone born at sea is registered in this parish.

Ragged School Museum ⊘ – *46 Copperfield Road.* Two Victorian warehouses (cranes and school bell on the façade) beside Regent's Canal, once occupied by one of Dr Barnado's Ragged (free) Schools, now house a small museum about the schools and their founder: Victorian schoolroom in which today's children can experience school at the end of the last century.

BOW ⊖ Bow Rd; DLR Bow Church

The district takes its name from the single arched 'bow' bridge built by Queen Matilda in the 12C over the River Lea.
In the 18C the medieval village of Bow, then surrounded by market gardens, was transformed into a residential suburb of the City.
Stranded on an island in the middle of Bow Road sits the 14C **St Mary, Stratford Bow Church.**

WEST HAM ⊖ *Bromley by Bow*

West Ham early developed into a manufacturing town owing to its position near the confluence of the navigable River Lea and the Thames and its proximity to London, where noxious industries were banned by the City authorities. As early as the 11C the Domesday Book recorded eight mills on Bow Creek. From the 17C onwards industrial activity diversified into calico and paper making, distilling and the manufacture of gunpowder at Congreve's rocket factory. In the 18C Bow Pottery was the largest porcelain factory in England; to its original blue and white pieces copied from Chinese porcelain, it added figures taken from mythology and natural history. At the end of the 19C there were about 300 companies in the area engaged in various industries: chemicals, engineering and metals, food, drink and tobacco, textiles, leather and clothing, timber and furniture, brick, pottery, cement and glass.

Three Mills ⊙ – At the north end of Bow Creek there is an attractive group of early industrial buildings. The **House Mill**, built in 1776 by Daniel Bisson, spans two waterways and four mill races and as such is the largest tide mill known in the country. It still contains six pairs of mill stones and four undershot water wheels which were driven by releasing the head of the water impounded at high tide. Some of the more modern equipment was removed in 1941 when work ceased because of the war. The original **miller's house** (demolished in the 1950s) has been reconstructed as part of the restored Georgian street front.
Granite setts and flagstones mark the path across to the **Clock Mill** which dates from 1817. The ornate clock tower, which is earlier, is surmounted by an octagonal turret, containing a bell and a weathervane. The conical caps of the two **drying kilns** are Victorian. Barge stands are visible in the river at low tide; they prevented the grain barges from being trapped in the mud at low water.

Abbey Mills Pumping Station – The impressive cruciform building, which houses sewage pumping machinery, was designed (1865-68) by Sir Joseph Bazalgette and Vulliamy in the Venetian Gothic style with an octagonal lantern above the crossing.

ELTHAM PALACE ★

Map p 297 **(UY)**
Overground: Eltham or Mottingham from London Bridge

South of Eltham and off Court Yard nestles a historical country retreat, a house of radical contrasts. Nine miles as the crow flies from London Bridge stands Eltham Palace, which is documented as being in the possession of Odo, Bishop of Bayeux and half-brother of William the Conqueror in 1086. From 1295 it was owned by Bek, Bishop of Durham who ceded it to Edward Prince of Wales (later Edward II) – the first of several monarchs to live there preferring it to Windsor which they found to be draughty by comparison, especially at Christmas time (Twelfth Night). By all accounts it would have been quite a large complex in the 14C, set amongst well stocked mature forest described by the chronicler Froissart as 'a very magnificent palace'. In 1390, under Richard II, Geoffrey Chaucer was Clerk of the Works here. Edward IV added the Great Hall in 1479-80; only foundations of Henry VI's royal apartments still remain; Henry VIII met Erasmus there, happy to live there until his interest in ships spurred him to move to Greenwich. During the Commonwealth, according to John Evelyn, it fell into 'miserable ruins' and was finally valued only as building material (£2 754). During the late 18C and 19C the place was more or less abandoned – painted as a Romantic folly by Turner and Girtin.
In 1931, it was leased to Mr Stephen Courtauld who restored the Great Hall and built his own distinctive 1930s country residence. When the Courtaulds moved to Scotland, the place was occupied by the Royal Army Corps (1945-92). It is now in the hands of English Heritage.

★**Eltham Palace** ⊙ – The house is approached over a fine stone bridge straddling the fish-filled moat. To the right of the Tudor House would have stood the chapel and 'My Lord Chancellor's lodging' *(34-38 Courtyard)* or the occasional residence of Cardinal Wolsey, who was installed as Lord Chancellor in the palace chapel.
The **Great Hall** (101ft long, 36ft wide and 56ft to the roof apex) is built of brick, faced with stone. Its chief glory, in all but the technical sense since the posts are tenoned, is the sweet-chestnut hammerbeam roof with a central hexagonal louvred section that once would have served to expel smoke from the large open hearth. Earlier than the roof at Hampton Court, Eltham narrowly predates that of Crosby Hall in Chelsea, and was almost certainly constructed by the king's master mason Thomas Jordan and carpenter Edmund Gravely. The windows are placed high in the wall, allowing for heavy tapestry hangings to insulate the lower sections. The wooden reredos was installed in the 1930s. Beyond the dais, reached via the oriels or bay-windows once lay the king's and queen's separate apartments.

Courtauld House – The task of redeveloping the site fell to the architects John Seely and Paul Paget. The five principal entertainment rooms with the bedrooms above, are accommodated in the south wing, extending eastwards in line with the Great Hall. The service wing meanwhile is orientated at an angle pivoting on the entrance hall.

All 'mod cons' pervade the house: soft American-style uplighting, a centralised vacuum cleaner in the basement collected dust from hoses fitted in each and every room, underfloor heating was boosted in the bedrooms with single bar electric fires, synchronised clocks and a loud-speaker system worked throughout. It is, however, the unique quality of the 1930s internal decoration that is particularly remarkable: fine wooden veneer (flexwood) panelling is fitted in all the main bedrooms, stylishly fashioned like the inside of a Cunard cruise liner – golden-satin coloured aspenwood, weathered sycamore, bird's eye maple, Japanese chestnut, Indian mahogany...

Sir Stephen Courtauld (1883-1967), brother of Samuel the benefactor of the Courtauld Institute, was an avid horticulturalist. Together with his wife, Virginia (1885-1972) – Ginnie for short, he moved from 47 Grosvenor Square taking their famous art treasures and favourite fittings (fireplace, grills, doors) with them to Eltham. In 1944 they moved to Scotland as the war continued, and emigrated finally to Rhodesia where Stephen might study his beloved orchids. Mrs Courtauld later returned to live with a niece in the Isle of Wight. There were no children.

Notable peculiar features of the house include the entrance-hall inlaid panels of Venice and Sweden (Roman gladiator and Scandinavian Viking) and the Alice in Wonderland reliefs set between the windows; Mrs Courtauld's legendary lemur's centrally-heated cage; her personal bathroom furnished with an onyx basin sur-round, gold-plated taps and gold-leafed mosaic alcove (designed by the then ever-so fashionable Peter Malacrida); the locally-made leather patchwork map in her sitting-room that features London's first airport at Croydon and the cardinal points as an Eskimo, Chinaman, African warrior and Red Indian chief; the dining-room fitted with its square-coffered silver-leafed ceiling, distinctive doors – with panels commissioned from Narini who studied the animals at London Zoo, and '30s black marble fireplace set with mother-of-pearl ribbon bands and polished Art Deco grate.

The house has been lovingly furnished in Art Deco style based on photographs of the interiors and on a detailed inventory; there are replicas of carpets, furniture and some of the paintings as well as fabrics in the style.

Gardens – Lovingly landscaped and planted by the Courtaulds, the gardens boast beautiful mature trees and beds of fragrant flowers (Seringa, wistaria, honeysuckle, roses). A perfect pleasure ground for visiting guests welcomed with warm hospitality to the house (hence the relief figure over the front door of the house).

Well Hall – *Well Hall Road; 1 mile north.* The Well Hall estate was the home of the Roper family, descendants of Thomas More *(see CHELSEA)*, until 1733. All that now remains are the site of the medieval house surrounded by a moat and reached by a 16C bridge, a Tudor barn *(restaurant and art gallery)* and the Pleasaunce – a garden surrounded by old red brick walls.

FULHAM

Map p 296 **(TY)** – ⊖ Putney Bridge

Fulham, Parsons Green, Walham Green, all within a wide loop of the river were once separate riparian villages with the odd large mansion in its own grounds which ran down to the water's edge. Market gardens covered the fertile marshlands. The Bishop of London was the lord of the manor, a property of vast extent, a mere four miles from Hyde Park Corner. Urbanisation came within a period of 50 years: in 1851 the population numbered 12 000; in 1901, 137 000.

The **Charing Cross Hospital** *(Fulham Palace Road)* moved from the Strand in 1973 into more modern cross-shaped premises equipped with state-of-the-art facilities.

Downstream from the bridgehead, **Hurlingham House**, an 18C mansion in its own wooded grounds, is the last of the big houses which once lined the river bank. It is now a private club with extensive tennis courts.

Fulham Palace ⊙ – *Bishop's Avenue.* The **palace**, which retains the appearance of a modest Tudor manor, was the official summer residence of the Bishop of London from 704 to 1973. The gateway, a low 16C arch with massive beamed doors,

Fulham Palace

leads through to the courtyard (1480-1525) graced by a large central fountain (1885). The two-storey red brick walls, except in the south range (restored), are strongly patterned with a black diaper design. The chapel (1866), added on the south side, was designed by William Butterfield in mock Tudor style.

The **museum** is housed in the east wing, in the Dining Room and Library (formerly a chapel); it traces the history of the site, the buildings and the gardens: archeological finds, souvenirs and portraits of past bishops, the ecclesiastical and political role of the Bishop of London, ecclesiastical vestments, stained glass.

The **grounds** consist of lawns shaded by a copper beech and an ancient evergreen, possibly planted by Bishop Grindal who sent grapes to Elizabeth I. The first magnolia to be grown in Europe and several other exotic species were planted here by Bishop Compton. The old walled kitchen garden contains beech hedge screens, a herb garden and a **wistaria walk**, enclosing the old vinery and clipped box hedges. The remains of a moat (1 mile long), filled in the 1920s, may date from the Roman period. Traces have been found of prehistoric and Roman settlements.

Fulham Pottery

At 210 New King's Road, one disused bottle kiln still stands on the site of the seven or nine kiln pottery established by **John Dwight** in 1671 by special permission of Charles II (1671) and soon known for its stoneware – 'vulgarly called Cologne ware', and salt-glazed earthenware so suited to modelling commemorative busts and statuettes.

All Saints Church ⊘ – Fulham parish church has been a landmark at this bridging point of the river since the 14C, its square Kentish stone tower a twin to Putney church on the south bank, although the vessel was rebuilt in Perpendicular style in the 19C.

Inside there is a rich collection of monuments and brasses: note the tombstones in the chancel floor to William Rumbold, standard bearer to Charles I in the Civil War, and Thomas Carlos, whose coat of arms, an oak tree and three crowns, was granted to his father after he had hidden in the oak tree at Boscobel with Charles II after the Battle of Worcester, 1651. Fourteen Bishops of London are buried in the yew-shaded churchyard.

Close to the church note the 19C **Powell Almshouses** with steep pitched roofs over a single storey, forming an L-shaped building around a quiet garden.

In town, unless otherwise indicated, our itineraries are walking tours.

GREENWICH ★★★

Map p 9 (KLZ) and p 11 (UY)
⊖ North Greenwich; Overground: Greenwich from Charing Cross, Waterloo,
London Bridge or Cannon Street; DLR: Island Gardens (north bank) and Footway to
Greenwich; by boat from Westminster, Tower Bridge.

The small town beside the Thames has a world wide reputation owing to the
Greenwich meridian and Greenwich Mean Time. The Royal Observatory stands on a hill
overlooking an attractive park sloping down to the river. Greenwich has many associations with the Royal Navy and British maritime history and its days as a royal
residence are recalled in the delightful Queen's House.

The **antique market** *(see INTRODUCTION – Shopping)* is well known and there are other
shops selling antiques and second-hand books.

A **footway tunnel** *(lift or 100 steps)* leads under the Thames *(10min)* to the Isle of Dogs,
from where there is a fine **view★★** of Greenwich Palace, painted by Canaletto in 1750
and now in the National Maritime Museum Collection.

Bella Court – Greenwich has been in the royal domain since King Alfred's time. It was
Humphrey, Duke of Gloucester, brother of Henry V, who first enclosed the park and
transformed the manor into a castle, which he named Bella Court; it was he also who
built a fortified tower upon the hill from which to spy invaders approaching London up
the Thames or along the Roman road from Dover. On Duke Humphrey's death in
1447, Henry VI's queen, Margaret of Anjou, annexed the castle, embellished it and
renamed it **Placentia** or Pleasaunce.

Tudor Palace – The Tudors preferred Greenwich to their other residences and
Henry VIII, who was born there, enlarged the castle into a vast palace with a tiltyard
and a royal armoury where craftsmen produced armour to rival the Italian and
German suits *(see TOWER OF LONDON)*.

Henry also founded naval dockyards upriver at Deptford and downstream at Woolwich
which he visited by sumptuous royal barge to inspect his growing fleet. The docks
were also accessible by a road skirting the wall which divided the extensive and quite
magnificent royal gardens from the park. Overlooking the thoroughfare was a two-
storey gatehouse which, legend has it, Queen Elizabeth was approaching one day in
1581 when Walter Raleigh, seeing her about to step into the mire, threw down his
cloak so that she might cross dryshod.

Palladian House and 'Pretty Palace' – Rich as the Tudor palace was, in 1615
James I commissioned **Inigo Jones** *(see INTRODUCTION – Architecture)* to build a
house for his queen (Anne of Denmark) on the exact site of the gatehouse, straddling the busy Woolwich-Deptford road. Jones, then aged forty-two (b 1573), was
known rather for his revolutionary stage settings, but he proved equally inventive
in his design for the Queen's House. Based on the principles of the Italian architect, Palladio (1508-80), it is a compact and well proportioned house despite its
'bridge room' over the road. Work stopped on Anne's death and was resumed only
when Charles I offered the house to his queen, Henrietta Maria, whose name and

Old Royal Naval College and Queen's House

the date (1635) appear on the north front; her initials are also inscribed over the fireplace in the queen's presence chamber, so 'furnished, that it far surpassed all other of that kind in England'.

During the Commonwealth the Tudor palace was despoiled, cleared for use as a barracks and prison while its collections were sold. At the Restoration, the Queen's House alone emerged relatively unscathed allowing Henrietta Maria to return there to live from time to time until her death in 1669 (in France). Charles II meanwhile, disliked the derelict palace, finding the Queen's House too small for his court: in 1665 he commissioned a King's House to be built by John Webb, a student of Inigo Jones. This resulted in what is now known as the King Charles Block of the Old Naval College, endowed with groups of four giant pilasters at either end and at the centre where they are crowned by a pediment. With the exception of the Observatory, however, all construction had to cease for lack of funds long before Charles' 'pretty palace' was complete.

Royal Hospital to Royal Naval College – Work at Greenwich was resumed in 1694 when William and Mary, who preferred Hampton Court as a royal residence, granted a charter for a Royal Hospital for Seamen at Greenwich founded on the lines of the Royal Military Hospital in Chelsea, appointing **Christoper Wren** as Surveyor of Works. Wren, as usual, submitted numerous plans before proposing the one we know today: at Queen Mary's insistence this incorporated the Queen's House and its 150ft wide river vista (acquired only when the Tudor palace was demolished), the King Charles Block alongside the construction of three additional symmetrical blocks, the King William (SW), Queen Mary (SE) and Queen Anne (NE, below which exists a crypt, sole remnant of the Tudor palace; *closed to the public*). To complete the scheme emphasis was focused by projecting cupolas before the refectory and chapel and the course of the Thames was modified and embanked – the only major vista design by Wren to be properly realised. The project took more than half a century to complete and involved Vanbrugh, Hawksmoor, Colen Campbell, Ripley, 'Athenian' Stuart... John Evelyn recorded in his diary that on 30 June 1696 he 'laid the first stone of the intended foundation at five o'clock in the evening... Mr Flamsteed the King's Astronomer Professor observing the punctual time by instruments'. By June 1704 he observed that the hospital had begun 'to take in wounded and worn out seamen... the buildings now going on are very magnificent', but as treasurer he also noted that by 1703 the cost already amounted to £89 364 14s 8d (the list of donors in the entrance to the Painted Hall shows that the King gave £6 000, the Queen £1 000, Evelyn £2 000).

In 1873 when the buildings were transformed into the Royal Naval College, a centre of scientific instruction, steam and steel had just replaced wood and sail. In 1998 the naval university moved out and most of the premises have now been taken over by the University of Greenwich.

The Queen's House, extended by colonnades and two wings in 1807, first accommodated the Royal Hospital School before becoming part of the National Maritime Museum (1937).

★★Old Royal Naval College ⊘ – Work is now underway to accommodate the campus of the University of Greenwich. The King Charles block will be occupied by the Trinity College of Music and buildings overlooking the Thames will house a new Greenwich Maritime Institute. The former Dreadnought Hospital designed in 1764 by James 'Athenian' Stuart, is being restored as the university library.

★Painted Hall – Wren's domed refectory designed as a pair with the chapel, was completed in 1703. In 1805 it was the setting for Nelson's lying in state before his burial in St Paul's. The hall and upper hall were painted in exuberant Baroque by Sir **James Thornhill:** William and Mary, Anne, George I and his descendants, celebrate Britain's maritime power in a wealth of involved allegory. The artist portrayed the current monarch as he worked through each new reign (1708-27) and was paid £3 a sq yd for the ceilings, £1 for the walls.

★Chapel – Wren's chapel was redecorated after a fire in 1779 by 'Athenian' Stuart and William Newton in Wedgwood pastel colours. Delicate Rococo swags and panelled rosettes cover the upper walls and ceiling; corbels and beams are masked by a lacework of stucco. Set up across the apse is *St Paul after the Shipwreck at Malta* by Benjamin West (1738-1820) who also designed the Coade stone medallions for the pulpit made from the top deck of a 3 decker.

★★National Maritime Museum ⊘ – *Tour: 2hr.* The fabulous historical collection of things maritime (fine art, precious prizes, rare instruments, treasures and mementoes) is proudly displayed by this large and beautifully organised museum. After the redevelopment of Neptune Court with a large free span glass roof 16 new galleries have been created.

The development of Britain's might as a sea power is traced from Henry VIII's early Tudor fleet through voyages of discovery (Captain Cook's travels in the South Seas and Pacific Islands, Sir John Franklin's Polar exploration) to 20C naval warfare in the Falklands and in the Gulf. Attention is also focused on the impact of modern life (travel, cargoes, pollution) on the sea.

A yacht, a 1930s speedboat, a gilded barge, a figurehead set the scene at the entrance. The theme of **Explorers** is the quest of early navigators and the exploits of intrepid men in search of new frontiers. The depths of the sea, the polar regions and space provide further challenges. Migration, tourism and transport of goods and mail brought about the age of cruise liners presented in **Passengers**. **Cargoes** examines the profound effect of sea transport, a cheap and efficient way of moving energy products, raw materials and finished goods round the world (container ships, oil tankers), on industrial activity and trade patterns. The style of uniforms and functional outfits (diving and survival suits) is dictated by climate and rank as illustrated in **Rank and Style**. **Global Garden** tells the story of the world's natural resources: tropical plants (potato, tomato, sugarcane, rubber, cotton, tobacco), medicinal plants (quinine, morphine) and exotic flowers and trees (orchids, azaleas, dahlias, rhododendrons) which are now an intrinsic part of everyday life.

Maritime London has held a prominent place in Britain's economic and social development: financing of trading ventures, chartering and insurance of ships and cargoes, setting up of Lloyd's, the Bank of England, the Stock Exchange and commodity exchanges. The city grew with the thriving docks, warehouses and related industries. Modern issues include safety standards at sea. The British Empire spread to the four corners of the world; the complex story of balances of power and cultural influences unfolds in **Trade and Empire**: slave trade, opium wars, American independence, transportation of convicts, reverse emigration from Asia and the Caribbean. Maritime rivalry between France and Britain in 18C-19C, world conflicts and nuclear-powered vessels and missiles are the themes of **Sea Power**. Banks of video monitors illustrate the conditions on modern ships; screens show how pilots use computerised navigation information picked-up from automated lighthouses and buoys.

Attractions for children

All Hands Gallery: interactive exhibits on diving, propulsion, signalling etc, model of 74-gun ship.
The Bridge: ingenious solutions to navigation problems.
Ship of War: exquisite models of warships.
It is best to visit the Royal Observatory at the top of the hill first.

Horatio **Nelson**'s military campaigns during the French Revolution wars, battles with Napoleon are illustrated with contemporary paintings, portraits, uniforms, logs, guns, maps and navigational instruments, models and a large collection of decorated china memorabilia. Personal artefacts include his bullet-pierced uniform worn at Trafalgar, his cabin furniture and items from his house at Merton *(see Outer London: WIMBLEDON – MERTON)*.

There are also presentations on the story of the water cycle, the fragile ecology and the future of the sea and exhibitions of paintings and photographs.

In the gardens at the rear are a **Dolphin Sundial** and the mast of the **Great Britain** (1863).

★★**Queen's House** ⊘ – *Open for special exhibitions only.* This elegant white Palladian villa (1616), the first Classical building in England, was designed by Inigo Jones *(see above)*. Distinctive features included its colour, the beautiful horseshoe-shaped staircase descending from the terrace on the north front and the loggia on the south front facing the park.

Inside the house is designed according to 17C protocol (Presence Chamber, Anteroom, Privy Chamber, Bedroom, Closets etc).

The **Tulip Stairs**, a cantilevered spiral stair (1630) named after the tulip motif on the wrought-iron balustrade, lead upstairs to the King's Apartments and the Queen's Suite.

The **Great Hall** consists of a cube (40ft) surrounded by a gallery. This provides a good view of Nicholas Stone's fine black and white marble paving (1636-7) below, the white and gold decor reaching up to Jones' gilded pine ceiling beams that once would have framed painted panels representing Peace surrounded by the Muses and the Liberal Arts. The originals by Gentileschi having been removed to Marlborough House in the 18C and cut to fit their new home, are here replaced by reproductions.

★**Royal Observatory Greenwich** ⊘ – *Tour 45min.* In 1675 Charles II directed Sir Christopher Wren to 'build a small observatory within our park at Greenwich, upon the highest ground, at or near the place where the castle stood' for 'the finding out of the longitude of places for perfecting navigation and astronomy'. Wren, who was a former astronomer as well as an architect, designed a house of red brick with stone dressing, an upper balustrade and miniature canted cupolas 'for the Observator's habitation and a little for pompe'; it is named Flamsteed House after John Flamsteed the first Astronomer Royal, appointed in 1675.

The **Meridian Building**, a mid 18C addition of the same brick, was built to house the observatory's growing **collection**★★ of instruments.

At the main gate are clocks showing world time, the 24 hour clock and British Standard Measures. The **tour** begins in the Meridian courtyard where visitors may record the exact time at which they stand on the Greenwich Meridian, the brass meridian of zero longitude linked in a straight line to the north and south poles.

On the south face of Flamsteed House are sundials. The red time ball on the roof was erected in 1833 to serve as a time check for navigation on the Thames; the ball rises to the top of the mast and drops at exactly 13 00 hours GMT.

Within **Flamsteed House** the first rooms trace the foundation and purpose of the Observatory, the various interpretations of the stars invented by early civilisations and the evolution of man's understanding of the heavens. Some of the usual small 17C rooms are furnished as they were in Flamsteed's day. The lofty and beautifully proportioned **Octagon Room** has been restored to its original 17C appearance, when, according to John Evelyn, it was equipped 'with the choicest instrument'.

The other displays trace the discovery of latitude and longitude: Parliament's prize (£20 000) offered to anyone who might invent a reliable way of charting a ship's position at sea; its award in 1773 to John Harrison for the H-1; the early practice of map and chart makers who fixed the zero meridian where they chose (Greenwich, Paris, the Fortunate Islands); the gradual adoption of the British reading with the inauguration in 1767 of the annual publication, *The Nautical Almanack*, which in combination with the marine chronometer and sextant enabled navigators to find longitude in relation to the Greenwich meridian; the standardisation of the meridian in 1884 at the Meridian Conference in Washington. The development of the railways and the telegraph had produced anomalies and even legal disputes: the time lag between London and Plymouth was 16 minutes. The six-pip time signal was introduced in 1924.

The **Meridian Building** contains the **Quadrant Room**, the Airy Transit Circle through which the meridian passes *(video)*, a collection of **telescopes** of all sizes and the Telescope Dome which contains Britain's largest (28in) refracting telescope *(video of the moon landing)*.

A variety of lectures on the moon and stars are given *(up 42 steps)* in the **Planetarium** at different times ⊘.

J Harrison's marine timekeeper No 1

Greenwich Park – Greenwich Park, palisaded in 1433 and surrounded by a wall in Stuart times, is the oldest enclosed royal domain. It extends for 180 acres in a great sweep of chestnut avenues and grass to a point 155ft above the river crowned by the Royal Observatory and the **General Wolfe** monument. On the slope below the Observatory there are traces of the giant grass steps designed by Le Nôtre in 1662.

A pioneering clockmaker

John Harrison (1693-1776) was born the son of a carpenter, little otherwise is known of his early life until 1713 when he completed his first pendulum clock made entirely of wood: oak for the wheels and box for the axles (Worshipful Company of Clockmakers Museum – see CITY – Guildhall).

In 1722 Harrison installed a unique clock at Brocklesby Park made from lignum vitae, a tropical hardwood that naturally exudes its own oil thereby keeping its mechanisms lubricated; this continues to keep accurate 'mean' time today. His next important invention was the bi-metallic gridiron-grass-hopper pendulum (1725-27) which maintained a more consistent swing by having a brass and steel rod and weight that expanded and contracted less with changes in temperature; the grasshopper mechanism provided a friction-free means of clocking the units of time.

At this time, an age of increasing maritime activity, it was critical for sailors to be able to determine longitude in order to chart the oceans that divided land-masses accurately. One means depended upon measuring time at sea from a pitching vessel against time at a constant meridian on land. In 1730 Harrison journeyed to London with drawings and calculations for a reliable clock that would be seaworthy: pendulum-less, resistant to corrosion or rust and resilient to extremes in weather. There he met Dr Edmond Halley, who introduced him to the clockmaker George Graham FRS who endorsed the manufacture of Harrison's No 1 (H-1). Tried on a journey to Lisbon in 1737, the clock proved itself accurate and the Board of Longitude convened for the first time: unconvinced, Harrison returned to Barrow to improve his invention; H-2 was never tested by the navy as its inventor remained dissatisfied... Described by Hogarth in his *Analysis of Beauty* as 'one of the most exquisite movements ever made' (1753) H-1 equipped the English with the technology to begin their colonisation of the high seas.

Beyond the Roman Villa and Great Cross Avenue are a **flower garden**, before ancient cedars of Lebanon, a pond with wild fowl and a Wilderness with a small herd of fallow deer.

Parkside east – In Park Vista are the early 18C plain two-storey **Manor House** *(no 13)*, the **Vicarage** *(no 33)*, a rambling 18C house incorporating Tudor fragments, and the 18C public house, the Plume of Feathers.

Vanbrugh Castle, a caricature of a medieval fortress, stands at the top of Maze Hill. It was built and lived in by the architect and playwright himself, Sir John Vanbrugh, from 1717-26 while he was Surveyor to Greenwich Hospital. Gothic towers, turrets, high walls, crenellations and all – it preceded Strawberry Hill *(see Outer London: TWICKENHAM)* by some 30 years.

For BLACKHEATH see separate listing in Outer London section.

★Ranger's House ⊙ – *Chesterfield Walk, West Parkside*. The mansion was originally a small brick villa with a stone balustrade lining the roof and steps leading up to an elegant stone frontispiece decorated with a mask. Rounded wings in pale yellow brick were added during the house's ownership by Philip, 4th Earl of Chesterfield (1694-1733), politician, diplomat and wit. The resultant south gallery, 75ft in length with a compartmented ceiling and three fine bow windows commands, its satisfied owner declared, 'three different, and the finest prospects in the world'; the gardens are still as beautiful.

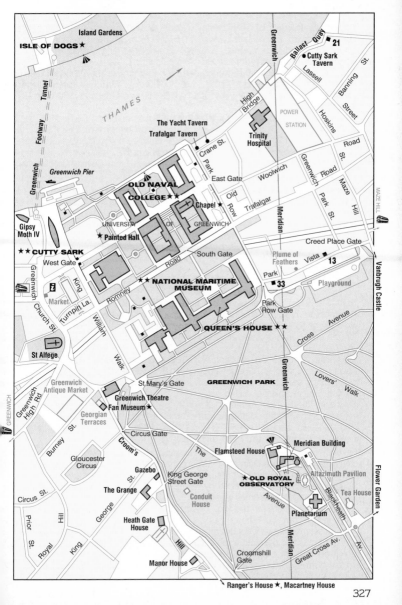

Riverside downstream

The area has preserved its historic heritage.

The **Trafalgar Tavern** of 1837 recollects the personalities and events of Nelson's time. Its bars and restaurant overlook the river from cast-iron balconies resembling the galleries of a man o'war. In the early 19C the tavern was the setting for the Liberal ministers' 'whitebait dinners' *(see Outer London: DOCKLANDS: Blackwall)* and later was described in *Our Mutual Friend* by Dickens who used to meet there with Thackeray and Cruikshank. Also overlooking the river and backing onto the old and narrow Crane Street, is **The Yacht Tavern** which is at least a century older.

The **Trinity Hospital** (f 1613) is a small white, importantly gabled and crenellated charity building.

Ballast Quay is a terrace of neat 17C early Georgian houses (note the 1695 Morden *(see index)* estate marks).

The **Cutty Sark Tavern** was rebuilt with a great bow window in 1804 on the site of earlier inns, while at the end stands the four-square Harbourmaster's Office *(no 21)* which for 50 years, until the 1890s, controlled colliers entering the Pool of London.

For Thames Barrier see Outer London: WOOLWICH – CHARLTON.

The **Suffolk Collection** of 53 paintings includes an outstanding series of full lengt family portraits by William Larkin (fl 1610-20) all in the finest clothes of th period, embroidered, slashed, jewelled, lace-collared and ruffed. Note the 17 Lotto rug displayed over a table as in the paintings.

The panelled rooms on the ground and first floor house the **Dolmetsch Collection** **Musical Instruments**: spinet (1709), lute clavichord, flute, a green harpsichor (1896). The topographical view of Croom's Hill were painted 150 years ago b T Hofland.

The **Architectural Study Centre** in the old coach house presents a collection, begun 1905, of items rescued from buildings in London which have been converted demolished: wrought and cast-iron work (firemarks, opercula, balconies), ceramic (delft tiles, Coade stone and other terracottas), bricks, metalwork, plaster work woodwork, fanlights, glass, staircases (spiral steps from Covent Garden market street names.

Croom's Hill – The winding lane was already an established local thoroughfare the 15C, when the park was enclosed, and thus became its natural wester boundary.

Macartney House *(private flats)*, a large rambling building of mellow brick and stone with a roof balustrade and tall rounded windows overlooking its own garden an the Ranger's house, was built by Andrew Snape, Serjeant Farrier to Charles II an according to Evelyn, 'a man full of projects', who in 1674 filched the land from th royal domain.

The **Manor House**, two storeys of red brick, is typical of 1697, even to the hoode porch with a finely carved shell motif.

Heath Gate House is a relatively low brick mansion with large gabled dormers an pilasters on brackets supporting the upper floor. The house (1630s) is a rar example of so early a domestic building with its exterior unaltered.

On the east side is a row *(nos 3-11)* of modest 17C tenements, weatherboarded the rear.

The Grange, an early 17C building with 18C additions, stands on a site recorded having been given to Ghent Abbey in 818 by a daughter of Alfred the Great overlooking the road and the park is a small square **gazebo** (1672) with a pyrami roof and carved plaster ceiling.

Gloucester Circus *(side turning)*, designed by Michael Searle in the 1700s, ha retained some of the original houses on the east and south sides.

The Georgian terrace *(nos 6-12)* dates from 1721-23. The Poet Laureate, C Da Lewis lived at no 6 from 1968 to 1972.

★**Fan Museum** ⊘ – *10-12 Croom's Hill*. This delightful museum owns some 2 000 fan Permanent displays explain how fans are made, the different materials used and th different types and sources of fans.

Temporary shows are organised by theme – children, feathered fans, flowered fan – which change three times a year.

Demonstrations on fan-making, construction, conservation and restoration tak place in the craft workshop.

The museum occupies two Georgian terrace houses (1721), scrupulously restore the garden is laid out with a fan-shaped terrace, a pool, Japanese style planting an a reproduction of a Georgian orangery.

At the bottom of Croom's Hill, on the corner, is the **Greenwich Theatre**, built in 196 in the shell of a Victorian music hall.

St Alfege Church ⊘ – The somewhat gaunt church (1718) with an elegant Doric portico is by **Nicholas Hawksmoor**, the superimposed tower by John James. Inside there are no pillars, although the span measures 65ft by 90ft. The murals *(east end)* are by Thornhill and the carving by Grinling Gibbons.

On the site where Alfege, Archbishop of Canterbury, suffered martyrdom at the hands of Danish invaders in 1012, churches were erected which witnessed Henry VII and his queen at worship, the baptism of Henry VIII, heard the father of English church music **Thomas Tallis** playing the organ for 40 years (console in SW corner) and saw his burial and also that of **General Wolfe**, parishioner and Commander of the British Army at the capture of Quebec (d 1759). Two other parishioners were Lavinia Fenton, the original Polly Peachum in *The Beggar's Opera* and John Julius Angerstein. The registers which date back to 1615, vividly portray the large families, child mortality, the decimation of plague years and contrasting, usual, longevity.

Greenwich Pier – A rounded pavilion, echoed by another on the north bank of the Thames, provides access to the **foot tunnel** to the Isle of Dogs *(10mins)*.

★**Cutty Sark** ⊘ – Launched at Dumbarton in 1869 for the China tea trade, the *Cutty Sark* became famous as the fastest clipper afloat: her best day's run with all 32 000 sq ft or 1/2 acre of canvas fully spread was 363 miles. In her heyday she brought tea from China and later wool from Australia, chasing before the wind like the cutty sark or short chemise of the witch Nannie, 'a winsome wench' in Robert Burns' poem *Tam O'Shanter*, hence the boat's distinctive figurehead. In 1922 she was converted into a nautical training school and transferred to dry dock at Greenwich in 1954. In her hold are papers, charts, mementoes and models, illustrating the history of the clipper trade *(see also BERMONDSEY – Bramagh Tea and Coffee Museum)* and her own story in particular. In the lower hold is a lively collection of boldly coloured 19C figureheads.

Cutty Sark

Gipsy Moth IV ⊘ – *Greenwich Pier*. The ketch (11 ton, 53ft), in which the late Sir Francis Chichester circumnavigated the world alone in 1966-67, stands nearby looking incredibly small.

Millennium Dome – Riverside walks, parkland and lakes to attact wildlife have transformed the Greenwich peninsula where the site of a former gas works has been extensively redeveloped to include roads, housing, stores and other amenities for the local population. However, the focal point of the regenerated area is the Millennium Dome, a vast domed structure with a spectacular glass fibre roof designed by Sir Richard Rogers, built to mark the third millennium.

Cutty Sark is also the name of a pale, most delicate blend of Scotch whisky branded by Berry Bros & Rudd of St James's. The name was suggested by the clipper which had just returned to British waters having traded under the Portuguese flag: the whisky meanwhile, was especially blended for the export market – destined for America and supplied throughout Prohibition (1920-33) via Nassau in the Bahamas; 'the real McCoy', a certain Captain William McCoy, was one such boot-legger there. Today the Cutty Sark Tall Ships' Race organised annually by the Sail Training Association is sponsored by the wine and spirit merchants.

DEPTFORD *Overground: Deptford from London Bridge*

The riverside village expanded during the reign of Henry VIII as a ship-building yard; later several Deptford-built vessels numbered among the fleet which defeated the Armada (1588). It was in Deptford Creek that Queen Elizabeth boarded the *Golden Hinde* in 1581 to dub Francis Drake knight for his circumnavigation of the globe and where Christopher **Marlowe** was stabbed to death in a tavern brawl (1593). In the 17C the diarist John **Evelyn** lived at Sayes Court where he cultivated a fine garden and which briefly, in 1698, and to his regret since the Russian was a bad tenant, he leased to Peter the Great while the latter learnt the art of shipbuilding in the yards. The dockyard closed in 1869.

St Paul's Church ⊙ – *East of Deptford High Street.* Thomas Archer's church (1712-30) has a lofty semicircular stone portico supporting an impressive steeple inside, great columns with gilded Corinthian capitals uphold a richly sculpted plaster ceiling above an extensive gallery. Nearby, in Albury Street, some 18C houses with elaborately carved doorcases have been preserved.

St Nicholas's Church ⊙ – *Corner of Deptford Green and Stowage Lane.* St Nicholas stands on a site occupied by Deptford parish churches since Saxon times. Of particular interest in the post-war reconstructed interior are the extended reredos by St Nicholas' 17C parishioner, **Grinling Gibbons** *(see INTRODUCTION)*, with swags of leaves, flowers and fruit, a peapod, the ciphers and coat of arms of William and Mary. There is also a weird carved relief, an early work by Grinling Gibbons, known as the *Valley of Dry Bones.* The Jacobean pulpit is supported on a cherub believed to have been a ship's figurehead.

The laurel-wreathed skulls on the gate posts originally dominated crossed bones and since so many privateers sailed from Deptford, it is claimed that the carving inspired the traditional skull and crossbones flag. More honourably, the church so long associated with Sir Francis Drake and his descendants, and steeped in naval history has the privilege of flying the White Ensign. It is here that Christopher Marlowe lies buried, 'slaine by Francis Frezer, the 1 June 1593' (tablet on west wall).

HACKNEY

n the 16C Hackney was a country village where wealthy city merchants established a second country residence away from the congestion and plague of the City. In the following century it was famous for its many schools; there were so many girls' boarding schools that Hackney was dubbed the 'Ladies University of Female Arts' and Pepys records attending Hackney Church in order to admire the young ladies.

Sutton House ⊘ – The house, which was probably built for Ralph Sadleir, who later became Principal Secretary of State to Henry VIII, dates from c 1535; it had gable ends and mullion windows and was originally known as the 'bryk place' as most buildings then were timber-framed structures. Early in the 18C the gable roofs were cut back to make room for the parapet, the present sash windows were inserted and a second entrance was made to the west wing. The cement rendering on the east wing dates from about 1870 and the porches from 1904.

The interior contains one of the **original Tudor transom windows**, now in the Lobby. The Parlour is entirely lined with **oak linenfold panelling** dating from the early 16C and has retained its original stone fireplace, surmounted by an overmantel with typical Renaissance fluted pilasters. The **painted staircase** is decorated with coloured oil painting directly on to plaster showing coats of arms, animals on pedestals bearing shields and a frieze with *trompe l'œil* work. The Little Chamber is lined with **Baltic oak panelling** dating from the late 16C.

The house was named in 1951 after Sir Thomas Sutton (d 1611), founder of Charterhouse School *(see CLERKENWELL)*, who lived in the neighbouring Tanhouse but had been thought to have lived in Sutton House.

Hackney Town – The ragstone tower is all that remains of the medieval Church of St Augustine: the present church, **St John-at-Hackney**, dates from the 1700s.

Hackney Empire – The theatre (1901) was designed by Frank Matcham and is a fine example of the variety palaces which were popular at the turn of the century. The Rococo auditorium has excellent acoustics.

Hackney Museum ⊘ – The chief exhibit of this museum of local history is an **Anglo-Saxon longboat** hollowed out from the trunk of an oak tree (c AD 900) abandoned during a Viking invasion.

Dalston – **Holy Trinity Church** ⊘ (1849) in Beechwood Road is the Clowns' Church as it holds an annual memorial service for Joseph Grimaldi (1779-1837) on the first Sunday in February. The tradition of clowns meeting once a year in church was started in the days of Grimaldi, the most famous British clown, the first to paint the face, who lived in Islington and is buried in the churchyard of St James' Church in Pentonville. When St James' Church was demolished, the clowns' service moved to Dalston.

> **Clowns International** ⊘ is a charitable organisation set up by clowns for clowns: its aims are to provide these special entertainers with an annual festival that celebrates their historical art and organises a convention at which to meet, exchange ideas, support others and encourage the talented young and hopeful, worldwide. It maintains a small gallery and archive ⊘ at 1 Hillman Street which is open to all, the curious, the interested, the circumspect and its professional and amateur members. Museum curator ☎ 020 7723 3877.

HAM HOUSE ★★

Ham House was at its prime under **Elizabeth Dysart, Duchess of Lauderdale**, 'a woman of great beauty but greater parts... a wonderful quickness of apprehension and an amazing vivacity in conversation... (who) had studied... mathematics and philosophy; but... was restless in her ambition, profuse in her expense and of a most ravenous covetousness; she was a violent friend, and a much more violent enemy'.

She lived in dangerous times – her father, William Murray first Earl of Dysart, had literally been youthful 'whipping boy' for Prince Charles, future Charles I. Elizabeth, it was said, became for a time the Protector's mistress.

Her first husband, Sir Lyonel Tollemache, was the first in the line of Earls of Dysart, who remained owners of Ham House until it was presented to the National Trust.

Her second husband, the Earl, later Duke of Lauderdale, favourite of the Stuart restoration, was a learned, ambitious, vicious character. A double portrait, *Both ye Graces in one picture*, by Sir Peter Lely in the Round Gallery, presents them graphically; the toll of years is clearly evident in the duchess of whom there is an earlier portrait on the same wall.

HAM HOUSE

The Lauderdales, according to their contemporaries, 'lived at a vast rate'. They enlarged the house, which had been built to the conventional Jacobean plan in 1610 and modified the front to give a continuous roof line with a horizontal emphasis. A family idiosyncrasy for making inventories and for hoarding furniture, paintings hangings and bills for structural and decorative alterations, has enabled the house to be returned to its 1678 appearance when it was described by John Evelyn as 'furnished like a great prince's'. The gardens have been relaid to the 17C plan.

Exterior – The fabric is brick with stone dressings; the building, three storeys beneath a hipped roof with a five bay centre *(north side)* recessed between square bays and typical, canted Jacobean outer bays. The fine iron gates and piers date from 1671; previously the house had been approached by a tree-lined canal from the river to a watergate near the main door; the present forecourt, with the Coade stone figure of **Father Thames** by John Bacon, was laid out in 1800.

Interior – Paintings, in this house, bring to life the period of Charles II, the Cavalier generals, the women at court – young, fair, delicately complexioned and far from innocent. Furniture, doors, doorcases, fireplaces and ceilings display the craftsmanship of the period, frequently Dutch for Dutch craftsmen were well established long before the accession of William III. The remarkable ceilings show the progress from geometrical type plasterwork to garlands and spandrels (compare the original, north and later, south rooms).

Long Gallery, Ham House

Ground Floor – The house has an impressive entrance in the Great Hall, increased above by the Round Gallery with a decorated plaster ceiling by Kinsman (1637). Lely portraits adorn the gallery; below are portraits of Dysarts (17C-18C) by Kneller and Reynolds.

The most notable features of other rooms on the ground floor are the gilt leather wall hangings and the 1679 cedar side tables in the Marble Dining Room (parquetry replaced the marble paving in the 18C), the artificially grained and gilded panelling, fashionable in the 1670s, the chimney furniture of silver, considered very ostentatious by contemporaries. In the Duchess's Bedchamber are damask hangings; in the Yellow Bedroom or Volury Room the bed (note the carved cherub feet) is hung with purple and yellow; in the White Closet are an oyster work veneered writing desk and picture of the south front of the house in 1683 *(fireplace)*. The altar cloth of 'crimson velvet & gould & silver stuff' in the chapel is original.

The **Great Staircase** of 1637, built of oak round a square well and gilded, has a singularly beautiful balustrade of boldly carved trophies of arms.

Upper Floor – Lady Maynard's suite contains 17C Flemish tapestries after Poussin below a wooden frieze and family portraits.

The Museum Room displays examples of the original vivid upholstery, an 18C toilet set, a prayer book of 1625, ledgers and bills of the alterations to the house and the 1679 inventory which has enabled the rooms to be arranged as in Elizabeth Dysart's day. The Cabinet of Miniatures presents a collection of miniatures by Hilliard, Oliver and Cooper.

The North Drawing Room is sumptuous, epitomising the Lauderdale passion for luxury and display in a plaster frieze and rich ceiling (1637) above walls hung with English silk tapestries (woven by ex-Mortlake workers in Soho), carved and gilded wainscoting, doorcases and doors; furniture is carved, gilded and richly upholstered; the fireplace is exuberantly Baroque...

Equally opulent is the Queen's Suite, rich with late 17C garlanded plaster ceilings, grained wainscoting and carved wood swags above the fireplaces; the furniture includes then fashionable Oriental screens, English japanned chairs, a small Chinese cabinet on a gilded stand and 18C tapestries.

In the heavily ornate closet with painted ceiling and the original satin brocade hangings, note the carved 'sleeping chayre'.

HAMMERSMITH

Map p 296 (**TY**)
⊖ Hammersmith Broadway

The district, which is predominantly residential, began as a riverside settlement on the north bank of the Thames and has gradually extended north. It is now bisected by the Great West Road (A/M4) to Bristol and South Wales and the Westway (A/M40) to Oxford.

Riverside – The most attractive part of Hammersmith is along the waterfront. Upstream from the bridge the embankment developed gradually from the early 18C with modest houses built singly or in terraces, adorned with balconies or festooned with wistaria; in the past the view included sailing barges making for harbour; now there are yachts or oarsmen in training.

Two big houses once stood on the riverbank below the bridge. **Craven Cottage** was an 18C cottage *orné* with Egyptian-style interiors, which burnt down in 1888; its name is now perpetuated in the name of Fulham football ground *(Stevenage Road)*. **Brandenburgh House** (17C) was the residence of Queen Caroline of Brunswick when she attempted to claim the rights of consort on the accession of her husband as George IV; it was demolished after her death in 1821.

Hammersmith Bridge – The present suspension bridge (1884-87), designed by Joseph Bazalgette, replaced the first Thames suspension bridge (1827).

Riverside Studios – *Crisp Road.* The studios comprise two theatres, an art gallery, bookshop, restaurant and bar; they opened in 1977 in a building which started life at the turn of the century as an iron foundry and was converted into film studios between the wars.

Temporary exhibitions and recitals are held in the lofty studio adjoining the house *(51 Temple Lodge, Queen Caroline Street)* where Frank Brangwyn, apprentice to William Morris *(see below)* from 1882 to 1884, took up residence in 1899; he built the studio to accommodate the large canvases which brought him fame.

Lower Mall – Among the 18C-19C buildings are the Amateur Rowing Association (no 6), which has a canopied balcony and a bow window supported on slender iron columns over the entrance to the boathouse; Kent House *(no 10)*, which is late 18C with symmetrical bay windows, yellow brickwork decorated with medallions after Adam and contemporary ironwork; the **Blue Anchor** pub; the **Rutland**, a Victorian pub. Westcott Lodge *(Furnival Gardens)* consists of two storeys beneath a plain brick coping, embellished with a canopied balcony supported by an Ionic pillared porch protecting the front door in the last of the six bays. Near the pier is a plaque which indicates the site of the creek and 'harbour where the village began'.

Upper Mall – Sussex House (1726) has stone urns at the corners of the brick coping and segmentally pedimented doorways flanked by Doric pilasters. The **Dove** pub has had a licence for 400 years, although the present building goes back only a couple of centuries; in the 18C it was a coffeehouse where James Thomson is said to have written the words of *Rule Britannia* in the upstairs room; from 1900 it housed the Doves Press and Bindery.

Kelmscott House, a plain three-storey house with five bays and dormers behind the brick coping, dates from the 1780s. In the 19C it was occupied by George Macdonald, poet and novelist (1867-77) before it became home to **William Morris** and his family until his death in 1896. There Morris installed a loom in his bedroom and held meetings in the stables; in the studio he drew the illustrations and designed founts for the fine books he printed in the nearby no 14 and published under the imprint of the **Kelmscott Press** *(see VICTORIA & ALBERT MUSEUM)*, named after Kelmscott Manor in Oxfordshire where Morris is buried.

Rivercourt House (now a school) dates from the early 19C.

The London Corinthian Sailing Club is housed in Linden House, which has Ionic pillared doorways and dates from the 18C (much refurbished); opposite, above the riverside wall, looking like a glassed-in crow's nest, is the race officers' box.

At the end of the Mall are two pubs: the *Old Ship Inn* and the *Black Lion;* the latter is set back from the river behind a garden with a brick arcade from an old riverside factory.

Hammersmith Terrace – The very urban terrace of 17 almost identical brick houses of three and four storeys, built as a single unit facing the river, dates from the mid 18C when all around were fields, market gardens, vineyards and famous strawberry fields. Philippe de Lotherbourg, artist and scenic designer at the Drury Lane Theatre *(see COVENT GARDEN)* in the 18C, lived at no 13; Sir Emery Walker, antiquary and typographer, who collaborated with Morris at the Kelmscott Press, lived at no 7; for more than 50 years Sir Alan Herbert (APH) (1890-1971), writer, lover and ardent protagonist of the Thames, occupied nos 12 to 13.

Other sights – North of the Great West Road the focal point of St Peter's Square with its substantial houses adorned with bay windows and pillared porches, is **St Peter's Church** ⊘ (1829), a yellow stock-brick landmark with pedimented portico and square clock tower; before it is a sculpture of a reclining woman by Karel Voge (1959).

St Paul's ⊘ – Between the bridge and the Broadway stands the parish church, grand in size, pink stone in fabric, neo-Early English in style with a tall tower surmounted by high pinnacles. It dates from 1882 when it replaced a 17C chapel of ease which, although restored and enlarged in 1864, proved too small to accommodate the fast expanding population (6 000 in 1801, 25 000 in 1861, 72 000 in 1881, 112 000 in 1901). The furnishings include late 17C chairs in the chancel and a 17C pulpit, carved with cherub's heads and garlands, from the Wren church of All Hallows, Thames Street. Among the 17C and 18C monuments is one erected by the church benefactor, Sir Nicolas Crispe before his death in 1665 to 'that Glorious Martyr King Charles I of blessed Memory' in the form of a bronze bust by Le Sueur.

The Ark – *Talgarth Road.* Moored alongside the Hammersmith flyover, this ship-like development has been described as 'an ecologically sound office building' conceived as it is by Ake Larson to challenge the building practices blamed for Sick Building Syndrome. Special air-conditioning systems diffuse fresh air that has been cooled across water-cooled batteries, stale air is exhaled through ventilators in the timber-lined atrium roof; central heating is delivered through a radiant system mounted in the ceiling, discharging air that has been warmed by gas-fired boiler heated water; heat and sound insulation is provided by triple glazing; light streams through from the outside and from a central core. The building is structurally supported by a steel frame, its shell sealed by bands of copper cladding that in time, should oxidise greens.

Brook Green – St Paul's Girls' School has been in situ since its foundation in 1903-04 in a red brick and stone building designed by Gerald Horsley with a formal entrance, carvings and segmental pediments.
The music wing (1913) is named after the composer, **Gustav Holst**, who was once music master at the school and wrote *St Paul's Suite for Strings.*

HAMPSTEAD ★★ – HIGHGATE

Map pp 296-297 (**TUX**)
⊖ Hampstead

Hampstead Village developed from a rural area with a few substantial houses, manors and farms into a fashionable 18C spa when the chalybeate springs were discovered in what became Well Walk. It was 4 miles only from the centre of London and, by the time enthusiasm for taking the waters had subsided, builders had begun the erection of houses and terraces, which continues to this day. In 1907 came the tube. Throughout its history this pleasant district has attracted writers, artists, architects, musicians, scientists.
The village, irregularly built on the side of a hill, has kept its original street pattern; main roads from the south and southeast meet and continue north; between is a network of lanes, groves, alleys, steps, courts, rises, places... At the foot of the hill lie Hampstead Ponds. On the north side of the Heath is Kenwood *(see separate listing).*

West side – One flank of **Church Row** is lined by a fine 1720 terrace of brown brick houses with red dressings, tall windows, straight hoods on carved brackets shading the Georgian doors. The range along the north pavement, older, younger and more varied, includes cottages, a weatherboarded house with oversailing bay, full style town houses of 3 storeys with good ironwork...
The Parish Church of **St John** ⊘ at the row's end, obscured in summer by the trees, was built boldly on an ancient site in 1744-47 with a spire rising from a battlemented brick tower, banded in stone. The interior, with giant pillars supporting arches in the tunnel roof, galleries on three sides and box pews, was twice enlarged in the 19C to accommodate Hampstead's rapidly growing population: 4 300 in 1801, 47 000 in 1881.

Hampstead residents – old and young

In the cemetery lie Kate Greenaway and Laszlo Biro, the inventor of the ball-point pen. Temporary residents of the neighbourhood have included John Constable, John Keats, Ian Fleming, Agatha Christie, Sid Vicious, Sting, Boy George, Elizabeth Taylor, Tom Conti, Emma Thompson, Rex Harrison, Peter O'Toole, Jeremy Irons...

Frognal – The district to the west, once a manor, hence all the roads of similar name, presents some distinctive buildings: University College School, large and neo-Georgian with Edward VII in full regalia standing above the entrance door; Kate Greenaway's house *(no 39)* designed in 1885 by Norman Shaw in true children's story book appearance with rambling gables and balconies; and the Sun House *(no 9 Frognal Way)* by Maxwell Fry at his 1935 best, in stepped horizontals in glass and gleaming white.

Holly Walk – The path north from the church, bordered by the 1810 cemetery extension crowded with funeral monuments, rises to the green and pink washed, three-storey houses of Prospect Place (1814) and delightful cottages of Benham's Place (1813).

Holly Place, 1816, is another short terrace flanking **St Mary's**, one of the earliest RC churches to be built in London, founded by Abbé Morel, refugee from the Revolution who came to Hampstead in 1796. From the top of the hill a maze of steps and alleys leads down to Heath Street.

Mount Vernon junction – The triangular junction of Windmill Hill, Hampstead Grove and Holly Bush Hill, weighed down by the late 19C National Institute for Medical Research, is redeemed by **Romney's House** (plaque), picturesquely built of brick and weather-boarding in 1797, and the tall 18C group: Volta, Bolton, Enfield and Windmill Hill, all of brown brick.

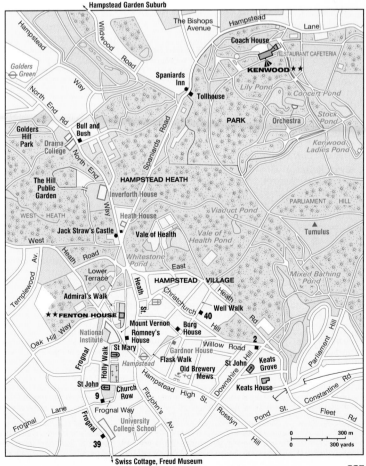

★★ **Fenton House** ⊙ – An iron gate (1707) by **Tijou** gives access to a red brick house, built in 1693; it is Hampstead's finest besides being one of its earliest and largest. The east front, with a recessed porch, is less attractive than the south front of seven bays beneath a hipped roof with a central pediment.

In the original design a self-contained closet was attached to every room but the dividing walls in all but one have now been removed. The original main pine staircase, with its twisted balusters and wide handrail, has survived as well as some doorcases, panelling and chimney pieces. In 1793 the house was bought by a Riga merchant, Philip Fenton, after whom it is still named; in 1952 it was bequeathed to the National Trust.

Collection – The furniture and pictures form a background to 18C porcelain – English, German and French – and the Benton-Fletcher collection of early **keyboard instruments**, some 18 in number ranging in date from 1540 to 1805, plus an early 17C Flemish harpsichord lent by HM the Queen Mother, an Arnold Dolmetsch clavichord (1925) and some stringed instruments. The instruments are for the most part kept in good playing order and are accessible to students. There are frequent concerts.

On the ground floor are harpsichords (1770 English, 1612 Flemish), the most important part of the English porcelain collection (Bristol, Plymouth, Chelsea, Bow, Worcester), some of the German figures, and an Oriental room (porcelain, lacquer pierglass, enamelled ware); on the landing Staffordshire figures and a Trubshaw grandmother clock.

On the first floor are German figurines, teapots; Worcester apple green porcelain in satinwood cabinets, the most important piece of English porcelain in the collection, a Worcester pink-scale vase and cover probably decorated in London (Drawing Room), 17C-18C Chinese blue and white porcelain, 18C English harpsichords, a 16C Italian and an early 18C English spinet, and a 17C virginal; on the top floor 18C square pianos, 17C and 18C harpsichords, 17C and 20C clavichords, and a 17C spinet and virginal. The 17C needlework pictures (Rockingham Room); the bird and flower pictures by the 18C artist Samuel Dixon (Porcelain Room) and the works of Sir William Nicholson (Dining Room) are noteworthy.

Admiral's Walk – The road leads to Admiral's House, built in the first half of the 18C and given its nautical superstructure including, in his time, a couple of cannon with which to fire victory salutes, by the colourful Admiral Matthew Burton (1715-95) after whom the house, now resplendent in 'tropical whites', is named. It was the home of Sir George Gilbert Scott from 1854-64, he made no alteration. The adjoining Grove Lodge also white, probably older, was Galsworthy's home from 1918 until his death in 1933 where he wrote all but the first part of the *Forsyte Saga*. Lower Terrace, at the end of Admiral's Walk, is where Constable lived from 1821-25 before moving to Well Walk.

Eastside – Downshire Hill going east from the foot of Hampstead High Street has some good Regency houses.

Flask Walk, which begins as a pedestrian street with a Victorian pub and tea merchant, continues east past Gardnor House, built in 1736, with a full height rounded bow window at the rear, to New End Square.

Burgh House ⊙ – This dignified house, with its south facing terrace, was built, probably by Quakers, in 1703 when Hampstead was becoming popular as a spa. The local physician, Dr William Gibbons, lived there in the 1720s; the wrought-iron gates bear his initials. The house takes its name from the Revd Allatson Burgh, vicar of St Lawrence Jewry in the City, who was so unpopular that his parishioners petitioned Queen Victoria to have him removed. A frequent visitor from 1934-37 was Rudyard Kipling whose daughter and son-in-law rented the house.

The panelled rooms, still served by the original oak staircase, are now used for poetry and music recitals, exhibitions by local artists and the Hampstead Museum; one room is devoted to the artist, John Constable *(see index);* information on the history, architecture and natural history of Hampstead and the Heath is available from the bookstall.

It was at no 40 Well Walk that **John Constable** lived from 1826 to his death. Christchurch Hill with its Georgian cottages leads to the mid 19C Church with a soaring spire visible for miles.

2 Willow Road ⊙ – Erno **Goldfinger** (1902-87) was born in Hungary; in 1920 he went to Paris and studied architecture at the École des Beaux Arts; five years later, he and a number of fellow students persuaded Auguste Perret, a pioneer in the use of reinforced concrete and 'structural rationalism', to set up a studio. In Paris he met and married the striking Ursula Blackwell (of the Crosse & Blackwell family), who then began painting under Amédée Ozenfant, a former collaborator of Le Corbusier. The three houses they built replaced a run-down terrace, but despite causing early controversy, its discreet, modern, functional design is sympathetic to the Georgian brick houses around. Inside, the central block is spacious, airy, light, practical, homely and full of individual mementoes, art collected by the couple (Ernst, Penrose, Miller, Picasso) and personal possessions (including a particularly long bath!). A central stairwell provides the main axis and access to the three floors; partition walls allow space to be transformed to accommodate great parties or enclose the warmth of intimate gathering; colour and texture are also significant.

Old Brewery Mews – Off Hampstead High Street on the east side, the former brewery building overlooking a well protected by a wrought-iron cage, has been converted into offices and a row of modern town houses.

St John's Church marks the Keats Grove fork, white and upright with a small domed bell turret, Classical pediment, large name plaque and square portico, a chapel of ease dating from 1818.

Keats Grove is lined by early 19C houses and cottages irregular in height, detached and terraced, bay windowed, balconied with canopies, many with flowered front gardens.

Keat's House, Hampstead

Keats House ⊘ – Two small semi-detached Regency houses with a common garden, known as Wentworth Place, were erected in 1815-16 by two friends with whom Keats and his brother, in lodgings in Well Walk, soon became acquainted. In 1818, Keats came to live with his friend Brown in the left hand house; shortly afterwards Mrs Brawne and her children became tenants of the right hand house. He wrote poems, including the *Ode to a Nightingale*, in the garden; he journeyed; he became engaged to Fanny Brawne; he became ill; in September 1820 he left to winter in Italy and in February 1821 he died.

'His short life' in Edmund Blunden's words 'was of unusual intensity; it insisted on being recorded in many ways'. These records are now assembled, chiefly in the Chester Room added in 1838-39 when the second house was acquired. The original rooms are furnished much as Keats and Fanny Brawne must have known them.

The **Keats Memorial Library** (*available to students by appointment only*) is in the local library next door.

John Keats (1795-1821) was the eldest of three sons. From an early age he showed a keen talent for poetry by translating Virgil's *Aeneid* into prose when still at school. In 1810, after losing both his parents (his father in a riding accident and his mother to consumption), he was apprenticed to a surgeon; four years later he transferred to St Thomas' and Guy's Hospitals in Southwark. By 1817, then living in the City, Keats decided to devote himself to the study of Elizabethan literature and to writing poetry, adopting the free form of the heroic couplet. When his brother and sister-in-law resolved to sail for America, Keats travelled to Liverpool to see them off and onwards on an extensive tour of the north (Lancaster, Lake District, Carlisle, Dumfries, Ireland, Ayr, Glasgow...); spent by the exertion and exposure, Keats began to display the symptoms of his fatal malady. His other brother died that December and Keats returned to Hampstead where he met Fanny Brawne not long before he too was to die in Rome.

Hampstead Heath – Hampstead Heath was the common of Hampstead Manor, an area where laundresses laid out washing to bleach in the 18C and, since earliest times, a popular place of recreation (vast one-day fairs; *Easter, Spring and Summer holiday Mondays*).

Whitestone Pond – The pond and the milestone (Holborn Bars 4 1/2 in the bushes at the base of the aerial) from which it takes its name, are on London's highest ground (437ft). The flagstaff is thought to stand on the site of an Armada beacon, the link with the signal south of the river on Shooter's Hill, Blackheath, visible on a clear day, and even more distinct at night. In the 18C and 19C military and admiralty telegraphs stood on Telegraph Hill (west).

Jack Straw's Castle – The white weatherboarded inn, rebuilt in 1962-64, was first mentioned in local records in 1713. The name is thought to be derived from the possibility that supporters rallied on the spot before going to join Straw in Highbury and Wat Tyler in central London in the Peasants' Revolt of 1381. Standing on its own at the junction of the two roads, Heath House, a plain early 18C mansion of brown brick is chiefly remarkable for its commanding position and the visitors received by its 18C-19C owner, the Quaker abolitionist, Samuel Hoare: William Wilberforce, Elizabeth Fry and the leading politicians of the day.

Vale of Health – The Vale, a cluster of late 18C-early 19C cottages, mid-Victorian and now a few modern houses and blocks, built in a dip in the heath and connected by a maze of narrow roads and paths, has at various times been the home of Leigh Hunt, the Harmsworth brothers, Rabindranath Tagore, D H Lawrence, Edgar Wallace, Compton Mackenzie. The origin of the Vale's name is said to derive from the fact that the area was unaffected by the plague in 1665; until 1677 it was a marsh; the houses began to be named from 1841.

To the west of North End Way stands Inverforth House, rebuilt in 1914 and now an annexe to Manor House hospital. Lord Leverhulme's extensive newly restored pergola, sweet with wistaria, rambling roses, clematis and honeysuckle, now forms part of **The Hill Public Garden**, formally laid out on a steeply sloping site and framed by the natural beauty of the trees of the West Heath. Nearby on the northern edge of the West Heath lies **Golders Hill Park**, its landscaped lawns and shrubberies sweeping down to two ponds past bird and animal enclosures.

Bull and Bush – The 1920s building with a modern inn sign, turn of the century paintings of Florrie Forde and a verse of the music hall song outside, reputedly stands on the site of a 17C farmhouse. In the 18C it became for a brief time Hogarth's country retreat, then a tavern, patronised by the painters Joshua Rey-

Hampstead Garden Suburb

The suburb was conceived by Dame Henrietta Barnett, living in what is now Heath End House, as a scheme for rehousing London slum dwellers in the early 20C. Raymond Unwin, the principal architect, designed an irregular pattern of tree-lined streets and closes converging on a central square with its Institute and two churches (one Anglican and one Nonconformist) by Sir Edwin Lutyens. The houses are in varied architectural style.

nolds, Gainsborough, Constable, Romney... Opposite is the gabled brick house (now a speech and drama college) where Anna Pavlova lived from 1921-31.

Spaniards Inn and Tollhouse – The inn and tollhouse have slowed traffic on Spaniards Road into single file since they were built in the early 18C. The small brick tollhouse marks an entrance to the Bishop of London's Park; the white painted brick and weatherboard pub stands on the site of a house said to have been the residence of a 17C Spanish Ambassador. In 1780 the Gordon Rioters, having sacked Lord Mansfield's Bloomsbury town house, stopped to ask the way to Kenwood nearby but were so plied with drink by the publican that they had not moved by the time the military arrived.

HIGHGATE

⊖ *Archway; Highgate*

The area began to be developed in the 16C-17C when one or two decided it was the place to build their country seats; in the 17C rich merchants built mansions there; in the 18C the prosperous, their houses... Highgate remains a village in character, centred on Pond Square and the High Street.

Pond Square – Small houses and cottages line three sides of the irregularly shaped Pond Square – from which the ponds disappeared in the 1860s. Along the south side runs **South Grove** lined with various houses: the early 18C Church House *(no 10)*, the Highgate Literary and Scientific Society *(no 11)* and Moreton House *(no 14)* a brick mansion of 1715. Opposite, **Rock House** *(no 6)* retains its over-hanging wooden bay windows (18C); on the far side of Bacon's Lane stands the late 17C **Old Hall**, built in plain brick with a parapet and at the back a great bow window, topped by a pierced white balustrade. **Bacon's Lane** honours the philosopher who was a frequent guest (and died) at Arundel House which used to be where Old Hall now stands.

The Flask (1721) on Highgate West Hill corner is a period country pub.

The tree-lined **North Road** runs past the 19C red brick buildings of Highgate School (f 1565) on the right and opposite a late Georgian terrace, nos 1-11, followed by individual houses of the same period *(nos 15, 17 plaque to A E Housman 19)*, and at 47, 49 another early Georgian group. Beyond stand the clean lined buildings, Highpoint One and Two, designed by **Lubetkin** and Tecton in 1936 and 1938; the first has two Erechtheon caryatids supporting the porch; one facing front, but the other (fed up perhaps)? at the half turn!

The Grove – This wide tree-planted road, branching off to the north, presents behind open railings late 17-early 18C terrace housing at its satisfying best; rose brick in colour, of dignified height, with segment-headed windows and individual variations.

The poet and critic S T Coleridge lived at no 3 from 1823 till his death in 1834 and is buried in St Michael's Church discernable by its tapering octagonal spire (1830) overlooking Highgate Cemetery.

Highgate Cemetery ⊘ – *Swain's Lane*. The Eastern Cemetery is still in use; here lie George Eliot (1819-80) and **Karl Marx** (d 1883) – bust (1956) by Laurence Bradshaw. The Western Cemetery (opened 1838) contains some remarkable 19C monumental masonry and the tombs of Michael Faraday (1791-1867), Charles Cruft who started the dog shows in 1886, and Gabriel and Christina Rossetti *(see TATE GALLERY)*.

Highgate High Street – The **Gate House Tavern** stands on the site of a 1386 gate house to the Bishop of London's park (18C house at the rear); no 46, with a small paned bay window, dates from 1729; no 23 opposite, Englefield House with straight-headed windows and modillion frieze and nos 17, 19 and 21 are all early 18C.

Highgate Hill – Just inside **Waterlow Park** stands **Lauderdale House**, 16C in origin but remodelled in the 18C in small country house style. This is the house about which the tale is told that in 1676, **Nell Gwynne** not yet successful in obtaining recognition for her princely 6-year-old son, dangled him out of a window before his father threatening to drop him, whereupon Charles called out 'Save the Earl of Burford' (the future Duke of St Albans). It is now used as a cultural and educational centre.

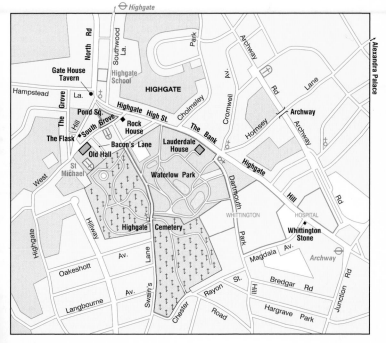

Opposite, high above the road, is **The Bank,** a row of brick houses; nos 110, 10 and 106, Ireton and Lyndale Houses are early 18C, no 104 Cromwell House (s called for uncertain reasons since 1833) of now mellow red brick with a sol parapet is 16C and has an octagonal domed turret (1638).

West of Highgate Hill is the **Archway,** a viaduct built to allow the road north (A1) pass through the hill 80ft below Hornsey Lane. The original structure by John Nas was replaced in 1897 by a metal construction designed by Alexander Binnie.

Whittington Hospital has grown out of the original 'Leper spytell' of 1473. Th **Whittington Stone** (1821), a marble cat sitting on a stone, marks the spot wher according to tradition **Dick Whittington** *(see index)* heard Bow bells telling him t 'turn again'.

Highgate Wood *(north of Archway and Muswell Hill junction)* comprises 70 acres (28 hectares) and is classified an ancient woodland, a remnant of the larger Ancient Forest of Middlesex, mentioned in the Domesday Book. Archeological surveys have revealed that potteries were active in the area around the time of the Roman Conquest (AD 43). Between 16C to 18C hornbeam would have been coppiced, while oak would have been grown to provide the Crown with timber for shipbuilding. In 1885, under threat of development, the wood was acquired by the Corporation of London. Today it is protected by an active conservation policy and equipped with children's recreation facilities.

Alexandra Palace ⊙ – ⊖ *Wood Green.* Set atop a hill in a 480 acre park, th People's Palace known as 'Ally Pally', was built in 1873 as a counterpart to Cryst Palace and twice burned down (1873, 1980). The Great Hall with its single-spa glass roof and rose window, the West Hall and Palm Court have been carefull restored and provide a venue for exhibitions, concerts and sporting events. Grea sweeping views of the city extend from the top of the hill.

The first live television transmissions were made in 1936 by the BBC fron Alexandra Palace.

In the 18C a number of **London spas** developed round mineral springs where people could take the waters in rural surroundings. They were frequented by the less wealthy, who could not afford the elegance of Bath. Among the most popular were Hampstead and Islington and also Sadler's Wells, which offered dancing, pantomimes and rope dancing, accompanied by the consumption of cold meat and wine.

Help us in our constant task of keeping up-to-date.
Send us your comments and suggestions to

Michelin Travel Publications
38 Clarendon Road
Watford
Herts WD1 1SX
Tel: (01923) 415000
Web site: www.michelin-travel.com

HAMPTON COURT ★★★

Map p 296 (TZ)
Overground: Hampton Court from Waterloo
Boat: Hampton Court (see PRACTICAL INFORMATION)

Hampton Court Palace ⊘ was begun in the 16C, an age of splendour and display, which is reflected in the magnificent and extensive Tudor buildings. It was extended in the late 17C with two ranges of handsome state apartments designed by Sir Christopher Wren for William and Mary.

Wolsey's Mansion – In 1514 the manor of Hampton was sold by the Knights of St John of Jerusalem to Thomas Wolsey, the son of an Ipswich butcher. While still in his early thirties, Wolsey was appointed to a chaplaincy in the household of Henry Tudor; under Henry VIII he rose to be Archbishop of York (1514), Lord Chancellor (1515), Cardinal (1515) and Papal Legate (1518). He celebrated his wealth and position with his houses in Whitehall, at Moor Park in Hertfordshire and at Hampton-on-Thames, which he chose for its 'extraordinary salubrity' attested by eminent English physicians and doctors from Padua.

In 1515 he enclosed the estate (1 800 acres) and began to construct a fine mansion according to the usual Tudor plan of consecutive courts bordered by buildings: Base Court, Clock Court, Carpenter's Court, hall and chapel (300ft by 550ft overall). The mansion was richly furnished throughout with painted and gilded ceilings and panelling and tapestries on the walls. It was staffed by the cardinal's personal household of 500 and contained some 1 000 rooms of which 280 were kept prepared for guests. Spring water was brought from Coombe Hill three miles away and carried under the Thames in leaden pipes. The palace was well supplied with waterclosets and great brick sewers which drained into the Thames and lasted until 1871.

Wolsey's wealth, it was said, exceeded the King's; the magnificence of his mansion outshone the royal palaces and attracted the eye and envy of the King. After 15 years Wolsey fell from power; within months of his disgrace he died (1530).

Tudor Palace – Despite its magnificence, Henry VIII enlarged and rebuilt much of the palace. He added a moat and drawbridge and wings to either side of the central gateway. He constructed the Great Hall, the Great Watching Chamber, the annexes around the Kitchen Court, including the Haunted Gallery, the Fountain Court, the tennis court wing and the south front overlooking the Pond Garden. A painting of this palace seen from the Thames, now in the Renaissance Picture Gallery *(see below)*, shows a forest of pinnacles and turrets and chimneys. Henry also built a tiltyard and planted a flower garden, kitchen garden and two orchards.

Edward VI, who was born and christened (1537) at Hampton Court, his two sisters, Mary and Elizabeth, and the early Stuarts resided at the palace in fine weather or when the plague was rife in London.

Unlike other royal residences, Hampton Court was reserved for Cromwell and was therefore preserved with its contents, particularly the wood carvings and paintings. When Charles II was restored to the throne he initiated the modern garden layout but the buildings remained largely unaltered and unmaintained until the late 17C.

Renaissance Reconstruction – Hampton Court entered its third and last phase of construction in the reign of **William and Mary**, who wished to make Hampton Court their main residence outside London. They engaged the talents of an unrivalled team of artist-master-craftsmen: Grinling Gibbons, Jean Tijou, Antonio Verrio, Morris Emmett, C G Cibber, Daniel Marot, the King's Dutch architect, and the great gardeners, George London and Henry Wise.

Initial schemes for the total demolition of the Tudor palace were discarded. Instead Wren rebuilt the east and south ranges of the Fountain Court to provide two suites of State Apartments, each comprising a guardroom, presence and audience chambers, drawing room, state bedroom and closet. The King's Side was in the south range overlooking the Privy Garden and the Queen's Side was in the east range overlooking the Fountain Garden. Wren also rebuilt the smaller informal royal apartments facing into the **Fountain Court★** and added a colonnade and a new south range to the Clock Court. The buildings were executed in brick in the classic Renaissance style of the 17C with stone centrepieces, enrichments and window surrounds; the long rows of tall, circular or square windows emphasise the horizontal lines of the building and the roof-level balustrade. The Banqueting House overlooking the river was built in the last years of William's reign after the death of Mary.

The decoration and furnishing of the State Apartments was begun under Queen Anne and completed under George II, the last monarch to reside at the palace, who also commissioned William Kent to decorate the Cumberland Suite. When the Great Gatehouse was rebuilt (1771-73), it was reduced in height by two storeys. In 1838 Queen Victoria opened the State Apartments, the gardens and Bushy Park to the public.

★★★ Palace

The **Trophy Gates** were built as the main gates in the reign of George II with lion an
unicorn supporters.

The **moat and bridge** were constructed by Henry VIII; the bridge, buried by Charles
when the moat was filled in, was excavated in 1910 when the parapet w
renewed and fronted by the King's Beasts.

The **Great Gatehouse** built by Wolsey was flanked in the reign of Henry VIII wi
wings decorated with 16C diapered brickwork. The **stone weasels** on the battlemen
date from the same period.

The **Arms of Henry VIII** appear in a panel *(renewed)* beneath the central oriel in th
Great Gatehouse and also on Anne Boleyn's Gateway *(see below)*. The **terraco**
roundels depicting Roman emperors, which appear on the turrets and elsewher
were bought by Wolsey for Hampton Court in 1521; they cost 6 guineas each an
were originally painted and gilded.

Anne Boleyn's Gateway is so called because it was embellished by Henry VIII during h
brief period as Queen; the bell turret is 18C. The Base Court side bears Elizabeth I
badges and initials, dating from 1566; on the other side are Wolsey's arms
terracotta (restored) and his cardinal's hat.

Caius Cibber carved the window surrounds in the Fountain Court, as well as man
of the palace's finest window and arcade ornaments.

*The interior of the palace is divided into six separate tours, each with a different then
(site plan below).*

Tudor Royal Lodgings – *30min; entrance in Anne Boleyn's Gateway.* The **Great H**
(1) (106ft × 40ft × 60ft), used by Henry's men for dining and sleeping, was bu
in 5 years (1531-36): Henry VIII was so impatient to see it finished that wor
continued by candlelight. The magnificent hammerbeam roof is ornamented wi
mouldings, tracery, carving and pendants relieved with gilding and colours. Th
walls are hung with 16C Flemish tapestries made by van Orley to illustrate th
Story of Abraham. At the west end is the Minstrels' Gallery.

The **Horn Room (2)**, from which the stairs led down to the kitchens, was the servir
place for the upper end of the hall: it takes its name from the deer antlers whic
were hung there for many years.

The **Great Watching Chamber (3)** was built in 1535-36 at the entrance to the Tud
State Rooms *(demolished)* with an elaborately panelled ceiling set with coloure
bosses displaying Tudor and Seymour devices between ribs which curve down t
form pendants. The 16C Flemish tapestries depicting the *Vices and Virtues* wer
possibly purchased by Wolsey in 1522; three others illustrate scenes fro
Petrarch's *Triumphs.*

The **Haunted Gallery (4)**, which is said to be haunted by the ghost of Catherin
Howard (dragged off because of her infidelity), looks on to the Round Kitche
Court. The Flemish tapestries are probably from Queen Elizabeth's collection.

The **Royal Pew (5)** was designed for Queen Anne with a ceiling by Sir Jame
Thornhill.

The **Chapel Royal (6)** was built by Wolsey but lavishly transformed by Henry VIII wh
inserted the fan vaulted wooden ceiling and gilded pendants. The reredos, a wrea
of cherubim above drops on either side of a framed oval, is by **Gibbons**; it is frame
by Corinthian pillars and a segmental pediment by **Wren**.

Queen's State Apartments – *45min; entrance in Clock Court.* The **Queen's Stairca**
(7) was the ceremonial approach to the Queen's State Apartments. The beautif
wrought-iron balustrade is by **Tijou** and the lantern by Benjamin Goodison (1731
The walls and ceiling were decorated by Kent (1735); on the west wall is a
allegorical painting by Honthorst (1628) depicting Charles I and Henrietta Maria a
Jupiter and Juno, and the Duke of Buckingham as Apollo.

The **Queen's Guard Chamber (8)** contains a monumental chimney-piece carved b
Grinling Gibbons.

The **Queen's Presence Chamber (9)** contains a bed and furniture made for Queen Ann
(1714). The elaborate plaster ceiling is by Sir John Vanbrugh, carvings by Gibbon
and the paintings by Tintoretto *(The Nine Muses)*, Gentileschi and Vasari.

The **Public Dining Room (10)** was decorated by Sir John Vanbrugh c 1716-18 for th
future George II and Queen Caroline. The cornice and royal arms above th
fireplace were carved by Grinling Gibbons. The paintings are by Sebastiano Ricc
Pietro Liberi and G Knapton *(Augusta, Princess of Wales with her family).*

The **Astronomical Clock** was made for Henry VIII in 1540 by Nicholas Oursian;
on the dial (8ft) are indicated the hour, month, date, signs of the zodiac,
year and phase of the moon. It pre-dates the publication of the theories of
Copernicus and Galileo and the sun therefore revolves round the earth. It
was transferred in the 19C from St James's Palace to its present site in the
Clock Court which was the main Court of Wolsey's house.

HAMPTON COURT PALACE

FIRST FLOOR

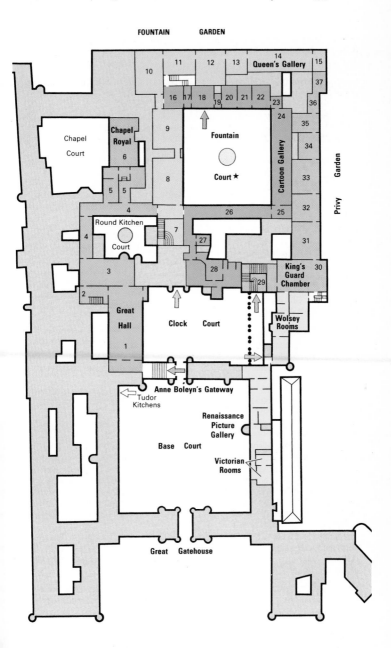

Tudor Royal Lodgings

Georgian Rooms

Wolsey Rooms and Renaissance Picture Gallery

Queen's State Apartments

King's Apartments

Entrance point (ground floor)

0   50 ft
0   20 m

FOUNTAIN   GARDEN

Chapel
Court

Chapel
Royal

10   11   12   13   14   Queen's Gallery   15

37

16 17 18 19 20 21 22 23   36

9   Fountain   24   35

6   Court ★   34

8   33

Cartoon Gallery

5   5   4   26   25   32

Round Kitchen   7   31

4   Court   27

3   28   King's
Guard
Chamber   30

2   29   Wolsey
Rooms

Great
Hall   Clock   Court

1

Anne Boleyn's Gateway

Tudor
Kitchens

Renaissance
Picture
Gallery

Base   Court

Victorian
Rooms

Great   Gatehouse

Privy   Garden

*To find the description of a sight, a historical event, a monument ... consult the index at
the end of the guide.*

The **Queen's Audience Chamber** (**11**) is hung with a 16C tapestry illustrating the Sto of Abraham and contains the canopied Chair of State. Portraits of the *Duke a Duchess of Brunswick* and of *Anne of Denmark*.

The **Queen's Drawing Room** (**12**) is decorated with wall and ceiling paintings by Ver (1703-05) commissioned by Queen Anne: *The Queen as Justice* (ceiling), *The Que receiving homage* (west wall), *Prince George of Denmark as Lord Admiral* (nor wall), *Cupid drawn by sea-horses* (south wall).

From the central window there is a splendid **view★** of the Fountain Garden (s below).

The **Queen's Bedroom** (**13**) contains State bed, chair and stools (1715-16) in crims damask; portrait of *Queen Anne as a child* by Sir Peter Lely. The ceiling by James Thornhill (1715) contains medallions of George I, the Prince and Princess Wales.

The **Queen's Gallery** (**14**) is hung with five early 18C tapestries depicting the histo of Alexander the Great and two cartoons by Carlo Cignani (1628-1719). The Tu vases were made for William and Mary. The mantelpiece was designed by Jo Nost and the carvings are by Grinling Gibbons.

The adjoining chamber (**15**) is decorated with embroidered wall coverings.

Georgian Rooms – *30min; entrance in Fountain Court.* In contrast with the pub state rooms, these private apartments are more intimate and comfortable. Mo have been restored to recreate interiors from 1737.

The **Queen's Private Chapel** (**16**) has a domed ceiling with a lantern. Religious paintin by Fetti surmount the doors here and in the following rooms.

The **Bathing Closet** (**17**) has no locks, instead a curtained screen would have be used. Note how the wooden bath is lined with linen to safeguard against splinter The **Private Dining Room** (**18**) is hung with works by Pellegrini. The large silv service is on loan from a private collector.

The next room is a second **Closet** (**19**).

The **Queen's Private Chamber** (**20**) is hung with paintings by Ruysdael, Brueghel a van de Velde. The painting of Friars in a nunnery was a particular royal favourite

The **King's Private Dressing Room** (**21**) contains a small early 18C bed.

George II's Private Chamber (**22**) is notable for its 1730 flock wallpaper and a por-trait of Cardinal Richelieu by Ph de Champaigne. There follows a small **lobby** (**23**).

> Etiquette dictated that the king visit the queen as she had fewer servants liable to be listening at the keyhole, rather than vice-versa. In order to protect privacy, a special lock was contrived: a silk cord within reach of Queen Caroline's bed.

The **Cartoon Gallery** (**24**) was designed by Wren (1699) to display seven of the ten tapestry cartoons drawn Raphael (1515) and depicting scenes from the lives of St Peter and St Paul; th were purchased by Charles I in 1623 and are now displayed in the Victoria a Albert Museum. The cartoons hanging here are copies.

The four doorcases and the very long drops framing the tapestry over the firepla were carved by Grinling Gibbons. The panel below the mantel shelf is by Jo Nost.

The **lobby** (**25**) is hung with a view of Hampton Court in George I's reign and a 1 hunting scene.

The **Communication Gallery** (**26**), which links the King's and Queen's Apartments, hung with the famous *Windsor Beauties* of Charles II's court by Lely; originally was hung with Mantegna's cartoons which are now in the Orangery *(see below)*.

Wolsey's Closet (**27**) contains its original furnishings: linenfold panelling *(restore* painted wall panels; frieze with Tudor badges, mermaids and Wolsey's motto as running motif; ceiling of timber with plaster and lead mouldings, a coloured a gilded combination of Tudor roses, Prince of Wales' feathers and Renaissan ornament.

The **Cumberland Suite** (**28**) was designed by William Kent (1732) for George II's thi son: elaborate plasterwork and chimney pieces; portraits of some of the roy children; paintings by Ricci, Carracci, Allori *(Judith with the head of Holoferne*. Giardano, Vouet *(Diana)*, Balestra, Strozzi and Le Sueur.

King's Apartments – *45min; entrance in Clock Court.* The **King's Staircase** (**29**), t ceremonial approach to the King's Side, is decorated with allegorical scenes paint by Verrio c 1700 and stylised wrought-iron balustrade by Tijou.

In the **King's Guard Chamber** (**30**) the upper walls are decorated with over 3 000 ar arranged by John Harris, William III's gunsmith.

The **First Presence Chamber** (**31**) contains William III's canopied chair of state. The o door-cases and limewood garlands are by Grinling Gibbons. A picture of the Ki by Kneller (1701) hangs in its original place; the portrait of *The Marquess Hamilton* is by Mytens.

The smaller **Second Presence Chamber** (**32**) sometimes served as a dining-room. Note the pier-glasses and the portrait of *Christian IV of Denmark* over the fireplace.

The **King's Audience Chamber** (**33**) contains the state canopy and 17C chair. The portrait of *Elizabeth of Bohemia* is by Honthorst. Note the pier-glasses and carving. View of the Privy Garden.

In the **King's Drawing Room** (**34**) note the elaborate carved frame above the fireplace, headed by a crown of fruit and flowers and descending in drops including garlands, putti and birds.

In the **King's State Bedroom** (**35**) the ceiling was painted by Verrio. The tapestries are from the 16C Abraham series. The state bed was used only for the formal *levée* and *couchée*.

The King slept in the **King's Dressing Room** (**36**) which is furnished in yellow taffeta; the ceiling by Verrio depicts *Mars in the Lap of Venus.*

The **King's Writing Closet** (**37**) was used for formal business, signing important documents. The mirror over the fireplace provides a view through the whole suite of rooms.

The **King's Private Apartments** on the ground floor are panelled and hung with portraits of courtiers by Kneller, Lely and Rigaud; they display architectural drawings of the Palace, a silver-gilt toilet service (c 1670) by Pierre Prévost, Dutch and Italian paintings, furniture.

The **Orangery** provided winter accommodation for the orange trees which grew in tubs and stood out of doors in summer.

The **Oak Room** is furnished with bookcases and a writing table.

The **King's Private Dining Room** is hung with portraits of the *Hampton Court Beauties* (Queen Mary's Court) by Kneller; the table is laid with pyramids of fruit and meringues; gold plate is on display in the alcove.

Wolsey Rooms and Renaissance Picture Gallery – *30min; entrance in Clock Court*. The Wolsey rooms, which were probably used by guests rather than by the cardinal himself, are ornamented with 16C linenfold and later plain panelling and an elaborate ceiling decorated with Wolsey's badges.

The Renaissance paintings, from HM the Queen's collection, include a family group of *Henry VIII and his children* including a posthumous portrait of *Jane Seymour* after Holbein, portraits of *Charles I and Henrietta Maria*, and *Charles I as Prince of Wales* by Mytens; *Charles V; The Field of the Cloth of Gold*; mid 17C view of Hampton Court; *Elizabeth I, Henry VIII, François I, Edward VI* attributed to William Scrots.

Hampton Court

There are also paintings by Tintoretto, Titian, Savoldo, Lotto, Bronzino, Bassano
Dosso Dossi, Corregio *St Catherine*, Salviati *The Virgin and Child with an Ange*
Bellini, Parmigianino, Raphael; Quentin Massys *Erasmus*; Cranach *Judgment c*
Paris; Breughel the Elder *Massacre of the Innocents*; Joose van Cleeve; Har
Baldung.
The two **Victorian Rooms** are furnished in the style of the 1840s.

Tudor Kitchens – *45min; entrance in Clock Court; sound guide available.* The 16
kitchens are the largest and most complete to survive from this period. When th
court was in residence they served two meals a day to some 600 people an
employed about 230 staff. They are laid out as for the preparation of the feas
served on Midsummer's Day in 1542. The tour begins in the cellar beneath th
Great Hall (**model** of the kitchens), proceeds to the main gates, where the produc
entered the palace, and passes through the **Butchery**, the **Boiling House**, the **Fles**
Larder and the **Fish Court** to the **Great Kitchens**, where the meat was cooked on spit
turned by boys known as gallopines, and sauces were prepared over charcoa
stoves; the dishes were then dressed or transferred directly to the **Servery**. Th
Wine Cellar is one of three in which home-brewed ale and imported wine wer
stored.

★★★Gardens

The gardens (50 acres) bear the imprint of their creators: the Tudor, Stuar
Orange monarchs, their designers and great gardeners. Over the years feature
have been raised and levelled; 17C and 18C box-edged parterres have bee
converted into lawns or woodland in line with fashion; new species have bee
introduced.
Wolsey planted a walled flower garden between the south front and the rive
under Henry VIII the area was converted into the Pond Garden and Privy Garder
The Privy Garden began as squares of grass, coloured brick dust and sand, dotte
with heraldic beasts on poles and topiary; a gazebo was erected on a raised moun
by the river, with a spiral approach flanked by gaudily painted King's Beasts; ther
was a watergate to welcome visitors who usually travelled by river in those days
Between 1599 and 1659 the heraldic garden was replaced with four simple gras
plats containing fine statuary; the beasts were transferred to stand in the cour
before the main entrance and the mound was levelled and the soil used t
construct the terraces which now flank the Privy Garden.
Under Charles II the land overlooked by the east front was laid out in the fashion
able French style practised by Le Nôtre; a vast semicircle of lime trees enclose
three radiating avenues, laid out in a giant goosefoot *(patte d'oie)*; the central claw
was represented by a canal, the Long Water, which pierced the rows of lime trees
The layout of the gardens today has been restored to that of 1702, designe
largely by William III, a 'Delighter' in gardening, and Mary, his queen, who wa
'particularly skill'd in Exoticks', for which she sent botanists to Virginia and th
Canary Islands.

South Side – The **Knot Garden**, a velvety conceit of interlaced ribands of dwarf bo
or thyme with infillings of flowers, was replanted this century within its walle
Elizabethan site. The royal cipher **ER 1568** appears on the stonework of the ba
window in the **South Front** overlooking the Knot Garden; the lead cupola an
octagonal turret date from the 16C.
The **Lower Orangery**, a plain building by Wren, now houses the Mantegna Cartoor
(c 1431-1506), possibly the earliest pictures on canvas to survive, which wer
bought by Charles I early in the 17C. *The Cartoons of the Triumph of Caesa*
consists of nine giant paintings, showing a triumphal procession, ending with th
portrait of an ashen withered Caesar, high in his chariot.
The **Great Vine★** produces an annual crop of 500-600 bunches of Black Hambur
grapes *(on sale late August to early September)*; it has a girth of 78 inches and wa
planted in 1768 by Capability Brown for George III.
The massive wistaria, near the Vine House, dates from 1840.
The **Banqueting House** *(for access, see plan)*, attributed to William Talman unde
William III, contains an important Baroque interior, the Painted Room by Verrio.
The **Privy Garden** was reserved for the monarch and his guests; each monarch altere
the layout to conform with contemporary fashion. The last major redesign too
place under William and Mary when Queen Mary's Bower, a hornbeam alley, an
the Queen's Terrace were built; the Tudor Water Gallery was demolished and th
garden extended to the river; it was screened from the towpath by 12 delicat
wrought-iron panels with English, Welsh, Scottish and Irish emblems designed b
Jean Tijou; the centre was laid out to a sophisticated 'broderie' design with pyr
amidal yews and clipped round-headed hollies. In the late 18C informal plantin
was introduced, the statuary was removed and the trees were allowed to grov
unclipped. The gardens have now been restored to their former glory, complet
with the bowered walkway.

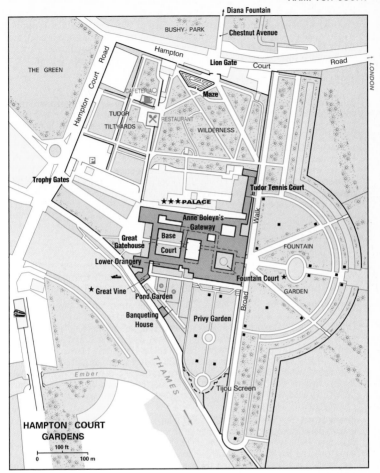

Diana Fountain

BUSHY PARK

Chestnut Avenue

Hampton

Lion Gate Court Road

LONDON

THE GREEN

Hampton Court Road

CAFETERIA

Maze

TUDOR
TILTYARDS

RESTAURANT

WILDERNESS

Trophy Gates

P

Tudor Tennis Court

★★★ PALACE

Anne Boleyn's
Gateway

Walk

**Great
Gatehouse**

Base
Court

FOUNTAIN

Lower Orangery

Fountain Court ★

GARDEN

★ Great Vine

Pond Garden

**Banqueting
House**

Privy Garden

Broad

THAMES

Ember

Tijou Screen

HAMPTON COURT
GARDENS

100 ft

0   100 m

East Side – The entablature (1694-96) of the east front of the palace was carved by Caius Cibber combining the William and Mary cipher with crown, sceptres, trumpets.

The **Broad Walk** was planned by Wren and Queen Caroline to separate the Privy Garden from the Fountain Garden.

The **Fountain Garden** was created under William III by retaining the radiating avenues created by Charles II and reducing the Long Water to its present length (3/4 mile); 13 fountains were installed in a formal scrollwork setting of dwarf box hedges (a Dutch fashion), obelisk-shaped yews and globes of white holly. Under Queen Anne eight fountains at the circumference were removed, the box hedge arabesques were replaced by grass and gravel; in Queen Caroline's time the fountains were reduced to the present singleton. In the late 20C the yews, which grew as they would in the 19C, were trimmed to their present conical shape to make room for flower beds and to reveal spectacular vistas from the east front. The double semicircle of lime trees was replanted in the 1980s.

The **Tudor Tennis Court** *(for access, see plan)*, which is still played on regularly, was built by Henry VIII; the windows are 18C.

North Side – The **Tudor tiltyards,** surrounded by six observation towers, of which one remains, are now walled rose gardens – roses cost 4 pence for 100 bushes in Tudor times.

The **Wilderness,** now an area (9 acres) of natural woodland, includes a triangular **maze** *(access see plan)* which dates from 1714. The site, originally occupied by Henry VIII's orchard, was formally laid out by William III with espaliers, clipped yews, hollies, box hedges and a circular maze.

The **Lion Gates** were part of Wren's grand design for a new north entrance and front to the palace.

The **Chestnut Avenue** in Bushy Park is another feature of Wren's plan. Four rows of lime trees flank the double row of chestnut trees (274 trees planted 42ft apart extending for over a mile) which are particularly striking when they are in flower in mid May. The **Diana Fountain** was commissioned by Charles II from Francisco

347

Fenelli for the Privy Garden. Northwest of the fountain is a **Woodland Garden** (100 acres) where rhododendrons and azaleas of every hue flourish beneath the trees on either side of the stream which is home to waterfowl and a black swan. Bushy Park was first enclosed by Charles I as a deer park; he also had a tributary of the Colne River diverted to form the Longford River (9 miles).

HAMPTON COURT GREEN

Opposite the palace gates and along the south side of the green are houses associated with the court, particularly in the late 17C and 18C: early 19C hotel on the bridge road, Palace Gate House, The Green, **Old Court House**, the home (1706-23) of Sir Christopher Wren, Paper House, Court Cottage, **Faraday House** *(18C with a bow window)* where Michael Faraday lived in retirement (1858-67), and Cardinal House behind a high fence. Hidden behind the last two houses are Old Office House, with a hipped roof, and small square **King's Store Studio**, with white weatherboarding (George III plaque). Facing the Green is the long brick range of the Tudor **Royal Mews**, built round a courtyard.

HARROW

Map p 296 **(TX)**
⊖ Harrow-on-the-Hill

Harrow, which has two distinct centres, derives its name from 'hearg', a pagan shrine which may have stood on the steep hill (406ft), the focal point of the conurbation.

Harrow-on-the-Hill – The village clings to the steep slopes below the parish church with a fine view of northwest London on all sides.

Little remains of the original **St Mary's Church** ⊙ begun by Lanfranc and consecrated by St Anselm in 1094; later visited by Thomas Becket and Cranmer. As Rector of Harrow Thomas Wolsey entertained Henry VIII at Headstone Manor *(see below)*.

Inside, there are interesting brasses, a 12C font and an early 18C pulpit. In the churchyard, where **Byron**'s daughter Allegra lies buried, is the Peachey tomb where Byron used to sit; it was restored by his publisher John Murray with a marble tablet engraved with four lines from his poem *'Written beneath an Elm in Harrow churchyard'*.

Harrow School ⊙ – Founded in 1571 by John Lyon *(monument in church)*, the well known public school occupies a group of high quality 19C buildings including the Old School of 1611 which was twinned in 1818-20 by C R Cockerell. The Chapel in flint and stone and the Vaughan Library in polychromatic red brick are by G G Scott. Also represented are Decimus Burton (Headmaster's house), Charles Hayward (boarding houses, labs, sanatorium and gymnasium) and William Burges who designed the New Speech Room (1874-77) in a D-shape.

Harrow Museum and Heritage Centre ⊙ – *Pinner View*. The museum and heritage centre, housed in **Headstone tithe barn★** (150ft long by 30ft wide), built in 1506 for £44 11s 8 1/2d, traces local history.

Famous former pupils include Byron, Robert **Peel**, Lord Palmerston, R B Sheridan who lived at the Grove in the 1780s piling up debts, Anthony Trollope a miserable day boy who walked from his home nearby which later inspired his novel *Orley Farm*, Lord Shaftesbury, John Galsworthy, Sir Winston **Churchill** and Nehru.

Headstone Manor itself consists of part of a great hall, built in 1344, a 14C timber-framed cross wing and 17C and 18C extensions, surrounded by a garden and enclosed on four sides by a **moat** fed by Yeading brook. The property belonged to the see of Canterbury until 1545 when Thomas Cranmer was obliged to hand it over to Henry VIII, who sold it to Sir Edward North, one of his officials.

Grim's Dyke – *Old Redding, Harrow Weald*. The earthwork, a rampart and a ditch some 5 miles long, is probably of Saxon origin. It gave its name to a mansion (now a hotel) designed in Tudor style by Norman Shaw in 1875, where the composer W S Gilbert lived from 1890 to 1911. The Music Room is graced by the original pink alabaster fireplace (15ft high).

The most important sights in this guide can be found on the Principal Sights map, and are described in the text. Use the map and plans, the Calendar of events, the index, and read the Introduction to get the most out of this guide.

ISLINGTON – HOLLOWAY

In the 19C **Cruikshank**, who lived in Highbury Terrace, was commenting graphically in *London going out of Town* or the *March of Bricks and Mortar* on the new builder-developers, among them Thomas Cubitt, who were laying out squares, terraces and 'meaner streets' which were soon inhabited by workers from the new light industries invading the neighbourhood (pop 1801 - 10 000; 1881 - 283 000; 1901 - 335 000). By the 20C Islington and Angel in particular had become a synonym for slums, grime and grinding poverty, raucous children, rough pubs, the Caledonian Market (Cally Market), the gas-lit glories of Collins Music Hall.

Since the Second World War restoration and repainting have returned terraces and squares to their precise well-groomed lines – notably **Duncan Terrace**, **Colebrooke Row**, built in 1761, and **Charlton Place**, with their Tuscan column framed front doors and lanterns, or rounded doorways and ground floor windows and shallow iron balconies; slums have been largely replaced by four to eight-storey blocks of brick, reminders of the locality's past as a major London brickfield.

Angel – Five main thoroughfares converge on the ancient crossroads – named after the Angel Inn which once stood on the corner.

Crafts Council Gallery ⊙ – *44a Pentonville Road.* The Crafts Council is a government-funded body dedicated to sustaining and encouraging a strong tradition in the decorative and applied arts. Besides publishing a magazine, it holds major exhibitions of contemporary (Chelsea Craft Fair) and historical work in its own collections. Further information is provided through its bookshop and slide index. It is housed in a deconsecrated Dissenters' Chapel known as Claremont Hall (1818-19).

Islington – 'A pleasantly seated country town' as it was styled by John Strype (1643-1737), became a suburb in the 17C when people fled the City after the Plague (1665) and the Fire (1666); the better-off removed to Islington while the poor, numbering some 300 000, erected shacks and tenements on Finsbury and Moorfields. Islington became fashionable: tea gardens were set up around the wells (Clerkenwell, Sadler's Wells etc); taverns marked the stages on the old well-trodden roads from the north, which had been used for centuries, until the coming of the railways, by farmers and herdsmen driving cattle, sheep and swine south, resting them in fields and pens around the village which became known as one of London's dairies, before going on down St John Street to Smithfield or, in the 19C and 20C, to the Caledonian Market.

Camden Passage – *Upper Street.* The quaint old alley is lined with small shops, arcades, restaurants, two Victorian pubs, and the newly built 'Georgian Village'. The small specialist shops can be searched for antique furniture, *Art Nouveau* ornaments in china and opalescent glass, Sèvres porcelain, heavy plate cameras, silver, military mementoes, and jewellery.

Business Design Centre – *Between Upper Street and Liverpool Road.* The former **Royal Agricultural Hall** (1861-62) was used successively for cattle shows, military tournaments, revivalist meetings, bullfighting (1888) and Cruft's Dog Show (1891-1939). After many years of dereliction it has been restored and modernised for trade exhibitions.

Islington Green – The shaded triangular green is pinpointed at its centre by a statue of Sir Hugh Myddelton *(see index)*. A plaque marks the site (north side) where from 1862 until the middle of this century Collins Music Hall was boisterous with song.

The Little Angel Theatre ⊙ – *Dagmar Passage.* A former temperance hall, north of St Mary's church, has since 1961 been a flourishing theatre devoted to puppetry. Marionettes, rod and shadow puppets, costumes and settings for the productions are made in the adjacent workshop.

Canonbury – Canonbury is served by a network of streets and squares lined by early 19C terraced houses of which **Canonbury Square★**, one time home of George Orwell and Sir Francis Bacon, since it is complete and beautifully proportioned, is the prime example. Minor connecting roads, such as Canonbury Grove with small country cottages overlooking a New River backwater *(towpath walks)*, and others, like Alwynne Road in which later 19C villas and semi-detached houses stand in the shade of tall plane trees, add to the atmosphere.

Estorick Collection of Modern Italian Art ⊙ – *Northampton Lodge, 39a Canonbury Square.* Giacomo Balla *(Rhythm of the Violinist)*, Umberto Boccioni *(Modern Idol)*, Carlo Carrà *(Leaving the Theatre)*, Gino Severini *(The Boulevard)*, Luigi Russolo *(Music)* together with the poet Filippo Tommaso Marinetti became fascinated with the concept of universal dynamism: in the words of the Futurist manifesto of 1910, 'a clean sweep should be made of all stale and threadbare subject-matter in order to express the vortex of modern life – a life of steel, fever, pitch and headlong speed.' Energy is boldly represented as electric light, cinematic movement and music: colour is irridescent, scintillating; space exists as a series of contrasted shadows. Besides the **Italian Futurists,** Estorick collected works by De Chirico (*The Revolt of the Sage,* 1916), Rosso, Modigliani, Morandi, Marini...

Canonbury Tower – A square dark red brick tower (60ft high) is all that remains of the manor rebuilt in 1509 on land owned in the 13C by St John's priory. In 1570 Canonbury was acquired for £2 000 as his country residence by Sir John Spencer, Lord Mayor and owner of Crosby House in Bishopsgate who largely rebuilt his out-of-town house. Buildings which now abut the tower date from the 18C-19C. Of the five late 18C houses overlooking Canonbury Place, the most imposing is the pedimented two-storey **Canonbury House**, with a central door framed by slender Ionic pillars. Today the tower is leased to a repertory drama company, the Tower Theatre.

Highbury – By the 19C Highbury had fallen into the hands of undistinguished developers except for **Highbury Place** (1774-79), Highbury Terrace (1789), Highbury Crescent (1830s), where detached and semi-detached villas had been erected for the more opulent.

Holloway – The villages of Lower and Upper Holloway, which are linked by the Holloway Road, merged in the 19C.

Caledonian Market Tower – *Caledonian Road, west side.* The tower, a white, Italianate structure, rising to a square loggia with a pointed roof, is now surrounded by a still life of undulating lawns, overlooked by the low red brick ranges of borough apartment blocks and the new hall of residence of the North London Polytechnic. In the 18C the site was occupied by the Copenhagen Tea Garden and Tavern.

The 'Cally'

The tower and the distinctive 18C to 19C square brick pubs the Lamb, the Lion and the White Horse which marked 3 of the 4 corners of the site (7 acres) are all that remains of the Caledonian Meat Market which flourished from 1876 to 1939 when the general meat market closed down; the wholesale market continued until 1963. For over half a century farmers, drovers, butchers thronged the market, the banks, post office, shops and offices, the vast sheds; each week 10 000 head of cattle and 8-10 000 sheep and pigs arrived at the market, driven along the two main roads or transported by rail.

The Prisons: Pentonville *(Caledonian Road, east side)* dating from 1840 is now hemmed in by neighbouring flats. The most famous of those executed in the prison were Dr Crippen (1910) and Roger Casement (1916). **Holloway Gaol** *(Parkhurst Road, north side),* founded in 1849, became a women's prison in 1903. In 1978 the famous twin towers, modelled on Warwick Castle, were replaced by an unobtrusive complex of terracotta brick buildings.

Sobell Sports Centre ⊙ – *Hornsey Road (junction with Tollington/Isledon Road).* The circular centre, massively built of ribbed rough cast and brown tinted glass opened in November 1973 offering facilities to local residents for cricket, judo, badminton, weight-lifting, squash, snooker, skating – the glass and lighting transforming the figures on the ice into a silent, Lowry-like scene.

KENWOOD ★★

Map p 296 **(TX)** and area map under HAMPSTEAD – HIGHGATE
⊖ Hampstead

'**A great 18C gentleman's country house with pictures such as an 18C collector might have assembled**' – William Murray, younger son of a Scottish peer, acquired Kenwood ⊙, then a 50-year-old brick house, in 1754, two years before he was appointed Lord Chief Justice and created Earl of Mansfield. He intended Kenwood as his country retreat, where he could relax and entertain, and in 1764 invited his fellow Scot, Robert Adam, to enlarge and embellish the house. The architect transformed it both outside and in and left so strong an imprint that all subsequent additions were in his style.

Iveagh Bequest – Kenwood was purchased by Lord Iveagh in 1925 and bequeathed to the nation in 1927. The house's contents, including much Adam furniture, had previously been sold and he filled it instead with the remarkable collection of pictures he had formed at the end of the 19C.
Efforts to recover the original furnishings (Adam side-table and pedestals (1775) in the Parlour) have been painstaking.

Exterior – The pedimented portico with giant fluted columns, frieze and medallion was Adam's typical contribution to the north front; on the south front, from which there is a splendid view down to the lake, Adam raised the central block to three floors (decorating the upper floors in his own style with pilasters and stucco), refaced the existing Orangery and designed the Library to the east to balance the façade.

Interior – Of the rooms on either side of the hall, the most remarkable are the Music and Dining Rooms (cornice and doorcase related in motif to the preceding enriched columns and entablatures), the Adam Library and Orangery.

★★**Adam Library** – The 'room for receiving company' as Adam described it, is richly decorated with Adam motifs and painted in blue and old rose, picked out in white and gold. The oblong room, beneath a curved ceiling, leads into two apsidal ends, each lined with bookcases and screened off by a horizontal beam supported on fluted Corinthian columns. Arched recesses, fitted with triple mirrors, flank the fireplace and reflect the three tall windows opposite.

★★**Paintings** – A Rembrandt, *Self-portrait in Old Age*, the lusty *Man with a Cane* by Frans Hals, the ringletted young girl *Guitar Player* by Vermeer, and works by Bol, Rubens, Cuyp and Crome hang in the Dining Room. Van de Velde seascapes and a Turner, *The Iveagh Seapiece* are found in the Parlour; the Vestibule is mostly hung with Angelica Kauffmann. Portraits by the English school people other rooms: beautiful Gainsborough women, including *Mary, Lady Howe* in pink silk with that special flat hat, *Lady Hamilton* by Romney; children – sentimental, patient, delighted – by Raeburn *(Sir George Sinclair)*, Reynolds *(The Brummell Children, The Children of J J Angerstein)* and Lawrence *(Miss Murray)*. Gainsboroughs of unusual character hang in the Breakfast Room and Orangery: *Going to Market, Two Shepherd Boys with Dogs Fighting* and the dramatic *Hounds coursing a Fox*; the portrait of *J J Merlin* is also noteworthy. A portrait of special interest is that by John Jackson of the *Earl of Mansfield, Lord Chief Justice*, creator of Kenwood.

Coach House – The restaurant contains the 19C family coach capable of carrying 15 people.

ENGLISH HERITAGE

KEW ★★★

Royal Residence – The Old Deer Park, which belonged to Richmond Palace *(see Oute London: RICHMOND)*, was guarded by a keeper's lodge, built on the site occupied since 1769 by Kew Observatory. In 1721 the lodge, which had been rebuilt, was sold to the future George II and his consort, Queen Caroline, who laid out around the renamed **Richmond Lodge** elaborate gardens in which she included typical 18C ornamental statues and follies.

In 1730, Frederick, Prince of Wales, although on unfriendly terms with George I leased a house only a mile away. The residence, the **White House**, 'an old timber house built in the late 17C, was redeemed in the diarist Evelyn's eyes only by the 'garden (which) has the choicest fruit of any plantation in England'. Frederick and Augusta rebuilt the house (known also as Kew House) on a site now marked by a sundial, in which the princess continued to reside after Frederick's death in 1751, devoting herself particularly to the garden.

King George III (1760-1820) and Queen Charlotte found with a growing family o 15 children that Richmond Lodge was too small, and on Princess Augusta's death in 1772 moved into the White House. This also rapidly proved too small and, in 1773 the **Dutch House** was leased for the young Prince of Wales (the future George IV) and his brother as well as other houses on Kew Green. Not satisfied, however, George II commissioned **James Wyatt** to design a new 'Gothic' enterprise to be sited on the riverbank. The **Castellated Palace**, as it was known, was never completed, but like the White House was demolished, leaving alone of all the cousin-hood of royal residences just the Dutch House or Kew Palace *(see below)*, which was occupied by Queen Charlotte until her death in 1818. In 1899 it was opened as a museum.

★★★ROYAL BOTANIC GARDENS ⊘

Kew Gardens are pure pleasure. Colour and the architecture of the trees, singly the weeping willow, the stone pine or in groups, delight at all seasons. The layman wil spot common-place flowers and shrubs and gaze on delicate exotics, gardeners check their knowledge against the labels for this 300 acre garden is the superb offshoot of laboratories engaged in the identification of plants and plant materia from all parts of the world and in economic botany.

The curatorship of the biggest herbarium in the world, a wood museum, a botanical library of more than 100 000 volumes and the training (3 year course) o1 student gardeners are also within the establishment's province.

The botanical theme of the gardens, as opposed to the purely visual, began under Princess Augusta who was personally responsible for the inauguration of a botanic garden south of the Orangery and the enlargement of the gardens from seven to more than 100 acres. On moving into the White House *(see below)*, Prince Frederick had employed William Kent not only to rebuild the house but to landscape the garden. On the prince's death in 1751, the Dowager Princess of Wales, guided by the Earl of Bute, a considerable botanist if no politician, appointed William Aiton as head gardener (1759-93) and William Chambers as architect (1760). Under Aiton, a Scot who had worked at the Chelsea Physic Garden, his son who succeeded him (1793-1841), and **Sir Joseph Banks** (d 1820), voyager, distinguished botanist, naturalist, biologist, and finally director, plants began to be especially collected from al parts of the world for research and cultivation. By 1789, 5 500 species were growing in the gardens.

In 1772 on the death of Princess Augusta, George III combined the Kew and Richmond Lodge gardens and had them landscaped by 'Capability' Brown. The Palace, Orangery, Queen's Cottage, Pagoda remain as colophon to the royal epoch.

Gardens – Major plantings and flowering seasons are indicated on the map overleaf, colour keyed to draw your attention to flowers in outlying areas. Many fine specimens of trees, some over 200 years old, were uprooted in the storm in October 1987 but most of the damage has been repaired.

★★**Palm House** – The house was designed by **Decimus Burton** and the engineer, Richard Turner, as a purely functional building (362ft long, 33ft high in the wings and 62ft at the centre). It is constructed entirely of iron and glass, has curved roofs throughout, took four years to erect (1844-48). Inside are tropical plants both useful (coffee, cocoa) and ornamental. The Chilean runner lizards in residence were given to Kew by Customs and Excise after having been smuggled into Britain.

Outside *(west)* is a semi-circular rose garden; the pond *(east)* is watched over by the Queen's Beasts (stone replicas of those designed by James Woodward to stand outside Westminster Abbey at the coronation in 1953).

★**Temperate House** – The house, again by Burton, but 20 years later and including crested ridges, octagons, wings, ornamentation, epitomises Victorian conservatory construction. The **Evolution House** recreates the climate of change affecting the Earth.

KEW GARDENS

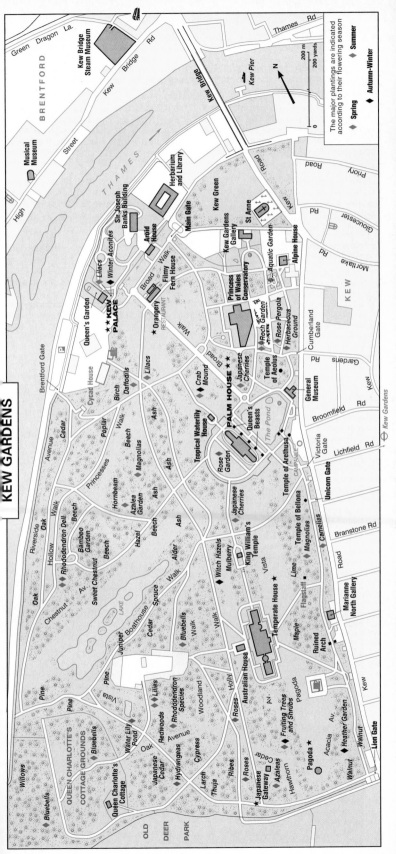

BRENTFORD

Green Dragon La.

Kew Bridge Steam Museum

Thames Rd

Musical Museum

High Street

THAMES

Kew Bridge

Kew Pier

N

0   200 m
0   200 yards

The major plantings are indicated according to their flowering season

◆ Spring   ◆ Summer
◆ Autumn-Winter

Brentford Gate

Cycad House

Queen's Garden

Sir Joseph Banks Building

Arold House

Herbarium and Library

Main Gate

Kew Green

St Anne

Kew Gardens Gallery

★★ KEW PALACE

Lilacs
◆ Winter Aconites

Broad Walk

Filmy Fern House

Orangery
RESTAURANT

Princess of Wales Conservatory

Aquatic Garden

Alpine House

Kew Road

Mortlake Rd

Gloucester Rd

Priory Road

KEW

Riverside

Oak

Hollow

Walk

Rhododendron Dell

Cedar

Avenue

Bamboo Garden

Poplars

Princesses

Birch

Daffodils

Lilacs

◆ Crab Mound

Rock Garden

Rose Pergola

Herbaceous Ground

Cumberland Gate

Gardens

Rd

Beech

Hornbeam

Azalea Garden

Hazel

Magnolias

Ash

Beech

Ash

Beech

Ash

Alder

Ash

★★ Japanese Cherries

Temple of Aeolus

PALM HOUSE

Tropical Waterlily House

Queen's Beasts

The Pond

CAMPANILE

Temple of Arethusa

General Museum

Broomfield   Rd

Lichfield Rd

Kew Gardens ⊖

Willows

Bluebells

QUEEN CHARLOTTE'S COTTAGE GROUNDS

Queen Charlotte's Cottage

Bluebells

Water Lily Pond

Japanese Cedar

Hydrangeas

Ribes

Larch

Thuja

Roses

Japanese Gateway ★

Azaleas

Hawthorn

Cedar

Walnut

Pagoda ★

Acacia Av.

Heather Garden ◆

Walnut

Lion Gate

Pine

Pine

Vista

Lilies

Redwoods

Avenue

Oak

Cypress

Rhododendron Species

Woodland

Holly

Roses

Fruiting Trees and Shrubs ◆

Kew

Pagoda

Ruined Arch

Marianne North Gallery

Maple

Flagstaff

Temperate House

King William's Temple

Vista

Mulberry

Witch Hazels ◆

Lime

Temple of Bellona

Camellias

Magnolias ◆

Branstone Rd

Road

Australian House

LAKE

Juniper

Boathouse

Cedar

Spruce

Bluebells

Walk

Walk

Walk

Sweet Chestnut Av.

Chestnut

Pine

Rose Garden

Japanese Cherries

Victoria Gate

Unicorn Gate

Broad Walk

Magnolias

353

Alpine House – Beneath a glass pyramid, built in 1981, from which rainwater drains into the surrounding moat, is a rock landscape including a refrigerated bed.

Other specialist houses (Aroid, Fern, Tropical Waterlily and Australian) present creepers from rain-forests, cacti, gourds and wattles, mimosas and eucalyptus.

Princess of Wales Tropical Conservatory – In this modern steel and glass diamond-shaped structure are recreated ten different tropical habitats ranging from the extremes of mangrove swamp to desert – from ferns and orchids to carnivorous and stone plants (Lithops), cacti and succulents set against a Mohave desert diorama. In 1996, a titan arum or 'corpse flower' which blooms every 30 years attracted great attention: the Sumatran native has flowered at Kew in 1889, 1926 and 1963.

Marianne North Gallery – In a building (1882) specially designed by her architect friend, James Ferguson, are exhibited paintings by Miss North of plants, insects and general scenes from the many countries she visited between 1871 and 1884.

Sir Joseph Banks Building – *First show at 10am.* The Thread of Life Exhibition is a multi-media show telling the remarkable story of cellulose.

★★**Kew Palace (Dutch House)** ⊘ – The terracotta brick building complete with Dutch attic gables and notable for the richness and variety of the brick laying, cutting and moulding, was built by Samuel Fortrey, a London Merchant of Dutch parentage, who commemorated his house's construction in a monogram and the date 1631 over the front door.

At the rear is the **Queen's Garden,** a formal arrangement of pleached alleys of laburnum and hornbeam, *parterres* (formal symetrical beds), a gazebo and plants popular in the 17C. The nosegay garden which dates from the 17C has been replanted with contemporary herbs.

> **Pioneering work** – Kew has practised biological control (Integrated Pest Man-
> agement) throughout its premises tailored to 40 000 txa (specific species) of
> plant and 750 000 specimens of fungi since 1991. Efforts to save some of
> the world's rarest orchids have led scientists at Kew to evolve a way of
> germinating plants from seed without the symbiotic fungus required in more
> natural habitats. Some 5 000 species (about 20% of the total known num-
> ber) are now propagated at Kew, having been accumulated over the last
> 200 years. The seed bank, founded to provide scientists and conservationists
> with the practical means of research will expand at Wakehurst Place in West
> Sussex courtesy of the National Lottery.

Inside, the house reflects the standard features of a small George III country house.
The rooms downstairs are all panelled: the King's Dining Room in white 18C style,
the Breakfast Room in early 17C style and the Library Ante-Room in re-set 16C
linen-fold. Upstairs, apart from the white and gold Queen's Drawing Room, formally set out with lyreback chairs for a musical evening, the rooms are wallpapered
with new paper printed from the delightful original blocks and intimate with family
portraits by Gainsborough and Zoffany. In the King's rooms note the embossed
terracotta paper in the Anteroom and in the bedroom a russet red paper patterned
in dark green with matching hangings. Downstairs in the Pages' Waiting Room, is
an exhibition of minor royal possessions: silver filigree rattles, alphabet counters,
snuff boxes, lists of Prince Frederick's gambling debts, the Queen's code of bell
pulls...

Queen Charlotte's Cottage ⊙ – The two-storeyed thatched house, typical of
'rustic' buildings of the period (1772) was designed by Queen Charlotte as a picnic
house: the cottage is furnished including tea for two upstairs.

Other buildings and monuments – Under Princess Augusta, William Chambers
set about constructing typical 18C garden follies: temples, a ruined arch, an
Orangery★ (1761) and a **Pagoda★** (1761), a garden ornament 163ft and ten storeys
high, still the climax to a long vista: now alas without its gilded dragon finials, this
folly had its floors pierced by the RAF during the Second World War to give them a
100ft vertical drop to test model bombs.

The **Main Gates** are by Decimus Burton (1848 the lion and unicorn on the original
gate are now above gates in Kew Road). By the pond stands the **Museum of Victorian
Plant Oddities**, formerly the General Museum, which dates from 1857-58, when it
replaced the original Museum of Economic Botany, the first in the world in 1847.
The **Japanese Gateway★** was imported for the Anglo-Japanese Exhibition of 1912.

OTHER SIGHTS

Kew Village – The most attractive houses on the green are those by the main
gates to the gardens. Dominating the north (river) side are Kew Herbarium
(collection of 5 million dried plants and library – *open to specialists*), a three-storey
Georgian house and extensive annexe, followed by an irregular line of 18C-19C
houses of brick with canted bays, canopied balconies, rounded doors and windows
in arched recesses... *(nos 61-83)*. On the far side of the gates backing onto the
gardens, are a line of one-time royal 'cottages', including, at no 37 Cambridge
Cottage, now the Wood Museum and Kew Gardens Gallery *(enter from inside the
gardens)*.

St Anne's Church – The west end is adorned by a triangular pediment and peristyle and
crowned by a bell-turret. The nave and chancel were constructed of brick in
1710-14 on the site of a 16C chapel once frequented by Tudor and Stuart courtiers.
In 1770 the church was lengthened, a north aisle built on, books and furnishings
were presented by George III, who in 1805 added the royal gallery (note the fine
Queen Anne arms and hatchments). In the rose-filled churchyard lie Gainsborough
(d 1788) and Zoffany (d 1810).

Public Record Office – *Ruskin Avenue*. The *Domesday Book (see index)*, Shakespeare's will, Guy Fawkes's confessions, Captain Cook's charts, Bligh's accounts of
the mutiny on the Bounty are just a few of the precious historic charters, accounts,
maps, seals, reports, registers, government papers and old chests (including the
Million Bank with multiple locks) entrusted to the PRO, founded in 1838 and
formerly in Chancery Lane. In their new premises, fragile papers are kept in
temperature and humidity-controlled environments.

Kew Bridge – The 18C bridge, also known as King Edward VII's Bridge, was
replaced in 1903 by the present structure of three spans of stone by Wolfe Barry
and Brereton.

ENVIRONS

Kew Bridge Steam Museum ⊙ – *Brentford. Entrance in Green Dragon Lane.* This museum of water supply demonstrates the development of James Watt's basic idea through over a century of improved efficiency and increased scale. There are six Cornish Beam Engines – the Boulton and Watt (1820), the 90" (1846), the Easton and Amos (1863), the Dancers End (1867), the Maudslay (1938), the Hathorn Davey Triple (1910) – and the Waddon Engine, the last steam-powered water pumping engine used commercially until 1983. A variety of smaller steam engines, traction engines and steam lorries, a narrow gauge railway, a water-wheel (1702), a forge, machine shop and a collection of relics connected with London's water supply complete the display.

Buildings in the 19C were, for the most part, erected round the engines with no provision for bringing in replacement parts so confident were our forefathers that their engines would last indefinitely. Exteriors were functional, the interiors dominated by giant columns, slender pillars and staircases enabling one to climb to cylinder and beam levels. The standpipe tower outside is a local landmark nearly 200ft high.

Musical Museum ⊙ – *368 High Street, Brentford (150yds west of Kew Bridge).* Inside an acoustically rewarding neo-Gothic church (19C) is a collection of some 200 mechanical music-makers – pianolas, organs, a wurlitzer...

Boston Manor ⊙ – ⊖ *Boston Manor.* The red brick house was begun in 1623 by Lady Mary Read who had acquired the property by settlement from Sir Thomas Gresham through marriage to his stepson; the magnificent moulded plaster ceiling in the State Room is dated 1623; the staircase with its *trompe l'œil* balustrade is also original.

In 1670 James Clitherow bought the property for £5 136 17s 4d, adding the bold entablature, window architraves and garden door, and landscaped the grounds with cedars and a lake.

William MORRIS GALLERY

Map p 297 **(UX)**
⊖ Walthamstow Central

The museum ⊙ is accommodated in a house that was home to the Morris family between 1848 and 1856, built c 1750 and named Water House after the moat which still exists in the grounds.

The displays are connected with the work of **William Morris** (1834-96) and of the firm Morris & Co (1861-1940) which he co-founded under the definition: 'Fine Art Workmen in painting, carving, furniture and the metals'. Although destined for the church Morris tried architecture and painting under the influence of Ruskin and the Pre-Raphaelites, before finding expression for his talents in the decorative arts.

The career of the designer and the history of the firm are traced in parallel and illustrated by examples of stained glass, tiles, furniture, wallpapers, fabrics and embroidery; Morris' own work includes his poetry and books published by the **Kelmscott Press**: Folio Edition of the Works of Geoffrey Chaucer (1896).

Two smaller rooms display work produced by members of the **Arts and Crafts Movement** *(ground floor)* and the work of the **Century Guild** *(first floor)*, founded by Arthur MacMurdo, who was influenced by Ruskin and Morris. Etchings and oils by **Sir Frank Brangwyn** ⊙ are exhibited *(first floor)* with paintings and drawings by the Pre-Raphaelites and their contemporaries.

For additional information see VICTORIA & ALBERT MUSEUM and Outer London: HAMMERSMITH.

OSTERLEY PARK ★★

Map p 296 **(TY)**
⊖ Osterley

Osterley Park ⊙ is the place to see **Robert Adam** interior decoration at its most complete. Room after room is as he designed it: ceilings, walls, doorcases, doors, handles, carpets, mirrors and furniture down to chairs standing in the exact positions for which they were designed.

A country seat for City gentlemen – **Sir Thomas Gresham** bought Osterley Manor in 1562 and immediately began to build a country house adjoining the old manor house, a late 15C Tudor brick building surrounding three sides of a courtyard. When Gresham's mansion was complete, Queen Elizabeth honoured her financier and merchant adventurer by a visit to the 'house beseeming a prince' (1576), which on his death in 1579, passed to his stepson Sir William Read, husband of Lady Mary of Boston Manor *(see Outer London: KEW – Environs).*

n 1711 the mansion was purchased by another City grandee **Francis Child**, although the old banker never lived there. His grandchild, namesake and heir, began transforming he place in 1756, work which was to continue for more than twenty years by which ime the house was owned by Francis Child's great niece, Sarah Sophia who in 1804 narried the future 5th Earl of Jersey.

n 1773 Horace **Walpole**, visiting from nearby Strawberry Hill, wrote: 'The old house is o improved and enriched that all the Percies and Seymours of Sion must die of envy... There is a hall, library, breakfast room, eating room, all *chefs d'œuvre* of Adam, a jallery 130ft long, a drawing room worthy of Eve before the Fall.'

)sterley was presented to the nation by the 9th Earl in 1949.

> **Francis Child**, a clothier's son from Wiltshire, came to seek his fortune in London in the 1650s, had found it, been knighted, elected Lord Mayor (1698) and become banker to Charles II, Nell Gwynne, Pepys, John Churchill, future Duke of Marlborough, King William and Queen Mary... He had started as a gold-smith's apprentice; moved to a second house where he married the owner's daughter, inherited the family fortune and business which he transformed to suit the times. Gold coinage was accumulating rapidly through increased trade in Tudor and Stuart times but was easily stolen; after finding that even deposits in the Tower were vulnerable (Charles I seized £130 000 from the vaults in 1640!) merchants placed their bullion with goldsmiths usually for a fixed time; the smiths with Francis Child as a forerunner began to lend the cash out at interest and became the City's first bankers. **Child's Bank** (now Royal Bank of Scotland) 'at the sign of the Marigold' after the premises they occupied when there were no street numbers can still be seen at No 1 Fleet Street *(see CHANCERY LANE – Fleet Street)*.

Exterior – The square form with corner towers of Sir Thomas Gresham's house remains, though enlarged and encased by new bricks and stone quoins in the 18C by the first of the two architects employed on the transformation. Sir William Chambers in addition reduced the courtyard to provide a hall and continuous passage round the house and completed the Gallery and Breakfast Room before being superseded in 1761 by the more fashionable Robert Adam. The latter made two contributions to the exterior, the grand, theatrical six-columned portico at the front and, at the rear, a horseshoe staircase with delicate wrought-iron and brasswork (1770).

Interior – The wide **Hall** is apsed at either end, the fine ceiling filled with floral scrolls is echoed in the two-tone marble pavement. Distinctive relief panels with trophies of war fill the spaces between pilasters. Classical statues nestle in niches on either side of the curved fireplaces and grisaille paintings. Each detail, save the statues and elegant marble urns on pedestals after the Antique, is designed by Adam, including the door handles.

Leave the Hall by the north door – on the right when entering the house and follow past a cabinet filled with fine porcelain, to the far end of the passage.

The **Breakfast Room** is painted in a strong lemon yellow contrasted with touches of blue to highlight the delicate ornamental detailing. The ceiling is by Chambers; tables and pier-glasses, however, were designed by Adam and the lyre back mahogany armchairs probably by Linnell.

The distinctive feature of the **Library**, painted in creamy-white to emphasise the leatherbound books and set off the painted panels, is the furniture: the lyre-back armchairs, a pedestal desk veneered with harewood (stained sycamore) and inlaid with motifs matched in the side tables are all made in about 1775 by John Linnell, the leading cabinet maker of his day, probably to his own designs under Adam's supervision.

The **staircase**, begun by Chambers, has a fine iron balustrade, and delicate stucco decoration added by Adam who also designed the three lamps hanging between the Corinthian columns. The ceiling painting is particularly Rubensesque.

At the top, turn right.

The **State Bedroom** or Yellow Taffeta Bedchamber is furnished with painted taffeta curtains and bed hangings, and ornate gilded mirrors. The bed, surmounted by cupped acorns, was designed by Adam (1779).

Beyond the stairhead is the suite of less extravagant rooms designed by Chambers for Mr and Mrs Child. None of the furniture in his **dressing room** is original but most pieces date from the mid 18C. The **bedchamber** has window curtains and bed valances made of cotton imported from India in the 1760s. The lacquer dressing-table and French ebony cabinet on a stand were among the furniture in the 1760s. The cornice, doors and shutters of her **dressing room** are the distinctive work of

State Bed, Osterley

Chambers. The chimneypiece and mirror were designed by Linnell; the portrait i Robert Child's daughter, Sarah Anne, who eloped with the 10th Earl of Westmorland The only original pieces are the 17C Japanese lacquer cabinet and the 18C Chines porcelain.

Return downstairs; turn right.

The **Eating Room** is an all Adam room: motifs from the pink and green ceiling decoration, notably the honeysuckle and pineapples are most typical. According to 18C custom the carved mahogany lyre-back chairs are set against the wall wher not in use, gate-leg tables would be brought in for dining.

The light and airy **gallery** boasting a fine view of the garden across the width of the house, was designed by Chambers. Marble chimney-pieces, Classical doorcases and 18C Chinese pieces and lacquered furniture are contrasted by the delicate Rococo-style frieze against the ochre and green colour-scheme introduced by Adam. As in the 18C the room is sparsely furnished and hung with pictures. Other fixtures including the five-seater sofas are by Adam; the pier-glasses and girandoles, garlanded and sup ported by nonchalant mermaids, are the Scotsman in his lightest vein.

The somewhat over gilded **Drawing Room** is dominated by the low, heavy coffered ceiling studded with flowering paterae and ostrich feathers. Pale pinks and greens gold and red are picked out in cornice and carpet (made at Moorfields) while motifs from the doorcases are echoed in the fireplace, the inlaid design and ormolu decoration of the two harewood veneered commodes. The serpentine sofas and chairs are after the early French neo-Classical style. The pier glasses and perfume burners are French.

In the **Tapestry Room**, the Adam motifs for ceiling and fireplace fade into insigni ficance beside the richness of the Gobelins' tapestries woven for the room, signed and dated by (Jacques) Neilson, 1775, an artist of Scots origin in charge of the works in Paris from 1751-88. On a rich crimson ground, framed in gold, is the Boucher series, *The Loves of the Gods*, and between are flower filled urns garlands, cupids at play... Chairs and sofa are in the same style.

The **State Bed Chamber** is decked in cool green. The Child crest of an eagle with ar adder in its beak features on the eight poster valance. The gilded chairs, their ova backs supported on reclining sphinxes, are one of Adam's most graceful design (1777). The chimney glass, surmounted by the Child crest, is declared in the house inventory of 1782 to have been the 'first plate made in England'. The walls would originally have been covered in green velvet.

The **Etruscan Dressing Room**, which helped to launch a fashion for the Antique demonstrates Adam's application to an 18C interior of what he took to be Etruscar decorative themes derived in fact from Ancient Greek pottery; even the chairs are made to conform to the theme in colour and patterning, though not in shape According to surviving inventories from 1782, it was here that the japanned Chippendale 1773 lady's writing desk was situated – a decorative mix that would not have offended or jarred 18C tastes or sensibilities.

The Demonstration Room is hung with plans and drawings of house and garden by Adam and others. The two 18C views of Osterley by Anthony Devis *(in the corridor to the hall)* are the only works from the original picture collection.

The **Stables**, built in 1577 by Sir Thomas Gresham were altered and refitted early in the 18C.

The **Pleasure Grounds** *(west of the house)*, which are being restored according to old maps and prints, contain Chamber's Doric temple to Pan and Adam's semi-circular garden house (c 1780). The cedar trees on south lawn were planted in the 1760s. The chain of lakes was created in the 1750s.

For Boston Manor, see Outer London: KEW – Environs.

PUTNEY – WANDSWORTH

Map p 296 **(TY)**
⊖ Putney Bridge; East Putney

The area's transformation was precipitated by the arrival of the railway in the mid 19C. In its wake came the builders. Evolution previously had been gradual, from settlement beside the ford to substantial village where Oliver Cromwell held a council of war round the communion table in St Mary's in 1647. Even the erection of a wooden toll-bridge in 1729 – the first above London Bridge – had little effect. The early association with the river remains: rowing clubs still line the Surrey bank, oarsmen practise in midstream; the **Boat Race** between Oxford and Cambridge Universities is rowed each spring over the four and a half mile course to Mortlake, as it has been ever since 1845.

Putney Bridge – The bridge, which marks the beginning (just upstream in line with the Universities' Stone by the Star and Garter pub) of the Oxford and Cambridge boat race, was designed in Cornish granite by Joseph Bazalgette in 1884 and replaced a wooden toll-bridge of 1729.

St Mary's Parish Church ⊘ – The church at the approach to Putney bridge was burnt out in 1973 and reopened after restoration in 1982. The 16C chantry chapel and 15C tower were preserved when the church was rebuilt in 1836.

Lower Richmond Road – Near the bridgefoot, low lying between the Lower Richmond Road and the river bank road which serves the club boat houses, is 18C **Winchester House**, dwarfed by the surrounding buildings.

Lower Richmond Road itself winds upriver past a straggling line of village and antique shops and small Victorian houses, punctuated by pubs of varying vintage: the **White Lion**, a flamboyant Victorian pub (1887) flaunting two caryatids like a ship's figurehead opposite the church, the **Duke's Head**, late Georgian overlooking the river and, just before the common, the Georgian French Revolution and the 19C gabled Spencer Arms.

On the Lower Common is **All Saints Church** (1874), notable for its Burne-Jones windows *(open for services only)*.

Oxford and Cambridge Boat Race, Putney

Putney High Street, Putney Hill — The bustling High Street with, halfway along a Tudor style, gargoyle decorated pub, the Old Spotted Horse, still includes tall 19C house-fronts. At the start of Putney Hill, near the crossroads, are to left and right no 11, The Pines, a monstrous tall grey attached Victorian House where **Swinburne** lived and no 28A, a pink washed Georgian villa with a firemark set like a beauty patch on its pale wall.

WANDSWORTH

Wandsworth began as a Surrey village straggling along the banks of the River Wandle (10 miles long), which rises west of Croydon and neither dries up in summer nor freezes in winter; its 'fishful qualities' were noted by Izaak Walton.

As early as 1602 its waters were harnessed to work corn and iron mills. Others who needed a constant water supply — potters, calico bleachers, fullers, launderers, printers, coppersmiths swelled the population. In the late 17C they were joined by silk weavers and felt hat makers, whose workshops are recalled in Factory Gardens off the west side of Streatham Common. Many of these workers were Huguenot refugees, whose presence is recalled in Huguenot Place *(Trinity Road, Wandsworth Common Northside)* and the **Huguenot Burial Ground** *(by, but independent of, St Mary Magdalene RC Church at 42 Wandsworth Common)*, which formerly served English and French Protestants and contains tomb stones dating from 1697.

All Saints Parish Church, an 18C building with 19C additions, stands on an ancient site. St Ann's Church *(St Ann's Hill)*, known as the Pepperpot church, dates from the 1820s. The Friends' Meeting House (1778) stands on the site of an earlier building (1697) with its own burial ground.

The Huguenots specialised in making felt hats, in particular **cardinals' hats:** only a cardinal in possession of a Wandsworth red hat could be sure of avoiding a red face when it rained.

The '**1723 House**' *(Wandsworth Plain)* is a terrace of six fine, three-storey brick houses with short flights of steps up to Corinthian pilastered front doors, a central pediment and wall sundial. Armoury Way, at the back, recalls Tudor times when every parish had its armoury.

According to a comment made in 1851, **Wandsworth Prison** *(Heathfield Road)* had 'nothing to recommend it to the eye'.

Still today the beer from **Young's Ram Brewery** ⊘ *(High Street)* is delivered to local public houses within a three-mile radius by drays drawn by beautiful black Shire horses.

RICHMOND★★

Map p 296 (TY)
⊖ Richmond; Overground: Richmond from Waterloo Station

Richmond, possessing what has been called the most beautiful urban green in England, grew to importance between the 12C and 17C as a royal seat and, after the Restoration, as the residential area of members of the court: Windsor, Hampton Court and Kew are easily accessible. In the courtiers' wake followed diplomats, politicians, professional men, dames and their schools, and with the coming of the railway in 1840, prosperous Victorian commuters.

On the east side of the main road are reminders of the growing village in the parish **Church of St Mary Magdalene** with its 16C square flint and stone tower, early brasses and monuments (actor Edmund Kean), 18C houses (Ormond and Halford Roads), 19C cottages (Waterloo Place), the Vineyard dating back in name to the 16C to 17C when local vines were famous, and the rebuilt almshouses of 17C foundation — Queen Elizabeth's, Bishop Duppa's and Michel's. In Paradise Road stands Hogarth House built in 1748, where Leonard and **Virginia Woolf**, who lived there from 1915 to 1924, founded the Hogarth Press.

Richmond Palace: royal residence through six reigns — The first residence, a manor house, erected in the 12C, was extended and embellished by Edward III, who died in it in 1377, was favoured by Richard II, his grandson while his queen, Anne of Bohemia was alive but demolished at her death in 1394. A new palace, the second, was begun by Henry V but completed only forty years after his death in the reign of Edward IV who gave it with the royal manor of Shene to his queen, Elizabeth Woodville, from whom it was confiscated by Henry VII; in 1499 it burned to the ground. Henry VII, parsimonious where his son was prodigal, nevertheless, 'rebuilded (the palace) again sumptuously and costly and changed the name of Shene and called it Richmond because his father and he were Earls of Rychmonde' (in Yorkshire). This palace, the third on the site, was to be the last.

The new Tudor palace conformed to standard design: service buildings of red brick, preserved today in the gateway, enclosed an outer or Base Court, now Old Palace Yard, from which a second gateway led to an inner or Middle Court, lined along one side by a Great Hall of stone with a lead roof.

The Privy Lodging, which included the state rooms, surrounded another court. Domed towers and turrets crowned the construction, which covered ten acres and was by far the most splendid in the Kingdom. Henry VII died in his palace; Henry VIII and Catherine of Aragon frequented it; Queen Elizabeth held court in it, particularly in springtime, and died there; Prince Henry, James I's son, resided there and added an art gallery to house the extensive collection of royal paintings, increased after the prince's death (in the palace) by the future Charles I who also resided there notably during the plague of 1625. At the king's execution the palace was stripped and the contents, including the pictures, were sold. By the 18C little remained and private houses: the Old Palace, Gatehouse, Wardrobe, Trumpeters, were constructed out of the ruins on the site.

Richmond Green – The Green, once the scene of Tudor jousting, has been a cricket pitch since the middle of the 17C.

Richmond Theatre, which overlooks the Little Green, was designed by Frank Matcham in 1889 and refurbished in 1991 more or less in accordance with its original appearance.

Along the east side of the Green are 17C and 18C houses and two narrow lanes opening into George Street. In the south corner in Paved Court are two pubs, the Cricketers and the Prince's Head; behind are narrow lanes with small shops.

Along the west side is **Old Palace Terrace** (1692-1700), six two-storey brick houses with straight hooded doorways, built by John Powell (who lived in no 32 which he also built).

Oak House and **Old Palace Place** date back to 1700. **Old Friars** (1687 date on a rainwater head) is so named as it stands on part of the site of a monastery founded by Henry VII in 1500; the

Richmond Theatre

house was extended in the 18C to include a concert room for the holding of 'music mornings and evenings'.

★★**Maids of Honour Row** – The famous row dates from 1724 when the future George II gave directions for 'erecting a new building near his seat at Richmond to serve as lodgings for the Maids of Honour attending the Princess of Wales'. There are four houses in all, each three storeys high with five bays apiece, pilastered, with friezed door cases, and small gardens behind 18C wrought-iron gates and railings. The brick is mellow, the proportions perfect.

The Old Palace and the Gatehouse – On the south side are two houses: the first – castellated, bay-windowed and with a central doorway incorporating Tudor materials, notably brickwork, from Henry VII's palace; the second is the original outer gateway of the palace (note the restored arms of Henry VII over the arch).

The Wardrobe – *Old Palace Yard*. Note the blue diapered Tudor walls incorporated in the early 18C building, and the fine 18C ironwork.

★**Trumpeters' House** – *Old Palace Yard*. The main front of this house converted c 1701 from the Middle Gate of Richmond Palace, overlooks the garden and can be seen through the trees from the riverside path. The giant pedimented portico of paired columns was formerly guarded by stone statues after which the house is still named. For a brief period in 1848-49 it was occupied by Metternich.

Richmond Riverside – Old Palace Lane, lined by modest, wistaria-covered 19 houses and cottages, leads from the southwest corner of Richmond Green to th river.

★**Asgill House** – Standing at the end of the lane overlooking the river from a site onc within the palace walls, is a house that was built c 1760 as a weekend and summe residence for the City banker and sometime Lord Mayor, Sir Charles Asgill. In pa golden stone with strong horizontal lines and a central bay advanced and canted fo the full three storeys, it was one of the last of its type to be built overlooking th Thames.

Take the towpath upstream past Trumpeters' House and Friars Lane to Whittake Avenue.

Museum of Richmond ⊘ – *Old Town Hall.* Displays relate to the local history c Richmond, Ham, Petersham and Kew: model of Richmond Palace in 1562.

Flanking the Old Town Hall is a new complex of offices, shops and restauran (1988), designed by Q Terry to complement the neighbouring buildings.

★★**Richmond Bridge** – The bridge, a classical, stone structure of five arches and parape designed by James Paine was built in 1774 to replace the horse ferry and widened i 1937; tolls were levied until the 19C. There is a milestone-obelisk at the north enc The towpath continues beyond the bridge as a riverside promenade below Terrac Gardens (between Petersham Road and Richmond Hill).

Richmond Hill – The view★★ gets ever better as one climbs the steep road lined by balconied terraces, immortalised through the ages by many artists includ- ing Turner and Reynolds. The **Wick** and **Wick House** on the west side of the road, built in 1775 and 1772 –

> *This lass so neat, with smiles so sweet,*
> *Has won my right good-will,*
> *I'd crowns resign to call thee mine,*
> *Sweet lass of Richmond Hill.*
>
> Leonard Macnally (1752-1820)

the latter by Sir William Chambers for Sir Joshua Reynolds, both enjoy view across the bend in the river towards Marble Hill.

At the top, overlooking the park stands Ancaster House, a brick mansion with b bow windows, built in 1722 principally to designs by Robert Adam. The house now attached to the Star and Garter Home for disabled sailors, soldiers and airme opposite, which stands on the site of an inn famous in the 18C and 19C an opened in 1924. (The British Legion poppy factory is at the Richmond end c Petersham Road.)

The park gates which mark the hilltop are dated 1700 and are attributed t Capability Brown.

★★**Richmond Park** – The countryside had been a royal chase for centuries whe Charles I enclosed 2 470 acres as a park in 1637. It is the largest of the roy parks, and is famous for its varied **wildlife** – most notably its herds of almost tam red and fallow deer, its majestic **oak trees** and the **spring flowers** (rhododendrons) c the Isabella Plantation.

On a fine day from the top of the Henry VIII mound (said to have been raised t allow the King to survey the field) there is a dramatic **panoramic view**★★★ extendin from Windsor Castle to the dome of St Paul's – look out for Telecom Towe Battersea Power Station, Canary Wharf...

Among the houses in the park are **Pembroke Lodge** ⊘ *(cafeteria),* a rambling lat 17C-18C house at the centre of colourful walled and woodland gardens adapted b John Soane from a molecatcher's cottage and later used by Lord John Russe (Prime Minister 1846-51 and 1865-66) and his grandson, the philosopher Ber rand Russell; Thatched House Lodge, the home of Princess Alexandra, and Whit Lodge, built by George II in 1727 as a hunting lodge and since 1955 the junic section of the Royal Ballet School.

ROYAL AIR FORCE MUSEUM ★★

Map p 296 (TX), Grahame Park Way
Buses: 226 along Edgware Road
⊖ Colindale

Affiliated to the Imperial War Museum *(see LAMBETH)*, this museum ⊙ is dedicated to the history of aviation and of the RAF and is presented in several hangars on the historic site of Old Hendon Airfield, where Grahame-White established his flying school before the First World War.

Lancaster bomber

Historical Galleries – *First floor.* The displays recount the history of the Air Force: early experiments with balloons and bi-planes; early trophies including the two British Empire Michelin Trophies awarded to the British pilot flying the greatest distance in a British plane: No 1 was awarded to Moore-Brabazon in 1910 for a distance of 19 miles; Von Richthofen's flying helmet; uniforms worn by Lord Trenchard, Chief of Air Staff; VCs and GCs won in combat; escape equipment; ejector seats; audio-visual display on life in the RAF today.

Main Aircraft Hall – The World War I hall presents a unique collection of aircraft in chronological order from a Blériot monoplane and a Sopwith Camel through a Supermarine Stranraer flying boat, a Westland (Bristol) Belvedere helicopter and a Sikorsky hoverfly to a Lightning Mach 2.
The **Flight Simulator** offers three programmes: flying with the Red Arrows in a Tornado; an aircraft carrier strike; a 1918 dog-fight in which the cockpit pitches and rolls as if at the mercy of the elements.
Visitors can sit in the cockpit of a **Jet Provost Trainer** and try the controls.

Bomber Command Hall – This hall contains a Lancaster, a Heinkel He 162A-2, a Handley Page Halifax, a Vickers Valiant, Vimy and Wellington, a B17 Flying Fortress, Mosquito and a Vulcan. There are static displays on the USAAF in Britain and the history of the RAF Factory at Farnborough and a replica of the office of Sir Barnes Wallis who invented the bouncing bomb.

Battle of Britain Experience – The Battle is announced by tableaux on the Munich Crisis, the Declaration of War and Evacuation.
The forces involved are represented by an impressive array of aircraft: Junkers 87 and 88, Heinkel 111, Messerschmitt against Gloster Gladiators, Tiger Moths, Spitfires and Hurricanes. In addition to the machines are an operations room, uniforms, medals, documents, relics and other memorabilia. The far end of the hall presents a V2 Rocket, Short Sunderland V, Westland Lysander and a Supermarine Seagull.

For historical background on the region see the Historical Table and Notes in the Introduction

ST JOHN'S WOOD

Map pp 6-7 (BCV)
⊖ St John's Wood

St John's Wood developed rapidly in the first half of the 19C. Its rural character, dating back to the Middle Ages when it was the property of the Knights Hospitallers of St John, whence its name, was swept aside as Marylebone began to overflow and Nash's development of Regent's Park made it a potentially desirable residential area. It was, moreover, within three miles of the City and Westminster – a perfect place for wealthy Victorians resident in Belgravia to keep their mistresses *(see TATE GALLERY – Holman Hunt)*. Cleverly the developers departed from the current urban styles and erected Italian type villas, broad eaved, often in pairs. By 1824 when Edwin Landseer (d 1873) moved into a house in St John's Wood Road, a colony of artists had begun to gather which much later included Sir Lawrence Alma-Tadema (d 1912) and W R Frith *(Derby Day:* d 1909).

The villas have now largely disappeared, replaced by apartment blocks and neo-Georgian houses; the small High Street has been modernised. Two landmarks, however, do remain.

St John's Wood Church ⊙ – *Prince Albert Road.* The church is of the same date, 1813, and by the same architect, Thomas Hardwick, as St Marylebone Parish Church *(see MARYLEBONE)* and like it has a distinctive, cupolaed turret.

Lord's Cricket Ground ⊙ – *St John's Wood Road.* Lord's is a private gentlemen's club. The best introduction to the ground, its history and its aura is by guided tour through the inner sanctum, the famous Long Room in the Pavilion (open to MCC members only during matches), the 'real' tennis court, the adjacent **MCC Museum** founded in memory of all the cricketers who lost their lives in the First World War which displays the famous **Ashes**, portraits (talking head of Dr WG Grace) and cartoons, cricketing dress, memorabilia from batting lists to snuff boxes, the Lord's shop and the award-winning Mound Stand. The Library is perhaps the world's most important Cricket archive – alas incomplete as the earliest records were destroyed by a fire in 1825.

The club, originally at the White Conduit in Islington, moved to Marylebone and altered its name accordingly in 1787 when Thomas Lord leased a site in what is now Dorset Square. In 1811 Lord lifted the sacred turf first to a field, which proved to be in the course of the Regent's Canal, and then to what, by purchase, has become the permanent ground.

The first match MCC played at the original Lord's ground (Dorset Fields) was against Essex on 1 June 1787. The present ground was inaugurated with a match against Herts on 22 June 1814. The first Test Matches at Lord's were played in 1884. The main gates were erected in memory of **Dr W G Grace** (d 1915) in 1923 Father Time, removing the bails, was placed on the grandstand in 1926.

The much acclaimed **Mound Stand** combines various building techniques: the ground level 1898 brick stand designed by the Verity brothers is preserved below decks of cantilevered steel-framed units (1985/6) sheltered by a marquee-like PVC-coated roof (1986/7). In accordance with MCC stipulations, the architect Michael Hopkins has differentiated public terraces from privately sponsored corporate boxes (including one reserved for Paul Getty Junior who funded half the project) and an upper promenade section exclusively for club members and debenture ticket holders. The futuristic design of the Media Centre (1999) an elliptical aluminium structure, breaks new ground.

Just around the corner from Lord's and up Grove End Road beyond the junction with **Abbey Road** is the particular zebra crossing immortalised by the Beatles album called Abbey Road and recorded at the EMI studios nearby. Nostalgic fans continue to come here to read the penned inscriptions and graffiti.

The Ashes urn contains the precious ashes of a pair of wicket bales. It is competed for in a series of test matches bi-annually by Australia and England but remains at Lord's irrespective of the winner. It was first awarded to the England captain the Hon Ivo Bligh in 1883 when on tour in Australia.

Saatchi Gallery ⊙ – *98a Boundary Road* – ⊖ *St John's Wood, Swiss Cottage, Kilburn.* Housed in a converted warehouse, the gallery holds temporary exhibitions of works from the Saatchi Collection of Modern Art, with a focus notably on young British artists (Damien Hirst, Marc Quin, Rachel Whiteread, Richard Wilson). The collection comprises paintings and sculpture by A Keifer, A Warhol, M Morley, C André, F Stella and other artists.

SWISS COTTAGE ⊖ *Swiss Cottage*

The chalet was built as the latest style in tavern design in 1840 and was so novel that it gave its name to the small locality beginning to develop between Hampstead and St John's Wood. First buses – it became a terminal in 1856 – then the tube (1868) brought transformation to a Victorian suburb now replaced by modern apartment blocks. The chalet, more brightly painted than a stage set, still exists (pub and restaurant) at the centre of an island site.

The attractive, irregular buildings of **Swiss Cottage Civic Centre** *(Avenue Road by Swiss Cottage Station)*, designed by **Sir Basil Spence**, include a library and swimming pool, opened in 1964. A temporary building houses the Hampstead Theatre Club.

Freud Museum ⊙ – *20 Maresfield Gardens.* The house to which Sigmund Freud escaped from Nazi persecution in Vienna in 1938 and where he lived until his death in 1939, has been turned into a museum devoted to Freud's life and work and to the history and development of psychoanalysis. On the ground floor are his study and working library with his famous couch and collection of books, pictures and **antiquities**★★, kept intact by his daughter Anna.

SILVERTOWN – NORTH WOOLWICH

Map p 297 **(UY)**
Overground: Silvertown, North Woolwich from Stratford East

Silvertown is named after S W Silver & Co, a rubber manufacturer founded in 1852. The district is dominated by the **Royal Docks**: Victoria Dock which opened in 1855, the Royal Albert Dock, the first to be lit by electricity, which was opened in 1880 by the Duke of Connaught on behalf of Queen Victoria, and King George V Dock, known during construction as the Royal Albert Dock Extension, which opened in 1921. The district is changing in character under the Docklands redevelopment plan.

Lyle Park – This small park overlooking the river was created for their employees by Tate & Lyle, sugar processors, whose works occupy the adjoining river-bank site.

Thames Flood Barrier – *Visitor Centre on the south bank (see Outer London: WOOLWICH – CHARLTON).* A small park on the north bank provides a fine **view** of this attractive feat of modern engineering. As the southeast corner of England is slowly sinking, the barrier was built to protect London from flooding in the event of a particularly high tide.

St Mark's Church, Silvertown – *Deconsecrated.* The church (1862) was designed by S S Teulon; it is scheduled to be converted into a Victorian Museum.

London City Airport – When the airport opened in 1987, providing easy access from the City to several European cities, it was the first STOL (short take-off and landing) airport; jet services were introduced at the end of March 1992. The runway is situated on a strip of land between the Royal Albert and George V Docks.

North Woolwich Old Railway Station Museum ⊙ – The Italianate style building (1847) has been converted into a museum featuring historical displays on the Great Eastern Railway and locomotives standing at the station platform.

Royal Victoria Gardens – The old North Woolwich Gardens, where dances used to be held, provide views of the Thames Barrier and the Woolwich Ferry, which carries vehicles and passengers across the river. There is also a foot tunnel for the rare occasions when the ferry is not operating.

SYON PARK★★

Map p 296 (TY)
Overground: Syon Lane from Waterloo Station

Artistic patronage – On the walls inside are portraits of the men and women who built up the house and their royal patrons by Gainsborough, Reynolds, Van Dyck, Mytens, Lely and by unknown artists of the English 16C school. Two men were principally responsible for the construction: the Lord Protector, Duke of Somerset, brother of Henry's queen, Jane Seymour, in the 16C and Hugh Percy, 1st Duke of Northumberland in the 18C. Somerset was given the former monastery site in 1547 by his nephew Edward VI and erected a Tudor mansion in the plan of a hollow square, dined his monarch there in 1550, laid out gardens, including the first physic garden in England... but in 1552 he was charged with conspiracy and executed.

For the next two centuries Syon was a political storm centre as the owners intrigued, conspired and often died brutally: John Dudley was beheaded (1553) for promoting his daughter-in-law, Lady Jane Grey, as Queen; Percys, Earls of Northumberland, were executed for supporting Mary Queen of Scots (1572), were found dead in the Tower (1585) and imprisoned for association with the Gunpowder Plot... With the marriage in 1682 of Elizabeth Percy to Charles, 6th Duke of Somerset, Syon returned to a descendant of its earlier owner, who also held office under the crown. In the 18C the new heirs, the Duke and Duchess of Northumberland, considered the house and grounds were in urgent need of remodelling: they commissioned **Robert Adam** and **Capability Brown** to produce designs.

The house ⊘ – The colonnaded east front of Syon House is visible across the river from Kew Gardens, the Northumberland Lion with outstretched tail silhouetted against the sky; a second beast, also from the model by Michelangelo, crowns the Lion Gate and graceful Adam screen on the London Road (A 315). The plain castellated main front gives no hint of the rich ornamentation within.

In the **Great Hall**, Adam is at his most formal: the high ceiling echoes the patterns laid into the black and white marble pavement; in the apses at either end nestle statues of the *Apollo Belvedere* and the *Dying Gladiator*.

The **Ante-Room**, by contrast, gleams darkly with heavy gilding, reds, blues, yellows in the patterned *scagliola* floor, and green marble and *scagliola* pillars (dredged from the Tiber), which line the walls on three sides and stand forward from the fourth to 'square' the room. Gilded statues gaze down from the entablature.

State Dining Room – The long apartment with column screened apses at either end was the first to be remodelled by Adam: deep niches with copies of antique statues along the left wall were reflected in pier mirrors; frieze, cornice, ceiling, decorated half domes, beautiful doorcases and doors, afforded a perfect setting for the banquets given by the Duke and Duchess in the late 18C.

Great Conservatory, Syon Park

Red Drawing Room – Scarlet Spitalfields silk, blooming with pale gold roses, on the walls and at the windows, a carpet, signed and dated 1769, woven at Moorfields, door pilasters with ivory panels covered with ormolu, gilded ceiling studded with Cipriani painted medallions, provide great richness; the room is, however, dominated by its Stuart portraits: Charles I (Lely), his queen, Henrietta Maria (Van Dyck); his sister Elizabeth of Bohemia (Van Honthorst); his elder brother who pre-deceased him, Prince Henry (van Somer); his daughter, Princess Mary of Orange (Hanneman), Henrietta, Duchess of Orleans (Mignard), Princess Elizabeth (Lely), his sons, Charles II and his wife Catherine of Braganza (Huysmans) and James II as Duke of York (Lely). The elegant mosaic-topped side tables are noteworthy.

Long Gallery – The long gallery of the Tudor house was transformed by Adam into a ladies' withdrawing room (far enough away from the dining room not to hear any masculine after dinner ribaldry!). It is 136ft long, 14ft wide and has a crossline decoration on the ceiling, grouped pilasters, wall niches, pier mirrors, so arranged as to disguise the length. Much of the furniture was designed, as throughout the house, by Adam, notably the veneered chest of drawers made by Chippendale.

The furniture in the **Print Room** includes two remarkable walnut, marquetry inlaid cabinets of the late 17C; the walls are again hung with family portraits.

★**Gardens** – Capability Brown assisted in designing the gardens, which extend to the river and maintain a tradition begun by Protector Somerset who planted many rare and imported trees; two of his mulberries still survive. In 1837 the gardens, world famous for their botanical specimens, were opened to the public. A vast **rose garden** *(separate entrance south of the house)* is in bloom from May to August.

The **Great Conservatory,** a beautiful semicircular building of white painted gun metal and Bath stone, with a central cupola and end pavilions was designed by Charles Fowler in 1820-27. Inside are cacti and an aquarium.

London Butterfly House ⊘ – In a tropical greenhouse visitors may stroll among many varieties of brilliant butterflies. All stages of breeding may be observed. Another section displays live spiders and insects: locusts, crickets, ants and scorpions.

Riverside – The **Isleworth Parish Church of All Saints** on the south outskirts of Syon Park has a square crenellated west tower of ragstone dating back to the 15C. The church was bombed and on the site since 1970 has stood a well-proportioned modern vessel of brick, wood and plain glass, with only small brasses rescued from the fire.

The London Apprentice pub dates back centuries although the present building is a mere 200 years old; the name is said to derive from the apprentices who in the 16C to 19C rowed up the river on their annual holiday and made the inn their own for a day.

Through-roads and access roads are shown in red or yellow on town plans.

TWICKENHAM

Map p 296 **(TYZ)**
Overground: Twickenham, St Margaret's, Strawberry Hill from Waterloo Station

Twickenham nowadays draws visitors rather to its rugby matches than to its riverside *(see INTRODUCTION – Sport).* In the 19C, Louis-Philippe, cousin of Louis XVI and future King of France (1830-48), three of his five sons, several descendants and a number of sympathisers all lived in as many as nine houses in Twickenham. Of these three remain: **Bushy House** was the home of the Duke of Clarence, later Wiliam IV who lived there first with his mistress Dorothea Jordan *(see index)* and their ten illegitimate children, and later with his wife, the future Queen Adelaide until her death in 1849; now leased by the Crown Estates to the National Physical Laboratory (Teddington); **Morgan House** on Ham Common, now part of the Cassel Hospital, and York House. In the grounds of Upper Lodge is the most complete 18C water garden in London.

York House – *Richmond Road.* The Yorke family lived on and worked a farm on the site in the 15C and 16C; successors, who from 1700 altered and rebuilt the house, retained the name including, in the 19C, members of the exiled French royal family and, this century, an Indian merchant prince. Today, the house accommodates Council offices.

The house has a terrace at the rear overlooking the walled garden. A footbridge leads to a cascade and rose garden preceding a shrubbery and grass terrace beside the Thames.

Sion Road – The road leading down to the river is joined halfway down, at the rounded Waterman's Lodge, by Ferry Road, a close of 'two down, two up' cottages. Beyond is **Sion Row**, a terrace of twelve three-storey houses built in 1721, in ordered lines with a uniform cornice, three lights and off centre entrances, personalized by individual doorways. At the end, parallel to the river, is a straggling line of houses of all periods: a pub, all corners and balconies, the Ferry House, three floors of white stucco with a slate roof, and Riverside House (1810), a rambling two storeys beneath broad eaves.

For details of the passenger ferry to Ham House, see PRACTICAL INFORMATION.

Orleans House Gallery ⊘ – Orleans House itself was demolished in 1926, only the **Octagon**, added in 1720, ten years after the house was first built, remains. This wing by James Gibbs has a brick exterior and splendid plasterwork, including fireplace, door pediments, figures and ceiling.

★**Marble Hill House** ⊘ – Marble Hill House was built in 1729 by Henrietta Howard (a mistress of the Prince of Wales, later George II), with monies settled on her by her royal lover, the future George II. She acquired a parcel of land beside the river; plans were sketched by Colen Campbell, Architect to the Prince of Wales. It was 1731, however, before Henrietta, now Countess of Suffolk and Mistress of the Robes, could 'often visit Marble Hill' and several years more before she took up residence there with her second husband, George Berkeley. She was an active hostess and received politicians, lawyers, and men of letters, including Alexander Pope and Horace Walpole. The most famous of later residents was another royal mistress, Mrs Fitzherbert, who lived there briefly in 1795.

The gardens, now disappeared but in the 18C considered integral to the house's design, were, from 1724, the preoccupation of **Alexander Pope** whose adages included 'in all let Nature never be forgot', a near neighbour at Crossdeep: of his house and gardens nothing remains save a grotto.

The house – The Palladian style, stucco house is three storeys high with the centre advanced beneath a pediment and an insignificant 18C entrance.

From the small hall, the square mahogany staircase leads directly to the Great Room, a 24ft cube splendidly rich in white and gold with carved decoration and copies of Van Dyck paintings upon the walls. Lady Suffolk's bedchamber *(left)*, divided by Ionic pillars and pilasters to form a bed alcove, is completed, like the other rooms, by a rich cornice and ceiling decoration. Though the actual furniture and furnishings were dispersed, an almost exact reconstruction has been achieved from a detailed inventory made on her ladyship's death in 1767. Some original items have been successfully traced: overmantel and overdoors by Panini and carved table in the Great Room. Fine collection of 18C paintings (Hogarth, Wilson, Hayman, Kneller).

A stone staircase leads to the restored second floor *(access on conducted tours only)* where is displayed a collection of chinoiserie.

The stable block *(north east)* dates from 1825-27. Close by is an 18C terrace, Montpelier Row.

★★**Strawberry Hill** ⊘ – *St Mary's College, Waldegrave Road.* In 1747 Horace Walpole, historian, antiquarian, bibliophile (15 000 volumes), diarist and letter-writer (48 volumes), acquired a modest 50-year-old cottage with ample grounds and a fine prospect of the river. He announced that as 'Grecian... columns and all their beautiful ornaments look ridiculous when crowded into a closet or a cheesecake house... I am going to build a little Gothic structure.'

'**A Little Gothic Castle**' – From 1748 to 1792 Walpole transformed and enlarged his house with battlements, round tower, turret, cloister and gallery – a remarkable creation which, though not the first instance of the 'Gothick', became the chief influence in the Gothic Revival. The fanciful interior, much of the ornament was derived from original medieval sources, was designed by the *Committee of Taste* (Walpole and John Chute assisted first by Richard Bentley and then by Thomas Pitt). Here Walpole set up the **Strawberry Hill Press** and displayed his 'profusion of rarities', which included a very fine **collection** of enamels and miniatures: a missal illustrated by Raphaël, a Holbein portrait of Catherine of Aragon as well as Cardinal Wolsey's hat. When the collection was auctioned in 1842 the sale lasted 32 days, was attended by 50 000 people and realised £33 468. On his death in 1797 Walpole left Strawberry Hill with an endowment of £2 000 a year to his cousin from whom it passed in 1815 to the Waldegrave family and to neglect. Strawberry Hill returned to fame under Frances, Countess Waldegrave (1821-1879), the 7th Earl's wife and a prominent political hostess, who restored and refurbished the house (1855) and herself designed a new wing for her grand receptions.

'**Prettiest bauble**' – The asymmetrical array of towers, battlements and chimneys are best viewed from the gate arch facing the road. The oratory and mini-cloister which flank the main entrance sound the monastic note which pervades the house.

The **staircase** links Walpole's additions with the small, low-ceilinged rooms in the old cottage; the balustrade is derived from the library staircase of Rouen Cathedral; the triple-arched vestibule and the niches were filled with military trophies. The low dado in the **eating room** was intended to create the effect of height; the ornate fireplace bristles with Gothic arches and pinnacles.

In the **library** the upper shelves are screened by arched openwork wooden doors, copied from the choir screen of Old St Paul's; the chimney-piece was inspired by a 14C canopied tomb; the heraldic ceiling is Walpole's own design. First editions and other precious volumes were kept in a locked cupboard.

Walpole's breakfast room was converted by Lady Waldegrave into a **Turkish Boudoir** with a velvet-lined ceiling; it contains two of Walpole's collections of miniatures (Ignatius Loyola and Francis Xavier).

The **Holbein Chamber**, once hung with paintings of Holbein, has a ribbed ceiling copied from the Queen's dressing room at Windsor. Inspiration for the screen and fireplace came from Rouen Cathedral (choir gates and high altar). The original crimson damask silk covers the walls of the **Gallery**, which is 'all Gothicism and gold, and crimson and looking glass'. The *papier maché* ceiling was derived from the fan vaulting in Henry VII's Chapel in Westminster Abbey.

The **Treasure Cabinet** was designed to resemble a Catholic chapel.

The **Round Drawing Room** is the work of **Robert Adam** guided by Walpole. The chimney-piece was modelled on the tomb of Edward the Confessor in Westminster Abbey and the ceiling is an imitation of the rose window in Old St Paul's Cathedral.

Grounds – St Mary's College and suburbia have invaded the grounds and the river prospect which Walpole enhanced with fawn and white cattle specially chosen for their colour. The only surviving ornament is the **Chapel-in-the-Woods**, modelled on a 16C chantry tomb in brick and Portland stone.

VAUXHALL – KENNINGTON

Map p 8 (**EFZ**)
⊖ Vauxhall, Oval

The construction of Westminster Bridge in 1750 to replace the horse-ferry led to the transformation of Kennington and Vauxhall from a rural hinterland of marshes, manorial estates, market gardens and even vineyards, into a prosperous and later densely-populated inner London suburb.

Property of the heir to the throne – In 1339 Edward III granted the manor of Kennington and Vauxhall to his son, the Black Prince. His name is preserved in Black Prince Road but the splendid palace he is said to have built was pulled down in 1531 by Henry VII *(plaque on Edinburgh House, 160 Kennington Lane)*. James I vested the manor in the royal heir as Duke of Cornwall and so it remains to this day.

By the time the Prince Regent was passing through on the way to his new Pavilion in Brighton (1815), Kennington Road was paved and provided easy access to the capital for those who preferred to live out of town; others were tempted to move to Kennington by the increased commercialisation of the riverside. Kennington Road, Kennington Park Road, Kennington Lane and the intervening network of streets were lined at first by Georgian houses and terraces *(Kennington Road: nos 104, 121 (1770), 150; Kennington Park Road: no 180)*, later by Victorian houses and bay-windowed cottages.

Vauxhall Bridge – The iron and stone bridge (1900) was designed by Maurice Fitzmaurice to replace an earlier iron bridge; the high iron parapet bears figures – Engineering, Science – against the piers. The bridgefoot, also known as Vauxhall Cross, is a junction where six main roads meet.

Vauxhall Gardens

The gardens, which occupied a site north of Harleyford Road, were greatly favoured by Evelyn and Pepys, who frequently 'took water to Foxhall, to the Spring Garden and there walked an hour with great pleasure'. In the 18C the garden of flowers, arbours, shaded walks, supper-boxes painted by Francis Hayman for light refreshments and simple pleasures was modernised and provided music, sophisticated meals and pastimes, including nightly firework displays; the atmosphere was caught by a number of artists, including Thomas Rowlandson (V & A collection). As the crowds thickened, however, knavery increased; the gardens became notorious and in the 19C they closed.

Vauxhall Cross – The striking purpose-built headquarters of MI6 are designed to project the Secret Service's new image. Nine floors of offices are screened from public gaze partly by green glazed curtain walling, partly by coloured pre-cast concrete panels – either way equally opaque from the open walkway outside. It is also protected by a fine metallic mesh that insulates the concrete from any electro-magnetic signal, inwards or outwards, called Faraday's Cage.

New Covent Garden Market – In Nine Elms Lane (south) stands London's main wholesale fruit and vegetable market, transferred from central London in 1974.

Kennington Lane – At nos 225-229 is an early 19C terrace beneath a central pediment, with apple green doors against white frames and window sashes; next to it stands **Imperial Court** (1836) which was the Licensed Victuallers' School until 1921 and the NAAFI HQ until 1992. In **Courtenay Square** (north side), planted with spring-flowering trees, the two-storey brick houses (1837-39) are delightfully transformed by white painted, summerhouse-shaped canopies supported on iron-work trellis pillars before each modest front door. **Cleaver Square** (across Kennington Lane east of the crossroads via Cleaver Street) is late Georgian.

KENNINGTON

Principal thoroughfares – **Kennington Park Road** is bordered *(east side)* by a very long, late 18C terrace *(nos 91-165)*, appealing as a unit and for the fanlights *(no 125)*. On the west side are the City and Guilds of London Art School and a Georgian house *(no 180)*. At the north end is a long terrace *(nos 121-143)*, dating from the 1770s; nos 104 and 150 date from the Georgian period. Charlie Chaplin lived at no 287 *(blue plaque)*.

Black Prince Road runs west, past **Woodstock Court** *(west)*, a model, two-storey precinct constructed around a fountained court (1930), and **Lambeth Walk** (north side), lined by grass verges and modern flats, far removed from the old market (1860s), aged housing and cockney gusto of the war time song, to the Albert Embankment (1866-69), where the horse-ferry used to land.

Kennington Park – The park was enclosed in 1852, after centuries as common grazing and a popular meeting ground, where some 200 000 Chartists gathered in 1848 intending to march on Westminster.

Halfway along the road frontage stands a prototype workman's cottage which the inscription in gold letters identifies as a 'model house for families erected by HRH Prince Albert'; it was commissioned by the Prince for the 1851 Exhibition.

The Oval – The famous cricket ground was a market garden when it was acquired in 1845 by the newly-formed Surrey County Cricket Club. At the east end are iron gates erected in memory of Sir Jack Hobbs (d 1963).

WIMBLEDON – MERTON

Map p 296 **(TZ)**
⊖ Wimbledon

The earliest known inhabitants of Wimbledon occupied the Iron Age hill fort on the south west side of the Common known erroneously as **Caesar's Camp**. The village developed in Saxon times along the High Street and around the church, first coming to prominence in 1588 when Thomas Cecil, Lord Burghley, then Lord of the Manor, built a mansion with turrets and gables, set amid terraced gardens on a slope north east of the church. Before its destruction in 1720 it was visited by Queen Elizabeth and King James I. The only building surviving from this period is **Eagle House** (1613) in the High Street which was built by Robert Bell, a native of Wimbledon and a founder of the East India Company. The Manor subsequently passed to Queen Henrietta Maria, to Sir Theodore Janssen, a financier who built a new house west of the church but was ruined in the South Sea Bubble, and then to Sarah, Duchess of Marlborough, who also built a new house linked to detached servants' quarters by an underground passage.

Wimbledon Common – In 1871, after 7 years of legal dispute with Earl Spencer, Lord of the Manor, who wanted to enclose the Common and develop some 300 acres for housing, Wimbledon Common was transferred to the Conservators to preserve in its natural state. Whereas Lord Spencer asserted that the land was boggy with noxious mist and fogs arising from it, Leigh Hunt wrote of the 'furze in full bloom making a golden floor of all that fine healthy expanse'. The horse racing, duelling and drilling of soldiers of earlier days have given way to horse riding, cricket, rugby and golf. 'Every person playing golf' is required by the Conservators 'to wear a red outer garment'. From 1860 the National Rifle Association held their annual shooting competitions on the Common, even setting up a horse-drawn tramway for the spectators, before moving to Bisley in 1889.

The 18C saw several large mansions rise round the Common; **Lauriston House** (1724; destroyed 1959), home of William Wilberforce; **King's College School** (1750) with adjoining Great Hall in Gothic Revival style (note the hexagonal pillar-box of 1872); **Southside House** ⊙ (1776) *Woodhayes Road*; **Gothick Lodge** (1760) *Woodhayes Road*, owned by Captain Marryat in the 1820s; **Crooked Billet** and **Hand-in-Hand**, 17C public houses; **Chester House** (1670) famous for the Sunday parties of the Revd John Horne Tooke whose election to Parliament in 1801 provoked the Act which made the clergy ineligible; **Westside House** (1760); **Cannizaro** ⊙ (1727, rebuilt in 1900) owned by Viscount Melville from 1887 who laid out the gardens and entertained William Pitt, Edmund Burke and Richard Sheridan; **Stamford House** (1720) and **The Keir** (1789). The **Round** or **Old Central School** (*Camp Road*), an octagonal building, was built in 1760 to educate 50 children of the deserving poor and is now incorporated in a primary school.

Wimbledon Windmill Museum ⊙ – The windmill, a hollow post mill built on the Common in 1817, has been converted into a museum illustrating the story of windmilling in pictures, models and the machinery and tools of the trade.

In the neighbouring miller's house Lord Baden-Powell *(see SOUTH KENSINGTON)* began to write *'Scouting for Boys'* in 1907.

Wimbledon Village – Stage coaches set out from the **Rose and Crown** and later from the **Dog and Fox** in the High Street, although the road over Putney Heath was infested with highwaymen.

The **Well House** in Arthur Road dates from 1761.

Wimbledon Museum ⊙ – *Ridgeway*. The local history museum is housed in the **Village Club**, which was built in 1858 to provide the working and middle classes with enjoyment and improvement through a reading room, library, lectures and instruction.

St Mary's Church ⊙ – Wimbledon church was mentioned in *The Domesday Book*; parts of a 13C rebuilding remain in the chancel. The present nave, tower and spire were designed in 1843 by Sir Gilbert Scott. Several famous people – William Wilberforce, Sir Theodore Janssen and J W Bazalgette *(see index)* are buried in the churchyard. To the north stands the **Old Rectory** (1500) the oldest house in Wimbledon and probably a priest's house until the Reformation. Near the churchyard entrance stands a small white house, **Stag Lodge**, with the hinges on which the gate to the later Manor House was hung still visible on a post at the side.

Wimbledon Lawn Tennis Museum ⊙ – *Church Road*. Displays depict the development of tennis and include sections on dress, equipment and the Wimbledon Champions from the early days in Worple Road to the modern era.

Tennis on grass demands greater exertion from players: the balls bounce less high off the ground and have to be hit harder than on hard courts. Furthermore, the Lawn Tennis Association contracts Slazenger to vary the quality of balls supplied for the Wimbledon championships in terms of size, colour, weight and consistency for a slower or faster game, always within approved guidelines set by the International Tennis Federation.

The **Open Championships** are usually held at the end of June. The Centre Court is exclusively reserved for the Championships; use of the No 1 court is limited to special events such as the occasional Davies Cup match.

Polka Theatre for Children ⊙ – *240 The Broadway*. A full programme, with performances and workshops for children, is supplemented by exhibitions of puppets etc. and a playground.

MERTON *Overground: Merton Park*

The village of Merton dates back to 1114 when Merton manor was granted to Gilbert the Knight. In 1117 he founded an Augustinian priory which was dissolved in 1538. On land known to have belonged to Sir Walter Raleigh stands Eagle House, a privately-owned, perfect example of a Queen Anne house.

From 1801 to his death in 1805 Nelson lived at **Merton Place**, now built over by rows of houses: Hamilton, Hardy, Nelson, Victory and Trafalgar Roads.

The arrival of the railway in 1838 transformed the village into a London suburb in fifty years. From 4 600 in 1861 the population grew to 55 000 in 1911. Rows of mainly small terraced houses covered parts of the Manor House park and the area round the station.

Merton Park – In 1867 John Innes, a successful business man, began to develop Merton Park, the original garden suburb, with tree-lined roads, holly hedges and interestingly varied houses. He was a keen farmer and in his will endowed an agricultural institute which has since produced composts and fertilisers bearing his name.

St Mary's Church – The church was built by Gilbert the Norman in the 12C; it has a stunted shingled steeple above a fine medieval roof and contains the seat from Nelson's box pew and his funeral hatchment. The south aisle windows, a memorial to John Innes, are by the firm William Morris & Co which occupied premises at Merton Abbey.

The **Norman Arch** *(west of the church)* is probably the gateway (re-sited 1935) of the guest house of Merton Priory where Thomas Becket and Walter de Merton, founder of Merton College, Oxford, were educated and where royal courts were held; the Statute of Merton, the oldest in English law, was drawn up here in 1236.

WOOLWICH – CHARLTON

Map p 297 (**UY**)
Buses: 51, 177, 180
Overground: Charlton from Waterloo
Boat: Thames Barrier from Westminster Pier, Greenwich

The fishing village of Woolwich began its naval and military career in the Tudor period. In those days it was the most important naval dockyard in the country. The *Great Harry*, built in 1512 during the reign of Henry VIII, was the first four-master to be launched in England; it had square sails on the fore and main masts, top sails on all four masts and top gallants on the first three. In 1717 the gun casting works were transferred from Moorfields and became the **Royal Arsenal** which reached its maximum output during the First World War when it extended over 1 200 acres and employed 80 000 men and women.

Royal Artillery HQ – The grandiose home of the RA comprises the arcaded buildings of the former **Royal Military Academy** (founded in 1741 and amalgamated with Sandhurst in 1964) and its regimental barracks (720ft long).

Museum of Artillery in the Rotunda ⊙ – The display traces the development of artillery from the Middle Ages to the present.

This most elegant of small museums began as a campaign tent designed by John Nash for the somewhat premature celebration of the defeat of Napoleon organised by the allied sovereigns in St James's Park in 1814. In 1819 the Prince Regent ordered the tent's re-erection at Woolwich 'to house military curiosities'.

Thames Barrier ⊙ – *Unit Way.* Construction of the barrier at Woolwich was undertaken in 1972-82 to protect central London from the threat of inundation by a surge tide. London is sinking on its bed of clay and Britain itself tilting: Scotland and the northwest are rising, the southeast is dipping by about a foot a century; tide levels have risen by 2ft at London Bridge in the last 100 years. The barrier is composed of 4 falling radial gates (3 to the north and 1 to the south) and 6 rising sector gates, the 4 larger being 61m (200ft) long and weighing 3 300 tonnes and the 2 smaller being 31.5m (103ft) long and weighing 900 tonnes. Each sector gate is raised, rotating through 90° from its concrete sill in the riverbed, by two arms projecting from the barge-shaped piers in which the lifting machinery is housed beneath huge stainless steel cowls. Further information is provided in an audiovisual presentation in the Visitor Centre.

Thames Barrier

CHARLTON

The Village – The parish church, the big house, the Bugle Horn Inn, a rebuilt post-house, the 18C White Swan, mark the length of the main street still characteristically rural and appropriately named.

St Luke's Church – *Charlton Church Lane*. The brick church with its square tower and Dutch gable doorway, dates, in the main, from 1630 when it was rebuilt by Sir Adam Newton *(see below)*. Inside are a memorial tablet to Master Edward Wilkinson (d 1567), Yeoman of the Mouth to Henry VIII and Edward VI and Master Cook to Queen Elizabeth, a 17C heraldic north window, the hatchment (west wall) of the Spencer Percevals and Spencer Wilsons, who in the 18C owned Charlton House, the royal arms of Queen Anne and the tablet and bust of Spencer Perceval, assassinated in the House of Commons when prime minister in 1812. The church, a landmark from the Thames, served as a navigational aid in the early 18C and still flies the white ensign on St George's and St Luke's days.

Charlton House ⊙ – The house, the finest extant example of Jacobean architecture in London, was built between 1607 and 1612 for Adam Newton, Dean of Durham and tutor to Prince Henry, eldest son of James I. Characteristically of deep red brick with stone dressings, it has a shallow H shaped plan with symmetrical bays at the end of each wing and balustrades lining the crest and terrace. At the centre is the door with a surround dated 1607, and two-storey bay above in stone, exuberantly decorated in an inexplicable German style.

Features inside include the plasterwork, particularly the ceiling with pendants in the Grand Saloon over the two-storey hall, the fireplaces, Long Gallery and typical staircase with square well and carved newel posts. The gateway, stranded on the front lawn, is the original Tuscan pillared entrance with an added 18C crest. In 1608 at James I's request a mulberry tree was planted in the north-east corner of the garden near the gazebo.

> The **Woolwich Free Ferry** dates from the 14C and is the last regular service of the hundreds which once crossed the Thames. It is now operated by three roll-on roll-off vessels each capable of carrying 1 000 passengers and 200 tons of vehicles on the 5 minute crossing.

On the cover of Michelin Green Guides,
the coloured band on top indicates the language:
blue for French
pink for English
yellow for German
orange for Spanish
green for Italian, etc.

WINDSOR CASTLE ★★★

Overground from London Waterloo

Windsor Castle ⊙ is the oldest royal residence to have remained in continuous use by the reigning monarchs and the largest castle in England. It was originally intended by **William the Conqueror** (c 1080) as one of several defensive strongholds built around London, and as such was constructed on the only elevated point in that stretch of the Thames valley. Norman castles conformed to a standard plan with a large tower or keep dominating the complex from an artificially raised earthen mound or *motte;* at Windsor this is flanked by the Upper and Lower Wards. The castle covers an area of thirteen acres.

Royal residence – As early as 1110 **Henry I** is known to have had quarters in Windsor to which he would retire after a day's hunting in the forest (now Windsor Great Park). His successor **Henry II** began building the stone castle as a royal residence equipped with State apartments in the Lower Ward and with more intimate, private lodgings on the north side of the Upper Ward for use by his close family (1165-79). Further expansion was undertaken by **Henry III** (1216-72) and by **Edward III** (1327-77) a century later.

Royal residents – Used by the Parliamentarians during the Civil War as a prison for Royalist supporters it became **Charles II**'s favourite (defensible) home outside London. In 1673 the architect Hugh May was appointed to manage a series of ambitious renovations that included the reconstruction of St George's Hall and the King's Chapel: he turned his attention not so much to changing the exterior appearance and crenellated walls but to the interior. He turned the draughty rooms into sumptuous apartments befitting a king: walls were insulated with oak wainscoting and festooned in Grinling Gibbons carvings, the ceilings decorated by the Italian painter Verrio (much of whose work was unfortunately destroyed by Wyatville in 1829) and gilded by a French master-craftsman René Coussin.
William III preferred Hampton Court to Windsor, but this situation was reversed with the accession of **George III** who had the Queen's Lodge (1777) designed by William Chambers; he modernised Frogmore in Home Park as a retreat for Queen Charlotte and revived the formal institution of the Order of the Garter in 1805. Additional plans for major improvements to other domestic apartments were laid after his first bout of illness, but work was halted as the king suffered a relapse in 1811.

Alterations to provide ever greater comfort were begun by **George IV** who appointed Jeffrey de Wyatville to oversee the transformations: mock Gothic renovations were implemented that included the addition of turrets, chimney stacks and battlements, the heightening of the Round Tower by 33ft, while extensions were remodelled to accommodate the large and complicated extension of the royal family. For this reason, Windsor was popular with **Queen Victoria** who received endless visits from her extended family in Europe and chose to receive heads of state there (King Louis Philippe in 1844; Emperor Napoleon III in 1855; King Victor Emanuel I of Italy; Emperor William I of Germany). She started the 'dine and sleep' practice maintained by Queen Elizabeth II where guests might be invited to spend an evening and stay overnight. The principal change made by Victoria was the creation of a private chapel in honour of Prince Albert who died at Windsor on 14 December 1861.
With the turn of the century came a change in spirit: **George V**'s Queen Mary began careful restoration of the castle which became the childhood home of HRH The Princesses Elizabeth and Margaret during the war, since which it has remained the Royal Family's principal home. The Court is in official residence throughout April and for Ascot Week in June when the annual Garter Day celebrations are held.

PRECINCTS
Enter from Castle Hill and proceed into the Upper Ward.

Round Tower – Henry II built this impressive section as a main defence feature surrounded by a dry (chalk) moat in c 1170; it was later heightened by Wyatville (1828-39). In fact oval (103ft × 94ft – 31.5m × 28.5m), it now houses the Royal Archives *(closed to the public)*.
From the North Terrace there is a fine **view** over Eton and the River Thames.

---

20 November 1992

The devastating fire which broke out in the Queen's Private Chapel at the northeast angle of the upper ward is thought to have been provoked by a spotlight on a curtain high above the altar. Major losses included the wooden ceiling of the St George Hall and Grand Reception room. Work was completed in November 1997, six months ahead of schedule, to coincide with the Queen's 50th wedding anniversary. It was the largest project of its kind this century, costing in excess of £37 million and calling on the skills of some of the finest craftsmen in the country.

Queen Mary's Doll's House ⊙ – Conceived by Sir Edwin Lutyens as an accurate record of contemporary domestic design on a scale of 12:1, it was presented to Queen Mary in 1924. The contents include standard amenities in working order (water system, electric lights and two lifts), a gramophone, vintage bottles of wine (supplied by Berry Bros in St James's), vintage cars, original paintings, leather-bound books including works by Kipling, G K Chesterton, Sir Arthur Conan Doyle, Thomas Hardy and J M Barrie.

Wall cases also display another time capsule comprising a remarkable travelling 'trousseau' of designer fashion-wear provided by the French and presented to the Princesses Elizabeth and Margaret after King George VI's official visit to France (1938). This includes hand-stitched kid gloves and a suite of period suit-cases.

Windsor Castle from the Long Walk

© The Royal Collection H M Queen Elizabeth II

★★State Apartments ⊙ – When the apartments were remodelled by George IV, Gothic was used for processional spaces (lobbies, halls, staircases) and an eclectic form of Classicism for the main reception rooms.

The **Gallery,** a vaulted undercroft designed to serve as the principal entrance hall to the State Apartments was cut off when the Grand Staircase was remodelled during the reign of Queen Victoria. Today it accommodates temporary exhibitions of prints, drawings and books from the Print Room and Royal Library. The **China Museum** displays fabulous pieces from services in the Royal Collection: Sèvres, Meissen, Copenhagen, Naples, Rockingham, Worcester... still used occasionally at banquets.

The **Grand Staircase** leads up to the first floor. The full-size statue is of King George IV. On the walls is arranged a collection of trophies, arms and armour (fine suit made for Henry VIII at Greenwich) as an introduction to the array in the fan-vaulted **Grand Vestibule.** In the cases are displayed various 18C and 19C trophies acquired after the Battle of Seringapatam (1799) and the Napoleonic Wars (the lead shot that killed Lord Nelson in the Battle of Trafalgar).

The **Waterloo Chamber** used to celebrate the anniversary of the Battle of Waterloo on 18 June, is hung with a series of portraits commissioned from Sir Thomas Lawrence by George IV; these depict the Allied leaders, political and military, who assisted in defeating Napoleon. Today the chamber is used for the annual luncheon given by the Queen for her Knights of the Garter and their consorts, for balls, receptions and concerts. The carved limewood panels (c 1680) from the workshop of Grinling Gibbons were retrieved from the King's Chapel.

The **Garter Throne Room** and the **Ante Throne Room** is used by the queen to confer upon her newly chosen knights the Order of the Garter (echoed in the plaster ceiling) before they adjourn to St George's Chapel. The **Grand Reception Room** particularly reflects George IV's personal francophile taste. The ceiling and walls badly damaged in the 1992 fire have been fully restored as well as the four huge chandeliers.

Public Rooms – The **King's Drawing Room** was once used by Queen Victoria for private theatrical performances, for which a stage was built up in the window alcove. Note the finely carved dado rail and Grinling Gibbons cornice; the five paintings by Rubens and his followers; the beautiful Boulle kneehole desk reputedly acquired by William III; the carpet presented to Edward VII by the Shah of Persia in 1903; the porcelain is all Chinese.

The **King's Bedchamber** has been considerably altered through history. The marble fireplace was designed by William Chambers and transferred from Buckingham Palace; the grandiose '*polonaise*' bed is attributed to the French furniture designer George Jacob and given its furnishings for the occasion of a visit from Emperor Napoleon III and his wife Eugénie in 1855, whose initials appear at the foot of the bed. The early 19C Aubusson carpet was presented to H M The Queen by President de Gaulle in 1960. Note the Canaletto views of Venice.

The **King's Dressing Room** is lined in red damask as intended by George III; the ceiling bears the initials of William IV; the carved cornice and panelled dado, however, survive from the times of Charles II. On the walls hang a number of **masterpieces★★**: works by Dürer (*Portrait of a Young Man*), Hans Memlinc, Jean Clouet, Hans Holbein, Andrea del Sarto, Rembrandt (*The Artist's Mother*), Rubens (*Portrait of the Artist*), Jan Steen, Van Dyck (*Charles I in Three Positions*). The Boulle marquetry bureau (c 1680) and cabinet (c 1695) are noteworthy.

The **King's Closet** is similarly furnished with exquisite pieces, mainly French, made of exotic woods (mahogany or satinwood) set with Japanese lacquer panels and bronze mounts.

The **Queen's Drawing Room** was substantially altered by Wyatville in 1834; the plate-glass windows being some of the first to be installed in England. The room is adorned with early 16C and 17C paintings (Holbein: *Sir Henry Guildford*, Mytens, Van Somer, Dobson: *Charles II*, Lely: *Mary II*) and furniture.

The **Octagon Lobby** is panelled in oak with splendid oval garlands by Gibbons. The **King's Dining Room** retains much of the character imparted to it by Charles II: Verrio's ceiling depicts a banquet enjoyed by the gods, while below, lovely still-life panels illustrate fruit, (lobster) fish and fowl; intricate limewood garlands of fruit and flowers carved by Grinling Gibbons and Henry Phillips tumble down the oak panelling. There is an interesting portrait by Sir Godfrey Kneller entitled *The Chinese Convert*.

The **Queen's Ballroom** or Queen's Gallery serves as a meeting room in which visiting heads of state may greet members of their diplomatic staff. Three English cut-glass chandeliers made for George III hang from Wyatville's plaster ceiling. The 17C silver pieces of furniture between the windows are rare vestiges of contemporary taste – similar pieces once made for Louis XIV had to be melted down to pay for military campaigns. On the walls hang a number of portraits by Sir Anthony van Dyck – the most notable being *Charles I in Robes of State*.

The **Queen's Audience Chamber**, together with the **Queen's Presence Chamber** next door, preserve the skilled artistry of craftsmen employed by Hugh May during the reign of Charles II. On Verrio's ceiling Queen Catherine of Braganza crosses the heavens in a chariot drawn by swans; Gibbons' crisply carved surround highlight the portraits; carved oak frames set off the Gobelins tapestries acquired by George IV in Paris in 1825. Note the fine sculpted bust by Roubillac (Handel) and Coysevox. In the second chamber, now used by the Knights of the Garter as robing room, Charles II's queen is seated below a canopy as Justice banishes Envy and Sedition from the kingdom.

The **Queen's Guard Chamber** was remodelled at the behest of George IV as a museum of British military achievement: replica French banners, the tricolour and the gold fleur-de-lys are presented each year to the queen by the current Duke of Wellington and the Duke of Marlborough as quit-rents for their estates at Stratfield-Saye and Blenheim, granted to their ancestors on perpetual leases by the grateful nation.

St George's Hall – This long room (180ft – 55m) claimed by remodelling Charles II's chapel and hall, was decorated by Wyatville in the neo-Gothic style inspired by the novels of Sir Walter Scott so admired by George IV. Completely gutted in the fire the hall has been magnificently restored with a hammerbeam oak roof (instead of previous painted plaster ceiling), complete with the 700 coats of arms of past Knights of the Garter.

Quadrangle – The equestrian statue is of Charles II. In the south-east corner is the Sovereign's Entrance which leads directly to the private royal apartments.

Lower Ward – Much of this section of the Castle precincts is given to the **College of St George** founded on 6 August 1348 by Edward III and comprising a dean, twelve canons, thirteen vicars and 26 'Poor Knights' on whom was conferred the Order of the Garter. On the left are the mid 16C lodgings of the Military Knights built by

Queen Mary. At the bottom stands the Guard House (1862). To the right sits St George's Chapel and beyond, a maze of cloisters and buildings attached to the chapel and choir school; the brick and timber-framed Horseshoe Cloister is reserved for the lay clerks (adult choristers).

★★**St George's Chapel** ⊘ – The spiritual headquarters of England's prime order of chivalry, the Most Noble Order of the Garter, is also the final resting-place of ten sovereigns including Charles I brought here after his execution at Whitehall in 1649.

The building was initiated by Edward IV (1475); the choir was finished in 1484; the stone-vaulted nave had been added at the death of Henry VII (1509); work was completed in 1528 in the reign of Henry VIII: a glorious expression of Perpendicular Gothic architecture *(see INTRODUCTION – Architecture)*. On the outside, the **Royal Beasts** (modern replacements) above the flying buttresses of the west end trace the royal descent from Edward III – the Lancastrians on the southside, the Yorkists on the north.

Interior – The 1790 Gothic-style Coade stone **organ screen** by Henry Emlyn was installed at the same time as the Samuel Green organ presented by George III. The splendid 75-light **west window** (36ft high and 29ft wide) survives in part from 1479, 1503, 1509 and 1842.

George VI Memorial Chapel was built in 1969, the first structural addition to the Chapel since 1504. The windows were designed by John Piper.

Quire – So called at Windsor to differentiate it from the body of choristers or choir, the Quire is separated from the nave by John Tresilien's magnificent wrought-iron gates (1478). The glorious east window (30ft high, 29ft wide; 52-lights) commemorates Prince Albert with incidents from his life illustrated in the lower tier, below the *Resurrection* (painted by Benjamin West) and the *Adoration of the Kings*. The carved alabaster reredos was also given by the Dean and Canons in memory of Prince Albert.

The woodwork executed largely by English and Flemish craftsmen dates from 1478-85 and includes a fine set of *misericords* or mercy seats and *popeyes* illustrating incidents from the lives of Christ (north side); the Virgin and St George (south side). The desk fronts of the front row are 19C.

Garter Stalls – On installation each knight is granted a stall marked with a numbered enamel name-plate (North 1 marks the Prince of Wales' stall), over which he/she will display their banner (5ft square of heavy silk bearing the arms approved by the College of Arms in the City of London), crest, helm, mantling and sword (made of cloth or wood and depicted half-drawn in readiness to defend the sovereign) and which they will keep until death when the accoutrements are all removed.

Other stalls are reserved for the Military Knights of Windsor (formerly the 24 Poor Knights appointed by Edward III, impoverished by ransoms paid to the French for their freedom) and the Naval Knights of Windsor (now dissolved).

Memorials – Emperor **Napoleon III** and his wife Eugénie of France, the close friends of Queen Victoria who withdrew from the international scene in 1870 when the Third Republic was born, and died at Chislehurst in 1873. Statue of **Leopold I**, King of the

---

Order of the Garter

The highest order of chivalry in the land is also the oldest to survive in the world. It was established by Edward III in 1348 when England was engaged in the 100 Years War with France and may have been modelled on the legendary story of the 5C King Arthur and his Knights of the Round Table: not only was the order to reward men who had shown valour on the battlefield, but also to honour those who manifested the idealistic and romantic concept of Christian chivalry. Tradition relates how at a ball fêting the conquest of Calais in 1347, the king retrieved a fallen garter and returned it to its rightful owner, the young and beautiful Joan of Kent, Countess of Salisbury, with the words 'Honi soit qui mal y pense' *('Shame on him who thinks evil of it')* – the emblem and motto of the Order. A more likely derivation is a strap or sword-belt from a suit of armour to denote the bond of loyalty and concord. At its initiation, Edward III nominated 25 English **Companion Knights**, including the Heir Apparent (the Black Prince): thereby providing himself with his own jousting team and one with which to do battle! Today there are still 25 Companion Knights including the Prince of Wales and at least one representative of each force (Navy, Army, Air Force). Additional '**Royal Knights**' may also be appointed by the sovereign following amendments made to the statutes by George I. Stranger, Foreign or '**Extra Knights**' may also be appointed; since 1905 this has been conferred upon regents or monarchs only (not necessarily Christian as they have included two Sultans of Turkey, two Shahs of Persia, four Emperors of Japan).

Belgians, the uncle of both Queen Victoria and Prince Albert – his first wife, **Princess Charlotte Augusta,** who would have succeeded her father George IV had she not died in childbirth, is commemorated by a sculptural group in the Urswick Chapel where the tomb of **George V** (d 1936) and Queen Mary (d 1953) by Lutyens is situated. In the Rutland Chapel *(open by special permission only),* founded in 1481, lies the particularly fine early 16C alabaster tomb of George Manners, Lord Roos, and his wife Anne, the daughter of the founders of the chapel. In the north aisle, but despoiled of its effigy and jewels during the Commonwealth is the tomb of **Edward IV** and Queen Elizabeth Woodville (when the pavement was relaid in 1789, the vault was broken by accident revealing the two coffins: that of the king revealed that he had been 6ft 4in tall!).

The **Royal Vault,** excavated by order of George III (1804-1810) extends from the High Altar to the Albert Memorial Chapel; in it rest George III, George IV, William IV and many of their direct descendants. In a second vault (memorial stone inserted by William IV in 1837) lie **Henry VIII,** Jane Seymour, **Charles I** (his embalmed body having been exposed to public view for at least a week at St James's Palace) and one infant of 17 children borne by Queen Anne (1702-1714). In the south aisle are the tombs of Edward VII (d 1910) and Queen Alexandra (d 1925) with their dog Caesar; Henry VI, founder of Eton College and King's College, Cambridge.

Albert Memorial Chapel – Built by Henry III (1240), this was the original chapel of the Order of the Garter at its foundation; left to decay, it was renovated by Henry VII as mausoleum for Henry I and intended by Cardinal Wolsey as his ultimate resting-place; fragments carved by Benedetto da Rovezzano were subsequently integrated into Lord Nelson's memorial in St Paul's Cathedral. It was given its magnificent Victorian embellishment by Sir George Gilbert Scott after the death of Albert, the Prince Consort, at the age of 42; it stands as a supreme expression of the 19C revivalist age complete with Venetian mosaics, inlaid marble panels and statuary. Note the four elaborate bronze candlesticks intended originally for the tomb of Henry VIII. Prince Albert's tomb was later removed to Frogmore.

Home Park – This section outside the Castle precincts but within the private grounds of Windsor Castle includes **Frogmore House** ⊙ which was built in 1684 and used by various members of the Royal household, most notably by Queen Charlotte and her unmarried daughters; today it is furnished largely with possessions accumulated by Queen Mary (black papier maché furniture, wax and silk flowers). Other buildings nearby consist of follies (Gothic ruin, Queen Victoria's Tea House and an Indian kiosk built of white marble) and the **Royal Mausoleum** ⊙, purpose-built (1862) by Queen Victoria after the untimely death of her husband Prince Albert. In the **Royal Burial Ground** *(closed to the public)* at Frogmore rest the Duke (Edward VIII) and Duchess of Windsor.

★WINDSOR GREAT PARK ⊙

A 4 800 acre park, once the hunting ground of Saxon leaders and medieval knights is today linked to the castle by the **Long Walk** (3 miles) planted by Charles II with elms in 1645 and substantially replanted with planes and chestnuts in 1945. At the top of the hill stands the **Copper Horse,** an equestrian statue of George III (1831).

Nestling in the park are two additional secluded former royal residences: **Royal Lodge** used by George IV as a retreat and now by Queen Elizabeth, the Queen Mother; and **Cumberland Lodge** where George II's son William Duke of Cumberland resided while charged with landscaping the park.

Smith's Lawn is a stretch of lawn reserved for polo matches, while beyond stretch the **Valley Gardens** ⊙, planted by the Duke of Cumberland with shrubs and trees that extend to **Virginia Water,** an area of 130 acres arranged around an artificial lake.

On the far side of the lake stand the **Ruins** which consist of Roman fragments brought in 1817 from Leptis Magna in Libya.

Savill Gardens ⊙ are another, independent set of landscaped wooded gardens laid in 1932 and endowed with a fine Temperate House in 1995. Glorious show in the spring when rhododendrons, azaleas, camellias and magnolias burst into symphonies of colour; highlights include broad varieties of lilies and roses in summer.

★★ETON COLLEGE ⊙

Royal antecedent – 'The King's College of Our Lady of Eton beside Windsor' was founded by Henry VI in 1440; a year later he founded King's College Cambridge where the young men might continue their studies. In 1443 accommodation was provided along the north side of the **School Yard** (now dominated by a statue of the founder and the 16C **Lupton's Tower**) comprising a class room **(Lower School)** and a dormitory **(Long Chamber)** where boys would have slept two or three to a bed; College Hall was built as a refectory for priests, Headmaster and scholars.

Henry's grand intentions for an almshouse and pilgrimage church were thwarted when he was deposed by his Yorkist rival Edward IV who promptly withdrew funding; the existing choir building was roofed and completed in 1482, a fine example of Perpendicular Gothic. Henry's provision for 70 scholars however was left intact.

★★ Chapel – At the heart of the college (originally meaning a community of priests rather than an educational establishment) is the chapel, endowed with many significant works of art.

The oldest are the Flemish-style wall paintings (1479-87), executed by at least four masters. On the north side are scenes associated with the chapel's patron the Virgin Mary, the south side ones depict the medieval story of a mythical empress.

In 1940 a bomb landed on the Upper School thereby destroying all the glass in the chapel save that above the organ. The east window was designed by Evie Hone in 1952 to complement panels designed by John Piper (four miracles on the north side and four parables on the south side). The modern roof is of stone-faced concrete, hung from steel trusses.

Collegers and Oppidans – Originally 70 scholars were to be entrusted to the care of a headmaster. In addition to the scholars, the school had a number of fee-paying Commensals who were lodged either in the Cloisters with the Fellows or in town. In the early 18C the system was reformed: accommodation was built to house such pupils who earned the name of 'Oppidans' from the Latin *oppidum* meaning *of the town*. Today the 24 Oppidan houses are managed by a housemaster and assisted by a Dame. Rivalry is maintained by a traditional contest on St Andrew's Day when the Wall Game is played between the Oppidans and the Collegers.

> Famous pupils have included several kings including George III; statesmen, of whom 19 Prime Ministers, such as Walpole, Gladstone, Pitt the Elder, Charles James Fox, Wellington, Macmillan, Douglas-Hume; the writers Fielding, Shelley, Thomas Gray, Aldous Huxley, George Orwell...

School Dress – Tailcoats and pin-striped trousers are still the norm. Senior boys wear wing collars (stick-ups) and white bow-ties. Top hats survived to the 1940s. Scholars wear gowns as they have since the College's foundation.

The Michelin on-line route planning service is available on a pay-per-route basis, or you may opt for a subscription package. This option affords you multiple route plans at considerable savings. Plan your next trip in minutes with Michelin on Internet: www.michelin-travel.com.

Bon voyage!

Canary Wharf DLR Station

Practical
information

Planning a trip

Seasons – There is no season of the year when the weather is too bad to permit visitors to enjoy the sights. Spring and autumn are the best seasons for visiting parks and gardens when the flowers are in bloom or the leaves are turning colour. The summer season is marked by traditional events: the Grand National, Ascot Week, Henley Royal Regatta, Trooping the Colour and Royal Garden Parties. Autumn and winter are the best time for visiting museums or for shopping as places are less crowded, except in the weeks before Christmas. At Christmas baubles flash in the windows of Selfridges, Hamley's Toy Shop, Harrods and Harvey Nicholls while the streets ring with the sound of carol singers and their charity collection boxes.

Documents – Despite the law, which came into force on 1 January 1993, authorising the free flow of goods and people within the European Union, it is nonetheless advisable for EU nationals to hold some means of identification, such as a **passport**. Non-EU nationals must be in possession of a valid national passport. Loss or theft should be reported to the appropriate embassy or consulate and to the local police.

A **visa** to visit the United Kingdom is not required by nationals of the member states of the European Union and of the Commonwealth (including Australia, Canada, New Zealand, and South Africa) and the USA. Nationals of other countries should check with the British Embassy and apply for a visa if necessary in good time.

The brochure *Safe Trip Abroad* (US$1.25) provides useful information for US nationals on obtaining a passport, visa requirements, customs regulations, medical care etc for international travel; it is published by the government printing office and can be ordered by telephone ☎ 1-202-512-1800 and ordered or consulted via the Internet on website www.access.gpo.gov

Customs – Tax free allowances for various commodities are governed by EU legislation except in the Channel Islands and the Isle of Man which have different regulations. Details of these allowances and restrictions are available at most ports of entry to Great Britain. It is prohibited to import into the United Kingdom any drugs, firearms and ammunition, obscene material featuring children, counterfeit merchandise, unlicensed livestock (birds or animals), anything related to endangered species (furs, ivory, horn, leather) and certain plants (potatoes, bulbs, seeds, trees). It is also an offence to import duty-paid goods (to a maximum value of £145) from the EU other than for personal use.

A Guide for Travellers outlines British customs regulations and "duty free" allowances; it is available from HM Customs and

> Remember to take some passport-size photos with you if you want to purchase a public transport and museum pass on arrival.

Excise, Dorset House, Stamford Street, London SE1 9PS. ☎ 020 7928 0533.

A booklet *Know before you go* is published by the US Customs Service; its offices are listed in the phone book in the Federal Government section under the US Department of the Treasury or can be obtained by consulting website www.customs.ustreas.gov

Christmas decorations in Regent's Street

Tourist Information Centres

The **British Tourist Authority (BTA)** provides assistance in planning a trip to London and an excellent range of brochures and maps. The addresses and telephone numbers of local Tourist Information Centres are given in the chapter on Admission Times and Charges.

United States:

625 North Michigan Avenue, Suite 1510, **Chicago**, Illinois 60611, ☎ 312-787-0490.

551 5th Avenue, Suite 701, **New York**, NY 10176, ☎ 212-986-2266.

World Trade Center, 350 South Figueroa Street, Suite 450, **Los Angeles**, CA 90071, ☎ 213-628-3525.

Canada:

111 Avenue Road, Suite 450, **Toronto**, Ontario, M5R 3J8, ☎ 416-961-8124.

France:

Maison de la Grande Bretagne, 19 rue des Mathurins, 75009 **Paris**, ☎ 1 44 51 56 20 (information).

Australia:

210 Clarence Street, **Sydney**, NSW 2000, ☎ 612-267-4666.

New Zealand:

Suite 305, 3rd Floor, Dilworth Building, corner of Customs and Queens Streets, **Auckland**, ☎ 649-3031-446.

Britain Visitor Centre is located at 1 Lower Regent Street, London SW1Y 4NS. ☎ 020 8846 9000.

London Tourist Board – Glen House, Stag Place, London SW1E 5LT: Written enquiries only.

Refunded VAT – In Great Britain a sales tax of 17.5 % (Value Added Tax) is added to almost all retail goods. Non-Europeans may reclaim this tax from accumulated purchases when leaving the country; paperwork should be completed by the retailer at the time of purchase (Harrods, Selfridges, Liberty's etc).

Tourism for the Disabled – Many of the sights described in this guide are accessible to disabled people; see Admission Times and Charges.

The *Michelin Red Guide Great Britain and Ireland* indicates hotels with facilities suitable for disabled people; it is advisable to book in advance.

The Royal Association for Disability and Rehabilitation (RADAR) publishes an annual guide with detailed information on hotels and holiday centres as well as sections on transport, accommodation for children and activity holidays. Apply to RADAR, 12 City Forum, 250 City Road, London ECIV 8AF, ☎ 020 7250 3222.

Other organisations such as the British Tourist Authority, National Trust and the Department of Transport publish booklets for the disabled.

Embassies and Consulates in London

Australian High Commission: Australia House, Strand, WC2B 4LA. ☎ 020 7887 5118.

> It is important to take out medical insurance prior to departure as treatment in Great Britain may be extremely expensive.

Canadian High Commission: Macdonald House, 1 Grosvenor Square, W1. ☎ 020 7258 6600.

Republic of Ireland: Irish Embassy, 17 Grosvenor Place, SW1X 7HR. ☎ 020 7245 9033.

New Zealand High Commission: 80 Haymarket SW1Y 4TQ. ☎ 020 7930 8422.

South Africa Embassy: South Africa House, Trafalgar Square, WC2N 5DP. ☎ 020 7930 4488.

United States Embassy: 24 Grosvenor Square, W1A 1AE. ☎ 020 7499 9000. Passport affairs ☎ 020 7491 3506.

Michelin Green Guides cover the world's great cities:
New York, London, Paris, Rome, Brussels, Berlin, Vienna, Washington DC, San Francisco, Chicago, Venice, Amsterdam

Travelling to London

By air

London is served by five airports. Enquiries on how to get to the airport may b directed through the London Tourist Board Visitorcall service ☎ 0839 123 433.

London Heathrow – Heathrow handles all major airline scheduled flights. It situated 20 miles west of London off the A4 / M4 and equipped with short an long-term car parks at the airport.
Terminal 1 handles British Airways / British Midlands flights; Terminal 2 handles Eu ropean destination flights; Terminals 3 and 4 handle long-haul flights to America Australia, New Zealand and the Far East.

Airport Information – ☎ 020 8759 4321.

Heathrow London Tourist Board Information Centre at Terminals 1, 2, 3 and Undergroun Station Concourse: open daily 8am to 6pm (7pm Jun to Sept). Terminal 3 Arriva Concourse: open daily 6am to 11pm.

Access to city centre – Taxis are subject to road traffic conditions (40min on a good day t Marble Arch but it is best to allow an hour) at an approximate cost of £43 – £48 Services may be booked in advance on ☎ 020 8745 5325.

Tube / Underground services to Central London are provided by the Piccadilly Lir between 5am and 12midnight *(see Underground map inside back cover)*. Averag journey time from Heathrow to Piccadilly Circus: 40/50 minutes. Cost: £3.40 (single £6.80 (return). At night the N87 bus shuttles between Heathrow and Trafalga Square every hour. London Transport Information ☎ 020 7222 1234. The **Heathro Express** (15-20min) link provides a fast alternative rail link into Paddington Statior Express class £10 (£13 peak hours), First class £20, free for under-16 ☎ 0845 600 1515.

Airbuses operate two different services. Tickets are purchased from the driver, Touris Information Centre at Victoria, London Regional Transport Travel Information Centre and many hotels: **A1** – Heathrow Air Terminals to Victoria Coach Station via Cromwe Road, South Kensington, Harrods, Victoria Rail Station. It runs every 30 minutes fror Heathrow 6.45am to 8.30pm; from Victoria 5.30am to 8.50pm. Approximate journe time 60/75 minutes. Cost £7 (single), £12 (return). **A2** – Heathrow Air Terminals t Russell Square via Holland Park, Notting Hill Gate, Bayswater Road, Lancaster Gate Paddington Station, Marble Arch, Baker Street, Great Portland Street, Euston Statio runs every 20 minutes from 5.30am to 8.50pm. Approximate journey time: 60/7 minutes. Cost £7 (single), £12 (return).
Information and reservations: ☎ 020 8400 6655/6 (from 6am to 10pm).

London Gatwick – 30 miles to the south down the M25/M23 (short and long-term car parks at the airport). Two, 'North' and 'South', terminals handle flights to destina tions worldwide, charters and short-haul flights to the Channel Islands. For genera and flight enquiries ☎ 01293 53 53 53.

Access – The Rail link **Gatwick Express** shuttles to and from Victoria Station (30min) Departures every 15 minutes at peak times (Mondays to Fridays 8.30am-7.30pm) Trains run from Gatwick between 1.35am and 12pm; from Victoria between 00.05am (except Mondays) and 11.32pm. Cost £9 (single), £16.40 (return). ☎ 0990 30 15 30 www.gatwickexpress.co.uk

Thameslink trains also operate from King's Cross and Blackfriars Stations ☎ 0345 48 49 50.

Taxis are subject to traffic conditions. Allow 90mins journey at an approximate cost o £60 – £65.

National Express Speedlink – Buses operate daily services from Gatwick North and Sout Terminals to Victoria (60-70min) via the Arndale Shopping Centre and Wandswort between 5.15am and 10.52pm. Return journeys from London Victoria Coach Station bay 9 to Gatwick South Terminal between 6.35am and 11.25pm. £7.50 (single), £1 (return); concessions and discounts available. ☎ 0990 80 80 80, 020 8668 7261 o 0990 747 7777 for National Express/Flightline services. www.speedlink.co.uk/

City Airport (Docklands) – 2 miles from Canary Wharf; 6 miles from Bank o England; 8 miles from the West End. Services from European business centre destina tions. 10minute check-in time.

General airport enquiries – ☎ 020 7666 0000.

London Executive Aviation (Executive private charters) ☎ 020 7474 3344.

Access – Courtesy airport bus to Canary Wharf (10min, Yellow Route) for transfer ont the DLR, and to Liverpool Street station (25min, Red Route) for services on th underground and mainline railway services to Cambridge. Reduced services at week ends. ☎ 020 7666 0000.

Luton Airport – Located in Bedfordshire. ☎ (Luton) 01582 405 100.
Access – **Thameslink trains** from St Pancras or King's Cross (35min) and airport bus or **Green Line** bus from Victoria Coach Station.

Stansted Airport – Located in Essex. ☎ (Bishop's Stortford) 01279 680 500.
Access – **SkyTrain** from Liverpool Street Station to Bishop's Stortford (50min) and bus.

By rail

London has 9 main-line termini connected by the underground and in some cases by special inter-station single-decker buses. Tickets and information are available from the termini.

Rail passes – Check eligibility for the Network Card, Family, Young Persons (16-25 yrs), Senior Railcard (over 60s) and Disabled Persons schemes. **Note:** It is important for disabled travellers to check procedures and facilities before undertaking their journey ☎ 020 7918 3015.
Special deals are also available for unlimited travel or group travel in Europe: check with travel agents or contact National Rail Enquiries for information on fares and timetables ☎ 0345 48 49 50.

Charing Cross – **South Eastern** network: Southeast England.

Euston – **North London Railways:** West Midlands; north Wales; northwest England; Scotland via the west coast; Northern Ireland; Republic of Ireland.

King's Cross – **Thameslink** services and West Anglia Great Northern Railway: East and northeast England; Scotland via the east coast.

Liverpool Street – **West Anglia Great Northern Railway** and **Great Eastern** services: Essex, East Anglia.
London Tourist Board – *Liverpool Street Underground Station.* Open daily, 8am to 6pm (7pm Jun to Sept).

Marylebone – **Chiltern Lines** to Birmingham.

Paddington – **Thames Trains:** West of England; south Wales, south Midlands.

St Pancras – **Thameslink:** East Midlands.

Victoria – **Network SouthCentral, Gatwick Express, South Eastern** services: Southern England. European destinations (including the Orient Express) 0207 834 2345.
London Tourist Board – *Victoria Station Forecourt.* Open Mondays to Saturdays, 8am to 7pm (8pm May, 10pm Jun to Sept); Sundays 8am to 6pm (7pm Jun to Sept).

Waterloo – **South West Trains, South Eastern** services: South western England and Windsor. ☎ 0207 928 5151.
Eurostar runs regular departures from Paris (Gare du Nord ☎ 015 12 21 22; Minitel 3615 / 3616 SNCF) and Brussels (☎ 02 224 58 90) to London (Waterloo International Station ☎ 0990 186 186/Special Services Unit 0207 928 0660).
London Tourist Board – *Waterloo International Terminal Arrivals Hall.* Open daily 8.30am to 10.30pm.

Paddington Station

By road

Coach – There are many companies offering coach services from London to all part of the British Isles. Most depart from Victoria Coach Station *(see Inner London Ma, page 7 DY)* in Buckingham Palace Road (next to Victoria Railway Station) or from Marble Arch. Remember to check for special season ticket rates such as the Nationa Express Familysaver coach cards and Tourist Trail passes.

City Link Oxford ☎ 01865 785 400.
Greenline Coaches ☎ 020 8668 7261.
National Express Coaches ☎ 0990 808 080.

Car – Nationals of EU countries require a valid **national driving licence**; US driving licence valid for 12 months; a permit (US$10) is available from the National Auto Club Touring Department, 188 The Embarcardero, Suite 300, San Francisco CA 94105 o from the local branch of the American Automobile Association. Other nationals requir an international driving licence.

For the vehicle it is necessary to have the **registration papers** (log-book) and a **nationalit plate** of the approved size.

Insurance – Insurance cover is compulsory and although an **International Insurance Certificate** (Green Card) is no longer a legal requirement in Britain, it is the mos effective proof of insurance cover and is internationally recognised by the police and other authorities.

Certain UK motoring organisations *(see below)* run accident insurance and breakdown service schemes for members. Europ-Assistance has special schemes for members. The American Automobile Association publishes a free brochure *Offices to Serve You Abroad* for its members.

Highway Code

The **minimum driving age** is 17 years old. Traffic drives **on the left** and overtakes on the right. Headlights must be used at night even in built-up areas and at other times when visibility is poor. There are severe penalties for driving after drinking more than the legal limit of alcohol.

Important **traffic signs** are shown at the end of the **Michelin Red Guide Great Britain and Ireland**, and in general correspond to international norms.

Seat belts – In Britain the compulsory wearing of **seat belts** includes rear seat passengers when rear belts are fitted and all children under 14.

Speed limits – Maximum speeds are:

70mph/112kph	Motorways or dual carriageways
60mph/96kph	other roads
30mph/48kph	in towns and cities.

Parking Regulations – Off-street parking is indicated by blue signs with white lettering (Parking or P); payment is made on leaving or in advance for a certain period. There are also parking meters, disc systems and paying parking zones; in the last case tickets must be obtained from ticket machines (small change necessary) and displayed inside the windscreen. Illegal parking is liable to fines and also in certain cases to the vehicle being clamped or towed away. The usual restrictions are as follows:

Double red line = no stopping at any time (freeway)
Double yellow line = no parking at any time
Single yellow line = no parking for set periods as indicated on panel
Dotted yellow line = parking limited to certain times only.

Resident parking: Different boroughs operate varying restrictions and since en-forcement has been granted to independent operators ticketing, clamping and removal are common. In Covent Garden, for example, parking on a yellow line is permitted in some areas after 6.30pm and after 8.30pm in others.

No stopping or parking on white zigzag lines before and after a zebra crossing at any time. Remember to give way to pedestrians on zebra crossings and when traffic lights flash amber. Arrangements providing additional space for special occasions are announced by the police in the press; information also from the London Tourist Board *(see above)*.

Do not leave anything of value in unattended vehicles at any time.

Bus lanes: blue road signs indicate the hours between which channels are reserved for buses and taxis. Most will bear a symbol permitting use by cyclists.

Petrol/Gas – In many service stations dual-pumps are the rule with **unleaded pumps** being identified by green pump handles or a green stripe. Leaded two-star petrol is no longer available in Britain, only unleaded two-star.

Motoring Organisations – The major motoring organisations in Great Britain are the Automobile Association and the Royal Automobile Club. Each provides services in varying degrees for non-resident members of affiliated clubs.

Automobile Association, Fanum House, Basingstoke, Hants, RG21 2EA; ☎ 0990 448 866; website: www.theaa.co.uk/theaa

Royal Automobile Club, RAC House, 1 Forest Road, Feltham, Middlesex TW13 7RR; ☎ 0202 917 2500; 0990 275 600 (travel information); Fax 020 8587 0168; website: www.rac.co.uk

Car Rental – There are car rental agencies at airports, air terminals, railway stations and in all large towns throughout Great Britain. European cars usually have manual transmission but automatic cars are available on demand. An international driving licence is required for non-EU nationals. Most companies will not rent to those aged under 21 or 25. The following firms operate on a national basis:

Avis	020 8848 8733
Budget	0800 181 181
Eurodollar	01895 256 565
Europcar	0345 222 525
Hertz	020 8679 1799

Check that parking facilities are available with the hotel before deciding to collect a car from the airport.

Ceramic tiles, Michelin House

Getting around

London Transport – Zoned tube and bus tickets are sold singly on buses or at tube stations. Books of ten Underground tickets (carnet) valid for travel within zone 1 may be purchased for £10 from Underground stations, TIC etc; they are also valid on the DLR: these are not valid on buses or overground services (National Rail). All children under the age of 5 years travel free on the Underground, only two accompanied by an adult on the buses may travel free of charge. Passengers must have a valid ticket for their complete journey or they may be liable to pay on-the-spot penalties (£5 buses, £10 underground).

London Transport Enquiries 55 Broadway, SW1H 0BD. ☎ 020 7222 1234.
Docklands Travel Hotline ☎ 020 7918 4000.

Travelcards – Multi-journey zoned passes are more economical for a stay in the capital valid for **One Day** or a 'season' (two-day **Weekend**, 7-day **Weekly**, 1 month, more than a month or 1 year).

A **Photocard** is required by adults and children using a Weekly Travelcard. It is also required by 14 and 15 year old children as a qualifier for the under 16 child fare One Day Travelcard and by youths applying for the 16-17 and student cards.

Family Travelcards are available for a group comprising two adults and one to fou children for travel after 9.30am Mondays to Fridays, all day weekends and publ holidays. Prices vary according to the number of zones covered by the ticket. Thes are available from Underground stations, National Rail stations and appointed news agents.

One Day Travelcards may be used Mondays to Fridays from 9.30am and 3am (th following day), weekends and public holidays from any hour for travel on the Under ground, Docklands Light Railway, National Rail overground trains and most Londo bus services (except night services), nearly everywhere within the designated 6 Londo zones. Adult £3.80 for zones 1 and 2, £4.50 for zones 1 to 6.

The **LT Card,** also valid for one day, is for use on the Underground, DLR and buses (n overground train services) only within the specified 6 London zones and not subject t any restriction during the morning rush-hour. Adult £4.80 for zones 1 and 2, £7.5 for zones 1 to 6.

Underground – Single or return tickets may be purchased from tube stations only. D keep them once you have passed through the electronic barrier as you will need to pas them through a second barrier at your station destination. Inspectors may also spo check them so do not destroy or deface them. Single zone ticket extensions must b purchased before you travel.

Note: To calculate an estimated journey time, count three minutes between stations an an average of fifteen minutes to change lines. Trains run from Central London unt 0.50am Mondays to Fridays and until 12midnight on Sundays.

The Underground Map is located after the Index.

DLR – The Docklands Light Railway includes 5 lines: **line A** runs from Beckton; **line B** fro Island Gardens; **line C** from Stratford; **line D** from Tower Gateway; **line E** from Bank Services are reduced at weekends.

Buses – Bus-routes are displayed in bus shelters as well as inside the buses themselves note that most bus-stop signs will bear the name of the stop, but if in doubt ask passenger or the conductor. Reduced services on some routes operate through the nigh – special rates may apply.

Note: White signs with the red logo indicate bus stops at which all listed buses mus stop – red signs with the white logo are request stops at which passengers must wav to the bus to stop and make a pick up. Night buses (signed with an owl perched on crescent moon) will only stop on request.

Doubledecker buses in Oxford Street

Public transport

Roads that once had been used only by walkers, riders, costermongers with their barrows and an occasional coach soon became congested with sedan chairs and hackney carriages (17C), curricles and gigs, phaetons and barouches, landaus and broughams (18C and 19C). By 1870 tram services were in operation and by 1886 there were some 7 020 hansom cabs plying for hire.

Commuting, which began in 1836-38 with the inauguration of the London Bridge Deptford Greenwich Railway, increased with every new line laid to a London terminal, taking on phenomenal proportions when the connecting Metropolitan Railway (Paddington to Farringdon Street) opened in 1863. On its first day the line carried 30 000 passengers and in the first year 9.5 million in open carriages drawn by steam engines through the tunnels. London Transport was established in 1933 as a public corporation to co-ordinate and modernise the underground, railway and bus companies then in existence. It was under the overall policy and financial control of the GLC from 1970 to 1984 when a new body, London Regional Transport, was set up under the Secretary of State for Transport.

Since then under a policy of deregulation and privatisation, bus services have been put out to competitive tender. The traditional red double-decker bus is still in operation but some routes are now serviced by private bus companies with distinctive liveries and smaller buses more suitable for narrow streets.

Taxis – The traditional London cab is available at railway termini, Heathrow airport, taxi ranks and cruising the streets. An orange roof-light displays whether or not it is available for pick-up. Minimum charge £1.40. Special fares operate after midnight, at weekends and on public holidays. Gratuities are discretionary but 10% is usual. Journeys beyond the limits of the Metropolitan Police District (MPD – an area broadly corresponding to but slightly less extensive than Greater London) are subject to negotiation. Taxis are not

Black London Cab

R. Besse/MICHELIN

obliged to go outside the MPD nor more than 6 miles from the pick-up point within the MPD.

Look out for the green refuges (Sloane Street, Pembridge Road, Bedford Square) run by a special charity that caters exclusively to cab drivers. Taxis can usually be hailed from thereabouts.

Note: unlicensed taxis, car-services or mini-cabs are to be used at the passenger's discretion: they are not subject to the same stringent standards enforced on the more distinctive London cabs and should be open to negotiation on long distance journeys.

Useful numbers – Radio Taxis 020 7272 0272. Dial-A-Cab 020 7253 5000. Data Cab 020 7727 7200. Computer Cab 020 7286 0286.

London cabs

All of London's 20 000 licensed taxi cab drivers have to pass stringent medical checks and demonstrate their 'knowledge' of London before being able to operate on the London streets. Vehicles must conform to three different front-wheel drive models: the original 1958 Fairway, the 1986 fibreglass Metrocab licensed to carry 6 passengers, the modern replica of the 1930s styled Asquith. Distinctive features include the doors, wheelchair straps, vinyl seats and lino floor (to allow the interior to be hosed out), a turning circle of 25ft and a rear luggage compartment capable of accommodating a hay bale, an archaic rule that backdates to the days of Hackney Carriages. All are subjected to exacting MOTs and regular on-the-spot controls on tyres, cleanliness and safety features by the Metropolitan Police.

Lost property: To claim property left in a licensed taxi contact the Public Carriage Office, 15 Penton Street, London N1 9PU. ☎ 020 7833 0996 Monday to Friday, 9am to 4pm.

Sightseeing

Tourist Information Centres – The main information centres operated by the **London Tourist Board** are located as follows (others are listed under section Admission times and charges):

Head Office – Glen House, Stag Place, London SW1E 5LT. **Victoria Station Forecourt** – Open Mondays to Saturdays, 8am to 7pm (8pm May, 10pm Jun to Sept); Sundays 8am to 6pm (7pm Jun to Sept).

City of London Information Centre – *St Paul's Churchyard, EC4.* Open May to October daily 9.30am to 5pm; otherwise Mondays to Saturdays 9.30am to 5pm (12.30pm Saturdays). ☎ 020 7332 1456/7.

Selfridges – Basement Services Arcade, Oxford Street, W1. Open during shop hours.

Britain Visitor Centre – *1 Regent Street, SW1Y 4NS.* Open all year, Mondays to Friday 9am to 6.30pm, Saturdays and Sundays 10am to 4pm; July to September Saturday 9am to 5pm.

Telephone Guides – **Visitorcall** – **the Phone Guide to London** is a recorded message service revised daily by the London Tourist Board *(49p per minute, plus any hotel/payphone surcharge).*

Dial 09064 123+ one of the following numbers:

400 What's On this week
403 Current Exhibitions
407 Sunday in London
411 Changing of the Guard
422 Rock and Pop Concerts

416/434 London Theatre
424 Where to take children
431 Guided Tours and Walks
432 River boat services
480 Popular attractions

Kidsline answers individual queries about activities for children ☎ 020 7222 8070 *(During school holidays and half-term holidays: Mondays to Fridays 9am to 4pm; otherwise Mondays to Fridays 4pm to 6pm).*

A **Weather Forecast** for Greater London is provided by the Meteorological Office on ☎ 09062 500 951.

London Line 2000: information on the millennium in London. ☎ 09068 66 33 44.

Discount facilities – Certain schemes are available for local visitors and to travellers from abroad.

English Heritage – Membership of this organisation provides free access to over 400 venues nationwide including the country houses of London (Kenwood, Chiswick House, Ranger's House). An **Overseas Visitor Pass** valid for 7 or 14 days at an initial cost of Adult £12 / £16, Family (2A+2C) £26 / £35. Contact English Heritage Customer Services, Portland House, Stag Place, London SW1E 5EE. ☎ 020 7973 3434.

Go See – The London White Card – This consists of a 3 or 7-day pass for unlimited access to London's museums, art galleries and exhibitions, validated at the first venue visited. Cost: £16 for individual adult 3 day card, £26 for individual adult 7 day Card; £32 for the Family (2A+4C under 16) 3 day card; £50 for the Family 7 day card. Available from participating museums and galleries, Victoria Coach Station, Waterloo International Terminal, in over 200 Top London hotels, TIC, BTA, London Visitor Centre, London Transport Information Centre and in Global Ticketing Systems worldwide. ☎ 020 7923 0807. e-mail: 101606.3626@compuserve.com
www.london-gosee.com

London for Less – Valid for 4 persons over a period of 8 days, the card offers holders a variety of discounts on hotels, major attractions, restaurants, pubs, theatres, concerts, telephone calls and foreign currency exchanges. Subscription to the scheme costs £12.99 for 4 persons for 8 days and is available from Metropolis International (UK) Ltd, 222 Kensal Road, W10 5BN ☎ 020 8964 4242 or through American distributors on ☎ 1 800 244 2361. Payment may be transacted by credit card and arrangements made for the cards and information pack to be sent either to you at home prior to departure or to the first hotel ready for your arrival in London. Parallel schemes in operation for Bath, Edinburgh and York.

London doubledecker buses

Further to the deregulation of the London Transport bus operator system and terrorist bomb in the City of London, bus routes have been subjected to change. With 17 500 vehicles on the road, however, buses provide an economical means of exploring the capital and admiring garden layouts and details of buildings above street level. Classic routes include numbers 11 (King's Road, Palace of Westminster, Whitehall, Trafalgar Square, Fleet Street, St Paul's, Mansion House) and 15 (Paddington, Marble Arch, Oxford Street, Regent Street, Trafalgar Square, Strand, Fleet Street, St Paul's, Monument, Tower of London, Whitechapel).

Sightseeing on the river

Thames Cruises – For information the 24 hour recorded message for the **London Tourist Board Riverboat Information Service** ☎ 09064 123 432 or contact service points direct.

Westminster Pier downstream:

to the **Tower**(25min): daily, 10.20am to 9pm, every 20min in summer; 10.30am to 3.45pm, every 45min in winter; £4.60 one way, £5.80 round trip . City Cruises Ltd ☎ 020 7930 9033.

to **Greenwich** (45min): daily 10am to 4pm/5pm every 30min in summer, 10.40am to 3.20pm every 40min in winter; £6 one way, £7.30 round trip. Westminster Passenger Services ☎ 020 7930 4097.

to **Thames Barrier** (75min): daily at 10.15am to 2.45pm, every 60-75min in summer; 11.15am, 1.30pm, 2.45pm in winter; £4.30. Tidal Cruises ☎ 020 7839 2164.

to **Millennium Dome**: the Millennium Express (from January 2000). For timetable and fares: City Cruises ☎ 020 7930 9033.

Charing Cross Pier:

to the **Tower** (20min) daily 10am to 4pm/4.30pm every 30min; £6.10. Catamaran Cruisers ☎ 020 7987 1185, 839 3572/2349.

to **Greenwich** (45min) and the **Thames Barrier** daily 10.30am to 4pm/4.30pm every 30min; £7.50.

Tower Pier:

to **Greenwich** (30min) and the **Thames Barrier** all year daily 11am to 4.30pm every 30min; £3.50. Catamaran Cruisers ☎ 020 7987 1185, 839 3572/2349.

to **Westminster** (20min) all year daily 11am to 4pm/6pm every 20min, £4.50 one way, £5.80 round trip. City Cruises ☎ 020 7488 0344.

Greenwich Pier:

to the **Tower** (30min) all year daily 11.30am to 4pm/4.30pm every 30min

to **Charing Cross** (40min) all year daily

to **Westminster** (45min) all year daily 11am (11.30am in winter) to 3.30 every 30min; £6 one way, £7.30 round trip. ☎ 020 8858 3996

to **Thames Barrier** (30min) March to November daily 11.15am to 4.45pm every 75min; £3.25 one way, £4.75 round trip. Campion Launches ☎ 020 8305 0300.

to **Millennium Dome**: Greenwich Shuttle(from January 2000). For timetable and fares: White Horse Fast Ferries ☎ 01774 566 220.

Westminster Pier upstream: Summer (April to September) only. WPSA ☎ 020 7930 4721/2062.

to **Putney** (45min) daily at 10.15am, 10.30am, 11am, 11.15am, 12pm, 2pm, 2.30pm

to **Kew** (90min) daily at 10.15am, 10.30am, 11am, 11.15am, 12pm, 2pm, 2.30pm.

to **Richmond** (2 hr) daily at 10.30am, 11.15am, 12pm.

to **Hampton Court** (3 1/2 hr hours) daily at 10.30am, 11.15am, 12pm.

The Thames

Ph. Gajic/MICHELIN

St Helena Pier, Richmond:
to **Hampton Court** (1 1/2 hours) Tuesdays to Sundays 11am to 4.15pm; return 11.15am, 2.35pm, 4.45pm. From £5.40. Turk Launches Ltd ☎ 020 8546 2434.
Mid April to mid June, weekends only 11.30am to 2.30pm, return 1pm, 4pm; 25 May to mid September daily 11.30am, 2.30pm; return 11am to 5pm, hourly. Colliers Launches ☎ 020 8892 0741.
to **Turks Pier, Kingston** mid April to September, Tuesdays to Sundays 11am to 6.15pm, every 60-75min. From £4,40. Turk Launches Ltd ☎ 020 8546 2434.
to **Teddington Lock** (no landing) mid April to 24 May, weekends, 11am to 5pm, hourly; 25 May to September, daily, 11am to 5pm hourly; Colliers Launches ☎ 020 8892 0741.

Evening cruises – Music and/or a meal contact: Mainstream Events ☎ 020 8940 3311. Catamaran Cruisers ☎ 020 7987 1185 / 7838 3573 (May to September, at 8pm. Disco cruises Saturdays from 7pm to 11pm or 8pm to 12midnight).

Canal Cruises and Boat Services – The **London Waterbus Company** operates a regular service along the Regent's Canal between Little Venice and Camden Lock via London Zoo – operates April to September daily 10am to 5pm, every hour; in October (daily) and November to March (weekends) from Little Venice at 10.30am, 12pm, 1.30pm, 3pm; from Camden Lock every hour . £3.90 one way, £5.40 round trip.
It also organises special day trips on the Regent's Canal from Camden Lock: east to Limehouse (£16.50); west to Brentford (£16). Booking essential for day trips. ☎ 020 7482 2550, 7482 2660.
Other operators include **Jason's Trip** ☎ 020 7286 3428 and **Jenny Wren** ☎ 020 7485 4433/6210.

Further information – For details on boating, canoeing, cycling and angling activities along the canals and the permits necessary (British Waterways boating license, National Rivers Authority, Thames Division, rod license) contact:
Lee & Stort Navigations, British Waterways, Enfield Lock, Ordnance Road, Enfield, Middx EN3 6JG. ☎ 01992 764 626; Fax 01992 788 226.
London Canals, British Waterways, The Toll House, Delamere Terrace, Little Venice, London W2 6ND. ☎ 020 7286 6101; Fax 020 7286 7306.

Guided tours – Most museums and art galleries organise guided tours and lectures. For information see the individual museum or gallery.
Official 'Blue Badge' guides permitted to operate in London may be contacted through the Tourist Information offices; they may be hired for the day or for a series of visits.

City Cruises Red Fleet – Commentary along the riverside from Westminster Pier to Tower Pier. April to October every 20 minutes between 10.20am and 5pm (6pm in summer). £4.60 single, £5.80 round trip, children half-price. ☎ 020 7930 9033 or 020 7488 0344.

Bus tours – Sightseeing tours on open-topped double-decker buses (weather permitting) are an excellent introduction to London for those who are not familiar with the capital.
Departure points vary but include: **Victoria** (near the Underground Station or Grosvenor Gardens or Buckingham Palace Road); **Green Park** (by the Ritz Hotel); **Piccadilly; Coventry Street; Trafalgar Square; Haymarket; Lower Regent Street; Marble Arch** (subway exit 7); **Baker Street** (Underground Station); **Tower Hill.**

Some tours are non-stop; some allow passengers to hop on and off and continue on a later bus with the original ticket. Ticket prices vary accordingly (from £10).

Note: Ensure the following sights are included on the various routes on offer: Bank of England, Fleet Street, Houses of Parliament, Hyde Park Corner, London Bridge, Piccadilly Circus, St Paul's Cathedral, Strand, Tower Bridge, Tower of London, Trafalgar Square, Victoria Embankment, Westminster Abbey, Whitehall.

The Original Sightseeing Tour – Hop-on-hop-off service, recorded commentary in 8 languages, 20 stops. Every ten minutes between 9am and 6pm in summer (at 15 minute intervals between 10am and 5pm in winter). £12.50, £7.50 (child). Starting points at Baker Street Underground, by Speaker's Corner at Marble Arch, Victoria Station, Piccadilly Underground station in Haymarket.

Evan Evans Tours also do Big Value Tours to Windsor, Oxford, Stonehenge and Bath. ☎ 020 8332 2222, Fax 020 8784 2835.

London Pride Sightseeing – Hop-on-hop-off service, 90min or 120min journey options. Service in operation daily from 9am to 9pm in summer (6pm in winter). Starting point from Piccadilly Circus outside Trocadero. Tickets from driver. £12, £6 child (including river cruise). ☎ 01708 631 122.

Visitors Sightseeing Tours – Half-day and full day tours of London and for tours outside London. ☎ 020 7636 7175.

The London Experience – Contact Frames Rickards ☎ 020 7837 3111; coach tours 020 7637 4171.

Black Taxi Tours of London – Personal two hour tours day or night in the comfort of a black cab. £65 per taxi. ☎ 020 7289 4371 or 0956 384 124.

Original London Walks – For information on guided walking tours consult the London Tourist Board, press listings or write to PO Box 1708, London NW6 4LW. ☎ 020 7624 3978 / 7794 1764 / 7911 0285, Fax 020 7625 1932, Email: london-@walks.com; website: www.walks.com , http://london.walks.com
Guides include trained actors, historians, professional Blue Badge holders, botanists, authors, etc. Themes available include: The City of London, Fleet Street, Legal London, Bloomsbury, Covent Garden Pubs, London theatres, Soho, the West End, Mayfair, Belgravia, Chelsea, Westminster, East End, Jewish East End, Docklands, Thames Pubs, Greenwich, Regent's Canal, Little Venice, Hampstead pubs, Royal London, Literary London, Shakespeare's London, Dickens' London, Sherlock Holmes' London, Beatles' London, the Swinging '60s...

The London Ghost Walk – Details from Thomas Bodie, 41 Spelman Street, E1. ☎ 020 7256 8973. Departure from Blackfriars Underground Exit 1, daily at 8pm, duration 2 hours irrespective of weather conditions.

Walkways – The London Tourist Board Information Centres provide maps *(charge)* of the **Silver Jubilee Walkway** (1977), 10 miles in the heart of London, marked by special pavement markers and including eight **viewpoints** with indicators identifying the neighbouring buildings: Leicester Square – Parliament Square – South Bank – Jubilee Gardens – Southwark Cathedral – St Katharine Docks – Tower Hill – St Paul's Cathedral – Barbican – Leicester Square.
The **London Wall Walk** (under 2 miles – 2.8km long) is marked by 21 panels and follows the line of the City wall between the Tower of London and the Museum of London.
The **Thames Towpath**, a 180-mile National Trail marked by 1 200 acorn signposts, runs from the Cotswolds to the Thames Barrier. For a free leaflet contact the Countryside Commission, PO Box 124, Walgrave, Northampton NN6 9TL.
The *Financial Times* have sponsored a series of walks in **Docklands**: Isle of Dogs (1, 2, 3 & 4); Rotherhithe and Bermondsey (5 & 6); Wapping and Limehouse (7 & 8); Limehouse and Poplar (9).

Rollerblading and cycling – Even the courier companies have resolved to beat the traffic by resorting to man-powered-wheels. Cycle routes run throughout the capital, across the Royal Parks (speed restrictions apply in Hyde Park) and along many bus routes. Special permission must be sought from London Canals / British Waterways for use of selected portions of the canal towpaths *(see above)*.

Omnibuses were introduced to London from Paris on 4 July 1829 by the coach-builder George Shillibeer. This was a 'handsome machine', as the papers called it, drawn by three horses abreast and capable of carrying 16-18 passengers. Long and short stage coaches were not licensed however to take up or set down passengers 'on the stones' (ie the pavements of central London), so Shillibeer discreetly ran his first omnibuses outside the central limits from Paddington Green to the Bank of England along Marylebone (then New) Road. By the 1830s there were so many company horse buses that they blocked the streets or charged through them in fierce rivalry.

Services

Money

Currency – The decimal system (100 pence = £1) is used throughout Great Britain. Scotland has different notes including £1 and £100 notes, which are valid outside Scotland; the Channel Islands and Isle of Man have different notes and coins, which are not valid elsewhere.
The common currency – in descending order of value – is £50, £20, £10 and £5 (notes); £2, £1, 50p, 20p, 10p, 5p (silver coins) and 2p and 1p (copper coins). *See Notes and Coins.*

Banks – Banks are generally open from Mondays to Fridays, 9.30am to 3.30pm; some banks offer a limited service on Saturday mornings; all banks are closed on Sundays and bank holidays *(see below)*. Most banks have cash dispensers that accept international credit cards.
Exchange facilities outside these hours are available at airports, bureaux de change, travel agencies and hotels.
Some form of identification is necessary when cashing travellers cheques or Eurocheques in banks. Commission charges vary; hotels usually charge more than banks.

Credit Cards – The main credit cards (American Express; Access/Eurocard/Mastercard; Diners Club; Visa/Barclaycard) are widely accepted in shops, hotels, restaurants and petrol stations. Most banks have cash dispensers which accept international credit cards.
In case of loss or theft, phone:

Amex   020 7222 9633   Access/Eurocard   01702 364 364
Barclay Card   01604 230 230

The loss should also be reported to the Police who will issue a crime number for use by the insurance or credit card company.

Post

Post Offices are generally open Mondays to Fridays, 9.30am to 5.30pm and Saturday mornings, 9.30am to 12.30pm. Late collections are made from Leicester Square and throughout the night (and on Sundays) at the principal sorting offices at Paddington, Nine Elms, Mount Pleasant, St Paul's. Stamps are also available from many newsagents and tobacconists. Poste Restante items are held for 14 days; proof of identity is required. Airmail delivery usually takes 3 to 4 days in Europe and 4 to 7 days elsewhere in the world.

Within GB	first class post 26p; second class post 20p.
Within EU	letter (20g) 30p (+ 13p for each extra 20g); postcard 30p.
Non-EU Europe	letter (20g) 30p (+ 13p for each extra 20g); postcard 30p.
Elsewhere	letter (20g) 63p (+ 33p for each extra 20g); postcard 37p; aerogrammes 36p.

Medical treatment

Visitors to Britain are entitled to treatment at the Accident and Emergency Departments of National Health Service hospitals. For an overnight or longer stay in hospital payment will probably be required. It is therefore advisable to take out adequate insurance cover before leaving home.

Telephone box

Visitors from EU countries should apply to their own National Social Security Offices for Form E111 which entitles them to medical treatment under an EU Reciprocal Medical Treatment arrangement.
Nationals of non-EU countries should take out comprehensive insurance. American Express offers a service, "Global Assist", for any medical, legal or personal emergency – call collect from anywhere ☎ 202 554 2639.
In case of an emergency, dial the free nationwide emergency number (999) and ask for Fire, Police or Ambulance.
To contact a doctor for **first aid, emergency medical advice** and **chemist's night service** ☎ 07000 37 22 55 or Medicentre ☎ 0870 600 0870. Do not hesitate to ask for a photocopy of any prescription. This may be important if follow-on treatment is required back home.

Telephone

Prepaid **British Telecom** phonecards, of varying value, are available from post offices and many newsagents; they can be used in booths with phonecard facilities for national and international calls. Some public telephones accept credit cards.

R. Bessol/MICHELIN

Rates vary: daytime, Mon-Fri, 8am-6pm; evening, Mon-Fri, before 8am and after 6pm; weekend midnight Friday to midnight Sunday.

100	Operator
192	Directory Enquiries within the UK
999	Emergency number (free nationwide); ask for Fire, Police, Ambulance, Coastguard, Mountain Rescue or Cave Rescue.

International Calls – To make an international call dial 00 followed by the country code, followed by the area code (without the intitial 0) followed by the subscriber's number. The codes for direct dialling to other countries are printed at the front of telephone directories and in codebooks.

00 61	Australia
00 1	Canada
00 353	Republic of Ireland
00 64	New Zealand
00 44	United Kingdom
00 1	United States of America
155	International Operator
155	International Directory Enquiries; there is a charge for this service

Rates vary: daytime, Mon-Fri, 8am-6pm; evening, Mon-Fri, before 8am and after 6pm; weekend midnight Friday to midnight Sunday.

Notes and coins

£50 note featuring
Sir John Houblon
(1632-1712),
Gatekeeper to the
Bank of England.

£20 note featuring
Michael Faraday (1791-1867),
physicist and inventor of the
Magneto Electric Spark
Apparatus.

£10 note featuring
Charles Dickens (1812-1870),
author of Pickwick Papers,
Oliver Twist, A Christmas
Carol etc.

£5 note featuring
George Stephenson (1781-1848),
engineer, inventor of the Rocket
Locomotive and builder of
the Stockton-Darlington Railway.

All notes and coins bear an image of the sovereign on one side. A metal strip is
threaded through the paper of the bank notes. The reverse side of the £1 coin
features different symbols: Royal coat of arms and Three Lions rampant (England),
Thistle (Scotland), Prince of Wales feathers (Wales) among others.
The Bank of Scotland issues £1 notes which are legal tender throughout the United
Kingdom.

Conversion tables

Weights and measures

1 kilogram (kg)	2.2 pounds (lb)	2.2 pounds
1 metric ton (tn)	1.1 tons	1.1 tons

to convert kilograms to pounds, multiply by 2.2

1 litre (l)	2.1 pints (pt)	1.8 pints
1 litre	0.3 gallon (gal)	0.2 gallon

to convert litres to gallons, multiply by 0.26 (US) or 0.22 (UK)

1 hectare (ha)	2.5 acres	2.5 acres
1 square kilometre (km²)	0.4 square miles (sq mi)	0.4 square miles

to convert hectares to acres, multiply by 2.4

1centimetre (cm)	0.4 inches (in)	0.4 inches
1 metre (m)	3.3 feet (ft) - 39.4 inches - 1.1 yards (yd)	
1 kilometre (km)	0.6 miles (mi)	0.6 miles

to convert metres to feet, multiply by 3.28 . kilometres to miles, multiply by 0.6

Clothing

Women							Men
	35	4	2½	40	7½	7	
	36	5	3½	41	8½	8	
	37	6	4½	42	9½	9	
Shoes	38	7	5½	43	10½	10	**Shoes**
	39	8	6½	44	11½	11	
	40	9	7½	45	12½	12	
	41	10	8½	46	13½	13	
	36	4	8	46	36	36	
	38	6	10	48	38	38	
Dresses &	40	8	12	50	40	40	**Suits**
Suits	42	12	14	52	42	42	
	44	14	16	54	44	44	
	46	16	18	56	46	48	
	36	08	30	37	14½	14,5	
	38	10	32	38	15	15	
Blouses &	40	12	14	39	15½	15½	**Shirts**
sweaters	42	14	36	40	15¾	15¾	
	44	16	38	41	16	16	
	46	18	40	42	16½	16½	

Sizes often vary depending on the designer. These equivalents are given for guidance only.

Speed

kph	10	30	50	70	80	90	100	110	120	130
mph	6	19	31	43	50	56	62	68	75	81

Temperature

Celsius (°C)	0°	5°	10°	15°	20°	25°	30°	40°	60°	80°	100°
Fahrenheit (°F)	32°	41°	50°	59°	68°	77°	86°	104°	140°	176°	212°

To convert Celsius into Fahrenheit, multiply °C by 9, divide by 5, and add 32.
To convert Fahrenheit into Celsius, subtract 32 from °F, multiply by 5, and divide by 9.

General information

Accommodation agencies – Contact the **London Tourist Board Visitorcall** for general advice ☎ 0839 123 435 (not accessible outside the UK; for charge rates see Sight-seeing) or turn to the fee-charging accommodation agencies at Victoria Station, Heathrow Airport and Gatwick Airport.

Visitorcall Accommodation Booking Service (TABS) – Booking by Visa or Access / Mastercard (administration fee charged) Mondays to Fridays 9am to 6pm, Saturdays 9am to 1pm. ☎ 020 7604 2890.

Electricity – The electric current is 240 volts AC (50 HZ); 3-pin flat wall sockets are standard. An adaptor or multiple point plug is required for non-British appliances.

Standard Time – In winter standard time throughout the British Isles is Greenwich Mean Time (GMT). In summer clocks are advanced by an hour to give British Summer Time (BST). The actual dates are announced annually but always occur at the weekend in March and October.
Time may be expressed according to the 24-hour clock or the 12-hour clock.

12.00	noon	19.00	7pm
13.00	1pm	20.00	8pm
14.00	2pm	21.00	9pm
15.00	3pm	22.00	10pm
16.00	4pm	23.00	11pm
17.00	5pm	24.00	midnight
18.00	6pm		

Public holidays – The table below gives the public (bank) holidays in England and Wales, when most shops and municipal museums are closed.

> 1 January
> Good Friday (Friday before Easter Day)
> Easter Monday (Monday after Easter Day)
> First Monday in May (May Day)
> Last Monday in May (Spring Bank holiday)
> Last Monday in August
> 25 December (Christmas Day)
> 26 December (Boxing Day)

In addition to the usual school holidays in the spring and summer and at Christmas, there are mid-term breaks in February, May and October.

Tipping – When a service charge is automatically included in the price of meals, it is not necessary to tip in restaurants and hotels. Gratuities given to taxi drivers, bellboys, doormen, hairdressers, tour guides are at the customer's discretion.

Lost property – Do not despair, sometimes precious possessions do get handed in: for property lost in the **street** enquire at the local police station; left in a **taxi** contact the Metropolitan Police Lost Property Office, 15 Penton Street, N1 9PU *(written enquiries only)* or ring ☎ 020 7833 0996.
For property left on **buses** ring ☎ 020 7222 1234; on an **underground train** enquire in person at the London Regional Transport Lost Property Office, 200 Baker Street, NW1 5RZ *(Mondays to Fridays 9.30am to 2pm);* enquiry forms also available from any LRT bus garage or station. ☎ 020 7486 2496 (recorded). Fax 020 7918 1028.
For property left on **trains** enquire at station of arrival or contact National Rail enquiries, ☎ 020 7928 5151.

Press

Time Out, published weekly (Thursdays) contains up to date information on venues and reviews for the theatre, cinemas, exhibitions, concerts, discos, restaurants, guided walks, cycle hire etc. Other listings appear in the **London Evening Standard** and the broadsheet newspapers. Information about local events is available from Town Halls and public libraries.

Shopping

Opening hours – The big stores and larger shops are open Mondays to Saturdays from 9am to 5.30pm or 6pm, Sundays from 10am or 11am to 4pm. Some are open late (8pm) one day a week – Wednesdays in Knightsbridge, Thursdays in Oxford Street and down Regent Street. Some supermarkets open round the clock and certain food (Indian or Arab) shops stay open until 10pm or later in Bayswater Road and Earl's Court Road.

The winter sales at Christmas and New Year and the summer sales in June and July are a popular time for shopping, as prices are reduced on a great range of goods.

Great Britain is a good place to buy clothes. There is a wide choice of woollen articles in cashmere or lambswool, particularly in Scotland. Classic styles are sold by well-known names such as Jaeger, Burberry, Marks and Spencer, John Lewis, Debenhams and House of Fraser. Made to measure clothing for men is available in London in Savile Row (tailors) and Jermyn Street (shirt-makers).

The best makes of porcelain – Wedgwood, Royal Worcester, Royal Doulton – are available in London and elsewhere; seconds can be bought at the factory or in Reject Shops.

Food (smoked salmon, Stilton cheese, pickles, marmalade) and drink (tea, gin and whisky) are also favourite items.

Ph. Gajic/MICHELIN

Albert Bridge by night

Calendar of events

Listed below are some of the most popular annual events. For specific dates and full details consult the national press and Tourist Information Centres.

January
First Thursday . . . . Boat Show at Earls Court Exhibition Centre

. . . . Start of Five-Nation Rugby Triple Crown at Twickenham

Charles I Commemoration held in Trafalgar Square

February

Chinese New Year in Soho

First Sunday . . . . Clowns' Service at Holy Trinity, Dalston

March

Chelsea Antiques Fair, Old Town Hall, Chelsea

Head of the River Race from Mortlake to Putney (420 crews leaving at 10 second intervals)

Oxford and Cambridge Boat Race from Putney to Mortlake

Easter
Good Friday . . . . Service and distribution of Hot Cross buns at St Bartholomew-the-Great

Easter Sunday. . . . . Carnival Parade in Battersea Park

Easter Monday . . . . London Harness Horse Parade in Battersea Park

Easter weekend . . . . Kite Festival on Blackheath

April

RHS Spring Flower Show at Westminster

London Marathon from Docklands to Westminster

May

Royal Windsor Horse Show held in Home Park, Windsor

Chelsea Flower Show at the Royal Hospital, Chelsea

F A Cup Final at Wembley

29 May . . . . Chelsea Pensioners' Oak Apple Day Parade at the Royal Hospital, Chelsea

June

Beating Retreat at Horse Guards Parade, Whitehall

Queen's Birthday. . . . . Trooping the Colour at Horse Guards Parade

Hampton Court Music Festival at Hampton Court Palace

Spitalfields Annual Music Festival

Regent's Park Open Air Theatre Season

Stella Artois Grass Court (Tennis) Championships held at Queen's Club

Antique Fairs at Grosvenor House, Piccadilly and Olympia Exhibition Halls

Ascot Racing Week

British Polo Open Championships at Cowdray Park

Royal Academy Summer Exhibition at Burlington House, Piccadilly

All England Lawn Tennis Championships at Wimbledon *(2 weeks)*

Cricket Test Matches at Lord's and The Oval

Last Sunday. . . . . Kite Festival on Blackheath

July

Hampton Court Palace Flower Show

Royal Tournament at Earls Court

Sir Henry Wood's Promenade Concerts at the Royal Albert Hall *(8 weeks)*

Glyndebourne Opera Festival at Glyndebourne in Sussex

The City Festival is celebrated in the City Churches and Halls Swan Upping on the River Thames

Doggett's Coat and Badge Race rowed by 6 new freemen of the Watermen and Lightermen's Company from London Bridge to Chelsea Bridge

Opera and ballet at the Holland Park Outdoor Theatre

Ladies' Day at Ascot

ANGUS TAVERNER

August

RHS Summer Flower Show in Westminster

Bank Holiday Weekend . . . . . . Hampstead Heath Fair

Notting Hill Carnival in Ladbroke Grove

September

First Saturday . . . . NatWest Trophy Final at Lord's Cricket Ground

Chelsea Antiques Fair held at Chelsea Town Hall

October

First Sunday . . . . Pearly Harvest Festival service for the Pearly Kings and Queens at St Martin-in-the-Fields *(Afternoon)*

First week . . . . Goldsmith's Show, Goldsmiths Hall

Chelsea Crafts Fair held at Chelsea Town Hall *(two consecutive one-week shows)*

Opening of the Michaelmas Law Term: Procession of Judges in full robes carrying nosegays to Westminster Abbey

November

First Sunday . . . . London to Brighton Veteran Car Run departing from Hyde Park Corner

London Film Festival organised by the National Film Theatre *(three weeks)*

Saturday nearest to the 9th . . Lord Mayor's Show held in the City

Sunday nearest
11 November . . . . Remembrance Sunday Cenotaph, Whitehall *(11am service)*

State Opening of Parliament by the Queen at Westminster

Regent Street Christmas lights are switched on

December

Lighting of the Norwegian Christmas Tree in Trafalgar Square

Carol Services throughout the capital's churches

Further reading

Reference

AZ London Street Atlas
Survey of London John Stow 1603 (1980)
The Faber Book of London A N Wilson 1993
Georgian London John Summerson 1945 (1991)
In Search of London H V Morton 1951 (1988)
Docklands, Phaidon Architecture Guide Stephanie Williams 1990 (1993)
The Blue Plaque Guide to London Caroline Dakers 1982
Notting Hill and Holland Park Past Barbara Denny 1993
The London Market Guide Metro Publications 1994
Access in London Couch Forrester and Irwin 1996
Artists' Houses in London 1794-1914 Giles Walkley 1996
Impressionist London Eric Shanes
The Aesthetic Movement Lionel Lambourne
Kew, the History of the Royal Botanic Gardens Ray Desmond 1995
Curious London Robin Cross
London – A guide to recent architecture Samantha Hardingham

Biography

The Compleat Angler Izaak Walton 1653
The Shorter Pepys Robert Latham 1985
Diary John Evelyn 1818
All Done from Memory Osbert Lancaster 1963
Down and Out in Paris and London George Orwell 1933 (1982)
84 Charing Cross Road Helene Hanff 1978
In Camden Town David Thompson 1983
Three Men in a Boat Jerome K Jerome 1889
Six Wives of Henry VIII Antonia Fraser
Mrs Jordan's Profession Claire Tomalin 1995
William Morris Fiona MacCarthy 1995
Longitude Dava Sobel 1996

Fiction

The History of Pendennis W M Thackeray 1849/50
Our Mutual Friend Charles Dickens 1864/5
Picture of Dorian Gray Oscar Wilde 1891
The Adventures of Sherlock Holmes Arthur Conan Doyle 1892 (1993)
The Golden Bowl Henry James 1904 (1983)
Jeeves Omnibus P G Wodehouse
Mrs Dalloway Virginia Woolf 1925 (1972)
The Girl of Slender Means Muriel Spark 1963
The London Embassy Paul Theroux 1984
Hawksmoor Peter Ackroyd 1985 (1988)
Taste for Death P D James 1986
London Fields Martin Amis 1989 (1990)
The Secret Agent Joseph Conrad 1907 (1983)
The Buddha of Suburbia Hanif Kureishi 1990
Journal of the Plague Year Daniel Defoe 1722 (1992)
Liza of Lambeth W Somerset Maugham 1897
The Collected Stories of Muriel Spark 1994

Admission times and charges

As admission times and charges are liable to alteration, the information printed below – valid for 2000 – is for guidance only. Where it has not been possible to obtain up-to-date information, the admission times and charges from the previous edition of the guide are printed in italics.

⊘ *– Every sight for which times and charges are listed below is indicated by the symbol* ⊘ *after the title in the Sights section.*

Order *– The information is listed in the same order as in the Sights section of the guide.*

Facilities for the disabled *– ♿ (♿) mean full or partial access for wheelchairs. As the range of possible facilities is great (for impaired mobility, sight and hearing), readers are advised to telephone in advance to check what is available.*

Dates *– Dates given are inclusive. The term weekend means Saturday and Sunday. The term holidays means bank and public holidays, when shops, museums and other monuments may be closed or may vary their times of admission. The term school holidays refers to the breaks between terms at Christmas, Easter and during the summer months and also to the short mid-term breaks (one week), which are usually in February and October. See PRACTICAL INFORMATION.*

Admission times *– Ticket offices usually shut 30min before closing time; only exceptions are mentioned below. Some places issue timed tickets owing to limited space and facilities.*

Charge *– The charge given is for an individual adult. Reductions may be available for families, children, students, senior citizens (old-age pensioners) and the unemployed; it may be necessary to provide proof of identity and status. Large parties should apply in advance as many places offer special rates for group bookings and some have special days for group visits.*

Foreign languages *– Where foreign languages are mentioned, an English language version is also available.*

Abbreviations *– EH = English Heritage*

> *CADW = Welsh Historic Monuments*
> *HS = Historic Scotland*
> *NACF = National Art Collections Fund*
> *RSPB = Royal Society for the Protection of Birds*
> *NT = The National Trust (for England, Wales and Northern Ireland)*
> *NTS = The National Trust for Scotland*
> *NTJ = The National Trust for Jersey*
> *NTG = The National Trust for Guernsey*

There are reciprocal arrangements among the NT, NTS, NTJ, NTG and the Royal Oak Foundation in the USA.

Tourist Information Centres 🛈 *– The addresses and telephone numbers are given for local Tourist Information Centres, which may provide information advice and booking services and information about local amenities, local market days, early closing days etc.*

INNER LONDON

B

BAKER STREET

Madame Tussaud's – ♿ Open daily, 9am (10am Sept to May) to 5.30pm (last admission). Closed 25 Dec. £11.50, £8 (concession), no charge (child u 5); combined ticket with the Planetarium £13.95, £10.80 (concession), £8 (child u 16). Brochure (French, German, Italian, Spanish). Wheelchair users must book in advance for safety reasons. ☎ 0870 400 3000; Fax 020 7465 0862.

Planetarium – ♿ Open daily. Performances from 10am to 5pm. Closed 25 Dec. £6.30, £4.80 (concession), £4.20 (child); combined ticket with Madame Tussaud's Exhibition £13.95, £10.80 (concession), £8 (child u 16), no charge (child u 5). Wheelchair users must book in advance for safety reasons. ☎ 0870 400 3000; Fax 020 7465 0862.
Access: by bus 2, 13, 18, 27, 30, 74, 82, 113, 159, 176, 274; ⊖ Baker Street.

Sherlock Holmes Museum – Open daily, 9.30am to 6pm. £6, £4 (child over 7). Brochure (French, German, Italian, Japanese, Russian, Spanish). ☎ (020) 7935 8866; Fax (020) 7738 1269; sherlock@easynet.co.uk; www.sherlock-holmes.co.uk

Drawings Collection RIBA *– Open by appointment only, Tues-Thur, 10am-1pm, 2-5pm. ☎ (020) 7307 3605, (020) 7307 3634; Fax: (020) 7486 3797.*

RIBA Heinz Gallery *– (♿) Open during temporary exhibitions, Mon to Fri, 11am to 5pm; Sat, 11am to 2pm. Closed public holidays. Leaflets available on exhibitions. ☎ (020) 7307 3634; Fax: (020) 7486 3797.*

Tate Modern – &. Open Sun to Thur, 10am-6pm, Fri and Sat, 10am-10pm (galleries open at 10.15am). No charge. Disabled parking only. Baby care room. Restaurants. Shop. ☎ 020 7887 8000, 020 7887 8008 (recorded information); www.tate.org.uk Access: by bus: 45, 63,100, 381. ⊖ Southwark, Blackfriars.

Bankside Gallery – (&.) Open Tues to Fri, 10am to 5pm (8pm Tues), Sat and Sun, 1pm to 5pm. £3.50, £2. Bookshop. ☎ (020) 7928 7521; Fax (020) 7928 2820.

International Shakespeare Globe Centre – &. Open daily, May to Sept, 9am to 12.30pm (theatre tours, every half hour), 1pm to 5pm (exhibition only); Oct to Apr, 10am to 5pm. Closed 24, 25 Dec and 1 Jan. £6, £4 (child), £5 (concessions), £16 (family 2A+3C). Shop, refreshments. ☎ (020) 7902 1500; Fax (020) 7902 1515; www.shakespeares-globe.org
Access: by bus 11, 15, 17, 23, 26, 45, 63, 76, 149, 172, 344, P11; ⊖ Mansion House, London Bridge.

The Rose Theatre Exhibition – Open all year, daily, 10am to 5pm. £3, £2 (child), £ 2.50 (concession), £8 family ticket (2A+3C). Audio-visual presentation (90min) on the hour and half past. ☎ 020 7593 0026, Fax 020 7633 0367; www.rdg.ac.uk/Rose
Access: by bus 45, 63, 172 to Blackfriars Bridge; 15, 17 to Cannon Street, 11, 15, 23, 26 to Mansion House; 146, 344, P11 to Southwark Street. ⊖ Mansion House, Cannon Street, London Bridge. BR Waterloo, London Bridge.

Clink Exhibition – Open daily 10am to 6pm. Closed 25 and 26 Dec. £4, £9 (family 2A+3C), £3 (children, concession). Guided tour, telephone for details. ☎ 020 7378 1558; Fax 020 7403 5813.

Golden Hinde – Open daily 9.30am to 5.30pm. Telephone first to confirm availability. Self-guided tour with leaflet: £2.50, £1.75 (child), £2.10 (concession), £6.50 (family ticket 2A+3C). Guided tour: £3, £2.25 (child), £2.60 (concession). Corporate entertainment, overnight stays, Pirate Parties for children: bookings ☎ 0541 505 041, 020 7403 0123; Fax 01722 333 343; info@goldenhinde.co.uk; www.goldenhinde.co.uk

HMS Belfast – (&.) Open daily, 10am to 6pm, last admission 5.15pm (5pm Nov to Feb, last admission 4.15pm). Closed 24 to 26 Dec. £5, no charge (children), £3.80 (concessions). Brochure (French, German, Spanish). Shop, snack bar. ☎ (020) 7940 6320; Fax (020) 7403 0719. www.hmsbelfast.org.uk; www.iwm.org.uk

London Dungeon – &. Open daily, 10am-6.30pm (5.30pm Oct to Mar); last admission 1hr before closing. Closed 25 Dec. £9.95, £8.50 (concession), £6.50 (child). Leaflet (French, German). Refreshments. ☎ (020) 7403 7221; Fax (020) 7378 1529. Access: by bus 17, 21, 22A, 35, 40, 43, 47, 48, 133, 344, 501, 505, 513, D1, D11, P3.

Winston Churchill's Britain at War – (&.) Open daily, 10am to 5.30pm (4.30pm Oct to Mar). Closed 24 – 26 Dec. £5.95, £3.95 (concessions), £2.95 (child), £14 (2A+2C). ☎ (020) 7403 3171; Fax (020) 7403 5104; britainatwar@dial.pipex.com; www.britain-at-war.co.uk ⊖ London Bridge.

Bayswater Road Art Exhibition – &. *Open Sun, 10am to 6pm.* ⊖ Lancaster Gate or Queensway.

Sir Alexander Fleming Laboratory Museum – Open Mon-Thur, 10am-1pm (last admission noon), otherwise, Mon-Fri, by prior appointment. Closed public holidays. £2, £1 (concessions). Leaflet (Chinese, Czech, Dutch, French, German, Greek, Gujerati, Italian, Japanese, Kannada, Polish, Russian, Spanish, Urdu). ☎ (020) 7886 6528; Fax (020) 7886 6739.
Access: by bus 7, 15, 27, 39.

Regent's Canal – (&.) Boat services: London Waterbus Company operates between Little Venice (Warwick Crescent) and Camden Lock (off Chalk Farm Road) via London Zoo, including the 272yd long Maida Hill Tunnel. Services: daily, 10am to 5pm on the hour, every hour. One way £4, £2.60 (children); return £5.50, £3.50(children); special rates to include admittance to London Zoo. Written information available (French, German) on application. ☎ (020) 7482 2550 or (020) 7482 2660 (information line).

The Foundling Museum – &. Open to groups only by prior arrangement with the curator. £2. Leaflets and guide books available. ☎ (020) 7841 3600; Fax (020) 7837 8084; janet@foundlingmuseum.org.uk

National Museum of Cartoon Art – *Open Mon to Fri, 12 pm to 6pm. Donation.* ☎ *020 7278 7172, Fax 020 7278 4234.*

The Dickens House Museum – Open Mon-Sat, 10am-5pm. Closed Sun and 1 Jan. £4, £3. Brochure and gallery cards (French, German, Japanese). ☎ (020) 7405 2127; dhmuseum@rmplc.co.uk; www.dickensmuseum.com

Access: by bus 17, 18, 19, 45, 46, 171, 171A, 196, 243, 259, 503, 505. ⊖ Chancery Lane, Russell Square, Holborn, King's Cross.

St George's Church, Bloomsbury – Open Mon to Fri, 9.30am to 5.30pm; Sun, 9.30am to 5pm (subject to change). Closed public holidays. Recitals: certain Tuesday lunchtimes. Services: Sun at 10.30am. ☎ (020) 7405 3044. stgeorg@aol.com

Contemporary Applied Arts – ⅄ Open Mon to Sat, 10.30am to 5.30pm. Closed public holidays. ☎ (020) 7436 2344; Fax (020) 7436 2446. www.caa.org.uk

Pollock's Toy Museum and Shop – Open Mon to Sat, 10am to 5pm. Closed Sun and public holidays. £3, £1.50 (child). Brochure (French, German, Japanese, Spanish). ☎ (020) 7636 3452.

Petrie Museum of Egyptian Archaeology – Open Tues to Fri, 1pm to 5pm; Sat, 10am to 1pm. Closed 1 week at Christmas. ☎020 7579 2884, Fax 020 7579 2886; kbines@vam.ac.uk; www.vam.ac.uk

Brunei Gallery – Open Mon-Fri, 10.30am-5pm. Closed weekends and Bank Holidays. Admission free. ☎ (020) 7898 4046; Fax (020) 7898 4949; gallery@soas.ac.uk; www.soas.ac.uk/gallery

Percival David Foundation of Chinese Art – (⅄) Open Mon to Fri, 10.30am to 5pm. Closed bank holiday Mon, Maundy Thur to Easter Mon, 2 weeks around Christmas and New Year. Reference library: 10.30am to 1pm; 2pm to 4.45pm (use of library chargeable). Guide book and information leaflet available. ☎ (020) 7387 3909; Fax (020) 7383 5163.

Access: by bus 7, 10, 24, 29, 30, 38, 68, 73, 91, 134, 168, 188; ⊖ Russell Square.

Chapel of Christ the King – *Open Mon to Fri, 7am to 4pm.*

BRITISH MUSEUM

British Museum – ⅄ Open Mon to Sat, 10am to 5pm; Sun, noon to 6pm. Closed 1 Jan, 21 Apr, 24 to 26 Dec. Open all other bank holidays, 10am to 5pm. No charge to main galleries, variable rates for temporary exhibitions. Guided tour (90min); lectures, gallery talks and films. Guide (Chinese, French, German, Italian, Japanese, Korean, Spanish). Restaurant, café. Wheelchairs available for hire. Please note restricted disabled access during current building work (telephone for details prior to visit, (020) 7323 8299). ☎ (020) 7636 1555; (020) 7637 7384 (recorded information for disabled visitors); Fax (020) 7323 8614.

BUCKINGHAM PALACE

Buckingham Palace – ⅄ Open (timed ticket) early Aug to end Sept, daily, 9.30am to 5.30pm; last admission 4.30pm. £10.50, £5 (child), £8 (concession). Brochure (French, German, Italian, Japanese). No photography. No smoking. ☎ (020) 7799 2331 (recorded information), (020) 7839 1377 (Visitor Office), (020) 7321 2233 (credit card line).

Royal Mews – Open Oct-July, Mon-Thur, 12noon-4pm; Aug-Sept, Mon-Thur, 10.30am-4.30pm (last admission 30min before closing time). £4.30, £3.30 (senior citizen), £2.10 (child), £10.70 (family). Photography permitted. ☎ (020) 7799 2331 (recorded information), (020) 7839 1377 (Visitor Office).

St James's Park

Queen's Gallery – Closed for major redevelopment. Reopening in 2002, the Queen's Golden Jubilee year.
Changing of the Guard – Usually May to early Aug, daily at 11.30am; otherwise, every other day, at 11.30am. ☎ 020 7414 2497.

Guards Museum and Chapel – ♿ *Open first Mon in Feb to 20 December, daily, 10am to 4pm; subject to closure on some ceremonial days – check by phone. £2, £4 (family ticket).* ☎ *020 7414 3271; Fax 020 7414 3411.*

C

CHANCERY LANE

St Etheldreda's Church – Open daily 8am to 6pm. Services: Mass, Sun, 9am, 11am, Mon-Fri, 8am-1pm, Sat, 9.30am. Café at the Crypt, Mon-Fri, 12noon-4.30pm. ☎ (020) 7405 1061.

St Andrew Holborn – *Open Mon to Fri, 8.30am to 4.30pm.* ☎ *(020) 7583 7394; Fax (020) 7583 3488.*

Gray's Inn – Gardens: Open Mon to Fri, noon to 2.30pm. Closed on Bank Holidays. Squares: open Mon to Fri 9am to 5pm.

London Silver Vaults – ♿ Open Mon to Sat, 9am to 5.30pm (9am to 1pm Sat). Closed public holidays, Good Fri to Easter Mon. No charge. Information Bureau. ☎ (020) 7242 3844.

Lincoln's Inn – Grounds: Open Mon to Fri. Closed weekends and public holidays. Chapel: Open Mon to Fri, noon to 2.30pm. Sun service: during legal terms at 11.30am.
Old Hall, New Hall and Library: Guided tour (minimum 15; £2 per head) on written application to the Assistant Under Treasurer, Lincoln's Inn, London WC2A 3TL. Fax (020) 7831 1839; mail@lincolnsinn.org.uk; www.lincolnsinn.org.uk

Hunterian Museum – Open Mon to Fri, 10am to 5pm. No charge. ☎ (020) 7973 2190, (020) 7312 6694 (recorded information); Fax (020) 7405 4438. museums@rcseng.ac.uk; www.rcseng.ac.uk. Access: by bus 1, 4, 6, 7, 8, 9, 11, 13, 15, X15, 19, 22B, 23, 25, 30, 38, 55, 68, X68, 76, 77A, 98. ⊖ Holborn.

Sir John Soane's Museum – (♿) Open Tues-Sat, 10am-5pm; first Tues of each month, 6pm-9pm. Closed public holidays, Good Friday and Christmas Eve. No charge. Guided tour available, Sat at 2.30pm (22 tickets (at £3) given out from 2pm; no advance booking). Groups by appointment only. Library and drawings collection available to scholars by appointment. ☎ (020) 7430 0175 (recorded information), (020) 7405 2107; Fax (020) 7831 3957; www.soane.org

St Dunstan-in-the-West – Open Tues, 10am-4pm, otherwise, by appointment. ☎ (020) 7405 1929.

Dr Johnson's House – Open Mon to Sat, 11am to 5.30pm (5pm winter). Closed public holidays. £4, £3 (concession), £1 (child). Guide book (French, Italian, Japanese). Guided tour (£3, 50min) by appointment. ☎ 020 7353 3745; curator@drjh; dircon.co.uk; www.drjh.dircon.co.uk

Prince Henry's Room – *Open Mon to Sat, 11am to 2pm. Closed public holidays.*

Temple Church – Open Wed to Sun, 11am to 4pm. Services: Sun (except Aug and Sept) at 8.30am and 11.15am. Guide book (English).

Middle Temple Hall – (♿) Open Mon to Fri, 10am to 11.30am and 3pm to 4pm. Closed public holidays and during Law Vacations.
Access: bus 168, 171, 171A, 176, X177, 188, 196, 501, 505, 521; ⊖ Holborn, Temple.

CHELSEA

Lindsey House – *Open by written appointment only, to: R. Bourne, 100 Chayne Walk, London SW10 0DQ.*

Holy Trinity Church – *Open throughout the year, Mon to Fri, 9.30am to 5.30pm, Sat 10.30am to 4.30pm. Services: Wed at 6pm, Sun at 8.45am and 11am. Concerts.* ☎ *(020) 7730 7270; Fax (020) 7730 9287.*

St Luke's Church – (♿) Open by appointment. ☎ (020) 7351 7365; Fax (020) 7349 0538.

Royal Hospital – Open Mon to Sat, 10am to noon and 2pm to 4pm; Sun, 2pm to 4pm. Grounds: usually open daily, 10am to 4pm. No charge. Leaflet (Arabic, Dutch, French, German, Italian, Japanese, Spanish). ☎ 020 7881 5224.
www.chelseapensioner.org.uk

National Army Museum – ♿ Open daily, 10am to 5.30pm. Closed 1 Jan, Good Fri, May Day holiday, 24 to 26 Dec. Recommended visit time: 2-3 hours. No charge. ☎ (020) 7730 0717; Fax (020) 7823 6573; pr@national-army-museum.ac.uk; www.national-army-museum.ac.uk
Access: by bus 11, 19, 22, 211 to King's Road; 137 to Pimlico Road; 239 (Mon to Sat only, stops immediately outside museum). ⊖ Sloane Square; BR to Victoria Station.

Chelsea Physic Garden – ♿ Open Apr to Oct, Wed, noon to 5pm; Sun, 2pm to 6pm. Chelsea Flower Show week: Open Mon to Fri, noon to 5pm. £4, £2 (concessions). Guide books (Arabic, French, German, Italian, Japanese); plants for sale; refreshments. No dogs. ☎ (020) 7352 5646; Fax (020) 7376 3910. www.cpgarden.demon.co.uk
Access: by bus 11, 19, 22, 211, 239, 319; ⊖ Sloane Square, Victoria (then take relevant bus).

Carlyle's House – (NT) Open Apr to Oct, Wed to Sun and holiday Mon, 11am to 5pm. Closed Good Fri. £3.50. Language boards (French, German, Italian, Japanese, Russian, Spanish). No interior photography. ☎ (020) 7352 7087. Access: by bus 11, 19, 22, 49, 239, 249, 319.

Chelsea Old Church – Open Tues-Fri, 2pm-5pm; Sun, 1.30pm-6pm. ☎ (020) 7701 4213 (parish office), 7352 8693 (administrator); Fax (020) 7795 0092; www.domini. org/chelsea-old-church

CITY

City of London Information Centre – *St Paul's Churchyard, EC4. Open May to Oct, daily, 9.30am to 5pm; otherwise Mon to Sat, 9.30am to 5pm (12.30pm Sat).* ☎ *020 7332 1456, Fax 020 7332 1457.*

Bank of England Museum – ♿ Open Mon to Fri, 10am to 5pm. Closed public holidays. No charge. Brochure (Arabic, Chinese, Dutch, French, German, Italian, Japanese, Spanish). ☎ 020 7601 5545; Fax 020 7601 5808.

Dutch Church – Open Tues to Fri, 11am to 3pm. Guided tour (Dutch/English) available. Brochure (Dutch/English). ☎ (020) 7588 1684; Fax (020) 7374 0790; dutchchurch@cs.com; www.dutchchurch.org.uk (Dutch).

All Hallows London Wall – *Open Fri, 11am to 3.30pm. Lunchtime talk at 1.10pm (40min) on last Fri of each month.* ☎ *(020) 7496 1680. Fax (020) 7496 1684.*

St Helen's Bishopsgate – ♿ Open Mon to Fri, 9am to 5pm via Church office entrance. Guide book (English only). Services: Sun at 10.15am and 7pm; Tues at 12.35pm and 1.15pm. ☎ (020) 7283 2231, Fax (020) 7626 8184.

London Metal Exchange – *Open by appointment only.* ☎ *(020) 7264 5555; Fax (020) 7680 0505.*

Leadenhall Market – *Open weekdays.*

St Botolph-without-Bishopsgate – Open Mon to Fri, 8am to 5.30pm. ☎ (020) 7588 1053/7588 1053; Fax (020) 7638 1256.

St Michael's Church – Open Mon to Fri, 8am to 5.30pm. Services: Holy Communion, Wed and Fri, 1.10pm; Choral Eucharist, Sun (except Aug), 11am; Organ recital, Mon (except bank holiday), 1pm. ☎ 020 7248 3826; citychurches@pmullen.freeserve. co.uk; www.st-michaels.org.uk

St Peter-upon-Cornhill – *Visit by appointment. Apply to St Helen's Bishopsgate Church Office* ☎ *(020) 7283 2231.*

St Andrew Undershaft – Open by appointment only: apply to St Helen's Bishopsgate Church Office. ☎ (020) 7283 2231.

St Katharine Cree – *Open daily except Sat, 10.30am to 4pm. Services: Thur at 1.05pm (Mass with hymns), Sun at 10am (Marthoma Syrian Church Liturgy).* ☎ *(020) 7283 5733.*

Spanish and Portuguese Synagogue – Open Sun, Mon, Wed and Fri 11.30am to 1pm; Tues, 10.30am to 4pm. £1. Guided tour Sun and Tues at 11.30am; Mon, Wed and Fri at noon; groups of more than 10 by appointment. ☎ (020) 7626 1274

St Botolph Aldgate – Open Mon to Fri, 10am to 3.30pm. ☎ (020) 7283 1670; Fax (020) 7623 5730.

St Mary Woolnoth of the Nativity – Open Mon to Fri. Closed public holidays. ☎/Fax (020) 7626 9701.

St Edmund the King and Martyr – Open Mon to Fri. Closed public holidays. ☎/Fax (020) 7626 9701.

St Olave's Church – *Open Mon to Fri, 9am to 5pm. Concerts: Wed (Hart Street) and Thur at 1.05pm.* ☎ *(020) 7488 4318; Fax (020) 7702 0811. www.sadds. demon.co.uk/hartst*

St Mary Abchurch – Open Mon to Fri, 9.30am to 2.30pm. Guided tour (French and German): Mon to Thur. Services (Holy Communion): Wed at 12.30pm, Thur at 1pm. Lunch-time talks: Wed at 1pm. Music recitals: Mon and Fri at 1pm.

St Clement Eastcheap – Open Mon to Fri, 9am to 4pm. ☎ (020) 7626 0220. nisuk@aol.com

Monument – Open daily, 10am to 5.40pm. Closed 1 Jan, 25 and 26 Dec. £1.50, 50p (child u 16). ☎ 020 7626 2717.

St Magnus the Martyr – ♿ Open Tues to Fri, 10am to 4pm; Sun, 10am to 2pm. Brochures and guide sheets. ☎ (020) 7626 4481.

St Mary-at-Hill – *Open all year, Mon to Fri, 10am to 3pm.*

St Margaret Pattens – *Open Mon to Fri, 8am to 4pm. Closed public holidays.* ☎ *(020) 7623 6630.*

Mansion House – Guided tours for small groups only on Tues, Wed, Thur at 11am and 2pm on written application to the Principal Assistant-Diary, Mansion House, London EC4N 8BH. Closed Aug, Christmas and Easter. No charge. ☎ (020) 7626 2500; Fax (020) 7623 9524.

St Stephen Walbrook – *Open Mon to Fri, 10am to 4pm (3pm Fri). Guide book. Services: Sung Eucharist (Lassus, Byrd, Palestrina) Thur at 12.45pm. Organ recital: Fri, 12.30pm to 1.30pm, no charge.* ☎ *(020) 7283 4444*

St Michael Paternoster Royal – Open Mon to Fri, 9am to 5pm. ☎ 020 7248 5202; Fax 020 248 4761; general@missiontoseafarers.org; www.missiontoseafarers.org

St James Garlickhythe – Open Mon to Fri, 10am to 4pm. Closed holiday Mon. Service: Sun (Sung Eucharist) at 10.30am. ☎ (020) 7248 7546.

St Mary Aldermary – Open Mon to Fri, 11am to 3pm. Leaflet. Guided tours available on Thur and Fri. www.mothersole.freeserve.co.uk

Cole Abbey Presbyterian Church – Open by appointment. Services: Sun at 11am and 6.30pm. Prayer meetings: Sun at 6pm, Thur at 7pm. ☎ (020) 7248 5213.

College of Arms – Open Mon to Fri, 10am to 4pm. Closed public holidays, State and special occasions. Brochure available in English; shop. ☎ (020) 7248 2762; Fax (020) 7248 6448. Access: ⊖ Blackfriars, St Paul's.

St Benet's Welsh Church – Open by appointment. Services: Sun at 11am and 2.30pm. ☎ (020) 7723 3104 (residence); ☎ (020) 7489 8754 (church).

St Andrew-by-the-Wardrobe – *Open every day, 8am to 6pm.* ☎ *(020) 7248 7546.*

St Bride's Church – Open Mon to Sat, 8am (9.30am Sat) to 4.45pm. Closed public holidays. Services: Sun (Choral) at 11am and 6.30pm; Mon to Fri at 8.30am, also at 1.15pm on Thur. Recitals: Tues, Wed and Fri (except Aug, Advent, Lent) at 1.15pm. No charge. Brochure (French, German, Spanish). ☎ (020) 7353 1301, (020) 7583 0239; Fax (020) 7583 4867; info@stbrides.com

St Bride Printing Library – Open Mon to Fri, 9.30am to 5.30pm. Induction loop. ☎ (020) 7353 4660; Fax (020) 7583 7073.

St Mary-le-Bow – Open Mon to Fri, 7.30am to 6pm (4pm Fri). Closed public holidays. Dialogues: Tues in term time at 1.05pm. Concerts: Thur in term time at 1.05pm. Brochure (French, German). ☎ (020) 7248 5139; Fax (020) 7248 0509.

St Vedast's Church – *Open Mon to Fri, 8am to 6pm. Closed public holidays. Services: (Sung Mass) Sun at 11am; Mon to Fri at 12.15pm. Guide book (French, German).*

St Martin-within-Ludgate – Open Mon to Fri, 11am to 3pm; Sun, 2.30pm to 4pm. Music recitals: Tue and Wed at 1.15pm. Services: Thur at 1.15pm. Brochure. ☎/Fax (020) 7248 6054.

St Margaret Lothbury – *Open Mon to Fri, 8am to 4.45pm. Closed public holidays. Services: daily at 8.15am; Bible teaching, Mon at 1.15pm; Holy communion, Tues at 1.10pm; informal worship, Wed, at 1.10pm. Organ recitals: Thur at 1.10pm. Guide book available in English.* ☎ *(020) 7606 8330; Fax (020) 7606 1204. Access:* ⊖ Bank.

St Lawrence Jewry – Open Mon to Fri, 7.30am to 2.00pm. Recitals: Mon at 1pm (piano); Tues at 1pm (organ); daily throughout Aug. Guide book available. ☎ (020) 7600 9478

Guildhall – Open (civic functions permitting), May to Sept, daily, 10am to 5pm; Oct to Apr, Mon to Sat, 10am to 5pm. Closed 1 Jan, Good Friday, Easter Monday, 25 to 26 Dec. ☎ (020) 7332 1463; Fax (020) 7332 1996.

Guildhall Crypt – Guided tour only; apply to the Assistant Remembrancer. ☎ (020) 7332 1463 (Mon to Fri).

Guildhall Library – ♿ Open Mon to Sat, 9.30am to 5pm. Print room closed on Sat. Closed public holidays and Sat preceding bank holiday Mon. ☎ (020) 7332 1868/ 1870; printedbooks.guildhall@corpoflondon.gov.uk

Guildhall Clock Museum – Open Mon to Fri, 9.30am to 4.45pm. Closed public holidays and part of Mon morning for maintenance work.

Guildhall Art Gallery – Open Mon to Sat, 10am to 5pm; Sun, 12pm to 4pm. Closed 1 Jan, 25, 26 Dec and on special occasions. ☎ 020 7332 1632/1856, 020 7332 3700 (recorded information), Fax 020 7332 3342; guildhall.artgallery@corpoflondon.gov.uk; www.guildhall-art-gallery.org.uk

City Business Library – 🦽 Open Mon to Fri, 9.30am to 5pm. Closed all public holidays. ☎ 0207 332 1812; Fax 0207 332 1847. ⊖ Moorgate.

St Anne and St Agnes – *Open Sun, all day; Mon to Fri, 10am to 3pm. Services: Sun (except in Aug) at 11am and 7pm; Wed at 1.10pm. Concerts: Mon (except bank holidays) and some Fri at 1.10pm. ☎ (020) 7606 4986; Fax (020) 7600 8984.*

Museum of London – 🦽 Open daily, 10am (noon Sun) to 5.50pm. Closed 1 Jan and 24-26 Dec.£5, £3 (concession), £9.50 (family 2A+3C), no charge (child, disabled), no charge after 4.30pm. Leaflets available (French, German, Italian, Japanese, Spanish). ☎ (020) 7600 3699; Fax (020) 7600 1058; info@museumoflondon.org.uk; www.museumoflondon.org.uk

Roman Fort – Open by appointment, first Tues of each month, 10.30am to noon; 3rd Fri of each month, 2.30pm to 4.30pm. No charge. Access via the Museum of London (see above). ☎ (020) 7600 3699.

St Botolph Aldersgate – *Open Wed to Fri, 11am to 3pm (later in summer); open on Tues at 1.10pm (prayer group) and 6.30pm (Bible group); open for Lord Mayor's Show Day (Sat nearest to 9 Nov), Open House weekend; other times by appointment. Service: worship and teaching, Thur at 1.10pm. Holy Communion on 1st and 3rd Mon of each month at 1.10pm. ☎/Fax (020) 7606 0684 (Churchwarden).*

St Giles Cripplegate – 🦽 Open Mon to Fri, 9.30am to 5.15pm; Sat 9am to noon; Services: Sundays at 8am, 10am and 6pm (4pm in winter) Guided tour: Tues, 2pm to 5pm. ☎ (020) 7638 1997 (admin); stgiles@globalnet.co.uk; www.users.globalnet.co.uk/stgiles

St Bartholomew the Great – 🦽 Open Mon to Fri, 8.30am to 5pm (4pm in winter); Sat, 10.30am to 1.30pm; Sun, 2pm to 6pm. Closed bank holiday Mon and Mon in Aug. Guide. ☎ (020) 7606 5171; Fax (020) 7600 6909; st bartholomew@btinternet.com

St Bartholomew's Hospital – *Guided tour (including St Bartholomew the Less, St Bartholomew the Great and Cloth Fair) April to November, Friday at 2pm. Charge. ☎ 020 7837 0546 (City of London Guides Association); Archives Department ☎ 020 7601 8152.*

St Bartholomew-the-Less – Open daily, 7am-10pm. Services: Sun, 8am, 11am. Prayers: Mon to Fri, 12noon. Roman Catholic Mass: Sun, 4pm.

St Sepulchre-without-Newgate – Open Tue, 12noon-2pm; Wed, 11am-3pm; Thur, 12noon-2pm. Organ Recital, Tue at 1pm, no charge. Music Recital, Thur, 1.15pm. Holy Communion Thur, 12.30pm. ☎/Fax (020) 7248 3826; citychurches@pmullen.freeserve.co.uk; st-michaels.org.uk/sepulchre

City Temple – 🦽 Open Mon to Fri. Chapel: Open for prayer 7am to 7pm. Services: Sun at 10.30am, Mon and Thur at 1.15pm. ☎ (020) 7583 5532; Fax (020) 7353 1083. city. temple@btinternet.com

Central Criminal Court, Old Bailey – 🦽 The public are admitted when the Courts are sitting, Mon to Fri, approximately 10am to 4.30pm with an adjournment for lunch. Bags, cameras, recording equipment, mobile telephones, food and drink prohibited.

CLERKENWELL

Charterhouse – Open for guided tour, Apr to July, Wed at 2.15pm; otherwise in groups by appointment. Unsuitable for disabled visitors. £3. Guide books. ☎ (020) 7253 9503; Fax (020) 7251 3929; tregistrar@aol.com

The Museum of the Order of St John – (🦽) Open Mon to Sat, 10am to 5pm (4pm Sat). Closed public holidays. Guided tour (1hr) Tues, Fri and Sat at 11am and 2.30pm. Donation: £4, £3.50 (concessions). ☎ (020) 7253 6644; Fax (020) 7336 0587; www.sja.org.uk/history
Access: by bus 4, 5, 55, 243, 279. ⊖ Farringdon.

Companies House – *Open Mon to Fri, 9am to 5pm. Closed public holidays. ☎ (020) 7253 9393 (answering service only).*

Wesley's House and Chapel – 🦽 Open Mon to Sat, 10am to 4pm; Sun after 11am service to 2pm. Closed bank holidays, 25 and 26 Dec. House and museum £4, £2 (concessions), no charge on Sun. Audioguides, videoshow, brochures and guidebooks available in English. ☎ (020) 7253 2262; Fax (020) 7608 3825.

Bunhill Fields – Garden: Open Mon to Fri, 7.30am to 7pm (4pm Oct to Mar); weekends, 9.30am to 4pm. Graveyard: apply in writing to the Superintendent of Parks and Gardens, West Ham Park, Upton Lane, Forest Gate, E7 9PU. Guide book available. ☎ (020) 8472 3584; Fax (020) 8475 0893; parks.gardens@corpoflondon.gov.uk; www.cityoflondon.gov.uk

COURTAULD INSTITUTE GALLERIES

Courtauld Institute Galleries – ♿ Open daily, 10am (12pm Sun) to 6pm. Closed 1 Jan, 24 to 26 Dec. £4, £3 (concession). Coffee shop. Bookshop. ☎ (020) 7848 2526; Fax (020) 7848 2589; galleryinfo@courtauld.ac.uk; www.courtauld.ac.uk

COVENT GARDEN

London Transport Museum – ♿ Open daily, 10am (11am Fri) to 6pm. Last admission 5.15pm. Closed 24 to 26 Dec. £5.50, £2.95 (concession), £13.95 (family 2A+2C). Interactive display (French, German, Italian, Spanish); fun bus for under-5s; kid-zones for children 7-12yrs. Café, shop. ☎ (020) 7379 6344, (020) 7836 8557 (24hr information); Fax (020) 7836 4118; www.ltmuseum.co.uk

Theatre Museum – ♿ Open daily except Mon, 10am to 6pm. Closed public holidays. £4.50, £2.50 (concession), £8 (family). Guided tours, visitor notes (English, German, French, Italian, Spanish and Japanese). Make-up demonstrations and costume workshops: daily. ☎ (020) 7943 4700; c.wright@vam.ac.uk; www.theatremuseum.org.uk

St Giles-in-the-Fields – Open Mon to Fri 9-4pm. Services: Sun, see notice-board; Wed at 1pm, Thur, (lunch-time service) at 1.25pm, Saints Days (Holy Communion) at 1pm. ☎ (020) 7240 2532

H

HYDE PARK – KENSINGTON GARDENS

Serpentine Gallery – ♿ Open daily for temporary exhibitions, 10am to 6pm. No charge. See press for details of exhibitions. ☎ (020) 7402 6075, Fax (020) 7402 4103. Access: by bus 9, 10, 12, 52, 94. ⊖ Lancaster Gate, South Kensington.

The Golden Lion

Kensington Palace – ♿ Open Mar to Nov daily, 1st admission 10am, last admission 5pm; Nov to Mar, Wed to Sun, 1st admission 10am, last admission 4pm. Closed 1 Jan, Good Friday, 24 to 26 Dec. Guided tours. £8.50, £6.10 (child), £6.70 (concession), £23 (family 2A+3C). Disabled visitors should telephone in advance. ☎ 020 7937 9561. www.hrp.org.uk Access: by bus 9, 10, 33, 49, 52, 52A, C1; ⊖ Queensway, High Street Kensington.

K

KENSINGTON

Roof Garden – *(♿) Open daily 9am to 5pm (call to view). Closed during private functions.* ☎ *(020) 7937 7994; Fax (020) 7938 2774.*

Linley Sambourne House – Open Mar to Oct, Wed, 10am to 4pm (last entry 3.30pm); Sun, guided tours (45min) only, 2.15pm, 3.15pm, 4.15pm; otherwise by appoinment (groups of 12 or more). £3.50, £2 (child), £2.50 (senior citizens). ☎ 020 7937 0663 (answering machine), 020 8994 1019 (Victorian Society).

Holland Park – Park: Open daily 8am to sunset. Brochures. Café. Sports facilities (tennis, cricket, football, squash). Holland Park and Holland House, £1; Kyoto Garden, £2. ☎ (020) 7471 9813 (reception); Fax (020) 7602 6130.
Open Air Theatre – Open June to August. Box office ☎ 0171 602 7856.

Leighton House – Open Mon to Sun, 11am to 5.30pm. Closed Tue and public holidays. No charge. Guided tours Wed and Thur at 12 noon, £3. Brochure (Arabic, French, German, Italian, Japanese, Spanish). Programme of concerts, lectures and exhibitions. ☎ 020 7602 3316; Fax 020 7371 2467.
Access: Bus 9, 9A, 10, 27, 33, 49 to Odeon Cinema/Commonwealth Institute. ⊖ High Street Kensington.

KNIGHTSBRIDGE – BELGRAVIA

Oratory of St Philip Neri – ♿ Open daily 6.30am to 8pm. ☎ (020) 7808 0900; Fax (020) 7584 1095.

St Columba's Church – ♿ Open Mon to Fri, 9am to 5pm. Services: Sun at 11am and 6.30pm. ☎ (020) 7584 2321; Fax (020) 7584 5446; office@stcolumbas.org.uk; www.stcolumbas.org.uk

L

LAMBETH

Museum of Garden History – (♿) Open Mar to mid Dec, Mon to Fri and public holidays, 10.30am to 5pm, Sun, 10.30am to 5pm; exhibitions throughout the year; lectures; courses; outings. Donation. Leaflet (French, German, Italian, Japanese, Russian, Spanish). Refreshments. ☎ (020) 7401 8865; Fax (020) 7401 8869; www.museumgardenhistory.org

Florence Nightingale Museum – ♿ Open Mon-Fri, 10am to 5pm, Sat, Sun and bank holiday Monday, 11.30am to 4.30pm. Last admission 1hr before closing time. Closed Good Fri, Easter Sun, 24 Dec-2 Jan. £4.80, £3.60 (concession), £10 (family). Film (20min). Refreshments. ☎ (020) 7620 0374.

St George's RC Cathedral – (♿) Open daily, 7.30am to 8pm, guided tours by appointment. Brochure (English). Temporary disabled access to cathedral. Disabled toilet facilities in Parish Hall (adjacent). ☎ (020) 7928 5256; Fax (020) 7787 8923; www.southwark-rc-cathedral.fsnet.co.uk

Imperial War Museum – ♿ *Open daily, 10am to 6pm. Closed 24 to 26 Dec. £5, £2.50 (child), £4.00 (concessions). Parking for the disabled. Leaflets (French, German). Café, shop. ☎ (020) 7416 5320; Fax (020) 7416 5321; www.iwm.org.uk*

M

MARYLEBONE

St Marylebone Church – ♿ Open Mon, 12.30pm to 1.30pm. Services: Sun at 8.30am (Holy Communion), 11am (Choral Eucharist), 6.30pm (Choral Healing Service, first Sun in the month); Wed at 1.10pm (Holy Communion in the Crypt, combined with Healing Service third Wed in the month). Leaflet available in Dutch, English, French, German, Spanish. ☎ (020) 7935 7315; Fax (020) 7486 5493; st.marylebone@ukgateway.net

St Peter's Church – *Open Mon to Fri, 9.30am to 5pm. Guide books. ☎ (020) 7629 3615; Fax (020) 7629 1284; contemporary–christianity–edu@msn.com*

MAYFAIR

Grosvenor Chapel – *Open Mon to Fri, 9am to 5pm.*

Church of the Immaculate Conception – Open daily, 7am to 7pm. Mass: Sun at 8am, 9.30am, 11am, 12.30pm, 4.15pm, 6.15pm; Mon to Fri at 7.30am, 8.30am, 12.05pm, 1.05pm, 6pm; Sat at 7.30am, 8.30am, 11am and 6pm. Mass in Czech 10.30am each Sun; in Japanese each 3rd Sun of month. Texts for Sun Mass in French, German, Italian, Spanish. ☎ (020) 7493 7811; Fax (020) 7495 6685.

St George's Hanover Square – Open Mon to Fri, 8.30am-3.30pm. Guide book. Handel Festival: Apr to May. ☎(020) 7629 0874; Fax (020) 7629 0874.

N

NATIONAL GALLERY

National Gallery – ♿ Open daily, 10am to 6pm (9pm Wed). Closed 1 Jan, Good Fri, 24 to 26 Dec. No charge to main galleries. Micro Gallery – Open daily 10am to 5.30pm (8.30pm Wed). Guided tour: (1 hour), daily, at 11.30am and 2.30pm (6.30pm Wed): meet in Sainsbury Wing Vestibule. Gallery Guide Soundtrack for hire from entrances (French, German, Italian, Japanese, Spanish). Brochure (French, German, Italian, Japanese, Spanish). Restaurant, café. Photography prohibited. ☎ (020) 7747 2885; Fax: (020) 7747 2423; information@ng-london.org.uk; www.nationalgallery.org.uk
Access: by bus 3, 6, 9, 11, 12, 13, 15, 23, 24, 29, 53, X53, 77A, 88, 91, 109, 139, 159, 176. ⊖ Charing Cross, Leicester Square, Embankment, Piccadilly Circus.

NATIONAL PORTRAIT GALLERY

National Portrait Gallery – &. Open daily, 10am-6pm (9pm, Thurs and Fri). Closed 1 Jan, Good Fri, 24 to 26 Dec. No charge except for special exhibitions. CD-Rom sound guide (French, Spanish, Japanese). Gallery Bookshop. Café. Restaurant. ☎ (020) 7306 0055; Fax (020) 7306 0056; www.npg.org.uk
Access: ⊖ Leicester Square, Charing Cross.

NATURAL HISTORY MUSEUM

Natural History Museum – &. Open daily, 10am (11am Sun) to 5.50pm (last admission, 5.30pm). £7.50, no charge (child), £4.50, (concessions); no charge (senior citizen); no charge for entry after 4.30pm, Mon to Fri and after 5pm, weekends and public holidays. Map and guide (French, German, Italian, Japanese, Spanish) available from the information desks and shops. Changing programme of special events. Activity sheets for children (30p). Book shop, gift shops. Restaurant, café, coffee bar, snack bar and picnic area. ☎ (020) 7942 5000; www.nhm.ac.uk
Access: bus 14, 49, 70, 74, 345; ⊖ South Kensington.

P

PICCADILLY

Rock Circus – &. Open daily, 10am (11am Tues) to 8pm (9pm, Fri and Sat). Closed 25 and 31 Dec, 1 Jan. £8.25, £6.25 (child), £7.25 (concessions). Guide books (French, German, Italian). ☎ (020) 7734 7203; Fax (020) 7734 8023; www.rock-circus.com
Access: by bus 3, 6, 9, 12, 13, 14, 15, 19, 23, 38, 53, 88; ⊖ Piccadilly Circus, Leicester Square.

Trocadero – Open daily, 10am to 1am. Closed 25 Dec. Multi-ride tickets from £5.90, £14.90 (family). ☎ 0906 888 1100 (premium rate).

Royal Academy – &. Open daily, 10am to 6pm; Fri, 10am-8.30pm. Closed 25 Dec. £6-£8 according to the exhibition. Restaurant; shop. ☎ (020) 7300 5760 (recorded information), (020) 7300 8000 (switchboard); Fax (020) 7300 8001; www.royalacademy.org.uk

Burlington Arcade – Open Mon to Sat, 9am to 6pm. ☎ (020) 7493 8939; www.pickett.co.uk

Michael Faraday Laboratory and Museum – Open Mon to Fri, 9am-6pm. £1 (adult/child). Guided tour by appointment with The Royal Institution of Great Britain, 21 Albemarle Street, London W1X 4BS. £5. ☎ (020) 7409 2992; Fax (020) 7629 3569; ril@ri.ac.uk; www.ri.ac.uk

Apsley House, Wellington Museum – (&.) Open Tues to Sun and holiday Mon 11am to 5pm (last admission 4.30pm). Closed 1 Jan, Good Friday, May Day holiday, 24 to 26 Dec. £4.50, £3 (concession); no charge (over 60s, child); free of charge 18 June: Waterloo Day. Soundguide available in English, French, German, Spanish. ☎ (020) 7499 5676; Fax (020) 7493 6576.
Access: by bus 2, 8, 9, 10, 14, 16, 19, 22, 36, 38, 52, 73, 74, 82, 137. ⊖ Hyde Park Corner.

R

REGENT'S PARK

Holy Trinity Church – *Open Mon to Sat, 9.30am to 6pm. Service: Tues at 12.30pm. SPCK Christian bookshops (including Charles Higham's bookshop for second-hand and antiquarian books).* ☎ (020) 7387 5282; Fax (020) 7388 2352.

Danish Church – Open Mon-Fri, 9am-1pm and 6.30pm-10pm (except Fri); Sat and Sun, 12noon-5pm. Services: Sun at 11am. Keys available at 5 St Katharine's Precinct. ☎ (020) 7935 7584; Fax (020) 7487 4029.

London Zoo – &. Open daily, 10am to 5.30pm (4pm Oct to Feb); last admission 1hr before closing time. Closed 25 Dec. £9, £7 (child), £8 (concessions). Restaurant, refreshments. ☎ (020) 7722 3333; Fax (020) 7586 5743; www.londonzoo.co.uk; www.weboflife.co.uk

REGENT STREET

BBC Experience – &. Open daily. First tour, 10am (11am Mon), last tour, 4.30pm. Closes 6pm. £7.50, £6.50 (concession), £4.95 (child), £19.95 (family, 2A+2C). Wheelchair users should call in advance. ☎ 0870 603 0304 (charged at national rate); Textphone: 0870 903 0304. Access: ⊖ Oxford Circus.

All Souls Church – Open Mon to Fri, 9.30am to 6pm (8pm occasionally); Sun, 9am to 8.30pm. Services: Sun at 8am, 9.30am, 11.30am and 6.30pm. ☎ (020) 7580 3522; Fax (020) 7436 3019; vestry@allsouls.org

ST JAMES'S

St James's Church – Open daily. Services: Sun at 9.15am and 11am, Tues at 1.05pm and 5.45pm (Evening prayer), Wed at 8.30am; Silent prayer and meditation on other mornings. Recitals: Wed to Fri at 1.10pm. Concerts: Usually Thur to Sat at 7.30pm. Lectures, seminars. Market: Tues 10am to 6pm (antiques also); Weds to Sat, 10am to 5pm (craft market only).

Spencer House – ♿ Guided tour (60min) Sun, 10.30am to 4.45pm every 20min. £6, £5 (concessions to students, Friends of the Tate, the Royal Academy and the V&A - all with cards – and children under 16 accompanied by an adult). No children under 10yrs. For group bookings contact The Administrator, Spencer House, 27 St James's Place, London SW1A 1NR. Guided tours in Dutch, French, German, Italian, Japanese, Spanish by prior arrangement. No photography. No smoking. ☎ (020) 7499 8620 for recorded information); Fax (020) 7409 2952; www.spencerhouse.co.uk

Chapel Royal, St James's Palace – *Services: Oct until Good Friday, Sun at 8.30am (Holy Communion), 11.15am (Choral Eucharist/Matins).*

Queen's Chapel, St James's Palace – Services: Easter Day until end July, Sun at 8.30am (Holy Communion), 11.15am (Choral Eucharist/Matins).

ST PANCRAS

London Canal Museum – (♿) Open Tues–Sun and bank holiday Mon, 10am–4.30pm. Closed 24–26 Dec. £2.50, £1.25 (concession). ☎/Fax 020 7713 0836; info@canalmuseum.org.uk; www.canalmuseum.org.uk
Access: by bus 10, 17, 30, 45, 46, 63, 73, 91, 214, 259, A2, C12; ⊖ Kings Cross.

British Library – ♿ *Exhibition Galleries: Open Mon to Fri, 9.30am to 6pm (8pm Tues), Sat 9.30am to 5pm, Sun 11am to 5pm. Reading rooms only open to readers with a Readers Pass.* ☎ *(020) 7412 7222 (Box office), (020) 7412 7332 (Visitor Services). www.bl.uk*

St Pancras Parish Church – Open Wed-Fri, 9am-5pm, Sat, 9am-12noon. Brochure French, German, Italian, Portugese, Spanish). Concert: Thur at 1.15pm; no charge. ☎ (020) 7388 1461.

The Wellcome Trust – ♿ *Science for Life Exhibition: Open, daily except Sunday, 9.45am to 5pm (1pm Saturday). Closed public holidays and previous Saturdays. No charge.* ☎ *0171 611 8727 (recorded information).*

Jewish Museum – ♿ Open Sun to Thur, 10am to 4pm. Closed Fri and Sat, Jewish Festivals, public holidays. £3, £2 (concessions), £7.50 (family), £1.50 (child). ☎ (020) 7284 1997; Fax (020) 7267 9008; www.jewmusm.ort.org; admin@mus.org.uk
Access: ⊖ Camden Town

ST PAUL'S CATHEDRAL

St Paul's Cathedral – ♿ Open daily, although Sun are reserved for services. Cathedral visiting: Mon to Sat, 8.30am to 4pm. Galleries: 9.30am to 4pm. £5, £4 (concession), £2.50. Guided tours (90-120min) at 11am, 11.30am, 1.30pm, 2pm. Audio guide (French, German, Italian, Japanese, Spanish); leaflets (Dutch, French, German, Italian, Japanese, Polish, Russian, Spanish); guide books (English, French, German, Italian, Japanese, Spanish).
Services: Sun at 8am (Holy Communion), 10.15am (Matins), 11.30am (Sung Euchar-st), 3.15pm (Evensong), 6pm (evening service), Mon to Fri at 7.30am (Matins), 8am (Holy Communion), 12.30pm (Holy Communion), 5pm (Evensong); Sat at 8am (Holy Communion), 8.30am (Matins), 12.30pm (Holy Communion), 5pm (Evensong). The choir sings at 11.30am and 3.15pm on Sun, and at Evensong on weekdays. ☎ (020) 7246 8350; (020) 7248 3104; reception@stpaulscathedral.org.uk

SCIENCE MUSEUM

Science Museum – ♿ Open daily, 10am to 6pm. Closed 24 to 26 Dec. £6.95, £3.50 (concessions), no charge (child, senior citizen); season ticket available; no charge for entry after 4.30pm. Brochure (French, German, Italian, Japanese, Spanish). Bookshop; restaurant; picnic area. ☎ (020) 7942 4455, 4454 (information desk), (020) 7942 4000 (switchboard); Fax (020) 7942 4447; sciencemuseum@nmsi.ac.uk; www.sciencemuseum.org

SOHO

Half-Price Ticket Booth *(tkts)* – Open (for evening performances) Mon-Sat, 10am to 7pm; (for matinée tickets) Sun noon to 3.30pm. Payment in cash, credit or debit card, or Theatre Tokens; service charge of about £2.50 per ticket, maximum 4 tickets per person.

Swiss Centre Glockenspiel – *Plays Mon to Fri at noon, 6pm, 7pm, 8pm; weekends and bank holidays at noon, 2pm, 3pm, 4pm, 5pm, 6pm, 7pm, 8pm.* ☎ *020 7734 1291.*

Notre Dame de France – *Open daily, 9.30am to 8.30pm. Brochure (French). RC Services: in French, Sun at 10am, 11.30am (11am only in July and Aug); Sat at 6pm in English, Mon to Fri at 12.15pm, 6pm. Holy days at 12.15pm (English) and 6pm (French). Hearing loop available.* ☎ (020) 7437 9363; Fax (020) 7437 9364.

Our Lady of the Assumption – Open daily 7am (10am Sat) to 7pm. RC Services Sun at 9am, 10am, 11am, noon, 5pm; Sat at 6pm; Mon to Fri at 8am, 12.45pm 5.45pm; Holidays at 8am, 12.15pm, 12.45pm, 5.45pm. ☎ (020) 7437 1525.

House of St Barnabas – *Open Wed, 2.30pm to 4.15pm; Thur, 11am to 12.30pm Closed Easter and Christmas. Donation.* ☎ (020) 7437 1894.

SOUTH BANK

London Aquarium – Open daily, 10am to 6pm (5pm last admission). £8.50, £6.50 (concession), £5 (child), £24 (2A+2C). ☎ 020 7967 8000, Fax 020 7967 8029 info@londonaquarium.co.uk; www.londonaquarium.co.uk

British Airways London Eye – ♿ Open daily, 9.30am-10pm (summer) 10.30am-6pm (winter, Sept onwards). £8.50, £5 (child u 16), £6.50 (OAP), no charge (child u 5). ☎ 0870 5000 600. www.ba-londoneye.com

Hayward Gallery – ♿ Open daily 10am to 6pm (8pm Tues and Wed). £6, £4 (concessions), £14 (family). Coffee shop; bookshop. ☎ (020) 7261 0127 (recorded information); ☎ 020 7960 4242 (advance booking); visual–arts@hayward.org.uk; www.hayward-gallery.org.uk

National Theatre – ♿ Backstage tour (75min), Mon to Sat. £4.75, £3.75 (concession). Book in advance in person at the Lyttelton Information Desk (10am to 11pm) or by telephone. 'Platforms' (early evening discussions, readings, interviews, debates 45min) as advertised. Bookshop; restaurant; refreshments; free concerts in Lyttelton foyer, daily (except Sun), 6pm . ☎ 020 7452 3400. www.nt-online.org
Access: by bus 1, 4, 26, 68, X68, 76, 168, 171, 171A, 176, 188, 501, 505, 521 (Waterloo Bridge); 76, 77, 171A, 211, 507, D1, D11, P11 (York Road); 149, P11 (Stamford Street): by car – reduced rate between 10am and 5pm if National Theatre car park ticket is stamped at reception.

Gabriel's Wharf – Open Tues to Sun, 11am to 6pm (designer-maker workshops).

SOUTH KENSINGTON

Royal Geographical Society – ♿ ☎ (020) 7591 3000; Fax (020) 7591 3001. Map Room and Library: Open Mon to Fri, 11am-5pm. ☎ (020) 7591 3050, £10.
Picture Library: Mon to Fri, 10am to 5pm by appointment only. ☎ 01715913060; Fax (020) 7591 3061.

Royal College of Music – *Museum of Instruments: Open in term time, Wed, 2pm to 4.30pm. Closed throughout Jan. £1.20, £1 (concessions). Group tour by appointment only (additional charge).* ☎ (020) 7591 4346; Fax (020) 7589 7740; museum@rcm ac.uk

Baden-Powell House – ♿ Open daily 7am to 11pm, manned 24hrs a day. Closed 24 Dec to 2 Jan. Hostel (180 beds). Restaurant. ☎ (020) 7584 7031; Fax (020) 7590 6902; bph.hostel@scout.org.uk

SOUTHWARK

Southwark TIC – London Bridge, 6 Tooley Street, SE1. Open summer, daily, 10am to 6pm; winter, daily, 10am to 4pm. ☎ 020 7403 8299.

Southwark Cathedral – ♿ Open daily, 8am to 6pm. Guide book. Donation (£2.50). Access: by bus 21, 35, 40, 47, 48, 149, 344, P3, P11; ⊖ London Bridge.

Old Operating Theatre, Museum and Herb Garret – Open (most Mon), Tues to Sun, 10.30am to 5pm. Closed 20 Dec-5 Jan. Leaflet (German). £3.25, £1.60 (child), £2.25 (concessions), £8 (family 2A+2C). Special lecture: first Sun of every month at 2.30pm. ☎ (020) 7955 4791; Fax (020) 7378 8383.
Access: bus 17, 21, 35, 40, 43, X43, 47, 48, 133, 149, 344, 501, 505, 513, D1, D3, P11.

George Inn – (NT) Bar food: daily. Restaurant: Open Mon to Fri (lunchtime and evenings), Sat, evenings only (please telephone for restaurant reservations). ☎ (020) 7407 2056 (during licensing hours); Fax (020) 7403 6613.

St George the Martyr – (♿) Open Sun, 10am to 4pm; Wed, noon to 1.30pm; Thur, (except holiday periods) noon to 2pm. Guide book. Induction loop. tonyslucas@ btinternet.com

Christchurch – Ring for admission. ☎ 020 7928 4707; Fax 020 7928 1148; slim@dswark.org

London Fire Brigade Museum – Open by pre-booked guided tour only: Mon to Fri (excluding bank holidays); tours at 10.30am, 12.30pm and 2.30pm. ☎ (020) 7587 2894; Fax (020) 7587 2878; esther.mann@ifcda.org.uk

STRAND

Queen's Chapel of the Savoy – Open Tues to Fri, 11.30am to 3.30pm. Closed Aug to Sept, also at certain times without notice. Guided tour by arrangement. Services: Wed at 12.30pm (Holy Communion), otherwise as advertised. ☎ (020) 7836 7221.

Gilbert Collection – Open daily, 10am (12pm Sun and holidays) to 6pm. Closed 1 Jan and 24-26 Dec. £4, £3 (concession); free to all Mon (except holiday Mon) 10am to 2pm. Combined ticket with Courtauld Gallery £7, £5 (concession). Audio guide. ☎ (020) 7240 4080; Fax (020) 7240 4060; info@gilbert-collection.org.uk; www.gilbert-collection.org.uk
Access: buses 6,9,11,13,15,23, 77a, 91, 176; BR to Charing Cross, Waterloo, Blackfriars. ⊖ Temple, Covent Garden, Charing Cross.

The Hermitage Rooms – ♿ Open Mon-Sat, 10am-6pm; Sun and bank holiday, 12pm-6pm (last admission 5.15pm). Closed 1 Jan, 24-26 Dec. £6, £4 (concession). Timed ticket, advanced booking recommended. Audio-guide. Shop. ☎ 020 7845 4630; Fax 020 7845 4637; info@hermitagerooms.com; www.hermitagerooms.com

St Mary-le-Strand – Open Mon to Fri, 11am to 4pm; Sun, 10am to 1pm. Leaflets (French, German, Italian, Japanese). Services: Tue and Thur, 1.05pm. Recital: Wed, 1pm. ☎ (020) 7836 3126 (Church), (020) 7836 3205 (Parish office).

Roman Bath – *(NT) Open by appointment May-Sept, Weds, 1pm to 5pm. 50p, 25p (concessions).* ☎ 020 7641 5264.

St Clement Danes – Services: Sun at 11am; Wed and Fri at 12.30pm in Crypt Chapel (Eucharist). Oranges and lemons carillon: Daily at 9am, noon, 3pm, 6pm (Sun 9am and 6pm only). Leaflets (Danish, Dutch, French, German, Italian). ☎ (020) 7242 8282, Fax: (020) 7404 2129.

Wig and Pen Club – *Guided legal tour (including the Club, the Royal Courts of Justice and the Inns of Court) on application (48hr notice), early Apr to late Oct on Mon except public holidays from 10am. Whole or half day (including meals) from £40.* ☎ *(020) 7353 6864.*

Royal Courts of Justice – ♿ Open when the Courts are sitting, Mon to Fri, approximately 9.30am to 4.30pm with an adjournment for lunch. No cameras are allowed into the building. ☎ (020) 7947 6000. Access: bus 4, 11, 15, 23, 26, 76, 171A, x15.

T

TATE BRITAIN

Tate Britain – ♿ Open daily, 10am to 5.50pm. Closed 24 to 26 Dec. No charge for permanent collection; variable fee for temporary exhibitions.

St Clement Danes

Guide books available (French, German, Italian, Japanese, Spanish). Telephone for details of current events. Restaurant; self-service café: Open daily, 12noon-3pm (4pm, Sun). Audio guide, £3, £2 (concessions). ☎ (020) 7887 8008 (recorded information), (020) 7887 8000; Fax (020) 7887 8007; information@tate.org.uk; www.tate.org.uk
Access: by bus 2, 3, 36, 77A, 88, 159, 185, 507, C10; ⊖ Pimlico, then 5min walk (follow the signs); BR Vauxhall Station.

TOWER OF LONDON

Tower of London – (♿) Open Mar to Oct, daily, 9am (10am Sun) to 6pm; Nov to Feb, daily, 9am (10am Sun and Mon) to 5pm; last admission 1hr before closing. Closed 1 Jan, 24 to 26 Dec. £11, £7.30 (child), £8.30 (concession), £33 (family 2A+3C). Tickets are also available from London Underground stations.
Guided tour (1hr) by Yeoman Warders from the Middle Tower (exteriors only).
Chapel of St Peter-ad-Vincula: open for guided tour only and for services on Sun at 9.15am (Holy Communion), 11am (Matins and sermon). ☎ 020 7709 0765.
Jewel House: queues tend to be shorter early in the day. Audio guides (Prisoners' Trail) in English, German, Italian, Spanish and French; guide books and leaflets in English, German, Italian, Spanish, French, Japanese and Russian.
Royal Fuseliers Regimental Museum: 50p. ☎ 020 7488 5611.

Tower Bridge – ♿ Open Apr to Oct daily 10am to 6.30pm (last admission 5.15pm); Nov to Mar daily 9.30am to 6pm (last admission 4.45pm). Closed 24 and 25 Dec, 17 Jan. £6.25, £4.25 (concession). £18.25 (family 2A+2C). Audio-guide (English,

TOWER OF LONDON

French, German, Italian, Japanese, Spanish). Guide books (English, French, German, Japanese, Russian). ☎ (020) 7378 1928; Fax (020) 7357 7935; enquiries@towerbridge.org.uk; www.towerbridge.org.uk
Access: by bus 15, 42, 47, 78, 100, D1, P11; River boat to Tower Pier. ⊖ Tower Hill, London Bridge.

All Hallows-by-the-Tower – Open daily, 9am to 6pm. Brass rubbing and audio tours: daily 11am to 4pm; Guide book available. ☎ (020) 7481 2928.

TRAFALGAR SQUARE

St Martin-in-the-Fields – ♿ Open daily, 8am to 6.30pm. Brochure (French, German, Italian, Japanese, Spanish). ☎ (020) 7930 0089, Fax (020) 7839 5163. Choral services: Sun at 10am, 12noon, 5pm; Wed at 1.05pm, 5pm.
Lunchtime recitals: Mon, Tues and Fri at 1.05pm; no charge. Evening concerts: Thur to Sat at 7.30pm; tickets available from ☎ (020) 7839 8362; Fax (020) 7839 5163, or the Crypt box office (Mon to Sat, 10.00am to 5pm).
Café in the Crypt – Open daily, 10am (noon Sun) to 8pm. ☎ (020) 7839 4342. Outdoor market: daily.

London Brass Rubbing Centre – Open daily, 10am (noon Sun) to 6pm. Closed Good Fri, 25 Dec. Exhibition, no charge; brass rubbings including all materials £1.90 to £15 according to size. ☎ 020 7930 9306.

VICTORIA AND ALBERT MUSEUM

Victoria and Albert Museum – ♿ Open daily 10am to 5.45pm, late view (seasonal) 6.30pm to 9.30pm. Closed 24 to 26 Dec. £5, no charge for students, under 18s, unwaged and after 4.30pm.
Brochure/map (26 languages), Gallery talks (French, German, Spanish, Italian). Guided tour (1 hour): Mon at 12.30pm, 1.30pm, 2.30pm, 3.30pm, Tues to Sun at 10.30am, 11.30, 12.30pm, 2.30pm and 3.30pm from the Information Desk in Main Entrance, no charge. Guided tours of particular sections: everyday at 12.30pm and 3.30pm; check at the Information Desk. Gallery talks: Mon to Sat at 2.00pm (in French, Spanish, Italian and German); no charge. Photography permitted; no flash, no tripods. Restaurant. Entrances in Cromwell Road and Exhibition Road. ☎ 020 7942 2000
Print Study Room: Tues to Fri, 10am to 4.30pm. ☎ 020 7942 2563, (recorded information on current exhibitions ☎ 020 7942 2530). www.vam.ac.uk
Access: by bus C1, 14, 74, ⊖ South Kensington.

WALLACE COLLECTION

Wallace Collection – ♿ Open Mon to Sat, 10am to 5pm; Sun 12noon to 5pm. Closed 1 Jan, Good Friday, May Day holiday, 24 to 26 Dec. No charge. Guided tours (1hr). Leaflet. Guide book (French, Japanese). ☎ (020) 7563 9500; Fax (020) 7224 2155; admin@the-wallace-collection.org.uk; www.the-wallace-collection.co.uk

WESTMINSTER

London Visitor Centre – Victoria Station Forecourt, SW1. In May, Mon to Sat, 8am to 8pm, Sun, 8am to 6pm; Jun to Sept, Mon to Sat, 8am to 10pm, Sun, 8am to 7pm; Oct to Easter, daily, 8am to 7pm; Easter to Apr 25, Mon to Sat, 8am to 7pm, Sun, 8am to 6pm.

Houses of Parliament – Guided tour on application to a Member of Parliament only.

House of Lords Record Office – ♿ Open by appointment, Mon to Fri, 9.30am to 5pm; Closed certain public holidays and last two weeks of Nov. Leaflet (English only) ☎ (020) 7219 3074; Fax (020) 7219 2570.

Jewel Tower – (EH) Open Apr-Oct, daily, 10am-6pm; Nov-Mar, daily, 10am-4pm. Closed 24-26 Dec; subject to closure at short notice. £1.50, £1.10 (concessions), 80p (child). ☎ (020) 7222 2219.

St Margaret's Church – *Open daily, 9.30am (Sun, 1pm) to 5.30pm. Service: Sun at 11am (Sung Eucharist).*

Blewcoat School – National Trust Shop and Information Centre: Open Mon-Fri, 10am-5.30pm. Closed bank holiday Mon, 25 Dec-1 Jan. ☎ (020) 7222 2877.

Westminster Cathedral – ♿ Open daily, 7am to 7pm (5.30pm public holidays). Audio tour; brochure (French, German, Italian, Japanese, Spanish). Belltower: Mar-Nov, daily, 9am to 5pm; Dec-Mar, Thur-Sun, 9am-5pm. ♿ entrance at southwest side of Cathedral. ☎ (020) 7798 9055; Fax (020) 7798 9090; bpalmer@westminster-cathedral.org.uk; www.westminstercathedral.org.uk

WESTMINSTER ABBEY

Westminster Abbey – ♿ Open Mon to Fri, 9.30am to 4.45pm; Sat, 9.30am to 2.45pm; last admission 1 hour before closing time. Refer to schedules at Christmas and Easter when additional services are held.
£5, £3 (concessions), £2, £10 (family 2A+2C).
Leaflet (French, German, Italian, Japanese, Russian, Spanish, Dutch).
Audio-guide (available in French, German, Italian, Spanish, Russian, Japanese; £2 surcharge on admission price).
☎ (020) 7222 5152; Fax (020) 7233 2072; press@westminster-abbey.org; www.westminster-abbey.org.
Guided tours by Vergers (maximum 90min): Apr to Oct, Mon to Fri at 10am, 10.30am, 11am, 2pm, 3pm (Fri 2.30pm); Sat at 10am, 11am, 12.30pm. Nov to Mar, Mon to Fri at 10am, 11am, 2pm, 3pm (except Fri); Sat at 10am, 11am, 12.30pm. £3 surcharge on admission charge. 020 7222 7110.
Services: Sun at 8am (Holy Communion), 10am (Matins), 11.15am (Sung Eucharist), 3pm (Evensong), 5.45pm (Organ recital), 6.30pm (Evening Service); Mon to Fri at 7.30am (Matins), 8am and 12.30pm (Holy Communion), 5pm (Evensong); Sat at 8am (Holy Communion), 9.20am (Matins), 3pm (Evensong).
Cloister: open daily 8.00am to 6pm.
Chapter House – (EH) Open daily, Apr to Oct, 10am to 5.30pm (last admission 5pm); Nov to Mar, 10am to 4pm (last admission 3.30pm); subject to closure at short notice on State occasions. Closed 1 Jan, 24 to 26 Dec. ☎ 020 7222 5897.
Chapel of the Pyx and Westminster Abbey Museum – (EH) Open daily, 10.30am to 4pm. Reduced charge for those who have paid Abbey admission charge. ☎ 020 7233 0019.
Chapter Library – Open May to Sept, Wed, 11am to 3pm. Admission on production of a Chapter House/Chapel of the Pyx/museum ticket.
College Garden – ♿ Open Tues, Wed, Thur, 10am to 6pm (4pm Oct to Mar). Donation. Brass Band concerts: July and Aug, 12.30pm to 2pm. ☎ 020 7222 5152.

WHITEHALL

Cabinet War Rooms – ♿ Open daily, 10am to 6pm; last admission 5.15pm. Closed 24 to 26 Dec. Audio guide (8 languages). £5.50, £4.50 (concession), no charge (child, senior citizen). Café; shop. ☎ 09001 600 140 (recorded information); (020) 7930 6961; Fax (020) 7416 5374; www.iwm.org.uk
Access: by bus 1, 3, 12, 45, 53, 59, 63, 58, 100, 159, 168, 171, 172, 176, 188, 344, C100, by train: Waterloo or Elephant and Castle BR Stations. ⊖ Lambeth North, Waterloo, Elephant and Castle

Banqueting House – ♿ Open (Government functions permitting; it is best to check by phone in advance), Mon-Sat, 10am-5pm. Closed 1 Jan, Good Friday, 24-26 Dec and all public holidays. £3.80, £2.30 (child), £3 (concession); includes audio guide. ☎ 020 7930 4179 or 020 7839 8919.
Access: by bus 3, 11, 12, 24, 29, 53, 77A, 88, 159

Horse Guards – Ceremonial mounting of the Guard daily at 11am (10am Sun) in summer on Horse Guards Parade; dismount ceremony daily 4pm in the Front Yard of Horse Guards; the Guards (Queen's Life Guards) ride along the Mall between Horse Guards and their barracks in Hyde Park. ☎ (020) 7414 2353.

OUTER LONDON

B

BARNES – ROEHAMPTON

St Mary's Parish Church – Open daily 10.30am to 12.30pm; otherwise key available from the Parish Clerk. ☎ (020) 8748 2708 (Parish Clerk), ☎/Fax: (020) 8741 5422 (church office).

Church of St Mary the Virgin – *Open Tues to Sat, 9.30am to noon.* ☎ *(020) 8876 1630.*

BATTERSEA

Battersea Old Church, St Mary's – Open June to Oct, Tues and Wed, 11am to 3pm. Services: Sun at 8am, 11am, 6.30pm. Guide book (English).
office@stmarysbattersea.org.uk; www.stmarysbattersea.org-uk

De Morgan Foundation – (♿) *Open by prior appointment, usually Wed afternoon. £2. Apply to 56 Bradbourne Street, London SW6 3TE.* ☎ *(020) 7371 8385.*

Battersea Dogs' Home – Open daily (except Thur), 10.30am to 4.15pm (3.15pm weekends and public holidays). 50p, 20p (concessions). ☎ (020) 7622 3626; Fax (020) 7622 6451; info@dogshome.org; www.dogshome.org

BERMONDSEY – ROTHERHITHE

Design Museum – 🔥 Open daily, 11.30am (10.30am weekends) to 6pm. Guided tour by appointment. £5.50, £4 (concession), £15 (family). Shop. Coffee shop Restaurant. ☎ (020) 7403 6933; Fax (020) 7378 6540; enquiries@designmuseum. org.uk; www.designmuseum.org Access: ⊖ Tower Hill, London Bridge, Bermondsey bus 15, 78, 100 (to Tower Hill); 42, 47, 188, P11 (to Jamaica Road/Tooley St).

Bramah Museum of Tea and Coffee – 🔥 Open daily, 10am to 6pm. Closed 25 to 26 Dec. Guide book (French, German, Japanese), private lectures and presentations. £4, £3 (concession). Tearoom. ☎ 020 7378 0222; Fax 020 7378 0219. e.bramah@virgin.net; www.bramahmuseum.co.uk

Church of St Mary Magdalen – 🔥 Services: Sun at 10.30am. Open otherwise by appointment. ☎ (020) 7407 5273.

St Mary's Church – Services: Sun at 9.30am and 6pm; Mon to Thur at 7.30am; Sat at 9.45am. Guided tours by arrangement, leaflets. ☎ (020) 7231 2465 (Rector), Fax (020) 7394 9683.

Brunel Engine House – Open all year, Sun, 1pm to 5pm; May-Oct, Sat, 1pm to 5pm; Mon-Fri, by arrangement. £2, £1 (concession), £5 (family ticket). ☎ (020) 7831 8545 (administrator); (020) 7231 3840 (museum); www.museumweb. freeserve.co.uk/brunel.htm

CHISWICK

Chiswick House – (EH) (🔥) Open Apr-Sept daily, 10am-6pm, 1-28 Oct daily 10am-5pm, 29-31 Oct, 10am-4.30pm, Nov-Mar, Wed-Sun, 10am-4pm. Closed 4 to 17 Jan, 24 to 26 Dec. £3.30, £2.50 (concessions), £1.70 (child). Guided tour available on request. Audio guide (English, French and German) available. Picnic area. ☎ (020) 8995 0508.

Hogarth's House – (🔥) Open Tues to Fri, 1pm to 5pm (4pm Nov to Mar); Sat and Sun, 1pm to 6pm (5pm Nov to Mar). Closed Mon, Good Friday, 25 and 26 Dec and Jan. No charge. Guided tour (30min) on request. Parking. ☎ (020) 8994 6757.

Fuller, Smith and Turner Griffin Brewery – Guided tours Mon, Wed, Thur and Fri at 11am, noon, 1pm and 2pm. £5, £3.50 (child, 14-18). No admission to children under 14 yrs. Tours must be booked in advance. ☎ (020) 8996 2063; Fax (020) 8996 2079; julie.knight@fullers.co.uk; www.fullers.co.uk Access: by bus 27, 237, 267, 391, E3; ⊖ Turnham Green.

St Nicholas Parish Church – Open Sun, 2.30pm to 4.30pm; Tues and Thur, 10am to noon; otherwise key available from the Vicarage. ☎/Fax (020) 8995 4717.

DOCKLANDS

Coronarium Chapel – *Service: Thur at 1.30pm.*

International Financial Futures & Options Exchange – *Closed for reasons of security* ☎ (020) 7623 0444; Fax (020) 7588 3624.

Tobacco Dock – *In process of redevelopment; telephone for details.* ☎ (020) 7702 9681

Tobacco Dock, Wapping

St George-in-the-East – Open (usually) Tues to Sun, 9am to 5pm. For confirmation ☎ (020) 7481 1345; Fax (020) 7680 0665.

St Paul's Church – Services: Sun at 9.30am. Key available from The Rectory, 298 The Highway, Shadwell.

St Anne's Limehouse – Open Thurs, 1pm-2pm; Sun 10.30am-12.30pm; 5pm-7.30pm. Also open first Thurs of each month, 10.30am-4pm. ☎ (020) 7987 1502; gordon.warren@dlondon.org.uk

Mudchute Park – *Park: Open permanently. Farm: Open daily, 10am to 4pm. Nature study centre; riding school.* ☎ *(020) 7515 5901; Fax (020) 7538 9530.*

Island History Trust – Open Tues and Wed, 1.30pm to 4.30pm; 1st Sun of each month, 1.30pm to 4.30pm. ☎ (020) 7987 6041.

DULWICH

Dulwich Picture Gallery – ♿ Open Tues to Fri, 10am to 5pm; Sat and bank holiday Mon, 11am to 5pm; Sun, 11am to 5pm. Closed Mon except bank holidays. £4, £3 (concessions), no charge (child, student, disabled, unemployed), no charge on Fri. ☎ (020) 8693 5254.
Access: by car from the South Circular, A205, A23, A21, follow signs to Camberwell Green, Dulwich, Dulwich Village, Dulwich Picture Gallery; 12min by train from London Bridge to North Dulwich or Victoria to West Dulwich; by bus P4 from Brixton underground Station.

Horniman Museum – ♿ Open daily 10.30am (2pm Sun) to 5.30pm. Closed 24 to 26 Dec. ☎ (020) 8699 1872; Fax (020) 8291 5506; enquiry@horniman.demon. co.uk; www.horniman.demon.co.uk
Access: by bus 176, 185, 312, 352, P4 (stop outside the museum), 122 (stops in Forest Hill), 63, P13 (stop in Sydenham Hill).

Crystal Palace National Sports Centre – ♿ *Open daily 8am to 10pm (8pm Sat, 6pm Sun, 5pm public holidays). Cost according to sport from £1.95; 65p (spectator). Parking. Restaurant. Refreshments.* ☎ *(020) 8778 0131; 776 7744 ext 231 (event details); Fax (020) 8676 8804.*
Palace Farmyard: Open Apr to Sept, daily, 11am to 5pm (5.30pm weekends and holidays), otherwise, daily, 11am to 3.30pm (4pm weekends and public holidays).
Boating: Apr to Sept.
Coarse fishing: Mid June to mid Mar. Contact Crystal Palace Park. ☎ *(020) 8778 9496.*

EALING

Pitshanger Manor and Gallery – Mattock Lane. Open Tues to Sat, 10am to 5pm. Closed 1 Jan, Easter, Christmas. ☎ (020) 8567 1227; Fax (020) 8567 0595; pitshanger@ealing.gov.uk Access: ⊖ Ealing Broadway.

EAST END

Tower Hamlets TIC – 18 Lamb Street, E1. Open Mon to Fri, 9.30am to 4.30pm; Sun, 11am to 2.30pm. ☎ 020 7375 2549, Fax 020 7375 2539.

St Leonard's Church – ♿ *Open Sun, 10am to noon; Mon to Fri, 10am to 5pm; Sat by request.* ☎ *(020) 7739 2063.*

Geffrye Museum – ♿ Open Tues to Sat, 10am to 5pm; Sun and holiday Mon 12pm to 5pm. Closed 1 Jan, Good Fri, 24 to 26 Dec. No charge. Guided tour by appointment. Restaurant; shop. Herb garden and period garden rooms: Open Apr to Oct. ☎ (020) 7739 9893, (020) 7739 8543 (recorded information); Fax (020) 7729 5647; info@geffrye-museum.org.uk; www.geffrye-museum.org.uk

Christ Church – ♿ Undergoing restoration: telephone for opening times. Services: Sun at 10.30am. ☎ (020) 7247 7202. Annual Music Festival: June and December. ☎ (020) 7377 0287.

Whitechapel Art Gallery – ♿ Open during exhibitions, Tues to Sun, 11am to 5pm (8pm Wed). Closed Mon. Charges for certain exhibitions only. Talks, tours and film screenings take place at various times. Telephone for details. Café. ☎ (020) 7522 7878 (recorded information), (020) 7522 7888 (general enquiries Tues to Fri only); Fax (020) 7377 1685; www.whitechapel.org
Access: by bus 5, 15, 15A, 25, 40, 67, 78, 253; ⊖ Aldgate East.

St John's Church – Open Sat, 10am to 11am. Services: Sun Mass at 10am. Daily mass times advertised at the church. Key available at the Rectory, 30 Victoria Park Square.

Bethnal Green Museum of Childhood – (♿) Open daily except Fri, 10am to 5.50pm. No charge. ☎ 020 8980 2415 (recorded information); Fax 020 8983 5225.

St Dunstan and All Saints Church – (♿) Services: Sunday, 8am, 10am, 6pm (prayers), 6.30pm; Monday to Friday, 8am, 5.30pm, Wednesday, 7.30pm, Thursday, 11am, Saturday, 9am, 6pm. Church open at other times by arrangement. No charge. ☎ (020) 7791 3545; Fax (020) 7791 0346; christopher.chessun@dlondon.org.uk

EAST END

Ragged School Museum – Open Wed and Thur, 10am to 5pm; First Sun in the month, 2pm to 5pm. No charge. Temporary exhibitions. Refreshments. ☎ (020) 8980 6405; Fax (020) 8983 3481. www.ics-london.co.uk/rsm
Access: by bus 25, 277, 309, 333 (summer only), 106, D5, D6, D7; ⊖ Mile End then follow signs across Mile End Park.

Three Mills – ♿ Open May to Oct, Sun, 2pm to 4pm; otherwise by appointment for groups. Guide Books (English only). Visitor Centre. £2, £1 (concessions), children free ☎ (020) 8980 4626; (020) 8472 2829 (bookings).
Access: by bus 25, 86, 108, 276, D8, S2; ⊖ Bromley-by-Bow.

ELTHAM PALACE

Eltham Palace – Open Apr to Sept, Wed to Fri, Sun, 10am to 6pm; Oct to Mar, Wed to Fri, Sun, 10am to 4pm (5pm Oct). Closed 1 Jan, 24 to 26 Dec. House and grounds: £5.90, £3 (child), £4.40 (concession); grounds only £3.50, £1.80 (child) £2.60 (concession). No dogs allowed. ☎ 020 8294 2548; www.english heritage.org.uk

FULHAM

Museum of Fulham Palace – Grounds: Open daily. Museum: ♿ Open Mar to Oct, Wed to Sun and bank holiday Mon, 2pm to 5pm; Nov to Feb, Thur to Sun, 1pm to 4pm. £1, 50p (concession), children free if accompanying adult. Guided tour £3: 2nd Sun in the month at 2pm, otherwise by appointment. Education service available ☎ (020) 7736 3233.
Access: by bus 74, 220 (to Fulham Palace Road); C4 (to Bishops Park Road); ⊖ Putney Bridge.

All Saints Church – ♿ Open Mon-Fri, 12pm to 3pm. Guide Book. ☎/Fax: (020) 7736 6301.

GREENWICH

Greenwich TIC – 46 Greenwich Church Street, SE10 9BL. Open Apr to Sep, daily 10.15am to 4.45pm; reduced hours in winter. ☎ 020 8858 6376, Fax 020 8853 4607.
Guided walks: From TIC (see above), daily: Meridian Walk and Royal Greenwich (90min) at 12.15pm and 2.15pm, £4, £3 (concession).

Old Royal Naval College – Painted Hall and Chapel and Special Exhibitions: Open daily, 10am (Sun, 12.30pm) to 5pm. £3, £2 (concession), no charge on Sun. Service Sun, 11am. ☎ 020 8269 4750; Fax 020 8269 4757; info@greenwichfoundation org.uk; www.greenwichfoundation.org.uk

National Maritime Museum – ♿ Open all year, daily, 10am to 5pm. Closed 24-26 Dec. £7.50, £6 (concession), no charge (child, senior citizen); combined ticket with Royal Observatory: £10.50, £8.40 (concession), no charge (child). Licensed café and restaurant. Giftshop. Play area. ☎ 020 8858 4422; 020 8312 6565 (24hr recorded information); www.nmm.ac.uk

Queen's House – Queen's House – Open for special exhibitions. Charge. ☎ (020) 8312 6608/6647. Fax (020) 8312 6522; bookings@nmm.ac.uk; www.nmm.ac.uk

Royal Observatory Greenwich – (♿) Open all year, daily, 10am to 5pm. Closed 24, 26 Dec. £5, £4 (concessions), no charge (child, senior citizen). Leaflet (English, French, German, Italian, Spanish). Parking. Café. ☎ 020 8858 4422; 020 8312 6565 (24hr recorded information). astroline@nmn.ac.uk (astronomy enquiries); www.rog.nmm.ac.uk

Ranger's House – (EH) (♿) Closed until 2002. ☎ (020) 8853 0035.

Fan Museum – Open Tues to Sun, 11am (noon Sun) to 5pm. Closed 1 Jan, 24 to 26 Dec. £3.50, £2.50 (concessions), no charge for senior citizens on Tues from 2pm. Fan-making workshop: by appointment only 1st Sat in every month. Audio guide. Brochure (English); Leaflet (French). ☎ 020 8305 1441; Fax 020 8293 1889.
Access: by bus 1, 177, 180, 188; Greenwich BR Station; Cutty Sark DLR Station. www.fan-museum.org; admin@fan-museum.org

St Alfege Church – Open Mon–Sat, 10am (Sun, 1pm) to 4pm. Leaflets (22 languages). Greenwich Festival: July. Thomas Tallis Society Concerts.

Cutty Sark – (♿) Open daily, 10am to 5pm. Closed 24 to 26 Dec. £3.50, £2.50 (concessions), £8.50 (2A+3C). Leaflet (Czech, Dutch, English, French, German, Greek, Hebrew, Hungarian, Italian, Russian, Spanish, Arabic, Danish, Finnish, Japanese, Korean, Norwegian, Polish, Portuguese, Slovakian, Swedish, Thai); guide book (French, German). ☎ (020) 8858 3445. Fax (020) 8853 3589; info@cuttysark. org.uk; www.cuttysark.org.uk

Gipsy Moth IV – Closed until further notice. ☎ (020) 8858 3445.

St Paul's Church, Deptford – Services: Sun at 9am, 10.30am, 6pm; Mon-Wed, 6pm; Thurs, 10am; Sat, 10am. Also open Wed, Fri and Sat, 2pm to 4pm. Guidebook. ☎ (020) 8692 1419 (Church Office), (020) 8692 0989 (Rectory).

St Nicholas' Church, Deptford – Services: Sun at 10am (adventurous all-ages liturgical worship). Viewing by arrangement with vicar. Guided tours by arrangement with Don Price ☎ 020 7639 4048, or Chris Shinn ☎ 020 8692 6919. wgcorneck@tesco.net.

HACKNEY

Sutton House – (NT) (&) Open Feb to Nov, Wed, Sun and bank holiday Mon, 11.30am to 5.30pm. Closed Good Fri. No photography or dogs. £2.10, 60p (child), £4.80 (family). Gallery; shop, café. ☎ (020) 8986 2264; Fax (020) 8525 9051.
Access: by bus 30, 38, 242, along Homerton High Street; 52, 236, 276, W15, from underground stations; 253 from Bethnal Green; 106 from Whitechapel.

Hackney Museum – *Closed to public until 2001.*

Holy Trinity Church (Clowns' Church) – & Memorial service: first Sun in Feb at 4pm. Otherwise open by appointment. ☎ (020) 7254 5062 (Vicarage).

HAM HOUSE

Ham House – (NT) & House: Open Apr to Oct, Sat to Wed, 1pm to 5pm. Garden: Open Sat to Wed, 10.30am to 6pm (or sunset if earlier). Closed 1 Jan, 25 and 26 Dec. No dogs. £5, £2.50 (child), £12.50 (family). Parking; refreshments. ☎ (020) 8940 1950; Fax (020) 8332 6903.
Access: by bus via Petersham Road, 371 to Royal Oak, Ham or 65 to Fox and Duck, Petersham then 20min on foot; ⊖ /BR Richmond. By foot ferry from Marble Hill House, Twickenham, daily Mar to Oct, 10am to 6pm. ☎ (020) 8892 9620 (ferry).

HAMMERSMITH

St Peter's Church – Services: Sun at 8am (Holy Communion), 10.30am (Parish Eucharist), 6.30pm (Evensong); Wed at 9.30am (Holy Communion). Otherwise open by appointment. ☎ (020) 8741 4848 or 748 1781; Fax (020) 8748 6610.

St Paul's Church – *Services: Sun at 8.30am, 11am, 5.30pm; Thur at 1pm.*

HAMPSTEAD – HIGHGATE

St John's Church – Open Mon to Sat, 8.45am to 4.30pm (4pm Sat); Sun, 1pm to 5.30pm. Services: Sun at 8am, 10.30am. 12.15, 6pm; Mon to Sat, see notice-board. ☎ (020) 7794 5808; Fax (020) 7794 5979; vestry@hampstead-parish.co.uk; www.hampstead-parish.demon.co.uk

Fenton House – (NT) (&) Open Mar, Sat and Sun only 2pm to 5pm, Apr to Oct, weekends and bank holiday Mon 11am to 5pm, Wed to Fri, 2pm to 5pm. Last admission 30min prior to closing. £4.20, £10.50 (family). Guide book (French, German, Japanese). Braille guide. No photography. ☎/Fax (020) 7435 3471. Access: bus 46, 268.

Burgh House – Hampstead Local History Museum and Community Arts Centre: Open Wed to Sun, noon to 5pm; 1 May – 31 Oct, Sat by appointment only; public holidays, 2pm to 5pm. Closed Christmas to New Year, Good Friday and Easter Monday. No charge. Brief leaflets (French, German, Italian, Japanese). ☎ (020) 7431 0144; Fax: (020) 7435 8817. Licensed Buttery: Wed to Sun, 11am to 5.30pm. ☎ (020) 7431 2516.
Access: by bus 46, 268; ⊖ Hampstead; BR Hampstead Heath station.

2 Willow Road – (NT) Open Apr-Oct, Thurs-Sat, 12noon-5pm. Last admission 4pm. Closed bank holidays. Guided tour (60min) every 45min from 12.15pm. £4.20, £2.10 (child). ☎ (020) 7435 6166.

Keats House – (&) Closed until May 2001. ☎ 020 7435 2062; Fax 020 7431 9293.

Highgate Cemetery – This is a private burial ground, run by a charity. Since it is closed during funerals, please telephone in advance for information. ☎ 020 8340 1834.

Alexandra Palace – & Palm Court: Open daily 9.30am to 5pm. Café, Phoenix Pub. Playground. Pitch and putt: Open in summer. Ice rink: Open daily. Telephone for opening times and special events. ☎ (020) 8365 2121; Fax (020) 8883 3999; alexandrapalace@dial.pipex.com; www.alexandrapalace.com
Boating lake: ☎ (020) 8889 9089.

Outdoor concerts in Grove: early July to early Sept, Sun, 3pm to 5pm; no charge. Access: by bus W3; ⊖ Wood Green, then take the free shuttle bus (show days) or W3 bus; BR Alexandra Palace Station

HAMPTON COURT

Hampton Court Palace – ♿ Open daily, 9.30am (10.15am Mon) to 6pm (4.30pm mid Oct to mid Mar). Closed 24 to 26 Dec. Guided tours and family trails available throughout the day. Audio guide. £10.50, £2.30 (child), £8 (concessions), £31.40 (family 2A+3C); Privy Garden or Maze only, £2.50, £1.50 (child); Parking (£3) restaurant, café; carriage rides (summer only). ☎ (020) 8781 9500; www.hrp.org.uk
Tudor Tennis Court and Banqueting House: Open in summer as for palace.
Chapel Royal – Services: Sun at 8.30am (Holy Communion); 11am (Sung Eucharist or 1st Sun – Choral Matins on other Sun); 3.30pm (Choral Evensong).
Gardens: Open daily 7am to sunset or 9pm (4pm winter). The Great Vine produces an annual crop of 500-600 bunches of Black Hamburg grapes (on sale late Aug to early Sept).

HARROW

St Mary's Church – Open Mon-Sat, 8am-6pm; Sun, 7.30am-8pm.

Harrow School – Old Speech Room Gallery: Open daily during term time, except Wed 2.30pm to 5pm – variable during holidays and exeats. No charge. ☎ (020) 8869 1205 or (020) 8422 2196.
Harrow School Tours: Guided tour (1hr, 90min, 2hr) by prior appointment, Mon to Sat, 9.30am to 5pm. £4.15 to £5.20, £3.30 to £4.35 (concession). French and German speaking guides available. Apply in advance to Mrs P Shyrane, 57 High Street Harrow on the Hill, HA1 3HT. ☎/Fax (020) 8423 1524.
Access: ⊖ South Harrow, Harrow-on-the-Hill

Harrow Museum and Heritage Centre – Open Wed to Fri, 12.30pm to 5pm (sunset in winter); weekends and bank holidays, 10.30am to 5pm (sunset in winter). Closed Christmas week. No charge. Guided tour of buildings by appointment; £1. Music events: Sun lunch-times. ☎ (020) 8861 2626; Fax (020) 8863 6407; www harrowarts.org.uk

ISLINGTON – HOLLOWAY

Islington TIC – 44 Duncan Street, N1. Open Apr-Nov, Tues-Sat 10am to 5pm, Mon 2pm to 5pm, (closed Sat 1.30pm to 2.30pm). Reduced hours during winter. ☎ 020 7278 8787, Fax 020 7833 2193; vic@islvic.demon.co.uk; www.discover-islington.co.uk

Crafts Council Gallery – ♿ Open Tues to Sun, 11am (2pm Sun) to 6pm. Closed 25 to 26 Dec. No charge. Reference library, picture library. Telephone to check exhibition programme. Crafts shop, café. ☎ (020) 7278 7700; Fax (020) 7837 6891; crafts-@craftscouncil.org.uk; www.craftscouncil.org.uk
Access: by bus 4, 19, 30, 38, 43, X43, 56, 73, 153, 171A, 214.

Camden Passage – *Market days: Wed and Sat, 8am to 5pm (4pm winter).*

Little Angel Theatre – Open weekends. £7.50/£5.50, £5/£4.50 (children and concessions). For details ☎ (020) 7226 1787; Fax (020) 7359 7565.
Access: by bus 38, 56, 73, 171A (to Essex Road), 4, 19, 30, 43, 236A (to Upper Street); ⊖ Angel, Highbury & Islington; BR Highbury & Islington.

Estorick Collection of Modern Italian Art – ♿ Open Wed to Sat, 11am to 6pm, Sun, 12pm to 5pm. £3.50, £2.50 (concession). Library by appointment; café; shop; garden. ☎ 020 7704 9522, Fax 020 7704 9531. curator@estorickcollection.com; www.estorickcollection.com
Access: by bus 271 to Canonbury Road; 4, 19, 30, 43 to Upper Street; 38, 56, 73, 171a to Essex Road; ⊖ Highbury & Islington.

Sobell Leisure Centre – *Open Mon to Fri, 9am to 11pm; Sat, 9am to 6pm; Sun, 9am to 10pm. Ice rink, gym, sauna, sunbeds, therapy rooms, function suite, football, netball, badminton, sqash, trampolining, climbing, exercise classes, , table tennis, junior activities, courses and parties.* ☎ (020) 7609 2166; Fax: (020) 7700 3094. www.aquaterra.org

KENWOOD

Kenwood – (EH) (♿) House: Open Apr to Oct, daily, 10am to 6pm (5pm in Oct); Nov to Mar, daily, 10am to 4pm. (Upper Hall on first floor currently closed.) Closed 24, 25 Dec. No charge. First floor exhibitions: charges, free to children under 12yrs. Audio-guide available (additional charge). ☎ 020 8348 1286; Fax 020 7973 3891.
Grounds: Open daily, 8am to sunset. Lakeside concerts: July to early Sept, Sat evenings (occasionally Sun). ☎ 020 7973 3893. Gypsy caravan: open by appointment only. Parking. Restaurant. Picnic area.
Access: by bus 210 (from Golders Green or Archway).

Royal Botanic Gardens – &. *Open daily, 9.30am to 3.30pm (variable according to season: 6.30pm in summer and 7.30pm weekends). Closed 1 Jan, 25 Dec. Glass houses and galleries close earlier than the Gardens.* £5, £3.50 *(concessions)*, £2.50 *(child)*, £13 *(family 2A+4C). Orientation Centre at Victoria Gate. Guided tour from Victoria Gate, daily at 11am and 2pm, £1. Maps available (French, German, Japanese, Spanish). Refreshments.* ✆ 020 8940 1171. www.kew.org

Kew Palace (Dutch House) – Closed for restoration until 2000.

Queen Charlotte's Cottage – Open weekends and bank holidays throughout summer; no additional charge for visitors to Royal Botanic Gardens; opening times as for Royal Botanic Gardens.

Public Record Office – *Admission by ticket only.* ✆ 020 8876 3444.

Kew Bridge Steam Museum – (&.) Open daily, 11am to 5pm. Closed Good Fri, 16 to 26 Dec. Weekends (engines in steam) £4, £3 (concession), £2 (child), £10.50 (family 2A+3C); weekdays (engines static) £3, £2 (concessions), £1 (child), £7 (family 2A+3C). Guide book and brochure (Dutch, French, German, Spanish, Italian). Large print guide available. Parking. Café (weekends). Bookshop. ✆ 020 8568 4757; info@kbsm.org.uk; www.kbsm.org.uk
Access: by bus 65, 237, 267, 391; ⊖ Gunnersbury, then 237 or 267 bus; Kew Gardens, then 391 bus; BR Kew Bridge.

Musical Museum – &. Open Apr to Oct, weekends, 2pm to 5pm; July and Aug, Wed, 2pm to 4pm. £3.20, £2.50 (concessions). Guide books, recordings available. ✆ (020) 8560 8108.
Access: by bus 65, 237, 267; ⊖ Gunnersby, then 237 or 267 bus; South Ealing, then 65 bus; BR Kew Bridge.

Boston Manor – House: Open early Apr to late Oct, weekends and bank holiday Mon, 2.30pm to 5pm. No charge. ✆ 020 8560 5441. Grounds: Open daily.

William MORRIS GALLERY

William Morris Gallery – (&.) Open Tues to Sat and 1st Sun of each month, 10am to 1pm, 2pm to 5pm. Closed Mon and public holidays. No charge. Leaflets (English only). ✆ (020) 8527 3782; Fax (020) 8527 7070; www.lbwf.gov.uk/wmg
Access: ⊖ Walthamstow Central and then by bus or on foot (10min) up Hoe Street to Bell Corner, turn left down Forest Road, Lloyd Park is third block on right, beyond Bedford Road.

OSTERLEY PARK

Osterley Park – (NT) House: &. Open Apr to Oct, Wed to Sun and bank holiday Mon 1pm to 4pm; Closed Good Fri. £4.20, £2.10 (child), £10.50 (family). Guided tour by appointment. No photography. ✆/Fax 020 8568 7714.
Park: Open daily, 9am to 7.30pm (or sunset if earlier); closes early during major events; no charge. Car park closed 25 and 26 Dec. Parking £2.50 (coaches free). Tea room. Gift shop.
Access: ⊖ Osterley (Piccadilly Line) then 20min walk.

PUTNEY – WANDSWORTH

St Mary's Church – Services: Sun at 10am and 6pm; also Thur at 12.30pm. Guide books available. ✆ (020) 8788 4575 (Vicar), (020) 8788 7164 (Curate), (020) 8788 7335 or (020) 8789 0953 (Churchwardens), ✆/Fax (020) 8788 4414 (Parish offices).

Young & Co's Ram Brewery – (&.) Open Mon to Sat (excluding bank holidays), 11am to 5.30pm (noon to 5pm Sat); scheduled tours: Tue, Wed, Thur, Sat at noon and 2pm (must pre-book). Evening visits by arrangement. £5.50, £4.50 (concessions), £3 (14-17yr olds, must be accompanied by adult), £9 (family). ✆ 020 8875 7005; Fax 020 8875 7006; thebrewerytap@youngs.co.uk; www.youngs.co.uk

RICHMOND

Richmond TIC – *Old Town Hall, Whittaker Avenue, Richmond TW9 1TP. Open Mon to Sat, 10am to 6pm (5pm Sat), also May to Oct, Sun 10.15am to 4.15pm.* ✆ 020 8940 9125, Fax 020 8940 6899.

Museum of Richmond – &. Open all year, Tues to Sat, 11am to 5pm; Sun (May-Sep) 1pm to 4pm. £2, £1 (concessions), children free. Guided walk in Richmond (90min) daily at 11am; £2. Coffee shop. ✆ (020) 8332 1141; Fax (020) 8948 7570; musrich@globalnet.co.uk; www.museumofrichmond.com
Access: by bus 33, 65, 190, 391, 415, H22, H37, R61, R69, R70; ⊖ District line; BR Waterloo and North London lines.

ROYAL AIR FORCE MUSEUM

Royal Air Force Museum – &. Open daily, 10am to 6pm. Closed 1 Jan, 24 to 26 Dec. £7, £4.50 (concessions), £5.50 (senior citizen), £15.50 (family). Flight Simulator £1.50. Guided tour available. Parking; licensed restaurant. ☎ 0891 600 5633 (recorded information, premium rate), (020) 8205 2266; Fax (020) 8200 1751.
Access: by car from M1 (Junction 4), A41, A5 and North Circular; ↔ Colindale Station then 303 bus; BR Mill Hill Broadway;

ST JOHN'S WOOD

St John's Wood Church – (&.) Open daily, 9am to 5pm. Services: Sun at 8am, 9.30am, 11am, 6.30pm. Concerts. ☎ (020) 7586 3864.

Lord's Cricket Ground – Guided tour (including museum) daily at noon, 2pm; or summer days at 10am. Telephone for exact schedule. Closed during test matches, cup finals, preparation days and certain public holidays. £6, £4.40, (concession). Museum only: Open match days to match ticket holders only, £2, £1 (concession). Leaflet (French, Italian). ☎ (020) 7432 1033; Fax (020) 7266 3825.
Access: by bus 13, 46, 82, 113, 139, 189, 274; ↔ St John's Wood, Marylebone.

Saatchi Gallery – *Open Thur to Sun, 12pm to 6pm. £4, £2 (concessions).* ☎ *(020) 7624 8299; Fax (020) 7624 3798.*
Access: by bus 16, 31, 139, 189; ↔ St John's Wood, Swiss Cottage, Kilburn.

Freud Museum – (&.) Open Wed to Sun, noon to 5pm. Closed Easter bank holidays, 24 to 26 Dec and over New Year (telephone for details). £4, £2 (concessions), no charge for under 12s. Limited parking. Brochure (English, French, German, Spanish, Portugese). Shop. ☎ (020) 7435 2002; Fax (020) 7431 5452; freud@gn.apc.org www.freud.org.uk
Access: by bus 13, 31, 82, 113, 268; ↔ Finchley Road

SILVERTOWN – NORTHWOOLWICH

North Woolwich Old Station Museum – Open Jan-Nov, Sat and Sun, 1pm-5pm. Additional opening during school holidays, Mon-Wed, 1pm-5pm (Wed activity days). Closed December. Engines in steam: Apr to Sept, first Sun in the month. Gift shop. ☎ (020) 7474 7244.
Access: by bus 101, 473; Silverlink North London Link Line to North Woolwich connections at Stratford with Central Line, Docklands Light Railway.

SYON PARK

Syon Park – House: (&.) Open mid Mar-Oct, Wed, Thur, Sun and bank holiday Mon, 11am to 5pm. Audio-guide, guide book, leaflets. Gardens: Open all year, daily, 10am to 5.30pm (or sunset). Closed 25 and 26 Dec. House and gardens £6, £4.50 (concession), £15 (family); gardens only, £3, £2.50 (concession), £7 (family). ☎ (020) 8560 0883; Fax (020) 8568 0936.

London Butterfly House – &. Open daily, 10am to 5pm (3.30pm winter). Closed 25 and 26 December. £3.30, £2 (children), £2 (concession). Parking. ☎ 020 8560 7272 (recorded information), 020 8560 0378; Fax 020 8560 7272. www.butterflies org.uk

TWICKENHAM

Twickenham TIC – *The Atrium, Civic Centre, York Street. Open Mon to Fri, 9am to 5.15pm (5pm Fri).* ☎ *020 8891 7272.*

Orleans House Gallery – House: &. Open Tues to Sun, 1pm (2pm Sun and public holidays) to 5.30pm (4.30pm Oct to Mar). No entry charge. Garden: Open daily, 9am to sunset. Parking. ☎ (020) 8892 0221; Fax (020) 8744 0501. leisure@ richmond.gov.uk; www.guidetorichmond.co.uk/orleans.html
Access: by bus 33, 490, H22, R68, R70, 290 (alight at The Crown public house or at Lebanon Park); ↔ Richmond; BR St Margaret's Station or Twickenham Station from Waterloo.

Marble Hill House – (EH) (&.) Open Apr-Sept, daily, 10am-6pm (5pm Oct); Nov-Mar, Wed-Sun, 10am-4pm. Closed 4-17 Jan, 24-26 Dec. £3.30, £2.50 (concessions), £1.70 (child). Guided tour (1hr, by appointment); audio guide available. Parking. Restaurant (summer), picnic area. ☎ 020 8892 5115.

Strawberry Hill – Guided tour (90min; minimum age 14) Easter to Oct, Sun at 2pm, 2.30pm, 3pm, 3.30pm; otherwise in groups by appointment. £4.75, £4.25 (concessions). ☎ (020) 8240 4114, (020) 8240 4311; Fax (020) 8255 6174.

WIMBLEDON – MERTON

Southside House – Open New Year's Day to Midsummer's Day. Guided tours (90min) Wed, Sat, Sun and bank holiday Mon at 2pm, 3pm, 4pm. £5, £3 (child). ☎ 020 8946 7643 (guides).
Access: by bus 93 to Wimbledon War Memorial; ↔ Putney Bridge, Wimbledon.

Cannizaro Gardens – Open daily, 8.30am to sunset (5pm to 9.30pm). ☎ (020) 8946 7349.

Wimbledon Windmill Museum – (&) Open Easter or Apr to Oct, weekends and public holidays, 2pm to 5pm (Sat), 11am to 5pm (Sun and public holidays). £1, 50p (concessions). Parking. Café. ☎ (020) 8947 2825.

Wimbledon Museum – Open Sat, 2.30pm to 5pm. No charge. Parties at other times by arrangement. ☎ (020) 8296 9914. Access: ⊖ Wimbledon; by bus 93, 200. mail@wimbledonmuseum.org.uk

St Mary's Church – & Open weekdays, usually 9am to 4pm. Closed sometimes during school holidays. ☎ (020) 8946 2605; Fax (020) 8946 6293.

Wimbledon Lawn Tennis Museum – & Open daily throughout the year from 10.30am – 5pm. Closed the Fri, Sat and Sun immediately before the Championships, the middle Sun of and the Monday immediately after the Championships, as well as 24 – 26 Dec and 1 Jan. £5, £4 (concessions). Leaflet (French, Dutch, German, Italian, Japanese, Spanish). Parking (end of Aug to May only). Tea room. ☎ (020) 8946 6131; Fax (020) 8944 6497.
Access: by bus 39, 93, 200; ⊖ Southfields then 15min walk; BR Wimbledon Station, then 25min walk.

Polka Children's Theatre – & Open all year (except Sept), Tues to Fri, 9.30am to 4.30pm; Sat, 11am to 5.30pm. Closed throughout Sept and 25 Dec. Workshops; exhibitions; playground; shop; café. ☎ (020) 8543 4888 (box office), (020) 8542 4258; Fax (020) 8542 7723; polakabox@hotmail.com; www.polkatheatre.com
Access: by bus 57, 93, 131, 155, 156, 163, 200; ⊖ South Wimbledon, Wimbledon; BR Wimbledon Station.

WINDSOR CASTLE

Windsor TIC – *24 High Street, Windsor.* ☎ *01753 852 010.*

Windsor Castle – & Open daily 9.45am to 5.15pm (4.15pm from Nov to Feb). Closed Good Friday, 19 June, 25 and 26 Dec. Last admissions March to Oct 4pm, Nov to Feb 3pm. Ticket prices include access to the Queen Mary's Dolls' House, the State Apartments and St George's Chapel (closed on Sun): £10.50, £8 (concession), £5 (child), £25.50 (family). Reduced rate when the State Apartments are closed. Telephone before visit to check all parts of the castle are fully open. ☎ 01753 869 898 (information office), 01753 831 118 (recorded message).
Changing of the Guard – Weather permitting, takes place daily, Apr to June, Mon to Sat at 11am; alternate days at other times of the year.
St George's Chapel – Open Mon to Sat, 10am to 4.15pm. Subject to closure at short notice. Last admission at 4.05pm. ☎ 01753 865 538.
Frogmore House, Gardens and Royal Mausoleum – Open on selected days in May and Aug bank holiday weekend. Variable charges. ☎ 01753 869 898. Royal Mausoleum only – Open 24 May only, 10am-4pm. No charge.

Windsor Great Park – *Open daily from sunrise to sunset.*

Valley Gardens – Open daily from dawn to dusk. Local (paying) car park open 8am to 7pm/sunset. ☎ 01753 847 518.

Savill Gardens – & Near Englefield Green, off the A 30. Open daily, 10am-6pm (dusk in Oct; 4pm Nov-Feb). Closed 25-26 Dec. April and May: £5, £4.50 (concession), £2 (child); June-Oct: £4, £3.50 (concession), £1 (child); Nov-Mar: £3, £2.50 (concession), £1 (child). No charge for accompanied children under 5. Guided tour by appointment. No dogs. Parking. Licensed restaurant, picnic area; plant and gift shop. ☎ 01753 847 518; Fax 01753 847 536. www.savillgarden.co.uk

Eton College – School Yard, College Chapel, Cloister Court and the Museum of Eton Life: Open Apr-early Oct, 10.30am (2pm mid Apr-late June, early Sept-early Oct)-4.30pm. Closed 15 and 31 May. College Chapel closed weekdays, 1pm-2pm, Sun, 12.30pm-2pm. £2.70, £2 (child). Guided tour (1hr) daily, at 2.15pm, 3.15pm; £4, £3 (child). ☎ 01753 671 177; Fax 01753 671 265.

WOOLWICH – CHARLTON

Museum of Artillery in the Rotunda – (&) Open Mon-Fri, 1pm-4pm. Closed bank holidays. Guided tour (60min) by appointment. Parking. ☎ (020) 8316 5402; (020) 8781 3127.

Thames Barrier Visitor Centre – & Open daily. Telephone to check opening times. Closed during the Christmas period. £3.40, £7.50 (3A+2C). Exhibition with video and working model. Guide book and information sheets (Dutch, French, German, Italian, Spanish). Parking. Cafeteria. ☎ (020) 8305 4188; Fax (020) 8855 2146.
Access: by bus 177, 180, 472; by train to Charlton Station from Charing Cross, Waterloo East, London Bridge and Dartford; by boat from Greenwich (25min) ☎(020) 8305 0300 and Westminster (75min) ☎ (020) 7930 3373; ⊖ North Greenwich.

Charlton House – (&) Open Mon to Fri, 9am to 10pm; Sat, 9am to 5pm (library only). £2. Guided tour (1hr) for parties by appointment. Leaflet. Refreshments. ☎ (020) 8856 3951; Fax (020) 8856 4162.

Index

The following subjects have been grouped together for easy reference: Almshouses, Churches and places of worship, Clubs (private), Guards, Hospitals, Markets, Museums and art galleries, Parks, Prisons, pubs and taverns (see Public houses), Registers, Theatres.

436

437

438